Tapping the Government Grapevine

Tapping the Government Grapevine

The User-Friendly Guide to U.S. Government Information Sources
Third Edition

by Judith Schiek Robinson

Oryx Press
1998

The rare Arabian Oryx is believed to have inspired the myth of the unicorn. This desert antelope became virtually extinct in the early 1960s. At that time, several groups of international conservationists arranged to have nine animals sent to the Phoenix Zoo to be the nucleus of a captive breeding herd. Today, the Oryx population is over 1,000, and over 500 have been returned to the Middle East.

© Copyright 1998 by The Oryx Press
4041 North Central at Indian School Road
Phoenix, Arizona 85012-3397

Published simultaneously in Canada

Printed and bound in the United States of America

∞ The paper used in this publication meets the minimum requirements of American National Standard for Information Science—Permanence of Paper for Printed Library Materials, ANSI Z39.48, 1984.

Library of Congress Cataloging-in-Publication Data
Robinson, Judith Schiek, 1947–
    Tapping the government grapevine : the user-friendly guide to U.S. Government information sources / by Judith Schiek Robinson. —3rd ed.
    Includes bibliographical references and index.
    ISBN 1-57356-024-3 (alk. paper)
    1. Government information—United States.   I. Title.
ZA5055.U6R63   1998
025.04—dc21   98-20618
                                                                         CIP

CONTENTS

PREFACE

Do not fold, spindle, or mutilate.
—Directive on computer punch cards [c. 1930s]

It's difficult to pinpoint exactly when the door opened and "let the future in."[1] Perhaps it was more than a century ago, when young Herman Hollerith convinced the government to use his electric machines to tally the 1890 census. Or possibly it was in 1966, when MEDLINE's precursor, MEDLARS, lumbered through an experiment in computerized medical indexing. Or perhaps it occurred during the summer of 1976, when the octogenarian *Monthly Catalog* shook off its idiosyncratic mantle to adopt machine-readable bibliographic standards. Whatever the spark, the resultant explosion toppled the status quo: In the late 1990s, government information was reborn. Agency publications ceased to exist in paper, only to be regenerated on the World Wide Web. Online dissemination of Government Printing Office products became the law of the land. Depository libraries redefined themselves. The result is the most exciting juncture in the history of government information access.

The endless tide of change is both dazzling and intimidating. This edition of *Tapping the Government Grapevine* mirrors the magnitude of this sea change. Draped across the skeleton of the first two editions is a completely new work, more than 90 percent fresh material. Focus on government Web sites is interwoven into the traditional documents knowledge base: genres of government documentation, access options, and agency concentrations. This exploration of the government information amalgam includes electronic resources, publications, maps, audiovisuals, archival collections and museums, as well as some of the personalities, events, and ironies behind them.

This book is a guided tour of the government information landscape. It identifies idiosyncrasies and potential pitfalls, differentiates between similar titles, and suggests effective search strategies. Practice exercises following most chapters provide not only answers, but also the thought processes for retrieving them. Sample entries from documents are not simply reproduced, they

are explained. Chapters feature search and access tips, quick-reference tables, information boxes, and illustrations. Appendixes stockpile URLs, abbreviations, and sample citations. The book is written for users and potential users of government information: librarians, library school students, researchers, butchers, bakers, candlestick-makers—anyone needing government information. It may be browsed to answer specific questions (key information is highlighted in summary tables for quick referral or review) or read cover to cover. United States federal resources are emphasized, but information about international, foreign, state, and local information sources is also provided in chapters 14 and 15. Karen F. Smith, coordinator of the Business and Government Documents Reference Center in Lockwood Library at the University of Buffalo, contributed chapter 15, focusing on foreign and international documents.

NAVIGATING THE INTERNET

The third edition of *Tapping the Government Grapevine* is immersed in Internet resources. The URLs (Uniform Resource Locators) referenced in this book are prefaced by http://, ftp://, gopher://, or telnet://. These "Internet addresses" transport users to either HTML documents at Web sites (http://), file transfer protocol sites and files (ftp://), remote computers (telnet://), or hierarchical menus of files and text (gopher://). The simplest way to access them is to type the URL (minus the angle brackets) into your Web browser. For example, to access LC MARVEL, type <gopher://marvel.loc.gov/> into the browser's location box (omitting the <>). Or, from your UNIX host or Internet access account start-up screen, type the command followed by the destination: gopher marvel.loc.gov

Describing Web sites is like narrating action at a bird feeder. Flux is frequent and without fanfare. If a URL becomes inoperative, pare it to its kernel and use the site's search engine or menus to track down the relocated Web page. For example, if the URL for "Copyright Basics"<http://lcweb.loc.gov/copyright/circs/

circl.html> becomes dormant, pare the URL to <http://lcweb.loc.gov/copyright/> or <http://lcweb.loc.gov/> to pick up its trail. To discover government publications added to Web sites since publication of this book, check the home page of the issuing agency and scout the GPO Access Web site.

Some Web sites present publications in Adobe Acrobat PDF (Portable Document Format), which resembles snapshots of the print publication. The Census Bureau's Web site PDF offering of *Census and You*, for example, replicates the fonts, formatting, colors, and images of its paper twin. To view PDF documents, download the free Adobe Acrobat Reader from <http://www.adobe.com/homepage.shtml>.

NAVIGATING THIS BOOK

Addresses for agencies discussed in the text appear at the end of individual chapters, while publishers' addresses and Web sites have been corralled into Appendix 1. Lists of free publications follow individual chapters, along with suggestions for further reading. Superintendent of Documents classification (SuDocs) numbers and URLs are provided throughout and URLs also appear in Appendix 5 for quick referral. Additional appendixes decode abbreviations, popular names, and commonly encountered citation formats. Some government products discussed in the book are also available through commercial vendors: These vendors have not been itemized but can be identified using sources such as the *Gale Directory of Databases*.

> *No idea is so modern that it will not someday be antiquated.*
> —Ellen Glasgow, Address to the Modern Language Association, 1936

I welcome your suggestions for the next edition. Contact me at the School of Information and Library Studies, 534 Baldy Hall, Buffalo, NY 14260-1020; (716) 645-3327; Fax (716) 645-3775; e-mail: lisrobin@acsu.buffalo.edu.

ACKNOWLEDGMENTS

My thanks to Kristen Wilhelm and Ted Hull, both from the National Archives, and to my colleagues David J. Nuzzo and Jill Ortner, University at Buffalo. Thanks also to the University at Buffalo School of Information and Library Studies students who performed library and Internet searching in support of this book: Guy Bennett, Charles Bernholz, Angela Button, Rosemarie Casseri, Molly Chatt, Calmer Chattoo, Pui Yan Chung, Rachael Covington, Michael Curtis, Marcia Daumen, Carol Dichtenberg, Robert Difazio, Andrew Dutka, Katherine Ellsworth, Kerrie Fergen, Carrie Golombek, Mary Jo Grundle, Dorchell Harris, Thomas Healy, Rhonda Hoffman, Suzanne Jacobs, Karenann Jurecki, Debbie Kinsella, Wendy Kramer, Puiyan Lee, Yanqing Li, Nicolette Lodico, Darlene Lysarz, Kathryn Maragliano, Gail Mates, Katherine Mattison, Terry Morris, Michael Murphy, Janice Norris, Adrienne Pettinelli-Furness, Kit Pitkin, Jennifer Reis-Taggart, Jeanne Riccardi, Kathryn Rickerson, Margaret Sacco, Patricia Sanders, Patricia Sarchet, Ted Sherman, Dennis Smolarek, Margaret Spiesz, Steve Sposato, Christine Stocklader, Elise Torre, Jennifer Trigilio, David Valenzuela, and Carol Veach.

Karen Smith wishes to thank Linda B. Johnson from the University of New Hampshire for her support and assistance in selecting readings on foreign and international documents.

NOTE

1. There is always one moment in childhood when the door opens and lets the future in. Graham Greene, *The Power and the Glory*. Mattituck, New York: Amereon House, 1940, chapter 1.

Tapping the Government Grapevine

CHAPTER 1
Introduction to Government Information Resources

The advent of government information is an excellent example of the Feds doing something right.
—Robert Schwarzwalder, *Database* magazine

The U.S. government, the world's most prolific information machine, has plugged itself in. In a climate of shrinking budgets, government restructuring, and alluring technological possibilities, federal agencies have surrendered to computers. Increasingly, government-produced information has leapt from the printed page onto the computer screen. A celebration of CD-ROMs in the early 1990s was followed by a rickety spin with Telnet and Gopher. By 1995, government agencies had mass migrated onto the World Wide Web. GPO Access, THOMAS, and the Web *Monthly Catalog* were launched. With each revolution of the globe, agencies spawned new Web pages: one mid-1997 survey identified 4,300 Web sites and 215 computer bulletin boards tethered at 42 departments and agencies.[1] In homes and offices from coast to coast, Internet surfers stumbled across government information. And the nation's best kept secret finally seeped into the public consciousness: Uncle Sam is the most benevolent information provider in the nation.

Offering Internet sites for nearly every agency and a nationwide network of depository libraries, the government also maintains primary research collections in the National Archives, 12 presidential libraries, and four national libraries (the Library of Congress, National Agricultural Library, National Library of Education, and National Library of Medicine). Harnessing this wealth of information is complicated by the government's array of sites, protocols, formats, and delivery options. Information is often duplicated in parallel offerings: legislative information for example, is available on the Web via the Library of Congress's THOMAS, through GPO Access, and by way of the House of Representatives Internet Law Library (which routes visitors back to THOMAS and GPO Access), as well as in traditional print and microfiche resources stockpiled in depository libraries.

GOVERNMENT GESTALT

Navigating this information terrain is expedited by "cognitive maps": visualizations that provide orientation, direction, and shortcuts. Cognitive maps that are used for government information-seeking demand knowledge of agency concentrations, reconnoitering access options, constant adaptation, and familiarity with documentation genres, such as regulations or laws. Navigating by trial-and-error is inefficient, especially on the Internet, where capricious results masquerade as credible. The adept seeker of government information distrusts global Internet search engines, bypasses general indexes and abstracts, and foregoes browsing. These trusted standbys can be inadequate for government searches, which rely instead upon a unique corps of Internet gateways, catalogs, and indexes to pilot the gentle reader. Half the battle is selecting the right venue. Two kick-start tables are provided in this chapter to keep you afloat until you learn more: Hot Buttons and Getting Started: Government Locators.

Federal government information activity is decentralized. That means sometimes the right hand doesn't know what the left hand is doing. In this case, instead of two hands, the federal government has around 5,800—that's the approximate number of departments and agencies currently in existence. While no single agency regulates all government information activity, a "Big Two" oversee federal information production and dissemination: (1) Congress's Joint Committee on Printing (JCP), which steers the Government Printing Office (GPO), and (2) the Office of Management and Budget (OMB), authorized by the Paperwork Reduction Act[2] to oversee the life cycle of government information from collection to dissemination. Besides these agencies, two major printing and distribution organs are the afore-mentioned Government Printing Office and the National Technical Information Service (NTIS). In addition, numerous clearinghouses, depository programs, archival collections, and information centers all provide government information.

GPO: The Mother Lode

While the Government Printing Office is not the sole source of federal publications, it is the federal government's primary information reproducer and distributor. GPO's responsibilities include not only printing for the federal government, but also disseminating government information to the public through the Superintendent of Documents and Depository Library Program. Since federal law mandates that agencies send copies of any federally funded information products to GPO for depository distribution, GPO is positioned to monitor government information production and to oversee its bibliographic control. The Government Printing Office is, therefore, one of the primary indexers and distributors of federal publications.

GPO Access

http://www.access.gpo.gov/su_docs/

GPO Access, a government information smorgasbord, is the embodiment of cybergovernment. Its panoptic sweep is tamed by ease of use, consistent search protocol, and an orderliness that helps even the uninitiated survive. This omnibus site offers the full text of cardinal government publications such as the *Federal Register* and *Congressional Record*, the Federal Bulletin Board (a source for downloading files), and links to agency Internet sites.

NTIS: The Other Lode

The National Technical Information Service (NTIS) is the nation's clearinghouse for unclassified technical reports of government-sponsored research. NTIS collects, indexes, abstracts, and sells U.S. and foreign research reports, not just on scientific and technical subjects, but also in the behavioral and social sciences. Most of these titles can be reproduced indefinitely, never going out of print. Unfortunately though, many NTIS titles are unavailable for depository distribution and are not listed in the *Monthly Catalog*. Instead, they must be traced using specialized indexes and databases.

FedWorld

http://www.fedworld.gov/

This "electronic marketplace" of U.S. and foreign government information is NTIS's gateway to agency databases, files, documents, and federal job listings. The FedWorld File Libraries, containing much of FedWorld's "meat," are accessible through FTP or Telnet (be prepared for grey backgrounds). FedWorld offerings sometimes duplicate other sites, loop back to more user-friendly hubs, or merely hawk subscription services off-limits to nonpaying Internet surfers. NTIS's reticence about its legal obligation to provide depository copies of its own electronic products means they are often off-limits to depository libraries, too.

Government Information Locator Service (GILS)

A government-wide, comprehensive information index has been a dream ever since the Commission on Federal Paperwork proposed the idea in 1977. The original Paperwork Reduction Act of 1980 tapped the Office of Management and Budget to pursue this ideal, now envisioned as a Web card catalog of federal information resources. A GILS home page describes the project <http://info.er.usgs.gov/gils/index.html>. After Congress and OMB directed all agencies to create public GILS records describing their information holdings, GILS became not one giant database, but a means of searching numerous agency information servers for decentralized agency collections. The most global incarnation of GILS is the GPO Access GILS site, which points to agency records and Privacy Act systems and to other federal GILS sites <http://www.access.gpo.gov/su_docs/gils/gils.html>. The GPO Access GILS site speaks our language, often noting SuDocs stem and FDLP information, with links to MOCAT and agency home pages. In truth, the blossoming of federal sites on the Web has probably made GILS passe. In their evaluation of GILS, Moen and McClure insinuated as much, concluding that GILS has splintered into a conglomeration of disparate agency systems, and recommending that GILS be refocused and reengineered.[3]

Internet Tip

Official federal government Web sites have .gov or .mil (military) domain names.

Information is the currency of democracy.
—Thomas Jefferson

Governments have been part of civilization since pre-historic times, originally recording their activities on stone, animal skins, parchment, and clay tablets; later on paper, microforms, floppy disks; and more recently on CD-ROMs and the Internet. Some people enjoy characterizing government information production as frivolous and whimsical, an example of the randomness of the universe. But government information actually reflects agency missions: the statutory authority establishing a government agency also dictates its purpose and role. Information is generated as part of the daily business of government, to fulfill agency missions, and to serve the public. While some government information is targeted at the general public, much is issued to record actions or deliberations, to meet legal requirements, or to fulfill administrative needs. National, state, and local governments all publish records of their activities, with the U.S. government holding the distinction of being the world's most prolific publisher.

As deadly as this might sound, government information can be the richest of information sources. Whether you are a student, teacher, historian, librarian, lawyer, doctor, dog groomer, or consumer—you can use government information. Requests handled by the Consumer Information Center (CIC), a source of free and inexpensive government pamphlets, provide a glimpse at its range. The CIC fields requests for pamphlets about housing, health, federal programs, food, travel, hobbies, money management, cars, weight control, and exercise. Agency Web sites and depository libraries abound with free information on these topics and more, not just for research, but for everyday life: child care, nutrition, travel, gardening, business management, and hundreds of other subjects. Alongside these practical booklets await the historical and current records of our government: city maps from the turn of the century, addresses of government agencies, voting records of legislators, regulations on food additives, and transcripts of the Whitewater hearings.

Government Information in Action

Three weeks after connecting to the Internet, an American teenager in Guatemala fingered a bank robber who had lurked for six years on the FBI's Most Wanted List. It was the first time the FBI's Web page had triggered an arrest <http://www.fbi.gov/wanted.htm>. The thief, Leslie I. Rogge, had a record of 25 bank heists, along with convictions for armed robbery, assault, burglary, possession of controlled substances, grand larceny, and fraud. After being sentenced to 20 years in prison, Rogge had escaped a Seattle jail in 1985, leaving a note saying he was going fishing.[4]

GOVERNMENT INFORMATION DEFINED

DOCUMENT: A piece of paper that has been sanctified by a bureaucrat. —Hugh Rawson

[A government publication is] informational matter which is published as an individual document at government expense, or as required by law. —Federal Depository Library Act of 1962

Although the terms "government publication" and "government document" are usually used interchangeably in this country, some nations and intergovernmental organizations distinguish between them. When the distinction is made, "documents" are defined as internal-use-only records (such as minutes of meetings), while "publications" are those available to outsiders (such as informational pamphlets). Government documents and publications are subsets of the broader concept of government information, including not only print and electronic formats but also published and unpublished information and both restricted and publicly available information. In other words, not all government information is available to the public or published. This book focuses on publicly available government information, both published and unpublished (archival collections, for example), in numerous formats.

In 1895, when Congress passed a comprehensive printing act later consolidated into Title 44 of the *U.S. Code*, the sole way to publish was using a printing press to create ink-on-paper documents. Because Title 44 U.S.C. and the Depository Library Act of 1962 predate modern technology, the definitions they promulgate are anachronistic—like trying to fit an automobile with horseshoes. Contemporary publication modes have broadened the reality of "printing" and "publications" to the omnibus notion of government information products and services, shifting emphasis from format to access. Government information is now broadly (but not legally) defined as that created or compiled by government employees, at government expense, or as required by law. Although the terms "document" and "publication" connote a paper format, the proportion of federal information in hardcopy is diminishing while electronic products proliferate. Electronic media have already eclipsed microfiche, relegating it to a diminished role as a records storage and archival medium. And, although it's unlikely that electronic formats will ever supplant paper entirely, economical, efficient carriers like the Internet, CD-ROMs, electronic bulletin boards, online databases, magnetic tape, and floppy disks are gaining swiftly.

In the 1990s government publications are more properly called government information products, to encompass both tangible and electronic titles. "Tangible" products can be held and shelved—paper, CD-ROMs, diskettes, microfiche—while electronic information is "accessed." Tangible products range from flimsy single-sheet fliers to cumbersome boxes, from table-sized maps to CD-ROMs that can be cradled in the palm of a hand. This mix of formats may scatter tangible government information throughout library collections. And some government information products can't be held at all, such as Web pages, databases, and bulletin boards. Without notice or fanfare, tangible products are often supplanted by Internet-only access. Many other files on government Web sites and bulletin boards are never cloned as discrete documents.

Why are these definitions important? Partly because they determine what's available via depository libraries. In practice, the Government Printing Office, which administers the Depository Library Program, defines a depository "publication" as any informational matter produced by or for government for public dissemination, regardless of format. Unfortunately, GPO's liberal interpretation of ambiguous pre-electronic legal language is not always embraced by the issuing agencies creating information products. Many neglect their responsibility to provide their products to GPO for depository distribution, allowing thousands of government-produced materials to slip through loopholes in the depository library net.

THE IMPACT OF NEW TECHNOLOGIES

Who represents the public in a Bottom-line Information Era?
—Wayne P. Kelley,
Superintendent of Documents

Equity of access to government information is the polemic of the electronic age. New technologies, unforeseen when our information laws were drafted, have prompted concern about erosion of access for computer have-nots. Organizations like the American Library Association, the Association of Research Libraries, and the National Commission on Libraries and Information Science have issued policy statements championing public access to government information. The National Commission on Libraries and Information Science, for example, described public information as a "national resource" owned by the people, and expressed concern that "basic principles regarding its creation, use and dissemination are in danger of being neglected and even forgotten."[5]

Although the Office of Management and Budget oversees government information policies, the United States lacks a unified national information policy. As the only major industrialized nation without such a blueprint, the U.S. trails behind Japan, France, Brazil, and Canada. Instead, the U.S. operates under what has been called a "de facto national information policy," a legal composite emanating from a potpourri of regulations,

judicial opinions, circulars, budget priorities, bureaucratic decisions, congressional oversight, and laws. (Between 1970 and 1990 alone more than 300 information laws were enacted.) Several key laws reign over this national information policy mosaic: the Printing Act of 1895, the Depository Library Act of 1962, the Freedom of Information and Privacy Acts, Copyright Act, OMB Circular A-130, and the Paperwork Reduction Act of 1995.

Hi Ho, Government Information

They've been called the closest thing we have to sacred cows: wild horses and burros with the law on their side. Because the Wild Horse and Burro Act of 1971 halted the backwoods practice of shooting feral equines for dog food, some 36,000 horses and 8,000 burros flourish under government guardianship in 10 western states. Title 43, Part 4700 of the *Code of Federal Regulations* forbids eating, killing, saddling, riding, or even irritating one without risking the government's wrath.[6] To prune the patronized herds their steward, the Bureau of Land Management (BLM), operates the Adopt-A-Horse-or-Burro Program. Anyone meeting rigorous character and housing standards can drive away with a horse for $125 or a $75 burro. For information, contact BLM at <http://www.blm.gov/whb/> or consult *So You'd Like to Adopt: America's Wild Horses and Burros* (I 53.2:H 78/15) and *Adopt a Living Legend—A Caretaker's Guide* (I 53.7/2:L 52) in a depository library.

BIBLIOGRAPHIC CONTROL

Unfortunately, no one—not the GPO, the JCP, nor the OMB—can make more than an educated guess as to how many information products are issued annually by the federal government.
—David Brown, GPO

The quest for government information requires two steps: first, verifying its existence, sometimes called "intellectual access," and then obtaining it, or "physical access." This quest is symbolized by two questions: what information has the government generated, and where can I find it? Bibliographic control involves creating records of items so they may be identified and accessed, fostering both intellectual and physical access. Bibliographic control of government information involves a parallel universe that only sporadically overlaps with that of traditional bibliographic control. Bibliographic access tools for government publications include specialized Internet search engines, government and commercially published catalogs and indexes, and databases such as WorldCat (the Online Computer Library Center's [OCLC] Online Union Catalog), the world's largest database of library bibliographic information.

Government information that eludes bibliographic documentation hovers in an informational black hole, untraceable because it lacks a bibliographic record. Legions of other government titles enjoy intellectual access, but their physical access is thwarted. This situation occurs when a title is listed in the *Monthly Catalog*, for example, but is not distributed to depository libraries.

In local collections, online catalogs have allowed nine out of every 10 depositories to "mainstream" documents by listing government titles in the library's online catalog. However, both library users and librarians should be alerted that some libraries still own more documents than are represented in their public catalogs. Others catalog some, but not all. Ideally, librarians who understand documents cataloging gaps will intercede for hapless users, yet some librarians do not realize the limitations of their own library catalogs. Hernon and McClure found that library staff rebounded from fruitless author or title card catalog searches by incorrectly assuming their library did not own the requested document.[7] The fact that this misconception occurred even in libraries that rarely cataloged documents underscores the need for library staff to acquaint themselves with the idiosyncrasies of their own library's documents policies.

Falling through the Cracks: The "Non's"

We can lick gravity, but sometimes the paperwork is overwhelming.　　—Wernher von Braun

Nondepository publications are those not earmarked to be sent to federal depository libraries. Non-GPO publications are those not produced under the auspices of the GPO. Because both nondepository and non-GPO materials exist, neither GPO nor depository libraries provide access to all federal government information.

Since non-GPO publications do not grind through the GPO machinery, they are often missed by GPO's bibliographic net of catalogs and Internet crawlers. Although agencies are required to supply copies of non-GPO publications for depository distribution and *Monthly Catalog* documentation, noncompliance is common. As many as half of all tangible government information products elude the depository system. Such lost publications are sometimes called "fugitive" documents. One Department of Health and Human Services official estimated that 80 percent of HHS publications, including many grant-related technical reports, never passed through the GPO system. This situation is typical of sci/tech literature, much of which is not funneled through GPO nor furnished by the issuing agency for depository distribution. It will be available from NTIS, but at a cost. Not only will these information products fail to appear on depository library shelves, they often will not be listed in any of GPO's bibliographic control tools. To find out if they exist and to get copies to read,

one must go through different channels—for instance, NTIS.

Not funneled through GPO, not announced, and not listed in mainstream government publication catalogs, indexes, or databases, fugitive publications are available only to those who know to ask for them. They include products considered of limited interest, such as those of the National Cancer Institute, those printed in-house by agencies or produced by contractors or grantees, limited distribution titles such as Congressional Research Service reports, and many promotional brochures, leaflets, and press releases. Thousands of fugitive publications slip through the bibliographic net each year, many because they were not printed through GPO, others because they were never "printed" at all—electronic dispatches that evade GPO's machinery.

THE QUEST

If you think education is expensive, try ignorance.
　　—Derek Bok, Harvard University President

If you are unfamiliar with government resources, you are handicapping yourself in the race for information. From contemporary accounts of the Titanic disaster to the latest cancer research, government information products spin a historical and up-to-the-minute record of our nation that cannot be surpassed. Government reports on the proverbial UFO crash near Roswell, New Mexico, in 1947 are a good example. First, a 1995 General Accounting Office (GAO) investigation uncovered no hidden government records (GAO/NSIAD-95-187). Next, the Air Force published *The Roswell Report: Fact Versus Fiction in the New Mexico Desert*, hypothesizing that debris found was from Project MOGUL, a secret spy-balloon operation (D 301.82/7:R 73). Finally, *The Roswell Report: Case Closed*, greeted by true believers with a collective harrumph, explained away stories of four-fingered bodies at the crash site (D 301.2:R 73). All were preceded, of course, by Project Blue Book, long open to researchers at the National Archives. While the average American was satisfied reading two-column newspaper synopses or watching three-minute accounts on the evening news, few realized that the reports themselves can be checked out from many government depository libraries as easily as a library book. Or knew that the full text of the GAO report is available free on GAO's Web site. Or understood why diehard UFO researchers regularly visit the Truman and Eisenhower presidential libraries to dig for clues.[8]

Although the United States enjoys an openness of information unparalleled anywhere in the world, few citizens exercise it. The nation monitors its government through newspaper front pages and television screens, rather than through the elaborate system of libraries and laws set up to guarantee our right to the truth, if only we will dig for it. The public lets the "professionals" do that for them: the scholars, reporters, consumer advocates, and special-interest groups for whom tracking down facts is all in a day's work. But, as happens with gossip, when information is filtered through second and third parties, it risks simplification and distortion. By depending on others to interpret our nation's daily activities, we risk information helplessness and dependency. We as a society have a freedom that threatens to atrophy if not exercised. Tracking down government information requires a sophisticated literacy that transcends the basic skills of reading and writing. Government information literacy, the ability to find and use government information for research and daily life, is the portal to a treasure trove of research material.

Don't feel guilty if you haven't joined the ranks of the government-information literate. The quest for government information can make even seasoned library users and senior librarians cringe like vampires recoiling from sunlight. Why? Much user reluctance can be chalked up to a sketchy awareness that government information products are "different," coupled with a lack of practice in using them. Ranging from light, informative pamphlets to ponderous treatises, government information products are produced in familiar formats: Web pages, books, journals, pamphlets, indexes and abstracts, reference tomes, databases, and audiovisuals. They do share two key distinctions, however: they emanate from government agencies rather than commercial publishers, and traditional library and Internet skills do not always retrieve them. The apparatus of government information is specialized, but not difficult. The biggest danger is overlooking it altogether.

Hot Buttons		
Search For	In Source	Scope
Government publications in any format	*Monthly Catalog* http://www.access.gpo.gov/su_docs/	Since January 1994
GPO prices	SPC http://www.access.gpo.gov/su_docs/sale/prf/prf.html	Current
Internet publications	GPO Access, Browse Electronic Titles http://www.access.gpo.gov/su_docs/dpos/btitles.html	New Internet titles
Agency Web pages	GPO Access, Federal Agency Internet Sites http://www.access.gpo.gov/su_docs/dpos/agencies.html	A FedWeb directory
Legislation	THOMAS http://thomas.loc.gov/ GPO Access http://www.access.gpo.gov/su_docs/ House Internet Law Library http://law.house.gov/	Full text *Congressional Record*, history of bills and Public Laws
House or Senate Reports	THOMAS http://thomas.loc.gov/	Since 1995, 104–1
Congressional Record	THOMAS http://thomas.loc.gov/ GPO Access http://www.access.gpo.gov/su_docs/	Since 1991, 102–1 Since 1995, 104–1
U.S. Code	House Internet Law Library http://law.house.gov/ GPO Access http://www.access.gpo.gov/su_docs/	All 50 titles are being digitized
Supreme Court	Federal Bulletin Board http://fedbbs.access.gpo.gov/court01.htm	Decisions since early 1990s; also U. S. Court of Appeals for D.C.
Supreme Court decisions, retrospective	http://www.access.gpo.gov/su_docs/ http://supct.law.cornell.edu/supct/index.html http://www.fedworld.gov/supcourt/index.htm	1937–1975
Regulations	*Federal Register* http://www.access.gpo.gov/nara/index.html CFR http://www.access.gpo.gov/nara/cfr	Since 1995 (Volume 60) Latest edition

Hot Buttons *(continued)*		
Search For	In Source	Scope
Patents	PTO Web site http://www.uspto.gov/	Since 1976
Presidential Proclamations	*Federal Register* http://www.access.gpo.gov/nara/index.html	Since 1995
Presidential Executive Orders	*Federal Register* http://www.access.gpo.gov/nara/index.html	Since 1995
U.S. Budget	http://www.access.gpo.gov/su_docs/budget/index.html	Current

Getting Started: Government Locators		
Search For	In Source	URL
Subjects	GPO Access "Browse Topics" using Subject Bibliography terms to link to Internet sites	http://www.access.gpo.gov/su_docs/dpos/pathbrws.html
Documents in the news	GPO Access "Hot Topics"	http://www.access.gpo.gov/su_docs/dpos/pathbrws.html
Federal Web pages: by keyword	GPO Access "Pathway Indexer" (more detailed than Browse Topics)	http://www.access.gpo.gov/su_docs/dpos/searche.html
	Villanova Center for Information Law and Policy, Federal Web Locator	http://www.law.vill.edu/Fed-Agency/fedwebloc.html
	GovBot	http://cobar.cs.umass.edu/ciirdemo/Govbot/
Federal Web pages: by agency name	GPO Access "Federal Agency Internet Sites"	http://www.access.gpo.gov/su_docs/dpos/agencies.html
	Villanova Center for Information Law and Policy, Federal Web Locator	http://www.law.vill.edu/Fed-Agency/fedwebloc.html
	Yahoo's Government Information Metasite	http://www.yahoo.com/Government
Federal, state, local, and foreign governments	Library of Congress, "Explore the Internet. Browse Government Resources"	http://lcweb.loc.gov/global/explore.html
New electronic titles; online-only titles	GPO Access "Browse Electronic Titles"	http://www.access.gpo.gov/su_docs/dpos/btitles.html
Read or download agency products	Federal Bulletin Board (FBB)	http://fedbbs.access.gpo.gov/
Agency information products	GILS	http://www.access.gpo.gov/su_docs/gils/gils.html
Consumer health information	Healthfinder	http://www.healthfinder.gov
Statistics	FEDSTATS	http://www.fedstats.gov

FREEBIES

The following Subject Bibliographies are available free from: Stop: SSOP, Washington, DC 20402; U.S. Fax Watch: (202) 512-1716:

> 141. Federal Government
> <http://www.access.gpo.gov/su_docs/sale/sb-141.html>

FURTHER READING

"Best Feds on the Web." *Government Executive: The Independent Business Magazine of Government* <http://www.govexec.com/virtual/bestgov.htm> (May 13, 1998).

> Select the "Virtual Government" button to access this annotated list of best federal Web sites.

Congressional Quarterly, Inc. *CQ Guide to Current American Government*. Washington, DC: Congressional Quarterly, Inc. Semiannual.

> Clearly written overviews of the three branches of government.

Eschenfelder, Kristen R., John C. Beachboard, Charles R. McClure, and Steven K. Wyman. "Assessing U.S. Federal Government Websites." *Government Information Quarterly*. 14 (April 1997): 173–89.

> A critique of federal Web sites from the policy vantage point.

Herman, Edward. *Locating United States Government Information: A Guide to Sources*. 2nd ed. Buffalo, NY: William S. Hein & Co., 1997.

> A "how-to" guide to finding and using government publications.

Hernon, Peter, Charles R. McClure, and Harold C. Relyea. *Federal Information Policies in the 1990s: Views and Perspectives*. Norwood, NJ: Ablex Publishing Corp., 1996.

> Developments and challenges in government information policy in the electronic age.

McClure, Charles R. "Libraries and Federal Information Policy." *Journal of Academic Librarianship* 22 (May 1996): 214–18.

> The impact of the mosaic of national information policies on libraries and public access.

McLoone, Tracy, ed. *The Federal Internet Source*. Washington, DC: National Journal, 1994–. Semiannual.

> A tipsheet on federal, state, and political Web sites.

Maxwell, Bruce. *How to Access the Federal Government on the Internet*. Washington, DC: Congressional Quarterly Books, 1996.

> A guide to the best government sites.

————. *How to Access the Government's Electronic Bulletin Boards*. Washington, DC: Congressional Quarterly Books, 1997– .

> Descriptions of nearly 200 BBSs operated by federal agencies, departments, and courts.

————. "Internet Mailing Lists Help Track the Federal Government." *Database* 19 (October 20, 1996): 57–60.

> E-mail subscriptions trigger automatic receipt of notices, advisories, and other agency documents.

Notess, Greg R. *Government Information on the Internet*. Lanham, MD: Bernan Press, 1997.

> One of the best topical directories of government Web sites.

Wetterau, Bruce. *Congressional Quarterly's Desk Reference on American Government*. Washington, DC: Congressional Quarterly, 1995.

> Q&A format provides information about the three federal government branches, elections, the Constitution, and more.

NOTES

1. General Accounting Office. *Internet and Electronic Dial-Up Bulletin Boards: Information Reported by Federal Organizations*. (GGD-97-86). GAO, 1997.

2. The Paperwork Reduction Act of 1980 (P.L. 96–511) was reauthorized in 1995 (P.L. 104–13).

3. William E. Moen and Charles R. McClure. *An Evaluation of the Federal Government's Implementation of the Government Information Locator Service (GILS): Final Report*. GPO, 1997. (GS 1.2: L 78/2 or <http://www.unt.edu/slis/research/gilseval/gilsdocs.htm> [September 30, 1997]).

4. Shelton, Denise. "Fugitive Caught Through FBI Web Site." CNET News.Com <http://www.news.com/News/Item/0.4.1632.00.html> (October 1, 1997).

5. "Principles of Public Information" adopted by the U.S. National Commission on Libraries and Information Science, June 29, 1990. <http://www.nclis.gov/information/pripubin.html> (September 15, 1997).

6. Guy Gugliotta. "Nation's Wild Horses Feeling Their Oats." *The Washington Post* (August 30, 1994): A19.

7. Peter Hernon and Charles McClure, "Unobtrusive Reference Testing: The 55 Percent Rule," *Library Journal* 111 (April 15, 1986): 40.

8. What's the connection between UFOs and the Truman and Eisenhower presidential libraries? Nothing, say the archivists who work there. But Harry S Truman was president in 1947, when the proverbial UFO crashed near Roswell, New Mexico, and Eisenhower followed in 1954: Brian Burnes. "UFO Research Seeks That Official Touch: Presidential Libraries Hold Little That Believers or Debunkers Can Use." *Kansas City Star* (December 30, 1996): A-8 (The Star/Library/Search <http://www.kcstar.com/> [July 17, 1997]).

CHAPTER 2
Access to Government Information

A FREE AND OPEN SOCIETY

To secure these rights, Governments are instituted among Men, deriving their just powers from the consent of the governed.
—The Declaration of Independence

Access to government information is truly essential to the American way of life, which relies upon its citizens to make informed public decisions. The free flow of information between government and the public has been called "the mortar of our society."[1] Libraries, especially depositories, which archive government information in every state of the union, provide a vital link between citizens and their government.

A popular Government without popular information, or the means of acquiring it, is but as Prologue to a Farce or a Tragedy; or perhaps both. Knowledge will forever govern ignorance: And a people who mean to be their own Governors, must arm themselves with the power which knowledge gives.
—James Madison

The doctrine of government accountability to citizens emerged during our nation's infancy, but not without controversy. The colonies' closed legislative proceedings and the secrecy surrounding the constitutional convention incited public criticism. Opening congressional proceedings to the public was debated during the Continental Congress, but the Senate continued to meet in secret sessions until 1795, when the public galleries were opened to reporters. Until the early 1800s, newspaper articles were the public's only means of monitoring congressional activities.

Arguing for the public's right to an impartial record of government activities, proponents of the people's right to know eventually triumphed. Citizen access to government information was seen as a way to ensure government accountability and informed citizen decision making. The Government Printing Office and the depository library system were created in the late 1880s,

charged with printing and archiving government records. Government publishing was nurtured by a law exempting government publications from copyright restrictions.

The first federal publications documented official activities with a sober stream of laws, treaties, court rulings, and congressional proceedings. Later, as agencies plunged into their missions, popular and informational publications began to roll off the presses: reports of geological surveys, first-person accounts of the opening of the West, "how-to" guides for farmers, and navigational aids among others.

THE FREE FLOW OF INFORMATION

We tend to take our open government for granted until we compare it with more repressive societies. Many nations enjoy no Freedom of Information Act (FOIA) equivalent and automatically classify all government-funded research. In Russia, for example, the 1993 constitution guarantees information access, but there is no freedom of information law to ensure the eventual release of classified information. To awaken Russians to democratic values, activists distribute translated copies of the American Civil Liberties Union pamphlet, "Your Right to Government Information."

After decades of secrecy, Russian *glasnost*, or "openness," prompted the release of files about the execution of the Tsar and his family during the Revolution, the 1983 downing of a South Korean airline, and the Korean War. Boris Yeltsin opened the Russian State Archives, where fragments of Adolf Hitler's skull— stored in a cardboard box since 1945—were finally displayed, and a cooperative exhibit was launched with the Library of Congress at <http://lcweb.loc.gov/exhibits/archives/intro.html>.

China, one of the most secretive governments in the world, constricts access to "cultural rubbish," which includes information about human rights, democracy,

Taiwan's independence, and the occupation of Tibet. The Chinese government monitors Internet access and suppresses discussion lists that carp about the government. Internet providers must sign pledges not to "harm the nation," Internet users must register with the police, and in some areas, e-mail must be printed and reviewed by authorities. The grip on information includes banning satellite TV dishes and squelching foreign newspapers writing about dissidents or other sensitive topics.

In Burma, owning or using a modem or fax machine without government permission is punishable by up to 15 years in jail. Similar sanctions await any unauthorized Burmans who link to computer networks.

Great Britain has long been known as the world's most secretive democracy. Their Official Secrets Act routinely classifies even innocuous government information for at least three decades, and files on the Royal Family are traditionally sealed for a century. Such secrecy forced British scholars to research the 1956 Suez Crisis in America — their own country's records about Egyptian nationalization of the British/French-owned Suez Canal were sealed. Only in the late 1980s was the Official Secrets Act relaxed, opening nonsensitive internal records. And the UK's new Open Government Initiative administrative code allows citizens to request government records and to appeal denials. While it lacks the clout of a law, it's hailed as a big step toward open government.[2]

> *Those who expect to reap the blessing of freedom, must, like men, undergo the fatigue of supporting it.* —Thomas Paine

In sharp contrast to these countries is the United States, where libraries and the Internet expedite access to publicly available, unclassified information. In the 1980s, the "Decade of the Spy," the FBI estimated that 90 percent of Soviet intelligence about the U.S. was gathered from open, public sources. During the Cold War, a favorite KGB hangout was the Library of Congress, offering free use of unclassified reports and technical publications, comfortable seating, and modern rest rooms. KGB agents openly attended congressional hearings, educational seminars, and trade shows, devouring openly accessible public information. In an interesting sidelight, FBI employee Earl Edwin Pitts, arrested in 1996 for selling secrets to the Russians, had his first meeting with his Soviet contact at the New York Public Library.

A new breed of open-source spying evolved in the 1990s—industrial and economic espionage. These industrial "spies" used government information, such as Securities and Exchange Commission filings by companies, conferences, news reports, database searches, and government and defense-contractor bulletin boards and Web sites to glean information about competing companies. FBI Director Louis Freeh testified before the Senate Intelligence Committee that America has never faced a greater security threat. "Anyone with a computer and a modem can become a potential terrorist," reading documents on the Internet, stealing copyrighted material, spying, or hacking into computers. To identify and counter foreign intelligence threats, a National Counterintelligence Center was inaugurated at <http://www.nacic.gov/>.

People have two typical reactions to exploitation of our open society. Proponents of limited government information access argue that our government should not be "the world's largest free library-reference service."[3] Others contend that although abuses are distasteful, it would be equally distasteful for our democratic principles to be compromised. As columnist Kenneth C. Bass explained, "When it comes to spies, Americans hate the disease. But we hate the cure as well."[4]

Government Information in Action

On December 17, 1969, the Secretary of the Air Force announced the termination of Project Blue Book, which chronicled official investigations of unidentified flying objects. Of the 12,618 UFO sightings investigated between 1947 and 1969, 700 remained "unexplained," but not considered extraterrestrial. Project Blue Book is open to researchers at the National Archives, or by buying copies of the microfilm rolls of sighting reports and photographs for about $23 each.

THE COST OF FREE INFORMATION

> *The core principle is that the public has paid for the collection, compilation, and publication of Federal information—and should have access to it without further cost.* —Wayne P. Kelley, Superintendent of Documents

The proper balance between cost-effectiveness and citizen access to government information has been debated for decades. A writer in 1895 complained that junk shops were stacked with tons of public documents waiting to be ground into scrap while the Capitol's vaults were heaped with unused books and documents. At the turn of the century, the Superintendent of Documents contended that an abundance of documents made the public think of them as cheap and contemptible. He characterized the problem as "chronic document indigestion."

Almost a century later, the battle continues between government cost cutters and right-to-know advocates. Recommendations of the 1977 Commission on Federal Paperwork were incarnated in the Paperwork Reduction Act (PRA), which sought to reduce the public's burden of reporting to government, and tapped the Office of Management and Budget to oversee government information policies.[5] OMB's Circular A-130, "Management of Federal Information Resources," is a policy statement outlining a framework for executive agencies to carry out PRA requirements and can be found at <http://www.whitehouse.gov/WH/EOP/OMB/html/circular.html>.[6]

Unfortunately, attempts to defray publication costs have resulted in a blossoming of electronic-format-only government information, a flurry of government/private company dissemination contracts, a system of user fees, and a relinquishing of government publication to private publishers ("privatization"). Critics caution that while these actions appear to save taxpayers money, by restricting free information access, they also create other, incalculable, costs.

Federal information paid for by taxpayers has traditionally basked, copyright-free, in the public domain. Recently, several contractual agreements have abridged access by restricting distribution or granting copyright or "copyright-like" controls to commercial intermediaries. The Census Bureau's *Hispanic Population of the United States: March 1994*, traditionally a depository item in the P-20 series, was published under a different title and priced at $15 by a trade association. Although the Census Bureau provided the staff, data, and research assistance, the trade association now holds the copyright to the publication. When a cooperative agreement between the National Cancer Institute and Oxford University Press lobbed the *Journal of the National Cancer Institute* out of the depository system and into the private sector, it took intervention from the Joint Committee on Printing to elicit a promise that the National Cancer Institute would provide depository copies.

Wayne P. Kelley, Superintendent of Documents, has cited these "dangerous new precedents" as threats to basic precepts of public access. Privatization allows government publications to slip from the taxpayer's grasp by withdrawing them from the depository arena. This trend triple-charges taxpayers, who pay government employees to create a product only to face an inflated price to buy a copy, after being stripped of free access in depository libraries. Those who can't afford to pay are blocked from perusing government information.

NEW TECHNOLOGIES

Access is also impacted by changes in depository document formats. The shift from paper to microfiche that began in the late 1970s saved money, but scattered collections and bred user inconvenience and confusion. The 1980s witnessed a surge of electronic information, with a concomitant decline in printed publications. The newest challenge to public access is solely-electronic government information, with no paper counterpart. Federal agencies are opting to save money and time by disseminating information electronically through the Internet, databases, floppy disks, CD-ROMs, and online bulletin boards. Many of these communiques are never cloned as discrete documents and become "fugitives" from the Depository Library Program. Charts, graphs, tables, notices, and announcements are especially vulnerable to solely electronic incarnations. Although these files have historic value, they tend to be periodically purged from Web sites to recover computer memory.

FEDERAL AMNESIA

> *With the use of paper, the development of policies was simple to trace. Successive drafts indicated the evolution of decisions. With computers, though, drafts no longer exist. Instead, policy papers evolve and each new version is written over the previous one.*
> —Patricia Aronsson, National Archives and Records Administration (NARA)

Although electronic technologies allow faster, cheaper, and more efficient information handling, they also threaten historical documentation. Because electronic records can be ephemeral, the danger of losing the nation's "memory" greatly troubles historians, archivists, and researchers. The Congressional Research Service predicts that by the year 2000, three-quarters of federal government transactions will be handled electronically. Electronic records are vulnerable because of their fragility, rapid obsolescence, and ease of erasure or alteration, coupled with government employees' lack of "historical awareness" and low priority for records management. Electronic recordkeeping could extinguish historical documentation by erasing electronic policy and decision-making records, first drafts, marginal notes, and attachments. Some observers rank the danger of information loss as more grave than that of deteriorating acid-paper in books. Fearing "federal amnesia," they have urged that solutions be found "if our history is not to stop short in the 1980's."[7]

CLASSIFIED DOCUMENTS

> *Secrecy is a form of government regulation.*
> —Senator Daniel Patrick Moynihan

The national security classification system hearkens back to an executive order issued by President Truman in 1951. Since then, additional presidential executive orders have modified the formal secrecy standards used by the executive branch. The result has been a pervasive, nonstatutory national security apparatus sequestering information at a cost of more than five billion dollars annually. With several million new documents stamped "secret" each year, Congress has begun reexamining the foundations of the nation's secrecy system. A congressional Commission on Protecting and Reducing Government Secrecy reviewed the entire classification system, recommending laws to establish broad classification/declassification standards, a government declassification hub within the National Archives, training for classifying officials, and the creation of a single executive agency to coordinate classification policies. The commission's report can be viewed at <http://www.fas.org/sgp/library/moynihan/index.html>. Meanwhile, President Clinton's April 17, 1995, Executive Order 12958 launched the least restrictive classification standards since the Cold War, reducing the number of people authorized to classify, shortening the duration of classification, and ordering massive declassification of millions of World War II-era documents and secrets more than 25 years old.

To comply, agencies declassified some 200 million records in 1996 alone—more than in the previous 12 years combined (while simultaneously classifying almost 6 million records anew). Declassification champs included the National Archives, Department of Defense, U.S. Information Agency, and the State, Commerce, and Energy departments. Security-classified records are a significant part of NARA holdings, and NARA is already home base for the Information Security Oversight Office, which oversees the security classification programs in both government and industry, reporting to the president annually on their status.

Index to Declassified Documents

The Declassified Documents Reference System Abstracts and Index (from Primary Source Media) lists declassified documents released by government agencies or obtained from the National Archives and presidential libraries, plus materials declassified under the Freedom of Information Act. The index and abstract are available in print, on CD-ROM, and online, with a companion microfiche collection containing the full text of the declassified documents. Since titles are indexed after they are declassified, issue dates and indexing dates do not correspond.

PUBLIC ACCESS LEGISLATION

> *Secrecy is the bane of democracy because it is the enemy of accountability.*
> —Arthur Schlesinger Jr., historian

The Freedom of Information and Privacy Acts are key means of public access to federal government records. The Freedom of Information Act (FOIA) opens agency administrative files to the public, while the Privacy Act safeguards personal information amassed by government. Both laws are founded on the principle of the people's right to know what their government is doing.

The Freedom of Information Act

Originally enacted on Independence Day, 1966, after 11 years of congressional debate, FOIA (pronounced "foy-ah") provided a formal procedure for requesting access to federal executive agency records. The law was toughened in 1974, making it easier, quicker, and cheaper to get information from federal agency files. The amendments gave agencies 10 days to acknowledge requests, set reasonable photocopying charges, allowed for appealing denied access, and facilitated tracking down information by requiring indexes to be printed in the *Federal Register*. Three decades after FOIA's original passage, the Electronic Freedom of Information Act Amendments of 1996 (Public Law 104-231), broadened FOIA beyond filing cabinets to agency records in any format, including electronic. E-FOIA (pronounced "E-foyah") mandates that agencies honor petitions for electronic information, improve recordkeeping, and use electronic media, such as the Internet, to increase access. It also lengthened the agency's time limit for acknowledging requests from 10 to 20 days. The Freedom of Information Clearinghouse provides details about the E-FOIA amendments and can be accessed at <http://www.citizen.org/public_citizen/litigation/foic/foic.html>

Tip

FOIA focuses on active records still in agency files. Many historical records have been transferred to the National Archives, where they may be accessed without invoking FOIA.

Who Uses FOIA?

Businesses, journalists, consumer groups, and citizens all use FOIA. Ralph Nader's successful campaign against the carcinogenic Red Dye No. 2 was bolstered by documents acquired under FOIA. The sons of executed spies Julius and Ethel Rosenberg made dozens of FOIA requests in their quest to clear their parents' names. FOIA requests led to disclosure of the My Lai massacre, opened Oliver North's notebooks and the government's Supreme Court briefing on the "Pentagon Papers," and uncovered files on such diverse subjects as unsafe nuclear reactors, contaminated drinking water, CIA mind experiments, $600 military coffeepots, ineffective drugs, and hazardous television sets.

The Freedom of Information Act has been called "the bread and butter of investigative journalism," yet a 1989 survey by the Society of Professional Journalists uncovered widespread frustration over denials and delays that stalled some requests for years. More chilling was the admission by government officials that a silent FOIA backlash has likely left some agency actions undocumented and bred "electronic shredding" of sensitive material to avoid FOIA disclosure.[8]

In 1993, President Clinton addressed a memo to departmental and agency chiefs urging them to renew their commitment to FOIA and to trim bureaucratic hurdles for "customer-friendly" handling of requests. Clinton's appeal was bolstered by a policy memorandum from Attorney General Janet Reno suggesting that agency FOIA compliance be in both the letter and spirit of the law and encouraging agencies to make disclosure the rule.

Limitations of FOIA

The Freedom of Information Act unlocks only federal executive agency files: Congress, the judiciary, and state and local agencies are not covered by the law. Many states and localities have passed their own freedom of information laws, however. The Freedom of Information Act pertains to agency files, not to published documents. Access to published documents is through depository libraries, the Government Printing Office, and other sources described in this text.

The Privacy Act

At no time in the past has our government known so much about so many of its individual citizens. Government bureaucracies seem to thrive on collecting additional information. That information is now stored in over 7,000 government computers, and the names of over 150 million Americans are now in computer banks scattered across the country. In short, data banks affect nearly every man, woman, and child in the United States today. —Richard M. Nixon, 1974

The seeds of our "dossier society" were sown with those of government taxation and social welfare programs, making massive recordkeeping a necessity for bureaucratic accountability.[9] Computers revolutionized federal recordkeeping, making it possible for more agencies to keep tabs on "far more people at far less cost than ever was possible in the age of the manual file and the wizened file clerk."[10] More than three decades ago, Vance Packard was among those sounding an alarm about the government's "giant memory machines." In his 1964 book, *The Naked Society,* Packard wondered what the impact of computerized recordkeeping would be in 1984, two decades hence: "If information is power, Americans should be uneasy about the amount of information the federal government is starting to file on its citizens in its blinking memory banks."

Today the federal government is our nation's biggest recordkeeper. Uncle Sam maintains some 3 billion files on individuals—an estimated 12 files per person. Most government agencies collect personal information in the course of their duties, from names and social se-

curity numbers to data on personal finances, health, and occupation. Uncle Sam maintains computer systems of personal information, packed with details gathered from the subjects themselves; from federal, state, and local governments; and from third parties such as state motor vehicle departments, credit bureaus, and insurance companies.

For the fish swimming in the ocean, the comprehension of wetness is impossible. Wet requires the contrast of dry. In the same way, it is hard for most Americans to appreciate the intricate layering of computerized networks that have been built up around each of our lives during the last 25 years. Abrupt violent changes, like the revolution in Iran, are easy to see. Incremental changes, stretching over decades, are harder to perceive. —David Burnham, *The Rise of the Computer State*

Congressional concern about increased computer recordkeeping led to the passage of the Privacy Act in 1974, requiring agencies to keep their records about individuals accurate, confidential, and within legal restrictions. The act allows citizens to find out what federal files are being kept about them, to see the files, and to correct them. But, conceived when most federal records were stashed in filing cabinets, the Privacy Act has stumbled into the electronic era bereft of clauses specifying access to computerized files. Computers have unsnarled monitoring and correcting personal files, and expedited interagency exchange of personal data. Until the Privacy Act is modernized, requesters remain dependent on agency and judicial expansiveness in interpreting the spirit of the law.

Threats to personal privacy have been a hot issue throughout the 1990s. A de facto national database knitted from individual government files contains information on most Americans and is searchable using a de facto electronic I.D., your social security number.[11] In 1997, the American Civil Liberties Union launched its Take Back Your Data campaign to draw attention to unsecured personal information and new threats to privacy, and its Web site can be found at <http://www.aclu.org/action/tbyd.html>. Concern about a computerized Big Brother may be reflected in anti-census sentiments springing up across the globe. Response to the 1990 U.S. census was sluggish, and Holland hasn't had a census since 1971. West Germans boycotted their census for 17 years, partly from fear of government misuse of the computerized data. It didn't help that the Interior Minister announced a plan to issue each West German an identity card and a computer file. This prompted fears that detailed personal data would be transmitted to tax authorities, police, or other punitive government agencies.

Government Files on You

When you fill out a student loan application, detail your finances to the IRS, register for the draft, or even rent a post office box, personal information is recorded about you. This information can be exchanged or used as the law allows. This is true not just for criminals, but for average, honest citizens. How might the average, honest citizen show up in CIA files, for example? Easily, on CIA lists such as:

- Authors of articles or books on intelligence (spying)
- Attorneys in private practice
- CIA employees with parking permits
- People writing to ask if the CIA has files on them (This catch-22 is also true for the FBI, which automatically creates a "record" about anyone asking whether she or he is in FBI files.)

Even the postal service keeps files, at least 75 of them, including:

- People who have had their mail forwarded
- Members of carpools with postal service employees
- People who ask not to receive sexually oriented ads in the mail

Using the Privacy Act

The Privacy Act allows you to know what government agency records are being kept about you; to read, correct, or append corrections to them; and to prevent their use for other than original purposes without your permission.

Federal Files You May Be In	
Agency	File
Education	Student aid applicants
IRS	Income tax filers
Social Security	Social security number holders
State Department	Passport holders
Transportation	Motorboat registrants
Veterans Affairs	Blood donors

If this list piques your interest, you can read about thousands of other agency files kept about individuals in *Privacy Act Issuances Compilation*, available at <http://www.access.gpo.gov/su_docs/aces/PrivacyAct.shtml>. This hefty biennial (knee-high in five volumes in its former hardcopy days) describes files, agency rules for requesting information, and how the records are used. The GPO Access GILS site points to agency privacy act systems and can be viewed at <http://www.access.gpo.gov/su_docs/gils/gils.html>.

The Laws in Action

The cost of the Freedom of Information Act is the cost of carrying out a democratic government.
—Katherine A. Meyer, Director of the Freedom of Information Clearinghouse

Government agencies process some 600,000 FOIA requests yearly, at a cost of about $500 each. Government-wide FOIA processing costs are around $50 to $60 million annually, largely to pay the salaries of staff who review records to delete exempted information.

Agencies like the FBI, CIA, and FDA have been deluged with FOIA requests. Receiving about one FOIA request a minute, the FBI has a backlog of more than 15,000 requests, resulting in a wait of up to four years. The Food and Drug Administration devoted the equivalent of 130 staff years to compliance in 1996 alone. The State Department averages 11 months to handle a FOIA request; the Department of Energy, five years. Along with legitimate applications, plenty of kooky ones clog the pipeline: Elvis Presley and UFOs are favorites.

Using the Laws

Use of the Privacy Act to access personal files has been less than anticipated, in part due to public ignorance of Privacy Act rights, difficulty identifying records, and the time and cost of communicating with agencies. (It has been estimated that seeing all your files would mean writing 5,800 separate letters and spending more than $1,856 on postage.) Since no central clearinghouse is in place to handle all requests, each must be sent to an individual agency holding files. The children of Julius and Ethel Rosenberg, for example, filed FOIA requests with more than 18 agencies as part of their quest to clear their parents' names. Terry Anderson's quest for details about his 6½ years as a hostage in Lebanon led to more than 50 FOIA requests to 11 agencies.

You must do your homework to file a FOIA or Privacy Act request. Research on agency missions and activities is often necessary to determine which agencies hold the information needed. Helpful sources are the *U.S. Government Manual*, with its descriptions of agency responsibilities, the *Privacy Act Issuances Compilation*, the *Federal Register*, and the *Code of Federal Regulations* (CFR), all of which are now on the Internet. To find agency announcements of rules for processing requests, search the *CFR Index and Finding Aids* volume (AE 2.106/3–2:) or the Rules section on the Internet CFR under "Freedom of Information." The *Federal Register Index* publishes the "Guide to Freedom of Information Indexes," a quarterly listing of indexes to individual agency files describing index coverage and accessibility. Daily *Federal Registers* also include agency FOIA rules. Scanning the *Federal Register* for notices of "Privacy Act: Systems of Records" and "Privacy Act:

Computer Matching Programs" is another way to monitor personal records systems. (See chapter 9 for a detailed introduction to the *Federal Register* and CFR.) *Privacy Act Issuances* is a compilation of agency rules from the *Federal Register*.

The Request Letter

> *An unclassified document can be hidden just as deeply in a file drawer . . . as a classified document can. The Freedom of Information Act never even becomes relevant until someone knows enough to ask for an "identifiable" document.*
> —Stanley Futterman, Associate Professor, New York University Law School

FOIA requires requesters to "reasonably describe" the information sought. This means that requests for "everything" or "anything" on a subject are frowned upon. The more specific the request, the better. A proper request will delineate the records sought using newspaper clippings, articles, citations to congressional reports, or citations to portions of the records previously released—anything to help the agency track the record within its filing system. For example, the American Library Association's FOIA request for details on the FBI's Library Awareness Program asked for "all records pertaining to FBI investigations [that] have thoroughly documented the many ways that specialized scientific and technical libraries have been used by the Soviet intelligence services, and all other documents pertaining to the Bureau's Library Awareness Program." Remember that FOIA doesn't require the requester to reveal why the information is wanted or how it will be used. The American Civil Liberties Union's online "Step-by-Step Guide to Using the Freedom of Information Act" at <http://www.aclu.org/library/foialetr.html>, the Department of Justice's *Your Right to Federal Records: Questions and Answers on the Freedom of Information Act and the Privacy Act* at <http://www.usdoj.gov/oip/foia_rights.htm>, and the Freedom of Information Clearinghouse's "The Freedom of Information Act: A User's Guide" at <http://www.citizen.org/public_citizen/litigation/foic/foilguid.html> offer clear, concise instructions.

To identify files kept on individuals, consult *Privacy Act Issuances Compilation* at <http://www.access.gpo.gov/su_docs/aces/PrivacyAct.shtml>. First identify the agency maintaining the records and then follow the agency's request procedures. Privacy Act requests must include the requester's full name and address, plus proof of identity—a photocopy of a document that shows your signature or photograph, such as a passport. Requests should specify the type of list where the record is held plus any information required by the agency, such as dates, subject matter, and identifying numbers. Requests should be addressed to the official listed for the record system, and "Privacy Act Request" should appear on the front of the envelope.

The Federal Information Center

An automatic garage door began mysteriously opening and talking. The curious homeowner called the Federal Information Center, which relayed his question to the Federal Communications Commission, where the talking-door phenomenon was traced to a ham radio. The Federal Information Center is a switching center for questions, providing either an immediate answer or the name of a government expert. After telephone callers brave an initial recorded message, they are connected to reference librarians who answer their questions: (800) 688-9889, TDD/TTY (800) 326-2996. A first stop for Web visitors is the "Frequently Asked Subjects" section at <http://fic.info.gov/>.

FREE MATERIALS

> *The golden age of government publications is over.* —Nelson Fitton, head of the Department of Agriculture, Publications Division

While it's true that the "golden age" of printed documents has passed, we now enjoy the "zinc age," an era when patience, persistence, and knowledge of a few techniques can still lasso free government publications and information.

Technique One: Contact the Issuing Agency

Many agency Web sites offer full-text versions of their key publications. To locate them, use the Web site's search engine or publications list. Web sites also alert requesters to free materials, resource people, and useful telephone numbers.

Rising costs of maintaining mailing lists, postage, printing, and storing have forced more and more agencies to curtail free publication distribution. But even in tightfisted times, many agencies will happily send general information brochures, copies of annual reports, and publications lists, and may add you to their mailing lists for free newsletters. When you'd like a free copy of a specific document (preferably a recent one), you can try writing or e-mailing a request for a "single free copy" from the issuing agency or a local field office. The issuing unit can be ascertained from the agency's Web page or the document's bibliographic description in the *Monthly Catalog*, WorldCat, or *Sales Product Catalog* (SPC). Agency mail and e-mail addresses, telephone numbers, and field offices are listed on agency Web sites and in the *U.S. Government Manual* (although its telephone numbers are notoriously outdated).

Technique Two: E-Mails or Telephone Calls

Agency personnel tend to be friendly and helpful, especially if you get the person most knowledgeable about your question. To avoid a "merry-go-round of referrals" (Ann Landers was once kept on hold by the Immigration and Naturalization Service for 45 minutes), it's best to contact a specific subject specialist. Consult print or Web agency directories to identify specific names. E-mail correspondence is ideal since it gets you past clerical gatekeepers to the experts. Identify e-mail addresses on the agency's Web page or query the webmaster, who will forward your inquiry within the agency. A few agencies provide general, "canned" e-mail responses, but most are quick and informative.

To pick the brains of agency staff, a telephone call is best. Telephone numbers can be identified using the agency's Web page or listings of agency telephone directories in the *Monthly Catalog*. Once the appropriate person is found, she or he is invariably eager to help. It sometimes shocks the public to discover that so-called bureaucrats are real people like themselves: they pay taxes, enjoy sharing their knowledge, and occasionally wear mismatched socks.

Technique Three: Contact Legislators

Senators and representatives can sometimes provide free copies of popular or special materials (such as laws or bills), and their local staffs may help track down materials. Senators and representatives also broker access to Congressional Research Service publications. (See chapter 8.) Requesters should turn to legislators only for special problems or current materials—not for highly technical or scientific documents, retrospective titles, or repeated requests. This is not the quickest way to get materials and should be recommended to library users only with caution.

Technique Four: Depository Libraries

Depository libraries and document purchases (described in chapters 3, 4, and 6) are more reliable sources of government information. Although depositories don't sell documents or give away free copies, they provide free access to government information, with some boasting collections that span almost a century. They are equipped with specialized indexes and abstracts, Internet connections, and expertise. Regular users of government information should get to know their local depository staff. Not only can staff assist in using their local collection, they can also refer requesters to other libraries and agencies and expedite interlibrary loan requests.

ADDRESSES

The National Security Archive, Gelman Library, George Washington University, 2130 H Street, NW, Suite 701, Washington, DC 20037; e-mail: nsarchiv@gwis2.circ.gwu.edu; (202) 994-7000; Fax: (202) 994-7005; <http://www.seas.gwu.edu/nsarchive>.

A nonprofit library of declassified and unclassified government records, including materials released under FOIA.

FURTHER READING

American Library Association. *Less Access to Less Information By and About the U.S. Government.* Distributed as a supplement to the *ALA Washington Office Newsletter*, issues since June 1996 are on the Internet at <http://www.ala.org//washoff/lessaccess.html> (May 13, 1998).

Indexed 1981–1987 cumulation is $7; indexed 1988–1991 cumulation is $10; semiannual updates since January 1992 are $1 each. Orders must be prepaid, with self-addressed mailing label: ALA, Washington Office, 1301 Pennsylvania Ave. N.W., #403, Washington, DC 20004-1701; (202) 628-8410; Fax: (202) 628-8419; e-mail: alawash@alawash.org.

Armstrong, Scott. "Do You Wanna Know a Secret? One Court Case Lifts the Veil On the High Cost of Classification." *The Washington Post* (February 16, 1997): Page C01; <http://www.fas.org/sgp/eprint/armstrong.html> (September 20, 1997).

The U.S. government's secrecy system is expensive and ineffective.

David, Jim. "Declassification: Where Are We Today?" Federation of American Scientists Project on Government Secrecy, Government Web Site, Secrecy e-Prints (February 1997): <http://www.fas.org/sgp/eprint/jimdavid.html> (October 2, 1997).

How agencies are implementing President Clinton's Executive Order on Declassification.

The Freedom of Information Clearinghouse. *Freedom of Information Clearinghouse Guidebook.* FOIC, 1992. <http://www.citizen.org/public_citizen/litigation/foic/foilguid.html> (September 18, 1997).

A guide to making FOIA requests and appealing agency decisions.

House Committee on Government Reform and Oversight. *A Citizen's Guide on Using the Freedom of Information Act and the Privacy Act of 1974 to Request Government Records.* (H. Rept. 105–37) GPO, 1997. (Y 1.1/8:105-37). Also available in the U.S. House of Representatives Internet Law Library, Privacy and information access <http://law.house.gov/107.htm> (September 30, 1997).

One of the most widely read congressional committee reports in history, this is a guide to rights under the laws, with details about how to request information.

Smith, Robert Ellis. *Compilation of State and Federal Privacy Laws*, [year]. Washington, DC: Privacy Journal, annual.

State and federal laws related to confidentiality of personal information are described.

NOTES

1. Donna A. Demac, *Keeping America Uninformed: Government Secrecy in the 1980s* (New York: Pilgrim Press, 1984), p. 4.

2. Harry Hammitt,"UK Secrets Legacy Yielding." *Government Technology* 9 November 1996): 16.

3. "Pro and Con: Cut Access to Government Data?" *U.S. News and World Report* 92 (January 18, 1982): 69–70.

4. Kenneth C. Bass, "What Can the U.S. Do to Catch More Spies?" *Buffalo News* (June 29, 1986): F-15.

5. Originally enacted in 1980, newly amended with the Paperwork Reduction Act of 1995 (P.L. 104–13).

6. Revised June 25, 1993.

7. Senate, Committee on Governmental Affairs, *National Archives and Records Administration Act of 1983, Hearings before the Committee on Governmental Affairs, 98th Congress, First Session on S. 905 Entitled the National Archives and Records Administration Act of 1983, July 29, 1983* (S. Hrg. 98-488) (GPO, 1984), p. 38. (Y 4.G 74/9:S. Hrg. 98-488).

8. Society of Professional Journalists, *Report from the FOIA Front: A Study of Journalists' Usage of the Freedom of Information Act* (The Society, 1989), p. 40.

9. Arthur R. Miller, *The Assault on Privacy: Computers, Data Banks, and Dossiers* (Ann Arbor, MI: University of Michigan Press, 1971), p. 20.

10. David Burnham, *The Rise of the Computer State* (New York: Random House, 1983), p. 11.

11. Congress, Office of Technology Assessment, *Electronic Record Systems and Individual Privacy* (OTA-CIT-296) (GPO, 1986), p. 3. (Y 3.T 22/2:2El 2/6), pp. 10–33.

EXERCISE

1. *United States Government Information*, the GPO sales catalog, lists a "helpful tool for home buyers" called *Mortgage Money Guide* (FT 1.8/2:SM). You could buy it from GPO, but first would like to try requesting a free copy from the issuing agency. How do you proceed?

CHAPTER 3
GPO, The Mother Lode

Printing is the other half, and in real utility the better half, of writing—both assist in communication between people.   —Abraham Lincoln

WHAT

Although the Government Printing Office (GPO) is not the sole source of federal documents, it is the federal government's primary information reproducer and distributor.

WHY

Title 44 of the *U.S. Code* requires that GPO fulfill federal printing and binding needs, distribute publications to the public, and disseminate government information products online.

HOW

GPO fulfills its distribution responsibility by preparing catalogs and indexes of government publications, distributing and selling government information products, piping information across the Internet, and administering the federal depository library system.

Congress's Joint Committee on Printing (JCP) administers and oversees GPO, acting as its board of directors. The JCP has authority over all government printing and binding, including microfiche, audiovisual productions, and electronic media.

WHO

At GPO's helm is the Public Printer, nominated by the president and confirmed by the Senate. One of the Public Printer's subordinates is the Superintendent of Documents (SuDocs), who oversees depository libraries, the sale of documents, and compilation of the *Monthly Cata-*

log, GPO Pathway Services, and other bibliographic aids.

WHEN

In the year 2000, GPO will celebrate its 139th year. It opened for business in 1861, the year President Lincoln was inaugurated.

WHERE

GPO's central office is in Washington, DC, although not all GPO printing is done there. About three-quarters is contracted out to commercial printers, and some is done at GPO regional printing offices (all bearing the GPO imprint, however). GPO's mail-order sales program operates from Washington, DC, with the assistance of 24 GPO bookstores nationwide, consigned federal agents like the Congressional Sales Office, and in cooperation with the Consumer Information Center distribution centers.

PUBLICK PRINTING

Our early Congress had no permanent, official printer. For three-quarters of a century, government printing was assigned to a hodgepodge of private entrepreneurs called publick printers. Publick printing was an unstable vocation, with frequent turnover and heavy competition for contracts. Early printers tended to dawdle, and with printing still in its infancy, even a diligent typesetter might complete just two or three pages before calling it a day. Many of these printing pioneers were slow, inaccurate, and messy, and were regularly fired by a disgruntled Congress. Early printers are also remembered for bribery, lost manuscripts, overcharging, and inspiring scandals and congressional investigations.

The publick printers' steady stream of motley documents led to visions of an official government printer, but some factions argued against it. A Senate debate over printing led to a challenge to a duel in 1833 (mercifully halted by bystanders). One impassioned supporter of central government printing compared Congress's reliance on printed materials to people's need for food. "For ships you can wait; for guns you can generally wait," explained the congressman, "but you cannot be deprived of your printing for a single day without serious embarrassment and loss of time."[1]

> *Printing created a new relationship between people and their governments, involving the individual to a far greater extent in his national destiny than ever before.* —Robert E. Kling, Jr.,
> *The Government Printing Office*

The dream of an official government printer languished for about 40 years. Finally laws were passed to establish central government printing, which by 1860 evolved into the Government Printing Office, charged with federal printing and binding. GPO's creation ended corruption and favoritism by snatching public printing away from private printers and newspaper publishers. While GPO's original charge was solely printing, sale and distribution responsibilities were added in 1895, when Congress passed a comprehensive printing act which became Title 44 of the *U.S. Code* (chapters 13 and 19). In 1993, Congress amended Title 44 with the GPO Electronic Information Access Enhancement Act (P.L. 103-40), requiring online dissemination of information. The GPO Access suite of Internet services grew out of this legislation.

The Government Printing Office set up shop in 1861 in the red brick building it still occupies today. The quarters were fully equipped for modern typesetting by hand, and boasted a boiler house, coal house, wagon shed, and stables (for which government issue included one black horse, one bobtail bay horse, and a delivery wagon). Passersby were sometimes pelted with pieces of discarded metal type tossed from the windows. The surrounding neighborhood was known as "Swampoodle" because of its swamp and puddles. Swampoodle bustled with geese, pigs, and goats, and was bordered by a creek characterized as an "indescribable cesspool."

GPO genealogy recounts how employees entered their new quarters the morning Confederate guns opened fire on Fort Sumter. Soon after, they worked by gaslight to set type for the Emancipation Proclamation and, later, President Lincoln's eulogy. Today, GPO presses continue to document America's triumphs, tragedies, and drudgeries by printing the laws, reports, and proclamations that shape the nation.

This Is a Printing Office

Crossroads of civilization
Refuge of all the arts against the ravages of time
Armory of fearless truth against whispering rumor
Incessant trumpet of trade
From this place words may fly abroad
Not to perish on waves of sound
Not to vary with the writer's hand
But fixed in time
Having been verified by proof
Friend, you stand on sacred ground
This is a printing office

Beatrice L. Warde,
from a bronze plaque
in the lobby of GPO

GPO TODAY

> *The Government Printing Office publishes the proverbial something for everyone.*
> —Betsy Pisik, *The Washington Times*

As the federal government's primary information reproducer and distributor, GPO's responsibilities include not only printing and binding, but also disseminating government information to the public. By linking printing with distribution responsibility, Congress made GPO the nation's information nexus. The Superintendent of Documents fulfills GPO's dissemination role through distribution of materials to depository libraries (see chapter 4), selling government publications, and compiling catalogs and indexes to them, including the *Monthly Catalog, Sales Product Catalog,* and Internet locators. (See chapter 5.)

Although Title 44 of the *U.S. Code* mandates all government printing be funneled through GPO, loopholes allow smaller jobs to be printed elsewhere. Some agencies are granted waivers to do their own printing and distribution while others wrangle to publish independently of GPO. These exceptions, coupled with a shift toward decentralized electronic publishing and private vendor-dissemination, have threatened GPO's command over government information. As a printing and distribution hub, GPO has been well-situated to monitor government information products for Internet announcement and inclusion in the *Monthly Catalog* and depository libraries. The electronic era threatens to aggravate the "fugitive" document problem by insulating GPO from a large portion of information production. Fugitive documents produced outside the GPO procurement system are lost to the Depository Library Program and are not sold in the GPO sales program.

> *GPO is not just for printing anymore.*
> —Robert W. Houk, Public Printer

"Printing," the Government Printing Office's middle name, has modernized beyond traditional "ink-on-paper." GPO is evolving from a traditional graphic printing plant to an information-processing operation dominated by electronic creation, replication, and dissemination. GPO is simultaneously broadening its role beyond printing and physical dissemination to serve as a conduit for electronic government information.

The Government Printing Office Electronic Information Access Enhancement Act of 1993 (the "GPO Access law") required GPO to disseminate government information products online and provide online access free to depository libraries and to others at "incremental cost." GPO's response to this legislative mandate was speedy and enthusiastic—the *Congressional Record* and *Federal Register* went online the following year, in June 1994. Initially, access was by subscription, free only on-site in depository libraries or by remote connection to depository library "gateways." Astronomical use of these free depository options depressed paid online subscriptions, and in December 1995, subscription fees were scrapped altogether; the Public Printer announced free and open Web access for everyone. "Gateways" in depository libraries continued to allow users to connect to GPO Access through user-friendly depository library hosts.

The GPO Access law also required an electronic directory of federal electronic information, establishing GPO as a government information "yellow pages." (See chapter 5.) This government-wide federal locator service was a natural extension of GPO's Title 44 responsibility to issue the *Monthly Catalog*. The *Monthly Catalog*, now on the Web, continues to cite information products, but GPO's Pathway Services suite offers a more comprehensive directory of federal electronic information.

Although often called the nation's biggest "publisher," GPO is not a true publisher, but a printer. This distinction is made because GPO neither initiates nor editorially controls its publications. These responsibilities are shouldered by the agencies that issue the documents. As a service unit, GPO prints what agencies want printed, with no input regarding content, titles, or even accuracy. The real publishers of government documents are the government issuing agencies responsible for their intellectual content.

What's Wrong Here?
A newspaper article attacked GPO for selling an outdated air force manual that promulgated the same misinformation that had already caused a plane crash killing 92 people.
Answer: GPO was innocent. The issuing agency, not GPO, is responsible for the content and accuracy of its publications printed by GPO.

Sales

We're not in business to make money. But sometimes we do. —Carolyn Crout, GPO

Mail order is GPO's primary mode for selling some 10,000 government information products. As a matter of fact, GPO has been ranked among the top five mail-order houses in the country. While the bulk of sales are to businesses, one-quarter of GPO customers are individuals. GPO prices are established by law at cost plus 50 percent, with the average document priced at around $11. Formerly the government's primary sales outlet for paper publications, GPO now sells electronic media such as CD-ROMs, database tapes, and diskettes, including the *Congressional Record, Federal Register, Statistical Abstract*, and *Budget of the United States Government*. A list of electronic sales titles is provided in the free Subject Bibliography 314, available at <http://www.access.gpo.gov/su_docs/sale/sb-314.html>, while a list of CD-ROM titles is available on the SuDocs Web page <http://www.access.gpo.gov/su_docs/sale/sale300.html>.

Orders can be placed on the Internet, mailed, faxed, or telephoned to GPO or a GPO bookstore. (See "Addresses.") Order with the GPO stock number rather than SuDocs number. GPO stock numbers, configured as S/N 000-000-00000-0, are sometimes listed in agency catalogs without the S/N identifier.

GPO publishes several free current awareness publications to encourage sales. Each includes prices, stock numbers, and order forms. Remember that GPO sales catalogs are promotional tools meant to be scanned or browsed, not bibliographies or indexes equivalent to the *Monthly Catalog* or *Sales Product Catalog*. With their lack of indexes and limited coverage, *New Products, U.S. Government Information Catalog, Consumer Information Catalog*, and the Subject Bibliographies are not intended to serve as indexes to government documents.

Subject Bibliographies
GP 3.22/2:

http://www.access.gpo.gov/su_docs/sale/sale100.html

Subject Bibliographies (SBs) are lists of GPO sales titles on some 150 topics. They are free from GPO and also are available via GPO Access and on the Federal Bulletin Board. SBs are not comprehensive lists of government titles on a topic, but they do list titles currently for sale from GPO. Entries provide title, publication date, stock number, price, ISBN, and in some cases, SuDocs number and an annotation. Subject Bibliographies are regularly revised and reissued under recurring SB numbers. The free Subject Bibliography index, *Guide to U.S.*

GPO Access: Quick Tips[2] <http://www.access.gpo.gov/su_docs/index.html>		
Search Element	Rules	Example
Subjects, titles, names, places	AND, OR (the default), ADJ (adjacent words or within 20 characters), NOT should all be capitalized or they will be ignored as stopwords Enclose phrases in quotation marks	"department of education" department ADJ education solar AND energy "solar energy" "gpo access training booklet" *(exact title)*
Truncation	Asterisk, following (no front or middle truncation)	legisla*
Nesting	Use parentheses to consolidate related segments	legislation AND ("child abuse" OR "child labor")
Stopwords	Ignored in queries; consult "Default Stopword List"	"department of education" "department education" department ADJ education
Abbreviations	Database ID codes appear in the Search Results List; not searchable; see also "Congressional Bills Database Abbreviations"	fr2fe96N [*Federal Register* February 2, 1996, Notices section] cr31ja96H [*Congressional Record* January 31, 1996, House section]
Scanning	"Navigation Aids" provides an outline of the site, allowing visitors to bypass some of the menus; a hot-linked "What's New" page summarizes content updates	Example: In the site outline, jump to National Archives and Records Administration to search the *U. S. Government Manual*

Government Information, identifies SBs related to topical areas (GP 3.22/2:yr/IND and <http://www.access. gpo.gov/su_docs/sale/sale180.html>).

Tip

To find the full text of a Subject Bibliography on GPO Access, append the 3-digit SB number to the URL below (replace xxx's with the number):
<http://www.access.gpo.gov/su_docs/sale/sb-xxx.html>
SB 71, for example, translates into 071, searched as <http://www.access.gpo.gov/su_docs/sale/sb-071.html>

While the Subject Bibliographies are free, the titles listed in them are for sale. Someone who doesn't care to buy documents can peruse many of them in a depository library, using the SuDocs number given in the Subject Bibliography as an access key. Internet equivalents of paper titles are noted in neither the Subject Bibliography nor the SPC: both are sales tools, and most agency Internet documents are free. Use the *Monthly Catalog* or GPO Access Browse Titles to identify Internet versions of publications (chapter 5).

United States Government Information: Publications, Periodicals, Electronic Products
GP 3.17/5:

This free catalog lists information products for sale from GPO. Titles range from popular to technical, in numerous subject areas and many formats—including books, journals, CD-ROMs, decals, and posters. *U.S. Government Information* is embellished with illustrations and annotations, making it pleasant to browse. Citations include price, GPO stock number, and occasionally SuDocs numbers. Although published quarterly, this sales catalog remains essentially unchanged, with only a few new titles added each quarter. Since no mailing list is kept, each current issue must be requested anew.

Like the Subject Bibliographies, *U.S. Government Information* is not a comprehensive list of GPO sales titles, including only a handful for a few popular topics. Since SuDocs numbers are usually noted, *U.S. Government Information* does serve as an access key to depository collections, where many of the documents may be used free of charge. When a SuDocs number is lacking it can be retrieved using the *Sales Product Catalog* (SPC).

New Products from the U.S. Government

GP 3.17/6:

http://www.access.gpo.gov/su_docs/sale/
market/prod001.html

New Products is a free listing of new titles added to GPO's sales inventory during the previous two months. It offers a no-nonsense roster of essential bibliographic details for ordering (or borrowing from a depository)—without annotations or frivolity.

Consumer Information Catalog

GS 11.9:

http://www.pueblo.gsa.gov/textver/

What comes to mind when you think of Pueblo, Colorado? Almost one in five Americans associates the city with government consumer information.[3] Pueblo's Consumer Information Center distributes 10 million pamphlets yearly. Although the *Consumer Information Catalog* is issued by the General Services Administration, orders are processed by GPO, which operates GSA's Consumer Information Center in Pueblo. The handy *Consumer Information Catalog* is aimed at the general public, listing free and inexpensive pamphlets on popular topics. When an agency agrees to pick up the tab for printing and distributing a publication, it is offered free in the *Catalog*. About 40 percent of the *Catalog*'s titles are free. (The word "free" retains its 1980s flavor—you must enclose a $1 service charge when ordering freebies.) Priced booklets in the *Catalog* are GPO publications. In addition, some pamphlets are available for 50¢ as part of the Low-Priced Publications Project, in which issuing agencies shoulder some of the costs usually assumed by GPO.

The *Catalog* itself and full text of all the publications it describes (without graphics/illustrations) are available from the Consumer Information Center's Bulletin Board System (202) 208-7679 and on the CIC Web site <http://www.pueblo.gsa.gov/>, which has been lauded as "the best and most comprehensive government Web site for consumer information and feedback."[4] The *Catalog* is issued quarterly. Multiple copies for bulk distribution can be requested by educators, libraries, consumer groups, and other nonprofit groups.

U.S. Government Subscriptions

GP 3.9:

http://www.access.gpo.gov/su_docs/sale/
subs001.html

or download from the Federal Bulletin Board

This publication is a listing of government "magazines" (aka periodicals and loose-leaf subscriptions) for sale from GPO. Brief bibliographic information, including SuDocs number stem, is included along with sales information and annotations. Government magazines are listed alphabetically by title, with agency and subject indexes. Available free, with automatic quarterly updates, this handy pamphlet is an asset at any reference desk. Use it as a reference for quick verification of SuDocs number stems or to confirm frequency and scope of GPO periodicals. Note: unlike the print *Monthly Catalog*, the bullets in *U.S. Government Subscriptions* do not indicate depository status.

Catalogs and Indexes

GPO catalogs and indexes include the current awareness catalogs already described, along with major bibliographies such as the *Monthly Catalog* and *Sales Product Catalog* (SPC). It is important to recognize that these tools fall into two distinct categories: those limited to documents sold by GPO, and those with broader scope. Many titles listed in the *Monthly Catalog*, for example, are not sold by GPO. Because GPO sells only a small portion of federal documents, GPO promotional catalogs and the SPC are not comprehensive. Each of the GPO sales catalogs omits items sold by other agencies, out-of-print titles, and those not sold to the public. Because of their lack of comprehensiveness, the GPO sales catalogs do not fully reflect the scope of depository library collections. (The Depository Library Program offers about 10 times more publications than does the GPO sales program.) The *Monthly Catalog* should be used for a comprehensive search, along with special-subject indexes as appropriate. Also note that GPO sales catalogs tend to note the SuDocs number, GPO stock number, and price, but omit any reference to availability in depository libraries. *Monthly Catalog*, WorldCat, and SPC all provide information about depository status, indicated by item numbers (with or without the word "item") and depository shipping list notations. Both or either may show up in bibliographic records.

U.S. Government Bookstores

Imagine the thrill of browsing through hundreds of new, crisp documents in a bookstore atmosphere. GPO operates 24 walk-in bookstores where you can browse, ask questions, buy documents, and order GPO titles not in stock. (Fewer than one-quarter of available titles are stocked in the bookstores.)

Formerly cloistered in federal buildings, the GPO bookstores of the 1990s have been relocated and refurbished—many transferred to shopping malls and key downtown sites. A complete directory can be found on GPO Access at <http://www.access.gpo.gov/su_docs/sale/abkst001.html>, in the GPO sales catalogs, and in the *Monthly Catalog*. GPO also lists bookstores in the telephone book's yellow pages for each bookstore city, under "Book Dealers—Retail".

Sales Product Catalog (SPC)

GP 3.22/3:

http://www.access.gpo.gov/su_docs/sale/prf/prf.html

GPO's comprehensive catalog of sales titles is the *Sales Product Catalog* This can be found in microfiche, the *GPO Sales Publications Reference File*, and on the SuDocs Web page; no paper version is available. The SPC functions as a "GPO Books in Print," listing documents currently for sale by the Government Printing Office. It also lists forthcoming and recently superseded or out-of-stock publications. The microfiche version can be searched by GPO stock numbers, SuDocs numbers, International Standard Book Numbers, and alphabetically by subjects, titles, agency series and report numbers, keywords and phrases, and authors. Guidelines for searching the Web version are provided in the SPC table in chapter 5. Another Internet version of SPC is provided free by Claitor's Law Books at <http://www.claitors.com/prf/prfindex.htm>.

Use the SPC to identify bibliographic information about GPO documents for sale and for verifying current prices and stock numbers for ordering. The SPC may also be used to find out what GPO has printed on a topic and to identify documents available in depository libraries.

SUPERINTENDENT OF DOCUMENTS CLASSIFICATION SCHEME

Library classification systems allow arrangement of materials by placing books about the same subject together on the shelves. Most people are familiar with the Dewey Decimal and Library of Congress classification systems, which group books within major classes of knowledge. Identifying the classification number, or call number, leads the searcher to the shelves, where other books on the same topic await. Such a system facilitates browsing by eliminating the need for title-by-title searching of the catalog. The Superintendent of Documents (SuDocs) Classification Scheme is not like this. Unlike the Dewey and Library of Congress schemes, the SuDocs system is based on provenance, or source—the issuing agency. Titles are shelved according to their issuing agencies, not their subject matter.

A SuDocs number is an alphanumeric notation designating the document's issuing agency and its subunits using letters and numbers, periods, slashes, and dashes. Since full bibliographic information is available

elsewhere (in the *Monthly Catalog*, for example), being able to decode these elements within a SuDocs number is unnecessary. Just as you needn't understand electronics to use your television set, you can use SuDocs class numbers without understanding their derivation. (If you are determined to torture yourself, however, consult the references at the end of this chapter.[5])

The ability to simply recognize a SuDocs number is a handy skill: the knowledgeable person will be surprised how often others confidently identify another number (a GPO stock number, for instance) as a SuDocs number. Each SuDocs number has two distinguishing elements: a letter or letters at the beginning, and a colon in the middle. SuDocs classification numbers begin with a letter or letters to designate the agency issuing the document:

LC,   for the Library of Congress,
A,   for the Department of Agriculture, or
NAS,   for NASA

The part of the SuDocs number through the colon is called the class stem. The addition of an individual book number following the colon makes each SuDocs number unique. For example, the SuDocs class stem for each CD-ROM version of the *Statistical Abstract of the United States* is identical:

C 3.134/7:

The addition of three digits indicating the year distinguishes between different editions and creates a unique class number for each:

C 3.134/7:997 (1997 edition)
C 3.134/7:993 (1993 edition)

This straightforward practice can expedite bibliographic searching. When a SuDocs stem is known, it can be quickly searched in the SPC, the *Monthly Catalog*, or WorldCat to identify the most recent edition or other bibliographic information.

Similar techniques frequently designate revised editions of numbered publications:

A 1.35:381 (original edition)
A 1.35:381/2 (first revision)
A 1.35:381/986 (1986 edition)

Occasionally, format is indicated in a SuDocs number:

C 3.134/6:UN 3/1992/SOFT/FLOPPY (a floppy disk)
Y 3.2:C 17/IN 8/INTERNET (available via the Internet)

Internet titles are assigned SuDocs numbers in addition to URLs, to help connect them with their parallel "print antecedents."

The SuDocs Scheme in Action

In physical collections arranged by SuDocs classification, SuDocs numbers can serve as a link between bibliographies and indexes and the documents collection. SuDocs numbers are noted in many major documents reference tools, including the *Monthly Catalog*, SPC, and *CIS/Index*. These sources can function as subject indexes to documents collections, with the SuDocs number used like a call number to retrieve documents from shelves or microfiche cabinets.

The *Daily Depository Shipping List*, an invoice accompanying each shipment of depository documents, lists SuDocs numbers for depository titles (GP 3.16/3: and <http://libaix01.uta.edu/shiplist/>). This simplifies processing in libraries using the SuDocs scheme, since the SuDocs number can be quickly transferred to the document for immediate shelving. Because depository shipments should be processed and shelved quickly, a document may reach the shelves before a library catalog can cite it. There it may languish, with potential users unaware of its existence until bibliographic tools catch up. Knowledge of SuDocs number stems can help overcome catalog time lags: when the stem of the notation remains unchanged, new editions can be retrieved without bibliographic verification. For example, knowing that the stem for the paper *Budget of the United States Government* is

PREX 2.8:

allows you to locate the most recent edition on the shelves without waiting for it to be acknowledged in a local library catalog. Remember that when the year is part of a SuDocs number, the initial digit is dropped: 1998 becomes /998.

The *List of Classes of United States Government Publications Available for Selection by Depository Libraries* is an aid to quick identification of SuDocs number stems (GP 3.24: and <http://fedbbs.access.gpo.gov/libs/class.htm>). It lists all categories of depository publications by SuDocs number stems, and allows quick referral from SuDocs stems to their issuing agencies and documents series (or vice versa). Both *Monthly Catalog* and SPC can be searched by SuDocs number, and the SuDocs number is one of the search keys for accessing WorldCat. (See chapter 5.) When the stem or complete SuDocs number is known, a SuDocs number search is usually faster than an author or title search.

Because of its usefulness, the SuDocs number should be included whenever a government document is cited. Citations lacking SuDocs numbers are incomplete and a nuisance for the person wishing to retrieve cited titles. Since the documents seeker often needs a SuDocs number to locate documents within a depository collection (about 70 percent are physically arranged by SuDocs numbers), the researcher will be forced to complete bibliographic work neglected by the citing author.

Tip: Finding Documents on the Shelves
In SuDocs class numbers, the numbers following periods are integers, not decimals. Thus, A 1.9: precedes A 1.88: just as 9 precedes 88 when counting. (In a decimal system like the Library of Congress Classification, .88 would be shelved before .9, since 88/100 precedes 90/100). For an easy practice sequencing SuDocs numbers, review the *List of Classes* or pamphlet *Monthly Catalog*, both of which are arranged in SuDocs number order.

Browsers Beware

Scanning library shelves to find interesting titles relies upon subject arrangement of materials. While documents browsing may provide some serendipitous finds (after all, agency missions restrict them to certain topics and concerns), browsing alone should never be relied upon to locate documents. Guessing which agencies might publish on a topic is not recommended either. Browsing is impeded not only by arrangement according to provenance, but also by the predominance of depository documents in microfiche, overlooked by someone scanning bookshelves. Because of browsing limitations, knowledge of bibliographic tools such as the *Monthly Catalog* and SPC is essential for the documents seeker.

Government Musical Chairs

The federal government is constantly in flux, with departments merging, dissolving, and changing names, sometimes altering agency SuDocs numbers in the process. For example, when the Education Division was a subagency of the Department of Health, Education, and Welfare (HEW), the division's publications were issued under a SuDocs number beginning with HE. Since 1979, when a separate Department of Education was established, the SuDocs number for that department's publications has begun with the prefix ED instead of HE.

Two approaches are used to handle shelving problems caused by government reorganization: reclassifying older documents to conform to the new number, or allowing both class numbers to remain, leaving related titles physically separated. (This is another reason documents browsing is inefficient.)

ADDRESSES

Superintendent of Documents, U.S. Government Printing Office, Washington, DC 20402.

Mail orders to: Superintendent of Documents, Box 371594, Pittsburgh, PA 15250-7954, (202) 512-1800, 9 a.m. to 4 p.m. Eastern time weekdays; Fax: (202) 512-2250; or the nearest GPO bookstore. Mail orders should include the 12-digit stock number, with VISA/MasterCard/Deposit Account information (include expiration date) or check or money order payable to Superintendent of Documents; ship-to address, and daytime phone. Online ordering: <http://www.access.gpo.gov/su_docs/>, select the *Sales Product Catalog.*

GPO Access Office of Electronic Information Dissemination Services, 732 N. Capitol Street, NW, Mail Stop: SDE, Washington, DC 20401; User Support Team: gpoaccess@gpo.gov; Toll free (888) 293-6498; (202) 512-1530; Fax: (202) 512-1262; <http://www.access.gpo.gov/su_docs/>.

FREEBIES

The following Subject Bibliographies are free from: Stop: SSOP, Washington, DC 20402; U.S. Fax Watch: (202) 512-1716:

77. Graphic Arts <http://www.access.gpo.gov/su_docs/sale/sb-077.html>

244. Government Printing Office <http://www.access.gpo.gov/su_docs/sale/sb-244.html>

Also free from GPO:

New Products from the U.S. Government (GP 3.17/6:): Mail Stop, SSOM, Washington, DC 20402-9373

United States Government Information: Publications, Periodicals, Electronic Products (GP 3.17/5:): Stop SM, Washington, DC 20401

United States Government Information for Business (GP 3.22:B 96/11): Washington, DC 20401

U.S. Government Subscriptions (GP 3.9:): Superintendent of Documents, U.S. Government Printing Office, Stop: SSOP, Washington, DC 20402-9328

Consumer Information Catalog from Consumer Information Center, Pueblo, CO 81009; (800) 888-8 PUEBLO; <http://www.pueblo.gsa.gov/cicform.htm>; or download a copy from CIC's Bulletin Board: (202) 208-7679

FURTHER READING

Congressional Research Service. *The Joint Committee on Printing: A Brief Overview.* by Harold C. Relyea. (CRS Report 95-425 GOV) Library of Congress, 1995.

A summary of the history and authority of the JCP.

Government Printing Office. *Annual Report.* GPO, Annual. (GP 1.1:) Free from GPO's Office of Congressional, Legislative, and Public Affairs; also on the Federal Bulletin Board <telnet://fedbbs.access.gpo.gov>, from the main menu, type: s annual report <enter>.

GPO's annual reports provide a quick overview of government printing, trends, and statistics.

Government Printing Office. *Biennial Report to Congress on the Status of GPO Access: A Service of the Government Printing Office, Established under Government Printing Office Electronic Information Access Enhancement Act of 1993, Public Law 103–40—June 8, 1993.* GPO, 1995–. Biennial. GP 1.1/2: or <http://www.access.gpo.gov/su_docs/aces/biennial/index.html> (June 18, 1998).

The GPO Access law requires biennial status reports in odd-numbered years.

Kling, Robert E., Jr. *The Government Printing Office.* New York: Praeger, 1970.

A history of GPO, from its beginnings into the twentieth century.

Nelson, Gail K. and John V. Richardson, Jr. "Adelaide Hasse and the Early History of the U.S. Superintendent of Documents Classification Scheme." *Government Publications Review* 13 (January-February 1986): 79–96.

A profile of the woman who devised the SuDocs classification scheme and her work at GPO.

NOTES

1. Government Printing Office, *100 GPO Years, 1861-1961, History of United States Public Printing*, by Harry Schecter (GPO, 1961), p. x. (GP 1.2:G 74/7/861-961).

2. For detailed instructions, consult "User's Guide" and "Helpful Hints" at <http://www.access.gpo.gov/su_docs/aces/desc004.html/> (August 15, 1997); or in print: Office of Electronic Information Dissemination Services. *GPO Access*

Training Booklet. GPO, annual. (GP 3.2:AC 2/4/yr.) Also available on the Federal Bulletin Board: <http://fedbbs.access.gpo.gov/> Select #4 *GPO Access* WAIS User Documentation and Helpful Hints/1 User Documentation.

   3. Judith Waldrop, "Educating the Customer," *American Demographics* 13 (September 1991): 46.

   4. Cynthia Etkin. "WebWatch: Online Consumer Resources" Library Journal Digital (May 1, 1997): <http://www.ljdigital.com/multi.htm> (November 1, 1997).

   5. Superintendent of Documents, Depository Administration Branch, *An Explanation of the Superintendent of Docu-*

ments Classification System (GPO, 1990) (GP 3.2:C 56/8/990 or <http://www.access.gpo.gov/su_docs/dpos/explain.html). Many explications of SuDocs number intricacies are excerpted directly from this source; MacGilvray, Marian W. *GPO Classification Manual: A Practical Guide to the Superintendent of Documents Classification System* (GPO, 1993). (GP 3.29:Pr 88/993) is a detailed description of the SuDocs scheme for catalogers and other professionals.

   6. R. R. Bowker, "Women in the Library Profession," *Library Journal* 45 (August 1920): 635–40.

EXERCISES

1. What is the SuDocs number for the *Congressional Record*? (Use one of the GPO promotional catalogs to snag a quick answer.)

2. Sequencing SuDocs numbers: Arrange the SuDocs numbers in shelf order.

   J 21.22:1
   D 101.2:N 56
   LC 3.4/2:62/991
   J 21.2/10:988
   LC 3.4/2:62 a
   I 19.81:40121-B 3-TF-024/991
   PR 41.8:P 96
   Y 3.T 22/2:2 T 22/24/v.2/pt.2/China
   D 101.2.A 8
   PREX 2.2:C 86

CHAPTER 4
Depository Libraries: Federal Information Safety Net

WHAT

In return for receiving free federal information products, depository libraries accept responsibility for making them available to the public. Depositories can take two forms: selectives, with partial collections; and regionals, which take all depository titles and keep them permanently.

WHY

Federal depository libraries make federal government information accessible to the public. Depositories provide free access to government publications and ensure their preservation for future generations.

WHEN

Among the oldest right-to-know statutes, the laws establishing the depository library system date back to the late 1850s. Key legislation that solidified the system as we now know it can be found in the Printing Act of 1895 and the Depository Library Act of 1962.

WHERE

Depository libraries are located in each state and congressional district, in the Canal Zone, Guam, Micronesia, Puerto Rico, and the Virgin Islands. About 1,371 depositories are dispersed throughout the United States and its territories, in academic, public, state, and other types of libraries.

WHO

Since each depository is required to open its collection for the free use of the general public, anyone may use a depository anywhere. Depositories serve not only the library's indigenous clientele, but also any member of the public. Each week between 750,000 and 950,000 people across the nation use depository libraries.

HOW

The Depository Library Program is administered by GPO's Superintendent of Documents, at an estimated yearly cost of about 10 cents per person in the United States. A 15-member Depository Library Council serves as an advisory board to the Public Printer, meeting in Washington, DC, each spring and fall. The authority for the Depository Library Program (DLP) is in Title 44, Chapter 19 of the *United States Code* (44 U.S.C. 1901 et seq.).

ONE OF AMERICA'S BEST-KEPT SECRETS

More people know the closest star than are aware of depository libraries.
—Ralph E. Kennickell, Jr., Public Printer

The federal depository library system has been characterized as both "the nation's collective memory," and "one of America's best-kept secrets."[1] Although depository libraries exist to make government information accessible to the public, many Americans have no idea what depositories have to offer. Heisser found that three-quarters of a group of 46 people interviewed had never heard of depository libraries, and Hernon discovered GPO bookstore customers to be unaware of depository collections.[2] When asked to define a "federal depository library," people asked at random in Buffalo, New York, offered the following definitions: a bank; a library book drop; a library for government workers; where Lee Harvey Oswald shot President Kennedy; the Library of Congress; a storehouse for old federal books; and a library that gets all government documents. None of these responses was correct.

FIGURE 4.1: Depository Library Program Logo.

When shown the depository eagle logo, some people incorrectly guessed that it designated the U.S. Post Office; a sports team; a wildlife fund; censorship (an eagle guarding a book); federal accountants; or an airline. The logo was registered as a GPO trademark in 1992.

DESIGNATION

Depository libraries are designated by law or by members of Congress. Depository law specifies that certain types of libraries—accredited law school libraries and state libraries, for example—are automatically eligible for depository status. Additional depository locations in each state are determined according to provisions allowing for two in each congressional district (designated by U.S. representatives) and two within each state (designated by U.S. senators). Supplemental provisions allow depository status for land-grant colleges and state libraries. Chances are your nearest depository is in an academic library, since about half are in academia. Public libraries are the second most common locations, housing about two out of every 10 depositories. The remainder are in many other types of libraries, including state, court, federal, historical, and medical libraries.

To locate nearby depository libraries, use the "Locate Libraries" function on GPO Access <http://www.access.gpo.gov/su_docs> and the Web MOCAT. Input a 2-letter state postal abbreviation or 3-digit telephone area code to generate a depository list. If both state and area code are input, a list of all depositories in the state appears first, followed by those in the area code. To locate only nearby depositories, put in area code only. The *Federal Depository Library Directory* lists depositories and GPO bookstores by state and city, with addresses, telephone and fax numbers, and e-mail addresses, and it can be accessed at <http://www.access.gpo.gov/su_docs/dpos/ldirect.html>.

A librarian needn't work in a depository to help people connect with government information. Reference specialists in both depository and nondepository libraries should acquaint themselves with the addresses, telephone numbers, and scope of nearby depositories and be ready to refer patrons to them. Blind referrals can be avoided by telephoning ahead to verify whether the material sought is available, and to alert the depository staff to the patron's needs. For the names of depository librarians, consult the *Directory of Government Documents Collections and Librarians*, published by the Congressional Information Service. Reference specialists in nondepository libraries can expedite referral by familiarizing themselves with the core titles guaranteed to be included in every depository collection. (See the list under "Selective Depositories" below.)

A TWO-TIER SYSTEM

The federal depository system is composed of two types of depositories: selective and regional. Selectives choose which of some 7,000 categories of publications to receive and keep for at least five years. Regionals agree to receive all depository documents and keep them permanently.

Selective Depositories

Selectives are not required to collect every depository title, although they may opt to receive all of them. They are called selective because they select only those classes of documents meeting the needs of their clientele. In recent years, tight budgets have forced many depositories to reduce the percentage of item numbers they elect to receive. With selectives taking anywhere from 10 to 90 percent of all depository documents (about 40 percent select less than one-quarter), each selective's collection is unique, and every depository document will not necessarily be available in every collection. Appendix A of the *Federal Depository Library Manual* provides a "Suggested Core Collection" keyed to the needs of public, academic, and law libraries. All depositories, however, are expected to own the following 20 core tangible titles:

Budget of the United States Government PREX 2.8:
Catalog of Federal Domestic Assistance PREX 2.20:
Census Catalog and Guide C 3.163/3:

Census of Population and Housing (for state of
   depository only) C 2.223/-:
Code of Federal Regulations AE 2.106/3:
Congressional Directory Y 4P 93/1:1/*congress*
Congressional Record X/a. Cong.–sess.:
County and City Data Book 3.134/2-1:
Federal Register AE 2.106:
Historical Statistics of the United States C 3.134/
   2:H62/970
Monthly Catalog GP 3.8/7:
National Trade Data Bank (CD-ROM) C 1.88:
Slip Laws (public) AE 2.110:
Statistical Abstract C 3.134:
Statutes at Large AE 2.111:
Subject Bibliographies GP 3.22/2:
U.S. Code Y 1.2/5:
U.S. Government Manual AE 2.108/2:
United States Reports JU 6.8:
Weekly Compilation of Presidential Documents AE
   2.109:

Regional Depositories

Regionals have many responsibilities beyond those of
selectives. They automatically receive all depository
titles and must keep them permanently, serving as archival collections for their states. The insurance of a comprehensive regional collection makes it possible for
selectives to discard older materials (with the regional's
supervision). The regional must also provide interlibrary
loan and reference service to both depository and
nondepository libraries in its locale, as well as coordinate workshops, training, and consultations.

Designation as regional requires approval by the
state library and a majority of the local selectives before
it can be enacted by one of the state's U.S. senators. Only
selective depositories can be candidates for regional status. Nearly two-thirds of the regionals are academic libraries (61 percent), with almost a third (29 percent)
located in state agencies and 10 percent in public libraries. A regional may serve two or more states or may
share regional responsibilities with another library. Regional status is voluntary, and no state is required to
have one, although currently all 50 states are served by
regionals.

> We do not want the best public information sys-
> tem that money can buy because we will not be
> able to afford it.
> —Representative Jim Bates, Chair of the House
>   Subcommittee on Procurement and Printing

Although two regional depositories are allowed in each
state, most states have only one. That's because living
up to regional responsibilities is expensive. Neither
selectives nor regionals receive government subsidies
to run their depositories—the host library picks up the

tab. In exchange for receiving some $100,000 worth of
free materials yearly, each regional invests anywhere
from one-half to three-quarters of a million dollars each
year. Because they must collect all depository documents, regionals often face storage problems.

Federal Depository Library Gateways

http://www.access.gpo.gov/su_docs/aces/
aaces004.html

Before it was free to all on the Internet, the online GPO
Access service was fee-based. Because GPO was committed to providing a free venue, Federal Depository
Library gateways were established to provide cost-free
pipelines to GPO's online subscription services. Public
access gateways allowed users to connect to GPO Access through depository libraries volunteering to host
off-site access through Internet and dial-up connections.
GPO Access is now free, but gateway libraries still exist, providing support to both on-site and off-site users.
GPO's goal is to eventually have at least one gateway
per state. Any depository can become a gateway.

RESPONSIBILITIES

The Federal Depository Library Program (FDLP) is a
partnership between government and libraries to link
the public with government information. A depository
must maintain a tangible collection on-site, help in locating and using government information, and provide
electronic access through computer workstations with
graphical user interfaces, CD-ROM capability, Internet
connections, and the ability to access the World Wide
Web. The federal government subsidizes creating, reproducing, and distributing information to depositories,
while the cost of processing, housing, staffing, and ser-
vicing the depository collection comes from the library's
budget. The library also picks up the tab for supplementing the collection with commercial access tools,
such as *CIS/Index,* and plugging collection gaps. For
every government dollar invested, depository libraries
contribute at least four. Estimates place the selective
depository tab at around $280,000 annually; $306,000
for a regional.

As a "library within a library," a depository's operations parallel those of its host library. The
depository's accommodations should be of equal quality, with decent lighting, temperature, ventilation, and
noise control. The collection should be open during the
same hours as other major library departments. Shipments of depository documents should be processed
quickly. Although GPO dictates free access to depository collections "without impediments," individual circulation policies are determined by each depository.
Some elect not to loan materials for use outside the li-

brary. All, however, are required to open their collections for on-site use, and many allow documents to be borrowed.[3]

Government Information in Action

After a two-year-old boy was kidnapped by his father and expropriated from California to Iraq, his mother's sleuthing led her to her local depository library. There she determined names of Iraqi officials and discovered step-by-step instructions in a State Department International Parental Child Abduction publication. With the aid of these references and copies of forms such as the State Department's "Application for Assistance Under the Hague Convention on Child Abduction," the mother located and recovered her son.

LOOPHOLES

> *During [the last] 100 years, there is probably not one moment when the [depository library] system was ever perfect.*
>
> —Jeanne Isacco,
> Readex Microprint Corporation

Traditionally, depository copies were automatically siphoned as GPO printed for agencies, with the FDLP (GPO) picking up the tab to piggyback the extra depository copies. Although 44 U.S.C. 501 mandates that all government printing funnel through GPO, loopholes permit independent publishing if agencies bankroll the cost of extra copies for depositories. Unfortunately, this mandate frequently goes unheeded. For example, many agencies balk at sending multiple copies of their tangible electronic products to GPO for distribution to depositories. Agencies view the cost of providing up to 1,400 copies of a CD-ROM or floppy disk, coupled with the need for user-friendly indexing, software, and manuals as "disincentives." In practice, some agency CD-ROMs sent to depositories have been problematic because of ineffective support materials or software.

Hatched on CD-ROMs or agency Web pages, within electronic bulletin boards, or through private vendor contracts, many information products escape GPO's depository dragnet. These lost titles are known as fugitives—government information products eligible for, but missed by, the Depository Library Program. Produced outside the GPO procurement system, fugitives are not only excluded from the Depository Library System, but they are also never sold through the GPO sales program, or, in some cases, preserved in the National Archives. About half of all tangible government information products are suspected to be fugitives.

If paper fugitives are slippery, electronic fugitives are quicksilver. Some exist solely on the Internet, with no print counterpart to foreshadow their existence. Lack of standardization results in some material mounted in PDF, others in HTML or ASCII, and still others using word processing software. Links to an online site may not be straightforward: the product may not be easily found there, or may turn out to be a summary rather than full text of an original.

COLLECTIONS

Before 1962, depositories received only GPO imprints, accounting for only half of all government printing output. The Depository Library Act of 1962 rectified this weakness by broadening the definition of a government publication to encompass any "informational matter which is published as an individual document at government expense, or as required by law." Back in 1962, publishing was confined to ink on paper, but today GPO interprets "published" broadly as "publically disseminated." Any informational matter produced for public dissemination, regardless of format, is depository fodder. This incorporates books, reports, maps, atlases, charts, posters, photographs, and periodicals published in paper and microfiche, as well as electronic products. OMB Circular A-130 and 44 *U.S. Code* mandate that all agency publications and electronic products of public interest or educational value be submitted to GPO for physical distribution, or, in the case of online services, be accessible free of charge to the FDLP. So-called tangible products are shipped to depositories in boxes and are added to physical collections—paper, microfiche, CD-ROMs, diskettes—while solely electronic information is "accessed."

All information available through the Federal Depository Library Program is cataloged by GPO. The cataloging records are incorporated into WorldCat (the OCLC Online Union Catalog) and then published in the *Monthly Catalog of United States Government Publications* and made available for online searching as part of the GPO Access Federal Locator services. (See chapter 5.)

Electronic Formats

> *Electronic dissemination of information is suddenly seen as a method of saving federal dollars as well as a way of being technologically hip.*
> —Charles Seavey, library educator, 1996

Until the electronic revolution, about 60 percent of depository titles arrived on microfiche, with the remainder on paper. The electronic era has allowed the government to publish through the Internet, bulletin boards, CD-ROMs, online databases, and floppy disks. The depository amalgam of the future is expected to be about half electronic and half paper and microfiche. In 1996 alone, the FDLP distributed 56,000 titles on microfiche or paper, 639 on CD-ROMs, tapped into more than 70 databases through GPO Access, pointed to almost 1,000 agency titles through GPO locator services, and hot-linked 1,148 MOCAT records to agency Internet sites.

Nitty Gritties of Selection

A depository collection begins when the library assumes depository status, with no retrospective, start-up materials provided. If the library wants earlier titles it must purchase them. Instead of selecting title-by-title, selective depositories choose categories of documents called "classes," which are sent automatically from then on. Titles in the news, like the "Plum Book" (a catalog of federal jobs, issued after each presidential election), are automatically sent to all depositories, even those not selecting that class. Each depository class is assigned an item number (example: Item 0455-G-04), the key to determining which documents are available to depositories. Item numbers are noted in the SPC description paragraph, in field 074 in OCLC Passport records and the *Monthly Catalog*, and in numerous bibliographies, indexes, and abstracts.

The quarterly *List of Classes of United States Government Publications Available for Selection by Depository Libraries* itemizes the approximately 7,000 categories of materials available for depositories to select. In the print version, classes are listed in SuDocs stem order, along with the item number and a short title for each class. An unofficial HTML edition[4] is arranged similarly at <http://www.du.edu/~ttyler/locintro.htm>. GPO's Web version is arranged in item number order. The *List of Classes* serves as a handy referral from SuDocs number stem to issuing agency (in the paper and unofficial Web versions). The list is helpful not only to depository staff but also to anyone wanting quick verification of depository status or SuDocs number stem. It may be consulted in paper (GP 3.24:) or the file may be downloaded or viewed from the FDLP Administration page (the "electronic *List of Classes*"), available at <http://fedbbs.access.gpo.gov/libs/class.htm>.[5] The Federal Bulletin Board file is updated monthly. Updates to the *List of Classes* are published irregularly in the "Update to the *List of Classes*" column in *Administrative Notes: Technical Supplement*. A supplement, *Inactive or Discontinued Items from the 1950 Revision of the Classified List*, lists class stems and rudimentary information for ceased or altered titles (GP 3.24/2:). Item selections can be modified once a year in the "annual update cycle," which in 1997 evolved from 4 x 6 green postcards to an online Web form—<http://www.access.gpo.gov/su_docs/dpos/amendment.html>. Additions to a library's profile made in July take effect the following October 1st, while deletions are activated the next day (except for microfiche, which activate the following quarter).

Another source of information about depository item classes is the Item Lister service on the FDLP Administration page <http://www.access.gpo.gov/su_docs/dpos/itemlist.html>. Updated monthly, the Item Lister can create a custom list of item selection numbers, with total and percent of items selected, for individual depository libraries. The microfiche *GPO Depository Union List of Item Selections* (GP 3.32/2:) is organized by item numbers, noting the depositories receiving them.

The *Daily Depository Shipping List*

GP 3.16/3:

http://ublib.buffalo.edu/libraries/units/cts/acq/GPO/

or download from http://febbbs.access.gpo.gov/libs/shiplist.htm

The *Daily Depository Shipping List* (DDSL) is an inventory accompanying each depository shipment. Each shipping list is individually numbered, with an E, M, P, or S suffix to indicate a shipment of electronic, microfiche, or paper formats, or separates. Scanned shipping lists since January 1997 are available for downloading soon after their release via the Federal Bulletin Board at <http://febbbs.access.gpo.gov/libs/shiplist.htm> and also through GPO's U.S. Fax Watch Service. Another option is a searchable shipping list database with check-in enhancements and a SuDocs label-generating program available at <http://ublib.buffalo.edu/libraries/units/cts/acq/GPO/>. This enhanced shipping list service, searchable by title, keywords, and item and SuDocs numbers, was developed in a partnership between the University of Buffalo, the University of Texas-Arlington, and GPO. *Administrative Notes: Technical Supplement*'s "Shipping List Alert" column gives the last shipping list numbers of the year, unused shipping list numbers, numbering errors, and other miscellaneous information.

Doc Ex

Some types of government information are never earmarked for depositories: those perceived as irrelevant, lacking educational value, wholly administrative or operational, classified, and "cooperative" publications (which must be sold to be self-sustaining, such as the *National Union Catalog*). The Library of Congress's Documents Expediting Project (Doc Ex) is a vehicle for obtaining government publications not designated for depositories or sold by either GPO or the issuing agency. Doc Ex is a cooperative effort between the Library of Congress and a subscribing membership consisting of university, public, and special libraries. In addition to providing members with nondepository titles and congressional committee documents, the project enjoys a special arrangement with the CIA for acquiring CIA Reference Aids (a series that may be subscribed to by nonmembers of Doc Ex).

Prepackaged Collections

Readex (a division of NewsBank) sells all documents cited in the *Monthly Catalog*, both depository and nondepository, on microfiche. Readex microfiche collections cost about $50,000 yearly for the depository run, and about $23,000 for the nondepository cluster. Libraries subscribing to the Readex collection arrange their microfiche in either SuDocs number or *Monthly Catalog* entry number order.

The SIRS Government Reporter on CD-ROM includes selected full-text federal government analyses, country profiles, fact sheets, statistics, charts, tables, graphs and maps, information about the federal bureaucracy and elected leaders, selected decisions of the Supreme Court, and historic documents. Complete bibliographic citations and brief summaries accompany each document.

ORGANIZATION

Depository materials are not required to be a segregated collection. They may be kept separate or integrated with other library materials. Another option is a partially integrated collection, with government information housed in both a special documents department and within other library departments. Since many government publications are valuable reference or bibliographic tools, some may be transferred to a noncirculating reference collection. Others may be shelved with magazines, finding their way into the library's periodicals collection. Government pamphlets may be sent to the vertical file.

Thus, in a single library, depository materials may be scattered to facilitate access. This physical dispersion may result in documents being shelved according to various classification schemes. The Superintendent of Documents system may be used in the documents department, while documents shelved with the regular book collection may be assigned Library of Congress or Dewey Decimal numbers. Since many depository documents are received in microfiche, many will be in microfiche cabinets rather than on bookshelves. The same is true for Readex microfiche collections of depository and nondepository titles. Titles in electronic formats, such as CD-ROMs, floppy disks, and online databases, may be in yet another location. With computerized documents cataloging records available through vendors, more and more depositories are "mainstreaming" documents by listing document locations in their library online catalogs.

Wherever depository materials are housed, though, they remain government, not library, property. Examine a depository document, and you'll see a notice of government ownership, probably on the cover.

Disposal of Documents

Getting rid of depository documents is like getting rid of plutonium.
—David J. Nuzzo, University at Buffalo

A selective depository served by a regional may discard documents only after keeping them for five years. Even then it is not a matter of tossing the document into a wastebasket—the regional must supervise weeding. The selective asks the regional's permission to discard, submitting a list of documents to be canned. Since the regional serves as a state backup collection responsible for interlibrary loan, it may claim some of the discards to plug gaps in its own collection. Regionals' 100-percent collections were established in 1962 or later, so their retrospective holdings are not necessarily complete. Selectives not served by a regional may not discard, even after five years. They must keep all depository materials permanently, since they cannot resort to a backup regional collection.

Certain types of documents may be discarded before the normal five-year statutory retention period.

Internet Shipping List Tips			
Content	Time	Searching	URL
Searchable, with processing enhancements (check-in, print labels)	Since 1/1997	Search by title keywords, SuDocs and item numbers; view DDSLs listed in item number, SuDocs number, or title order; sort entries	http://ublib.buffalo.edu/libraries/units/cts/acq/GPO/
Downloadable raw data (FBB)	Since 1/1997	Select date listed in numerical order: DDSL # 998-0227-P is 980227p.dbf	http://fedbbs.access.gpo.gov/libs/shiplist.htm
Internet-only titles	Not listed on DDSLs		

Documents okayed for automatic discard are listed on *The Superseded List* (GP 3.2:Su 7/996 and <http://www.access.gpo.gov/su_docs/dpos/suplist.html>), which is periodically amended by the *Administrative Notes: Technical Supplement's* "Update to the Superseded List."

National Archives Backup Collection

The nation's most complete historical collection of federal documents is in the National Archives, designated as Record Group 287, "Publications of the U.S. Government." While most National Archives holdings are unpublished material from federal agencies, The National Archives and Records Administration (NARA) also archives historical copies of many government publications. The core of the collection is the former Public Documents Library that hearkens back to the 1890s, arranged in SuDocs number order. Thus, Record Group 287 serves as a "resource of last resort" for depository libraries, which may buy photocopies of materials. An introduction to the collection is given in the free General Information Leaflet No. 28, "Looking for an Out-of-Print U.S. Government Publication?" (AE 1.113:28). The *Cumulative Title Index to United States Public Documents, 1789–1975*, compiled by Daniel Lester (Historical Documents Institute), is a guide to the former GPO collection that was transferred to NARA for safekeeping. For more information contact NARA's Center for Legislative Archives at <http://www.nara.gov/nara/legislative/>.

Don't Make Me Come Up There!

Just as becoming a depository is voluntary, a depository may voluntarily relinquish its status (two did so in 1995). The privilege may also be withdrawn by the Superintendent of Documents if the library fails to live up to its legal obligations. Formerly, each depository was inspected at least once every seven years. This system has been replaced by a periodic self-study questionnaire.[6] The questionnaire is sometimes augmented by a telephone interview with GPO, or, when warning alarms go off, a traditional on-site inspection. A library neglecting its responsibilities receives a warning and six months on probation to correct deficiencies. If it does not, it may be stripped of depository status by the Superintendent of Documents. With 95 percent of inspected libraries in compliance with their depository responsibilities, such contravention is rare.

FDLP Partnerships

FDLP Partnerships are official agreements between GPO and individuals or depository libraries to pursue joint FDLP projects. The FDLP Administration Web site provides a Partnerships link to information about the Partnership Program, accessible at <http://www.access.gpo.gov/su_docs/dpos/fdlppro.html>.

ELECTRONIC EGRESS

The concept of an electronic FDLP was refined from a 1996 *Study to Identify a More Electronic Federal Depository Library Program*, framed by a think tank of representatives from government, librarianship, and the information industry. Their final report was submitted to Congress in 1996 as the *Study to Identify Measures Necessary for the Successful Transition to a More Electronic Federal Depository Library Program* (GP 3.2:EL 2/3/FINAL and <http://www.access.gpo.gov/su_docs/dpos/studyhtm.html>).[7] It set a five- to seven-year timetable for the electronic transition—by FY 2001. GPO will promote access to electronic information by directing users to agency electronic information services, mounting agency source files on GPO Access, and cataloging and indexing Internet products. When agency electronic data must be sold to be self-sustaining, depositories will provide access on-site or through Federal Depository Library gateways <http://www.access.gpo.gov/su_docs/aces/aaces004.html>. Historical material will continue to be accessible in pre-electronic, physical documents collections. The result will be a virtual FDLP superimposed over vigorous tangible collections.

By the year 2001, depository information will be predominately electronic—available through the Internet or dial-up connections, through "gateway libraries," or through CD-ROMs and diskettes housed in depository collections. Paper or microfiche versions will be phased out as soon as reliable electronic alternatives emerge, with only a few titles duplicated in paper incarnations. There will be two basic types of depository information: computer-accessible from a Superintendent of Documents or agency site, and physical/tangible format (CD-ROMs, microfiche, maps, core titles in paper). Emphasis will be on linking to SuDocs-operated online services rather than stockpiling geographically dispersed book and fiche collections. Depositories are alerted of online products through the *Administrative Notes: Technical Supplement's* "Update to the List of Classes" (URLs are provided in the Status column), and the GPO Access "Browse Electronic Titles" page <www.access.gpo.gov/su_docs/dpos/btitles.html>. A comprehensive listing of online-only titles is expected.

Transition to Electronic FDLP[8]	
From	To
Focus on products	Focus on services
Dissemination	Access
Shipping physical products	Electronic connections
Physical, tangible information formats	Online, Internet access
Short-term GPO responsibilities	GPO responsible for long-term access

There is a very good chance that neither the depository library system nor the GPO will survive this century.

—Charles Seavey, library educator

Despite fears that electronic information may render depositories obsolete, depositories are holding their ground as the nation's primary government-citizen conduit. Although focus has shifted from on-site physical collections to electronic linkage, the underlying ideology of permanent and equitable public access remains a FDLP hallmark. Depository libraries are government information sanctuaries. When government Internet offerings such as the Census Bureau's STAT-USA are saddled with subscription fees, GPO wangles free access for depository clientele. When people lack computers or computer literacy, depositories help them plug into cybergovernment. By championing audience-appropriate and use-appropriate formats, permanent preservation, and public access, the FDLP preserves the nation's oeuvre, providing all formats of government documentation.

DEPOSITORY LEGISLATION

The General Printing Act of 1895 combined several unrelated laws governing printing and distribution of government publications; made GPO's Superintendent of Documents responsible for the depository library system; and provided for one depository per congressional district, but not for disposal of documents—they had to be kept permanently.

The Depository Library Act of 1962, the first major revision of depository law since 1895, allowed two depositories per district and established regionals and a way for selectives to discard unwanted documents. To incorporate documents not printed by GPO, the law defined government publications as "informational matter which is published . . . at Government expense, or as required by law." Because the 1895 and 1962 laws did not spell out requirements for depository access to then-unforeseen electronic media, many factions are pushing for modernization of the depository laws.

In 1978, libraries of accredited law schools were allowed depository status with the enactment of Public Law 95–261.

The Government Printing Office Electronic Information Access Enhancement Act of 1993 required GPO to disseminate government information products online, spurring creation of GPO Access, GPO's electronic dissemination service.

OTHER DEPOSITORIES

The federal depository program is only one of numerous government deposit arrangements. Some federal agencies operate their own depository systems: the Patent and Trademark Office and the Census Bureau are two examples. Depositories are also maintained by state and local governments and for foreign and international organizations, such as the United Nations.

The Documents Prayer

Our Father who art in Washington,
SuDoc be thy name,
thy Depository come,
thy Publication be done,
in Microform as in Hard Copy.
Give us this day our Daily Shipment.
And forgive us our Class Numbers,
as we forgive those who number against us.
And lead us not into non-Depository status,
but deliver us from the Post Office.
For thine is the Census, and the Patents
and the Monthly Catalog, forever.

Amen

—Hal Hall, 1976

ADDRESSES

Doc Ex: Documents Expediting Section, Exchange and Gift Division, Library of Congress, Washington, DC 20540-4200; e-mail: dbloxsom@mail.loc.gov; (202) 707-9527; Fax: (202) 707-0380.

FREEBIES

The following Subject Bibliographies are free from: Stop: SSOP, Washington, DC 20402; U.S. Fax Watch: (202) 512-1716:

150. Libraries <http://www.access.gpo.gov/su_docs/sale/sb-150.html>

244. Government Printing Office <http://www.access.gpo.gov/su_docs/sale/sb-244.html>

FURTHER READING

GODORT Handout Exchange. Hosted by the University of Michigan Documents Center Web site. <http://

www.lib.umich.edu/libhome/Documents.center/ godort.html> (November 10, 1997).

Government information user guides from depository libraries.

Government Printing Office. *Fulfilling Madison's Vision: The Federal Depository Library Program*. Depository Library Council, 1996. (GP 3.2: M 26).

Testimonials show how depository libraries affect lives.

"Keeping America Informed; Federal Depository Library Program; a Program of the Superintendent of Documents, U.S. Government Printing Office (GPO)" <http://www.access. gpo.gov/su_docs/dpos/102years.html> (February 13, 1998).

Background, events, statistics, and laws behind depository libraries.

Superintendent of Documents. Library Programs Service. *Administrative Notes*. GPO, 1985– . Monthly. (GP 3.16/3–2: and <http://www.access.gpo.gov/su_docs/dpos/adnotes. html> [June 18, 1998]).

———. *Administrative Notes: Technical Supplement* GPO, 1994–. Monthly. (GP 3.16/3–3: and <http://www.access.gpo. gov/su_docs/dpos/techsup.html> [June 18, 1998]).

Depository library news organs with information about events, government information, and GPO. *Administrative Notes* (AN), the "parent" newsletter, offers news and articles. The *Technical Supplement* (ANTS) provides details and procedures, updating the *List of Classes*, FDLP manuals, depository listings, directories, and "The E-Report: Status of Federal Electronic Information," an irregular status report on the availability of electronic products to depositories. Tables of contents and keyword searching are available on the Web site. *Administrative Notes* is issued on the 15th of the month; *Administrative Notes: Technical Supplement* on the last day. A searchable, full-text version of AN since September 1995 is available at <http://www.lib.umich.edu/libhome/Documents. center/adnotes.html> [June 18, 1998].

NOTES

1. Donna A. Demac, *Keeping America Uninformed: Government Secrecy in the 1980's* (New York: Pilgrim Press, 1984), p. 136; GPO, the agency responsible for administering the Federal Depository Program, acknowledged that the program has long been "one of America's best-kept secrets." *Government Printing Office, Annual Report: Fiscal Year 1984* (GPO, 1985), p. 5.

2. David C. R. Heisser, "Marketing U.S. Government Depository Libraries," *Government Publications Review* 13 (January-February 1986): 55–65; Peter Hernon, "Use of GPO Bookstores," *Government Publications Review* 7A (1980): 362.

3. Depository responsibilities are detailed in the following documents, also available on the Federal Bulletin Board or the FDLP Administration Web page <http://www.access. gpo.gov/su_docs/dpos/fdlppro.html> (October 8, 1997). Unofficial versions are on "Basic Depository Library Documents: The Unauthorized HTML Editions" <http://www. du.edu/~ttyler/bdldhome.htm> (June 18, 1998). *Instructions to Depository Libraries*, official FDLP rules and regulations (GP 3.26:D 44/992); *Federal Depository Library Manual*, a how-to-run-a-depository guide (GP 3.29:D 44/993); *Federal Depository Library Manual, Supplement 1, "Collection Development Guidelines"* (GP 3.29:D 44/993/SUPP.); *Federal Depository Library Manual, Supplement 2, Guidelines for the Federal Depository Library Program*, recommended standards (GP 3.29:D 44/993/SUPP.2); *Federal Depository Library Manual, Supplement 3: Self-Study of a Federal Depository Library* (GP 3.29:D 44/993/SUPP.3); "Recommended Minimum Specifications for Public Access Work Stations in Federal Depository Libraries," *Administrative Notes* 17(May 15, 1996): 6–8: Each depository should provide public computer work stations with a graphical user interface, CD-ROM capability, and Internet and World Wide Web connectivity; "Spatial Data Supplement to Recommended Minimum Specifications for Public Access Work Stations in Federal Depository Libraries," *Administrative Notes* 17 (June 15, 1996): 14–15.

4. "Basic Depository Library Documents: The Unauthorized HTML Editions," coded and designed by Thomas G. Tyler, University of Denver Library.

5. Sometimes when the *List of Classes* on the Web interface of the Federal Bulletin Board is downloaded to a Netscape browser, major chunks seem to be missing. Use the following GPO tips for downloading the entire file and converting it into ASCII comma-delimited format to allow its retrieval in a database application: 1. On the Options pull-down menu select General Preferences; 2. Go to Helpers; 3. Highlight File type text/plain; 4. In Action select Save to Disk; 5. Click on OK, and then download. *Administrative Notes* 18 (August 15, 1997): 6 (GP 3.16/3-2:18/11 or <http://www. access.gpo.gov/su_docs/dpos/adnotes.html#6>) (September 5, 1997).

6. A template of "Self-Study of a Federal Depository Library" (*Federal Depository Library Manual, Supplement* 3; GP 3.29:D 44/993/Supp.3) is on GPO's Web site <http:// www.access.gpo.gov/su_docs/dpos/selfstud.html> (June 18, 1998) and in ASCII text via the Federal Bulletin Board.

7. First articulated in *The Electronic Federal Depository Library Program: Transition Plan, FY 1996—FY 1998* (1995), the concept of an electronic FDLP was refined in the Strategic Plan included in the 1996 *Study to Identify a More Electronic Federal Depository Library Program*.

8. Paraphrased from Gil Baldwin, "The Federal Depository Library Program in Transition" *Administrative Notes* 17 (February 15, 1996): 21 (GP 3.16/3-2:17/04).

EXERCISE

1. Is *General Information Concerning Patents* a depository title? (Use sources discussed in this chapter to answer this question.)

CHAPTER 5
Bibliographies and Indexes

WHAT

The *Monthly Catalog* is the most comprehensive list of information products from all federal agencies, although it does not list every government title. The *Sales Product Catalog* (SPC) lists titles for sale from GPO. Neither the SPC nor *Monthly Catalog* indexes the contents of government periodicals, a role fulfilled by commercially published indexes.

WHERE

You can find the SPC and the *Monthly Catalog* on the Internet (called the Catalog of United States Government Publications because it is updated more frequently than monthly) and on CD-ROM or online from commercial publishers.

WHEN

The Government Printing Office catalogs tangible products soon after shipping them to depositories, and catalogs remotely-accessible electronic titles shortly after being notified of their Web debuts. With a genealogy spanning back to 1895, the GPO Web *Monthly Catalog* is retrospective to 1994, while commercial subscriptions cumulate since July 1976. The SPC is updated daily online and monthly in microfiche (known by its original name, the *Publications Reference File* or PRF).

WHY

The Superintendent of Documents helps fulfill GPO's dissemination role by creating the *Monthly Catalog*, *Sales Product Catalog*, and Internet locators to serve as "yellow pages" for locating government information products.

THE MONTHLY CATALOG

http://www.access.gpo.gov/su_docs/

Its formal title is *Monthly Catalog of United States Government Publications*, but friends call it MOCAT. MOCAT provides both dynamic and historical records of federal agency products, either identifying physical documents or linking to electronic ones. As the most comprehensive federal bibliography available, the *Monthly Catalog* is among the FedWeb's "Big Three."[1] Although it falls short of listing every unclassified government product, it documents both depository and nondepository materials, both GPO and non-GPO products, and physical publications as well as agency products on the Internet.

MOCAT Plugged In

In 1976 the *Monthly Catalog* entered the electronic age by adopting machine-readable (MARC) format. Twenty years later that modernization enabled an Internet MOCAT and electronic cumulative versions, allowing the venerable *Monthly Catalog* Père to be laid to rest after 110 years. Since July 1976, it had sported a cleaner format and enhanced bibliographic documentation. The post-1976 *Monthly Catalog* incorporated MARC, Anglo-American Cataloging Rules, and Library of Congress subject headings, and it was fed into the OCLC cataloging network. The Web MOCAT goes further, hot-linking to digital publications moored at agency Web sites.

As a government information product, the *Monthly Catalog* is free of copyright restrictions, allowing commercial companies to reproduce their own versions. Numerous *Monthly Catalog* incarnations in varied formats are available from both government and commercial sources. It's important to remember that while commercial incarnations are clones of the GPO *Monthly Catalog*, each has been uniquely enhanced and has a distinct personality. Thorough searching demands

FIGURE 5.1: Web *Monthly Catalog* Search Results.

[1]
List of classes. [computer file]. Monthly. United States. GP 3.35:CLASS/(DATE). [[0554-A (online)]]. ① ②
   Rank: 1000 Locate Libraries , TEXT , HTML
         ③   ④   ⑤

[2]
List of classes. [computer file]. Monthly. United States. GP 3.35:CLASS/(DATE). [[0554-A (online)]].
http://fedbbs.access.gpo.gov/libs/class.htm ⑥
   Rank: 982 Locate Libraries , TEXT , HTML

[3]
List of classes of United States government publications available for selection by depository libraries /. Quarterly, 1977-. United States. GP 3.24:(DATE). GPO stock no.: 721-007-00000-6. [[0556-C]].
   Rank: 958 Locate Libraries , TEXT , HTML

[4]
List of classes of United States government publications available for selection by depository libraries /. Quarterly, 1977-. United States. GP 3.24:(DATE). GPO stock no.: 721-007-00000-6. [[0556-C]].
http://fedbbs.access.gpo.gov/libs/CLASS.htm ⑥
   Rank: 935 Locate Libraries , TEXT , HTML

Summary results show ① SuDocs number, ② depository status (item number in double brackets), plus links to ③ depositories selecting this item, ④ the full cataloging record, and ⑤ the same record with the URL hot linked (in this case, however, there is no URL and no hot link. Records **[2]** and **[4]** have hot links, indicated by URLS ⑥. Click the URL in the summary record or click HTML to unfold the full record with the URL hot-linked.

familiarity with the protocols for the variant being used. The descriptions that follow are based on the GPO-issued *Monthly Catalog*. Why learn the GPO version? Not only because it's the archetype for the commercial versions, but also because it is free on the Internet—independent of library subscriptions and other paid access. You never know when you might find yourself working in a weather station at the South Pole.

Commercial CD-ROM and online cumulations offer a single compilation of all *Monthly Catalog* entries since July 1976—when MOCAT went electronic. The commercial versions do not always broadcast their *Monthly Catalog* antecedents or sport the *Monthly Catalog* moniker, however—substituting names like Government Publications Index, GPO CAT/PAC, EZ-DOCS, and GPO on SilverPlatter. MARCIVE's GPO CAT/PAC, for example, is described as a "GPO database" of government publications since 1976. The clue that the MARCIVE product is the *Monthly Catalog* rather than SPC (also a GPO database) is the 1976 date: the year *Monthly Catalog* became machine readable.

Hernon and McClure have warned that reliance upon technology has not been balanced by technologi-

Monthly Catalog		
Version	Coverage	Searchable By
Web Catalog of United States Government Publications http://www.access.gpo.gov/su_docs/ GP 3.8/8:	Since January 1994 Full records	Any access points: Keywords, numbers, initials (See Web MOCAT: Search Tips, p. 40)
CD-ROM GP 3.8/7:	Since January 1996 Full records Includes Periodicals Supplement	Author Title, title keyword LCSH Contract no. Entry no. Item no. OCLC no. S/N Series/Report no. SuDocs no.
Abridged paper GP 3.8:	Since January 1996 Abbreviated records include agency, entry no., SuDocs no., title, date, paging, series, shipping list no., item no., OCLC no.	Title keyword
Monthly Catalog Père GP 3.8:	Ceased after December 1995	Author Title, title keyword LCSH Contract no. Series/Report no. S/N SuDocs no. (in semiannual and annual cumulations)

cal insight: failing to understand, for instance, that a CD-ROM index to GPO publications is the equivalent of *Monthly Catalog*.[2] To avoid being ensnared, searchers should begin by clarifying the electronic product's scope and protocols. Lack of understanding can lead to time-consuming search duplications: searching the same *Monthly Catalog* in multiple formats, for example. A benighted searcher could search four incarnations of essentially the same records: the Web, CD-ROM, an abridged MOCAT, and WorldCat. Such a search is duplicative rather than comprehensive, i.e., a big waste of time.

Interpreting MOCAT Records

The GPO Web MOCAT is swaddled in MARC tags—the librarian's vernacular, but gibberish to most laymen. (This is an advantage of commercial, electronic MOCAT subscriptions, which label MARC fields.)

MARC Fields

010	Library of Congress control number
020	ISBN
022	ISSN
027	Standard technical report number
035	OCLC number
037	Source of purchase; S/N
040	Cataloged by
049	Holdings data
074	Depository item number
086	SuDocs number
088	Report number
099	Local call number (takes precedence over others)
260	Publisher, date
500	Notes; nondepository titles may include the note "Not distributed to depository libraries"
650	Subject headings
856	URL
990	MOCAT entry number

Internet Documents

Online-only titles are initially found in GPO Access "Browse Electronic Titles," a potpourri of online titles not yet cataloged for MOCAT mingled with PDF and Web documents and titles not listed anywhere else <http://www.access.gpo.gov/su_docs/dpos/btitles.html>. Browse Titles is arranged in SuDocs number order, i.e., an agency/subagency listing. The Internet browser's Find command can be used to search page by page (note that the Find statement can be a SuDocs number). If an Internet version is not listed in Browse Titles, pick up strays by checking the agency Web site: identify the agency in WorldCat, MOCAT, or SPC, then use the Federal Agency Internet Sites directory on GPO Access to identify the agency's URL. Periodicals and serials converted to electronic format can also be identified by SuDocs number or by title on the University of

Memphis's Uncle Sam Migrating Government Publications site <http://www.lib.memphis.edu/gpo/mig.htm>.

MOCAT doubles as both catalog and locator service. In the GPO Web MOCAT record, clicking "TEXT" displays the full cataloging record, while clicking "HTML" reveals the same record with the URL hot-linked. Another way to connect directly to an electronic document is to click on the URL in the summary record (look for *http://*).

Tip

In the SPC and the Web MOCAT summary record, TEXT does not link to the document's full text—it merely unfolds the full MARC record.

When a tangible product predates its electronic clone, the original record is updated with a note in the 530 field and a URL in the 856 field. The record for a title that premiered on the Internet and later sprouted a tangible twin is updated with a 074 field and a 530 "other formats available" note. (Such records have multiple item numbers.)

How to Tell If a Title Is Online

Both the summary and full GPO Web MOCAT records show a URL for Web documents. The full record displays a hot-linked URL in the summary paragraph and in the series note (example: VII. Series: Online version: <http://www.access.gpo.gov/plumbook/toc.html>.

Depository Status. Learning to recognize item number configurations and fields is helpful since both the GPO Web MOCAT and OCLC Passport list item numbers without identifying them. In the GPO Web MOCAT, depository status is indicated in the summary record by an item number in double brackets, and in the full record in field 074, but without the word "item." OCLC Passport also notes depository item number in field 074 without labeling it an "item" number. In the GPO CD-ROM, look for the word "Item" (on the computer monitor, "item" is preceded by a black diamond, but the diamond does not appear on printouts). In the abridged pamphlet MOCAT, "Item" is preceded by a black bullet.

SuDocs Number. The SuDocs number is in field 086 in the GPO Web MOCAT, and centered above the entry in the abridged pamphlet and CD-ROM versions. Some government information products temporarily lack a SuDocs number in their initial bibliographic records, while others, often fugitives, are never assigned a SuDocs number. The presence of a SuDocs number does not guarantee depository status, since GPO assigns them to both depository and nondepository federal

FIGURE 5-2: Web *Monthly Catalog* Full Record.

```
List of classes. [computer file]. Monthly. United States. GP ①
3.35:CLASS/(DATE). [[0554-A (online)]].
* * * * * * * * * * * * * * * * * * * * * * * * * * * * * * * * * * * * * * * * * * * * * * * * * * * * * *
<001> ocm32171269
<005> 19950920165602.0
<040a> GPO                                    ②
<040c> GPO                                    ②
<040d> GPA
<043a> n-us—
<074a> 0554-A (online)                        ③
<086a> GP 3.35:CLASS/                         ④
<099a> GP 3.35:CLASS/(DATE)                   ④
<049a> GPAA
<245a> List of classes
<245h> [computer file].
<246i> LIB name:
<246a> CLASS
<246a> List of classes of United States government publications
available for selection by depository libraries
<260a> [Washington, D.C. :                    ⑤
<260b> U.S. G.P.O.,                            ⑤
<310a> Monthly
<362a> Began in 1993?
<538a> System requirements: PC; telecommunications software; modem.
<500a> Mode of access: via INTERNET, telnet to federal.bbs.gpo.gov
3001. Also, dialup by modem direct to telephone number (202)
512-1387.
<516a> Individual file in ASCII comma delimited format.
<500a> Description based on: Mar. 1995; title from LIB (library)
short description.
<520a> Contains item no., class no., type of publication (i.e.,
annual report, general handbook, serial title) and format
(i.e., paper, microfiche, electronic).
<580a> Online version of printed publication: List of classes of
United States government publications available for
selection by depository libraries (Supt. of Docs. class no.
GP 3.24:).
<650a> Government publications                  ⑥
<650z> United States                            ⑥
<650x> Bibliography                             ⑥
<650x> Periodicals                              ⑥
<650x> Databases.                               ⑥
<610a> United States.                                    ⑦
<610b> Superintendent of Documents.                      ⑦
<610b> Depository Administration Branch                  ⑦
<610x> Databases                                         ⑦
<610x> Periodicals.                                       ⑦
<710a> United States.
<710b> Government Printing Office.
<787t> List of classes of United States government publications
available for selection by depository libraries
<787x> 0882-4045
<856a> federal.bbs.gpo.gov
<856p> 3001
<856m> help@eids05.eids.gpo.gov
<856n> Office of Electronic Information Dissemination Services,
Mail Stop SDE, U.S. G.P.O., Washington, D.C. 20401
<990a> 96-00599
```

The unfolded record for [1] in Figure 1 shows ① the summary record again, ③ item number, and ④ SuDocs number. Two subject headings are indicated by ⑥ and ⑦. Note that the distributor is indicated in ⑤, not ②. GPO is sometimes mistakenly identified as distributor when Field 040, showing that GPO has cataloged a title ②, is misinterpreted.

GPO Web MOCAT: Search Tips		
http://www.access.gpo.gov/su_docs/		
Scope	Scout Report	
OCLC records since January 1994	Enclose phrases in quotation marks AND, OR, NOT, ADJ in caps ADJ retrieves words within 20 characters (OR is assumed when no operator is specified) truncation: * following word stem	
Search Type	Rules	Example
Full record	Select "Enter search term(s)": Words (including author, title, subject headings, format), numbers (including dates, SuDocs no., S/N, MOCAT entry no.), or initials; In summary record, select TEXT, HTML for full record; hot link for full text electronic version	legislation OR legislative legislat* "S 1.142/2:990-93" "721-021-00000-9" "94-3084"
Agency	Select "Enter search term(s)": Type words in order ("state dep*" will not retrieve Department of State) dept retrieves issuing agency entries only, spell out department to locate additional records (to retrieve both, use dep*) Word order matters - when unsure, truncate Stopword "of" is unnecessary	"Government Printing Office" "dep* housing development"
Fielded Search		
SuDocs number	Entire SuDoc number or stem Include punctuation and spacing Do not enclose in quotation marks	S 1.142/2:990-93 s 1.142/2:990-93 S 1.142/2 s 1.142/2:
Title	Exact title is enclosed in quotation marks	"Marketing U.S. Tourism Abroad"
S/N	Twelve digits Do not enclose in quotation marks	721-021-00000-9
Depository item number	Use to search for an agency publication category or, sometimes, for a specific publication Format suffix (MF, P, E, O) is optional, but omit parentheses if included	0557-A
Publication date	Fill both date fields	One year: From [1998] to [1998] Range of years: From [1996] to [1998]
Issuing agency	Enclose in quotation marks Stopwords can be omitted	"state dep*" OR "dep* state"
Reviewing Results		
Cataloging record only	Select TEXT	Full cataloging record with URLs noted but not hyperlinked
Cataloging record with hot link	Select the hot-linked URL or HTML	Full cataloging record plus hyperlink to full text of electronic document
Obtaining Titles		
Depository collections	Select Locate Libraries: Fill in state postal abbreviation or telephone area code to list depositories receiving that Item	"Not Physically Distributed to Depository Libraries" indicates electronic format only
Electronic documents	Select the hot-linked URL or HTML	http://www.
Purchase	Summary records for GPO sales titles include S/N (not hyperlinked)	GPO stock no.: 041-015-00175-1.

products. SuDocs numbers and item numbers are assigned to online resources to help associate new online products with their older physical equivalents. The SuDocs and item numbers also help libraries to add the online records to their online catalogs (OPACs) according to their item selection profile with a commercial vendor.

In a library where tangible documents are shelved by the SuDocs classification system, one can often go directly from the *Monthly Catalog* to the shelves or microfiche cabinets to retrieve a depository document. The *Monthly Catalog* also serves as an index to Readex full-text microfiche collections of depository documents, which are arranged either in SuDocs number or *Monthly Catalog* entry number order.

Keyword and Subject Searches

Subject headings are drawn from a controlled vocabulary (*Library of Congress Subject Headings* [LCSH]), while title keywords are skimmed from document titles. Full text searches in the GPO Web MOCAT trigger searches through each complete record for matches. These differences affect search strategy.

Full text searching on the GPO Web MOCAT offers the advantage of harnessing popular terminology, augmented by the power of truncation (* in GPO Access), to review the entire record. When using the abridged pamphlet MOCAT, remember that its keyword index is limited to words from document titles. If a searched word is not in a title, the keyword index will not locate that document. For example, searching for materials on "preschool education" would miss the unrevealing title *Even Start.* On the other hand, a subject search in the CD-ROM or online MOCAT subscription services under the Library of Congress subject heading "Education, Preschool—United States—Periodicals," snags *Even Start.*

Before searching the CD-ROM or online MOCAT subscription services by subject, determine the exact subject headings assigned to the topic, using *Library of Congress Subject Headings* (LC 26.7:). Subject headings can also be extrapolated by finding the headings assigned to any on-target document using the *Monthly Catalog* or the Cataloging in Publication (CIP) information inside the document itself. Never guess at subject headings. A successful subject search must use exact terminology. The LC subject heading for *How to Control Bed Bugs* (1976), for example, is "Beetles—Control—United States," an unlikely candidate for a lucky guess.

In GPO Web MOCAT records, subject headings are stacked, rather than written lengthwise. The record for *Survey of Current Business*, for example (MOCAT entry 97-00318), shows three headings in the 650 and 651 fields:

<650a> Commercial statistics
<650x> Periodicals.
<651a> United States
<651x> Economic conditions
<651x> Statistics
<651x> Periodicals.
<651a> United States
<651x> Commerce
<651x> Statistics
<651x> Periodicals.

Each is read as if the x's are connected to the a's with hyphens. A period after a subject term indicates the end of the heading. In the MOCAT CD-ROM, the abridged MOCAT, commercial subscriptions, and OCLC Passport records, the subject headings are written across, as they would be in a library catalog.

MARC Subject Headings	
GPO Web MOCAT Record	Translation
<650a> Commercial Statistics <650x> Periodicals.	Commercial statistics—Periodicals.
<651a> United States <651x> Economic conditions <651x> Statistics <651x> Periodicals.	United States—Economic conditions—Statistics—Periodicals.
<651a> United States <651x> Commerce <651x> Statistics <651x> Periodicals.	United States—Commerce—Statistics—Periodicals.

FIGURE 5.3: Sample CIP Form.

Rabbitt, Mary C.
The United States Geological Survey, 1879–1989.
  (U.S. Geological Survey circular; 1050)
  Bibliography: p.
  Supt. of Docs. no.: I 19.4/2:1050
  1. Geological Survey (U.S.)—History. 2. Geology—United States—Surveys—History. I. Geological Survey (U.S.) II. Title. III. Series.
QE76.R28 1989 353.0085′55 89-600109

The Cataloging in Publication information located on the verso (back) of the document title page usually notes the subject headings (numbered with arabic numbers 1. and 2. in this example) and SuDocs number for the document (labeled "Supt. Of Docs. no."). Each can be helpful in bibliographic searching.

Search Tip
When searching multiple indexes, remember that the LCSH terms productive in the *Monthly Catalog* are not necessarily the subject descriptors used in all indexes.

Entry Numbers. Entry numbers, also called MOCAT record ID numbers, are displayed in the Web records (field 990) and in the MOCAT abridged pamphlet and

CD-ROM editions. In both the abridged pamphlet *Monthly Catalog* and the historical MOCAT that ceased in 1995, short index entries point to the full record via entry numbers. Since mid-1976, entry numbers have included a prefix indicating the year, making each unique. Before 1976, entry numbers lacked year prefixes, reusing the same numbers year after year. You can affix a homemade year prefix to distinguish them yourself: (74)34552, for entry 34552 in the 1974 MOCAT, for example. Because entry numbers are assigned in the final MOCAT edit, new Web site records won't have them initially. In the CD-ROM version, the title and subject indexes provide not only a short title and entry number but also SuDocs number and author, making referral to the full bibliographic entry unnecessary if the SuDocs number is the only information sought.

FIGURE 5.4: MOCAT CD-ROM.

```
97-546     ❶
           ❷     GP 3.24:(DATE)
List of classes of United States government publications available
   for selection by depository libraries / Office of the Assistant
   Public Printer (Superintendent of Documents), U.S. Government
   Printing Office. Washington, D.C. : The Supt. of Docs.,        ❸
      v. ; 28 cm.
      Quarterly, 1977-
      Annual, 1960-1976
      Began with 1960. Spine title: List of classes Ordering address:
   Supt. of Docs., U.S. Govt. Print. Off., Washington, DC
   20402. Description based on: Dec. 1977; title from caption. Some
   issues combined. Also available online, via the Federal Bulletin
   Board, under title: List of classes. ~Item 0556-C ~Item          ❹
   0556-C (online) S/N 721-007-00000-6 @ GPO - $34.00
   (subscription) - $24.00 (single copy) - $12.00 (supplement) ISSN
   0882-4045 Has supplement: Inactive or discontinued items from the
   1950 revision of the classified list ISSN 0882-4037 Continues: List
   of classes of United States government publications distributed to
   depository libraries
      1. Government publications -- United States -- Bibliography --  ❺
   Periodicals. 2. *Government Publications -- United States --
   bibliography. I. United States. Superintendent of Documents. II.
   United States. Information Dissemination/Superintendent of Documents.
   Depository Administration Branch. III. United States. Superintendent
   of Documents. Depository Administration Branch. IV. Series: Online
   version: ftp://fedbbs.access.gpo.gov/gpobbs/CLASS V. Series: Online   ❻
   version: http://fedbbs.access.gpo.gov/libs/CLASS.htm §               ❻
   http Z1223.A7L57 90-649584 [J83] 015.73/053 /20 OCLC 05529709
           ❼              ❽              ❾              ❿
```

❶ Entry or ID number, ❷ SuDocs number, ❸ distributor (GPO), ❹ depository status (item number), ❺ subject headings, ❻ URL (not hotlinked), ❼ Library of Congress classification number, ❽ LC control number, ❾ Dewey classification number, ❿ OCLC number.

Periodicals

A component of the CD-ROM *Monthly Catalog*, the Periodicals Supplement lists government periodicals (magazines) issued at least three times yearly. The distinction between the Periodicals Supplement and GPO's *U.S. Government Subscriptions* sales catalog discussed in chapter 3 parallels differences between the *Monthly Catalog* and SPC. *U.S. Government Subscriptions* lists only serials sold by GPO, while the more comprehensive MOCAT Periodicals Supplement lists serials from

GPO and from other government agencies. Periodicals Supplement bibliographic records add notes telling where some government magazines are indexed.

Search Tip

The *Monthly Catalog* diligently records individual issues of many periodicals: for example, Title 30 of the *Code of Federal Regulations* (AE 2.106/3:30/P.700-END/996), in addition to CFR Titles 1–29 and 31–50, as they are released. To quickly locate general, open-entry records for periodicals in the GPO Web MOCAT, add *AND subscription* to the title in the full text search box: for example, "official gazette" AND subscription. Then use the browser's Find command to look for *NOS.* in SuDocs numbers.

Loopholes

Although the *Monthly Catalog* is the most comprehensive listing of federal information products, its omissions should be noted. The MOCAT does not index individual articles in government periodicals, provide abstracts, index federal specifications, or comprehensively document government audiovisuals, databases, technical reports, and some agency special publications, such as those of NASA or the Department of Defense. Nor are cooperative publications, which must be sold to be self-sustaining, always included in the *Monthly Catalog*.

> If the only tool you have is a hammer, you treat everything like a nail.   —Abraham Maslow

One danger of becoming overly fond of the *Monthly Catalog* is forgetting its flimsy coverage of technical reports. Overlap between the *Monthly Catalog* and NTIS has been estimated at only 10 percent (primarily depository titles).[3] The mistaken assumption that *Monthly Catalog* lists all government documents and that GPO is the government's sole distributor led to poor scores when 12 libraries were unobtrusively tested with NTIS-oriented reference questions. Only about four out of every 10 questions were answered correctly, even though the NTIS answer sources were sitting right on the libraries' shelves.[4] Reading chapter 6 will help documents users learn clues that steer a search away from the *Monthly Catalog* and toward the NTIS bibliographic apparatus.

WorldCat

WorldCat (the OCLC Online Union Catalog), is the world's largest database of bibliographic information. All *Monthly Catalog* records are first composed in OCLC, then replicated in the MOCAT CD-ROM, the abridged pamphlet edition, and the GPO Web MOCAT (within two days after OCLC production).

WorldCat offers two especially useful command-driven methods for searching at OCLC Passport workstations—by title or by SuDocs number—both of which are simple and quick. The SuDocs number search key is

gn:

followed by one or two letters, plus up to 10 numerals of the SuDocs number. For example, the SuDocs number E 1.28:TID-28163 may be searched as follows:

gn:e12828163 *or* fin gn e12828163

The WorldCat search key for government documents titles is the same as for other materials: 3,2,2,1 (the first three letters of the first word; first two letters of the second and third words; first letter of the fourth word). For instance, the *Handbook of Labor Statistics* is searched as:

han,of,la,s *or* fin dt han,of,la,s

If multiple records are available, choose those generated by DLC (Library of Congress) or GPO. WorldCat on OCLC Passport also offers the option of using an entry command of PRSMGOVT to limit the search to government publications and related materials (for example, *CIS/Index*, not a government publication, but given a government tag in the database).

Note a subtle differentiation between the professional, command-driven WorldCat on OCLC Passport workstations and the public-oriented WorldCat on FirstSearch. While both mirror the same data, WorldCat on OCLC Passport workstations is aimed at trained professionals, providing more search control but requiring an ability to decode MARC records. WorldCat on FirstSearch (OCLC/Passport's doppelganger) translates MARC fields because it is aimed at laymen, but sometimes dispenses more chaotic results.

Verifying a title on WorldCat offers the added advantage of identifying it as government-issued, redirecting the search toward the government documents collection. This prevents one of the pitfalls of federal searches—difficulty differentiating between government and nongovernment titles. Commercially published titles often have official-sounding names, but will not be included in federal bibliographies like *Monthly Catalog* or SPC. Falling back to WorldCat also provides orientation when a library's documents collection is uncataloged. Assuming the library doesn't own a document not listed in the library catalog could be a mistake: WorldCat will verify its source as federal and steer you toward the documents collection. And because

WorldCat entries often give SuDocs numbers (field 086) and note depository status (field 074 gives item number), the searcher may be able to go directly to the shelves or microfiche cabinets to retrieve a physical document.

Sales Product Catalog

http://www.access.gpo.gov/su_docs/sale/prf/ prf.html

GP 3.22/3: (the microfice PRF version)

Considered a GPO "Books in Print," the *Sales Product Catalog* (SPC) lists publications for sale from GPO. The SPC is available online through GPO Access and in microfiche, bimonthly with monthly supplements. In addition to the official GPO Web version, Claitor's Law Books offers a Web SPC at <http://www.claitors.com/ prf/prfindex.htm>.

The SPC is easy to use, and many prefer it to the *Monthly Catalog* for identifying current GPO titles. The SPC is useful for finding bibliographic information about GPO sales titles and verifying current prices and stock numbers. This step is a must when an older GPO title has been found in *Monthly Catalog* and the searcher wants to buy a copy. Verification in the SPC ensures the title is still for sale and confirms its current price. The SPC may also be used to determine what's available from GPO on a topic and to identify titles available to depository libraries (look for the word "Item" in the SPC Description paragraph or a Depository Shipping List number [DSL] in the Notes paragraph). The abbreviation NB (for New Books) in the Notes paragraph indicates the title appeared in GPO's *New Products* sales catalog. The Subject Bibliography paragraph guides searchers to Subject Bibliographies listing similar products.

The microfiche PRF is divided into three sections, searchable by:

Section 1. GPO stock numbers (includes ISBNs)
Section 2. SuDocs numbers
Section 3. Alphabetically interfiled: Report numbers, subjects, keywords and phrases, authors, titles, agency series

It is important to realize that a document's absence from the SPC does not mean it doesn't exist, or even that it's no longer in print or for sale. Absence from the SPC does indicate that the title is not currently sold by GPO. A futile SPC search should be followed by a search of the more comprehensive *Monthly Catalog*. Many titles appear in both SPC and MOCAT.

SPC/*Monthly Catalog* Comparison	
SPC	MOCAT
GPO publications	GPO, plus other issuing agencies
Sales publications only	For-sale, out-of-print, and not-sold titles
Current price	Prices may be out of date
Keywords, LIV	LCSH
Not input into OCLC	Input into OCLC

FIGURE 5.5: Sales Product Catalog.

```
PRF Online Via GPO Access

Title:                    List of Classes of United States Government
                          Publications Available for Selection by Depository
                          Libraries


Stock Number:             721-007-00000-6
Availability:             in stock / whse and/or retail / priced
Price:                    $36.00
Price (non-U.S.):         $45.00
List ID:                  LCGPD
Description:                          Quarterly periodical with a supplement.
                          Subscription              price covers issues for
                          1 year. Subscription                 service begins
                          with the first issues after the            order
                          is processed. Copies of the latest 2 quarterly
                          issues and the latest supplement are retained
                          in stock for individual purchase. The supplement
                          has the Title: Inactive or Discontinued Items
                          From the 1950 Revision of the Classified List.
                          Single copy, $24.00, supplement, $14.00; foreign
                          single copy, $30.00; supplement, $17.50. LCGPD.
                          File Code 2B.   ❶

Publisher:                Government Printing Office, Superintendent of
                          Documents   ❷

Note:                     Estimated single issue weight: 1 lb. 1 oz.; supplement,
                          7 oz. O/N 97-220.
Key Phrases:              Subscriptions, LCGPD, Government Publications,
                          United States Government Publications Available
                          for Selection by Depository Libraries, Depository
                          Libraries
SuDocs Class:             GP 3.24:
ISBN:                     0-16-011184-6
ISSN:                     0882-4045
Cross reference:          000-000-00000-1
Quantity Price:           discount
Binding:                  perfect binding
Cover:                    paper
Subject Bibliography:     150HR 244EE
Status date:              04-23-85
Unit:                     subscription
Unit (non-U.S.):          each
```

Since **[1]** in Figures. 5.1 is distributed by GPO, we can also find it in the *Sales Product Catalog*. Atypically, this record does not note depository status, which would be indicated by an item number concluding the Description paragraph (see ① for typical placement). The Publisher statement ② is also uncharacteristic, since the issuing agency (i.e. Publisher) is GPO. By definition, every title in SPC is distributed (sold) by GPO, but GPO-as-distributor is never mentioned in any record—it's a given. GPO is cited here as issuing agency (i.e. Publisher). Think of it this way: Distributor answers the question, "Who sells it?"; publisher/issuing agency identifies "Who wrote it?"

Sales Product Catalog	
To Search	Select
Words, initials, or numbers	Full text search Enclose phrases in quotation marks
SuDocs number	Fielded search Enclose in quotation marks
	Some citations initially lack SuDocs numbers. If a SuDocs number search is unsuccessful, try other clues, such as title.
Stock number	Fielded search: Stock number
Superseded stock number	Fielded search: Notes
Title, author, issuing agency, date	Fielded search: Select corresponding field
Alternate title (example: The Plum Book)	Fielded search: Description
Subject headings, series, place, organization, title keywords, and phrases	Fielded search: Key phrase Many subject headings are from LC's "Legislative Indexing Vocabulary" (LIV) <http://lcweb.loc.gov/lexico/liv/brsearch.html>
Annotation, series, report number, departmental or contract number, LC card number	Fielded search: Description
Depository item number	Full text search Fielded search: Description
Format (example: CD-ROM, posters, microfiche, multimedia, computer tapes, maps)	Fielded search: Year/Pages*
*Strange but true	

The annual *Out-of-Print GPO Sales Publications Reference File* (OPRF) was a cumulative listing of out-of-stock GPO sales titles (GP 3.22/3-3:). There have been two six-year OPRF cumulations: the *Exhausted GPO Sales Publications Reference File, 1980* (EPRF), covering 1972–78, and the *OPRF 1986*, covering 1979–84. Since the six-year cumulations do not supersede the earlier files, all should be kept for a complete record of out-of-stock titles since 1972.

HISTORICAL SOURCES

Pioneer Sources

Poor Benjamin Poore. In the early 1880s, he faced an awesome task. For a century, the nation's publications had eluded bibliographic control. The handful of existing indexes were unsatisfactory, leaving knowledge "virtually hidden, the benefits of the labors of the best minds of the country were diminished, and the lights of experience were obscured."[5] To fill the void, Congress commissioned a catalog of all government publications issued since the birth of the nation, and assigned its compilation to the Senate's Clerk of Printing Records, Benjamin Poore. Ben Poore surveyed the task before him, feeling like "Christopher Columbus when he steered westward on his voyage of discovery, confident that a new world existed, but having no knowledge of its distance or the direction in which it lay. No one could estimate how many publications were to be cataloged, where they were to be found, how long it would take . . . or . . . the probable cost."[6]

Despite the obstacles, it took Poore only two years to compile the catalog known today as Poore's Catalogue, the *Descriptive Catalog of the Government Publications of the United States, September 5, 1774–March 4, 1881* (Senate Miscellaneous Document 67, 48th Congress, 2nd Session, Serial Set 2268). Poore's Catalogue has its weaknesses—many departmental publications were omitted and the index is troublesome—but it is the sole documentation for many of the titles listed. Its brief entries and annotations comprise more than a retrospective bibliography—they sketch the nation's early history in entries like the one that follows:

> *Treaty with the Cherokee Indians. The whites not to settle on Indian hunting-grounds; The hatchet to be forever buried.* (p. 17)

In the decades that followed, several more catalogs were compiled, some documenting only congressional publications, others covering all branches of government. Thorough descriptions of these and other retrospective titles are provided in Schmeckebier and Eastin's *Government Publications and Their Use*, pp. 6–64. "Modern" documentation began in the late 1890s with the biennial Document Catalog (GP 3.6:), which recorded federal publications issued between 1893 and 1940, until it was eclipsed in 1947 by the *Monthly Catalog*. Historical searchers should not overlook the Congressional Information Service's (CIS) indexes to congressional hearings, committee prints, and the Serial Set (described in chapter 8), which are easy to use and retrospective to the 1700s and 1800s. (See Retrospective Searching table.) In *Using Government Information Sources*, Sears and Moody recommend using these CIS indexes rather than Greeley's *Public Documents of the First Fourteen Congresses, 1789–1817*, and the *Tables and Index*, which are "older, less sophisticated indexes."[7] The CIS's CD-ROM Congressional Masterfile 1 streamlines historical searching between 1789 and 1969 by merging CIS indexes for the Serial Set, published and unpublished committee hearings, committee prints, and Senate Executive Documents and Reports.

Pre-1976 *Monthly Catalog*

The pre-1976 *Monthly Catalog* used keywords rather than Library of Congress subject headings, with no keyword-in-title index. Since Library of Congress subject headings were not the authority, terms used in pre- and post-July 1976 searches may differ. For example, materials on the U.S.S.R. are currently indexed under the subject heading "Soviet Union," while in 1974 the heading was "Union of Soviet Socialist Republics," with no "see" references from new terminology to old.

Search Tip

Searches in the pre-1976 *Monthly Catalog* may locate documents available from the Clearinghouse for Federal Scientific and Technical Information (CFSTI), Publication Board, Technical Services Office, or OTS. All are former names of NTIS. (See chapter 6.) Because most NTIS publications remain perpetually in print, older titles cited in the *Monthly Catalog* can still be purchased (although at today's prices).

Cumulative Indexes

Commercial cumulations offer a single compilation of all *Monthly Catalog* entries since July 1976. The GPO Web MOCAT is retrospective only to 1994. Because the commercial CD-ROM or online versions cumulate the contents of dozens of printed MOCAT issues, they offer one-stop searches and harness the advantages of Boolean logic.

Carrollton Press has published two cumulative subject indexes covering 1895 to 1971: *Cumulative Subject Index to the Monthly Catalog of U.S. Government Publications, 1895–1899*, and *Cumulative Subject Index to the Monthly Catalog of U.S. Government Publications, 1900–1971*. These serve as subject indexes to the defunct Document Catalog and the *Monthly Catalog* through 1971. In addition to the ease of subject searching offered, the two cumulations provide SuDocs numbers for pre-1925 *Monthly Catalog* entries, something MOCAT itself didn't do. For this reason these two subject cumulations are called the "Classes Added" editions.

GPO issued decennial (every 10 years) and quinquennial (every five years) MOCAT index cumulations. For retrospective searches spanning several years, the cumulations are great time savers. Unlike the cumulative MOCAT indexes between 1941 and 1976, the GPO cumulations for 1976–1980, 1981–1985, and 1986–1990 were issued in microfiche rather than paper.

The *Cumulative Personal Author Indexes to the Monthly Catalog of U.S. Government Publications, 1941–1970* (Pierian Press) is especially helpful for accessing publications for which MOCAT itself had no personal authors indexed between mid-1946 and 1962. By indexing all personal names associated with each title, the Pierian Press cumulation solves another access problem, since between 1941–1946 and 1963–1975 MOCAT indexed only the first personal author. The Historical Documents Institute's *Cumulative Title In-*

dex to United States Public Documents, 1789–1976 is not restricted to *Monthly Catalog* listings, but represents titles in the historic GPO collection now housed in the National Archives. Another retrospective index is Kanely's *Cumulative Index to Hickcox's Monthly Catalog of United States Government Publications, 1885–1894* (Carrollton Press).

TRADE BIBLIOGRAPHIES

Some trade bibliographies offer selective coverage of government publications. Most notable is *Books in Print,* which lists many high-demand GPO sales titles, including publications in the news, like the Plum Book. In general, however, *Books in Print* and other mainstream bibliographies that include federal publications are most useful for alerting the uninitiated to the availability of government titles. Seasoned users will turn to more comprehensive government sources such as SPC and the *Monthly Catalog.* And since trade bibliographies focus on sales, they usually omit any notice of free access on the Internet, in depository libraries, or SuDocs numbers, frequently the keys to depository access.

PERIODICALS

Traditional periodical indexes offer only sketchy coverage of government periodicals. In 1997, the *Readers' Guide to Periodical Literature* indexed only five of the titles covered by the Congressional Information Service's *U.S. Government Periodicals Index;* PAIS covered 12. Nor can one turn to the *Monthly Catalog,* because it provides bibliographic snapshots of government periodicals but does not index their contents.

U.S. Government Periodicals Index (USGPI)

The Congressional Information Service's *U.S. Government Periodicals Index* is the equivalent of a *Readers' Guide to Periodical Literature* for government magazines. Entries include the SuDocs stem for the periodical. USGPI coverage is retrospective to 1988. For coverage from 1970–1987, consult the defunct *Index to U.S. Government Periodicals.*

Public Affairs Information Service (PAIS) International

http://www.pais.inter.net/

> *PAIS is like the nice little grandmother who used to give you cookies and tea and is now into nouvelle cuisine.* —Barbara M. Preschel, Public Affairs Information Service Executive Director

PAIS International selectively indexes literature about business, economic and social conditions, public administration, and international relations. While including federal documents, *PAIS International* also covers journal articles, books, serials, pamphlets, public and private organization reports, and state and foreign government publications. The only federal documents indexed are public policy-related titles that emphasize

Retrospective Searching	
Title	Coverage
General:	
Poore's Catalogue	All three branches of government; 1774–1881
Ames, John. *Comprehensive Index to the Publications of the United States Government, 1881–1893.* H.Doc. 754, Serial Set 4745, 4746 I 15.2:In 2/2-3.	Ames's Index continued where Poore left off; all three branches covered, 1881–1893; some departmental publications omitted
Catalogue of the Public Documents of the [53rd to 76th] Congress and of All Departments of the Government of the United States. GP 3.6:	The Document Catalog was the 1st systematic record of federal publications; covering 1893–1940, it continued Ames's Index
Monthly Catalog	Published since 1895 under various titles. Before 1925 no SuDocs numbers were given—Research Publications' cumulative indexes provide them
Hickcox's Monthly Catalog (*United States Government Publications. A Monthly Catalog,* John Hickcox, Ed.)	Covers 1885–1894; not a government document
Congressional:	
CIS Serial Set Index	Serial Set numbers, 1789–1969
CIS U.S. Congressional Committee Prints Index	Covers 1830–1969; continued by *CIS/Index*
CIS U.S. Congressional Committee Hearings Index	Covers 1883–1969; continued by *CIS/Index*

facts and statistics. Federal coverage is most thorough for congressional hearings and committee prints, agency reports, and studies. Congressional committee reports, appropriations documents, and annual reports are generally excluded. (See chapter 8.)

PAIS International provides abstracts and thorough bibliographic information for the documents cited, including report number, SuDocs number (identified as "SD cat. no."), and source of purchase. (Titles available free are identified also.) Since no indication of depository status is given, searchers should be reminded that federal publications may be available for free use in depository libraries or on the Internet.

PAIS International is available in print, online through commercial vendors, and on CD-ROM. (Note that although the PAIS accession number provided in online and CD-ROM records resembles a *Monthly Catalog* entry number, it is not.) Searching PAIS print and online indexes is streamlined by using *PAIS Subject Headings*, a thesaurus of PAIS index terms.

ERIC

http://ericir.syr.edu./

For three decades, the Educational Resources Information Center (ERIC) system has specialized in the literature of educational research and practice. The system comprises the ERIC database and a network of 16 subject clearinghouses and various adjunct subject clearinghouses that collect and analyze literature to be indexed, abstracted, and added to the ERIC database. While most of the titles cited in ERIC's database and indexes are not government-produced, ERIC itself is sponsored by the Department of Education, Office of Educational Research and Improvement, and is run by the National Library of Education. ERIC's Internet presence is maintained by AskERIC, an electronic question-answering service and virtual library available at <http://www.askeric.org>, and some 30 Internet sites linked by one megasite run by ACCESS ERIC <http://www.aspensys.com/eric/>.

The ERIC database is the largest and most frequently used education database in the world. It consists of two files: Resources in Education (RIE), emphasizing research reports, curriculum guides, conference papers, and program descriptions, and Current Index to Journals in Education (CIJE), with articles from education-related journals. The ERIC database since 1989 can be searched on the Internet (select "Search ERIC Database" from the AskERIC home page). Internet access to the database prior to 1989 is possible from sites listed in "Internet Access Points to ERIC" on AskERIC <http://ericir.syr.edu/ithome/networkers/networker8_1.html>. The database is also available on

locally mounted library systems and through private online database and CD-ROM vendors.

ERIC's major abstract journals are *Current Index to Journals in Education* (ED 1.310/4: and from Oryx Press) and *Resources in Education* (ED 1.310: and from Oryx Press). *Current Index to Journals in Education* (CIJE) announces journal articles, which are assigned ERIC Journal (EJ) numbers. *Resources in Education* (RIE) announces research reports, books, syllabi, manuals, bibliographies, and numerous other documents, each assigned an ERIC Document (ED) number. Both RIE and CIJE are searchable online using the ERIC database. Searches of ERIC indexes or the ERIC database are facilitated by using the *Thesaurus of ERIC Descriptors* (on microfiche, ED 1.310/3: and from Oryx Press), a controlled vocabulary of educational terms.

Journal articles announced in CIJE may be found in libraries, borrowed through interlibrary loan, or purchased as reprints from the UnCover Company, University Microfilms International, or the Institute for Scientific Information. Paper or microfiche copies of documents cited in RIE may be found in many depository collections (ED 1.310/2:), in libraries subscribing to the ERIC microfiche collection, or purchased in paper or microfiche from the ERIC Document Reproduction Service (EDRS). The titles distributed to depository libraries are Department of Education documents in the public domain and announced in *Resources in Education*. These comprise a subset (about 10 percent) of the ERIC microfiche collection and include only government-funded reports, not contractor reports. A pilot project to make more ERIC public domain reports available to depositories is underway in a cooperative effort between GPO, ERIC, and OCLC. Documents announced since January 1996 will soon be available from EDRS in full text on the Internet and through document faxback.

Access Tip

Monthly Catalog or WorldCat entries with SuDocs number ED 1.310/2: are ERIC documents. The number following the colon is the ED number. Example: ED 1.310/2:249504 = ED 249504. These titles may be found in many depository collections and in libraries owning the ERIC microfiche collection, or may be ordered from ERIC Document Reproduction Service.

Magazines on the Web

Many agencies mount their periodicals on their Web sites. To identify a Web version of a periodical, check GPO Pathway Browse Titles under the agency name. To pick up strays, use the search engine on the agency's Web site or check the lists of government Web periodicals maintained by the University of Louisville Ekstrom Library <http://www.louisville.edu/library/ekstrom/

govpubs/periodicals/periodical.html> and Auburn University Libraries Microforms and Documents Department (MADD) <http://www.lib.auburn.edu/madd/docs/govperiodicals.html>. Periodicals converted to electronic format can be identified by Sudocs number or by title on the University of Memphis's Uncle Sam Migrating Government Publications site <http://www.lib.memphis.edu/gpo/mig.htm>. Web periodicals are usually unindexed, accessed either by hopping blindly from issue to issue or by a preliminary scouting expedition in *U.S. Government Periodicals Index*. Note that *USGPI* is weak on alerting readers to parallel, Internet versions of periodicals. For example, a citation to an article on zip codes in *Census and You* gives SuDocs stem, volume number, and paging, but fails to point out an Internet clone of the tangible depository version.

Periodical Pitfalls

Ideally, indexes covering government periodicals should be used in tandem with traditional periodical indexes to ensure a thorough search of the wealth of topics covered by federal publications. Without a librarian's guidance, however, government periodical articles are easily overlooked. Intervention is especially urgent if the government-oriented indexes are segregated in a separate documents department. Proximity itself would not rectify user unfamiliarity, however. Direction and instruction from knowledgeable librarians is a must. Another potential difficulty is locating government periodicals: in many depository collections, government periodicals may be shelved by SuDocs numbers, separated from the mainstream periodical collection. In such situations, users will need guidance to find the government periodicals they need.

ADDRESSES

ACCESS ERIC, 1600 Research Blvd., 5F, Rockville, MD 20850-3172; e-mail: acceric@inet.ed.gov; (800) LET-ERIC; Fax: (301) 309-2084; <http://www.aspensys.com/eric/>.
Questions should be referred to ACCESS ERIC or to the appropriate ERIC clearinghouse. A list of ERIC clearinghouses with address, e-mail address, telephone and fax number, and URL is provided at <http://www.aspensys.com/eric/address.html>.

FREEBIES

The following Subject Bibliographies are free from: Stop: SSOP, Washington, DC 20402; U.S. Fax Watch: (202) 512-1716:

244. United States Government Printing Office Publications <http://www.access.gpo.gov/su_docs/sale/sb-244.html>

From ACCESS ERIC (see address and telephone number above under "Addresses"):

A Pocket Guide to ERIC (ED 1.308:Ed 8/6/yr)

FURTHER READING

Heinzkill, Richard. *Reading the OCLC Screen*. Eugene, OR: John Richard Heinzkill, 1989.
A quick reference guide for deciphering codes and abbreviations in OCLC records.

Lang, Elizabeth. "Government Periodicals and the Reference Librarian: Obstacles and Accommodations." *The Reference Librarian* no. 27–28 (1989): 305–12.
Suggestions for incorporating government periodicals into the reference librarian's repertoire.

Maxymuk, John, ed. *Government CD-ROMs: A Practical Guide to Searching Electronic Documents Databases*. Westport, CT: Mecklermedia, 1994.
This is a manual for manipulating popular government CD-ROMs, including ones from the Census, GIS, NTDB, TRI, and the National Health Interview Survey.

Sears, Jean L. and Marilyn K. Moody. *Using Government Information Sources: Print and Electronic*. 2nd ed. Phoenix, AZ: Oryx Press, 1994.
Chapter 53, "Historical Searches," discusses search strategies, describes sources, and explains ways to identify SuDocs numbers omitted from retrospective indexes.

Superintendent of Documents. *PRF User's Manual: A Guide to Using the GPO Sales Publications Reference File*. GPO, 1981. (GP 3.22/3: Manual/981).
A concise, helpful guide to using the microfiche PRF.

NOTES

1. The other two are GPO Access, which encompasses the Web MOCAT and more than 70 databases from all branches of government (discussed in chapter 3), and THOMAS, the Library of Congress's award winning legislative site (chapter 8).

2. Peter Hernon and Charles R. McClure, *Public Access to Government Information: Issues, Trends, and Strategies*, 2nd ed. (Norwood, NJ: Ablex Publishing Corp., 1988), p. 168.

3. Charles R. McClure, Peter Hernon, and Gary R. Purcell, *Linking the U.S. National Technical Information Service with Academic and Public Libraries* (Norwood, NJ: Ablex Publishing Co., 1986), p. 117.

4. McClure, Hernon, and Purcell, pp. 77–88.

5. Senate, *Descriptive Catalog of the Government Publications of the United States, September 5, 1774–March 4, 1881 by Ben Perley Poore*. (Senate Miscellaneous Doc. 67, 48th Congress, 2nd Session, Serial No. 2268), III.

6. Senate, p. III.

7. Jean L. Sears and Marilyn K. Moody, *Using Government Information Sources: Print and Electronic*. 2nd ed. (Phoenix, AZ: Oryx Press, 1994), p. 480.

EXERCISES

1. What's the official title of "the Plum Book," published after each new president takes office?

2. Is *Basic Facts about Patents* on the PTO's Web site?

3. How much does the latest edition of *Constitution of the United States of America: Analysis and Interpretation* cost?

4. How often is *Congressional Quarterly's Guide to Congress* published?

5. Identify full bibliographic information (including depository status and SuDocs number) for any of the core titles held in every depository library, listed on pp. 28–29 of chapter 4.

Retrospective Sources

6. Cite any USDA "Farmers' Bulletin" issued before 1976, noting SuDocs number and depository status.

7. Thomas Jefferson sold his personal library to Congress after the British burned Washington in the War of 1812. When Jefferson's books were loaded onto wagons for the trip from Monticello to Washington, he tucked his own handwritten catalog of his collection in with them. Long lost, a copy of the Jefferson catalog was rediscovered and published by the Library of Congress in 1989. Identify it bibliographically.

8. A magazine article about the FBI's Library Awareness Program mentions an FBI report called *The KGB and the Library Target, 1962–Present.* No additional information about the report was given in the article. Identify it bibliographically.

9. As part of its Library Awareness Program, the FBI asked librarians to alert them to "foreigners" seeking sensitive but unclassified information in libraries. After a flurry of unfavorable media attention, congressional hearings explored possible conflicts between the FBI program and individual privacy rights. Identify the hearing on FBI "counter-intelligence visits to libraries" which occurred in the late 1980s.

10. In the first national analysis of academic and public depository library users, Charles R. McClure and Peter Hernon estimated that at least 167,000 people used depository libraries weekly. Academic depositories were more heavily used than public, and users tended to be highly educated students, professionals, or managers. Identify Hernon and McClure's 1989 report.

CHAPTER 6
Scientific Information

WHAT

Scientific and technical information collected by or for the government is an important subset of all government information. The federal government takes science very seriously, spending about $69 billion yearly to support research and development.

WHY

Science and technology have been heralded as "pervasive determinants of modern life," instrumental in advancing our understanding of nature, achieving national goals, and solving societal problems. Government-generated scientific literature is useful not only to scholars and researchers, but also to businesspeople, students, hobbyists, homeowners, medical patients, and other members of the public who use sci/tech research results in their daily lives, often without realizing it.

HOW

As the nation's central clearinghouse for unclassified technical reports of government-sponsored research, the National Technical Information Service indexes, abstracts, and sells U.S. and foreign technical reports and federal government databases and software. Required by law to be self-supporting, NTIS recovers its costs through product sales. Numerous other agencies announce and disseminate sci/tech information through Web sites, special subject indexes and abstracts, databases, electronic bulletin boards, clearinghouses, and information analysis centers. A small percentage of scientific literature is funneled through GPO and federal depository libraries.

WHO

Most U.S. government research is conducted by corporations and universities under contract to government agencies that require technical reports for accountability. Four agencies support about 90 percent of government-sponsored research: the Department of Defense (48 percent), Health and Human Services (17 percent), NASA (12 percent), and the Department of Energy (11 percent).

SCIENTIFIC LITERACY

Although Americans are interested in science, their understanding of scientific concepts can be fuzzy. An estimated 94 percent of adults are scientifically "illiterate."[1] Not quite half, for example, know the Earth revolves around the Sun once yearly or realize that prehistoric humans did not live alongside dinosaurs (darn those cartoons).[2] Scholars estimate that "at least nine out of ten citizens lack the scientific literacy to understand and participate in the formulation of public policy on a very important segment of their national political agendas."[3] Or, expressed another way: "Do you want these people deciding where to stash leftover plutonium?"[4]

TECHNICAL REPORTS

They are called "technical" because they speak to experts within a discipline. They are called "reports" because they report to sponsoring organizations about the progress of funded research. National, state, and foreign governments, international organizations, and research institutions all sponsor research, and therefore spawn technical reports. Some are brief progress reports of a few typewritten pages, while others are bulky volumes crammed with details. More frequently than journal articles, technical reports document unsuccessful as well as successful research. They may be informally photocopied or typed, with most never passing through the Government Printing Office either for printing or bibliographic documentation. Instead they are channeled through a documentation system independent of GPO: the National Technical Information Service (NTIS), for more than a half-century the government's central clearinghouse for technical reports.

Tip

In citations to technical reports, the "sponsoring organization" is the government agency that funded the research. The "performing organization" conducted the research and prepared the technical report. Sometimes the performing and sponsoring organizations are the same government agency.

Before World War II, the federal government wasn't a major player in scientific research, most of which was privately funded and reported in scientific journals. Technical reports evolved after a flood of World War II government research money necessitated new ways to disseminate findings. The versatile technical report could be quickly and cheaply reproduced and easily classified, and partly eclipsed journal articles and books as conduits for scientific communication.

Technical reports have been characterized as "science right now," the leading edge of research disclosing the latest sci/tech findings.[5] As primary information sources, technical reports are raw rather than polished. Quickly released, they bypass traditional publication channels, including peer review and editing. As a result, new technical reports are more current than either books or journal articles (although some technical reports themselves are published in books or journal articles). Technical reports are unbound, interim, and ephemeral, usually in a numbered series. They enjoy minimal use initially, and that diminishes quickly. They are often categorized as "unpublished" or "grey literature," and many never appear in any nonreport format. If information seekers overlook national report collections and their announcement bulletins, they may miss key documents that are untraceable using traditional bibliographic searches.

Finding Government Grants

The giants for government grant-seeking are the *Catalog of Federal Domestic Assistance* (CFDA) and the *Federal Register* (government contracting opportunities are published in *Commerce Business Daily* at <http://cbdnet.gpo.gov/>). The CFDA, a general directory of federal grant programs, is available in print and in a searchable Web version. The print version has agency, function, subject, and eligibility indexes. Issued each June, with an update in December, it provides over-

views of programs, but not whether a program is currently funded. To pinpoint levels of funding available, application deadlines, and other current information, consult the *Federal Register*, primarily the Notices and separate parts for key agencies. (See Finding Grant Sources, p. 52.)

> *No one reads the literature.*
>
> —Dr. Rustum Roy,
> Pennsylvania State University

Government technical reports are underused. In fact, most U.S. scientists fail to survey the literature, even in their own research specialties.[6] Underuse stems partly from heavy reliance on electronic dissemination of sci/tech data, increasing the percentage of fugitives that elude both NTIS and GPO. GPO is especially vulnerable: many fugitives from the Depository Library System are sci/tech titles not printed by GPO but routed by the producing agency into NTIS's stockpile.

With the dissemination of sci/tech information shifting to electronic modes (and the concomitant displacement of paper and microfiche), an NTIS/University of California-Davis pilot project is testing free, online depository access to NTIS documents maintained in electronic image format. Converting paper documents into images allows the images to be indexed, edited, stored, routed, and retrieved by computer. With the exception of computer and audiovisual products, foreign documents, and copyrighted materials, virtually all government-generated NTIS documents will be included. Depository library clientele will be allowed to freely view, download, or print the PDF files, and depositories may print copies for their collections. Depository libraries could eliminate cataloging and shelving the reports, since images could be acquired on demand.[7] The service will be free to depositories and will allow NTIS to FTP (File Transfer Protocol) images to libraries more cheaply than it could print and mail them. Agency estimates for processing Freedom of Information Act (FOIA) requests provide a cost perspective: printing and sending a 3,800-page document (typical for FOIA requests) costs $120, while downloading it onto a computer disk costs a mere $1.06.

Technical Report Citations

Technical reports are tagged with multiple numbers, any of which may function as access points for bibliographic searching. Besides title, author, and agency information, a single technical report may boast contract numbers, grant numbers, accession numbers, report series codes, report numbers, project and task numbers, and the occasional SuDocs number. Although often not identified as such on the report itself, a standard technical report number (STRN) or a nonstandard technical report number may be included in the report's catalog-

Finding Grant Sources		
"Grants and Awards" SB 258 GP 3.22/2:258	Lists useful resources	GPO Access: http://www.access.gpo.gov/su_docs/sale/sb-258.html
GPO Access Browse Topics: "Grants and Awards"	Government Internet sites	http://www.access.gpo.gov/su_docs/dpos/topics/grants.html
Federal Register AE 2.106:	Grant announcements	http://www.access.gpo.gov/nara/index.html Select Notices section: (grant* OR fund*) "grant programs" grant ADJ programs AND *subjects* may be added with caution
Catalog of Federal Domestic Assistance PREX 2.20:	Directory of federal grant programs	http://www.gsa.gov/fdac/ Search terms: grants OR "project grants" OR "formula grants"
Federal Information Exchange, Inc.	Information from *Commerce Business Daily*, *Federal Register*, and other sources; register for automatic e-mailed announcements	http://web.fie.com/
Commerce Business Daily C 1.76:	Contracts and procurements, sales of government property	http://cbdnet.gpo.gov/
GrantsNet (DHHS)	Information about HHS and other federal grant programs	http://www.hhs.gov/progorg/grantsnet/grntinfo.html Select "Search for Funding" to identify Web sites for various topics
Agency Web pages	Information about funding opportunities	Identify agency concentrations through *U.S. Government Manual*: http://www.access.gpo.gov/nara/index.html Identify URLs through GPO Access "Federal Agency Internet Sites:" http://www.access.gpo.gov/su_docs/dpos/agencies.html
FEDIX	Links to educational and research opportunities	http://www.rams-fie.com/ Select FEDIX

ing record (MARC fields 027 and 088). Occasionally, a report sports a Report Documentation Cover Page, which specifies the STRN in the "Report No." box. Unfortunately, many authors cite technical reports sloppily, creating trauma for the poor souls who later try to track down references.

Each document added to the NTIS collection engenders a searchable bibliographic record of its existence: the NTIS product identification code (called an NTIS number in the NTIS Database). NTIS product IDs are in a PBYR-5 format, beginning with alphabetical prefixes designating the origin or processing agency, followed by a five- to eight-digit number and three alphabetic characters (example: PB97-856512INF). Some of the more common alpha prefixes are

   PB, for NTIS-processed reports
   AD or ATI, for Defense Department documents
   TT, for technical translations
   PR, for free brochures describing NTIS products and
      services

NTIS product IDs double as order numbers and should be provided when ordering from NTIS (quote the entire alphanumeric number, including the final three letters). They are also computer search keys within the NTIS Database (use only the first six digits, omit the final three letters).

Obtaining Technical Reports

Thousands of technical reports are for sale from NTIS, with others sold by GPO or scientific issuing agencies. In addition, some may be in library technical-report collections, while a small percentage are sent to federal depository libraries. Various libraries shelve technical reports differently, often by report numbers. To familiarize yourself with technical-report arrangement in a library, ask at the reference desk. To determine whether a particular title was sent to federal depository libraries, search the *Monthly Catalog* by title or report number, or search the title in WorldCat and check for a field 074 — depository item number.

Important MARC Fields

027 Standard technical report number
074 Depository item number
086 SuDocs number
088 Nonstandard technical report number
260 Publisher, date
500 Notes; if nondepository, may include the note "Not distributed to depository libraries"
650 Subject headings

The Library of Congress's Science and Technology Division maintains one of the world's largest, most accessible technical report collections, primarily on microfiche <http://lcweb.loc.gov/rr/scitech/trsover.html>. The division's Technical Reports and Standards Section includes reports from some 60 nations. The division also collects information on all aspects of science and technology except technical agriculture and clinical medicine (covered by the National Agricultural Library and the National Library of Medicine). A collection of historical materials includes first editions of Copernicus and Newton and the personal papers of the Wright brothers and Alexander Graham Bell. Inquiries flow into the division from all over the world and researchers are welcome in the division's Science Reading Room, which houses a collection of technical dictionaries, encyclopedias, handbooks, CD-ROMs, directories, standard scientific texts, journals, and indexes and abstracts.

The division's Science Tracer Bullets (LC 33.10:) are a series of free literature guides pointing to information resources on both popular and technical scientific topics. New Tracer Bullets are announced in the *Library of Congress Information Bulletin* (LC 1.18: or <http://www.loc.gov/loc/lcib/>). Individual Tracer

Bullets and a list of all titles are free from LC's Science and Technology Division at <http://lcweb2.loc.gov/sctb/>.

NATIONAL TECHNICAL INFORMATION SERVICE (NTIS)

http://www.ntis.gov/

NTIS was seeded with a collection of captured German World War II documents and formally established by executive order from President Truman in 1945. Today's NTIS has evolved into the broker for much of the nation's federally sponsored scientific, technical, engineering, and business-related information. NTIS spans both the "hard" and "soft" sciences, including disciplines such as management, information technology, state and local government problem-solving, and economics. NTIS products include audiovisuals, federally generated computer software and databases, and foreign technical reports. NTIS is also the central source for licensing U.S.-government-owned patents.

With more than 2.5 million titles, the NTIS inventory is the largest publicly available research pool in the world. These technical reports emanate from the sponsored research of more than 600 federal agencies, in addition to state, local, and foreign governments, international organizations, academic institutions, and private sector organizations. The bulk of the NTIS collection pours out of three agencies: the Departments of Energy and Defense and NASA, along with some 600 others, including the Environmental Protection Agency, National Institute of Standards and Technology, and Department of the Interior.

Despite its vast collection, NTIS does not have all technical reports. Until the American Technology Preeminence Act (ATPA) of 1991, agency submissions were voluntary, allowing one-third to one-half of federal technical reports to circumvent NTIS. The ATPA requires all federal agencies to deposit their federally funded scientific, technical, and engineering information at NTIS within 15 days of release. NTIS sells these reports in either paper or microfiche, imprinting copies on demand from the NTIS archival collection. Demand for paper and microfiche copies has been declining in deference to NTIS's fastest-growing product line—electronic products. Almost 90 percent of the titles in the database remain perpetually in print and can be ordered online, by mail, or purchased at the NTIS bookstore in Springfield, Virginia. There are caveats to the NTIS "perpetually in print" rule: the recently acquired Bureau of Mines legacy collection is only available in microfiche and older captured World War II documents are available from the Library of Congress and the National Archives.[8]

FedWorld

> *Nearly as large as the federal budget deficit, FedWorld is a hugely popular repository for government (and nongovernment) documents and files.*
> —Lycos, 1997

The National Technical Information Service introduced FedWorld in 1992 to provide a comprehensive central access point for locating and ordering U.S. government information. FedWorld is a conduit to agency FTP data files (FedWorld FTP Site—Access to the FedWorld File Libraries) and dial-up government bulletin boards (most unavailable via the Internet), federal job openings <http://www.fedworld.gov/jobs/jobsearch.html>, and hot links to government Web sites and information sources, arranged under NTIS subject categories. Most FedWorld files are free, but some require a subscription.

The Genesis of NTIS

During the denouement of World War II, Allied teams scrambled to capture Nazi war secrets before they could be destroyed. Many Germans had ignored Hitler's dying orders to scuttle all equipment and documents, instead secreting them away. In dynamited mountain caves, mine shafts, factories, labs, and hideaways, Allied search squads ferreted out tons of scientific documentation, German patents, Himmler's papers, machines, and even scientists themselves.

To process the flood of Nazi military, scientific, and industrial secrets, President Truman established the Office of the Publication Board. Each week some one thousand enemy documents were translated, abstracted, announced in the *Bibliography of Scientific and Industrial Research Reports,* and then sold without copyright restrictions at the cost of microfilm reproduction. The Russians reportedly bought everything, while American entrepreneurs "practically park[ed] on the . . . doorstep," vying to get a jump on production secrets for medicines, chemistry, aviation, plastics, textiles, synthetic rubber, synthetic fuel, rockets, insect repellents, and fire extinguishers.[9]

The Office of the Publication Board later became NTIS (but is memorialized in the PB-prefix of NTIS product IDs); its *Bibliography of Scientific and Industrial Research Reports* evolved into NTIS OrderNow; and technical reports became the predominant method for communicating research results.

Government-Produced Databases

NTIS serves as the prime vendor for government-produced data files and software, both bibliographic and nonbibliographic. Government databases can be purchased or leased directly from NTIS on magnetic tape, diskette, CD-ROM, videotapes, and optical discs; searched online through commercial vendors; or purchased on commercially produced CD-ROMs. NTIS's

Federal Computer Products Center sells government software and datafiles on diskette, CD-ROM, and magnetic tape <http://www.ntis.gov/fcpc/fcpc.htm>. The FCPC home page provides a searchable list of all computer products since 1990. The monthly NTIS Alert, *Computers, Control and Information Theory,* describes new software and data files added to the Federal Computer Products Center collection, with abstracts of research related to computers and information technology.

NTIS offers nonbibliographic databases in business and science, with statistical, numeric, and full-text data files from numerous federal agencies. These include health and vital statistics from the National Center for Health Statistics, nutrition and food intake data from the Department of Agriculture, and regulatory licensee data from the Federal Communications Commission.

Government software and data files can be identified by searching the NTIS Bibliographic Database, through the NTIS Web site, and FedWorld. To search the NTIS Database, add the terms "software," "computer programs," "datafile," and/or "model-simulation." To search for computer programs in machine-readable form, combine the terms "software" or "computer program" with "magnetic tape" or "diskette."

To limit a search of the NTIS Web site to computer products, add the term "ntiscomputer."

Government Bulletin Boards

Some agencies, such as the Departments of Agriculture and Commerce, pump massive amounts of data into bulletin boards, frequently "time sensitive" or perishable data that will be quickly superseded. FedWorld's Dialup/Telnet Site is NTIS's gateway to agency bulletin boards.

BIBLIOGRAPHIC SEARCHING

Computerized databases are handy for identifying technical reports because of their versatility. Any of several bibliographic elements—author, title, numbers—can quickly snag a specific citation from a database. Manual searching of specialized print indexes is another option. Many indexing and abstracting services list technical reports, and many are searchable online or in CD-ROM cumulations.

Technical report searches should begin with the most comprehensive source—the NTIS Database, NTIS Web site, or OrderNow (for two-year coverage)—followed by searches of scientific subject indexes and databases, FedWorld, and finally the *Monthly Catalog,* as appropriate.

FIGURE 6.1: German Documents Stashed in Mineshaft.

U.S. Army soldiers fish Nazi papers out of standing water in an 800-foot shaft of an abandoned Austrian potash mine, 1945.

NTIS Database

The NTIS Database is one of the most heavily searched databases in the world. It cites and abstracts every title added to the NTIS collection since mid-1964 (printed or microform indexes provide access to titles that pre-date the online database), including U.S. and foreign technical reports, periodicals, government patents and patent applications, federally generated data files and databases, and software programs, with an increasing proportion of citations to unpublished foreign material (about one-quarter of new titles). Currently, no list of the old collection of pre-NTIS Database resources exists. These titles are maintained in files and are being keyed into an electronic system.

The NTIS Database is searchable by title, personal and corporate authors, product ID, contract number, and subjects. The database is accessible online or on CD-ROM through commercial vendors, or it may be leased from NTIS. Online and CD-ROM providers are listed

at <http://www.ntis.gov/comserv.htm>. CD-ROM versions of the NTIS Database offer coverage from the early 1980s and differ from the online database in some search and display options. A user manual, *NTIS Database Search Guide* (PB96-153606KAR), can be downloaded free from the NTIS Web site <http://www.fedworld.gov/NTIS/prs/dbguide.htm>.

Subject Searching

Because numerous disciplines are represented in the NTIS collection, 13 thesauri are used to select subject terms (descriptors) describing the content of reports. A list of thesauri used to index the NTIS Database is provided in appendix A of the *NTIS Database Search Guide*.

After a useful NTIS document is identified, noting its descriptors and identifiers (or keywords in OrderNow) will help to locate similar titles. NTIS Database citations include a "descriptors" field, with asterisks indicating major descriptors. Keywords in the "identifiers" field are subject terms not yet represented in the thesauri, such as chemical compounds, cities, biological species, computer programs, research projects, and scientific instruments. Identifiers marked with asterisks have the same significance as asterisked descriptors. Citations are also classified according to 39 "subject categories," which can be combined with keywords to refine searches. Three-character subject category codes comprise two numbers and a letter, for example: 57Y (Toxicology). Particularly significant reports are flagged with an asterisk following the subject category code. Similarly, limit a search by appending an asterisk to the subject code in the search statement. Appendix B of the *NTIS Database Search Guide* provides a complete list of subject categories and subcategories.

NTIS OrderNow

http://www.ntis.gov/ordernow/

Skyrocketing print dissemination costs resulted in the December 1996 termination of the NTIS Database print counterpart, *Government Reports Announcements and Index*, after a 21-year run. GRA&I's annual index was discontinued with the 1994 edition. (See Appendix 6 for GRA&I search tips.) Enter NTIS *OrderNow Catalog on CD-ROM*, a quarterly sales catalog with rolling two-year coverage. (For retrospective searching turn to the NTIS Database.) NTIS considers OrderNow an alternative to the printed GRA&I, which represented a current subset of the NTIS Database. Updates for the last 90 days are available on the Web at NTIS OrderNow Update and searchable by keyword or fields such as title, abstract, or source.

OrderNow triggered a GPO/NTIS confrontation when NTIS denied any legal obligation to provide depository copies of its electronic resources (a dispute underscoring the need to modernize the language in Title 44 of the U.S.C.). Before allowing OrderNow to join the depository inventory, NTIS demanded that GPO pay licensing fees for its retrieval software. GPO declined on principle, citing OMB Circular A–130 and 44 U.S.C. requirements that agencies supply electronic copies for depository distribution and pay depository printing and binding costs for products produced outside GPO. NTIS finally agreed to make OrderNow available to the depositories that had been receiving the defunct GRA&I.

NTIS Search Tip

The NTIS Database cites journal articles, tagged with NTIS product IDs and available for purchase from NTIS. Purchase is unnecessary, however, if the journal is owned locally or the article is available through interlibrary loan. An entry for a journal article will provide clues in the Title field—for example: "Title: Journal of Nanjing University of Aeronautics and Astronautics, Vol. 29, No. 1, February 1997; Bimonthly Pub."

The NTIS Web Site

http://www.ntis.gov/

The NTIS Web site is a source for identifying price and availability of government manuals, handbooks, computer products, and audiovisuals from NTIS. One-third of the nearly 3 million titles in the NTIS collection are listed on the NTIS Web site. This subset includes titles added to the NTIS collection within the last decade, new titles, and best sellers, arranged according to subject and format. (Select the "Search for Products" option to search for a title, subject, or NTIS product ID.) The Web site includes a technical reports database since 1988 (the listings, modified from the NTIS Database, lack abstracts), and coverage of special collections such as the National Audiovisual Center and Published Searches. NTIS Published Searches are prepackaged selected bibliographies with abstracts on high-interest topics <http://www.ntis.gov/databases/psearch.htm>. The free Published Search Master Catalog (PR-186) describes published searches, each costing about $65, plus handling <http://www.ntis.gov/prs/pr186.htm>.

To access the NTIS Web site expanded database of information products, click on "Search by Keyword" or "Advanced Search" at <http://www.ntis.gov/search.htm>. This database will be enhanced with imaged document availability information from the NTIS/University of California-Davis pilot project, and used in conjunction with a new NTIS document ordering system as the document identification and ordering interface for depository library pilot project participants.

NTIS Alerts

These current awareness bulletins provide summaries of research, software, and data files in special subject fields. Each NTIS Alert gives full bibliographic citations, abstracts, and order forms. Many have annual subject indexes. The subjects are

> Agriculture and Food
> Biomedical Technology and Human Factors Engineering
> Building Industry Technology
> Business and Economics
> Civil Engineering
> Communication
> Computers, Control and Information Theory
> Electrotechnology
> Energy
> Environmental Pollution and Control
> Government Inventions for Licensing
> Health Care
> Manufacturing Technology
> Materials Sciences
> Ocean Sciences and Technology
> Transportation

Availability

Document source is noted in the Availability Field. Note that availability is sometimes from "Supt. of Docs." (i.e., GPO) or FedWorld (download only). Some titles, such as the *Statistical Abstract of the United States*, are listed both in *Monthly Catalog* and NTIS sources, are for sale from both GPO and NTIS, and are available for free use in depository libraries. Occasionally, documents go out of print at GPO only to be picked up by NTIS, which continues to sell them, although often at a higher price. The 1997 *Condition of Education*, for example, was farmed out to NTIS when GPO's stock was exhausted, jumping from $25 (GPO) to $57 for paper copy from NTIS (PB97–175590).

With pricing based on market demand rather than cost recovery, NTIS prices tend to exceed GPO's. In 1993, for example, GPO CD-ROMs cost between $13 and $40, compared to $13 to $1,200 for NTIS CD-ROMs. GPO titles are selected for their high sales potential, lowering the unit cost per copy and giving GPO publications an average cost of about $8. NTIS titles must be permanently archived regardless of sales potential, and NTIS enjoys fewer economies of scale in printing and sales. The average NTIS title sells only 5–10 copies, with one-quarter to one-third of the NTIS inventory never selling a single copy. NTIS has been faulted for repackaging and selling publically supported federal information at high prices, adding legal restrictions on reuse, and "thus magically creating a monopoly over public-domain government data."[10]

As illustrated in the table below, the GPO price is often lower.

Price Comparison: GPO and NTIS*		
	GPO	NTIS
Toxics Release Inventory	$38	$45
Basic Guide to Exporting	$12	$16.50
Standard Industrial Classification Manual	$29	$30
Statistical Abstract of the United States	$43	$33
World Factbook (CD-ROM)	$19	$40

*Titles among NTIS's Top 10 Best Sellers that are also sold by GPO (May 1997)

Sometimes NTIS prices are in code rather than dollar amounts. The alphabetic prefix of the code indicates document format—paper copy (PC), microfiche (MF), audiovisual (AV), magnetic tape (mag tape), CD-ROM, or diskette. To translate price codes in the NTIS Database, consult the price schedule in the free NTIS *Catalog of Products and Services*. OrderNow gives prices in dollar amounts.

NTIS and Libraries

When McClure, Hernon, and Purcell tested how well libraries linked users with technical reports, they found NTIS resources to be largely untapped. The six public and six academic libraries studied were ineffectual in alerting their users to NTIS products and services. Unobtrusive reference questions garnered an accuracy rate of about 42 percent, even though the libraries owned the NTIS answer sources and maintained federal depository collections.[11] (Academic libraries fared better than public, tallying about 53 and 30 percent correct answers, respectively).

> *If the assumptions are wrong, the conclusions aren't likely to be very good.*
> —Robert E. Machol, operations researcher

Clues in the test questions that should have telegraphed the need for NTIS sources were ignored, and staff failed to associate PB numbers with NTIS, or to consult NTIS sources to verify technical report citations. Some staff mistakenly assumed GPO was the only distributor of government publications, or that the *Monthly Catalog* would list all government titles.

Monthly Catalog

Because the roles of NTIS and GPO overlap, the *Monthly Catalog* offers partial coverage of technical reports, listing some that are available to depository libraries. Some technical-report series, including those from the Environmental Protection Agency and Nuclear Regulatory Commission, have been printed at GPO, sent to depositories, and listed in the *Monthly Catalog*. Overlap is hardly comprehensive, however: one comparison found that for every 20 EPA titles in the NTIS Database, only one was listed in the *Monthly Catalog*.[12]

Overlap between NTIS listings and the *Monthly Catalog* was 10 percent in the late 1980s (depository documents only) and 30 percent between NTIS and WorldCat (two-thirds were nondepository documents).[13] Often when a technical report is identified in OrderNow or the NTIS Database, it must be searched again in the *Monthly Catalog* or WorldCat to identify its SuDocs number for retrieval in a depository collection. McClure, Hernon, and Purcell recommend title searches as the best strategy for locating NTIS publications in the *Monthly Catalog*, as well as in WorldCat.[14]

NTIS and the *Monthly Catalog* often use different, even contradictory, subject terms to describe documents. The Library of Congress subject headings used in MOCAT tend to be more general, while the NTIS Database leans toward technical descriptors.

Specialized Sources

The Departments of Defense and Energy and NASA use NTIS to supply their reports to the public. Products from all three will be included in the NTIS/University of California-Davis pilot project testing free online depository access to NTIS documents in electronic image format. Each also has its own technical information center to serve personnel and contractors: the Defense Technical Information Center (DTIC), Energy's Office of Scientific and Technical Information (OSTI), and NASA's Scientific and Technical Information Facility (STIF).

Energy Literature

Energy Research Abstracts ceased after 1995 and is supplanted by the Web DOE Reports Bibliographic Database, containing citations to DOE-sponsored scientific and technical reports since 1994 <http://apollo.osti gov/dra/dra.html>. The database cites all DOE-sponsored reports sent to depository libraries in microfiche since 1994 (E 1.99:), noting SuDocs number (labeled "Sup.Doc.Num."), availability in depository libraries—labeled "GPO Dep. (Depository Libraries)"—and NTIS order numbers. The field identified as "GPO Subject Category Numbers" is actually depository item numbers.

Records for energy technical reports are duplicated in the NTIS database, where DOE titles are assigned subject category codes in the identifier field (for example: ERDA/123456 or EDB/662240). These numbers are defined in *International Energy Subject Categories and Scope. Revision 2* (NTIS ID number DE 92018520).

The citations are also available commercially on the DOE Energy Science and Technology database of worldwide energy-related information. It is available through commercial vendors identified in the free NTIS *Catalog of Products and Services*. Descriptors are listed in *International Energy: Subject Thesaurus* (E 1.55:).

In September 1996, DOE ceased depository distribution of unlimited-distribution DOE reports in microfiche (E 1.99:). Because DOE reports comprise about one-third of depository titles, DOE/OSTI (Office of Scientific and Technical Information) and GPO developed an electronic replacement to maintain DOE report content in depositories. DOE is sending TIFF image files to GPO and creating an electronic "Information Bridge" to link bibliographic citations to their full text or "image." This link will allow depository access to DOE files through GPO Access <http://www.doe.gov/bridge/>.

DOE OSTI Current Awareness Publications (CAP) sites provide links to citations and abstracts of new sci/tech reports on energy topics and nuclear reactors <http://www.doe.gov/html/osti/products/publics.

html>. As part of its Openness Initiative, the Department of Energy's OpenNet opens formerly classified information to the public <http://apollo.osti.gov/html/osti/opennet/opennet1.html>. The searchable OpenNet cites all declassified documents released since October 1994, plus older declassified document collections, and some "never classified" documents of historical interest.

The Department of Energy's Energy Information Administration (EIA) provides statistical and analytical energy publications and an Internet site. EIA's National Energy Information Center (NEIC) is a source of energy information and referral. EIA's CD-ROM, *Energy InfoDisc* (E 3.60: and <http://www.eia.doe.gov>) offers full text of EIA publications, databases, and software, with a search engine. The free, annual *EIA Publications Directory* contains abstracts of EIA publications (E 3.27: and <http://www.eia.doe.gov/index.html>). EIA also sells data files and modeling software, described in *Directory of Energy Information Administration Models* (E 3.48: and <ftp://ftp.eia.doe.gov/pub/pdf/other.docs/>) and *EIA Directory of Electronic Products* <http://www.eia.doe.gov/bookshelf/other.html>. Timely statistical reports from the Energy Information Administration are available through EPUB, the EIA electronic bulletin board, free at (202) 586-2557. Instructions are in *Electronic Publishing System (EPUB) Quick Start Users Guide* (E 3.8: El 2), which is free from EIA. To link to Internet sites, use the GPO Access "Browse Topics," and select "Energy" <http://www.access.gpo.gov/su_docs/dpos/pathbrws.html>.

Defense Technical Information Center

http://www.dtic.mil/

The Defense Technical Information Center (DTIC, pronounced "dee-tick") is the central point within the Department of Defense for U.S. government agencies and their contractors to get information about Defense-related research. Topics of interest to the Defense Department span the sciences: not only aeronautics, missile and space technology, navigation, and nuclear science, but also biology, chemistry, energy, environmental sciences, oceanography, computer sciences, sociology, and human factors engineering. Because much of DTIC's collections are classified, however, users must qualify for service from DTIC.

Fortunately, a good chunk of unclassified DTIC information is available to the public through NTIS (usually product ID series AD-xxx xxx), and DTIC's database of the last 11 years of unclassified, unlimited technical report citations. The database is open to the public through DTIC's Public-STINET service at <http://www.dtic.mil/stinet/str/index.html>.

Several Web sites offer additional public access to DOD resources, including DOD's home page, DefenseLINK, and anonymous FTP sites. These Internet services provide a wide array of information such as DOD press releases, directives and instructions, and photographs. DefenseLINK is the DOD Web hub for the public and the starting point for locating information on Defense servers around the world <http://www.dtic.mil/defenselink/index.html>. DefenseLINK provides a portal for information about the Department of Defense, with links to information services of each military department and organization. It also contains many Defense publications, answers to frequently asked questions, and a search interface.

NASA

http://www.sti.nasa.gov

STAR. NASA's electronic abstract journal, *Scientific and Technical Aerospace Reports* (STAR), has been in PDF format since 1996 and is available at <http://www.sti.nasa.gov/Pubs/star/Star.html>. STAR indexes and abstracts worldwide unclassified technical reports on aeronautics and astronautics, engineering, geosciences, physics, chemistry, mathematics, and the "sciences": computer, space, social, and life. STAR lists reports, translations in report form, patents and patent applications, and dissertations emanating from NASA, government, universities, industry, and research organizations worldwide. Analytics are provided for conference proceedings and other compilations of separate papers. STAR offers five indexes: subject (based on the *NASA Thesaurus*), personal author, corporate source, contract number, and report number. Citations are arranged in 10 subject divisions, subdivided into 76 specific, narrower categories, listed numerically in each STAR table of contents. When a document has been assigned a SuDocs number (NAS 1.[no.]:), it is included (unlabeled) as a "Report No." Older entries indicate availability for sale from NTIS and from GPO (abbreviated SOD or GPO) in the "Avail:" statement. (This is no longer noted.)

Tip

To access entries in the Web STAR, click on a Subject Division in the Table of Contents—then on its components, called "Subject Categories"—or on the subject or name indexes.

RECONselect. The NASA Center for AeroSpace Information (CASI) maintains several search engines for the NASA Scientific and Technical Information (STI) databases. NASA's internal online service, RECON, and its heir RECONplus, are accessible only to authorized

users. One database is publicly available, however: the NASA CASI Technical Report Server (TRS) or RECONselect at <http://www.sti.nasa.gov/RECONselect.html>.

RECONselect contains 2.2 million citations and abstracts to publicly available aerospace documents, journal articles, and conference proceedings from the NASA STI database and is a subset of the NASA Technical Report Server (NTRS), a source of recent full-text reports produced by the NASA centers. The experimental NTRS allows searching of the various abstract and technical report servers maintained by NASA centers and programs <http://techreports.larc.nasa.gov/cgi-bin/NTRS>. RECONselect includes citations from STAR, but is broader than STAR since it includes the file from NASA's predecessor organization, the National Advisory Council on Aeronautics, going back to 1915. STAR is actually culled periodically from the NASA STI databases, whereas RECONselect includes everything from the databases that is publicly available. Otherwise, the content of STAR and RECONselect is identical and the two databases can be used interchangeably. To link to Internet sites, use the GPO Access "Browse Topics," and select "Aerospace and Armed Forces" <http://www.access.gpo.gov/su_docs/dpos/pathbrws.html>.

Users of NASA information resources should consult the *NASA Thesaurus*, the controlled vocabulary used to index documents in the NASA scientific and technical information database (NAS 1.21: and <http://www.sti.nasa.gov/nasa-thesaurus.html>).

Environmental Literature

http://www.epa.gov/

Although the Environmental Protection Agency is attempting to reverse the trend, many EPA products have traditionally slipped through the depository library net. This slippage has been attributed to EPA's decentralization and reliance upon contractors, a common antecedent of fugitive documents.

Many EPA reports are sold by NTIS, and some are posted on the Federal Bulletin Board. EPA materials on the Federal Bulletin Board include *Federal Register* documents, *Access EPA*, and test guidelines. (Select "White House File Areas and Federal Agencies," then "Federal Agencies with Information Posted on the Federal Bulletin Board.") The National Center for Environmental Publications and Information is a central repository for all EPA paper and electronic documents available for distribution and can be reached at <http://www.epa.gov/ncepihom/index.html>. The Energy Information Administration's "EIA's Environmental Publications and Data" Web page offers links to publications of environmental interest <http://www.eia.doe.gov/environment.html>. The EPA Headquarters Information Resources Center (IRC) provides one-stop shopping for EPA information, including environmental research assistance, referrals to other EPA information sources, access to collections of EPA reports, assistance in locating materials on EPA's Web site, and coordination with the National Center for Environmental Publications and Information for distributing and mailing EPA documents <http://www.epa.gov/natlibra/hqirc>. To link to other Internet sites, use the GPO Access "Browse Topics," and select "Environmental Protection" <http://www.access.gpo.gov/su_docs/dpos/pathbrws.html>.

The EPA Toxics Release Inventory (TRI), mandated by the Emergency Planning and Community Right-to-Know Act of 1986, discloses information about toxic chemicals released into the environment <http://www.epa.gov/opptintr/tri/>. The complete text and tables from the public TRI data release documents are available on the Internet on EPA's Environmental Indicators Home Page <http://www.epa.gov/Indicator/> (select "EPA Data Aggregated Nationally or by State, County, Zip Code"), or on EPA's Envirofacts gateway to environmental databases <http://www.epa.gov/enviro/html/ef_home.html>. The cumulative TRI database since 1987 can also be searched on TOXNET in MEDLINE or consulted on CD-ROM in depository libraries (EP 5.22/2:).

EPA also publishes an annual report summarizing the TRI data and analyzing trends. A visual perspective is provided through the LandView mapping CD-ROMs (EP 1.104/4:CD-TGR 95-LV 3-*no*). The set contains database extracts from the Environmental Protection Agency, Census Bureau, U.S. Geological Survey, Nuclear Regulatory Commission, Department of Transportation, and Federal Emergency Management Agency. The data can be used to create maps showing demographic and economic data from the 1990 census, hazardous waste sites, and pollution. The maps show detail down to the street level for regions of the United States <http://www.epa.gov/swerosps/bf/html-doc/lv3_des4.htm>. Disc 11 covers the entire U.S., but depicts street-level detail only for counties in the 12 largest metropolitan areas.

EPA Publications Bibliography: Quarterly Abstract Bulletin (EP 1.21/7:) lists Environmental Protection Agency technical reports and journal articles added to the NTIS collection. Since it contains only documents sent to NTIS, it is not comprehensive. (No comprehensive listing of EPA documents exists.) Cumulations of the bibliography are available for 1984–1990, 1977–1983, and 1970–1976 (EP 1.21/7-2:). While all the publications cited are for sale from NTIS and are cited in the NTIS Database, some are also available in depository libraries and co-listed in the *Monthly Catalog*.

EnviroText, an environmental awareness organization's Web site co-sponsored by EPA, supports focused searches of databases of laws, executive orders, and regulations, including the current day's *Federal Register* <http://tamora.cs.umass.edu/info/envirotext/index.html>.

The EPA Library Network maintains a computerized union catalog, the Online Library System, which is accessible to the public through NTIS: (703) 487-4807. The *ACCESS EPA* Library and Information Sources pamphlet (EP 1.8/13: Ac 2/library) describes the special collections of EPA libraries and information centers. *ACCESS EPA* is a comprehensive directory of EPA information resources and services, functioning as a pathfinder to agency information (EP 1.8/13: Ac 2/yr or <http://www.epa.gov/Contacts/Access/>). The *National Publications Catalog* lists publications from EPA and the National Center of Environmental Publications and Information.

The National Environmental Data Index provides access to United States environmental data and information descriptions <http://nedi1.nedi.gov/>. The embryonic site allows composite searching for environmental data across several agencies, including the Environmental Protection Agency, National Oceanic and Atmospheric Administration, the Department of Energy's Office of Scientific and Technical Information, U.S. Geological Survey, National Biological Service, and National Aeronautics and Space Administration.

NATIONAL LIBRARY OF MEDICINE

http://www.nlm.nih.gov/nlmhome.html

> *Even with all our modern advances in health care, I still consider good information to be the best medicine.*
> —Dr. Michael E. DeBakey, M.D.

The world's largest medical research library, the National Library of Medicine (NLM), has an exhaustive health sciences collection and selective holdings in chemistry, physics, botany, zoology, and veterinary medicine (cooperating with the National Agricultural Library to collect veterinary science information). Its collections include books, journals, technical reports, theses, microfilm, pictorial and audiovisual materials, and the nation's largest medical-history collection, spanning the eleventh to mid-nineteenth centuries. Full descriptions of NLM databases are provided in the NLM Fact Sheet, "Online Databases and Databanks" <http://www.nlm.nih.gov/pubs/factsheets/online_databases.html> and in fact sheets for specific databases. NLM Fact Sheets, one- to two-page descriptions of NLM programs and services, are accessible on the NLM Web page <http://www.nlm.nih.gov/pubs/factsheets/factsheets.html>.

MEDLINE (MEDlars onLINE) is the National Library of Medicine's premier bibliographic database encompassing medicine, nursing, dentistry, veterinary medicine, health care, and preclinical sciences. The world's most extensive collection of published medical information, MEDLINE is essentially *Index Medicus* online, with citations and abstracts from world biomedical journals (retrospective to 1966).

MEDLINE is used to produce printed indexes and bibliographies, including *Index Medicus*, the monthly subject/author guide to current articles from about 2,500 of the world's biomedical journals (HE 20.3612:). *Abridged Index Medicus* is designed for small hospitals and clinics (HE 20.3612/2:). MEDLINE citations are incorporated into *International Nursing Index* and the *Index to Dental Literature*.

PreMEDLINE is an interim database that updates MEDLINE daily with new citations and abstracts. After Medical Subject Headings (MeSH) terms and other indexing data are added to the raw records, the full-blown citations are incorporated into MEDLINE and deleted from PreMEDLINE.

> *Last week, in a startling policy reversal that indicates the speed at which the information revolution is progressing, the government gave all Americans free and open Web access to MEDLINE.*
> —Peter Gorner, *Chicago Tribune*, June 1997

About half of all MEDLINE searches are performed by or for patients researching medical diagnosis or treatment. Until 1997, users registered and paid to search MEDLINE and other NLM databases. Launched with much fanfare, NLM's free access to MEDLINE over the Web joined Healthfinder, the consumer health information service, in a government push to deliver health information to the public.

To search MEDLINE free, select PubMed or Internet Grateful Med from the NLM home page <http://www.nlm.nih.gov/nlmhome.html> or go directly to PubMed <http://www4.ncbi.nlm.nih.gov/PubMed/>. PubMed allows free MEDLINE searching with links from MEDLINE abstracts to the full-text articles. Developed by NLM's National Center for Biotechnology Information in conjunction with biomedical publishers, PubMed blossomed from a collaboration between NLM and major science publishers such as the *New England Journal of Medicine, Science, Journal of Biological Chemistry*, and *The Proceedings of the National Academy of Sciences*. To canvass additional sources of free MEDLINE searching, consult Dr Felix's Free MEDLINE Page <http://www.beaker.iupui.edu/drfelix/>. MEDLINE is still searchable through numerous paid online services, on CD-ROM from several vendors, and through a nationwide network of universities, medical schools, hospitals, and government agencies <http://www.nnlm.nlm.nih.gov/>.

MeSH should be consulted before constructing medical subject searches (HE 20.3612/3-8:). A MeSH Fact Sheet is available at <http://www.nlm.nih.gov/pubs/factsheets/mesh.html>. Self-paced training for using MeSH and searching MEDLINE is available in MEDTUTOR, a microcomputer training package that may be downloaded from the NLM Web site <http://sis.nlm.nih.gov/tehpcl.htm>.

Grateful Med is a user-friendly software package for searching MEDLINE on a personal computer. The Grateful Med floppy disk helps inexperienced searchers create, submit, refine, and download MEDLINE searches. Full-text articles can be ordered through Grateful Med's Loansome Doc at <http://www.nlm.nih.gov/pubs/factsheets/loansome_doc.html>.

An Internet Grateful Med, providing free access to several databases in addition to MEDLINE, requires no additional software <http://igm.nlm.nih.gov.>. "Grateful Med" and "Internet Grateful Med" Fact Sheets are free from NLM and on NLM's Web site <http://www.nlm.nih.gov/pubs/factsheets/grateful_med.html> and <http://www.nlm.nih.gov/pubs/factsheets/igm.html>. The "New User's Survival Guide" on the Internet Grateful Med Web site is a guide to searching.

Profile: Dr. John Shaw Billings
Pioneering Medical Librarian

A century and a quarter ago, 27-year-old Dr. John Shaw Billings was assigned to spend his spare time overseeing the Surgeon General's fledgling library of medical books. Billings began by selecting books and journals for the library's collection, eventually devoting over a quarter of a century to developing the collection into today's National Library of Medicine, the world's largest medical library. As an admirer in a later century explained, John Shaw Billings "*was* the library between 1865 and 1895."

Through letters, personal charm, and an army of volunteer "book scouts," Billings garnered book and journal donations to fill gaps in the library's collections. Within a decade he had transformed a small reference collection into the best medical library in the world and had begun a journal-indexing project that was the genesis of NLM's *Index-Catalogue* and *Index Medicus*.

A student of chemistry, poetry, literature, fungi, crania, and vital and medical statistics, Billings was praised as "virtually an all-around superman, who has certainly had no equal." His impact was felt beyond the NLM: it was Billings who suggested a census-tabulating machine to Herman Hollerith, and Billings who wooed Adelaide Hasse (creator of the SuDocs classification scheme) from government service to the New York Public Library, where he was director.

Internet Health Resources		
MEDLINE (free)	http://www.nlm.nih.gov/nlmhome.html or http://www.4ncbi.nlm.nih.gov/PubMed/	Articles in biomedical journals
Information hubs	Healthfinder http://www.healthfinder.gov	Gateway to federal, state and local government, university, and non-profit consumer health information sites
	National Institutes of Health http://www.nih.gov/health/	Links to NIH clearinghouses, publications, and hotlines for patients and professionals
	Department of Health and Human Services http://www.os.dhhs.gov/	Select HHS Agencies to identify subject specialties
	Centers for Disease Control and Prevention http://wonder.cdc.gov/	CDC reports, guidelines, and data
Experts and organizations	National Health Information Center http://nhic-nt.health.org/	Referral to government and nongovernment agencies, and toll-free numbers
Patient education and professional health education	CHID http://chid.nih.gov/	AIDS; cancer; diabetes, digestive, and kidney diseases; arthritis and skin diseases
Substance abuse	PREVLINE http://www.health.org/	From Substance Abuse and Mental Health Services Administration; includes searchable bibliographic databases on drug use
Mental health	National Mental Health Services Knowledge Exchange Network (KEN) http://www.mentalhealth.org/	Prevention, treatment, and rehabilitation
Statistics	National Center for Health Statistics http://www.cdc.gov/nchsww/nchshome.htm	Select Frequently Asked Questions

CLEARINGHOUSES

Healthfinder

http://www.healthfinder.gov

Healthfinder is a Web portal to hundreds of federal, state, and local government health information sites; universities; and nonprofit groups producing reliable information for the public. Healthfinder is intended to escort the public to trusted consumer health information. It offers online dictionaries, publications, catalogs, and journals; links to clearinghouses, databases, Web sites, and self-help groups; and information packages for illnesses and age groups/populations (called Guided Tours). One user praised it this way: "This is the friendliest government Web site I've seen. It was so easy to use. It was downright exciting."

National Health Information Center

http://nhic-nt.health.org/

The National Health Information Center (NHIC) is an Internet health information referral service from the Office of Disease Prevention and Health Promotion of the U.S. Department of Health and Human Services, referring people with health questions to government and nongovernment organizations and to toll-free numbers. Its Health Information Resource Database lists organizations and government offices offering health information, with contact information, abstracts, and information about publications and services. The NHIC Web site also offers links to toll-free numbers for health information and to specialized federal health information centers and clearinghouses.

CHID

http://chid.nih.gov/

When you think patient education and professional health education, think CHID: the Combined Health Information Database. CHID combines information from various government agencies to serve as a central hub for hard-to-find information from Public Health Service (PHS) divisions, including the Centers for Disease Control and Prevention, NIH, and the Office of Disease Prevention and Health Promotion. Coverage includes AIDS; cancer; diabetes, digestive, and kidney disease; and arthritis and skin diseases. CHID complements

MEDLINE, focusing on obscure information resources from hospitals, voluntary health associations, government, pharmaceutical companies, and specialized health publishers, plus citations to selected journal articles.

INDEX TO HEALTH INFORMATION (IHI)

The Congressional Information Service's *Index to Health Information: A Guide to Statistical and Congressional Publications on Public Health* consolidates health-related citations and abstracts from *American Statistics Index, Statistical Reference Index, Index to International Statistics,* and *CIS/Index,* retrospective to 1988. Citations from the CIS statistical indexes point to an array of publications about the disabled, drugs, environmental health, epidemiology, family planning, health care and conditions, product safety, vital statistics, and other public health topics. Highly specialized medical literature, clinical studies, and medical journals are not covered. Citations from *CIS/Index* include transcripts of oversight and legislative hearings on health-related matters, congressional reports, and congressional documents with authoritative research on key issues.

DENTISTRY

A unit of the National Institutes of Health, the National Institute of Dental Research (NIDR) operates the National Oral Health Information Clearinghouse (NOHIC) to disseminate information from voluntary health organizations, research institutions, government agencies, and industry <http://www.nidr.nih.gov/>. NOHIC distributes patient and professional education materials and sponsors the Oral Health Database of bibliographic citations, abstracts, and availability information for print and audiovisual materials. NOHIC staff provide free searches on topics in oral health. NIDR's newsletter, *NIDR Research Digest,* is available on the Web <http://www.nidr.nih.gov/digest/digest.htm>. Ongoing dental research projects can be identified on the DENTALPROJ file of MEDLARS.

Index to Dental Literature is published by the American Dental Association in cooperation with the National Library of Medicine. It is not a government document, but the journal articles listed in the index are gleaned from MEDLARS.

NATIONAL AGRICULTURAL LIBRARY

http://www.nal.usda.gov/

The National Agricultural Library (NAL) is the world's largest agricultural library. On NAL's 48 miles of shelves are more than two million volumes, not only about agriculture but also veterinary science, entomology, botany, forestry, soil science, food and nutrition, rural

sociology, economics, physics, chemistry, biology, natural history, wildlife, ecology, genetics, natural resources, energy, meteorology, and fisheries. Bibliographic access to NAL's vast collections is available in print through the monthly *Bibliography of Agriculture* (Oryx Press) and online via the AGRICOLA database.

The *Bibliography of Agriculture* is an index to worldwide agriculture research and general periodical literature. AGRICOLA (pronounced "a-GRICKO-lah"—not "agri-COLA," a carbonated drink for farmers) comprehensively covers worldwide agriculture-related literature since 1970, including journal articles, monographs, proceedings, theses, patents, translations, audiovisual materials, computer software, and technical reports. It is accessible through commercial online vendors identified in the free NTIS *Catalog of Products and Services.* Search tips are given in *AGRICOLA User's Guide* (A 17.22:Ag 8; PB85-100618). Subject searching is based on the *CAB Thesaurus,* compiled by CAB International in cooperation with NAL and available at <http://www.nal.usda.gov/indexing/subjguid.html>.

NAL operates 10 information centers with specialties in agricultural trade and marketing, alternative farming, animal welfare, aquaculture, biotechnology, food and nutrition, plant genome, rural development, technology transfer, and water quality. The centers are described on NAL's Web page <http://www.nal.usda.gov/answers/answers.html>.

OCCUPATIONAL SAFETY AND HEALTH

http://ftp.cdc.gov/niosh/nioshtic.html

The National Institute for Occupational Safety and Health (NIOSH), part of the Centers for Disease Control and Prevention, is responsible for prevention of work-related illness and injuries. The National Institute for Occupational Safety and Health Technical Information Center Database (NIOSHTIC) indexes occupational safety and health literature back to 1973, with some key references from as early as the nineteenth century. Much of the literature indexed and abstracted in NIOSHTIC is from sources outside the core occupational safety or health journals. Subject areas covered include biochemistry, control technology, toxicology, epidemiology, occupational medicine, pathology, histology, physiology, metabolism, chemistry, health physics, behavioral sciences, ergonomics, safety, hazardous wastes, education, and training. Vendors for the database are listed on the NIOSH Web site.

NIOSH also produces the quarterly *Registry of Toxic Effects of Chemical Substances* (RTECS), known as the "Toxic Substances List" (HE 20.7112/3:). Considered the premier toxicological database, RTECS contains data on toxicity and effects of toxic chemicals on people and animals. *Registry of Toxic Effects of Chemi-*

cal Substances (RTECS): Comprehensive Guide to the RTECS is a guide to the data (HE 20.7108:T 65). RTECS is available through NLM's TOXNET, with additional vendors listed on the NIOSH Web site <http://ftp.cdc.gov/niosh/rtecs.html>.

WATER RESOURCES

The U.S. Geological Survey's Selected Water Resources Abstracts (SWRA) database comprehensively covers water-related literature since 1939 (microfiche, I 1.94/2:). Since July 1994 only USGS abstracts have been added. A Web interface is located at <http://water.usgs.gov/public/nawdex/swra.html>.

RESEARCH IN PROGRESS

Ongoing research information systems bridge the prepublication gap by alerting scientists to projects recently funded, in progress, or recently completed. Research-in-progress databases tell what research is being performed, where, and by whom, and identify funding sources, beginning and ending dates, and sources of additional information. They can be used to avoid duplication, identify funding sources, stimulate ideas, or locate subject specialists.

The National Technical Information Service has characterized its FEDRIP (Federal Research In Progress) database as "one of the government's best kept secrets," a cache of federally funded research summaries in the physical and life sciences and engineering. Particularly strong in health and medicine, FEDRIP includes research summaries contributed by 13 federal agencies, including the Environmental Protection Agency, National Science Foundation, Departments of Energy and Agriculture, NASA, National Institutes of Health, National Institute of Standards and Technology, U.S. Geological Survey, and the Nuclear Regulatory Commission. FEDRIP users should remember that many federal R & D agencies are not represented in the database, including the Department of Defense, a key funder of research. FEDRIP may be accessed through commercial vendors identified in the free NTIS *Catalog of Products and Services*. A free FEDRIP Database search guide can be requested from NTIS (PR–847).

Numerous agencies maintain their own research-in-progress databases. Some must be searched directly through the agency, while others are accessible through commercial database vendors. HSRPROJ (Health Services Research Projects in Progress) is available through MEDLARS. Ongoing dental research projects can be identified on the DENTALPROJ file of MEDLARS. The Department of Agriculture's CRIS summarizes agricultural, food and nutrition, and forestry research and is available at <http://cristel.nal.usda.gov:8080/>. The

National Institutes of Health and the Substance Abuse and Mental Health Services Administration maintains CRISP (HE 20.3013/2–4: and <http://www.nih.gov/grants/award/crisp.htm>; also available through FEDRIP).

FOREIGN SCIENTIFIC INFORMATION

The person who knows three languages is trilingual; two languages, bilingual; one language, American.   —German graffiti

The United States is responsible for only about one-third of the world's research and development, making access to the work of foreign scientists crucial. Unfortunately, many U.S. researchers "do not sense the need to consider foreign STI, and do not have the skills needed to do so even if they wanted."[15]

About one-quarter of the NTIS collection is foreign reports and translations, including many from Western Europe and Japan. The Japanese Technical Literature Act of 1986 requires NTIS to collect and translate Japanese technical reports. NTIS provides online access to some Japanese databases and oversees Japanese literature translation and exchange. NTIS's *Directory of Japanese Technical Resources and Technical Reports* lists businesses and government agencies that collect, abstract, translate, or disseminate Japanese technical literature, and cites translations of Japanese technical documents available through NTIS (PB91–100941).

Many citations in NTIS OrderNow are to non-English publications. Foreign-language titles can be identified by a notation in the language field, for example: "Language: Spanish." Foreign language reports list the foreign-language title first with the translated title in parenthesis. When the report itself has been translated into English, the English title is presented before the foreign language title. If only the abstract is in English, the language of the full document is identified, not the language of the abstract.

Some foreign documents are in English when received by NTIS. Others have been translated, like those from the CIA's Foreign Broadcast Information Service (FBIS, [pronounced "FIB-bis"]). FBIS, the world's premier media-monitoring service, gathers translated and English-language news and information marshaled from newspapers, magazines, broadcasts, and unclassified technical reports across the globe. Formerly issued as publications, FBIS compilations are now funneled into NTIS's World News Connection (WNC), a Web-only foreign news clipping service available for a fee at <http://wnc.fedworld.gov/>. The new incarnation has raised hackles: Internet accessibility can result in queuing at work stations, downloading is torturous, and photocopying is a glimmering memory. A weekly or monthly subscription to the WNC two-year backfile entitles users to unlimited interactive searches and automated searches or "profiles." NTIS plans an archival collection of material more than two years old. Readex/NewsBank's FBIS Index on CD-ROM, covering FBIS Daily Reports for 1978–1996, is now inactive. Readex still sells printed reports for individual geographical areas, with the retrospective documents also available on microfiche.

The *World Translations Index* (WTI), published by the International Translations Centre <http://www.library.tudelft.nl/itc/> in The Netherlands, indexes translations of technical reports, articles, patents, standards, and books published since 1979. WTI is available in print and through commercial database vendors.

The National Translations Center, formerly based in the Library of Congress, closed in 1993. Housed in LC for only four years after its move from Chicago's John Crerar Library, the center was in the red. After a period of limbo, the 1989–1993 NTC translation collection (translations numbered from 89–10001 through 93–17461) was transferred to the Canada Institute for Scientific and Technical Information, which maintains a Web site at <http://www.nrc.ca/cisti/>. The Canada Institute for Scientific and Technical Information (CISTI) is the information and technology diffusion service for National Research Council of Canada, the chief science and technology agency for the Canadian federal government. These NTC translations may be ordered from CISTI, but are not listed in CISTI's catalog. The NTC records are listed in DIALOG file 295, the International Translations Centre's WTI database, and in WorldCat (WorldCat records continue to show LC as the location, however). Earlier translations are archived in boxes at LC, and are inaccessible. A few earlier ones are also held at the British Library Document Supply Centre in the UK.

Numerous databases incorporate foreign sci/tech information. The National Library of Medicine's *Index Medicus* and MEDLINE cite non-English articles in biomedical journals and include English abstracts when available, and many MEDLARS databases include English abstracts to worldwide literature. The DOE Energy Science and Technology Database lists energy literature worldwide, including translations and foreign technical reports. About one-third of the National Agricultural Library collection is non-English, and NAL's translation collection is indexed in AGRICOLA. Copies of translations may be borrowed through land-grant university libraries or purchased from NTIS or CISTI. Foreign literature coverage in the *Bibliography of Agriculture* has been eclipsed by the Food and Agriculture Organization of the United Nations publications AGRINDEX (print) and AGRIS (online database).

REFERRAL: EXPERTS AND SPECIAL FACILITIES

Federally funded R & D centers are government-supported but are administered by industry, universities, or nonprofit organizations. Most focus on basic research in a single area, and many maintain unique research facilities for national use. Information analysis centers (IACs) repackage information for their clients, providing reference service and creating compilations, digests, state-of-the-art reviews, newsletters, and announcement services. IAC products are designed to be current and authoritative, and to review, summarize, and analyze information. Federally supported IACs tend to be related to science and technology, with IAC publications sold through typical sources like NTIS and GPO, and cited in their publications catalogs. To identify IACs, consult *Government Research Directory* (Gale Research Company). A directory of Department of Defense information analysis centers is available on the Internet at <www.dtic.mil/iac/iacdir.html>. General directories are located on the "TechExpo Directory Of Government Technical Sites On WWW" from the Online Exposition for High Technology at <http://www.techexpo.com/gov_data.html> and the Federal Laboratory Consortium's "FLC Laboratory Locator Network" at <http://www.zyn.com/flc/flclocat.htm>.

The National Referral Center database is maintained within the Library of Congress. A file of organizations, initially developed by LC's defunct National Referral Center, allows referral to organizations, groups, and experts in the sciences and social sciences. This is a referral rather than an answer-providing service. The database can be searched by subject, city, state, or country. Entries for government agencies, academia, think tanks, observatories, public interest groups, and associations describe location, interests, collections, publications, and information services. The referral database is searchable on the Library of Congress's LOCIS <http://lcweb.loc.gov> (password = organizations).

DIRLINE (pronounced "DUR-line") is the National Library of Medicine's online database of information about health and biomedicine organizations, research resources, projects, databases, and electronic bulletin boards. Entries locate and describe publications, holdings, and services. DIRLINE is also available using Grateful Med software and through NLM's Locator <http://locator.nlm.nih.gov>. An NLM Fact Sheet describes content and access and is located at <http://www.nlm.nih.gov/pubs/factsheets/dirlinfs.html>.

Also searchable through MEDLINE is the Directory of Biotechnology Information Resources (DBIR), an online directory of biotechnological referral information. Included are descriptions of databases, networks, publications, organizations, collections, contact people, and repositories of cells and subcellular elements.

STANDARDS AND SPECIFICATIONS

Standards and specifications for materials, products, or services are set by government, trade, learned, technical, consumer, labor, and other organizations. They set minimum performance, quality levels, optimal conditions, or methodology by standardizing dimensions, ratings, terminology and symbols, test methods, performance, and safety specifications. American National Standards are voluntary, unless adopted or referenced by government.

The National Institute of Standards and Technology (NIST, formerly the National Bureau of Standards) operates the National Center for Standards and Certification Information (NCSCI) Web site, the central inquiry point for standards and certification information, available at <http://ts.nist.gov/ts/htdocs/210/217/bro.htm>. The center provides information about United States, foreign, and international voluntary standards by responding to inquiries, maintaining a reference library, and serving as the U.S. switching center for information to and from foreign countries. The center does not provide copies of standards, but refers requesters to the appropriate standards organization.

The Library of Congress's Science and Technology Division archives U.S., foreign, and international standards in its Technical Reports and Standards Collection. The collection includes extensive holdings of U.S. standards issued by the American National Standards Institute (ANSI) <http://www.ansi.org/> and its affiliated industrial, standards-producing organizations, plus worldwide industrial standards, and military standards. The division's Science Reading Room is open to the public.

Several government agencies issue mandatory and voluntary standards and specifications. The *Department of Defense Index of Specifications and Standards*, or DODISS, lists unclassified federal, military, and departmental standards and specifications (D 1.76:). Although military standards and specifications are not yet available in full text electronically, DOD operates a single stock point for current military specifications and standards at <http://www.dodssp.daps.mil/>. The Federal Supply Service issues the annual *Index of Federal Specifications, Standards and Commercial Item Descriptions*, which lists federal specifications, standards, and handbooks and identifies qualified products (GS 2.8/2:). Copies of current federal standards and specifications needed by businesses for bidding and contracting are listed free from GSA Business Service Centers at <http://www.gsa.gov:80/regions/r8/busi.htm>. The *Code of Federal Regulations* lists many mandatory agency standards, while the *Monthly Catalog* cites standards and standards-related publications. To link to Internet sites, use GPO Access "Browse Topics," and select "Standards" <http://www.access.gpo.gov/su_docs/dpos/pathbrws.html>.

The American National Standards Institute (ANSI) is America's private, nonprofit, coordinating organization for private sector voluntary standardization. The National Standards Association offers several print, database, and on-demand services for tracing and obtaining standards.

ADDRESSES
Agriculture

National Agricultural Library, 10301 Baltimore Blvd., Beltsville, MD 20705-2351; (301) 504-5755. The D.C. Reference Center is in Room 1052, South Agriculture Building, U.S. Department of Agriculture, 14th & Independence Avenue, SW, Washington, DC 20250; dcrc@nalusda.gov; (202) 720-3434.

ALF (NAL's electronic bulletin board): For information and a free user's guide, write to National Agricultural Library, Public Services Division, Room 100, ATTN: ALF, 10301 Baltimore Blvd., Beltsville, MD 20705-2351.

Energy

National Energy Information Center, Energy Information Administration, Forrestal Bldg., EI-30, Room 1F-048, Washington, DC 20585; E-mail: infoctr@eia.doe.gov; (202) 586-8800; Fax: (202) 586-0727; <http://www.eia.doe.gov/index.html>.

Office of Scientific and Technical Information (OSTI), U.S. Department of Energy, Box 62, Oak Ridge, TN 37831, ATTN: Information Services; E-mail: usertalk@adonis.osti.gov; (423) 576-8401; Fax: (423) 576-2865; <http://www.doe.gov/html/osti/glance/about.html>.

Environmental Protection Agency

Public Access, EPA Headquarters Information Resources Center, operated by Garcia Consulting, Inc., 401 M St, SW (3404), Washington, DC 20460; E-mail: public-access@epamail.epa.gov; (202) 260-5922.

Library of Congress

Science & Technology Division, Library of Congress, Washington, DC 20540; (202) 707-5664; <http://lcweb.loc.gov/ss/scitech>

Technical Reports and Standards Section, Science and Technology Division, The Library of Congress, Washington, DC 20540-4750; (202)-707-5655; Fax: (202)-707-0253; <http://lcweb.loc.gov/rr/scitech/trsover.html>.

Medicine

National Library of Medicine, 8600 Rockville Pike, Bethesda, MD 20894; E-mail: mms@nlm.nih.gov;(888) FINDNLM (general information), (301) 594-5983; <http://www.nlm.nih.gov/>.

NTIS

National Technical Information Service, U.S. Department of Commerce, 5285 Port Royal Road, Springfield, VA 22161; E-mail: info@ntis.fedworld.gov; Sales Desk: (800) 553-NTIS, (703) 487-4650, Subscriptions: (703) 487-4630; Fax: (703) 321-8547, E-mail ordering: orders@ntis.fedworld.gov.

Standards

National Center for Standards and Certification Information, National Institute of Standards and Technology, Bldg. 820, Room 164, Gaithersburg, MD 20899; E-mail: joanne. overman@nist.gov; (301) 975-4040; Fax: (301) 926-1559.

Translations

CISTI, National Research Council Canada, Building M-55, Montreal Road, Ottawa, Canada K1A 0S2; E-mail: cisti.info@nrc.ca; (800) 668-1222 or (613) 993-1600; Fax: (613) 952-9112; <http://www.nrc.ca/>.

FREEBIES

The following Subject Bibliographies are free from: Stop: SSOP, Washington, DC 20402; U.S. Fax Watch; (202) 512-1716. Many others on sci/tech topics are listed in the free SB Index (SB-599).

22. Dentistry <http://www.access.gpo.gov/su docs/sale/sb-022.html>

162. Agriculture <http://www.access.gpo.gov/su_docs/sale/sb-162.html>

231. Specifications and Standards <http://www.access.gpo.gov/su_docs/sale/sb-231.html>

Agriculture

From National Agricultural Library:

Agricultural Libraries Information Notes, ALIN (A 17.23:) Back issues are available through NAL's Web page <http://www.nal.usda.gov/alin/>

A17.18/5: *List of Journals Indexed in AGRICOLA* (A 17.18/5:) <http://www.nal.usda.gov/indexing/ljitoc.htm>

Notes title and abbreviated title, NAL call number, ISSN, imprint, indexing coverage, and availability of abstracts; copies free with a self-addressed label from: LJI, Indexing Branch, Room 011, USDA, ARS, 10301 Baltimore Blvd., Beltsville, MD 20705-2351

Quick Bibliographies (QB's) are bibliographies culled from AGRICOLA <gopher://gopher.nal.usda.gov/1/nalpub/qb>

Special Reference Briefs (SRB) are copies of custom NAL bibliographies <gopher://gopher.nal.usda.gov/0/nalpub/bull10.alf>

Energy

From National Energy Information Center, EI-231, Energy Information Administration, Forrestal Bldg, 1000 Independence Ave, S.W, Washington, DC 20585; E-mail: infoctr@eia.doe.gov; (202) 586-8800; Fax: (202) 586-0727; <http://www.eia.doe.gov/index.html>

EIA New Releases (E 3.27/4: and <http://www.eia.doe.gov/neic/contents.html>)

EIA Publications Directory (E 3.27: and <http://www.eia.doe.gov/index.html>)

Energy Information Directory (E 3.33: and <http://www.eia.doe.gov/neic/contents.html>)

National Library of Medicine

For a complete list of NLM Fact Sheets: FACT SHEETS, Office of Public Information, National Library of Medicine, 8600 Rockville Pike, Bethesda, MD 20894; <http://www.nlm.nih.gov/pubs/factsheets/factsheets.html>

Catalog of Publications, Audiovisuals & Software (URLs are provided for electronic versions of titles)

DIRLINE <http://www.nlm.nih.gov/pubs/factsheets/dirlinfs.html>

Gratefully Yours, a bimonthly newsletter for Grateful Med users <http://www.nlm.nih.gov/pubs/gyours/gyours.html>

NLM News (HE 20.3619:) <http://www.nlm.nih.gov/pubs/nlmnews/nlmnews.html>

This bimonthly newsletter announces new publications, database products, and free materials. To be added to the mailing list, contact NLM News Editor, Melanie Modlin; e-mail: melanie_modlin@nlm.nih.gov.

Current Bibliographies in Medicine (CBM) <http://www.nlm.nih.gov/pubs/resources.html>

These current awareness bibliographies on biomedical topics (excluding AIDS, covered in *AIDS Bibliography*) are the first NLM publications to jettison print for Internet-only publication. All of the approximately 10 titles issued yearly since 1992 are free on the Web. Individual CBMs created in tandem with an NIH conference are also printed by GPO.

Library of Congress

From Science Reference Section, Science and Technology Division, Library of Congress, 10 First Street, S.E., Washington, DC 20540-5581; <http://lcweb.loc.gov/rr/scitech/>

Individual Tracer Bullets and a list of all Tracer Bullet titles; include a self-addressed mailing label.

NTIS

From National Technical Information Service, Technology Administration, U.S. Department of Commerce, Springfield, VA 22161; (703) 487-4650; Fax: (703) 321-8547

Newsline, an online quarterly newsletter announcing NTIS activities and new products (PR-660), is available on the NTIS Web site at <http://www.ntis.gov/newsline/newsline.htm>.

Published Search Master Catalog (PR–186)

NTIS *Catalog of Products and Services* (PR–827) <http://www.ntis.gov/prs/pr827.htm>

Search Guide to FEDRIP Database (PR–847)

FURTHER READING

Gimbel, John. *Science, Technology, and Reparations: Exploitation and Plunder in Postwar Germany.* Stanford, CA: Stanford University Press, 1990.

> The story behind the allies' "intellectual reparations" program to exploit Nazi know-how.

Hernon, Peter and Charles R. McClure. *Public Access to Government Information: Issues, Trends, and Strategies.* 2nd ed. Norwood, NJ: Ablex Publishing Corp., 1988.

> See Gary R. Purcell's chapter on "Technical Report Literature."

McClure, Charles R. and Peter Hernon. *Academic Library Use of NTIS: Suggestions for Services and Core Collections.* NTIS, 1986. (PB86–228871).

> A manual of practical suggestions for making NTIS products and services available in libraries, with an annotated bibliography of "core" NTIS collections for specific subject areas.

Moody, Marilyn K. "Technical Report Literature on the World Wide Web." *ISRQ: Internet Reference Services Quarterly* 1 (Issue 3, 1996): 7–21.

> An overview of technical reports and their electronic outlets.

Schwartz, John. "On the Web, It's Hard to Know What Health Information Is Reliable." *Washington Post*, April 22, 1997; Health Section, page 12.

> Good news about Healthfinder.

Sprehe, J. Timothy. "Are the National Technical Information Service's Prices Too High?" *Government Information Quarterly* 13 (October 1996): 373–91.

> The answer is "no." The study and the basis for this conclusion are described.

NOTES

1. Morris H. Shamos. *The Myth of Scientific Literacy.* (New Brunswick, NJ: Rutgers University Press, 1995) p. 90, 191. It should be noted that Shamos argues that seeking a scientifically literate citizenry is unrealistic and our educational efforts should be generalized and redirected.

2. National Science Board. *Science and Engineering Indicators 1996.* (NSB 96-21) GPO, 1996. p. 7–8. <http://www.nsf.gov/sbe/srs/seind96/startse.htm> (November 3, 1997).

3. "Scientific Illiteracy," *Society* 27 (July/August 1990): 3.

4. Judith Stone, "Ignorance on Parade," *Discover* 10 (July 1989): 102.

5. John Sullivan, "What's Going on in Sci-Tech," *LC Information Bulletin* 42 (January 17, 1983): 18.

6. House. Committee on Science, Space, and Technology, *OTA Report "Federally Funded Research: Decisions for a Decade" Hearing before the Subcommittee on Science of the Committee on Science, Space, and Technology, 102–1, March 20, 1991* (GPO, 1991), pp. 79, 97. (Y 4.Sci 2:102/7)

7. For further information about the project, contact Kristin Vajs at NTIS kvajs@ntis.fedworld.gov or (703) 487-4690 or Linda Kennedy lmkennedy@ucdavis.edu or (916) 752-1656.

8. See *Guides to German Records Microfilmed at Alexandria, VA.*, a series of finding aids for the National Archives collection of microfilmed records seized during World War II (AE 1.112:). All microfilm is available for use at the National Archives or may be purchased from the National Archives Publications Sales Branch.

9. C. Lester Walker, "Secrets by the Thousands," *Harper's Magazine* (October 1946): 336. Related articles are Groff Conklin, "The Publication Board—World's Biggest Publishing Project." *Publisher's Weekly* (August 10, 1946): 581–83; Julius C. Edelstein, "Science as Reparations," *Physics Today* 1 (December 1948): 6–14.

10. Robert Gellman. "NTIS is an Information Policy Disaster," *Government Computer News* (October 21, 1996): 29; <http://www.gcn.com/backissues/gcnnews/102196/GELCOL27.HTM> (October 28, 1997).

11. McClure, Hernon, and Purcell, pp. 78–88.

12. An unpublished study by Steve Hayes was described in *Government Information as a Public Asset Hearing before the Joint Committee on Printing, 102-2, April 25, 1991.* (S. Hrg. 102-114) GPO, 1991, p. 18 (Y 4.P 93/1:G 74/12)

13. Charles R. McClure, Peter Hernon, and Gary R. Purcell, *Linking the U.S. National Technical Information Service with Academic and Public Libraries* (Norwood, NJ: Ablex Publishing Co., 1986), pp. 116–17.

14. McClure, Hernon, and Purcell, p. 116.

15. Congress. Office of Technology Assessment, *Helping America Compete: The Role of Federal Scientific & Technical Information* (OTA-CIT-454) (GPO, 1990), p. 55. (Y 3.T22/2:2 Am 3/2)

EXERCISES

1. How much is a subscription to the NTIS *Environment Highlights* catalog?

2. Bibliographically verify any of the following titles.
   a. *How to Get It: A Guide to Defense-Related Information Sources* (Defense Department)
   b. *The Effects of Electronic Recordkeeping on the Historical Record of the U.S. Government: A Report for the National Archives and Records Administration, a Study by the National Academy of Public Administration*
   c. *Protection of Personal Privacy Interests Under the Freedom of Information Act* by T. J. Hasty
   d. *Managing Federal Information Resources: Annual Report Under the Paperwork Reduction Act of 1980* (OMB)

3. How can you get a copy of PR–1001, *Media Resource Catalog*?

CHAPTER 7
Patents, Trademarks, and Copyrights

The Patent System added the fuel of interest to the fire of genius. —Abraham Lincoln

WHO

Anyone may obtain a U.S. patent, trademark, or copyright, regardless of age or nationality.

WHAT

Patents, trademarks, and copyrights are known as "intellectual property." Although some people confuse them, the protection granted for each is completely different, and each serves a different purpose. Patents relate to inventions; trademarks to product names or symbols; and copyrights to literary or creative works. Both patents and copyrights grant exclusive rights for a limited time, after which the work or invention enters the public domain.

WHEN

Patents have been granted since 1790, when George Washington signed the first patent law and three patents were issued. The first copyright law was enacted the same year. Trademark protection was enacted in 1905.

WHERE

The Patent and Trademark Office (PTO) in the Department of Commerce grants patents, issues trademarks, and administers patent and trademark laws. Copyrights are registered by the Register of Copyrights within the Library of Congress. Protection for each is granted in the United States only—protection in other countries is granted by individual governments according to their laws.

WHY

The basis for patents and copyrights is embedded in the Constitution, which granted Congress the power to "promote the Progress of Science and useful Arts" by giving authors and inventors exclusive, temporary rights to their own writings and discoveries. Trademark protection is based on the commerce clause of the Constitution.

HOW LONG

In 1995, patent protection for utility and plant patents was extended from 17 to 20 years (from date of filing) if periodic maintenance fees are paid.[1] Design patents are protected for 14 years. The United States boasts the world's fastest patent examination process: 19.1 months. Copyright protects for the author's lifetime plus 50 years, while trademarks may be renewed indefinitely as long as they are being used.

PATENTS

We said, "What is it that makes the United States such a great nation?" And we investigated and found that it was patents, and we will have patents. —Japanese official visiting the United States in 1900

A patent holder receives exclusive rights to make, use, or sell an invention, design, or plant. To be issued a United States patent, the patentee must file a detailed description of the invention, which is then published by the government. The result is a mutually beneficial system that allows individuals to profit from their ideas while the nation accumulates what has been called a "depository of genius." Sometimes the public-disclosure requirement deters companies from seeking patents because they wish to protect secrets. The formulas for Coca Cola and Silly Putty are two examples of such "trade secrets," kept private to maintain a company's competitive edge.

Because U.S. patents are the world's greatest repository of technical information, they offer a means of keeping abreast of the latest technology and, conversely, reviewing technological history. By definition, patents report new ideas, since a patentable invention must be new, useful, and nonobvious. Patents also appear before other publication formats, with fully 80 percent never republished anywhere else, not even in journals.

Utility Patents

Most patents are utility patents, granted for a product, process, apparatus, or composition of matter. Utility patents chronicle the nation's technological growth: Alexander Graham Bell's telephone (no. 174,465), Thomas Edison's electric lamp (no. 223,898), the Wright brothers' flying machine (no. 821,393), television (no. 1,773,980), oral contraceptives (no. 2,744,122), and the artificial heart (no. 3,641,591). Standing shoulder-to-shoulder with these noble inventions is an army of more whimsical notions: the alarm clock bed (no. 1,293,102), a means to detect life from the grave (no. 1,436,757), a coat for two (no. 2,636,176), a shoe that makes backward footprints (no. 3,823,494), and a urinal target for men (no. 4,044,405).[2] One thousand and one uses, and all are documented in United States patent literature.

Living Patents

In 1980, a landmark Supreme Court decision ruled that a living microorganism could be patented, making life forms other than plants patentable for the first time. Ground was broken again when Harvard was issued a patent for a "higher" animal: their laboratory mouse. The "Harvard mouse," genetically engineered to be cancer-prone, illustrates the PTO's requirements for patentable animals: it is human-engineered, not found in nature, and nonhuman (the PTO won't patent people). Animal patents are utility patents.

* * * * *

America's first genetically engineered food was the Flavr-Savr tomato, enhanced with a gene that extends vine-ripening without softness in texture.

* * * * *

John Moore was a victim of a rare form of leukemia. Without Moore's knowledge, his doctors cultured his unusual spleen cells, obtained a patent on the cell line, and sold it for use in cancer and AIDS research. Although Moore's unique cells are expected to earn millions, Moore will not share the profits: he lost his suit for "royalties" from the sale of his cells.

Plant Patents

Winter-hardy flowering shrubs, disease-resistant dogwoods, thornless roses, an apricot/plum: all are among the 10,000 asexually reproducible cultivars on the plant patent rolls. Until the Plant Patent Act of 1930, few people bothered to breed plants in this country. Since breeders couldn't prevent others from reproducing or selling their discoveries, incentive for horticultural experimentation was nonexistent. After Thomas Edison urged Congress to give plant breeders the same status enjoyed by mechanical and chemical inventors, protection for plants was granted through a law allowing new varieties of asexually reproducible plants to join the list of patentable items. (Asexual reproduction is by means other than seed, such as rooting cuttings, layering, budding, or grafting). Eligible plants include roses, fruit, conifers, broadleaf trees, shrubs, vines, and flowers. (See figure 7.1.) Tuber-propagated plants—the Irish potato and Jerusalem artichoke—are not protected. Other types of plants, seeds, and plant parts may be patented under general patent laws, as long as they are "nonnaturally occurring . . . a product of human ingenuity." The first plant patent went to New Jersey resident Henry Bosenberg on August 18, 1931, for a champagne-colored rose. Today, both of PTO's plant patent examiners have descendants of Plant Patent Number 1, the New Dawn Rose, growing in their backyards.

Design Patents

The appearance of ornamental products can be protected by a design patent, which protects the "look" of an object rather than how it works or the way it is made. Offering the same legal protection as utility patents, design patents protect the appearance of objects like furniture, containers, games, toys, food, guns, and pet supplies. (See figure 7.2.)

Classification

Since the first patent was granted on July 31, 1790, more than 5 million descendants have been issued. Organizing this vast archive entails grouping inventions into broad technological categories called "classes," and specific technological categories, or "subclasses." The U.S. Patent Classification System (USPC), the world's most comprehensive system for categorizing patented technology, boasts more than 400 classes and 137,000 subclasses. A single patent may be assigned to more than one subclass (cross-referencing). Each patent is assigned first to broad classes and then to narrower subclasses. The Design Patent Classification System has 37 classes and more than 3,800 subclasses. Plant patents are classified under some 89 subclasses. Class and subclass

FIGURE 7.1: Plant Patent.

April 5, 1932. L. BURBANK Plant Pat. 15
PEACH
Filed Dec. 23, 1930

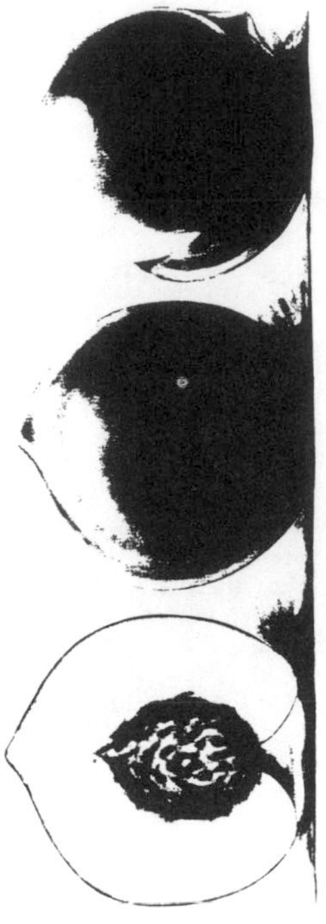

Patented Apr. 5, 1932 **Plant Pat. 15**

UNITED STATES PATENT OFFICE

LUTHER BURBANK, DECEASED, LATE OF SANTA ROSA, CALIFORNIA, BY ELIZABETH WATERS BURBANK, EXECUTRIX, OF SANTA ROSA, CALIFORNIA, ASSIGNOR TO STARK BRO'S NURSERIES & ORCHARDS COMPANY, OF LOUISIANA, MISSOURI

PEACH

Application filed December 23, 1930. Serial No. 504,399.

This invention relates to a new and distinct variety of peach.

This new variety of peach has resulted from years of experimenting with a definite objective in view, that is, to produce a satisfactory yellow freestone peach which ripens half way between the ripening periods of the known varieties, the June Elberta and the Early Elberta. It is similar to the Hale peach except that it has a large pit. Its blood and seed are similar to the Muir, but the fruit is more golden in color. It is a stronger growing tree than the Valient and is not subject to peach curl and disease (Bacteria impruni) as is the last named variety. This new variety produces a very large fruit which averages about one-half pound. Its golden color with maroon shadings modified by a grayish pubescence, adds to its effectiveness in size. Although the skin of the fruit is thin and tender, tests have proven it to be a remarkable shipper; coupled with its great size, impressive coloring, excellent quality, and being a freestone, it represents an outstanding commercial peach. When cut in half, a pleasing modified apricot yellow flesh is disclosed which has a peach red tinge near the pit.

The following specifications and attached drawing show the distinctions and general characteristics of this new variety which has been asexually reproduced.

Tree

Tree.—The tree, being of vigorous growth, is larger than other varieties of the same age. Its branches are stout, with strong, well knit forks, of divergent habit, with an average angle of 45° to 60°. The bark on the trunk of the young tree forms scales, curling in rather thin flakes, transversely around the trunk. The color is russet brown, modified by light olive gray scarfskin, which, on younger branches has a silvery gloss.

Twigs.—The new growth twigs are vigorous and stout, varying to rather slender on lower branches and becoming drooping as growth progresses. The color of the bark of the twigs is glossy courge green minutely dotted with lighter green and shaded van-

dyke red on exposed side, changing to buckthorn brown on earliest growth of the season. The internodes are short to medium. The dormant fruit buds are medium to large, prominent, free, and dull red-brown with grayish pubescence. The leaf buds are rather small and appressed.

Foliage.—The foliage is abundant. The leaves are medium to large, strongly incurved. The texture is thick, soft, and almost velvety. The base is tapering and acute. The blade is flat to distinctly folded, and wrinkled along the midrib. The margin is wavy with a crenate edge having minute reddish points strongly forward. The apex is acuminate to lanceolate. The upper surface is smooth, dull, with slight oily sheen on oldest leaves. The color is hellebore to courge green. The undersurface is smooth and deep grape green in color.

Glands.—There are from two to four large reniform glands, often with additional rudimentary glands on the base of the blade.

Petiole.—The petiole is rather short, and is stout. Its color is clear dull green-yellow, extending to midrib and often extensively tinged vandyke red as on the twigs. The upper side is deeply grooved.

Fruit

Form.—The form is globular with rather broad base and prominent apex producing a broad cordate outline in the longitudinal cross-section. The size is large and uniform, being about three inches axial diameter and three inches largest transverse diameter, and two and three quarters inches smallest transverse diameter, the sides being unequal. The stem is short and moderately stout. The cavity is wide and of medium depth. The suture begins in the cavity, being rather deep at first, becoming a line over the side of the fruit, again more distinct and deep, and ending at the apex which is prominent acute to mammiform.

Color.—The color is light orange yellow to capucine orange, largely tinged with minute dots of peach red shading to nopal red and maroon on exposed cheek. The general color

E. W. BURBANK
Executrix of
LUTHER BURBANK, Deceased

By Robb & Robb
ATTORNEYS

Luther Burbank, who died four years before the passage of the Plant Patent Act of 1930, was awarded 16 plant patents posthumously. His Plant Patent 15, Peach, earned him entry into the National Inventors Hall of Fame.

numbers can be used as access points for searching. The Patent and Trademark Office sells lists of patents or cross-referenced patents contained in subclasses.

Components of a Patent

A typical patent includes drawings, a brief "abstract" or summary, plus the patent "specification," a detailed description of how to make or use the invention. Every patent cover page provides similar information, as

shown in figure 7.3. The numbers in brackets, called INID Codes, are part of an international system that allows cover page elements to be identified even when written in an unfamiliar language.

Patent Numbers

Every patent is assigned a unique number. Since 1836, when number one was issued, the total has swelled to more than five million. (The first patent was issued much earlier, 1790, as noted previously.) Design patent num-

FIGURE 7.2: Design Patent.

United States Patent [19]

Everson

[11] **Des. 270,936**

[45] ** **Oct. 11, 1983**

[54] **COMBINED TOILET TANK AND AQUARIUM**

[76] Inventor: **D. Randall Everson**, 18615 Loree Ave., Cupertino, Calif. 95014

[**] Term: **14 Years**

[21] Appl. No.: **227,164**

[22] Filed: **Jan. 22, 1981**

[51] Int. Cl. .... **D23—02**
[52] U.S. Cl. **D23/49; D23/66;** D30/11
[58] Field of Search D23/49, 65–67; D30/11; 4/353, 661; 119/5

[56] **References Cited**

U.S. PATENT DOCUMENTS

D. 101,441	10/1936	Dreyfuss	D23/65
D. 179,484	1/1957	Lampkins	D30/11
D. 199,729	12/1964	Kaiser	D23/66
D. 229,766	1/1971	Kephart	D30/11
830,286	9/1906	Alexander	D23/66 X
918,456	4/1909	Marcellus	D23/66 X
2,238,699	4/1941	Levine	4/353
3,968,525	7/1976	Alexander	D23/66 X
4,364,132	12/1982	Robinson	4/661 X

Primary Examiner—James R. Largen
Attorney, Agent, or Firm—Thomas E. Schatzel

[57] **CLAIM**

The ornamental design for a combined toilet tank and aquarium, as shown and described.

DESCRIPTION

FIG. **1** is a perspective view taken from the top, front and left side of a combined toilet tank and aquarium showing my new design;
FIG. **2** is a front elevational view thereof;
FIG. **3** is a top plan view thereof;
FIG. **4** is a bottom plan view thereof;
FIG. **5** is a left side elevational view thereof;
FIG. **6** is a right side elevational view thereof; and
FIG. **7** is a rear elevational view thereof.
The broken line representation of plants and gravel in FIGS. **1** and **2**, a toilet bowl in FIG. **1** and plumbing hardware in FIG. **7** is for purposes of illustration only and form no part of the claimed design.

The ornamental design for a combined toilet tank and aquarium is protected by Des. 270,936, reproduced in its entirety on these two pages. Since design patents don't deal with how an invention works, the patent drawings need only hint at the answer to an obvious question: How do you prevent flushing the fish?

FIGURE 7.2: Design Patent (*continued*).

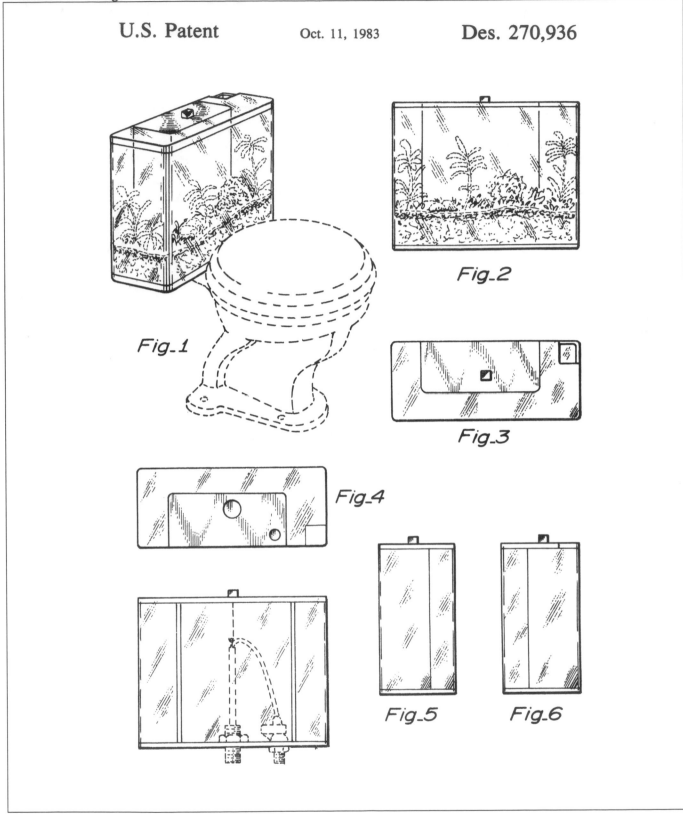

FIGURE 7.3: Cover Page of Patent.

Patent Front Pages

This brief explanation of the information available from a U.S. Patent is designed for the person unfamiliar with patents.

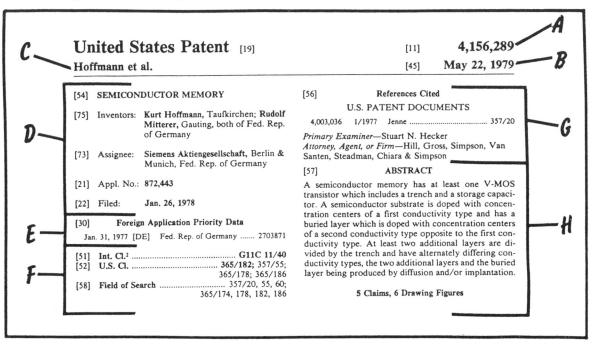

A. 4,156,289 is the U.S. Patent number.

B. **May 22, 1979** is the issue date.

C. **Hoffmann** is the last name of the inventor who is listed first.

C. **et al** indicates that there are other inventors.

D. **Semiconductor Memory** is the title describing the claimed invention.

D. The patent shows the name and city of residence of each of the **Inventors.** Unassigned patents show the full address of the Inventors.

D. **Assignee** refers to a company, organization or individual to which the inventors' rights to a patent are assigned. The name and city are shown.

D. **872,443** is the serial number given to the application, which was filed on **Jan. 26, 1978.**

E. **Foreign Application Priority Data** indicates corresponding applications which were filed in other countries, gives the filing date and foreign application number. By fulfilling certain requirements, an applicant filing in the U.S. may be entitled to the benefit of the filing date of a prior application in a foreign country.

F. **Int. Cl...G11C 11/40** is the International Patent Classification.

F. **U.S. Cl...365/182, 357/55, 365/178 and 365/186** are the four U.S. Classifications listed for this patent: Class 365, subclass 182, Class 357, subclass 55, Class 365, subclass 178 and Class 365, subclass 186. The classification listed in boldface on the patent is called the original classification (OR). The others are the cross-reference classifications (XR). Every patent has one and only one original classification. If disclosure of the patent falls into more than one subclass, additional copies of the patent are placed in those subclasses as cross-reference classifications.

F. The **Field of Search...** refers to the U.S. Classification where the Patent Examiner searched to compare the claimed subject matter to that disclosed in previous patents and articles.

G. **References Cited** refers to references which may be cited by the examiner and applicant to show the state-of-the-art or to indicate the prior art most closely related to the invention which is claimed in the application.

H. The Patent and Trademark Office (PTO) requires that the patent application include a brief **Abstract** of the technical disclosure in the specification. The purpose of the abstract is to enable the PTO and the public to determine quickly the nature and gist of the technical disclosure.

H. The front page also lists the number of **Claims** and the number of **Drawing Figures** in the patent. When appropriate, a representative drawing is also included on the front page of the patent.

Source: *Patent Profiles. Microelectronics - II.* GPO, 1983. (C 21.25:M 58/v.2)

bers are in a different numbered series, often preceded by the letter D or Des. (Example: Des. 270,936).

Claims

Claims are formally written phrases that precisely define the invention. Patent claims have been likened to land deeds, outlining the boundaries of the claimed invention. "Crossing [a claim's] boundary without the owner's permission is a trespass or, in intellectual property terms, an infringement."[3]

Patent Searches

Patent searching typically involves defining a "field of search" and identifying specific patents within that field. Patents are identified through Web, CD-ROM, manual, or online database searches, and examined in either of two formats: the patent summary (on the PTO Web page or *Official Gazette*) or a full text copy of the patent itself. The *Official Gazette* is available in many federal depository libraries and in Patent and Trademark Depository Libraries (PTDL), or may be purchased from the Government Printing Office. (See figure 7.4 for a sample patent from the *Official Gazette*.) The full patent can be examined in Patent and Trademark Depository Libraries, extracted from full-text online databases, or

FIGURE 7.4: Patent from *Official Gazette*.

2,026,082
BOARD GAME APPARATUS
Charles B. Darrow, Philadelphia, Pa., assignor to Parker Brothers, Inc., Salem, Mass., a corporation of Maine
Application August 31, 1935, Serial No. 38,757
9 Claims. (Cl. 273—134)

1. In a board game apparatus a board acting as a playing-field having marked spaces constituting a path or course extending about the board, said path affording a continuous track for the purpose of continuity of play, certain of said spaces being designated as by position or color so as to constitute a distinguishable group, there being a plurality of such groups each differing from the others and each having its spaces adjacent on the same side of the board, the apparatus having indications of the rentals required for the use and occupancy, by opponent players, of spaces of one or more such groups, which rentals are subject to increase by the acquisition of an additional space or spaces of the same group by the same individual player, thereby making it possible for the possessor to exact greater payments or penalties from any opponent resting or trespassing thereon.

The patent abstract and one drawing for a board game called MONOPOLY appeared in the December 31, 1935, *Official Gazette*.

	Is It Patented? A Search Strategy*	
Step 1	Identify patent class/ subclass	*Index to U.S. Patent Classification System* Patents ASSIST
Step 2	Review class/subclass hierarchy	*Index to U.S. Patent Classification System* Patents ASSIST
Step 3	Explore class/subclass scope	*Classification Definitions* Patents ASSIST U.S. Patent Bibliographic Database <http://patents.uspto.gov/ CLASSES/classes.html>
Step 4	Review patents in class/subclass; adjust inappropriate class designations by searching for keywords	Patents BIB Automated Patent System (APS) U.S. Patent Bibliographic Database <http://patents.uspto.gov/>
Step 5	Get patent numbers (in reverse chronological order)	Patents CLASS ("Patents by Subclass" file) Subclass Listings from PTO APS Text
Step 6	Cull by reviewing patent summaries	*Official Gazette*, in patent number order U.S. Patent Bibliographic Database <http://patents.uspto.gov/>
Step 7	Examine complete patents	PTDL collection APS Image

*Known as a "prior art" search.

purchased from the Commissioner of Patents and Trademarks. To link to Internet sites, use the GPO Access "Browse Topics," and select "Patents and Trademarks" <http://www.access.gpo.gov/su_docs/dpos/pathbrws.html>.

Patent and Trademark Depository Libraries (PTDLs)

Patent and Trademark Depository Libraries are designated by the PTO to ensure that copies of U.S. patents and patent and trademark reference sources are publically accessible. Older collections are in paper, with new patents arriving on microfilm (except plant patents, which are received in paper or microfiche). Some 80 PTDLs, scattered coast to coast in academic, public, state, and special libraries, put almost half of all Americans within commuting distance of a patent collection.

Patent libraries offer access to Cassis, a family of CD-ROM indexes to U.S. patent search tools, bibliographic information, classifications, application serial numbers, and images (USAPat). Selected PTDLs offer the Automated Patent System (APS), the same database used by patent examiners at the U.S. Patent and Trademark Office, offering all patent images and text back to 1790.

PTDLs also stock supplemental reference sources and provide assistance accessing patent and trademark information, free seminars, and toll-free telephone hook-ups with experts at PTO. PTDL staff can answer questions and help in constructing search strategies. Because service hours and the range of individual collections vary, users are advised to contact a PTDL before visiting. A PTDL directory is provided in issues of the *Official Gazette* and on PTO's Web page <http://www.uspto.gov/go/ptdl>. A free locator map may be requested from the Patent and Trademark Depository Library Program office.

Computer Searches

Hobbled by manual search techniques acknowledged to be among the slowest on the planet, PTO began automating its patent examination process in the early 1980s. Throughout PTO's two centuries, searching had been by hand through millions of sheaves of paper. PTO officials readily admitted that some seven percent of their 34 million documents were always missing or misfiled. With 3,500 new applications arriving weekly and manual patent examinations taking about two years, Congress ordered PTO to automate. After a troubled start, the $600 million Automated Patent System (APS) has rebounded and is searchable by the general public in PTDLs (text only) and on terminals in the PTO Public Search Room (text and image searching). This full text database incorporates patents issued since 1790, including abstracts of Japanese and European patents. The mammoth project made PTO the government's pioneer in optical-disc storage technology.

The two APS online databases are APS Text and APS Image. APS Text is a full text database of U.S. patents since 1971. APS Image has complete U.S. patent documents (including all drawings) since George Washington signed the first patent in 1790, searchable by classification or patent number. APS Text is available in many Patent and Trademark Depository Libraries, while APS Image is accessible only at the PTO in Arlington, Virginia, and via PTO "partnership libraries" in Sunnyvale, California, and Detroit, Michigan. Partnerships between PTO and selected PTDLs supplement the free PTDL services with specialized, fee-based services.

The full range of keyword and number searching can be done in both APS Text and APS Image back to 1971. Patents issued before 1971 are searchable only by patent or classification number. The primary difference between APS Text and APS Image is output: in Text, only the text portion of a patent can be printed, while Image allows printing full-page images of patent pictures and drawings.

APS also contains reexaminations, certificates of correction, and English language abstracts of unexamined Japanese patent applications published since 1980. Every Tuesday, PTO adds about 2,000 newly issued patents, making APS the most up-to-date service in the world. No other database can claim a complete, online collection of U.S. patents as of last Tuesday.

Patent Searching			
Content	File	Coverage	Access
Patent cover pages	U.S. Patent Bibliographic Database	Since 1976	http://www.uspto.gov Searchable with summaries; no drawings or claims
Full text of U.S. patents, with drawings	APS Image	Since 1790	PTO; Partnership libraries Classification or patent number; keywords (back to 1971)
Full text of U.S. patents	APS Text	Since 1971	PTDLs Keywords; patent or classification number
Patent drawings	USAPat	Since 1994	C 21.31: (CD-ROM) Not searchable: retrieve by patent number
U.S. patent cover pages and images	IBM Patent Server	Cover pages since 1971; images since 1978	http://patent.womplex.ibm.com/ Searchable by keywords, patent number
Subset of U.S. patent abstracts	STO's Internet Patent Search System	Currently the 1980s, #4242757–4890334	http://sunsite.unc.edu/patents/intropat.html Also searchable *Index to Classification* & *Manual of Classification*

The Patent Office Building

When the British burned Washington in 1814, the U.S. Patent Office building was the only government structure to survive. In a conflagration cliffhanger, torch-wielding British troops were dissuaded by the Superintendent of Patents himself, William Thornton, who threw himself before the building shouting, "Are you Englishmen or vandals?" Thornton argued that burning the U.S. patent depository would be as barbarous as burning the Alexandrian Library, "for which the Turks have been ever since condemned by all enlightened nations." Persuaded by the plucky stranger, the marauders spared the building.

Within 40 years, the Patent Office occupied a new building which attracted thousands of visitors to see displays of toy-sized patent models in its exhibition halls. Patent models were a major Washington tourist attraction until 1877, when a disastrous fire consumed the building and many models, including such treasures as Robert Fulton's original drawings for his steamboat. The loss was mourned as a national tragedy.

Today's Washington visitors may view the renovated remains of the Old Patent Office, which now houses two Smithsonian museums: the National Portrait Gallery and the National Museum of American Art.

Internet Searching

http://patents.uspto.gov/

On the PTO Web site resides the U.S. Patent Bibliographic Database of patent cover pages (cover pages = patent bibliographic data). The database contains patent cover page data for utility, design, reissue, plant, and SIR (Statutory Invention Registration, see p. 81.) patents issued since 1976, along with the AIDS Patent Database of the full text and images of AIDS-related U.S., European, and Japanese patents. Bibliographic information includes patent and application number, series code, patent type, filing date, title, assignee, attorney, related U.S. patent documents, classification, and abstract. Drawings and claims are excluded. The patent database can be searched by any bibliographic elements, such as inventor's or assignee's name, patent title, or abstract. Because this site was developed in cooperation with the Center For Networked Information Discovery and Retrieval, it is mirrored at CNIDR, the Web Patents Project <http://www.cnidr.org>. For online searching of pre-1976 patents, the PTO recommends using a commercial service. Patents can be searched online and on CD-ROM through numerous commercial vendors. (Descriptions can be found in sources such as the *Gale Directory of Databases.*)

Cassis

Cassis is a family of CD-ROM indexes of trademarks and U.S. patent search tools, bibliographic information, classifications, application serial numbers, and images (USAPat). Cassis helps identify which classes to search, generates lists of patent numbers issued within a classification, and allows word searching of classification titles and abstracts (patent bibliographic information). *USAPat: U.S. Patent Documents on CD-ROM* (full patent with drawings) is not a search tool: it requires a patent number. Originally available only in PTDLs, Cassis is now widely available in other libraries and for sale to the public.

Search Aids

Manual of Classification. The *Manual of Classification* lists class and subclass titles in the U.S. Patent Classification System. Sometimes subclasses are not listed sequentially (subclass 455, for example, might precede subclass 410): these line numberings are sometimes reshuffled on the list. The manual can be searched in print or on Cassis/Patents ASSIST. Its cousin, *Index to the*

Cassis: Patents		
Content	File	Coverage
Full text of search tools	Patents ASSIST	*Classification Manual, Definitions, Index*, IPC-USPC concordance, and more
Bibliographic information	Patents BIB C 21.31/2:	Data from patent cover pages since 1969, with references to drawings in USAPat
Assignments	Patents ASSIGN	Patent assignments since 1980
Patent drawings	USAPat C 21.31: (CD-ROM)	Full patent with drawings since 1994; not searchable: retrieve by patent number determined using Patents BIB
Classifications	Patents CLASS C 21.31/3:	Classification of utility, design, plant, reissue and X-numbered patents, defensive publications, and SIRs since 1790
USPC-IPC concordance	Patents ASSIST C 21.14/2:C 74/990	*U.S. Patent Classification to International Patent Classification*
Application serial numbers	Patents SNAP	Concordance: patent numbers/application serial numbers since 1977

U.S. Patent Classification System, serves as an index to the manual, listing the descriptive titles of each class and subclass. Design-patent classes are listed in the last volume of the manual and alphabetically in the index. Plant patent classification is also given in the manual and the index. (See figure 7.5.)

Translating Patent Language: *Index to the U.S. Patent Classification System.* Patent language is not like everyday language. Patent classes and subclasses emanate from the U.S. Patent Classification System, which technically describes the invention's use, function, or effect. In the world of patents, chewing gum becomes "food or edible material processes, compositions and products normally nondigestible chewable material" (Class 426/Subclass 3). The familiar pencil is transformed into "coating implements with material supply, solid material for rubbing contact or support therefore" (Class 401/Subclass 49); and lipstick becomes "drug, bio-affecting and body treating compositions, live skin colorant containing, lip" (Class 424/Subclass 64). This illustrates the need to use the *Index to the U.S. Patent Classification System* to construct a search according to "patent language" rather than everyday language.

The *Index to the U.S. Patent Classification System* is a gateway into patents' nomenclature (C 21.12/2:). The index is an alphabetical list referring from popular terminology to patent classes and subclasses. If, for example, you wanted to locate patents for mousetraps, you could search the index under "MOUSE, Traps" and be referred to Class 43 and Subclass 58+. (The + designates class 58 and all subclasses indented under it.) The index includes lists of utility and design patent class titles. The index can be searched in hardcopy or on Cassis/Patents ASSIST. For a quick and dirty fix on classification, try searching for words in class titles and patent abstracts on Cassis or the patent database on the PTO Web site.

Classification Definitions. More detailed definitions for classes and subclasses are given in *Classification Definitions*, which differentiates between similar classes and clarifies inclusions and exclusions (microfiche, C 21.3/2:). Regarding what most of us call a mousetrap, for example, *Classification Definitions* distinguishes between traps and vermin destroyers. The explanation is not always simple (or savory): Traps "lure animals not domesticated or take advantage of some habit of the same and which by reason of some voluntary action on the part of the said animals catch or wound or paralyze or kill the same or in general render them helpless, that man may work his will on them." Vermin destroyers, on the other hand entice vermin to approach of their "own free will, whether impelled by curiosity, hunger or habit" and (in the best tradition of Greek tragedy) force them "in spite of themselves, to destruction."

Classification Definitions can be searched (in spite of ourselves) in print, on the PTO Web site, or on Cassis/Patents ASSIST.

Patent Summaries

Each Tuesday issue of *Official Gazette of the United States Patent and Trademark Office - Patents* contains summaries and drawings for all patents issued during the previous week (C 21.5:). Published weekly since 1872, the *Official Gazette* (OG) does not reproduce the entire patent, only the patent abstract (actually, a single claim) and one drawing, except for plant patents which are not illustrated. (See figure 7.4.) OG patent summaries are arranged in patent number sequence and indexed by class and subclass numbers and by patentees (with separate indexes for utility, design, and plant patents). Plant patents precede utility patents in the *Gazette*; design patents follow. An annual separate issue, *Index of Patents* (C 21.5/2:), serves as a cumulative index to each year's *Official Gazette*, allowing searches by names of patentees and assignees, by patent class and subclass numbers, and by class titles.

Search Tip

To determine the OG issue where a particular patent number appears, consult the table in Part II of the annual *Index of Patents*, "List of Patent, Design, Plant Patent, Reissue and Defensive Publication Numbers Appearing in the Individual Issues of the Official Gazette for [year]."

Searching the Full Patent

For peripatetic searchers, the Patent and Trademark Office (PTO) in Arlington, Virginia, is considered "the greatest technical library in the world" and the best place to conduct a patent search. The PTO's Search Facilities archive copies of patents granted since 1790, with access to the APS Text and Image searching (fee-based). The paper backfile is arranged by class/subclass, with bound volumes and microfilm backfiles in numerical order. The Search Rooms open patent records and files to the public in a rambling warren of cubbyholes stacked with sheaves of paper. The PTO patent files are a source of technical information or can help in determining whether an invention has been patented. The PTO also opens its scientific library to the public, a wealth of scientific and technical books in numerous languages, scientific journals, the official patent journals of foreign countries, and copies of foreign patents.

Patent and Trademark Depository Libraries (PTDLs) are another source for examining the full patent. Each week, PTDLs receive a copy of every patent issued during the previous seven days. Since the breadth

FIGURE 7.5: Sample Page from *Manual of Classification*.

43-2   CLASS 43   FISHING, TRAPPING AND VERMIN DESTROYING   DECEMBER 1984

	FISHING
	.Line-attached bodies, hooks and rigs
	..Selectively free sliding or fixed on line
44.88	...Line strain or motion actuated, e.g., strike or pole tip released
44.89	..Bendable or deformable material for line connection, e.g., split shot
44.9	..With line passing through center of body
44.91	...With line-gripping means
44.92	..With relatively movable parts and/or resilient construction for attachment to line
44.93	...Movable wedge or collect ring type
44.94	...Spiral or pigtail line holder wrapped around stem
44.95	...Resiliently biased or elastic line clamping means
44.96	..Sinkers with ground-engaging means, e.g., trolley or surf anchors
44.97	..Sinkers with guards or retrieving features
44.98	.Lines and/or leaders
44.99	.Bait distributors, e.g., chumming devices
53.5	.Disgorgers and gags
54.1	.Holder
55	..Catch and natural bait
56	..Minnow buckets
57	...Aerating pump
57.1	..Hook
57.2	...Holder for snelled hook under tension
57.3	..Trotline holder
58	TRAPS
59	.Burglar
60	.Imprisoning
61	..Swinging or sliding closure
62	..Falling encaging member
63	..Jaw cage type
64	.Self and ever set
65	..Nonreturn entrance
66	...Victim-opened
67	...Victim-closed
68	..Sinking compartment
69	..Tiltable platform
70	...Trigger-released
71	..Rotatable platform
72	...Trigger-released
73	.Self-reset
74	..Rotating door or platform
75	..Smiting
76	.Victim-reset
77	.Impaling or smiting
78	..Rectilinear striker movement
79	...Impaling
80	....Burrow type
81	..Swinging striker
81.5	...Auxiliary striker holder
82	...Direct engaging latch
83	....Automatic catch
83.5	...Automatic set
84	.Explosive
85	.Choking or squeezing
86	..Movable loops
87	..Constricting noose
88	.Jaw
89	..Suspended
90	..Modified jaw
91	...Parallel oscillating
92	..Modified trigger mechanism
93	...Direct engagement
94	....Wedge or toggle
95	...Automatic catch
96	..Attachments
97	...Setting
98	.Electrocuting
99	..Body-removing or concealing

100	.Fish
101	..Weirs
102	..Elevatable cage
103	..Portable or floating
104	...Towable
105	..Foldable or collapsible
106	..Porpoise
107	.Insect
108	..Tree trunk
109	..Furniture
110	..Operator-controlled
111	..Mechanically operated
112	..Electrocuting
113	..Illuminated
114	..Adhesive
115	...Flypaper holders
116	...Flexible with drawable section
117	...Upright perch slidable receptacle
118	..Reticulate fabric
119	..Window screen or door
120	..Garbage can
121	..Crawling insect type
122	..Fly vases
123	..Bedbug type
124	VERMIN DESTROYING
125	.Fumigators
126	..Tree apparatus
127	..Smokers
128	...Bee type
129	..Vaporizers
130	...Steam
131	.Poison holders
132.1	.Insect
133	..Catchers
134	...Implements
135	....Spring-operated
136	....Adhesive
137	....Swatters
138	...Machines
139	....Suction
140	.....Traveling
141	....Blast
142	....Rotated agitator
143	....Oscillated agitator
144	..Burners

CROSS-REFERENCE ART COLLECTION

900	LIQUID INSECTICIDE SPRAYER

To locate mousetraps in the manual, the searcher must know the class. In Class 43, Fishing, Trapping and Vermin Destroying, Subclass 58, Traps, we find numerous types of mousetraps. The dots in the manual show levels of subclassification, with each level providing greater detail.

of their retrospective collections varies, not all patent depository libraries have patents back to number one, but all have at least a 20-year backfile. Unlike the collection at the Patent and Trademark Office, these collections are arranged in patent-number order, with many patents on microfilm rather than paper. People wishing to search a specific technology (class/subclass) will find this arrangement less convenient, but may identify patent numbers in specific classes and subclasses using Cassis or the Subclass Listings available on a diskette or printout from PTO. (Orders should specify subclasses and years needed.)

For examining individual patents, mail-order is another option. Copies of patents may be purchased by mail from PTO for $3.00 each.

Patent Models

Until 1880, each patent application was accompanied by a miniature working model. Some of these finely crafted models may have cost as much as $1,000 (in the 1800s) to custom-make, and models for unmanufactured inventions were the only effigies ever produced. Thousands of the models were destroyed in the Patent Office fires of 1836 and 1877, with even more lost during a clumsy PTO relocation and storage in a leaky tunnel. The neglected collection was finally auctioned off in 1908 for $1,550.

Although the model requirement was rescinded in 1880, patent models remain part of the American psyche. Gordon Gould's 28-year legal battle for the laser patent resulted partly from a patent model misunderstanding. Assuming he needed a working model, Gould postponed filing for two years. Meanwhile, Charles Townes scooped up the laser patent, became known as the father of the laser, and won a Nobel Prize.

Government Patents

Federal agencies also patent inventions, primarily related to health, agriculture, and forestry. Because NTIS licenses businesses to use government inventions, agencies notify NTIS of their patents for inclusion in the NTIS Bibliographic Database (no privately owned patents are listed). This procedure has made NTIS the clearinghouse for licensing government inventions.

NTIS does not grant licenses for government patents from NASA, the Department of Energy, or the Department of Defense, which handle their own licensing. The indexes and databases of the Departments of Defense and Energy list government-owned patents and patent applications. (See chapter 6.) *NASA Patent Abstracts Bibliography* (NASA PAB) provides abstracts and drawings for NASA-owned U.S. patents, along with abstracts of patent applications, and can be accessed at <http://www.sti.nasa.gov/Pubs/Patents/pat50.pdf>. It is in PDF only; the paper version was discontinued in

1995. The Abstract Section covers NASA-owned inventions cited in *Scientific and Technical Aerospace Reports* (STAR) during the last six months, while the Index Section lists STAR entries since 1969. Entries include NASA accession and case number, inventor, patent number or application serial number, and patent classification number. Patents may be searched by subject, inventor, inventing organization, or number.

NTIS report numbers for patents and patent applications have a PAT or PAT-APPL (pronounced "pat-apple") alpha prefix, followed by the patent or application number issued by PTO (example: "Report Number: PAT-APPL-8-693 816"). Government patents may be searched on the NTIS database using the keywords "Patents" or "Patent Applications" combined with the NTIS subject category 90, Government Inventions for Licensing. (Omit NTIS subject category 90 to also retrieve foreign patents). Notices of patents available for license or sale appear in the NTIS Alert titled *Government Inventions for Licensing,* the *Federal Register,* and OG (in the PTO notices section). Patent bibliographies and abstracts are included in NTIS's *Published Search Master Catalog,* serving as quick guides to patent information on a technology. NTIS sells copies of government patent applications; copies of patents themselves must be purchased from PTO.

Foreign Patents

Patents provide protection only in their country of issue. Almost half of U.S. patents are granted to foreign nationals to protect their inventions in this country. Likewise, Americans may seek not only a U.S. patent, but also patents in other nations. In fact, most of Europe's patent applicants are Americans. The United States and Japan are the only two patent offices in the world issuing the majority of patents to their own citizens. To protect an invention in any of about 120 countries offering patent protection, an inventor must file in each country under that country's laws.

International treaties such as the Paris Convention and the Patent Cooperation Treaty (PCT) provide reciprocal protection and filing rights in member countries. The Paris Convention for the Protection of Industrial Property requires its 100 member-countries to guarantee foreigners the same patent and trademark rights they give their own citizens. The Patent Cooperation Treaty came into force on January 24, 1978, and facilitates filing of patent applications for the same invention in 44 member-countries by providing for centralized filing and a standardized application. In countries served by a regional patent office such as the European Patent Office, a single application can be simultaneously registered in any member nation. Timing is important since most countries grant a patent to the first person to file an application. (The United States is unusual in granting the patent to the original inventor, the first-to-invent, rather than the first-to-file.) While U.S. patent applications remain secret until a patent is granted, European applications are often available before their U.S. counterpart is granted.

Foreign Patent Searching

A "patent family" is created when an inventor applies for multiple national patents. It includes all the applications and patents for the same invention from various nations. These are differentiated in patent databases as the "basic patent" (the first entered into the database, not necessarily the first published), and "equivalent patents," subsequent database entries for the same invention.

Online patent family (or patent equivalent) searches are useful when an English-language version of a non-English patent is sought, or for translating from a U.S. application number to a patent granted from another nation. Because non-U.S. patents and gazettes are difficult to locate in the U.S., it helps to identify the U.S. equivalent of a foreign patent. Numerous online database services offer U.S. and foreign patent searching, including the PTO Partnership Library in Sunnyvale, California, and Derwent's World Patents Index database (WPI).

The *United States Patent Classification to International Patent Classification* (C 21.14/2:C 74/990) is a concordance for relating the U.S. Patent Classification System (as revised through June 1989) to the 5th edition of the World Intellectual Property Organization's International Patent Classification System (IPC). The International Patent Classification number is listed on U.S. patents, designated by the INID Code [51]. (INID is the acronym for "Internationally agreed Numbers for the Identification of [bibliographic] Data".) The United Nations' World Intellectual Property Organization (WIPO) in Geneva, Switzerland, administers the Paris Convention and PCT and publishes the International Patent Classification. The WIPO Web site provides an introduction: "General Information on the Sixth Edition of the International Patent Classification (IPC) (WIPO Publication No. 409)" <http://www.wipo.org/eng/general/ipc/brochure/index.htm>. A detailed introductory manual is on the same site <http://www.wipo.org/eng/general/ipc/manual/index.htm>.

Most countries publish an official patent journal similar to our *Official Gazette,* many of which may be consulted in the Patent and Trademark Office's collection of official foreign patent-office journals. The WIPO Web site provides links to national intellectual property offices <http://www.wipo.org/eng/general/pcipi/otherwww/ipo_web.htm>. A helpful guide to foreign patent documentation is *Patents Throughout the World* (Rochester, NY: Clark, Boardman and Callaghan), a digest of national patent laws.

Because patent examiners consult patents issued by foreign countries to establish the validity of U.S. patents, the Patent and Trademark Scientific Library maintains a foreign patent collection. Some PTDLs also collect foreign patents. The Patent and Trademark Office also sells copies of some foreign patents. Under agreements with the Japanese and European Patent Offices, the PTO acquired digital cover page images of patents issued by key patent offices in Europe and Asia for APS. By the year 2001, PTO expects to have loaded the entire Japanese and European patent database.

Patent Glossary

Digest (Dig.)—a collection of cross-reference patents assembled to streamline patent examination searches; now called Cross-Reference art collections (X-art)

Disclosure Document—evidence of the date of an invention's conception, filed with the PTO and retained for two years; not to be confused with a patent application

Field of search—cross-referenced patent classes (OR and XR) examined when searching for similar patents

File wrappers—the documentation and cited art associated with a patent

Interference—a proceeding to determine the original inventor of a contested invention

Name and Date Patents—unnumbered patents issued between 1790 and 1836; some have been placed in the classified files with an x-prefix and are called the X-Numbered Patents; these patents are indexed in *Early Unnumbered United States Patents 1790–1836: Index and Guide to the Microfilm Edition* (Research Publications)

OR—a patent's primary [original] classification assignment; noted on the patent in bold type under [52] U.S.Cl., but not in OG

Patent family—all patents and patent applications for the same invention in various countries; sometimes called "patent equivalents"

Patent number equivalents—the U.S. equivalent of a foreign patent

Prior art—the technology related to an invention; searched to determine the novelty of a patent application

Reclassification—a change in class or subclass to reflect new technology; when a new number is created, previous patents may be reclassified

Reissue patent—a patent that corrects and replaces an unexpired patent reexamined by PTO for invalid claims

Shoes—PTO patent files; descendants of the original shoeboxes in which patents were stored

Statutory Invention Registration (SIR)—a defensive patent that prohibits a similar patent, but does not prevent others from making, using, or selling the invention

UX—unofficial cross-references, related patents consulted by the examiner

X-art collections (cross-reference art collections)—cross-reference patents in a class; listed in the *Manual* at the end of a class in numerical sequence, in the *Index* denoted with an asterisk

X-Numbered Patents—unnumbered Name and Date Patents (issued 1790–1836) placed in the classified files with an x-prefix

XR—cross-reference, or additional, classifications; noted on the patent under [52] U.S.Cl., but not in OG

The Patent and Trademark Office's Technology Assessment and Forecast (TAF) Program is a source of statistics on patent activity. TAF calculations show that almost half of U.S. patent applications are from foreign nationals, for example. (The Japanese are the most active, with Californians ranking as the most productive U.S. inventors.) TAF prepares statistical analyses showing patent activity by elements such as year, state, country, SIC, and patent class. TAF will also perform custom reports on a cost-reimbursable basis.

TRADEMARKS

Trademarks are words, names, symbols, shapes, slogans, or devices used to identify and distinguish goods. The Lanham Act, passed in 1946 and signed by President Truman, liberalized and strengthened trademark registration. Its broadened definition of a trademark paved the way for nearly two million product marks. Even colors, smells, and sounds can occasionally be registered as trademarks—Owens-Corning has a lock on the color pink for home insulation, the sounds of the NBC chimes and the MGM lion are protected, as is the

aroma of Clarke Company's perfumed embroidery thread.[4] Companies designate their trademarks in capital letters followed by an ® or ™, with the generic name of the product in smaller type (JELL-O® brand gelatin dessert; BAND-AID® brand adhesive bandages). The ᔆᴹ is a service mark, for services such as advertising, entertainment, or veterinary care.

How many trademarks will you encounter today? If you are an average American, as many as 1,500. These ubiquitous words and pictures are so much a part of our lives that we are not always conscious of them. Some trademarks are engraved in the public consciousness. (See figure 7.6.) Colonel Sanders died in 1980, but his face continues to identify products of the Kentucky Fried Chicken Corporation. The original canine model for Nipper, the RCA dog, has been dead for more than 90 years, but his image remains one of America's best-loved trademarks. Some of the oldest trademarks, issued between 1870 and 1899, are still active, including John Deere, Anheuser-Busch, Quaker Oats, Aunt Jemima, Lifebuoy, Coca Cola, and Hires.

Genericide

Have you ever "xeroxed" an article? The Xerox Corporation begs to differ: Actually you "photocopied" it. The distinction may seem unimportant, but company lawyers who see their trademark used as a verb or noun are likely to dash off a letter to offenders asking them not to repeat the error. It's called "genericide"—the loss of a trademark used generically too often. When the courts decide a trademark has become associated with a general product rather than a specific brand, the trademark enters the public domain for anyone's use. Webster's dictionaries abound because the courts de-

FIGURE 7.6: The Morton Salt Umbrella Girl.

The Umbrella Girl design is a registered trademark of Morton International, Inc. No one modeled for the Morton Salt umbrella girl's picture, designed in 1911 for the first national advertising campaign for salt. The original slogan under the picture was "Even in rainy weather, it flows freely." Both the revised slogan, "When it rains it pours," and the umbrella girl are protected by registered trademarks, and the round blue Morton Salt container sports a patented pouring spout. Courtesy Morton International, Morton Salt Division.

termined the name had become generic through customary usage. A trademark can lose its registration in one country, but not all. Aspirin lost its American trademark because Bayer used it as a noun ("Buy aspirin") instead of an adjective ("Buy ASPIRIN® brand analgesic"), but it remains a trademark in South America and Canada. Thermos is generic in the United States, but is still a British trademark. A more recent entry into the trademark graveyard is Monopoly, now in the public domain after Parker Brothers lost a legal battle with a rival game named Anti-Monopoly. Infringement battles of the 1990s often involve conflicts between established trademarks and identical Internet domain names.[5]

Trademark Graveyard
Former Trademarks Now in the Public Domain

aspirin	malted milk
brassiere	milk of magnesia
cellophane	mimeograph
celluloid	mineral oil
corn flakes	nylon
cube steak	phonograph
dry ice	pocket book
escalator	shredded wheat
harmonica	thermos
kerosene	trampoline
lanolin	vanilla
linoleum	yo-yo

Trademark Searching

The weekly *Official Gazette of the United States Patent and Trademark Office—Trademarks* (C21.5/4:) lists and illustrates trademarks and has an index of registrants (the companies, organizations, and people owning the trademarks). The *Index of Trademarks*, an annual index to the *Gazette*, is arranged alphabetically by registrants' names, with address and registration information (C 21.5/3:). To link to Internet sites, use the GPO Access "Browse Topics," and select "Patents and Trademarks" <http://www.access.gpo.gov/su_docs/dpos/pathbrws.html>.

Cassis, available in all PTDLs, allows searching of active, registered marks and trademark applications. Trademarks REGISTERED (C 21.31/7:) contains the text of all active, federally registered trademarks since 1884. Trademarks PENDING (C 21.31/8:) contains the text of pending trademark applications. Trademarks ASSIGN (C 21.31/9:) contains data derived from trademark assignment deeds recorded since 1955. Trademarks ASSIST (C 21.31/10:) consolidates the full text of trademark search tools such as *Trademark Manual of Examining Procedure*.

The most thorough trademark searches are conducted at the Patent and Trademark Office in Arlington, Virginia, where the PTO Trademark Search Library archives a copy of every registered trademark. Active trademarks are kept in cross-referenced alphabetical sections (for word marks) and design sections (for symbol marks such as birds, stars, flowers, etc.), with number-ordered trademarks available on microfilm and in bound volumes.

Paid online access to the PTO trademark examination database is available through PTO's Trademark X-Search service at the PTO Search Facilities in Arlington, Virginia, and in Partnership Libraries. X-Search is a fully indexed image and text search/retrieval database of more than 1.85 million live, pending, and dead marks, with images. Cost in the PTO Search Room was about $40 an hour in 1997. A second automated trademark system, TRAM (Trademark Reporting and Monitoring), tracks workflow, status, location, prosecution history, and bibliographic data for pending applications, active registered marks, and abandoned and expired registrations. TRAM is used for photo composition of the Trademark Gazette. Commercial sources of online and CD-ROM trademark searching are also available.

Trademark Searching		
Content	PTO Source	Coverage
Registered TMs	Cassis: Trademarks REGISTERED	Since 1884
TM applications	Cassis: Trademarks PENDING	Current
TM assignment deeds	Cassis: Trademarks ASSIGN	Since 1955
TM search tools	Cassis: Trademarks ASSIST	Full text of current editions
New registrations	*Official Gazette - Trademarks* (C 21.5/4:)	Illustrates TMs
TM registrants	*Index of Trademarks* (C 21.5/3:)	Annual index to the *Gazette*
Image and text search/retrieval	X-Search	Online access to the PTO trademark database for current trademarks

The Trademark Wars
Trademark Infringement Cases

"The Other White Meat" (pork) vs. "The Ultimate White Meat" (lobster)

YA-HOO! cakes vs. Yahoo! (search engine)

Mattel Inc. vs. *Miller's—An Independent Magazine for Barbie Doll Collectors* (for unauthorized use of the Barbie name and image)

Toys R Us vs. Roadkills R Us (Web site)

COPYRIGHT

http://lcweb.loc.gov/copyright/

Copyright protects authors, artists, and others from theft of their intellectual property. Copyright protects the way a work was expressed but not the ideas, systems, or facts conveyed. Books, music, plays, choreography, photographs, game boards and rules, art, motion pictures, sound recordings, computer programs, architectural blueprints, advertisements, labels, and maps can be copyrighted. (See figure 7.7.) Protection cannot be granted for slogans, processes, procedures, ideas, stan-

FIGURE 7.7: Copyrightable Works.

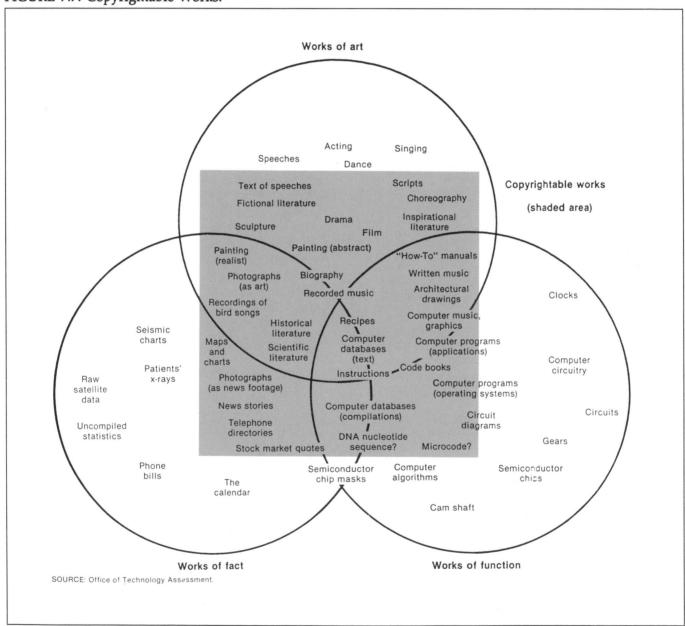

Congress's Office of Technology Assessment has identified three types of copyrightable works: works of art, of fact, and of function. Those deemed suitable for copyright protection are shown in the shaded area. Source: *Intellectual Property Rights in an Age of Electronics and Information.* GPO, 1986. (Y 3.T22/2:2 In 8/3)

dard calendars, blank forms, U.S. government publications, names, short phrases, expressions, or titles. (This book, for example, could legally have been titled *Gone with the Wind*.)[6] Since 1976, the duration of copyright protection has been the author's lifetime plus 50 years. Before 1976, protection was granted for 75 years. Thus, the copyright for *Gone with the Wind*, published in 1936, will expire in 2011; the song, "Happy Birthday to You," in 2010.[7] The full text of 17 U.S.C. (Copyrights) is available on the Web from the Cornell Law School's Legal Information Institute (ranked with three stars by Magellan) at <http://www.law.cornell.edu/uscode/17/> and on the House gopher.

Soon after Noah Webster (of dictionary fame) lobbied for the U.S. copyright protection that would safeguard his *American Spelling Book*, Congress enacted the 1790 copyright law. Since 1870, the Library of Congress has been in the copyright business, registering U.S. copyrights while accumulating free materials for its collections. Libraries of copyright deposit have been likened to collections of classified botanical specimens which hold definitive examples of plants. Copyright deposit has allowed the Library of Congress to gather a century of America's creative products. The results reveal themselves in the library's unparalleled collections: the world's greatest Civil War and Old West photograph collection and the only surviving copies of some nineteenth-century dance music, ballads, minstrel songs, and ragtime are examples.

Registering a copyright requires a $20 fee and depositing two copies (of a literary work) with the Library of Congress.[8] The Copyright Office's CORDS project (Copyright Office Electronic Registration, Recordation & Deposit System) seeks to develop a system for digital copyright registration and documentation and can be accessed at <http://lcweb.loc.gov/copyright/cords.html>.

The United States and other nations enjoy reciprocal copyright protection as members of the Universal Copyright Convention (UCC) and the Berne Convention for the Protection of Literary and Artistic Works.[9] Member nations honor each other's copyrights and allow infringement suits to cross national borders. A list of nations maintaining copyright relations with the United States is given in the free Copyright Office Circular 38a," International Copyright Relations of the United States," available at <http://lcweb.loc.gov/copyright/circs/circ38a>.

Copyright Searches

The free Copyright Office Circular 22, "How to Investigate the Copyright Status of a Work," is the best guide to copyright searching (LC 3.4/2:22/995 and <http://lcweb.loc.gov/copyright/circs/circ22>). The Copyright Office suggests three approaches for determining whether a work is protected: looking on the work itself for copyright notice, author, or imprint; searching Copyright Office records spanning back to 1870; or hiring the Copyright Office to search for you. The Copyright Office also cautions that a combination of the three methods may be needed and that, even then, results may be inconclusive. Registrations from 1870 to 1977 are in the Copyright Card Catalog in the Madison Building; those since 1978 are available via LOCIS (Library of Congress Information System) at <http://lcweb.loc.gov/copyright>. The *Catalog of Copyright Entries* (CCE), a Copyright Card Catalog in book—then microfiche—form until its discontinuance in 1996, includes registrations through 1982 (LC 3.6/6:). The fourth series of CCE, covering 1978–82, was the last released, after which the Copyright Office substituted Internet publication of copyright registrations and renewals via LOCIS. The free Copyright Office Circular 23, "Copyright Card Catalog and the Online Files" helps to make sense of these options (LC 3.4/2:23/993 and <http://lcweb.loc.gov/copyright/circs/circ23>). A LOCIS Quick Search Guide for copyright is available at <gopher://marvel.loc.gov:70/00/locis/guides/copyrigt.loc>. To link to other Internet sites, use the GPO Access "Browse Topics," and select "Copyright" <http://www.access.gpo.gov/su_docs/dpos/pathbrws.html>.

OVERLAPPING PROTECTION

Some works are eligible for both copyright and patent protection: computer programs, games, and designs for objects, both functional and aesthetic, are examples. (See figure 7.8.) A single game, for instance, may have patent protection for the game apparatus; copyright for the board, box, pieces, and rules; and trademark registration for the name. (Although Parker Brothers lost the trademark for the name "Monopoly," they still hold a copyright on the game itself). Other examples of overlapping protection are the Rolls-Royce hood ornament, which is protected by copyright as a piece of sculpture, a design patent, and a trademark; and the Coca-Cola bottle, which enjoys both patent and trademark protection.

FIGURE 7.8: Ghostbusters.

The GHOSTBUSTERS logo is protected both by trademark registration and copyright. Courtesy Columbia Pictures Industries, Inc.

THE COURTS

Patent infringement disputes and patentability appeals are heard first by U.S. district courts and then by the Court of Appeals for the Federal Circuit. The Bureau of National Affairs, Inc.'s (BNA) *United States Patents Quarterly* reports patent, trademark, and copyright cases; Patent Office tribunals; and Supreme Court opinions related to patents, trademarks, or copyrights. *Patent, Trademark & Copyright Journal*, published by BNA, reports intellectual property developments in the courts, Congress, the executive branch, PTO, and professional associations. The annual *Decisions of the United States Courts Involving Copyright* cites federal and state copyright and intellectual property cases since 1789 (LC 3.3/3:). Most citations are to West Publishing Company's National Reporter System and BNA's *United States Patents Quarterly. Shepard's Intellectual Property Law Citations* lists citations to litigated patents, trademarks, and copyrights.

ADDRESSES

Copyright

Copyright Office staff will perform copyright searches for $20 an hour (1997 cost). The free Circular 22, "How to Investigate the Copyright Status of a Work" (see "Freebies" below), describes information needed for search requests. Send requests to Reference and Bibliography Section, LM-451, Copyright Office, Library of Congress, Washington, DC 20559-6000; (202) 707-6850; <http://lcweb.loc.gov/copyright/>.

Individuals may search copyright records at the Copyright Office, Library of Congress, LM 455, James Madison Memorial Bldg., 101 Independence Ave., S.E., Washington, DC 20559-6000; for a map see <http://lcweb.loc.gov/copyright/cpyintro.html>; to speak to a Copyright Information Specialist, call (202) 707-3000.

Patents and Trademarks

PTO sells copies of any patent (identified by patent number) or trademark (identified by trademark registration number) for $3.00 (utility and design patents and trademarks) and $12.00 for plant patents (which include a color photograph). U.S. Patent and Trademark Office, Patent and Trademark Copy Sales, Box 9 PTCS, Washington, DC 20231; Fax: (703) 305-8716; E-mail order to ptcs@uspto.gov; click on the "Order Copy" icon on the PTO Web site; or order in person at the Crystal Plaza Public Service Window. An order form is available in PTO's *Products and Services Catalog* (C 21.30:) or on the PTO Web site <http://www.uspto.gov/web/offices/ac/ido/oeip/catalog.htm>. The PTO General Information Services Division: (800) PTO-9199, (703) 308-HELP; Fax: (703) 305-7786.

Patent and Trademark Depository Library Program, U.S. Patent and Trademark Office, Crystal Park 3, Suite 481, Washington, DC 20231; (703) 308-5558; Fax: (703) 306-2654; <www.uspto.gov/go/ptdl>.

The Patent and Trademark Office and its Scientific Library and Search Facilities are located at 2021 S. Clark Place, Crystal Plaza, Arlington, VA 22202; (703) 308-9800; <http://www.uspto.gov/web/offices/ac/ido/pssd/index.html>.

Technology Assessment and Forecast (TAF) Program, U.S. Patent and Trademark Office, PK-3, Suite 441, Washington, DC 20231; (703) 306-2600; Fax: (703) 306-2737; <http://www.uspto.gov/web/offices/ac/ido/oeip/taf/>. A detailed description of TAF products and services is in *Products and Services*, free from PTO and on the TAF Web site.

The Trademark Search Library, 2900 Crystal Drive, South Tower, Room 2B30, Arlington, VA 22202; (703) 308-2768.

PTDL Partnership libraries

Great Lakes Patent and Trademark Center at the Detroit Public Library, 5201 Woodward Ave, Detroit, MI 48202; E-mail: cburman@cms.cc.wayne.edu; (313) 833-3379 or 800-547-0619; Fax: (313) 833-6481; <http://www.detroit.lib.mi.us/glptc/>.

The Sunnyvale Center for Innovation, 465 S. Mathilda Ave, Sunnyvale, CA 94086; patents@sci3.com; (408) 730-7290, (408) 737-4945; Fax: (408) 735-8762; <http://www.sci3.com/>.

FREEBIES

The following Subject Bibliographies are free from: Stop: SSOP, Washington, DC 20402; U.S. Fax Watch (202) 512-1716:

> 21.   Patents and Trademarks <http://www.access.gpo.gov/su_docs/sale/sb-021.html>

> 126.   Copyright <http://www.access.gpo.gov/su_docs/sale/sb-126.html>

Copyright

From Publications Section, LM-455, Copyright Office, Library of Congress, Washington, DC 20559-6000 or by calling the Copyright Office Forms Hotline at (202) 707-9100 and leaving a recorded request; up to three items at a time through Fax-on-Demand (requires a touch tone telephone) at (202) 707-2600

> Circular 1, "Copyright Basics" (LC 3.4/2:1/996–2 and <http://lcweb.loc.gov/copyright/circs/circ01.html>)

> Circular 21, "Reproduction of Copyrighted Works by Educators and Librarians" (LC 3.4/2:21/995 and <http://lcweb.loc.gov/copyright/circs/circ21>)

> Circular 22, "How to Investigate the Copyright Status of a Work" (LC 3.4/2:22/995 and <http://lcweb.loc.gov/copyright/circs/circ22>)

Patents

From the World Intellectual Property Organization

> See titles listed as "Free of Charge" on their Web Catalogue of Publications <http://www.wipo.org/eng/catalog/index.htm>

From Patent and Trademark Office, Information Dissemination Organization, Crystal Park 3, Suite 441, Washington, DC 20231:

> PTO *Products and Services Catalog*
>
> "The U.S. Patent and Trademark Office Public Search Facilities: Arlington, VA" (pamphlet)

FURTHER READING

The Copyright Website <http://www.benedict.com/homepage.htm#home> (October 3, 1997).
> Fascinating copyright tips, facts, and background at this Web page ranked four-star by Magellan.

Elias, Stephen. *Patent, Copyright & Trademark: A Desk Reference to Intellectual Property Law.* Berkeley: Nolo Press, 1996.
> A self-help guide to the legalities of intellectual property.

European Patent Office "Where to Find Patent Information on the Internet" <http://www.epo.co.at/epo/online/index.htm> (October 3, 1997).
> A hot-linked list of databases, national patent offices, and patent classification systems.

Hogan, Donald W. "Unwanted Treasures of the Patent Office." *American Heritage* 9 (February 1958): 16–19, 101–103.
> You can't find more interesting reading about patent models.

International Trademark Association. The Lanham Act: Alive and Well After 50 Years <http://www.inta.org/lanham.htm> (October 18, 1997).
> The Lanham Act, which celebrated its 50th anniversary in 1996, was not the first U.S. trademark law.

Lubar, Steven. "'New, Useful, and Unobvious." *American Heritage of Invention & Technology* 6 (Spring/Summer 1990): 9-16.
> The rocky history of determining the patentability of inventions.

Morgan, Hal. *Symbols of America.* New York: Viking, 1986.
> An illustrated compendium of trademark stories.

Patent and Trademark Office. *Basic Facts About Trademarks.* GPO, 1996. (C 21.2:T 67/4/996).
> A brief introduction to trademarks and trademark applications.

———. *General Information Concerning Patents.* GPO, 1922– . Annual. (C 21.26/2:992-2 and <http://www.uspto.gov/web/offices/pac/doc/general/> [June 18, 1998]).
> An overview of patents and how to apply for them.

———. *The Story of the U.S. Patent and Trademark Office.* GPO, 1988. (C21.2:P 27/3/988).
> A history of inventions, inventors, and the patent system in America.

Peltz, James F. "Bright Lights, Big Money." *Discover* 9 (March 1988): 78–79, 81.
> The story of Gordon Gould's 28-year fight for the patent rights to the laser.

Stanford University Libraries, FindLaw, and the Council on Library Resources. "Copyright and Fair Use." <http://fairuse.stanford.edu/> (April 1, 1998).
> Practical pointers on copyright fair use, with primary materials, current legislation and cases, Internet resources, and an overview of the copyright law.

Stone, Judith. "Cells for Sale." *Discover* 9 (August 1988): 33–39.
> An account of the legal battle for rights to patented cells from leukemia patient John Moore's spleen.

Walsh, Mark. "Patently Amusing" *Internet World* 8 (April 1997): 56–58, 60.
> The article introduces Greg Aharonain's Internet Patent News Service <patents@world.std.com> in this way: "Armed with independent research and biting wit, Aharonain offers a mix of statistics, news, and gossip on high-tech patents that has become required reading for those on the cutting edge of law and technology."

Wherry, Timothy Lee. *Patent Searching for Librarians and Inventors.* Chicago: ALA, 1995.
> A guide to identifying a field of search and searching prior art, with interesting background information.

NOTES

1. Over 20 years, the fees total $3,500 for individuals and $8,000 for companies. A fee schedule is available on request or on the PTO Web site <http://www.uspto.gov/> (November 5, 1997).

2. Thanks to Charles Wilt, Patent Depository librarian in Philadelphia, who compiled a list of "crazy patents."

3. Sidney B. Williams, "Protections of Plant Varieties and Parts as Intellectual Property," *Science* 225 (July 6, 1984): 19.

4. Clarke's Needles of Goleta, California, received the first trademark on a scent for their floral-smelling OSEWEZ ("Oh-Sew-Easy") embroidery threads.

5. Domain names are assigned independently of PTO, by Network Solutions, Inc. in connection with the National Science Foundation, on a first-come, first-served basis, and added to registry known as InterNIC.

6. Although titles can't be copyrighted, they may be eligible for trademark protection.

7. Copyrighted in 1935, "Happy Birthday to You" was written by two kindergarten teachers. It earns more than $1 million yearly in royalties from companies that license it for use in products.

8. Although registration is not required to secure copyright, there are definite advantages to registering a work. Copyright is automatically seared into place when a work is created, i.e. when it is first fixed in a copy or phonorecord. Copyright protection is enhanced by including an optional but recommended copyright notice in the publication, and by formal registration with the Copyright Office. For details, consult Circular 3, "Copyright Notice," and Circular 1, "Copyright Basics," (LC 3.4/2:1/996-2 and <http://lcweb.loc.gov/copyright/circs/circ1.html> [June 18, 1998]), free from from the Copyright Office (see Addresses).

9. The United States was among the founding members of the UCC (the U.S. joined the 1952 convention in 1955), but did not join the 1886 Berne Convention until 1989.

EXERCISES

1. Patent number search
   Locate something with a patent number and identify the patent summary.

2. Patent name search
   Locate and cite the patent for any of the following:
   a. David Golde and Shirley Quan, cells from leukemia patient John Moore's spleen, 1984
   b. Gordon Gould, laser, 1987
   c. Philip Leder and Timothy Stewart, the "Harvard mouse," 1988
   d. Richard James, Slinky (toy), 1947
   e. Herman Hollerith, early computer, 1889
   f. Ananda Chakrabarty, living microorganism, 1981

3. What's wrong with this description of how Bartlett's *Familiar Quotations* protected its title?
   "As other editors took over, it became necessary to patent 'Bartlett' as a trademark protected by law, something that would have shocked its creator."*

4. Locate the National Technical Information Service's registered trademarks, NTIS® or FedWorld®.

---

*Peter Gorner. "From the Mouths of History—'Bartlett' Notes the Quotables." *Chicago Tribune* (October 16, 1980): Sect. 2, pp. 1,4.

CHAPTER 8
Legislative Information Sources

Incongruous: Where the laws are made.
—Bennett Cerf

WHAT

Congress's chief function is lawmaking.

WHY

The Constitution grants all legislative powers to "a Congress of the United States, which shall consist of a Senate and House of Representatives."

WHEN

A term of Congress lasts two years, incorporating a first and second session, each lasting one year. Congresses are numbered consecutively: for example in 1998, the 105th Congress was in the second of two one-year sessions (105–2).

HOW

The United States Congress is bicameral, comprising the Senate, with two members from each state, and the House of Representatives, with a membership of 435, apportioned according to state population. Three non-partisan congressional support agencies provide information and analyses: the Congressional Budget Office, Congressional Research Service, and General Accounting Office.

WHO

The legislative branch employs about 30,000 people, including senators, representatives, the staffs of the Library of Congress and Government Printing Office, plus congressional, committee, and congressional support agency staffs.

WHERE

Most legislation may be introduced in either the House or Senate, except revenue measures, which must originate in the House. The bulk of Congress's legislative work takes place in committees, including standing (permanent), select and special (ad-hoc), and joint (House-Senate) committees.

LEGISLATION ON THE INTERNET

Both the Library of Congress's THOMAS <http://thomas.loc.gov/> and the GPO Access <http://www.access.gpo.gov/congress/index.html> Web sites provide congressional documents free on the Internet. Although THOMAS and GPO Access share a common source—the electronic files GPO uses to print bills and the *Congressional Record*—they are fraternal rather than identical twins. Each undergoes different processing and uses different search engines (WAIS in GPO Access; INQUERY in THOMAS).

TYPES OF LEGISLATION

Bills, joint resolutions, concurrent resolutions, and simple resolutions are the four types of U.S. legislation. Bills are the usual form in which legislation is proposed. Although thousands of bills may be introduced each year, few are enacted into law, and most never receive serious consideration. If not enacted into law, both bills and resolutions die at the end of a Congress—the fate of about 95 percent of those introduced.

Basically equivalent to bills, joint resolutions usually pertain to more limited matters and are used for constitutional amendments and money measures. To become law, both bills and joint resolutions must pass both chambers and be approved by the president (except for constitutional amendments). If the president vetoes a bill, passage by two-thirds of both houses of Congress is required to override the veto and enact the legislation. Laws that emerge from joint resolutions are published in the *Statutes at Large*. Copies of bills and joint resolutions are available on GPO Access and THOMAS, in depository libraries (microfiche, Y 1.4/[no.]:), and through the Government Printing Office (for a price). Recent bills are often free from members of Congress or the Clerk of the House's Legislative Resource Center at <http://clerkweb.house.gov/lrc/lrc.htm>.

Concurrent resolutions are used to express facts, opinions, principles, or purposes jointly by both the House and Senate. Examples include fixing the time for congressional adjournment, appointing joint committees, or sending a congratulatory message to a foreign country. Concurrent resolutions passed by both chambers are published in the *Statutes at Large*.

A simple resolution is considered only by one chamber and is frequently used for procedural matters and rules. In September 1997, during the 105th Congress, both the Senate and the House of Representatives used resolutions to express condolences to the British people after the death of Diana, Princess of Wales. During the 100th Congress, the House of Representatives amended its rules to allow members to refer to the Senate by its name instead of as "the other body." The change was accomplished through a House resolution.

Public and Private Bills

Unlike public bills, which pertain to the public at large or classes of citizens, private bills affect only specific individuals or organizations. Examples are claims against the government, land titles, and immigration or naturalization. When passed, public bills become public laws; private bills become private laws. Public and private laws are numbered in separate sequences and printed in separate sections of the *Statutes at Large*.

A Sampling of Private Laws	
61–103	A farmer is reimbursed for a horse injured by a Weather Bureau kite.
88–82	Two boys are rewarded for finding a hoard of money willed to the government.
96–77	Unwitting participant in an LSD experiment is compensated.
100–15	A postman is compensated after being attacked by a dog.

THE LEGISLATIVE PROCESS

There are two things you don't want to see being made: laws and sausages.

—Otto von Bismarck

The Congressional Research Service reports that few Americans clearly understand how Congress executes its legislative responsibilities.[1] Knowledge of the legislative process is essential to tracing legislation and identifying the documents generated at each step. These documents deal with much more than Congress itself: they span the breadth of congressional legislation and oversight from apples to zoos, and are often the most current information available on a topic. The researcher who overlooks congressional publications may be missing definitive primary resources.

With 153 possible steps in the legislative process and undocumented political activities interwoven at every stage, the knowledgeable observer recognizes that outsiders can only glimpse what really happens in Congress. Eric Redman, junior staffer for a senator, described his personal research on the Senate: "The books I read seemed to describe a wholly different institution from the one I worked in and had come to know."[2]

Introduction and Preliminary Deliberations

Congress in its committee rooms is Congress at work.　　　　—Woodrow Wilson

A bill may be introduced by one or more legislators known as sponsors and cosponsors. The text of bills since 1994 are available on GPO Access and THOMAS. Preliminary deliberations occur in committee or subcommittee, where Congress's most important work is transacted. Committees have been called the nerve endings of Congress: collecting information, sifting alternatives, and refining legislation. To assess proposed legislation, a committee may hold hearings and may commission a study called a committee print. Hearings, committee prints, and reports are the three basic types of congressional committee publications. At the start of each month, the *Congressional Record* Daily Digest summarizes last month's committee activities in each chamber, with hot links in the THOMAS version to the full text of *Congressional Record* pages and legislation.

In their oversight role, congressional committees are "watchdogs of the executive branch," overseeing the execution of laws and conducting investigations for fact-finding or to expose incompetence or wrongdoing. Committees also consider executive communications, presidential nominations and treaties, and execute the congressional budget process. An index to department and agency reports required by law to be filed with Congress is *Reports Required by Congress: CIS Guide*

FIGURE 8.1: How a Bill Becomes Law.

This graphic shows the most typical way in which proposed legislation is enacted into law. There are more complicated, as well as simpler, routes, and most bills never become law. The process is illustrated with two hypothetical bills, House bill No. 1 (HR 1) and Senate bill No. 2 (S 2). Bills must be passed by both houses in identical form before they can be sent to the president. The path of HR 1 is traced by a solid line, that of S 2 by a broken line. In practice most bills begins as similar proposals in both houses.

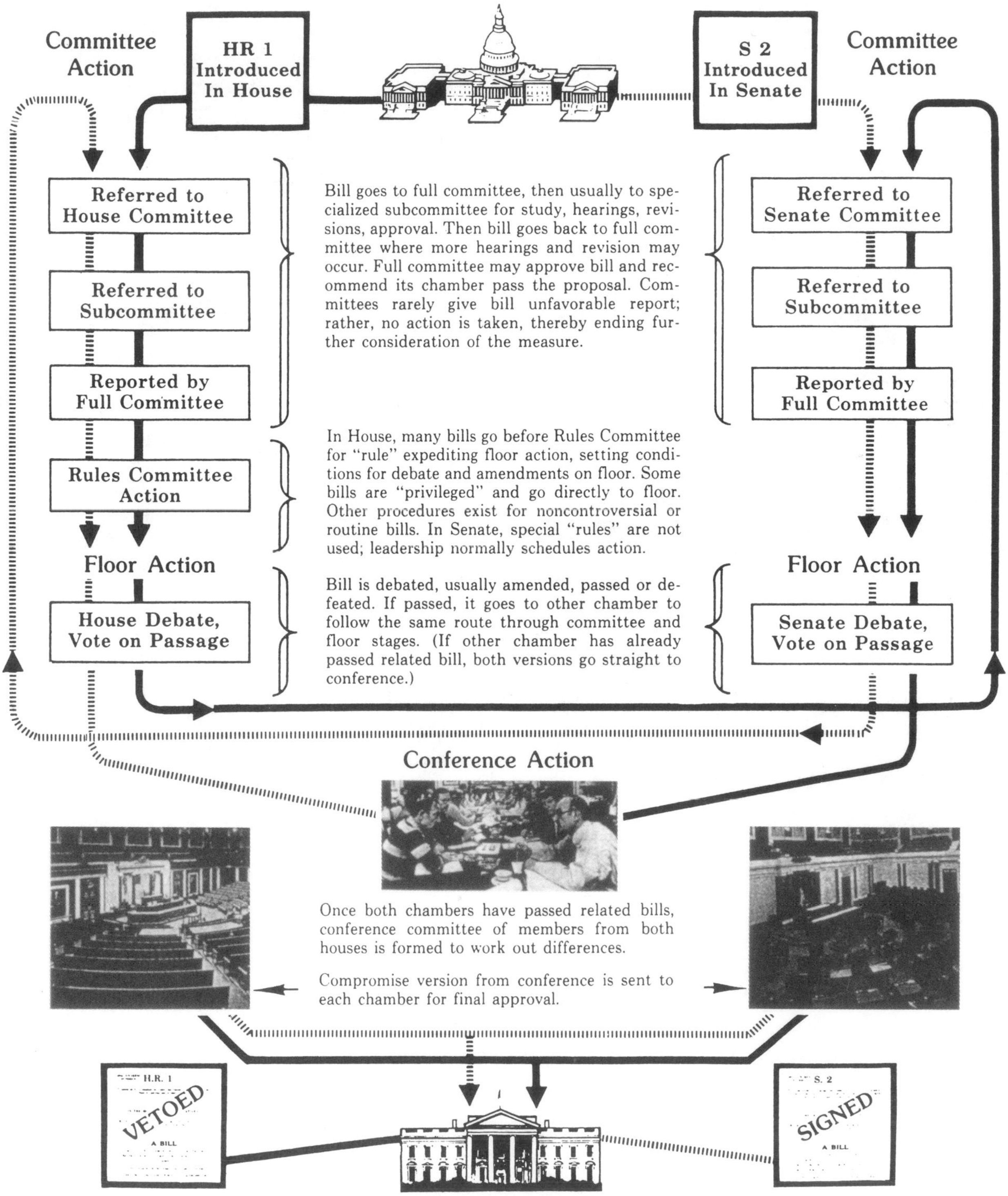

Committee Action

HR 1 Introduced In House

S 2 Introduced In Senate

Committee Action

Referred to House Committee

Referred to Subcommittee

Reported by Full Committee

Bill goes to full committee, then usually to specialized subcommittee for study, hearings, revisions, approval. Then bill goes back to full committee where more hearings and revision may occur. Full committee may approve bill and recommend its chamber pass the proposal. Committees rarely give bill unfavorable report; rather, no action is taken, thereby ending further consideration of the measure.

Referred to Senate Committee

Referred to Subcommittee

Reported by Full Committee

Rules Committee Action

In House, many bills go before Rules Committee for "rule" expediting floor action, setting conditions for debate and amendments on floor. Some bills are "privileged" and go directly to floor. Other procedures exist for noncontroversial or routine bills. In Senate, special "rules" are not used; leadership normally schedules action.

Floor Action

House Debate, Vote on Passage

Bill is debated, usually amended, passed or defeated. If passed, it goes to other chamber to follow the same route through committee and floor stages. (If other chamber has already passed related bill, both versions go straight to conference.)

Floor Action

Senate Debate, Vote on Passage

Conference Action

Once both chambers have passed related bills, conference committee of members from both houses is formed to work out differences.

Compromise version from conference is sent to each chamber for final approval.

H.R. 1 VETOED A BILL

S. 2 SIGNED A BILL

Compromise bill approved by both houses is sent to the president, who can sign it into law or veto it and return it to Congress. Congress may override veto by a two-thirds majority vote in both houses; bill then becomes law without president's signature.

to Executive Communications from the Congressional Information Service.

Sources of Information on Committee Membership*

"Senate Committee Assignments" <http://www.senate.gov/committee/committee.html>
House "Committee Office Web Services" <http://www.house.gov/CommitteeWWW.html>
CIS/Index (by members' names)
CQ Weekly Report annual supplement, "Committee Guide"
Congressional Staff Directory
Congressional Yellow Book
Congressional Index
Calendars of the House of Representatives (conference committees)
U.S. Code Congressional and Administrative News
Congressional Directory
Politics in America

---

*Arranged with the most current first

Hearings

A committee might hold hearings for numerous reasons, including fact-finding and political motivations. A common objective is gathering background information for legislation or oversight investigation of malfeasance, disaster, or crisis. Since the first congressional inquiry in 1792, a cavalcade of investigations has touched almost every conceivable subject, from "un-American activities" to Watergate and Whitewater. Other motivations for holding hearings may be to garner public opinion, provide an outlet for citizen frustration, foster support for a bill, work toward compromise, or delay action on a bill.

You have probably seen snippets of hearings on the evening news. The witness sitting before a congressional panel to deliver a statement and answer questions may be a government official, outside expert, scholar, special-interest group spokesperson, concerned citizen, celebrity, or sports figure. Ayn Rand, Gary Cooper, Walt Disney, Henry Ford, Mickey Mantle, Herbert Putnam (Librarian of Congress), Jackie Robinson, Eleanor Roosevelt, and Mark Twain all testified before Congress in their time. The epics of congressional documents, hearings can provide not just facts and opinions, but anecdotes, human interest, tragedy, and laughter (noted in the transcripts as [laughter]).

Testimony is transcribed verbatim and compiled, although members and witnesses are allowed to correct their grammar and syntax, called "smoothing." Off-the-record statements are excluded, and testimony about confidential matters discussed in closed sessions is noted but not divulged. Hearings provide a transcript of testimony, witness answers to committee questions,

discussion, and any supplementary material inserted into the record such as exhibits, related reports, statistics, letters, or magazine articles. With their insertions of reprinted articles, hearings can be mini-anthologies. For example, the FBI's *The KGB and the Library Target, 1962–Present,* printed by NTIS and not distributed to depositories, was inserted into the House hearings, *FBI Counterintelligence Visits to Libraries* (Y 4.J 89/1:100/123), which was sent to depositories.

Because about 60 percent of hearings are submitted to GPO in camera copy to capture nondigitized content like affidavits, newspaper articles, and exhibits, most hearings are not digitized for CD-ROM or online access. Electronic submission increased during the 105th Congress, allowing selected hearings to be added to THOMAS and GPO Access.

Search Tip

Note that "Supplementary Material" in hearings is not individually indexed in *CIS/Index.* Recalling an earlier example, the FBI's *The KGB and the Library Target, 1962–Present* was inserted on pages 244–78 in the House Committee on the Judiciary's 1989 *FBI Counterintelligence Visits to Libraries, Hearings* (Y 4.J89/1: 100/123). But because it was lumped amid supplementary material it cannot be identified by title in *CIS/Index* or Congressional Masterfile 2. How do you find it? You stumble across it in the table of contents. If the full text of the hearing had been online in THOMAS, a keyword search would have found it.

Each published hearing includes a table of contents identifying witnesses, but no index. *CIS/Index* indexes not only the hearing but also each witness's testimony, with abstracts. The *Monthly Catalog* lists but does not abstract hearings. The keys to the contents of hearings are THOMAS and *CIS/Index.* THOMAS and the House Internet Law Library <http://law.house.gov/10.htm> provide the full text of selected digitized hearings starting with the 105th Congress in 1997. The University of Michigan Documents Center has a guide to hearings available on the Internet at <http://www.lib.umich.edu/libhome/Documents.center/hearings.html>. The Congressional Information Service's Web subscription service, Congressional Universe, includes written submitted testimony for most hearings since 1993 and selected hearings between 1988 and 1992. Focusing on aspects of hearings not covered by *CIS/Index,* the *Congressional Hearings Calendar* (Hein) allows hearings to be identified from partial references that cite date of hearing, committee and subcommittee, chairperson, or title.

Public release of hearing transcripts is at the committee's discretion. Although most transcripts are available to the public—directly from the committee, via THOMAS, or through depository libraries (in one study of academic depository library circulation statistics, hearings accounted for one-third of documents circulated[3])—others are never mass produced for public distribution. Executive hearings (also called executive sessions) are the opposite of public hearings—they are closed to the public and rarely printed. The printing run for most hearings is typically only about one-thousand copies that are often quickly snapped up by journalists, lobbyists, and other eager readers. After that, requesters are referred to GPO or the Congressional Sales Office in Washington, DC, where copies can be purchased. C-SPAN Online offers Internet access to selected hearings in RealAudio at <http://www.c-span.org/>. Congressional committee documents are also available to libraries through Doc Ex, a source of publications not sent to depositories and not for sale.

Tips

Many agencies and special interest groups post transcripts of their hearings testimony on their Web sites.

To find transcribed testimony from a recent hearing, try NEXIS, "IN THE NEWS" section, under the witness's name.

Identifying Hearings Documents*

THOMAS
Congressional Index
CIS/Index Legislative Annual
PAIS
Monthly Catalog
CIS U.S. Congressional Committee Hearings Index (1833–1969)

---

*Arranged with the most current first

The *CIS Index to Unpublished U.S. Senate Committee Hearings* and *CIS Index to Unpublished U.S. House of Representatives Committee Hearings* identify "long-buried" hearings from the mid-1800s through the 1960s. CIS's Congressional Masterfile 1 on CD-ROM includes citations to these unpublished House and Senate hearings. Full text of the unpublished hearings is sold on microfiche by the Congressional Information Service. Some unpublished hearings since 1988 are available on LEXIS/CNGTST.

Committee Prints

A committee may commission a special background research report on proposed legislation, called a committee print. Prepared by committee research staff, the Congressional Research Service, or outside consultants, committee prints frequently provide highly valuable situation reports, statistics, historical background, and legislative analyses.

Committee prints have been characterized by the Congressional Information Service as "once the most private of public documents," because of their inconsistent distribution, limited printings, and frequent public unavailability. Some are not labeled "committee print" on their covers, and many are not identified by committee serial numbers. Most committee prints since 1970 can be identified using *CIS/Index* or the *Monthly Catalog*. They are included on Congressional Information Service's Web subscription service, Congressional Universe. Some are available in depository library collections or from the congressional issuing committee. Officially, committee prints are not available free, but are for sale from GPO or the Congressional Sales Office.

A key index for retrospective committee prints is the *CIS U.S. Congressional Committee Prints Index*, covering prints issued from the mid-1800s through 1969 (also included in CIS's Congressional Masterfile 1 on CD-ROM).

Identifying Committee Prints*

Congressional Index
CIS/Index
PAIS
Monthly Catalog
CIS U.S. Congressional Committee Prints Index (1833–1969)

---

*Arranged with the most current first

Committee Reports

The committee has several options for the disposition of a bill. It may fail to report it, causing it to "die" in committee, the fate of about 85 percent of bills. Occasionally, an unfavorable report may be issued, in which the committee recommends against the bill's passage. Most often, though, if a bill is "reported from committee" for consideration by the larger body, the report is favorable. The reported bill is sent to the chamber floor along with a written explanation called a report. The bill may be exactly as originally introduced or amended in committee ("marked up"). Committee mark-up sessions held to debate and vote upon proposed amendments are available commercially through LEGI-SLATE's Markup Reports. Changes are noted in the printed report by typographical comparison, with amendments explained at the beginning of the report. The reported bill is placed on a calendar and assigned a chronological calendar number (an internal control number bearing no relationship to when the bill will be considered).

The committee report can be meaty, containing much more than the proposed legislation. It often includes detailed analysis, committee rationale, issues disclosed in hearings, cost projections, and sometimes minority or supplemental views of committee members. The results of any committee roll-call votes on whether to report the bill are also given. (Their inclusion is noted on the report's cover.) Recorded committee votes are also noted in the annual index to *CQ Weekly Report.* The report's immediate function is to inform the larger body so members can evaluate the bill, but later the judicial and executive branches may consult it to determine "legislative intent"—the courts to help interpret the law, executive agencies to help draft regulations emanating from the law.

Each committee report is designated as "H." for House or "S." for Senate, and sequentially numbered by Congress (for example, "105" for the 105th Congress) followed by the individual report accession number:

H. Rpt. 105–342
S. Rpt. 105–16

The full text of committee reports since 1995 are available on THOMAS and GPO Access. Reports are sometimes free from the issuing committee, can be purchased from GPO, are available in depository libraries (Y 1.1/ 5: [Senate] and Y 1.1/8: [House]), and are included in the Serial Set. Issues of *U.S. Code Congressional and Administrative News* reprint portions of key committee and conference reports. Committee reports are cited in the *Monthly Catalog* and *CIS/Index* (which also abstracts their content). Neither MOCAT nor *CIS/Index* alert researchers to a cited report's full text availability on THOMAS/GPO Access, however.

Committee Reports on THOMAS: Quick Tips http://thomas.loc.gov/		
Scope	Scout Report	
Full text Since 104–1 (1995–96)	When multiple reports are retrieved, a brief display shows title and report number (hot-linked to full display); or select from the full display "option menu" A report selected from the brief display list has a clickable table of contents with links to the full text To continue, select "Forward" on the navigation menu or select an item from the table of contents display	
Search type	*Rules*	*Example*
Keyword/phrase	Lower case; space between words; select "House" or "Senate" or search all (the default)	ecology balanced budget line-item veto
Report number	Select "House" or "Senate," type report number in the search box	104–27
Bill number	With or without spaces and periods, in upper- or lowercase Type number in Committee Reports, Bill number search box "Chamber Action" in CR Daily Digest itemizes "Measures Reported," giving bill number (with link to legislative history), short title, and report number (no link)	h.r. 2408 S 1098 H. Res. 225 hjres 44 SRES 24 S. CON. RES. 5
Reporting committee	Click committee name from the House or Senate scrolling committee boxes	Committee on Environment and Public Works
Browse report titles	Choose chronological listing for House or Senate	*In the Matter of Representative Newt Gingrich* House Rpt. 105–1
Using Boolean, proximity, or relevance operators (in INQUERY)	Refer to THOMAS: Not-So-Quick Tips table at chapter's end	

Identifying Reports*

THOMAS/GPO Access
Calendars of the House of Representatives
Congressional Record Index
Congressional Index
CIS/Index
Monthly Catalog
CIS Serial Set Index (1789–1969)

---

*Arranged with the most current first

The weekly *Calendars of the House of Representatives* is a cumulative record of the status of bills reported from both the House and Senate (Y 1.2/2: or from the United States Congress page on GPO Access, select "Miscellaneous House Publications.") Its title is plural because the House maintains five calendars for various types of legislation.[4] Its scope (House and Senate), frequency (daily on GPO Access and weekly in print), price (free to depository libraries), and cumulative, detailed information combine to make the House *Calendars* a key resource for tracing legislation.

To retrieve the contents in the GPO Access version, search for "table of contents." The weekly Monday print issues and daily cumulations on GPO Access include an index and a History of Bills and Resolutions giving a complete chronological legislative history for all House and Senate legislation reported out of committee. Hearings and committee prints are omitted, however. To access the History of Bills section, search "history of bills and resolutions" or click on the Table of Contents listing under the type of legislation desired: for example, click on "*H.Cal. (October21) HOUSE BILLS*." The final first-session paper issue is a permanent reference until superseded by the second-session final issue, cumulating information on bills acted upon in both houses during the two-year Congress.

Floor Action

Debates and Amendments

> *It doesn't work efficiently. . . . It's a messy, untidy spectacle to watch. But I think it is vital to the nation.*
> —Senator J. Bennett Honston, describing Senate debate

A bill brought to the floor for consideration may be debated or amended. Floor action may take days, although most legislation is noncontentious and stimulates no more than half an hour's debate. Zwirn notes that although "the ideal functions of floor debate are to inform and persuade," most legislators have already made up their minds about the bill.[5] In these cases, the "debate" may actually be recitation of prepared statements.

The Heat of Debate

The floors of Congress are safer than they used to be. Until the Civil War, it was common for legislators to be armed with guns or Bowie knives. When a gun accidentally discharged inside a desk during one House debate, some 40 Members whipped out their pistols in response. Early floor action was punctuated by fistfights, spitting, blows to the head, toupee-snatchings, and pummelings. Such behavior has always been considered unparliamentary. Today, standards of unparliamentary behavior prescribe that shoving matches, profanity, obscenities, and insults be stricken from the *Congressional Record*. Only those watching the live proceedings from the galleries or on C-SPAN witness the fuller spectacle of floor action.

Identifying Dates of Floor Action*

THOMAS/GPO Access
Congressional Record Index via THOMAS/GPO Access
CIS/Annual (Legislative Histories volume)
Journals of the House and Senate
Slip law
Statutes at Large

---

*Arranged with the most current first

Voting

Some votes provide only a final tally, while others record how individuals voted. A member has the option of voting for or against, or being recorded either as present but not voting, absent, or pairing. Pairing is coordinated with another member wanting to vote the opposite way, so that the two votes negate each other. Unrecorded methods of voting provide only overall totals for and against the measure but not how individuals voted. Recorded votes (roll calls) document each member's vote and are numbered. Voting is documented in the *Congressional Record*, searchable on THOMAS and GPO Access. If the number isn't known, search "roll call vote no." as a Word/Phrase search.

Voting Records*	
Final Tallies	Recorded Votes
Congressional Record/ THOMAS/GPO Access House and Senate Journals	*Congressional Record*/ THOMAS/GPO Access *Congressional Roll Call* *CQ Weekly Report* *Congressional Index* *CQ Almanac*

*See also the Library of Congress Internet Resource Page, "Voting Records of Members of Congress" at <http://lcweb.loc.gov/global/legislative/voting.html#records>.

Action in Second Chamber

A bill approved in one chamber is conveyed to the other and thereafter may be called an "act." Additional documentation is generated in the second chamber as the act replicates its route through the first house: (1) assignment to committee; (2) possible hearings, committee prints; (3) report from committee; and (4) floor action. The act may be accepted as is, rejected, amended, or ignored while the second chamber pursues its own version (called a companion, similar, identical, or related bill). Companion bills are often introduced simultaneously in each chamber, with different bill numbers. Often one is allowed to die while the other continues through legislative channels. The House *Calendars* note this in the History of Bills and Resolutions by recording that one bill was "laid on table," and that the companion bill was "passed in lieu."

Congressional Record

X/a.Cong.-sess.:

http://thomas.loc.gov/

http://www.access.gpo.gov/congress/index.html

> *There simply is no first amendment right to receive a verbatim transcript of the proceedings of Congress.*
> —Gregg v. Barrett, 771 F.2d 539 (D.C. Cir 1985)

On October 18, 1972, Hale Boggs of Louisiana stood to address the House of Representatives in a 34-page speech praising his colleagues' legislative accomplishments. Or so it seems from reading the *Congressional Record*. Mr. Boggs had actually died 48 hours before his "speech," victim of a plane crash on October 16. Hale Boggs's speech is a classic metaphor for the paradoxical character of the *Congressional Record*, a publication mistakenly assumed by many Americans to preserve a verbatim transcript of congressional debates.

Characterized over the years as an "oratorical shell game," a "comic book," a "vanity press," a "fraud," and a "sham," the *Congressional Record* is an enigma of government documentation. Although mandated to be "substantially a verbatim" account of congressional proceedings, the *Record* has been legally altered throughout its history. Under the guise of correcting transcription errors, some legislators have changed, omitted, or added remarks, creating a fascinating, and often indistinguishable, blend of truth and fiction. The transformation began when each participant in debates was given a transcript of his or her remarks as recorded by official reporters. Those remarks could be edited—theoretically to correct grammar or mistakes, but actually in almost any way imaginable.

Speakers have changed the meaning of their words: for example, changing "My conscience demands that I vote against this measure," to "My conscience demands that I vote for this measure." Legislators experiencing second thoughts have withdrawn remarks actually spoken, excising a characterization of a distinguished colleague as being corrupt, for example. And finally, members have appeared to be speaking when no speech was actually delivered. This technique, called inserting remarks, allowed Hale Boggs to file the text of his "speech" before leaving for vacation. It's been estimated that fully half of the words in the *Record* were never spoken.

The weaknesses of such a system have not been overlooked. As an official record of the deliberations behind lawmaking, used by the courts and executive agencies to interpret legislative intent, the *Record* has its flaws. In the spirit of a substantially verbatim record, the House enacted a 1995 rules change to limit doctoring remarks spoken in debate. Members can still edit their own words by obtaining unanimous consent to revise and extend, but changes in meaning beyond technical, grammatical, and typographical corrections may be questioned by the parliamentarian, and the existence of C-SPAN encourages honesty.

To further combat the *Record's* documentary weaknesses, the House uses a different typeface to differentiate statements not actually delivered. The distinctive typographical style is distinguishable in the GPO PDF version of the *Record*. It does not yet appear in THOMAS, although it's imminent. And the Senate tags the beginning and end of inserted (undelivered) speeches with black bullets, visible in print, on THOMAS, and in GPO Access PDF files, and noted as <bullet> in GPO Access text files. Although both chambers have tightened rules about inserting undelivered remarks, a senator can still avoid bullets by delivering as little as one sentence of the speech. The bullet is also omitted by special request, even if none of the text was actually uttered on the floor.

The *Congressional Record* and its predecessors (the *Annals of Congress, Register of Debates*, and *Congressional Globe*) have been published since 1789. Early Senate debates were simply summarized in the third person in newspapers, and later in the *Annals of Congress*. Not until the mid-1800s did a new method called shorthand allow the Official Reporters of Debate to transcribe every word, paving the way for the premier issue of the modern *Congressional Record* in 1873. The Stenotype machine arrived in 1974, operated in 15-minute shifts by a team of six reporters.

The *Congressional Record* is available on THOMAS and GPO Access and in many depository collections. The GPO Access version offers a choice of viewing either a plain text or PDF version. The Library of Congress has digitized the debates and proceedings through 1873 as part of their National Digital Library program <http://memory.loc.gov/ammem/amlaw/lawhome.html>.

There are four *Congressional Record* sections, each with a different character and veracity: the proceedings of (1) the House and (2) the Senate; (3) extensions of remarks; and (4) the Daily Digest. Pages numbered "HL," known as the Lobby List, listed individuals and organizations registered under the Lobbying Disclosure Act of 1995 and Federal Regulation of Lobbying Act of 1946. The quarterly list was published in the *Congressional Record* in February, May, August, and November.

The House and Senate proceedings offer more than edited debates—they include records of votes and legislative actions, and full texts of many bills. The "Extensions of Remarks" are undelivered texts that members ask to have appended to the record. Senators and representatives sometimes send reprints from the *Record* to constituents as free, franked mail, which explains much of the "down-home" content of the Extensions of Remarks. This potpourri of speeches, book or magazine excerpts, poems, recipes, and songs must be examined to be appreciated. (At a cost of about $469 a

Congressional-Record page, this hodgepodge of Americana might be deemed extravagant by some readers.) The "Daily Digest," a summary of daily activities, is a concise factual record of committee and floor proceedings, including action on bills, votes, hearings, meetings, bill status, and, at week's end, the agenda for next week. At the start of each month, the digest offers a "Resume of Congressional Activity," with statistics on the number of days Congress has been in session, the number of pages in the *Record*, bills enacted into law, measures reported from committee, reports, quorum calls, votes taken, vetoed bills, and executive nominations. The Daily Digest may be browsed on THOMAS for a specific date. At session's end, the Daily Digest is issued as a separate part of the bound *Congressional Record*, with a subject index and a table of bills enacted into public law.

At year's end, a final permanent, bound *Congressional Record* for the entire annual session is published. The bound *Record*, not the daily issues, is considered the authority for interpreting legislative intent. The bound *Congressional Record* is not simply a compilation of the daily issues—it is smoothed by editorial work

Congressional Record on THOMAS: Quick Tips http://thomas.loc.gov/		
Scope	Scout Report	
Full text	Since 102–1 (1991–92); similar to the print version, each issue is divided into sections: Senate, House, Extensions, and Daily Digest; online version adds a Table of Contents; Daily Digest offers "Highlights" and itemized "Chamber Action"	
Search Type	*Rules*	*Example*
Keyword/phrase	Select numbered Congress; space between words, use lowercase; to limit by *Record* section (Senate, House, or Extensions of Remarks) or date, click radio button	line item veto
Speaker	In keyword/phrase search: a search or limit by member's last name retrieves speeches, insertions, or references to the member; to retrieve all references of the name, leave keyword search box blank	kennedy
Date	In keyword/phrase search: limit using date-range boxes; to search one day, leave 2nd date box empty; to search one month, type or abbreviate month (add year for other than current year)	9/30/96 09/30/96 9-30-96 Sept 30, 1996 September 30, 1996 Sept September 1996
Browse a date or section	Select "Browse Congressional Record Issues by Date/part," select date; can limit by Senate, House, Extensions, or Daily Digest	Scan listings
Committee reports	Browse Daily Digest, "Chamber Action" to find bill number (with link to legislative history), short title, and report number (no link)	
Daily Digest	Browsable but not searchable; summaries of legislative actions and documents are cited and hyperlinked to the full text	

Congressional Record Index on THOMAS: Quick Tips http://thomas.loc.gov/		
Scope	Scout Report	
An alternative to searching CR full text	An alphabetical list of subjects, people's and organization names referenced in the *Congressional Record* since 103–2 (1994)	
Search Type	*Rules*	*Example*
Keyword/phrase, name, year	Space between words, lowercase; select congress number; link from bill numbers to bill text, and from CR page number to the text of that page	office of technology assessment edward kennedy
Subjects, names, places, short titles of legislation	Select "Browse Alphabetical List of All Index Topics" or "Browse List of Major Topics" (the most searched terms); displays cites to relevant CR pages or bill numbers, which are hot-linked to the full text	Select "AARON-AEROSOL" Select "Animals"
Using Boolean, proximity, or relevance operators (in INQUERY)	Refer to the table: THOMAS: Not-So-Quick Tips	

and other processing, such as the integration of the Extensions of Remarks into the body of the text. As a result, the *Congressional Record* annual cumulations do not always reproduce every word from the daily issues.[6] The permanent, bound *Record* has a separate index. Because of differences between daily issues and the annual compilation, the bound index cannot be used with the daily issues, and vice versa.

A printing and funding backlog has dogged depository library receipt of the bound *Congressional Record* for years, causing some depositories to be missing daily or final issues since 1986. Since 1990, the bound *Record* has been sent in paper only to regional depositories. The "bound" *Congressional Record* since 1983 has been distributed to selectives only on microfiche (except for the Index and Daily Digest volumes, available in either paper or microfiche). In FY 1997, funding to publish the bound *Congressional Record* was terminated, and GPO was directed to replace the bound *Record* with CD-ROM, a format of unproven longevity. Printed volumes for 1985–1988 will still be sent to regional depositories before the new CD-ROM era begins.

Congressional Record Index

The *Congressional Record Index* itemizes the contents of daily *Records* and provides a "History of Bills and Resolutions" section detailing the status of legislation (select "History of Bills" on GPO Access). The final biweekly editions of the paper *Congressional Record Index* (X/a.Cong.- sess.:nos./ind.) and the THOMAS version cover only the previous two weeks, while on GPO Access, the *Congressional Record Index* cumulates from the beginning of the congressional session. On GPO Access, each year of the Index can be searched indi-

vidually, or the historical database can be selected to search comprehensively from 1983 to last year.

Both THOMAS and GPO Access provide legislative histories summarizing actions reported in the *Congressional Record*. The biweekly History of Bills and Resolutions in paper and on THOMAS chronicles only the status of legislation acted upon during the previous two weeks, and does not cumulate until the bound end-of-session edition. The History of Bills and Resolutions on GPO Access spans back to 1983. It cites *Congressional Record* page and the date of the daily issue in the format S1234 [19JA] = Senate section page 1234, January 19th. Legislative Indexing Vocabulary (LIV) is the thesaurus for searching "Bill Summary & Status" in THOMAS and is available at <http://lcweb.loc.gov/lexico/liv/brsearch.html>.

Congressional Television

I was impressed by the fact that it's a little more boring than you would actually think the House would be.   —Citizen viewer

The House began live radio and television broadcasts of its chamber proceedings in 1979, followed by a cautious Senate in 1986. Senate television coverage, initially proposed 39 years earlier, was preceded by heated debate (one senator cautioning that floor proceedings were "not a pretty thing to watch") and a two-month pilot test. Today, C-SPAN broadcasts live, gavel-to-gavel coverage of House and Senate floor action (and some hearings) <http://www.c-span.org/>. Video- and audiotapes of chamber proceedings may be purchased through the House or Senate clerks before being erased every two months and reused. Audio- and videotapes of chamber action are permanently archived in the Li-

Congressional Record on GPO Access: Quick Tips http://www.access.gpo.gov/congress/index.html		
Scope	Scout Report	
Legislative history capsules	Select the specialized search page for History of Bills	
Search Type	*Rules*	*Example*
Page number (Since 1995 only)	Enclose in quotes	"page h1234" finds [[Page1234]] embedded in text
Date (Since 1995 only)	date= date=> date=x/x/x TO x/x/x date=9/30/96 AND " "	date=9/30/96 date=>9/30/96 (after that day) date=9/18/96 TO 9/30/96 (inclusive) date=9/30/96 AND "birthdays"
Date (Since 1994 only)	"record *month date*"	"record January 26"
Multi-year	Each year is a separate file but more than one can be selected	To search since 1994, downgrade to 1994 techniques (less sophisticated)
Votes	"last name" AND "roll call vote"	"kennedy" AND "roll call vote"
Speeches	"mr, mrs, or ms, last name" AND "record *date*" finds a topic discussed; then search NAME in caps in browser's Find command, choosing the "match case" search option	"mr kennedy" AND "record june 21" KENNEDY
Bill number (since 103–2, 1994)	Enclose in quotes; if omitting periods, replace with spaces; to interpret preface status-code for bills, refer to "Abbreviations Used in GPO Databases"; results are listed according to relevance, not chronologically	"h r 1234" "h.r.1234" h r ADJ 1234 h.r. ADJ 1234 "s 1234" or "s.1234" "s j res 123" or "s.j.res 123"; etc.
Public law number (enacted since 1995, 104–1)	Enclose in quotes; if omitting periods or hyphens, replace with spaces	"public law 104 1" "public law 104–1" public ADJ law ADJ 104 ADJ 1
U.S. Code cite	Type as a single word; use truncation to find all subsections	42USC109*
Statutes At Large cite	Enclose in quotes	"109 stat 3"
Abbreviations	Database ID code appears in the Search Results List; not searchable; see also "Congressional Bills Database Abbreviations"	cr31ja96H [Congressional Record January 31, 1996, House section]

brary of Congress's Motion Picture, Broadcasting, and Recorded Sound Division[7], the National Archives[8], and the Public Affairs Video Archives at Purdue University. The existence of complete, unedited audio and video recordings of floor action creates dual records of congressional proceedings: the verbatim tapes and the printed *Congressional Record*, "a record of what we wish we would have said, if only we had said it right."[9]

Legislative Journals

Actually, the *Congressional Record* was never intended to be the official record of congressional proceedings. The official chronicles are the annual legislative logs of each chamber, covering either the first or second con-

gressional session. Because Article I of the Constitution commands Congress to publish a journal of its proceedings, the House *Journal* (XJH) and Senate *Journal* (XJS) record daily minutes, plus a concise record of legislative action, including motions and votes.[10]

The legislative journals omit the text of floor debate, but are useful for tracing action in either chamber. Each has a "History of Bills and Resolutions" section arranged by bill number, with name, title, and subject indexes. The Library of Congress Web site, A Century of Lawmaking for a New Nation, includes the Journals of the House and Senate, starting with 1789 <http://memory.loc.gov/ammem/amlaw/lawhome.html>. CIS sells microfiche collections of the House and Senate journals since the first Congress in 1789. *The National State*

Papers of the United States, 1789–1817 reprints the Journals of the first 14 Congresses (M. Glazier, publisher).

Bicameral Action

Before an act can be forwarded to the president, the House and Senate versions must be identical. When different versions emerge, one chamber may simply accept the other's amendments. If not, differences may be resolved through a conference committee. About 10 percent of laws have required conference committees. The committee of representatives from each chamber reconciles the two versions so that an identical bill can be approved by each. The paper House *Calendars* include information on the status and membership of conference committees in two tables: "Bills in Conference" and "Bills Through Conference," which also notes any presidential action or public law number. In the GPO Access version, search for "table of contents" and then select "Bills in Converence" or "Bills Through Conference."

The conference report, containing the text of the compromise legislation and background information, cannot be amended. Unless it is accepted in its entirety by both the House and Senate, the legislation dies. Approving the conference report means approval of the compromise bill. Conference reports are numbered and designated in the same way as other committee reports. They are cited in the *Monthly Catalog* and indexed and abstracted in *CIS/Index*. Like other congressional reports, conference reports are available on THOMAS and GPO Access, in depository libraries, from their issuing committee, and frequently reprinted in *U.S. Code Congressional and Administrative News*.

Historical Materials

Research in unpublished and original congressional documentation from 1789 to the 1980s is supported by the National Archives' Center for Legislative Archives. In 1937, the Senate transferred its historical records from the Capitol's attics and basements to the newly opened National Archives. House records followed in the 1970s. Although most of these official records of Congress (largely committee records) were dirty, water-damaged, and brittle, they were "perhaps the most valuable collection of records in the entire government,"[11] documenting all phases of government activity. The Senate cache of research material since 1789, along with that of the House of Representatives, now reside in the Archives' Center for Legislative Archives <http://www.nara.gov/nara/legislative/>.

The Senate Historical Office compiles information on important events, precedents, dates, statistics, and comparisons between current and historical Senate activities and can be accessed at <http://www.senate.gov/history/index.html>.

CIS/Index

CIS/Index to Publications of the U.S. Congress and its CD-ROM and online equivalents index and abstract the working papers of Congress since 1970. Widely respected as the most comprehensive index to congressional publications, *CIS/Index* indexes and abstracts committee reports, hearings, committee prints, and House and Senate Documents (but not the *Congressional Record*). *CIS/Index* provides availability information for every congressional publication cited: many are available in depository libraries or sold by GPO (the CIS abstract includes SuDocs and Item numbers); all may be purchased on microfiche from the Congressional Information Service; and some may be requested from issuing committees. *CIS/Index* is available in print, on CD-ROM (as the Congressional Masterfile 2), and also searchable online through commercial vendors. The Legislative History volume of *CIS/Index,* issued each spring, includes what has been lauded as "probably the most complete summaries of the legislative history of federal enactments."[12] These are also searchable on CIS's Web subscription service, Congressional Universe, since 1984.

Congressional Glossary[13]

Congressional Edition—the Serial Set
Executive document (Ex. Doc.)—an executive branch communication to Congress, printed as a House or Senate document (and included in the Serial Set)
Executive session—a congressional committee meeting closed to the public and press; the Senate frequently dissolves into executive session when considering presidential nominations and treaties
The Historical Series—another name for Senate executive sessions
Legislative day—the span of time before adjournment; the House tends to adjourn daily, but a Senate legislative day may last for several calendar days
Long title of a bill—preamble
Pamphlet print—slip law
Star print—a reprinted bill or amendment that supersedes earlier printings, indicated by a small black star in the lower left corner of the cover
Unanimous consent—enactment of a bill without debate in both chambers, usually with a voice vote

---

A 1994 study showed the following able to answer most congressional questions: House *Calendars,* Commerce Clearing House's (CCH) *Congressional Index*, the *Congressional Record*, and *Congressional Quarterly Almanac*.[14] CCH's *Congressional Index* summarizes the status of every pending bill and resolution. House and Senate measures are listed numerically in different sections, with sponsors, date of introduction, and committee assignment. Later, action is reported in tables. Laws can be identified by Public Law (PL) number, bill or resolu-

	THOMAS Databases http://thomas.loc.gov/
Search Type	Scope
Congressional Record Since 102nd Congress (1991–92).	Like the print version, each issue is divided into: Senate, House, Extensions of Remarks, and Daily Digest; online version adds a Table of Contents
Congressional Record Index Since 103–2 (1994).	Searchable by keyword, phrase, name, year; browse a list of major topics; links from bill numbers to bill text, and from CR page number to the text of that page
Bill Summary and Status Since 93rd Congress (1973) Provides overview and status, continuing *Digest of Public General Bills and Resolutions* (LC 14.16:)	Searchable by a combination of up to three: bill number, amendment or PL number (year or congress must be known), title, keyword, sponsor/co-sponsor, committee/subcommittee, index term (paste Legislative Indexing Vocabulary (LIV) terms into the "Search by Index Term" box <http://lcweb.loc.gov/lexico/liv/brsearch.html>); click on Digest and Status; links to full bill text and sections of the *Congressional Record*
Public Laws Since 93rd Congress (1973)	By PL number
Bill text (since 103rd Congress)	Searchable by bill number, keywords; may limit to either Senate or House or by sponsor (member name search box at the bottom of the screen)
Roll call votes	Select *Congressional Record* database from the THOMAS home page, type in date, click on Recorded Vote link at bottom of page; or select *Congressional Record* database from Full text of Legislation, click on References to This Bill in the *Congressional Record*; or browse the *Congressional Record* Daily Digest for a specific date, then search VOTE or ROLL NO. in your browser's Find command
Committee reports (measures reported from committee only) 104th Congress (1995–96)	Full text via THOMAS Brief records in CR Daily Digest, "Chamber Action" lists bill number (with link to legislative history), short title, and report number (no link)
Hot Legislation	Major bills receiving floor action in the current congress, searchable by bill number/type, title, keywords; links to the Bill Digest and to full bill text and sections of the *Congressional Record*
Committee reports	Full text of reports reported out of committee; cites in CR Daily Digest, "Chamber Action"

tion number, subject, sponsor, and popular title. *Congressional Index* is updated weekly while Congress is in session and for up to six weeks following final adjournment. The *Congressional Quarterly Almanac* compiles stories from the year's *CQ Weekly Reports*, grouping all articles by topic. Vote studies and roll call votes are organized in one section of the *Almanac* to expedite voting analysis.

PRESIDENTIAL ACTION

The enrolled version of the bill (enr.) is sent to the president, who has 10 days (excluding Sundays) to either sign or veto it. In either case, the president often issues a message, which is published in the *Weekly Compilation of Presidential Documents* and usually incorporated in the Serial Set as a House or Senate document. When Congress is in session, the president may opt for inaction, allowing the bill to automatically become law after 10 days, or to die on his desk if Congress adjourns before the 10-day time limit (a "pocket veto"). About four out of every 10 presidential vetoes are pocket vetoes.

Presidential Action*

Text of messages:
Congressional Record via THOMAS/GPO Access
CQ Weekly Report
Weekly Compilation of Presidential Documents
House and Senate Journals
Public Papers of the Presidents
Serial Set

References to text:
THOMAS/GPO Access
Congressional Record Index
House *Calendars*
CIS/Index
Slip law
Monthly Catalog
Statutes at Large
CIS Serial Set Index (through 1969)

*Arranged with the most current first

If Congress takes no action on a vetoed bill, it dies. To override a veto requires two-thirds majority vote of both the House and Senate. This is rare: overrides have occurred for only about four percent of presidential vetoes since George Washington.[15] In the case of a pocket veto, the bill is deader than a doornail, with no opportunity for an override. If a bill becomes law, a veto is part of its legislative history. For a comprehensive list of presidential vetoes from the 1st to 103rd Congresses, consult *Presidential Vetoes, 1789–1988* (Y 1.3:S.pub.102–12) and *Presidential Vetoes, 1989–1994* (Y 1.3:S.pub.103–13), covering through Bill Clinton's first term. Arranged chronologically by Congress and bill number, with name and subject indexes, these tabulations of vetoes note any subsequent congressional action and cite pages in the *Congressional Record*.

Congressional Votes on Vetoes*

Congressional Record via THOMAS/GPO Access
Congressional Index
CQ Weekly Report
CQ Almanac
Congressional Roll Call
House and Senate Journals

---

*Arranged with the most current first

LAW

Slip law → *Statutes at Large* → *U.S. Code*

A new law, or statute, is identified by a public or private law number, composed of the number of the Congress where it passed (for example, 105), followed by a chronological number (105–18). Often, however, it is referred to by a popular name, such as the Presidential Records Act of 1978, with no mention of its public law number at all. The law becomes effective on its enactment date unless a different effective date is specified. Figure 8.3 shows the components of a public law in slip-law form (and in the *Statutes at Large*). At the start of each month, the *Congressional Record* Daily Digest summarizes laws passed, with hot-links in THOMAS.

Individual public and private laws are published separately in pamphlet form as slip laws a few days after enactment, and are available since the 93rd Congress (1973) on THOMAS and GPO Access, in depository libraries (AE 2.110:), free from the House or Senate Document Rooms while supplies last, and are sold by GPO. The public (but not private) slip laws include a citation to their future location in the *Statutes at Large*, marginal notes, citations to the *U.S. Code*, and a brief legislative history. Later, individual slip laws join other laws: first in the *Statutes at Large*, where they are bound in chronological order for each session of Congress, then by subject in the *U.S. Code*.

FIGURE 8.2: Public Law 95–261 in THOMAS.

H.R.8358: A bill to amend title 44, United States Code, to provide for the designation of libraries of accredited law schools as depository libraries of Government publications.
Sponsor: Rep. Nedzi.- LATEST ACTION: 4/17/78 Public Law 95–261

A summary of P.L. 95–261 as it appears in THOMAS, Bill Summary & Status for the 95th Congress. Clicking on *H.R.8358* leads to links to a full legislative history.

United States Statutes at Large

AE 2.111:

A couple of years following each congressional session, the slip laws are accumulated chronologically in the *Statutes at Large*. *Statutes at Large* contains the text of all public and private laws, joint and concurrent resolutions passed during each single-year congressional session.

Statutes at Large Citation

97	Stat.	113
↓		↓
vol.		page

Like the slip laws it compiles, *Statutes at Large* cites the *U.S. Code* and provides a brief legislative history. The *Statutes* volumes are sometimes called session laws because they hold the laws enacted in a single congressional session, arranged chronologically by enactment date. The volumes also include federal agency reorganization plans, proposed and ratified Constitutional amendments, and presidential proclamations. Finding aids for *Statutes* volumes include subject and personal name indexes, a bill-to-law list, concurrent resolutions, and Laws Affected tables.

During each yearly session, laws are also compiled in the commercially published, monthly *U.S. Code Congressional and Administrative News* (USCCAN), which offers quicker access to laws than the official *Statutes at Large*. USCCAN provides the full text of every newly enacted public slip law, with the text of selected documents in its legislative history, such as committee and conference reports and statements in the *Congressional Record*, plus a legislative summary, subject index, and list of acts by popular names. USCCAN updates *United States Code Annotated*, which annually codifies the same material.

FIGURE 8.3: 92 STAT. 199.

 PUBLIC LAW 95–261—APR. 17, 1978 92 STAT. 199

Public Law 95–261
95th Congress

An Act

To amend title 44, United States Code, to provide for the designation of libraries of accredited law schools as depository libraries of Government publications.

Apr. 17, 1978
[H.R. 8358]

Be it enacted by the Senate and House of Representatives of the United States of America in Congress assembled, That chapter 19 of title 44, United States Code, is amended by adding at the end thereof the following new section:

Depository
libraries,
designation.

"§ 1916. **Designation of libraries of accredited law schools as depository libraries**

44 USC 1916.

"(a) Upon the request of any accredited law school, the Public Printer shall designate the library of such law school as a depository library. The Public Printer may not make such designation unless he determines that the library involved meets the requirements of this chapter, other than those requirements of the first undesignated paragraph of section 1909 of this title which relate to the location of such library.

"(b) For purposes of this section, the term 'accredited law school' means any law school which is accredited by a nationally recognized accrediting agency or association approved by the Commissioner of Education for such purpose or accredited by the highest appellate court of the State in which the law school is located.".

"Accredited law
school."

Sec. 2. The table of sections for chapter 19 of title 44, United States Code, is amended by adding at the end thereof the following new item:

"1916. Designation of libraries of accredited law schools as depository libraries."

Sec. 3. The amendments made by this Act shall take effect on October 1, 1978.

Effective date.
44 USC 1916
note.

Approved April 17, 1978.

LEGISLATIVE HISTORY:

HOUSE REPORT No. 95–650 (Comm. on House Administration).
SENATE REPORT No. 95–670 (Comm. on Rules and Administration).
CONGRESSIONAL RECORD:
    Vol. 123 (1977): Oct. 25, considered and passed House.
    Vol. 124 (1978): Mar. 6, considered and passed Senate, amended.
        Apr. 4, House agreed to Senate amendments.

The slip law in the *Statutes at Large* shows (1) Public Law number and date of enactment, (2) *Statutes* citation where the slip law will be reprinted, (3) the original bill from which this law emerged, (4) the *U.S. Code* citation where this amendment will be placed, (5) effective date (in this case, different from enactment date), (6) legislative history showing the House and Senate committees that considered the bill and their report numbers plus dates when action was documented in the *Congressional Record*, and (7) the text of the amendment.

United States Code

Y 1.2/5:

http://www.house.gov/Laws.html

http://www.access.gpo.gov/su_docs/dbsearch.html

The official compilation of active laws, the *U.S. Code* (USC) offers a subject compilation of public laws under 50 "titles" or categories. Codifying consolidates similar topics, incorporates amendments, and deletes repealed text. Private or temporary laws are not included. Unlike the *Statutes at Large*, the *U.S. Code* does not summarize legislative history, but refers to the slip law in the *Statutes at Large*. Figures 8.3 and 8.4 compare a public law as it appears in the *Statutes at Large* and the *U.S. Code*.

The printed *Code* is updated every six years, with annual cumulative supplements in the interim. The annual supplements contain all changes to the general and permanent laws since the last edition, accessible through the same indexes and tables. The *Code* contains subject, name, and popular-name indexes, along with conversion tables to translate citations from *Statutes at Large*, Revised Statutes, Public Laws, Executive Orders, and Proclamations into *United States Code* citations. The "Tables" volume of the *U.S. Code*, compiled by the House of Representatives Office of the Law Revision Counsel, lists all *U.S. Code* sections amended since the last *Code* issue and is also online at <http://law.house.gov/uscct.htm>. The Library of Congress Internet guide to "Judicial Branch Resources" links to the *U.S. Code* Classification Table in Public Law order and in Title and Section order and is available at <http://lcweb.loc.gov/global/judiciary.html>. The Tables translate from public law number to *U.S. Code* title and section number. For translating from USC citation to public law, consult the "Historical and Statutory Notes" following sections of the *Code* in the *United States Code Annotated*. These notes chronicle House and Senate report numbers, laws, amendments, and effective dates.

How to Find U.S. Statutes and U.S. Code Citations (GS 4.102:St 2/980) shows how to quickly locate current *Statutes* and *U.S. Code* citations from typical references that require further citing. These include references to the Revised Statutes section; date, name, or number of the law; *Statutes* citation; or *Code* citation. This short pamphlet is available for $2.75 from the Office of the Federal Register. Tables for translating *Statute* citations into *U.S. Code* citations are included in the USC, USCA, and USCS.

The House of Representatives Internet Law Library provides a searchable *United States Code* with all official notes and appendices, Supplements, the Table of Popular Names, and the Law Revision Counsel's U.S. Code Classification Table. In the House Internet Law

Library, searching is done by title, section, and keyword. Keyword searching uses AND, OR, NOT, ADJ, w/n, NEAR/n (within 5 words), with phrases in single quotation marks. For subject searches, use the equal sign and an exclamation mark: = topic!. Specific kinds of truncation are indicated by ?, *, and $.

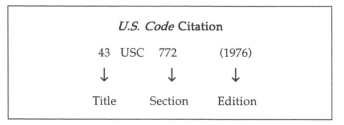

U.S. Code Citation

43	USC	772	(1976)
↓	↓		↓
Title	Section		Edition

Annotated Codes

Unofficial, annotated codes append cites to court decisions and *Code of Federal Regulations* to the text of statutes. These codes are *United States Code Annotated* (USCA) and *United States Code Service* (USCS). Both USCA and USCS offer speedier updating than the official *Code*, plus simpler supplements using pocket parts (annual paperback addendums inserted into a back-cover cavity that looks as if pages were cut out) and periodic pamphlet supplements. The two are differentiated by the fact that "the USCA purports to include all annotations, so that a single volume may encompass only two or three *Code* sections; while the USCS provides more selective but more detailed annotations, and also includes references to some law review articles."[16] Before being codified in USCA, session laws are compiled in the companion publication, *United States Code Congressional and Administrative News*. Another technique for identifying statutory changes and interpretations uses *Shepard's Citations* and is called "Shepardizing." *Shepard's Citations* covers all state and federal laws, major courts, and some government agencies.

Tip: Finding Laws on a Topic

Congressional committees often produce compilations of laws on topics under their oversight. Look for titles like *Compilation of Selected [topic] Legislation* when searching in sources such as *CIS/Index* or MOCAT.

LEGISLATIVE HISTORY

A law's legislative history is threaded in the documents generated during its legislative journey. A typical law has trekked through some 48 separate stages, and major legislation may be repeatedly regenerated before finally passing, its documentation snaking through several congressional sessions. This document trail-of-crumbs permanently records legislative intent, Congress's rationale for enacting the law. Legislative

FIGURE 8.4: 44 USC 1916.

§ 1912. Regional depositories; designation; functions; disposal of publications

Not more than two depository libraries in each State and the Commonwealth of Puerto Rico may be designated as regional depositories, and shall receive from the Superintendent of Documents copies of all new and revised Government publications authorized for distribution to depository libraries. Designation of regional depository libraries may be made by a Senator or the Resident Commissioner from Puerto Rico within the areas served by them, after approval by the head of the library authority of the State or the Commonwealth of Puerto Rico, as the case may be, who shall first ascertain from the head of the library to be so designated that the library will, in addition to fulfilling the requirements for depository libraries, retain at least one copy of all Government publications either in printed or microfacsimile form (except those authorized to be discarded by the Superintendent of Documents); and within the region served will provide interlibrary loan, reference service, and assistance for depository libraries in the disposal of unwanted Government publications. The agreement to function as a regional depository library shall be transmitted to the Superintendent of Documents by the Senator or the Resident Commissioner from Puerto Rico when the designation is made.

The libraries designated as regional depositories may permit depository libraries, within the areas served by them, to dispose of Government publications which they have retained for five years after first offering them to other depository libraries within their area, then to other libraries.

(Pub. L. 90–620, Oct. 22, 1968, 82 Stat. 1286).

HISTORICAL AND REVISION NOTES

Based on 44 U.S. Code, 1964 ed., § 84a (Pub. L. 87–579, § 9, Aug. 9, 1962, 76 Stat. 355).

SECTION REFERRED TO IN OTHER SECTIONS

This section is referred to in section 1911 of this title.

§ 1913. Appropriations for supplying depository libraries; restriction

Appropriations available for the Office of Superintendent of Documents may not be used to supply depository libraries documents, books, or other printed matter not requested by them, and their requests shall be subject to approval by the Superintendent of Documents.

(Pub. L. 90–620, Oct. 22, 1968, 82 Stat. 1286.)

HISTORICAL AND REVISION NOTES

Based on 44 U.S. Code, 1964 ed., § 85a (June 27, 1956, ch. 453, § 101, 70 Stat. 369).

§ 1914. Implementation of depository library program by Public Printer

The Public Printer, with the approval of the Joint Committee on Printing, as provided by section 103 of this title, may use any measures he considers necessary for the economical and practical implementation of this chapter.

(Pub. L. 90–620, Oct. 22, 1968, 82 Stat. 1287.)

HISTORICAL AND REVISION NOTES

Based on 44 U.S. Code, 1964 ed., § 81c (Pub. L. 87–579, § 10, Aug. 9, 1962, 76 Stat. 356).

§ 1915. Highest State appellate court libraries as depository libraries

Upon the request of the highest appellate court of a State, the Public Printer is authorized to designate the library of that court as a depository library. The provisions of section 1911 of this title shall not apply to any library so designated.

(Added Pub. L. 92–368, § 1(a), Aug. 10, 1972, 86 Stat. 507.)

§ 1916. Designation of libraries of accredited law schools as depository libraries

(a) Upon the request of any accredited law school, the Public Printer shall designate the library of such law school as a depository library. The Public Printer may not make such designation unless he determines that the library involved meets the requirements of this chapter, other than those requirements of the first undesignated paragraph of section 1909 of this title which relate to the location of such library.

(b) For purposes of this section, the term "accredited law school" means any law school which is accredited by a nationally recognized accrediting agency or association approved by the Commissioner of Education for such purpose or accredited by the highest appellate court of the State in which the law school is located.

(Added Pub. L. 95–261, § 1, Apr. 17, 1978, 92 Stat. 199.)

EFFECTIVE DATE

Section 3 of Pub. L. 95–261 provided that: "The amendments made by this Act [enacting this section] shall take effect on October 1, 1978."

TRANSFER OF FUNCTIONS

The functions of the Commissioner of Education were transferred to the Secretary of Education pursuant to section 3441(a)(1) of Title 20, Education.

CHAPTER 21—ARCHIVAL ADMINISTRATION

The amendment enacted as Public Law 95-261 appears in the *U.S. Code* without a legislative history, but with a citation to the *Statutes at Large* where the legislative history can be found. The same section can be found on the *U.S. Code* Online via GPO Access.

Internet USC		
GPO Access <http://www.access.gpo.gov/su_docs/dbsearch.html>	Scout Report	
	AND, OR, ADJ in caps Enclose phrases in quotation marks Truncate* to retrieve subsections	
Search Type	*Rules*	*Example*
U.S. Code citation	In quotes, no spaces	"44USC1916" "44USC19*"
Statutes at Large citation	In quotes, use spaces	"92 stat 199"
Public Law number	pub l cong-no.	"pub l 95-261" pub ADJ l ADJ 95 ADJ 261
Keywords	AND, OR , ADJ in caps, phrases in quotation marks	law AND accredited AND depository
House Internet Law Library <http://www.house.gov/Laws.html> or <http://143.231.180.66/usc.htm>	Scout Report	
	Includes all official notes and appendices, Supplements, the Table of Popular Names, and the Law Revision Counsel's *U.S. Code* Classification Table Specific kinds of truncation are indicated by ?, *, and $	
Search Type	*Rules*	*Example*
Subjects	equal sign and an exclamation mark: = topic!	=veterans!
Keywords	AND, OR, NOT, ADJ, w/n, NEAR/n (within 5 words), with phrases in single quotation marks.	law AND accredited AND depository

histories are important for both judicial and administrative interpretation in executing the law.

Bill or public-law numbers are keys to reconstructing legislative history. When the bill or law number is unknown, it may be identified through subject, short title or popular name, or other indexes provided in THOMAS, GPO Access, *Statutes at Large, U.S. Code*, the annotated codes, *CIS/Index*, or *Shepard's Acts and Cases by Popular Names*. To find a rescinded law plucked from the *U.S. Code*, use the tables of public law numbers in *Statutes at Large* or *United States Code Congressional and Administrative News*.

The *Digest of Public General Bills and Resolutions*, discontinued after the 101st Congress, summarized public bills and resolutions (LC 14.6:). An online version of the "bill digest" since 1973 (93rd Congress) is still available through Bill Summary & Status on THOMAS, and on LC's online database, LOCIS (pronounced "low-kiss") <telnet://locis.loc.gov>. (The telnet can also be linked from <http://lcweb.loc.gov/catalog/>.) Retrospective legislative histories may be traced with the help of Eugene Nabors's *Legislative Reference Checklist: The Key to Legislative Histories from 1789–1903* (Rothman).

Compiled Legislative Histories

In 1921, the General Accounting Office began preparing a legislative history for every bill that impacted GAO, expanding in 1931 to include all bills introduced in Congress. The GAO Legislative History Collection is open to researchers in the Legislative Section of the GAO Law Library and in the Federal Records Center. This full-text collection is considered the most comprehensive set of legislative histories of public laws enacted 1921 to 1977, including initial and companion bills, amendments, hearings, committee reports, and discussion recorded in the *Congressional Record*.

Nancy P. Johnson's *Sources of Compiled Legislative Histories: A Bibliography of Government Documents, Periodical Articles, and Books, 1st Congress–101st Congress* (AALL Publ. 1993–) is a guide to locating previously compiled legislative histories in print and online, with listings by subjects and by public law number, plus a bibliography of documents, finding aids, and compiling techniques.

Sources for Tracing Legislative History and Bill Status	
Title	Access Points
THOMAS <http://thomas.loc.gov/>	Subject, keywords, bill number, PL number, date, sponsors, committee
GPO Access <http://www.access.gpo.gov/congress/index.html> Select History of Bills	History of Bills and Resolutions section of the *Congressional Record Index* since 1983
U.S. Code Congressional and Administrative News	Keywords in public law titles, popular name, subjects, PL number
CIS/Index *CIS/Annual* (Legislative Histories volume) Congressional Masterfile 2 Congressional Universe	Title, bill number (if reported from committee), Report number, Document number, Senate hearing or committee print number, committee/subcommittee chairperson, PL number, SuDocs number
Slip law	Law text is followed by a concise legislative history citing presidential remarks in the *Weekly Compilation of Presidential Documents*
House *Calendars* Y 1.2/2: GPO Access <http://www.access.gpo.gov/congress/index.html> and select Miscellaneous House Publications	Only bills reported from committee Print: bill number in "History of Bills and Resolutions," PL number in "Public Laws" and "Private Laws" sections, subjects and names in the index On GPO Access, "History of Bills and Resolutions" retrieves cumulative legislative histories.
Congressional Record <http://thomas.loc.gov/> <http://www.access.gpo.gov/congress/index.html>	Biweekly print index covers only bills acted on during the previous two weeks. Subjects and names in the index; bill numbers (in "History of Bills and Resolutions" in print version). End-of-session print issue is cumulative.
Statutes at Large	Number of bill or law. Reprints the slip law's concise legislative history.

BIOGRAPHICAL SOURCES

> *The first six months it's "How did I get here?"*
> *The next six months it's "How did they get here?"*
> —Senator Robert Dole, Kansas

The *Congressional Directory* presents short biographies of House and Senate members, along with their committee memberships, terms of service, addresses, and telephone numbers (Y 4.P 93/1:1/cong and on GPO Access <http://www.access.gpo.gov/congress/index.html>). The Directory can be accessed by state, by committee, by member's name, and by subject. Also functioning as a general government directory similar to the *U.S. Government Manual*, the *Congressional Directory* lists government agency addresses and phone numbers, state and territorial governors, foreign diplomats, and news media personnel, plus maps of congressional districts.

For retrospective biographies, refer to the *Biographical Directory of the United States Congress, 1774–1989*, which profiles members since the Continental Congress, plus executive branch officers since George Washington's administration (Y 1.1/3:100–34; Serial Set 13849). This publication is introduced as a House or Senate document and is printed by a special congressional

resolution. The 1989 revision was the first since 1971, with the next expected by the year 2000. *Women in Congress, 1917–1990* provides biographies and photographs of women senators and representatives (Y 1.1/2:SERIAL 14004; H.Doc.101–238). *Black Americans in Congress, 1870–1989* is a compendium of biographical essays and portraits of African American senators and representatives since 1870 (Y 1.1/7:101–117; H.Doc.101–117; Serial Set 13947).

For photographs, turn to the *Congressional Pictorial Directory* with its black-and-white photos of House and Senate members, officials of the Capitol, chaplains, the president, and vice president (Y 4.P 93/1:1 P/cong and on GPO Access in Adobe Acrobat Portable Document Format [PDF] <http://www.access.gpo.gov/congress/index.html>. Photos of members are also provided in the *Congressional Yellow Book* and *Congressional Staff Directory*.

About 12,000 staffers do much of Congress's daily, behind-the-scenes work. The *Congressional Directory* helps to identify some of these aides by listing congressional administrative assistants and secretaries. Other sources are the *Congressional Staff Directory* and *Federal Staff Directory* published by CQ Staff Directories, Inc.

Information About Senators and Representatives	
State -> Senators/Representatives	THOMAS *Congressional Directory* *Who's Who in Congress* Roll Call's Hill Directory <http://www.rollcall.com/>
County/city -> Senators/Representatives	*Congressional Staff Directory*
Committee -> names of members	THOMAS *Carroll's Federal Directory* *Congressional Directory* *Congressional Record* *Congressional Staff Directory* *CQ Weekly Report* annual supplement, Committee Guide *Who's Who in Congress*
Names of members -> committee assignments	http://congress.org/ *Congressional Staff Directory* *Who's Who in Congress* *CQ Weekly Report* supplement, Committee Guide *Politics in America*
Web page and e-mail addresses	THOMAS http://www.house.gov/MemberWWW.html http://www.senate.gov/senator/members.html http://lcweb.loc.gov/global/legislative/email.html
Biographies	*Almanac of American Politics* *Congressional Directory* *Congressional Index* *Politics in America* *Who's Who in Congress*
Federal Election Campaign Act Reports	http://www.FEC.gov
Financial disclosure statements	*Financial Disclosure Reports of Members of the U.S. House of Representatives* (annual) Y 1.1/7:
Former senators and representatives	*Biographical Directory of the American Congress, 1774–1989* (Y 1.1/3:100-34) Senate Historical Office list <http://www.senate.gov/history/nameindex/a.htm>

CONGRESSIONAL DISTRICTS

One of a congressman's small pleasures is reading an angry letter from a person who says he'll never vote for you again—and then seeing from the address that the writer lives in another district. —Rep. Gilbert Gude, Maryland

Most representatives and senators have Web sites. The Library of Congress Internet Resource Page, "E-mail Addresses for Congress," is a handy linkage to them and can be accessed at <http://lcweb.loc.gov/global/legislative/email.html>. Web sites and e-mail addresses are also provided on the Clerk of the House page <http://clerkweb.house.gov/>.

> **Writing Senators and Representatives**
>
> Senators: The Honorable Robert/Roberta Slone
> U.S. Senate
> The Capitol
> Washington, DC 20510
> Dear Senator Slone:

> Representatives: The Honorable Robert/Roberta Slone
> U.S. House of Representatives
> The Capitol
> Washington, DC 20515
> Dear Mr./Ms. Slone:

Facts about congressional districts are available in the *Congressional Directory* and *Congressional District Atlas*, as well as in numerous privately published reference sources. The Atlas provides district maps and refers from county and incorporated municipality to the proper district (C 3.62/5:).

CONGRESSIONAL SUPPORT AGENCIES

Three agencies support Congress's legislative pursuits: the Congressional Budget Office (discussed in chapter 10), the Congressional Research Service, and the General Accounting Office. The agencies, which provide background information and analysis to support congressional decision making, withered from tetrad to trinity in 1995, with the demise of the Office of Technology Assessment. Because support-agency publications are created expressly for Congress, there "is no automatic presumption of public access to this material." Support agency publications reach only a small segment of the public "who know enough to use their congressional office contacts" and, to a lesser extent, to use the depository library program.[17]

General Accounting Office

http://www.gao.gov

The General Accounting Office (GAO) is Congress's auditor, overseeing the receipt and spending of public funds through audits, investigations, and evaluations. Most GAO reviews are triggered by congressional committee requests, while others are required by law. In July 1995, for example, GAO released *Government Records—Results of a Search For Records Concerning The 1947 Crash Near Roswell, New Mexico* (GAO/NSIAD-95-187) in response to Congressman Steven H. Schiff's (R-NM) 1994 request for an official study of the Roswell incident. Single copies of GAO "blue cover" reports describing GAO audits, congressional testimony, and governmental oversight are free by mail from GAO or in depository libraries (GA 1.13:). Those produced since 1995 are available through GPO Access using the specialized GAO database search page <http://www.access.gpo.gov/su_docs/dbsearch.html> or directly through GAO <http://www.gao.gov/>. They can be identified on the GAO Web page, or using the monthly *Reports and Testimony*, which summarizes individual "blue books" (GA 1.16/3: and <http://www.gao.gov/reports.htm>), or the *Annual Index: Reports Issued in FY [year]* (GA 1.16/3-2:), both free from GAO. For reports released since the latest *Reports and Testimony*, check Recent Reports on the GAO Web site <http://www.gao.gov/new.items/newtitle.htm>. Daily listings of GAO reports and testimony appear in the GAO Daybook on GAO's home page and via e-mail messages on GAO's Daybook listserv.

The Office of Technology Assessment

The Office of Technology Assessment (OTA) was Congress's "think tank," producing nonpartisan analyses of technological issues to help Congress in its planning process. The "tiny but much-admired" agency was shut down during budget cutting in the 104th Congress.[18] OTA's Web site, OTA Online, is now mirrored by Princeton University's Woodrow Wilson School of Public and International Affairs at <http://www.wws.princeton.edu/~ota>. OTA publications are still sold by NTIS and GPO, which sells *OTA Legacy*, an archival

CD-ROM set of all reports produced during OTA's lifespan, 1972-1995 (Y 3.T 22/2:2 L 52/V.1-5/CD). Archival collections of OTA reports and background papers will be available at the University of Maryland (College Park), George Mason University, and the University of California—Santa Barbara. The unpublished records of OTA are housed at the National Archives' Center for Legislative Archives, but will remain closed until 2015.

Congressional Research Service: "The Information Arm of Congress"

> *Go over to the Library of Congress. It has the most beautiful interior in the world. Also, the greatest and richest treasury of knowledge. Work those people to death. They like it. They will do research for you over the phone, and deliver books to you, marked right where you want them.*
> —Advice to new members of Congress from Rep. Maury Maverick of Texas, 1949

The Congressional Research Service (CRS) serves Congress exclusively and "in many ways is the present-day form of what the entire Library of Congress was when it began."[19] Without partisan bias, CRS staff research and analyze information for Congress, providing confidential services ranging from in-depth policy analyses, legal research, legislative histories, or speech writing, answering some 2,000 congressional inquiries daily, and providing materials requested by legislators for their constituents. Much CRS work remains unpublished and confidential, off-limits to the public: property of the legislators requesting it.

Public access to CRS publications produced solely for Congress is the exception rather than the rule. In fact, congressional offices are cautioned against distributing lists of CRS products to their constituents. The quarterly *Guide to CRS Products* and its monthly *Update* are printed in-house and stamped "For Congressional Office Use Only." Other CRS products printed in-house with restricted availability are CRS Reports for Congress (in-depth studies of legislative issues), Info Packs (packets of background information), and Issue Briefs (concise briefings on issues in the news). Some commercial vendors sell CRS materials, including Penny Hill Press and University Publications of America.

CRS reports sometimes emerge as committee prints or reports, House or Senate Documents, or speeches printed in the *Congressional Record*. These may be identified using THOMAS or GPO Access, the *Monthly Catalog*, *CIS/Index*, or the *Congressional Record Index*. Although CRS cannot respond directly to citizen requests, some CRS products are accessible through "back door" sources. A legislator can sponsor a constituent request, forwarding materials from CRS to the requester. The House of Representatives maintains an open-access Web page of selected CRS reports at <http://www.house.gov/rules_org/crs_reports.htm>. Some members of Congress place selected CRS reports on their Web pages to allow constituent access. The Joint Committee on the Library of Congress has appointed a task force to explore officially mounting selected CRS Reports onto the Internet.

Government Information in Action

In 1976, surrounded by news media, Librarian of Congress Daniel Boorstin opened a small box cradling the contents of President Lincoln's pockets the night he died. Entrusted to Lincoln's son, Robert Todd, and kept in the family more than 70 years, these mementos were donated to the Library in 1937 by Lincoln's granddaughter. For reasons no one remembers, they had rested in an LC vault for nearly four decades. The two pairs of eyeglasses—one repaired with string—pocketknife, button monogrammed with an "A," watch fob, wallet with newspaper clippings, and $5 Confederate bill can be viewed in LC's American Treasures of the Library of Congress exhibit at <http://www.loc.gov/exhibits/treasures/trm012.html>.[20]

THE LIBRARY OF CONGRESS

The Library of Congress is the world's greatest single repository of human memory and thought.
—James H. Billington, Librarian of Congress

The Library of Congress, the world's largest, most comprehensive library, began in 1800 as a parliamentary reference room boasting 740 volumes, four atlases, and three maps. When the British burned Washington 14 years later, British soldiers used the Library's books for kindling. After the collection was reduced to ashes, Thomas Jefferson offered his personal collection of 6,700 volumes to rebuild it. Jefferson's library, considered one of the country's finest, was purchased by Congress for $23,950 in 1815 to seed the Library of Congress's rebirth. Originally open only to members of Congress and the Supreme Court, the library has evolved from a private library to the de facto national library, but retains reference and research service for the Congress as its primary mission.[21]

Reigning as Congress's library and major research arm, the nation's copyright agency, and "one of the world's leading cultural institutions," the Library of Congress is among the most popular destinations on the Internet. When the Library of Congress threw its "electronic doors" open in 1994, it was the first U.S. institution to make its major exhibitions and computerized resources available electronically. The American Memory historical collections of the National Digital Library beamed LC's Americana collections previously available only to those who could visit Washington to the world and is now accessible at <http://lcweb2.loc.

gov/ammem/>. LOCIS, LC's online public access catalog, allowed remote access to the Library's catalog and copyright registrations and can be linked through <http://lcweb.loc.gov/catalog/>. The primeval MARVEL, LC's gopher, made text files available before the advent of the Web. During the 104th Congress, Jefferson's namesake, THOMAS, emerged as an elegant gateway to congressional information and is available at <http://thomas.loc.gov>.

Visitors will find LC's selective Experimental Web Catalog page easier to navigate than the comprehensive, command-driven LOCIS. Still under development, the Experimental Web Catalog provides access to more than 4.8 million of the Library's 27 million records and is available at <http://lcweb.loc.gov/catalog/>. Unlike LOCIS, this new format allows easy searching by keyword, author, title, ISBN, and LC class, as well as limiting by format, date, publisher, and language.

THE SERIAL SET

Y 1.1/2:

> *It will be difficult, if not impossible, to do historical documents research without having the Serial Set available.*
> —Jean L. Sears and Marilyn K. Moody,
> *Using Government Information Sources*

The Serial Set, America's longest-running series, is a serially numbered collection of House and Senate Reports and Documents dating back to 1789 in a documentary compendium considered without peer in Western representative democracies. The terms "reports" and "documents" are not generic, but refer to congressional historical records officially designated in either category. These are initially issued individually in the course of each Congress in paper or microfiche and, for two centuries, have been later compiled for posterity into the permanently bound and numbered Serial Set. The *Constitution of the United States of America: Analysis and Interpretation*, for example, is Senate Document 103–6 (Y 1.1/3:103–6) and also Serial Set volume 14152 (Y 1.1/2:Serial 14152). The conversion is slow: in 1995 (the 104th Congress) volumes for the 102nd Congress (1991–1992) were shipped to depositories. Distribution lags for around two years after the congressional session because no one can foresee how many parts a report will have. Thus, binding and serial number assignment are postponed until session's end to ensure inclusion of all the parts. Senate, House, and Executive Reports since the 104th Congress (1995–1996) are available on THOMAS (select Committee Reports) and on GPO Access (select Congressional Reports).

The House and Senate Reports included in the Serial Set are the familiar congressional committee reports on pending legislation, probably the most important publication group in the Serial Set. Traditionally confidential, Senate Executive Reports have been part of the Serial Set since the 97th Congress (1980). The record in *Monthly Catalog* and WorldCat will include an added entry similar to this one—I. Series: United States. Congress. Senate. Report; 104–229—in which 104–229 is the Senate Report number. In the initial, individual release, the report number appears as part of the SuDocs number: Y 1.1/5:104–229.

Documents in the Serial Set include not only congressional publications but also diverse noncongressional materials ordered printed by Congress and earmarked as House or Senate Documents. These materials include executive-agency issuances such as presidential messages to Congress, annual or special reports to Congress, special studies and background information, and annual reports of some veterans and patriotic groups (for example, the Boy and Girl Scouts, the Daughters of the American Revolution, and the American Legion). Senate Treaty Documents have been designated as Senate Documents and included in the Serial Set since the 96th Congress (1978–79). Documents since the 104th Congress are available on GPO Access (select "Congressional Documents"). Like the Reports, Documents are sequentially numbered within each Congress:

> H. Doc. 105–1
> S. Doc. 104–578

The record in *Monthly Catalog* and WorldCat will include an added entry similar to this one—I. Series: House document (United States. Congress. House); 104–113—in which 104–113 is the House Document number. In the initial individual release, the document number appears as part of the SuDocs number: Y 1.1/7:104–113.

The Serial Set offers a fascinating patchwork of primary American history documentation: background on the assassinations of Presidents Lincoln and Kennedy, accounts of the sinking of the *Titanic,* reports from the McCarthy-era House Committee on Un-American Activities, details of World War II rationing, records of the inquiry against President Richard M. Nixon, and 67 volumes from the Iran-Contra Investigations (Serial numbers 13810–13840).[22] It has been said of the Serial Set that "there has rarely been a published series of its depth and breath of coverage, and none in this country as long-lived."[23] The Library of Congress Law Library reports that the Serial Set is their second-most heavily used resource. (Law reviews are the most used.) The Serial Set offers more than two centuries of the following publication types:

- Congressional journals, administrative reports, directories, manuals, and other internal publications
- Congressional reports on public and private legislation

- Reports of congressional investigations
- Annual reports from federal executive agencies
- Executive agency survey, research, and statistical publications
- Annual and special reports from nongovernmental agencies[24]

The Serial Set's consecutive serial numbering—it began in 1817 during the 15th Congress—results in a roughly chronological arrangement of some 20,000 numbered, bound serial volumes. Earlier congressional publications for the first 14 Congresses and some later Congresses are included in the American State Papers, which have been numbered 01–038, and also been reprinted as the *National State Papers of the United States, 1789–1817* (M. Glazier, publisher). Copies of Serial Set documents may be purchased from GPO, CIS, and Readex, or consulted in depository libraries.

The Serial Set Study Group was established in 1994 to explore cost-saving alternatives for producing the bound *U.S. Congressional Serial Set,* which costs GPO $1,567,000 annually. The 102nd Congress, for example, generated 120 Serial Set volumes; the 101st Congress, 125 volumes. The Study Group's report recommended incremental pilot testing of techniques for saving money, improving operations, and expanding use of technology.[25] In FY 1997, funding cuts limited distribution of the bound *U.S. Congressional Serial Set* only to regional depositories or to one library in any state without a regional, and Congress directed GPO to produce a CD-ROM Serial Set starting with the 105th Congress. Bound volumes for the 104th Congress will continue to be distributed free to selectives until FY 1998 or 1999, when work for the 104th Congress will be completed. Distribution of bound volumes for the 105th Congress will begin around FY 2000. GPO is fighting for regionals to receive the Serial Set in paper as well as CD-ROM, and is considering offering selectives the option of buying a bound Serial Set.

Serial Set Catalog

GP 3.34:

Since the 98th Congress (1983–84), GPO has published the *United States Congressional Serial Set Catalog: Numerical Lists and Schedule of Volumes* (GP 3.34:). The biennial *Serial Set Catalog* includes a numerical list of congressional Reports and Documents, a schedule of Serial Set volume contents, and the original *Monthly Catalog* listings of individual reports and documents enhanced with Serial Set numbers added in bold type. It is indexed by author, title, subject, and series/report and bill numbers.

From 1895 to 1933 (54th to 72nd Congresses), the Document Index listed House and Senate documents and reports (GP 3.7:1–43). Issued at the end of each congressional session, the index contained numerical lists of reports and documents, plus a schedule of Serial Set volumes showing the reports and documents bound in each, along with a subject index. The *Checklist of United States Public Documents, 1789–1909,* known as "the 1909 Checklist," (GP 3.2:C 41/2) briefly describes on pages 5–169 the contents for Serial Set volumes 1–5561 from the 15th to 60th Congresses (1817–1909). Serial Set coverage in the Document Index was superseded by *Numerical Lists and Schedule of Volumes,* covering 1934 to 1980 (73rd to 96th Congresses). The *Numerical Lists and Schedule of Volumes of the Documents and Reports of Congress* (GP 3.7/2:) referred from document and report numbers to the Serial Set volume where the report or document could be found (numerical lists), and from serial numbers to the report numbers in each Serial Set volume (schedule of volumes). It was searchable by report, document, and serial numbers only, not by subjects or names. Next, for a short time, this finding aid was issued as a supplement to the *Monthly Catalog,* undergoing a name change to *Monthly Catalog United States Congressional Serial Set Supplement* (GP 3.7/2:). Issued following each Congress, this source had author, title, subject, series/report number, bill number, GPO stock number, and title keyword indexes.

CIS US Serial Set Index

Covering the American State Papers and the Serial Set from 1789 to 1969, the Congressional Information Service's *CIS US Serial Set Index* allows searching by subject, names of people and organizations, report and document numbers, numbers of bills for which reports were issued (1819–1969), and serial volume numbers. The set indexes House and Senate reports and documents (plus the House and Senate Journals through 1952). Omitted are hearings, debates, and committee prints. Part XIV of the *CIS Serial Set Index,* Index and Carto-Bibliography of Maps, 1789–1969, describes more than 50,000 maps embedded in Serial Set volumes. The Carto-Bibliography can be searched by subject/geographic area, map title, personal names, and corporate names. The Congressional Information Service's CD-ROM Congressional Masterfile 1 streamlines historical searching between 1789 and 1969 by merging CIS indexes to the Serial Set, published and unpublished committee hearings, committee prints, and Senate Executive documents and reports.

Finding Serial Set Numbers		
Report/Document Date	Title	
1789–1969	*CIS Serial Set Index*	
If *CIS Serial Set Index* is unavailable:		
1774–1881	Poore's Catalogue *Descriptive Catalogue of the Government Publications of the United States, September 5, 1774–March 4, 1881* Serial Set 2268.	
1881–1893	"Ames" *Comprehensive Index to the Publications of the United States Government, 1881–1893* Serial Set 4745, 4746.	
1895–1933	Document Index (*Index to the Reports and Documents of Congress*) GP 3.7:1–43	
Report/Document Date	Title	Title's Year of Issue
1933–80 73rd through 96th Congresses	*Numerical Lists and Schedule of Volumes* GP 3.7/2:	1933–82
1981–82 97th Congress	*Monthly Catalog Congressional Serial Set Supplement* GP 3.8/6:	1985
1983–84 98th Congress	*U.S. Congressional Serial Set Catalog: Numerical Lists and Schedule of Volumes*	1988 GP 3.34:983–84
1985–86 99th Congress		1989 GP 3.34:989–90
1987–88 100th Congress		1992 GP 3.34:987–88
1989–90 101st Congress		1994 GP 3.34:989–90
Since 102nd Congress	*Administrative Notes. Technical Supplement* GP 3.16/3–3: <http://www.access.gpo.gov/su_docs/dpos/techsup.html>	Irregular, interim coverage

LEGISLATIVE PROCEDURE

The Constitution allows each chamber to determine its own rules. These are published in manuals describing precedents, practices, organization, and operation. Mastering the bevy of congressional rules has been compared to learning a foreign language. House rules are adopted anew every two years (updated by an Interim House Rules Manual, a House Document), while the Senate's standing rules are rarely changed.

The *House Rules Manual*, the font of House parliamentary procedures, originally prepared by Thomas Jefferson and popularly known as Jefferson's Manual (Y 1.2:R 86/2/), is accessible on GPO Access <http://www.access.gpo.gov/congress/house/index.html>. This source contains the U.S. Constitution and House rules with notes showing history and interpretation. The House also has its own *Ethics Manual* (Y 4.St 2/3:Et 3/yr.).

The *Senate Manual* contains rules, the Articles of the Confederation and the U.S. Constitution, a list of presidents pro tempore since the first Senate, presidential election electoral votes since 1789, and lists of senators and Supreme Court justices since 1789 (Y 1.1/3: or <http://www.access.gpo.gov/congress/senate/index.html>).

ADDRESSES

The Congressional Sales Office, North Capitol and G. Streets, N.W., Washington, DC 20402; open for walk-in business between 8:00 a.m. and 4:00 p.m. at 710 N. Capitol, Washington, DC.

General Accounting Office, Box 6015, Gaithersburg, MD 20884-6015; information@www.gao.gov; (202) 512-6000; Fax: (301) 258-4066; <http://www.gao.gov>.

The Library of Congress, 101 Independence Avenue, S.E., Washington, DC 20540; general information (202) 707-5000; Fax: (202) 707-5844; Reference (202) 707-5522; Fax: (202) 707-1389.

Library of Congress, Motion Picture, Broadcasting, and Recorded Sound Divison, Motion Picture and Television Reading Room, James Madison Memorial Bldg., Room 336, Washington, DC 20540-4805; (202) 707-8572; Fax: (202) 707-2371.

Public Affairs Video Archive (PAVA), Purdue University, 1000 Liberal Arts & Education Building, West Lafayette, IN 47907-1000; E-mail: information@pava.purdue.edu; (800) 277-2698; Fax: (317) 423-4495; <http://pava.purdue.edu>.

FREEBIES

The following Subject Bibliographies are free from: Stop: SSOP, Washington, DC 20402; U.S. Fax Watch (202) 512-1716:

197.   United States Code <http://www.access.gpo.gov/su_docs/sale/sb-197.html>

228.   Congressional Directory <http://www.access.gpo.gov/su_docs/sale/sb-228.html>

Congress

Single free copies of all congressional publications except committee prints and hearings are often available from the issuing committee, or from the House or Senate Document Rooms.

Senate Document Room, Senate Hart Office Bldg., Room B-04, Washington, DC 20510; (202) 224-7860; Fax: (202) 228-2815. Limit is 12 requests daily. Group requests by document type (laws, bills, reports, documents) in numerical order.

Copies of recent laws, and House bills, reports, documents, and joint, simple or concurrent resolutions are available from House Document Room, H2-B-18 FHOB, Washington, DC 20515-6622; (202) 225-3456. Requests are limited to 12 different House documents daily, via walk-in (the Ford Building is at the corner of 3rd and D Streets, SW, across the street from the Federal Center SW Metro station), mail (include a self-addressed gummed label); Fax: (202) 226-4362; E-mail: hdocs@hr.house.gov, or telephone. To expedite handling, group requests by document type, in numerical order. The House Document Room does not stock hearings, committee prints, bill analyses, or the *Congressional Record*.

FURTHER READING

Bacon, Donald C., Roger H. Davidson, and Morton Keller, eds. *The Encyclopedia of the United States Congress*. NY: Simon & Schuster, 1995.
Considered the definitive work on Congress, its members, history, and operations, these four volumes offer comprehensive essays and an extensive legislative glossary.

Chiles, James R. "Congress Couldn't Have Been this Bad, or Could it?" *Smithsonian* 26 (November 1995): 70–82.
The "good old days" in our nation's capitol were rude, rowdy, and risky.

Christianson, Stephen G. *Facts about the Congress*. NY: H. W. Wilson, 1996.
A chronological history of Congress since 1789.

Civilization: The Magazine of the Library of Congress. NY: L.O.C. Associates, 1994–. Bimonthly.
LC's snappy membership magazine.

Cole, John Y. "Smithmeyer & Pelz: Embattled Architects of the Library of Congress," *Quarterly Journal of the Library of Congress* (October 1972): 282–307. LC 1.17:72/4.
You had to be there.

Congressional Quarterly. *Congress A to Z: A Ready Reference Encyclopedia*. 2nd ed. Washington, DC: Congressional Quarterly, Inc., 1993.
This companion to CQ's *Guide to Congress* is a dictionary of congressional lingo.

THOMAS: Not-So-Quick Tips http://thomas.loc.gov/		
Scout Report	Operators must be preceded by #	
Search Operators	*Rules*	*Example*
AND Each term must appear in the document	#band( )	#band(legislative appropriations 1996)
Relevancy, AND "fuzzy AND" The more terms found, the higher the document's weight	#and( )	#and(loans grants aid assistance Pell Stafford student education)
OR Any or all of the terms must appear in the document	#or( )	#or(loans grants)
NOT The first word must be present; the second word must be absent	#bandnot( )	#bandnot(wetlands public)
NOT (Relevancy) Documents lacking the terms receive higher weight Recommended for use with compound searches, #sum for example	#not( )	#sum(printing#not(budget debt appropriations authorization))
Weight minus Single term's weight is decreased, reducing weight of documents containing it	#-term	#sum(waste#-hazardous#-toxic#-nuclear)
Sum (Relevancy) Terms have equal weights	#sum( )	#sum(france french nuclear atomic testing)

Relevancy, Weighted Sum
Weights are assigned to terms to indicate their importance
	#wsum(tw x iw x)
	tw=total weight of the query
	iw=component's individual weight
		#wsum(1.0 0.4railroads 0.4 airlines 0.1trucks 0.1 automobiles)

Proximity, ordered First term precedes, and is within n words of the second term	#n( ) #odn( )	#3(library congress) #od3(library congress)
Proximity, unordered Terms are within a "window" of n words of each other, in any order	#uwn( )	#uw50(legislative appropriation government printing office)
Proximity, phrase Terms occur together	#phrase( )	#phrase(government printing office)
Proximity, passage Terms are within n words of each other, in any order	#passagenN (x . . .x)	#passage50(student financial aid assistance grants loans)
Field Search is limited to the specified field	#field(field x)	#field(TITLE wetlands)
Synonym Terms are weighted as if they were the same term	#syn( )	#syn(document publication)
MAX The highest weighted synonym (maximum weight) determines relevancy of each document	#max( )	#max(executive manager officer director)

THOMAS: Not-So-Quick Tips (continued) http://thomas.loc.gov/		
Scout Report	Operators must be preceded by #	
Search Operators	*Rules*	*Example*
Weight plus Term's weight is increased relative to other terms Good for refining search results	#+term	#sum(militia#3(domestic terrorism)#+wiretap)
Filter require Retrieves first set of documents only if second set is retrieved	#filreq(1 2)	#filreq(#uw10(defense appropriations)#uw10(defense authorization))
Filter reject Retrieves first set of documents only if no documents satisfy the second set "If there's nothing on the 2nd statement, give me the results of the 1st statement instead."	#filrej(1 2)	#filrej(#uw10(defense appropriations)#uw10(defense authorization))

———. *Congressional Quarterly's Guide to Congress.* 4th ed. Washington, DC: Congressional Quarterly, Inc., 1991.
> An overview of the history, development, and operations of Congress.

———. *CQ's Pocket Guide to the Language of Congress.* Washington, DC: Congressional Quarterly, Inc., 1994.
> This glossary of congressional procedures, organization, staff, and officers truly fits in a pocket, if you have a pocket this big.

———. *How Congress Works.* 2nd ed. Washington, DC: Congressional Quarterly, Inc., 1991.
> A detailed guide to the operations of Congress.

DeLong, Suzanne. "What is in the United States Serial Set?" *Journal of Government Information* 23 (March/April 1996): 123–35.
> A survey of serial set content from its beginnings to the trimmed-down set of the 1980s.

Kravitz, Walter. *Congressional Quarterly's American Congressional Dictionary.* Washington, DC: Congressional Quarterly, Inc., 1993.
> This guide to Congress, agencies of Congress, and the legislative process is a one-volume course on congressional jargon, procedures, and practice.

The Law Librarians' Society of Washington, DC, Inc. *Legislative Research SIS Membership Directory and Source Book: 1997.* LLSDC, 1997. $7.50 (includes shipping and handling) from Law Librarians' Society of Washington, DC, Inc., 669 South Washington Street, Alexandria, VA 22314-5092.
> Most of this 18-page pamphlet is organizational, but Rick McKinney's eight pages of "Sources of On-Line Legislative and Regulatory Information" tables (government and commercial database providers) make it worth buying.

Martin, Fenton S. and Robert U. Goehlert. *How to Research Congress.* Washington, DC: Congressional Quarterly, 1996.
> An introduction to tools for researching congressional procedures, committees, investigations, reform, foreign affairs, and legislative analysis.

Ross, Rodney A. "Field Notes: Using the U.S. Congressional Serial Set for the Study of Western History." *Western Historical Quarterly* 25 (Summer 1994): 209–13.
> A practical introduction to the Serial Set as a historical research tool.

Senate. Republican Policy Committee. *Glossary of Senate Terms: A Guide for TV.* GPO, 1986. (Y 1.3:S.Prt. 99–157).
> Although only 19 pages long, this short piece is a useful guide to common congressional parlance.

Smith, Steven S. and Christopher J. Deering. *Committees in Congress.* 3rd ed. Washington, DC: Congressional Quarterly, Inc., 1997.
> A treatise on the development and workings of "government by subcommittee" in the House and Senate.

The U.S. House of Representatives. "The Legislative Process—Tying It All Together." <http://www.house.gov/Tying_it_all.html> (June 17, 1998).
> A brief overview of the legislative process within the House of Representatives, with hot links.

Willet, Edward F. *How Our Laws Are Made.* (Bicentennial ed., 1789–1989) (House Doc. 101–139) GPO, 1990. (Y 1.2:97008167) <http://thomas.loc.gov/home/lawsmade.toc.html> (February 11, 1997).
> The standard citizen's guide to the legislative process is often available free from members of Congress.

Wines, Michael. "How the Record Tells the Truth Now." *New York Times* (January, 22, 1995): section 4, p. 7, col. 1.
> A tape-recorded speech is compared with the *Congressional Record* transcript and lets you be the judge.

The following titles are excellent introductions to legal research and materials:

Blackman, Josh. *How to Use the Internet for Legal Research.* NY: Find/SVP, 1996.

Cohen, Morris L. and Kent C. Olson. *Legal Research in a Nutshell.* St. Paul, MN: West Publishing Co., 1996.

Elias, Stephen. *How to Find and Understand the Law.* 4th ed. Berkeley: Nolo Press, 1995.

Herskowitz, Susan. *Legal Research Made Easy*. Clearwater, FL: Sphinx Publishing, 1995.

Jacobstein, J. Myron, Roy M. Mersky, and Donald J. Dunn. *Fundamentals of Legal Research*. 6th ed. Westbury, NY: Foundation Press, 1994.

McKinney, Ruth Ann. *Legal Research: A Practical Guide and Self-Instructional Workbook*. St. Paul, MN: West Publishing Co., 1996.

Maier, Elaine C. *How to Prepare a Legal Citation*. Woodbury, NY: Barron's Educational Series, Inc., 1986.

> A guide to proper citing according to *A Uniform System of Citation,* including sections on citing laws and legislative histories.

NOTES

1. *Congressional Research Service, Congress and Mass Communication: An Institutional Perspective, Prepared for Joint Committee on Congressional Operations. 93rd Congress, 2nd Session* (Committee Print) (GPO, 1974), p. v. (Y 4.C 76/7:C 73).

2. Eric Redman, *The Dance of Legislation* (New York: Simon & Schuster, 1973), p. 16.

3. Beth Postema and Terry L. Weech, "The Use of Government Publications: A Twelve-Year Perspective," *Government Publications Review* 18 (May/June 1991): 223.

4. House calendars: the Union Calendar, for legislation dealing with revenues, money, or property; the House Calendar, for legislation not involving money; the Consent Calendar, for noncontroversial measures on either the Union or House calendars; the Private Calendar, for private bills; and the Discharge Calendar, for motions to discharge committees. The Senate has only one calendar for legislation reported from committee.

5. Jerrold Zwirn, *Congressional Publications: A Research Guide to Legislation, Budgets, and Treaties* (Littleton, CO: Libraries Unlimited, Inc., 1983), p. 83.

6. Robert D. Stevens, "But Is the Record Complete? A Case of Censorship of the Congressional Record," *Government Publications Review* 9 (January-February 1982): 75–80.

7. To view videotapes at the Library of Congress, researchers must make an appointment two to three weeks in advance—the time required for transfer from storage. Holdings for the House begin January 25, 1983; for the Senate, May 5, 1986. Access is by date only: the requester must supply a marked photocopy of the *Congressional Record* indicating the exact segment. To buy copies of floor proceedings, contact the Library of Congress Public Services Office. The Library of Congress's Recorded Sound Reference Center houses audiotapes from the House only, February 21, 1979, through December 20, 1985.

8. The House videotapes since 1983; Senate tapes since 1986.

9. *Task Force on the Congressional Record, Prepared for the Committee on House Administration of the U.S. House of Representatives, August 1990*. (Committee Print) GPO, 1990. p. 2 (Y 4.H 81/3:C 76/3).

10. The Senate has two journals, the second being the *Senate Executive Journal,* a record of proceedings related to treaties and nominations. (See chapter 10.)

11. Senate. *Historical Almanac of the United States Senate: A Series of "Bicentennial Minutes" Presented to the Senate During the One Hundredth Congress* by Robert J. Dole. GPO, 1989. (S.Doc.100-35) (Serial Set 13850). Y 1.1/3:100-35. p. 228.

12. Morris L. Cohen, Robert C. Berring, and Kent C. Olson, *How to Find the Law*, 9th ed. (St. Paul, MN: West Publishing Co., 1989), p. 243.

13. See also A Glossary of Senate Terms <http://www.senate.gov/about/glossary.html> (June 17, 1998).

14. John Richardson. "A State Transition Model of United States Congressional Information." *Journal of Government Information* 21 (January/February 1994): 25–35.

15. Congressional Research Service. *Presidential Vetoes, 1789–1996: A Summary Overview*. (CRS Report for Congress 97-163 GOV) CRS, 1997. <http://www.house.gov/rules_org/97-163.htm> p. 2. (December 1, 1997).

16. *United States Law: Finding Statutory Material* (CRS Report for Congress, 90-110 A). Washington, DC: CRS, 1990. p. CRS-3.

17. Office of Technology Assessment, *Public Access to Congressional Support Agency Information in the Technological Age: Case Studies,* by Stephen E. Frantzich. NTIS, 1989. PB89-225221; *CIS/Index* microfiche no. 89-J952-25, p. v.

18. Carney, Eliza Newlin. "Losing Support" *The National Journal* 27 (September 23, 1995): 2353.

19. Library of Congress, *Guide to the Library of Congress* (LC, 1985), p. 37.

20. Library of Congress. *American Treasures in the Library of Congress: Memory/Reason/Imagination*. NY: Abrams, 1997. A catalog of the major exhibition mounted in 1997 provides a peek at the largest exhibit in the Library's history.

21. Good books about the Library of Congress include Carol Highsmith and Ted Landphair's crisp and dazzling *The Library of Congress: America's Memory*. Golden, CO: Fulcrum Publishing, 1994; also Goodrum, Charles A. *Treasures of the Library of Congress*. NY: Abrams, 1980; and Library of Congress. *Jefferson's Legacy: A Brief History of the Library of Congress* by John Y. Cole. LC, 1993. LC 1.2:J 35/8 and <http://lcweb.loc.gov/loc/legacy/>; and Cole, John Y. *On These Walls: Inscriptions and Quotations in the Buildings of the Library of Congress*. LC, 1995. LC 1.2:W 15.

22. In FY 1987 there were 660 Reports (30,930 pages) and 142 Documents (16,226 pages) of the House and Senate Iran-Contra Investigation; in FY 1988 there were 1,025 Reports (121,166 pages) and 116 Documents (25,444 pages). The 30 Iran-Contra Appendices volumes were issued both as Senate [S. Rept. 216] and House [H. Rept. 433] reports, but only the Senate Reports were bound in the Serial Set. The House reports were assigned a serial number and cross-referenced in the Schedule of Volumes to the Senate Reports, saving $500,000.

23. *Congressional Information Service, User Handbook: CIS U.S. Serial Set Index* (Washington, DC: CIS, Inc., 1980), pp. 2, 10.

24. Congressional Information Service, p. 10.

25. Government Printing Office. *Report of the Serial Set Study Group: Investigation of Alternatives for Production & Distribution of the Bound U.S. Congressional Serial Set; Submitted to the Public Printer, U.S. Government Printing Office, October 7, 1994*. GPO, 1995. GP 1.2:SE 6/3.

EXERCISES

1. Many Capitol watchers were stunned by Congress's decision to abolish its Office of Technology Assessment during the cost-cutting summer of 1995. Among those defending OTA was Rep. Amo Houghton Jr. (R-NY). Before OTA closed its doors on September 29, 1995, Houghton praised Congress's small but highly respected think tank in an OTA "memoriam" printed in the *Congressional Record.* Locate Houghton's speech.

2. Senate Report 104–114 called upon the Government Printing Office to develop a strategic plan for a rapid transition to an electronic Federal Depository Library Program. Locate the full text of this report.

3. I'd like to read the Paperwork Reduction Act of 1995,

4. Was H.R. 3802, the Electronic Freedom of Information Act Amendments of 1996, enacted into law?

5. Is this the most recent edition of *Citizen's Guide on Using the Freedom of Information Act and the Privacy Act of 1974 to Request Government Records* (H. Rept. 105–37) GPO, 1997?

6. Find the text of the law governing the Federal Depository Library Program.

Retrospective Searches

7. Smokey Bear, the forest fire prevention symbol, was created by the Forest Service in the 1950s. Government-produced, and thus in the public domain, Smokey was ineligible for trademark protection so Congress outlawed unauthorized use of Smokey's name or image. Identify this 1952 law and any background materials in its legislative history.

8. In early 1987, the Office of Management and Budget initiated a controversial push to privatize the National Technical Information Service, ordering it contracted out to the private sector. A self-sustaining agency, NTIS had paid its own way since its inception. Witnesses in House and Senate hearings cautioned that privatization would be costly and risky, characterizing the proposal as "a triumph of ideology over common sense." Identify one hearing on the topic. (The debate was resolved, by the way, when NTIS and the Commerce Department's new Technology Administration merged.)

9. In 1912, a Senate special subcommittee investigated the sinking of the *Titanic*, which had killed many prominent Americans among others. Although no legislation was pending, the investigation was authorized by a Senate resolution, broadening the precedent for Senate investigations beyond immediate lawmaking. Identify the committee's report. Helpful tip: 1912 was the 62nd Congress.

10. As part of its Library Awareness Program, the FBI asked librarians to alert them to Soviet citizens seeking "sensitive but unclassified" information in libraries. After a flurry of unfavorable media attention, congressional hearings explored possible conflicts between FBI counterintelligence visits to libraries and individual privacy rights. Identify the hearing, which took place in the late 1980s.

11. In 1925, Congress appropriated $10,000 to dispose of old patent models. A fire had already destroyed one-third of the model collection, leaving 150,000 survivors, each no larger than 12 square inches. Some were transferred to the Smithsonian Institution or returned to their inventors, while thousands were auctioned off. Identify any congressional document pertaining to the disposal of the models. Helpful tip: 1925 was the 68th Congress.

12. The Federal Information Resources Management Act of 1989 (S. 1742) was introduced to reauthorize the Paperwork Reduction Act. What was its status at the close of the 101st Congress?

CHAPTER 9
Regulations

Regulations are the engines of federal law.
　　　　　　　　　　　—Steven L. Katz, Attorney

WHAT

Administrative regulations and adjudications, along with statutes and judicial opinions, are our nation's three primary sources of law. Regulations, sometimes called quasi-legislation or bureaucratic law, are authorized by law or by presidential executive order to be written by executive agencies. Like laws, they are binding upon those to whom they apply.

HOW

Congress delegates the power to issue regulations and adjudicate disputes to executive agencies and independent administrative agencies. These agencies are sometimes called "the fourth branch" of government because they exhibit characteristics of all three branches of government.

WHY

Although it may be easy to imagine federal bureaucrats maniacally pounding out regulations in windowless rooms, regulations are not created by whim, but by law. They result from power granted to the president by the Constitution or power delegated by Congress.

REGULATIONS AND AMERICAN LIFE

According to a Gallup poll commissioned by the League of Women Voters, Americans are a little fuzzy on the details of the regulatory process.[1] The poll results, which a League official characterized as "appalling," showed many Americans to be unclear about what regulations are, where they come from, and why they are promulgated. Half could not name a single regulation affect-

ing their lives, and even more were unable to differentiate between regulations and laws. Only one in five Americans interviewed knew that executive agencies write regulations. Four out of five admitted they didn't know where regulations came from, or guessed incorrectly that they emanated from Congress or the courts.

Government regulations receive a lot of negative press. Read an article about regulations in a popular magazine, and you'll probably find complaints about "bureaucratic red tape," "strangulation by regulation," and other depictions of regulatory villainy. Most people don't realize the extent to which regulations affect their daily lives. The care tags on your clothes, nutritional labels on food, overhead storage on airplanes, the purity of the air, and the composition of many prepared foods—all are government-regulated. An understanding of the purpose and use of regulations leads to several conclusions: they have a daily impact on our lives; they are not written to torture us (although that is sometimes a result); and citizens have a say in regulation writing.

Nature's Buffet: Defects Allowable in Food[2]

CHOCOLATE: up to 60 microscopic insect fragments per 100 grams or 90 insect fragments in one sample; or one rodent hair per 100 grams

CANNED CITRUS JUICE: fewer than 5 fly eggs or one maggot per 250 ml

BAY LEAVES: up to 5 percent moldy or insect-infested pieces or 1 mg mammalian excreta per pound

FROZEN BROCCOLI: fewer than 60 aphids, thrips, and/or mites per 100 grams

FISH: less than one-quarter of their surface with a definite odor of decomposition in less than 5 percent of the sample

---

Rules and regulations (the terms are synonymous) are a means of implementing laws enacted by Congress. If every law spelled out the particulars of its administration, the shelves of statutes would overflow and Congress would be stalled in a quagmire of details (evidenced by the fact that the *Code of Federal Regulations* sprawls across three times the shelf space as the *U.S. Code*). Instead, lawmakers write laws as broad policy statements, with the expectation that specifics will be determined later by the executive agencies administering the laws day to day.

Laws often specify which agencies are required to write rules to carry out legislation. Look for language like:

> The Department of _____ shall. . .
> The Commissioner shall prescribe regulations which. . .

In this way Congress "delegates" authority to the executive administrative agencies to implement legislation by writing rules that itemize procedures and details. For this reason, regulations are sometimes described as "delegated legislation." Seen in this light, regulations are an extension of legislation in a logical evolution from general to specific.

The question of who controls the regulatory agencies is a long-standing constitutional debate. Is it the head of the executive branch—the president, or Congress—the watchdog of the executive branch? The Office of Management and Budget (OMB) carries out presidential oversight of rulemaking by approving regulations before their appearance in the *Federal Register*. OMB's Office of Information and Regulatory Affairs (OIRA) is the hub of this activity, overseeing the government's regulatory, paperwork, and information-management activities. OMB's annual *Regulatory Program of the United States Government* overviews and describes agency regulatory programs (PREX 2.30:). The "Unified Agenda of Federal Regulations," published in the *Federal Register* each April and October, projects regulatory activity in specific regulatory agencies.

The *Federal Register*

AE 2.106:

http://www.access.gpo.gov/su_docs/
dbsearch.html

> *While the* Federal Register *stands as the official organ of the government, it is a publication with limited circulation read by few ordinary citizens.*
> —Office of Technology Assessment

It all started with a merry mix-up. In July and August 1933, President Franklin D. Roosevelt issued six complicated executive orders on petroleum quotas. The real problem began when a seventh executive order revoked the first, but chaotic recordkeeping cloaked the blunder. When the president's first petroleum executive order (which no longer existed) prompted a refining company to sue the government, the case climbed all the way to the Supreme Court. Chief Justice Charles Evans Hughes, realizing the suit was predicated on a defunct executive order, issued a scathing denunciation of the plaintiffs, defendants, and lower courts for ignorance of the law, and the president and the secretary of the interior for failing to publicize their regulations. In response, Congress passed the Federal Register Act, mandating a daily publication to chronicle presidential proclamations, executive orders, and agency regulations.

The genesis of the *Federal Register* was Congress's stipulation that government regulations have no legal force until made public by publication. For the first time, Americans had a practical way to learn about the regulations affecting them. Supplemental legislation called for codifying the rules in the *Code of Federal Regulations*. The primary function of the resultant *Federal Register/Code of Federal Regulations* system is to inform the public about rules set by federal agencies.

Although "it graces few of America's coffee tables," the *Federal Register* is a major vehicle for regulating and governing the United States.[3] Several categories of documents must be announced in the *Federal Register* before they can be legally binding: presidential proclamations and executive orders, rules and regulations, proposed rules, notices, and Sunshine Act meetings (government meetings open to the public and requiring announcement in the *Federal Register*).

The *Federal Register* since January 2, 1994 (volume 59) is available through GPO Access <http://www.access.gpo.gov/su_docs/dbsearch.html>. This online version is the official government version, with full text and all graphics. On the GPO Access "General search page for all databases" page, the current year's *Federal Register* is automatically highlighted in the search box. Why? Because it's the most-searched database on GPO Access. The GPO Access specialized search page for the *Federal Register* offers more sophisticated searching than the GPO Access general database page, however. An alternate route to the GPO Access *Federal Register* database is through the Office of the *Federal Register* site at <http://www.nara.gov/fedreg/>. To view a daily table of contents and yearly cumulative indexes back to 1994, use <gopher://gopher.nara.gov/11/register/toc>, selecting issue date or cumulation range and searching by keywords.

Published Daily, Monday Through Friday, Damn It.

The Blizzard of '96 may have shut down the federal government, but it couldn't hobble the *Federal Register*. Intrepid staffers who trekked through 17 inches of snow to roll the regulation presses produced some of the slimmest issues on record. The reason: the worst blizzard to hit the East Coast in 70 years had forced most rule-writing agencies to close for the snow emergency.

Proposed Rules

The rationale goes like this: since regulations affect all of us, the public should have a say in regulation writing. After all, regulations are quasi-legislation, and citizen representation in the legislative process is an American tradition. Public participation broadens regulators' perspectives, ensures protection of citizen concerns, and balances the lobbying of self-interested industries. To achieve this, the law requires agencies to consider public input when writing regulations. This input occurs at the "proposed" rulemaking stage, when agencies must announce regulations being drafted and allow the public to comment on them. The vehicle for soliciting public input is the *Federal Register*.

In actuality, almost half of all regulations go on the books with no public comments at all.[4] The sheer volume of regulations and "regulatory gobbledygook" are hurdles to citizen understanding of both proposed and final rules. As a congressional report explained, "People cannot be expected to understand that which is incomprehensible."[5] Not only are regulations baffling to the general public, they can be unintelligible even to the people who wrote them. At a "plain-English" workshop, bureaucrats told to rewrite their regulations more clearly often could not decipher the original versions—that they wrote themselves.

An Example of Bureaucratese from a Regulation-Writing Workshop

We respectfully petition, request, and entreat that due and adequate provision be made, this day and the date hereinafter subscribed, for the satisfying of these petitioners' nutritional requirements and for the organizing of such methods of allocation and distribution as may be deemed necessary and proper to assure the reception by and for said petitioners of such quantities of baked cereal products as shall, in the judgment of the aforesaid petitioners, constitute a sufficient supply thereof.

Translation: *Give us this day our daily bread.*
—The Bible, King James version

The "Proposed Rules" section of the *Federal Register* announces early or final drafts of rules with names, addresses, and telephone numbers of contact people and guidelines for submitting comments. A comments deadline is announced, usually at least two months hence. The guidelines for comments should be followed because they are a part of the agency's plan for analyzing a flood of information. If the agency has to search for your point, there's the chance it will be missed or misunderstood.

What happens to the public comments? The agency does more than blindly tally comments for various points of view: it must address all issues raised in the comments. When a proposed rule is finalized, the final rule's "Supplementary Information" section in the preamble describes public comments and the agency's response to them. Public input does have impact. The 1981 "catsup-as-a-vegetable" regulation is a memorable example. The U.S. Department of Agriculture (USDA) made headlines by suggesting that catsup qualify as a required vegetable component of school lunches. The ensuing public furor convinced the USDA to recall their proposed rules, and catsup reverted to its former status as a condiment.

Final Rules

> *Regulation is the substitution of error for chance.*
> —Fred J. Emery, former director of the
> Office of the Federal Register

Like the Government Printing Office, the Office of the Federal Register has no control over the regulations it prints. The OFR does require, however, that each agency begin its text with a plain-English preamble concisely describing the regulation. (See figure 9.1.) The "Action" section of the preamble identifies a regulation as either final or proposed. The effective date (usually not the same as the publication date) is also noted in the preamble. Since final rules published in the *Federal Register* have the force of law, the effective date mandates when all affected parties will be required to comply.

The text of the actual rule is near the end of the posting. In the printed *Federal Register*, look for a section mark (§), and in the Internet version use the browser's Find command to search for "as follows." This command picks up the language that typically precedes the text of the rule: for example, "Accordingly, 26 CFR parts 1, 301, and 602 are amended as follows:..."

Federal Register Citation

Regulations published in the *Federal Register* are cited by volume and page, with the date sometimes added in parentheses.

FIGURE 9.1: Preamble Requirements.

tions, registrations, reports, contracts, and similar items, and the instructions for preparing the forms, may not be published in full. In place thereof, the agency concerned shall submit for publication a simple statement describing the purpose and use of each form and stating the places at which copies may be obtained.

§ 18.12   Preamble requirements.[1]

(a) Each agency submitting a proposed or final rule document for publication shall prepare a preamble which will inform the reader, who is not an expert in the subject area, of the basis and purpose for the rule or proposal.

(b) The preamble shall be in the following format and contain the following information:

> AGENCY: ——————————
> (Name of issuing agency)

reader who is not an expert in the subject area, or that a report of additional information is in the public interest, the agency shall include in the preamble the following information, as applicable:

(1) A discussion of the background and major issues involved;

(2) In the case of a final rule, any significant differences between it and the proposed rule;

(3) A response to substantive public comments received; and

(4) Any other information the agency considers appropriate.

[41 FR 56624, Dec. 29, 1976]

§ 18.13   Withdrawal of filed documents.

A document that has been filed with the Office of the Federal Register and placed on public inspection as required by this chapter, may be withdrawn from publication by the submitting agency only by a timely written instrument revoking that document, signed by a duly authorized representative of the agency. Both the original and the revoking document shall remain on file.

§ 18.14   Correction of errors in documents.

After a document has been filed for public inspection and publication, a substantive error in the text may be corrected only by the filing of another document effecting the correction.

§ 18.15   Correction of errors in printing.

Typographical or clerical errors made in the printing of the FEDERAL REGISTER shall be corrected by insertion of an appropriate notation or a reprinting in the FEDERAL REGISTER published without further agency documentation, if the Director of the Federal Register determines that—

(a) The error would tend to confuse or mislead the reader; or

(b) The error would affect text subject to codification.

§ 18.16   [Reserved][1]

§ 18.17   Effective dates and time periods.

(a) Whenever practicable, each document submitted for publication in the FEDERAL REGISTER should set forth dates certain. Thus, a document

> AGENCY: ——————————————
> (Name of issuing agency)
>
> ACTION: ——————————————
> (Notice of Intent), (Advance Notice of Proposed Rulemaking), (Proposed Rule), (Final Rule), (Other).
>
> SUMMARY: ——————————————
> (Brief statements, in simple language, of: (i) the action being taken; (ii) the circumstances which created the need for the action; and (iii) the intended effect of the action.)
>
> DATES: ——————————————
> (Comments must be received on or before: ————.) (Proposed effective date: ————.) (Effective date: ————.) (Hearing: ————.) (Other: ————.)
>
> ADDRESSES: ——————————————
> (Any relevant addresses.)
>
> FOR FURTHER INFORMATION CONTACT: ——————————————
> ——————————————
> (For Executive departments and agencies, the name and telephone number of a person in the agency to contact for additional information about the document [Presidential Memorandum, 41 FR 42764, September 28, 1976].)
>
> SUPPLEMENTARY INFORMATION: ——
> ——————————————
> (As required by the provisions of paragraph (c) of this section.)

19

Federal Register regulations (1 CFR 18.12) require agencies to include a preamble in plain English to explain proposed and final rules. Source: *The Federal Register: What It Is and How to Use It*, 1978 ed.

46 FR   3566   (1981)
Volume   Page   Date

Federal Register Finding Aids

The cumulative, monthly *Federal Register Index* is included with each *Federal Register* subscription and is also published separately (AE 2.106:vol./no./ind.). It is helpful for tracking regulations, but not overwhelmingly so, because of its broad indexing. The index is actually a consolidation of *Federal Register* tables of contents, supplemented with general subject headings. The result is an index of issuing agencies and very general topics. Terms used in the *Federal Register* and CFR indexes are based on the "Federal Register Thesaurus of Indexing Terms," free from the Office of the Federal Register, via the Office of the Federal Register home page, or directly at <gopher://clio.nara.gov/00/register/thes.txt>. The *Federal Register Index* also lists Privacy Act publications, a table of pages and dates referring from page numbers to *Federal Register* issues,

Internet *Federal Register*		
Source	*Coverage*	*Search Strategy*
GPO Access <http://www.access.gpo.gov/su_docs/>	Full text since 1994 (Volume 59)	Use the GPO Access specialized search page or enter through the OFR page; select FR sections to search; search by phrases, date, page number, or section
Search Tips		
Final rules	Select search field "Rules"	Search phrase is automatically enclosed in quotes
Contents of a specific issue	date=xx/yy/zz AND contents	date=01/31/97 AND contents

and a quarterly Guide to Freedom of Information Indexes.

The *CIS Federal Register Index* is a comprehensive weekly index to the daily *Federal Register*. Offering a different approach than searching the full text online through sources such as GPO Access, the *CIS Federal Register Index* allows searching document descriptions by subjects and names, CFR section numbers, agency docket numbers, and by effective dates and comment deadline dates to identify the subject of the rule and action taken, issuing agency, issue and page, and type of rule (proposed, final, etc.). A "Calendar of Effective Dates and Comment Deadlines" announces effective dates, along with deadlines for comments, hearings, and replies. The Congressional Information Service's Web subscription service, Congressional Universe, accesses the full text of the *Federal Register*.

Life Cycle of a Regulation

Stage	Published in
Proposed rule	*Federal Register*
Final rule	*Federal Register*
Codified final rule	*Code of Federal Regulations*

The *Code of Federal Regulations* (CFR)

AE 2.106/3:

http://www.access.gpo.gov/su_docs/
dbsearch.html

Publication in the *Federal Register* is only the first stop on a regulation's journey. (See figure 9.2.) The year's accumulation of new rules, amendments, and deletions to old rules, presidential publications, and other materials in the daily *Federal Register* totaled some 69,366 pages in 1996 alone. The final rules and presidential materials are funneled yearly into the *Code of Federal Regulations*. Here the general and permanent rules origi-

nally published in the *Federal Register* are systematically arranged under 50 subject titles (about half of which cover the same subjects as the *U.S. Code*).

The 50 CFR titles are divided into chapters (one for each rule-issuing agency), parts (general topics of regulation), and sections (the rules themselves), each with its own table of contents. The smallest component within the CFR is the "section," where the actual text of a regulation appears. The section is the basic unit of the CFR, with section numbers incorporating part and chapter numbers. CFR citations pinpoint the title (broadest division) and section (smallest division), referring the searcher to the beginning of the text of a regulation.

The official online edition of CFR on GPO Access will grow incrementally until all 50 titles are available. The House of Representatives Internet Law Library also provides access to the *Code of Federal Regulations*. The *United States Code Annotated* (USCA) includes references to the CFR, with some USCA titles providing full text of regulations. Several commercial vendors include the full text of the *Code of Federal Regulations*.

CFR Citation

The *Code of Federal Regulations* is cited by title and section numbers, with the date sometimes added in parentheses.

40 CFR	211.10	(1978)
↓	↓	↓
Title	Section	Date of Edition

CFR Revisions

The 50 CFR titles are revised annually, at staggered intervals throughout the year. This means that the revision date on the cover of a CFR title must be carefully noted—depending on the revision schedule, some titles will be more up to date than others. GPO releases the printed and online versions concurrently, releasing an online edition when a CFR title is printed.

FIGURE 9.2: STAT/USC Compared with FR/CFR.

Parallel Codification of Legislation and Regulation

LEGISLATION
is published first as

is compiled annually in the

is codified in the

Slip Law
(Public Law 94–142)

U.S. Statutes at Large
(89 Stat. 773)

U.S. Code *
(20 U.S.C. 1401 et seq.)

Legislation Is Implemented by Federal Agencies as Rules and Regulations

REGULATIONS
appear as
agency documents

which are published
daily in the

and codified annually in the

FR Doc. 77–36597

Federal Register
(42 FR 65082)

Code of Federal Regulations
(45 CFR 121a)

* Published by West Publishing Company under the direction of the Office of the Law Revision Counsel of the House of Representatives.

Source: *The Federal Register: What It Is and How to Use It,* 1978 ed.

Internet CFR	
Source	*URL*
House of Representatives Internet Law Library	http://law.house.gov/cfr.htm
GPO Access Use the specialized search page	http://www.access.gpo.gov/nara/cfr/index.htm. http://www.access.gpo.gov/su_docs/dbsearch.html

CFR Finding Aids

The approximately 200 volumes of the CFR span 15 feet of shelves and harbor some 60,000 pages of fine print. Several aids expedite searching this mass of information. The *CFR Index and Finding Aids* (AE 2.106/3–2:) is a separate volume of the CFR, included as part of the CFR subscription or purchased separately. Like the *Federal Register*, it indexes by agency names and broad subject headings, referring to CFR titles and parts (but not sections) where the regulation appears. Terms emanate from the "Federal Register Thesaurus of Indexing Terms" <gopher://clio.nara.gov/00/register/thes.txt>. Tables of laws and presidential documents cited as authority for regulations are included, along with tables by presidential document numbers. Using the finding-aids volume, one can use an authority table to translate a Public Law number into a CFR chapter and refer from laws that require publication in the *Federal Register* to *Statutes at Large* and *U.S. Code* citations. It also includes: (1) a list of agency-prepared indexes appearing in individual CFR volumes; (2) acts requiring publication in the *Federal Register*; (3) a list of CFR titles, chapters, subchapters, and parts; and (4) a list of agencies appearing in the CFR (also found in every CFR volume). The *CFR Index and Finding Aids* is not yet online.

Search Tip

In the Federal Register Thesaurus, a descriptor preceded by an *x* is not a valid term. Use the major heading under which it is indented.

The Congressional Information Service publishes an *Index to the Code of Federal Regulations*, which allows searching document descriptions (rather than the full text of the CFR) by subject, geographic entities and names, and CFR citations. Users are referred to both a CFR citation and to the CIS microfiche edition of the CFR. The Congressional Information Service's Web subscription service, Congressional Universe, accesses the full text of the *Code of Federal Regulations*.

Several commercial vendors provide the full text of the *Federal Register* in various formats. The *U.S. Code Service* (USCS) includes the texts of pertinent sections of the CFR. The *United States Code Congressional and Administrative News* reprints significant regulations from the *Federal Register*, and *United States Law Week* digests administrative-agency rulings. *Federal Register* and CFR excerpts are posted on the Federal Bulletin Board. (Select "Congress and Legislative Agencies Including Selected Federal Register and CFR Areas.") Some regulations are reprinted on the Web pages of regulatory agencies.

The *List of CFR Sections Affected* (LSA) serves as a bridge between newly published rules in the *Federal Register* and the CFR (AE 2.106/2:). As its title indicates, LSA lists CFR sections affected by rules and proposed rules published in the *Federal Register*. LSA can be used to answer the question: What new rules or proposed rules have been issued for this CFR title and section since its last revision?

LSA may be searched by CFR title, chapter, part, and section to identify *Federal Register* issues in which amendatory actions and proposed rules have been published since the last revision. It cannot be searched by subject—the searcher must know the CFR title and section to use LSA. Also included is a table of statutory authorities for regulations published in the *Federal Register*, updating the authority table in the *CFR Index*. The federal depository library gateway at the University of California <http://www.gpo.ucop.edu/> provides searching of "CFR Parts Affected": select "Search Fed. Register" and scroll down to the "CFR Parts Affected" box.

The monthly LSA is cumulative and comes as part of the *Federal Register* subscription or can be bought separately. Because of the staggered CFR revision schedule, four permanent issues of LSA must be saved during the year to ensure comprehensiveness until the next CFR revision. To identify CFR provisions in force between 1964 and 1983, use the cumulated LSAs for 1949–1963 (GS 4.108:List/949–63), 1964–1972 (GS 4.108:List/964–72/vol.), and 1973–1985 (AE 2.106/2–2:).

CFR, House Internet Law Library <http://law.house.gov/>		
To Search By	*Use*	*Example*
CFR Title & Section Example: 21 CFR 155.200	title#:cite w/3 section	21:cite w/3 155.200
CFR Title & Part Example: 21 CFR 155	title#:cite w/3 section	21:cite w/3 155
Keyword(s)	Connectors can be used in upper- or lowercase: AND, OR, NOT, ADJ. W/n (within n words to the right). NEAR/n (within n words in either direction).	wetlands wetlands AND federal federal ADJ wetlands federal w/3 wetlands wetlands near/3 federal
Phrases	Enclose in quotation marks	"Congressional Record"
Topics	Subject term followed by !	wetlands!
Truncation	? = one per missing character * = unlimited characters $ = 0-1 characters	wom?n? congress* lab$r (retrieves labor or labour)

REGULATION DETECTIVE WORK: SEARCHING THE LATEST VERSION OF A RULE

People often become aware of a rule through the media, which may describe agency actions without clearly identifying them as regulations. Usually the *Federal Register* and *Code of Federal Regulations* are not mentioned as sources for locating the rule, and no publication date is given. This presents several challenges for the researcher: first, recognizing that the action described is an executive agency regulation, and second, locating the text of that regulation.

To find the most up-to-date version of a regulation, search the CFR, followed by a search of the *Federal Register*, and, if the print versions are used, LSA. An excellent exercise that walks the reader through a complete search of paper publications in the *Federal Register* system is described in *The Federal Register: What It Is and How to Use It* (AE 2.108:F 31). Commercial publications may also be used to identify citations in the *Federal Register* and CFR.

TRACKING REGULATIONS	
If you know	Search these sources
CFR citation	Web CFR; LSA; *CIS Federal Register Index*; *Federal Register* ("CFR Parts Affected in This Issue," and "CFR Parts Affected during [current month]"); *CFR Index and Finding Aids* or "Finding Aids" section in CFR volumes; LEXIS; WESTLAW
Subjects and names	Web FR/CFR; *CIS Federal Register Index*; *Federal Register Index*; *CIS Index to the CFR*; *CFR Index and Finding Aids*; LEXIS; WESTLAW

TRACKING REGULATIONS (*continued*)	
If you know	Search these sources
Public Law number	*CFR Index and Finding Aids*, Parallel Table of Statutory Authorities and Agency Rules

ADJUDICATIONS

Administrative agency adjudications decide cases involving regulations. Like court opinions, agency opinions are issued first in slip form and advance pamphlets, and later cumulated into permanent, bound volumes of administrative reporters. Like laws and court opinions, they are issued either officially or unofficially (commercially). Some may be searched online using LEXIS or WESTLAW. Official administrative publications are listed in *A Uniform System of Citation* and in Sears and Moody's *Using Government Information Sources*; both official and unofficial reporters have been described by Maclay.[6]

Shepard's United States Administrative Citations cites decisions of many federal departments, along with those of courts (regulatory actions are subject to judicial review), boards, and commissions. The primary citator to administrative agency decisions and rulings is *Shepard's Code of Federal Regulations Citations*, a compilation of citations to the CFR from the Supreme Court, the *Statutes at Large*, various federal court reporters, and decisions of agencies, courts, boards, and commissions. It can be used to identify citations to judicial interpretation of CFR sections, presidential proclamations, executive orders, and reorganization plans.

FREEBIES

Free workshops on using the *Federal Register* and *Code of Federal Regulations* are offered in Washington, DC, and selected cities. Look for announcements on introductory page II of the *Federal Register*.

NOTES

1. League of Women Voters, *Survey of Public Awareness of and Interest in Federal Regulations* (Washington, DC: The League, 1982).

2. Center for Food Safety and Applied Nutrition. *The Food Defect Action Levels: Levels of Natural or Unavoidable Defects in Foods That Present No Health Hazards for Humans,* (FDA, 1995). (HE 20.4002:F 73/28). It should be noted that these levels pose no health hazard and are harmless, natural, and unavoidable.

3. *Federal Regulatory Directory.* 6th ed. (Congressional Quarterly, Inc., 1990), p. 18.

4. Senate, *Study on Federal Regulation. Vol. III Public Participation in Regulatory Agency Proceedings* (Senate Doc. 95-71) (GPO, 1977), p. viii. (Y 4.G 74/6:R 26/5/v.3). This comprehensive, six-volume report on federal regulations remains the most thorough review of the regulatory process ever conducted by Congress.

5. Senate, *Study on Federal Regulation. Vol. III,* p. 159.

6. Veronica Maclay, "Selected Sources of United States Agency Decisions," *Government Publications Review* 16 (May/June 1989): 271–301.

EXERCISES

1. Examine the content of any of the "snowbound" *Federal Registers* released January 9, 11, and 12, 1996, during and after the Blizzard of '96 federal government shutdown.

2. In the spirit of the National Performance Review, Federal media production and dissemination was consolidated by transferring the National Audiovisual Center from the National Archives to NTIS in 1994. Locate background information about this transfer.

3. Find the announcement in the 1997 *Federal Register* that the North American Industry Classification System (NAICS) had replaced the Standard Industrial Classification (SIC).

4. Locate last year's Thanksgiving or Mother's Day proclamation.

5. Find any of the following regulations in the FR or CFR, noting their proper citations:
   a. A regulation describing whether an inventor must submit a working model to secure a patent.
   b. The presidential libraries display gifts sent by well-wishers from all over the world. Their museum collections are bolstered by the fact that government employees must relinquish gifts worth more than $200 to the National Archives. Locate the regulation that dictates this.
   c. A regulation that prescribes the contents of mayonnaise.
   d. A regulation that prescribes the contents of cottage cheese.
   e. A regulation that prescribes the size limitations for carry-on baggage on airplanes.
   f. A regulation related to child safety seats in cars.

CHAPTER 10
Executive Branch Information Sources

The buck stops here.

—Harry S Truman

WHAT

The president is the nation's chief executive and the administrative head of the executive branch, composed of 13 executive departments plus numerous temporary and permanent agencies.

WHO

The president must be a citizen born in the U.S., who is no younger than 35 and has lived in the United States for at least 14 years.

WHY

Article III of the United States Constitution decrees that "the executive power shall be vested in a President of the United States of America." The constitutional powers expressly granted to the president include serving as commander in chief of the army and navy, granting of reprieves and pardons, making treaties (with Senate concurrence), nominating Supreme Court justices, and vetoing acts of Congress. The Constitution also directs the president to recommend legislation and to periodically update Congress on the state of the Union.

WHEN

The president's term commences at noon on January 20, every fourth year.

HOW

Thirteen executive departments and their agencies administer the laws enacted by Congress. The executive branch also includes independent agencies such as the Veterans' Administration, independent regulatory commissions such as the Federal Trade Commission, government corporations like the Tennessee Valley Authority, and federally aided corporations including Gallaudet College and Howard University. Many documents of legal effect and significance are issued by the president, executive agencies, and independent administrative agencies.

WHERE

Many presidential documents are published, while original materials are housed in the Library of Congress and presidential libraries, with some inaccessible to the public.

PUBLICATIONS OF THE PRESIDENCY

The papers of the presidents are among the most valuable sources of material for history. They ought to be preserved and they ought to be used.

—Harry S Truman

Arnold Hirshon has distinguished between four categories of presidential papers: public/published, executively controlled, official, and personal.[1] Of the four types, the public/published papers are the most accessible. These include materials issued by the White House, such as legally binding proclamations and executive orders, plus presidential messages, speeches, and statements. These are funneled into established sources of documentation, making them straightforward to trace. The bulk of this chapter will focus on this type of material.

Unlike the published papers, much presidential documentation is initially sealed from the public, including personal, executively controlled, and official papers. A president's personal papers are those not created in the course of official duties, such as personal letters, diaries and journals, or family mementos.

Executively controlled documents are "privileged" from disclosure to Congress or the courts (and the public) because they incorporate national secrets, classified or legal information, or policy-making records. President Richard M. Nixon cited executive privilege when he withheld the White House audiotapes subpoenaed by the Senate Watergate Committee in 1973, claiming the tapes contained frank and private Oval Office conversations extraneous to the committee's investigation. The Supreme Court later ordered the tapes released to the Watergate special prosecutor.

Another restricted category of presidential documents are National Security Directives (NSDs), issued by the president through the National Security Council. During the 1980s, for example, a National Security Directive authorized the U.S. invasion of Grenada. Characterized as the president's "secret laws," National Security Directives are not required to be published or released to Congress or the public. Of the estimated 1,042 NSDs issued since 1961, only about 247 have been declassified. The National Security Archive, a nonprofit research institute and library, sells a microfiche collection of *Presidential Directives on National Security from Truman to Clinton*, with an accompanying printed guide and index.

Official presidential papers are working documents generated in the course of daily presidential activities. Robert Goehlert and Fenton Martin, however, distinguish between unpublished working papers and final presidential decisions and actions, which are published. "Unlike the Congress and the Supreme Court, the decision-making process in the White House is closed to the public."[2] White House policy-making deliberations are internally documented in unpublished memos, drafts, notes, diaries, or tape recordings. In fact, until 1978, all official presidential records were considered the president's private property. Now the law mandates that they pass into the custody of the archivist of the United States at the conclusion of the president's term. As a result, official papers are unpublished, but not inaccessible. After the president leaves office, most are archived in the presidential libraries, where they are available to scholars.

Raymond Geselbracht has identified four eras in the history of presidential papers, beginning with a chaotic epoch ushered in by George Washington.[3] When Washington left office, he took his official letters, notes, drafts, and working papers home to Mount Vernon, primarily because there was nowhere to archive them. Washington's action established a precedent for personal, not public, ownership of presidential papers—a privilege exercised freely by every exiting president until Richard Nixon.

As a result, the destiny of official presidential papers was haphazard. Geselbracht notes that "the papers of many of the nineteenth-century presidents were

seriously damaged, and almost every collection suffered from neglect."[4] Some presidential papers simply vanished, while others were burned, loaned to biographers and lost, stashed in attics and basements, distributed as souvenirs, cut up for autographs, or destroyed during the Civil War. Many were even sold back to the government.

This tradition of neglect was reversed at the turn of the century when the Library of Congress (LC) began collecting presidential papers. In what marked the beginning of the second era of preservation, LC's Manuscript Division was established as a repository, giving presidents the first real alternative to carting off their papers after retirement. But because LC lacked legal authority to demand presidential papers, its preservation efforts were dependent upon voluntary donations.

Today the Library of Congress's Presidential Papers Collection houses the papers of most of the presidents from Washington through Coolidge <http://lcweb2.loc.gov/ammem/presprvw/23pres.html>. The collection is located in the Library's Manuscript Division and includes letters, financial records, speeches, notes, and writings—all for sale on microfilm. Several of these collections are slated to be placed online, beginning with those of George Washington, Thomas Jefferson, and Abraham Lincoln. Other presidents' collections will follow. An index accompanies each purchase of a microfilmed presidential collection, or one may be bought separately. Published indexes in the *President's Papers Index Series* serve as guides to each president's collection, providing descriptions of contents and an index to the microfilm (LC 4.7:). A list of U.S. and foreign libraries owning complete or partial sets of *Presidential Papers* microfilm is available from the Manuscript Division, while indexes to the series may be consulted in many depository libraries. *A Guide to Manuscripts in the Presidential Libraries*, by Burton, Rhoads, and Smock (Research Materials Corp.), provides descriptions of manuscript collections and microfilm resources (as well as oral histories in nine of the presidential libraries).

The Library of Congress Presidential Papers Collection*

Chester A. Arthur	Abraham Lincoln
Grover Cleveland	James Madison
Calvin Coolidge	William McKinley
James A. Garfield	James Monroe
Ulysses S. Grant	James K. Polk
Benjamin Harrison	Theodore Roosevelt
William H. Harrison	William Howard Taft
Andrew Jackson	Zachary Taylor
Thomas Jefferson	George Washington
Andrew Johnson	Woodrow Wilson

*Since Herbert Hoover, the presidents' papers have been in the custody of presidential libraries administered by the National Archives and Records Administration.

Franklin D. Roosevelt is the nation's answer to the historian's prayer.
—R.D.W. Connor,
first archivist of the United States

Franklin D. Roosevelt ushered in the third era of preservation in 1939 when he created the first presidential library. Roosevelt donated land, solicited private donations for construction, and then consigned the Roosevelt Library to the government to maintain. Harry S Truman followed suit, donating his papers to his own library in Independence, Missouri. Later, the 1955 Presidential Libraries Act formalized government maintenance of the presidential libraries with tax dollars. Like the Library of Congress's presidential papers program, presidential libraries were a compromise "between the competing private and public property claims to presidential papers."[5] Because the Presidential Libraries Act embraced the traditional view that presidents own their papers, depositing them in a presidential library remained voluntary.

The fourth era began after Richard Nixon's resignation rekindled questions about ownership of presidential papers. Exercising a two-century-old precedent, the departing President Nixon claimed his presidential papers and tapes as personal property. But, in the wake of Watergate, the nation was feeling cantankerous. To mollify objections, Nixon temporarily deposited his papers at the National Archives, restricting access and asserting his right to reclaim and even to destroy them. Congress then seized the Nixon materials by passing a law giving the government control over them (the Presidential Records and Materials Act of 1974), with a second law designating presidential papers in general as national, not private, property (the Presidential Records Act of 1978).

As a result of the Presidential Records Act, official records of any president after 1981 belong to the nation, not the president. The Presidential Libraries Act is still on the books, but to ease the taxpayers' maintenance burden, legislation has mandated that new libraries established after Ronald Reagan have endowment funds.

Public Statements

Official daily White House press releases announce administrative and presidential activities, providing the text of major addresses and remarks, proclamations, executive orders, communications to executive departments, messages to Congress, letters to foreign heads of state, fact sheets, nominations and appointments, and presidential statements. Most of these are published in the various sources discussed below.

FIGURE 10.1: The LBJ Library.

Four floors of archives are visible from the museum area of the Lyndon Baines Johnson Library behind glass walls rising above the second floor of the Great Hall. Behind the glass are four stories of red document boxes, each bearing a gold presidential seal. Courtesy LBJ Library.

Presidents on the Presidency

The job is interesting, but the possibilities for trouble are unlimited.
—John F. Kennedy

They're all my helicopters, son.
—President Lyndon B. Johnson to a corporal pointing out the presidential helicopter by saying, "This is your helicopter, sir."

I can get up at nine and be rested, or I can get up at six and be president.
—Jimmy Carter

Is the country still here?
—Calvin Coolidge after a nap

Presidential Proclamations and Executive Orders

Soon after he took office, George Washington issued the first executive order, asking his Cabinet for "a clear account" of the infant government of 1789. (The first proclamation was also issued in 1789—declaring Thanksgiving Day.) Executive orders were not issued uniformly or numbered until 1907, and, until the inception of the *Federal Register* in 1936, the only systematic organization and numbering of executive orders was done by the State Department. It was the State Department that collected them from agencies throughout the Capital and began numbering them in 1907, designating an 1862 order from President Lincoln as number one. (President Washington's 1789 order is the earliest unnumbered executive order.) The mandate for announcement in the *Federal Register* (FR) signaled a new era—never before had presidential proclamations and executive orders been publicly available immediately after issuance.

Since 1936, presidential executive orders and proclamations have been published in the *Federal Register*, where they must appear to be legally binding. Later they are codified in Title 3 of the *Code of Federal Regulations* (CFR). Presidential proclamations and executive orders are legal documents, issued under statutory authority or according to presidential powers granted by the Constitution. Proclamations are issued by virtue of the president's office, by law, or in response to congressional joint resolutions. Executive orders are authorized by the president's statutory or constitutional powers. When issued with legal authority, both executive orders and proclamations have the same effect as laws.

Legally, proclamations and executive orders are the same, and the best way to differentiate between them is simply to accept the designation they have been assigned. In actual use, most executive orders are working documents often used to command government agencies or officials, while proclamations address the general public. Our national security classification system, for example, is based on a series of executive orders that began with one issued by President Truman in 1951. Affirmative action in the workplace was instituted with Executive Order 11246 issued by President Lyndon Johnson in 1965.

Two types of proclamations are used—ceremonial, which announce special observances, holidays, or events, such as Mother's Day, Snow White Week, and National Rice Month; and the more substantive, nonceremonial proclamations, dealing with trade, imports and exports, and tariffs. Often triggered by a congressional joint resolution authorizing and requesting the president to issue a proclamation, almost one-third of all public laws between 1987 and 1995 were commemorative. Commemorations reduced to a trickle after a reform-minded House rule prohibited them in 1995. Now all congressional commemorations are sponsored by the Senate.

Depending on its recency, the text of a proclamation can be found in the *Federal Register*, *Weekly Compilation of Presidential Documents*, *U.S. Code Congressional and Administrative News* (under Proc. number), Title 3 of the CFR (Proc. number), *Codification of Presidential Proclamations and Executive Orders* (under subject or EO number), *Public Papers of the Presidents* (under issue date), or *CQ Almanac* (issue date).

Although proclamations and executive orders are numbered consecutively, they are often cited by the *Federal Register* volume and page where they first appeared. For example, Presidential Proclamation 4693 would be cited according to the FR volume and page where it was published: 44 FR 56669. Confidential or classified executive orders are issued but not published.

Internet Presidential Documents		
Proclamations since 1995	*Federal Register* AE 2.106:	http://www.access.gpo.gov/nara/index.html Limit to "Presidential Documents"
	Weekly Compilation of Presidential Documents AE 2.109:	http://www.access.gpo.gov/su_docs/dbsearch.html "proclamation 7029" "mother's day " *proclamation* (for a list)
	Code of Federal Regulations AE 2.106/3:	http://www.access.gpo.gov/nara/cfr/index.html Select "Search Your Choice of CFR titles and/or Volumes," and then select "Title 3 The President" Searches retrospectively through last December; use FR for current year
Executive orders since 1995	*Federal Register* AE 2.106:	http://www.access.gpo.gov/nara/index.html Limit to "Presidential Documents"
	Weekly Compilation of Presidential Documents AE 2.109:	http://www.access.gpo.gov/su_docs/dbsearch.html "executive order 13010"
	White House Virtual Library	http://www.whitehouse.gov/WH/html/library.html
	Code of Federal Regulations	http://www.access.gpo.gov/nara/cfr/index.html Select "Search Your Choice of CFR Titles and/or Volumes" "Title 3 The President" Searches retrospectively through last December; use FR for current year

They are numbered as executive orders, however, and are released to Congress. The *Statutes at Large* includes the text of proclamations but not executive orders. Some proclamations and executive orders issued under specific statutory authority are published with statutes in the *U.S. Code*. The *U.S. Code* has tables listing executive orders that implement laws, as well as tables of proclamations.

When searching the online *Federal Register* through GPO Access or the Office of the Federal Register, check the "Presidential Documents" box to limit the search. *Congressional Information Service (CIS) Federal Register Index* indexes presidential documents in the *Federal Register*. Monthly when Congress is in session, the *U.S. Code Congressional and Administrative News* provides the full text of new presidential proclamations, executive orders, and executive branch reorganization plans. Proclamations and executive orders are indexed by number, referring to the subject and date of each and the location of the text in the *U.S. Code Congressional and Administrative News*. Shepard's *Code of Federal Regulations Citations* compiles citations to proclamations, executive orders, and presidential reorganization plans from the Supreme Court, *Statutes at Large*, various federal court reporters, and other sources.

Retrospective Searching

Title 3 of the *Code of Federal Regulations*, The President, is the one CFR volume not superseded by the next year's issue. Each annual cumulation contains only the proclamations and executive orders issued during a single year. The *Codification of Presidential Proclamations and Executive Orders, April 13, 1945–January 20, 1989* (AE 2.113:945-89) can be used to fill in previously issued proclamations and executive orders from the Truman to Reagan administrations, and from 1989 on, refer to the annual Title 3 issues. The *Codification of Presidential Proclamations and Executive Orders, April 13, 1945–January 20, 1989* gives the text of many proclamations and executive orders with amendments incorporated, arranged in 50 subject chapters. The cumulative codification allows researchers to ascertain the status of issuances during its 45-year range, and provides referral from statutes, title, and the *U.S. Code* to presidential document number, with a table listing each proclamation and executive order issued between 1945 and 1989. This source is updated every four years and has been likened to "a USCA of official presidential action," a combination sourcebook, index, and finding aid.[6] The full text of presidential proclamations, executive orders, and other documents, with indexes, has been compiled in issues of the *Code of Federal Regulations. Title 3, The President* (GS 4.108/2:), released irregularly six times since 1938. The indexes from all six are combined in the *Code of Federal Regulations. Title 3, The*

President, 1936–1965, Consolidated Tables (GS 4.108/2:936–965/ind). The *CIS Index to Presidential Executive Orders and Proclamations 1789–1983* indexes numbered and unnumbered executive orders and proclamations, with a companion microfiche full-text collection. The index is searchable by subjects, names, organizations, geographic areas, and dates of issue, with cross-references to interrelated executive orders.

Between 1925 and 1936, when systematic publication commenced in the *Federal Register*, proclamations and executive orders were issued individually under SuDocs classification PR ___.7: and PR ___.5: (an individual number for each president followed the PR prefix), and they may be found in some older depository library collections. The *Statutes at Large* has included proclamations since 1791, and *A Compilation of the Messages and Papers of the Presidents, 1789–1897* (Y 4.P 93/1:3/1-10, H.Misc.Doc.210, Serial Set 3265/V.1-10) covers early issuances. Annual *Public Papers of the Presidents* volumes cover every president since Harry S Truman.

Nominations

At the start of each month, the *Congressional Record* Daily Digest offers a "Disposition of Executive Nominations," with statistics on executive nominations for the year, and a summary of the month's nomination hearings. In THOMAS, select "*Congressional Record Text*," then "Browse: Issues by Date and Section," there selecting "Daily Digest." In the Daily Digest use your browser's Find command to locate the word *nomination*. In GPO Access choose "Congressional Record," then select "Daily Digest" under "Congressional Record Sections." Enter the Search Terms *nomination* or keywords in the search box. The "Nominations" section in *Congressional Index* summarizes the status of nominations (confirmed or submitted), arranged by nominee's name.

Presidential Messages

http://www.whitehouse.gov/

> *Presidential footprints almost inevitably lead to Capitol Hill, for there is little that a modern president does that does not somehow involve the Congress.*
> —G. Calvin Mackenzie,
> *Studying the Presidency*

The president's oral and written communications to Congress and the public are called presidential messages. Messages to the public include speeches, radio addresses, press conferences, and press releases. Presidential messages to Congress may accompany bills introduced with the president's endorsement or treaties submitted for Senate consent, or may communicate the

Internet Executive Orders: Quick Tips	
Office of the FR http://www.nara.gov/fedreg/eo.html#top	Identify EO's since 1962 in chronological order by EO number/date
Weekly Compilation of Presidential Documents http://www.access.gpo.gov/nara/nara003.html	"executive order 13010"
House Internet Law Library, "Presidential Documents" http://law.house.gov/13.htm	Full text of key EOs and other presidential documents
FedLaw http://www.legal.gsa.gov/legal1geo.htm	By EO number (primarily 1993–1996); link to full text
White House, "Virtual Library" http://www.whitehouse.gov/WH/html/library.html	Search by keyword or EO number
U.S. Code via House of Representatives Internet Law Library http://law.house.gov/usc.htm	Proclamations and executive orders issued under specific statutory authority Two-step process: 1) EX W/2 ORD W/2 no. /F:EXEC Example: EX W/2 ORD W/2 11845 /F:EXEC 2) display text using browser's Find by entering no. Example: FIND 11845

president's rationale for signing or vetoing an act. Many of these are ordered printed by Congress as House or Senate Documents and then included in the Serial Set, *Congressional Record*, and the House and Senate Journals—making legislative search skills an asset for presidential research. Messages may be traced through the indexes listed below, as well as through the legislative history summarized in a slip law and *Statutes at Large*, both of which cite presidential statements published in the *Weekly Compilation of Presidential Documents*.

Weekly Compilation of Presidential Documents

AE 2.109:

http://www.access.gpo.gov/nara/nara003.html

http://www.access.gpo.gov/su_docs/dbsearch.html

Each week the White House releases transcripts of presidential news conferences and public speeches, messages to Congress, and statements. The text of presidential materials released during the preceding week is provided in the *Weekly Compilation of Presidential Documents*. The *Weekly Compilation* also includes a monthly dateline, lists of laws approved by the president, nominations submitted to the Senate, and a checklist of White House releases. Each Monday issue of the *Weekly Compilation* has a cumulative index for the year, with separate indexes appearing quarterly, semiannually, and annually.

Presidential Messages

PUBLIC MESSAGES

Text:
Weekly Compilation of Presidential Documents
White House Virtual Library <http://www.whitehouse.gov/WH/html/library.html>
Congressional Quarterly (CQ) Weekly Report
CQ Almanac
Newspapers

Indexes:
Cumulative index in each *Weekly Compilation of Presidential Documents*
Congressional Record Index History of Bills and Resolutions/THOMAS/GPO Access
Monthly Catalog
PAIS
Newspaper indexes

MESSAGES TO CONGRESS

Text:
Congressional Record/THOMAS/GPO Access
CQ Weekly Report
CQ Almanac
U.S. Code Congressional and Administrative News
House and Senate Journals
Serial Set

Indexes:
Congressional Record Index/THOMAS/GPO Access
Cumulative indexes in each *Weekly Compilation of Presidential Documents*
CIS/Index
CIS Serial Set Index
House and Senate Journals
Monthly Catalog
PAIS
Slip laws
Statutes at Large

Internet *Weekly Compilation of Presidential Documents* http://www.access.gpo.gov/nara/nara003.html http://www.access.gpo.gov/su_docs/dbsearch.html	
To Find	Search
Table of contents, specific issue	"contents" and "july 28, 1997" The date must be a Monday
Tables of contents for the year	"contents" On retrieved record, *pd15se97 Contents =* contents for September 15, 1997
Specific page	"page 1158" Identify page number through a contents search
Topics	"mother's day" mother's ADJ day "may 5, 1997" AND "mother's day"
Executive orders	"executive order 13010"
Proclamations	"proclamation 7029" Topics (see above)

The *Weekly Compilation of Presidential Documents* reprints speeches, remarks, and press conferences verbatim. A tape recording of the president's actual words is compared with prereleased transcripts to verify accuracy. When no tape is available, the *Weekly Compilation* notes that the published text is based on a press release rather than actual delivered remarks. The GPO Access database abbreviation for the *Weekly Compilation of Presidential Documents* is pd (for "presidential documents").

Public Papers of the Presidents of the United States
AE 2.114:

> *Once you get into the great stream of history you can't get out.* —Richard M. Nixon

Before 1957, a systematic official compilation of the presidential messages and speeches did not exist. Except for presidential executive orders and proclamations published in the *Federal Register*, publicly issued presidential materials had not been accumulated and published by the government for more than 50 years. The first compilation of presidential messages and proclamations for Presidents Washington through McKinley had been authorized by Congress and compiled by James D. Richardson in the 10-volume *A Compilation of the Messages and Papers of the Presidents, 1789–1897* (Y 4.P 93/1:3/1–10, H.Misc.Doc.210, Serial Set 3265/ V.l-10). Since then, the government had done nothing to organize and systematically record presidential materials released to the public.

This documentary gap was bridged in 1957 with the initiation of *Public Papers of the Presidents*, which

bound papers and speeches released from the White House by Herbert Hoover and every other president since Harry S Truman. This official series contains the text of each president's speeches, news conferences, messages, statements, communications to Congress, executive orders, proclamations, nominations, and appointments. For example, the last item in the Nixon volumes is a letter to Secretary of State Henry Kissinger, dated August 9, 1974:

> Dear Mr. Secretary:
> I hereby resign the Office of President of the United States.
> Sincerely,
> Richard Nixon

The John F. Kennedy volumes end with JFK's last speech, delivered on November 22, 1963, in Fort Worth before his flight to Dallas. Preceding the text of speeches Kennedy had prepared to deliver that same afternoon is a footnote explaining that the president was shot and killed while driving in an open motorcade toward downtown Dallas.

Since 1977, *Public Papers* has incorporated all the material originally published in the *Weekly Compilation of Presidential Documents*. Because the set contained only selected *Weekly Compilation* material between 1965 and 1976, many libraries have saved older issues of *Weekly Compilation*, but discard current issues after receipt of the annual *Public Papers*.

Public Papers volumes include subject and name indexes, with appendixes of supplementary material such as the president's public schedule, White House announcements, and a list of public and private laws. Individual volumes of *Public Papers* include indexes, but for a cumulated index to all the volumes, consult *The Cumulated Indexes to the Public Papers of the Presidents of the United States*, published by Kraus International Publications. Bernan Press publishes cumulated indexes for individual presidents since Truman.

THE FEDERAL BUDGET
PREX 2.8:

http://www.access.gpo.gov/su_docs/ dbsearch.html

http://www.access.gpo.gov/omb/

> *A billion here, a billion there—pretty soon it adds up to real money.*
> —Senator Everett Dirksen, Illinois

Although many people associate the federal budget with the thick, paperbound book displayed on the television news each January, the national budget is not a single document but a series of executive and legislative publications issued throughout the fiscal year, October 1– September 30. Initiated by the executive branch, the budget is finalized by Congress—not with the sweep of a single law, but piecemeal during the congressional budget process.

The federal budget odyssey begins with a proposed budget, forwarded from the president to Congress. (This document is the one that makes headlines each January.) The 1997 budget, for example, sprawled through five volumes and 2,424 pages (weighing 10 pounds, 13 ounces), a rationale for its parallel release in CD-ROM (PREX 2.8/1:). The proposed budget, the *Budget of the United States Government*, incorporates a Supplement (PREX 2.8:yr/SUPP.), an Appendix (PREX 2.8:YR/APP), Historical Tables (PREX 2.8/8:), Analytical Perspectives (PREX 2.8/5:), the Budget System and Concepts (PREX 2.8/12:), and A Citizen's Guide to the Federal Budget (PREX 2.8/5:yr/CITIZE).

The *Economic Report of the President* <http://www.access.gpo.gov/su_docs/aces/aaces002.html> (select "Economic Report of the President" from the scroll box) is transmitted to Congress within 10 days after the budget's release (numbered individually, PR__.9:). Each president's economic report is numbered sequentially: e.g., President Clinton's (our 42nd president) economic report is PR 42.9:. The *Economic Report of the President* summarizes the nation's economic health, discussing trends, numerical goals, and objectives. Congress holds annual hearings to review the president's economic report, and issues a *Joint Economic Report* (Y 1.1/8:), the Joint Economic Committee's critique of the president's report.

Beware Budget Blunders

Remember that the president's *Budget of the United States Government* is a proposal. This means that totals for the current and upcoming fiscal years are projected, not actual, amounts. Figures for the past year (budget year minus 2) are factual, but data for the current (budget year minus 1) and next fiscal years are estimates that may be modified during budget execution and the congressional budget process.

The Congressional Budget and Impoundment Control Act of 1974 established a congressional budget process for reviewing the president's budget proposals. Congress may approve, disapprove, or change the president's proposals, sending them through the same legislative machinery as any bill. The House and Senate budget committees react to the president's proposed budget with an overall budget plan establishing spending ceilings and broad priorities, using budget analyses and information (but no recommendations) supplied by the Congressional Budget Office. If the Senate and House adopt different budget plans, a conference committee resolves their differences. Finally, a budget plan in the form of a concurrent resolution designed to guide

Congress in its budget deliberations is agreed upon by both chambers.

During the congressional budget process, legislation is introduced, committee reports and prints are issued, and hearings are held. With the budget resolution as a guide, Congress enacts authorization bills to create federal programs, and appropriations bills to fund them. Tracing documents generated during the congressional budget process requires a legislative search using the resources discussed in chapter 8, including THOMAS (search "Budgets" under "Major Legislation by Topic"), the status tables in the House *Calendars,* and the *Congressional Record* Daily Digest, along with *American Statistics Index* to identify statistical budget documents. Congressional Budget Office (CBO) "scorekeeping" reports track action on revenue and spending bills. Scorekeeping is monitoring the status of individual authorization, appropriation, and revenue bills against budget resolution targets. The *CBO List of Publications* cites analyses of alternative fiscal, budgetary, and program policies and is free from the CBO Publications Office. The full text of recent titles is provided on the Congressional Budget Office Gopher <gopher://gopher.cbo.gov:7100/1>. CBO publications can be traced using *Monthly Catalog* or *CIS/Index.*

PRESIDENTIAL LIBRARIES

We have papers from my 40 years in public service in one place for friend and foe to judge, to approve or disapprove.... This library will show the facts, not just the joy and triumphs, but the sorrow and failures, too. —Lyndon Johnson, dedicating the Johnson Library, 1971

Modeled after FDR's library and administered according to Congress's ground rules, presidential libraries and museums are built with private donations and then turned over to the government to administer. Except for the Richard M. Nixon Library and Birthplace in Yorba Linda, California, they are maintained by the National Archives and Records Administration. The Nixon Library and Birthplace is not a true presidential library, since it is not maintained by NARA and houses no original presidential documents. It is privately operated and houses only Nixon's personal diaries and pre-presidential papers, embellished with some objects loaned by the National Archives. Nixon's official presidential papers and White House tapes remain national property, warehoused by the National Archives in the Nixon Presidential Materials Staff (the Nixon Project) at the National Archives <http://sunsite.unc.edu/lia/president/nixon.html>. The Bush Presidential Materials Project in College Station, Texas <http://csdl.tamu.edu/bushlib/bushpage.html> was opened to the public in 1997 as the Bush Presidential Library and Museum.

Presidential libraries preserve "the real stuff of history"—not only papers and personal mementos of the president, but also of his associates, friends, and relatives. Their collections include manuscripts, artifacts, photographs, films, recordings, microfilm, and gifts from foreign heads of state. "Perhaps the most confusing thing about [presidential libraries] is their name—for they are neither collections of books about Presidents nor collections of Presidents' books."[7] Presidential "libraries" are actually archives and museums "dedicated to educating the public about a former President, his administration, and the office of the President in the American system of government."[8] Their collections include John F. Kennedy's rocking chair, the draft of Franklin Roosevelt's Pearl Harbor speech, Harry Truman's "The Buck Stops Here" sign, and Jimmy Carter's cardigan sweater.

Visual and audio materials are important components of many of the collections. Some Nixon White House recordings, for instance, have been processed and opened to the public.[9] (A release schedule has been set for opening the remainder.) The John F. Kennedy Library, another example, houses thousands of photographs and films documenting nearly every day of Kennedy's term. Oyez Oyez Oyez, a multimedia Supreme Court database, provides selected audio materials from presidential libraries on their US History Out Loud site <http://oyez.at.nwu.edu/history-out-loud/>.

White House Tapes

The taping system in President Nixon's Oval Office and Cabinet Room snaked from hidden microphones to seven Sony 800B recorders secreted in the White House basement. The five-inch reels whirled for two and a half years, depositing 3,700 hours of conversations from the White House, the Old Executive Office Building, and Camp David onto 950 now-fragile tapes. The 264 hours open to the public can be heard only at the National Archives at College Park because the tapes are too delicate for duplication and are legally restricted to boot. To listen to them all, set aside two years of eight-hour days, and five-day weeks. Bring aspirin, since the conversations are often unintelligible. A 27,000-page conversation log will help you keep your place.

Conversations had been secretly recorded in the White House for three decades before tapes helped topple Nixon. Oval Office bugs preserved conversations of FDR, Truman, Eisenhower, Kennedy, and LBJ, and are now part of their presidential library audiovisual collections.

Although presidential libraries have their critics (some deride them as "paper pyramids"), their contributions go beyond the archival preservation of papers and artifacts. These libraries touch not only scholars but also thousands of ordinary Americans who file through their doors to tour their museums and attend conferences, exhibitions, and special programs. Each presidential library has its own personality. At the Truman Library in Independence, Missouri, for example, visitors can see the actual 1941 Chrysler coupe driven by Vice President Truman and a fireplace mantle from the White House. The Roosevelt Library boasts museum exhibits that include locks of Roosevelt's baby hair, his christening gown and cradle, his first pony saddle, and his cane. Eleanor Roosevelt's life is also reflected, in letters, personal papers, and photographs. The Kennedy Library has the papers of Ernest Hemingway, donated by Mary Hemingway, the author's widow. The Johnson Library displays George Foreman's heavyweight championship belt and robe, donated because Foreman credited the Job Corps, a Johnson Administration anti-poverty program, with redirecting his life. The Nixon Library and Birthplace shelters Julie and Tricia Nixon's wedding gowns, a chunk of the Berlin Wall, and the Colt .45 presented to the president by Elvis Presley.

Presidents may restrict access to materials in their libraries. The Iran-Contra documents in the Reagan Library, for example, will be sealed until at least 2002, to protect national security, foreign policy, and confidentiality. Restricted access can be appealed to the National Archives, and the bulk of material is quickly opened to the public. The "Accessions and Openings" section of *Prologue* lists new additions to library collections, as well as opened or declassified records (AE 1.111:).

Each presidential library has a Web page <http://www.nara.gov/nara/president/address.html>. *A Guide to Manuscripts in the Presidential Libraries*, published by Research Materials Corporation, describes manuscript collections, microfilm resources, and oral histories in the Hoover, Roosevelt, Truman, Eisenhower, Kennedy, Johnson, and Ford libraries, with an index that allows searching by names, subjects, government agencies, and countries. Frank L. Schick's *Records of the Presidency: Presidential Papers and Libraries from Washington to Reagan* (Oryx Press) describes legislation and agencies related to presidential records, bibliographic guides, plus the history and contents of sets of presidential papers. Fritz Veit's *Presidential Libraries and Collections* (Greenwood Press) and Pat Hyland's *Presidential Libraries and Museums, An Illustrated Guide* describe inventories of the collections.

FOREIGN RELATIONS

U.S. foreign relations are rooted in the constitutional powers of the president and are conducted by the executive branch. The Department of State advises the president on foreign relations and negotiates treaties and agreements with other nations. State Department materials are accessible through the State Department link on the GPO Access home page at <http://www.access.gpo.gov/state/index.html>, the Department of State Foreign Affairs Network (DOSFAN) <http://dosfan.lib.uic.edu/>, and the Federal Bulletin Board at <http://fedbbs.access.gpo.gov/statedpt.htm>.

Foreign Relations Publications

US Department of State Dispatch

S 1.3/5:

http://www.state.gov/

http://fedbbs.access.gpo.gov/libs/dos_disp.htm

The State Department's official documentary record is *US Department of State Dispatch*. In 10 yearly issues plus two supplements, *Dispatch* chronicles foreign policy, reprints speeches and congressional testimony of the president and secretary of state, and provides fact sheets, policy statements, maps, and profiles of countries in the news. Announcement of the latest *Dispatch* release and full text of selected State Department documents are available automatically by e-mail through subscription to State Department listservs at <http://www.state.gov/WWW/listservs.html>. To access *Dispatch* on the State Department's Web page requires knowing the issue needed. Indexes to *Dispatch* include the Congressional Information Service's *American Foreign Policy and Treaty Index*, and *Index to U.S. Government Periodicals*. The quarterly *U.S. Foreign Affairs on CD-ROM* (S 1.142/2:) is the most comprehensive State Department package, with the full text of *Dispatch*, presidential and State Department speeches, statements, testimony, briefings, *Background Notes*, and Daily Press Briefing Transcripts since 1990. GPO Access "Browse Topics" for Foreign Affairs of the United States links to Internet sites <http://www.access.gpo.gov/su_docs/dpos/pathbrws.html>.

DOSFAN (Department of State Foreign Affairs Network) is a Web collection of official U.S. foreign policy information and decisions since 1993, including *Dispatch* and *Background Notes* <http://dosfan.lib.uic.edu/index.html>. A partnership between the Department of State, the Library at the University of Illinois at Chicago, and GPO, DOSFAN provides country and topical information on sociopolitical situations, economic trends, democracy, human rights, culture, development assistance, environment, and terrorism, along with speeches, statements, testimony, and electronic versions of depository publications.

Foreign Relations of the United States

S 1.1:

Another source of diplomatic background information is the Department of State's *Foreign Relations of the United States* (FRUS), serving for more than a century as the documentary record of U.S. diplomacy and foreign policy. The policy of publishing the records of American diplomacy began in 1861, when Secretary of State Seward published his important diplomatic dispatches. Today, *Foreign Relations of the United States* is the oldest, most comprehensive publication of its kind in the world. It's been called "the world's most prestigious ongoing collection of government documents."[10] The annual volumes form the official record of U.S. diplomacy, including background documents like diplomatic communications, memoranda, diplomatic notes and telegrams, and other documents tracing the formulation of foreign-policy decisions. Concerns about the integrity and completeness of FRUS were addressed in 1991 in the Foreign Relations Authorization Act, which mandated that FRUS be compiled according to principles of historical objectivity and accuracy. The series was mandated by Congress to be free of alterations, unnoted deletions, or omissions aimed at concealing policy weaknesses.

Declassification procedures demand at least a 25-year time lag before publication of FRUS. Volumes covering U.S.-China relations during the Eisenhower administration in 1958–1960, for example, were not released until 1996. They chronicle the Taiwan Strait crisis, which in 1958 threatened to escalate into war with China. Special FRUS volumes are sometimes published for topics such as the Paris Peace Conference of 1919 and the summit meetings of World War II. A complete list of volumes for every president since Lincoln, including volumes available on the Web, is available on the State Department Web site <http://www.state.gov/www/about_state/history/frus.html>.

FRUS is indexed in the *Monthly Catalog* and volumes issued for 1958–60 forward are indexed in the Congressional Information Service's *American Foreign Policy and Treaty Index* (scan AFPTI accession number 7000–7 in the abstracts).[11] Coverage of volumes issued before 1958 is also provided by *CIS/Index*.

American Foreign Policy: Current Documents

S 1.71/2:

American Foreign Policy: Current Documents is a related series, published under several titles since 1950.[12] Unlike *Foreign Relations of the United States* and its publication lag, *American Foreign Policy: Current Documents* compiles publicly released contemporary materials. Included are foreign policy messages, addresses, statements, interviews, press briefings and conferences, plus congressional testimony by the president and representatives of the executive branch. Much of the contents was previously released in other official publications, while some segments were never before published. The Congressional Information Service's *American Foreign Policy and Treaty Index* and accompanying microfiche collection provide access to key policy documents from the executive branch, Congress, and independent federal agencies.

Treaties

Treaties are written agreements between nations, governed by international law. The U.S. Constitution identifies treaties as part of the supreme law of the land and grants the president power to forge them with the consent of Congress. The president may negotiate a treaty without Senate consent, but cannot ratify it without approval by two-thirds of the Senate. After ratification, treaties are proclaimed by the president and assume the same legal authority and force as statutes.

Stages in the Treaty Process

1. Negotiation by the president
2. Signature by the president
3. Transmittal to Senate
4. Ratification (after congressional approval)
5. Publication
6. Proclamation
7. Execution

The Treaty Process

The process begins when the president forwards a treaty to the Senate, where it is considered by the Foreign Relations Committee <http://www.senate.gov/committee/foreign.html>. The treaty, usually supplemented by a presidential endorsement, is designated a Senate Treaty Document (Y 1.1/4:) and numbered sequentially during each Congress: Treaty Document 105–5, for example, is Y 1.1/4:105–5. The Senate approves about 90 percent of treaties submitted by the president. Only 20 treaties have ever been killed by lack of a two-thirds vote. (The Treaty of Versailles, for example, was rejected twice, keeping the United States out of the League of Nations.)

Senate inaction is a more common tactic, sometimes inducing the president to withdraw the treaty. Unlike other legislation, treaties do not die at the conclusion of a Congress—they remain vital until either acted upon by the Senate or withdrawn by the president. Treaties have been known to stagnate for years,

even decades, awaiting Senate action. The Senate Web site, "Legislative Activities: Treaties" provides a summary of treaty status and actions at <http://www.senate.gov/activities/treaties.html>. The *Congressional Index* "Treaties (Summaries)" section capsulizes the status of treaties since the 81st Congress (1949), with treaty document number, title, summary, and any action (Senate Executive Report number/date and date Senate agreed to resolution). The *Congressional Index* "Treaties (Index)" section can be searched by keywords to identify entries in "Treaties (Summaries)." The State Department Treaty Affairs Office can explain the current status of a treaty (202) 647-1345. The commercial journal *International Legal Materials* publishes many treaty texts earlier than the Department of State.

The *Journal of the Executive Proceedings of the Senate*, called the Executive Journal, is the official record of Senate actions on nominations and treaties (Y 1.3/4:). The Executive Journal compiles presidential nomination and treaty messages and proceedings of Senate executive sessions. To locate consideration of President Bush's nomination of Clarence Thomas to the Supreme Court, for example, search the Executive Journal for the 102nd Congress, 1st session (1991), volume 133. The Executive Journal is arranged in topical sections by date and is searchable by names of nominees, places, and by executive department or agency. References are found to President Bush's July 8, 1991, nomination of Clarence Thomas to the Supreme Court, for example, and to the October 15, 1991, vote and confirmation. The *Senate Executive Calendar* (Y 1.3/2:, not depository), an agenda of treaties and nominations reported from committee, lists treaties in calendar number order, noting subject, committee action, and executive report number.

Although Senate Treaty Documents can technically be kept confidential, the injunction of secrecy is usually lifted, allowing them to be printed without classification. Senate Treaty Documents have been in the Serial Set since the 97th Congress (1980–81) and are available on microfiche from the Congressional Information Service. The Library of Congress Web site, A Century of Lawmaking for a New Nation, includes historical issues of the Senate Executive Journal beginning with the First through Eighth Congresses, 1789 to 1805 <http://memory.loc.gov/ammem/amlaw/lawhome.html> Senate Treaty Documents are searchable in the *Monthly Catalog, American Foreign Policy and Treaty Index, CIS/Index,* Congressional Masterfile 2, and other legislative indexes. (See chapter 8.) Before 1980, Senate Treaty Documents were called Senate Executive Documents and were sequentially lettered: Exec. Doc. A, 99–1; Exec. Doc. B, 99–1. The *CIS Index to U.S. Senate Executive Documents & Reports* indexes materials issued between 1817 and 1969 by subject, names, title, and Document or Report numbers (also searchable on CD-ROM through CIS's Congressional Masterfile 1). The Congressional Information Service also sells a Senate Executive Documents and Reports microfiche collection covering 1817–1969.

In the Senate Foreign Relations Committee, the treaty proposal is translated into a bill and treated as any legislative measure: it may die, remain unaltered, or be amended. In the process, it may generate public or executive hearings. Executive hearings (also called executive sessions) are the opposite of public hearings—they are closed to the public and rarely printed. When treaty hearings are public, transcripts are usually printed and distributed by the committee. The Foreign Relations Committee may report the treaty—favorably or unfavorably, with or without conditions. Treaty recommendations are reported from committee to the full Senate in Senate Executive Reports, which are numbered by congress and report number: Exec. Rept. 104–4, for example (Y 1.1/6:). The Senate can then ignore the treaty, amend it, or go on record with reservations against it.

Traditionally confidential, Senate Executive Reports have been part of the Serial Set since the 97th Congress (1980) and are depository items. Senate Executive Reports are indexed in *American Foreign Policy and Treaty Index*, the *Monthly Catalog*, and *CIS/Index*. A "Legislative Activities Report of The Committee on Foreign Relations" is submitted by March 31st of each odd-numbered year. (Similar reports are required of all Senate standing committees.) The full text is in THOMAS and provides Treaty Document numbers for approved treaties ("Treaties" section) and Executive Report and Treaty Document numbers ("Committee Publications" section). Currently, however, the full text of Senate Executive Reports themselves are not available on THOMAS. Senate, House, and Executive Reports since the 104th Congress (1995–1996) are available on GPO Access at <http://www.access.gpo.gov/congress/index.html> (select "Congressional Reports").

Most treaties receive Senate approval and then are ratified and made public by presidential proclamation. There are often three different dates: when a treaty was 1) signed, 2) ratified, and 3) entered into force. The treaty's final ratification is up to the president, not the Senate, with the formal treaty promulgation issued under the president's name. The president is not legally obligated to accept Senate treaty action, remaining free to withdraw the treaty from Senate consideration at any time, or to decline to ratify it even after Senate consent has been granted.

Treaty Searches

Legislative action → TIAS → UST

Cohen, Berring, and Olson identify four stages of treaty research: (1) locating the text, (2) determining whether the treaty is in force and its coverage, (3) interpreting the text, and (4) determining its status.[13] The first stage, locating the treaty text, is complicated by the fact that treaties can be elusive before ratification and entering into force. Treaty actions are announced in State Department press releases and in *Dispatch*. The *Dispatch* section called "Treaty Actions" is arranged by topic, providing treaty title and dates entered into force, signed, or ratified. Treaties can be obtained from the Senate Document Room (202) 224-7860 or from the Senate Executive Clerk.

About six months after its effective date, the treaty is numbered sequentially and issued in slip form as part of the *Treaties and Other International Acts Series* (TIAS) (S 9.10:no.). Each individually numbered TIAS pamphlet contains the text of a single treaty or agreement. The series began with number 1501 in 1946. The contents of TIAS are indexed in *Monthly Catalog*, *Treaties in Force*, the Congressional Information Service's *American Foreign Policy and Treaty Index* (search under topics or under "Treaties and conventions" in the index), Hein's *Current Treaty Index*, and—for older treaties—*World Treaty Index*, which covered 1900–1980. Selected treaties are summarized in the commercially published *International Legal Materials* (listed in the table of contents under "Treaties and Agreements"). In the U.S. House of Representatives Internet Law Library, Treaties and International Law provides full text of selected recent and historical treaties and agreements <http://law.house.gov/89.htm>.

The next stop for treaties originally published in TIAS is to be bound and cumulated in *United States Treaties and Other International Agreements* (UST) (S 9.12:). UST is a chronological arrangement of treaties, with country and subject indexes. (Subject headings are drawn from treaty titles rather than a controlled vocabulary.) UST citations resemble those in the *U.S. Code* or *Code of Federal Regulations*: 26 UST 1793 is UST volume 26, page 1793. UST began in 1950 with TIAS 2010, when treaties ceased being published in *Statutes at Large*.

Older treaty texts (before UST) are available in the *Statutes at Large* (until 1950), and *Treaties and Other International Agreements of the United States of America, 1776–1949* (S 9.12/2:v.1-13). This title, often cited as "Bevans" because it was edited by Charles Bevans, is considered "the definitive edition of U.S. treaties and international agreements for this time period."[14] Treaties weren't numbered until 1908, when the numbered "Treaty Series" was launched with number 489. The Treaty Series was issued singly as pamphlets by the Department of State until replaced in 1945 by TIAS. The Treaty Series did not include Indian treaties. The Executive Agreement Series was another precursor to

TIAS, issued singly as pamphlets by the Department of State until replaced in 1945. For a detailed history of treaty documentation consult Schmeckebier and Eastin's chapter on "Foreign Affairs" in *Government Publications and Their Use* (1969).

An ongoing series compiled by Igor Kavass and published by W. S. Hein includes *United States Treaty Index: 1776–1990 Consolidation*, indexing agreements, slip treaties, and treaties not published in TIAS by number and chronologically under countries or subjects. Its semiannual update is *United States Current Treaty Index* (in print and CD-ROM). The two sources index agreements and treaties numerically, chronologically, geographically, and by subject, giving TIAS number, title or description, and signature date. Unpublished and unnumbered treaties in *United States Current Treaty Index* are assigned KAV numbers (named after Igor KAVass; example: KAV 3901) by Hein until the State Department numbers them, with a cross-reference index from KAV to TIAS numbers. Peter Rohn's *World Treaty Index* covers twentieth-century (1900–1980) treaties registered in the League of Nations Treaty Series, the United Nations Treaty Series (UNTS), and national sources. Hein's *Current United Nations Treaty Index* is a source for identifying newly published UNTS agreements.

To determine whether a treaty is still in effect, check the annual *Treaties in Force* (TIF), which lists all treaties and other international agreements still in force on January 1 of each year (S 9.14: and <http://www.acda.gov/state/>). The walloping 3.2 MB version of TIF can be accessed through the State Department's Web site by selecting "International Policy." TIF is arranged by country and subject, furnishing a brief summary of the treaty and a list of countries party to it. Scanning through TIF, you'll find predictable topics like "Arms Control," along with the unexpected: "Astronauts" (an international pact for rescuing and returning them) or "Polar Bears" (Canada, Denmark, Norway, the U.S. and USSR agreed to protect them). TIF provides cites to the full treaty text in UST and TIAS, and for older treaties, the full treaty text in *Statutes at Large* and Bevans. Igor Kavass's annual *Guide to the United States Treaties in Force* (Hein) is meant to be used with TIF, supplementing it by providing additional access points for searching. *United States Current Treaty Index* (Hein) includes the full text of TIF.

Interpreting a treaty is aided by examining documents in its legislative history. Treaty Documents and Senate Executive Reports may be traced through *American Foreign Policy and Treaty Index, Monthly Catalog, CIS/Index, Congressional Index*, and *Congressional Record Index*. Although few can take advantage of it, most of the records of the Senate Committee on Foreign Relations are open to the public in the Capitol. Praised as the "most accessible [records] of any com-

Treaty Searches	
Title	Scope
Indexes:	
CIS *American Foreign Policy and Treaty Index*	Abstracts and bibliographic information
Congressional Index	Treaty summaries
CIS/*Index*	Cites Senate treaty documents and legislative history of legislation to implement treaties
Current Treaty Index	Slip treaties too recent to be in TIAS
Treaties in Force (TIF)	Cites source of treaty full text
Serial Set Catalog	The series/report index is searchable by treaty document numbers
CIS *Index to U.S. Executive Documents and Reports*	Senate Executive Documents and Reports issued 1817–1969
Congressional Masterfile I	Senate Executive Documents and Reports issued 1817–1969
Text:	
Treaties and Other International Acts Series (TIAS)	Individual treaties
Statutes at Large	Treaties before 1950
Bevans	Treaties before 1950
UST	Cumulated chronologically since 1950

mittee in Congress," they are available from 1816 through the early 1980s.[15]

Executive Agreements and Legislation

Most international agreements bypass the treaty process by taking the form of executive agreements or legislation. Unlike treaties, executive agreements are not mentioned in the Constitution. Executive agreements are understandings between the president and foreign governments, and they are more common than either treaties or legislative actions. In 1989, the United States had 5,117 executive agreements on the books, compared to 890 treaties. In fact, the treaty has been called "an all-but-discarded procedure."[16] Less binding and formal than treaties, executive agreements require no Senate consent, simplifying their handling. While treaties are considered laws and may supersede earlier laws or treaties, executive agreements must operate within the boundaries of existing law and cannot alter it. The 1981 release of 52 American hostages from Iran was negotiated by President Carter as an executive agreement, as was much of the United States' involvement in the Vietnam War and the Lend-Lease Agreement of World War II. Sometimes executive agreements are used to execute treaties. Executive agreements since 1993 are indexed in *American Foreign Policy and Treaty Index*.

The Senate may use joint resolutions for treaty action, with passage in both houses substituting for a two-thirds Senate approval. Texas and Hawaii were annexed to the United States this way. Congress occasionally tries to induce the president to negotiate a treaty by passing joint or concurrent resolutions.

THE EXECUTIVE OFFICE

The basic structure of today's presidency emerged in 1939 with the creation of the Executive Office of the President. The idea was to provide executive assistants to help the president work with agencies and departments. The burgeoning staff of the Executive Office resulted in a "dramatic expansion in the size of the Presidency."[17] The influential Office of Management and Budget is a subunit of the Executive Office of the President, as is the White House staff, the Council of Economic Advisors, and many smaller bodies. The *Federal Staff Directory* includes information about the Executive Office of the President. Executive Office publications can be identified using *Monthly Catalog, CIS/Index,* SPC, PAIS, and *American Statistics Index,* which despite its appellation, is "the best source of comprehensive information" for executive branch publications.[18]

Executive Branch Publications

It is estimated that half of executive agency documents are missed by the depository library system. *CIS Index to U.S. Executive Branch Documents, 1789–1909* covers departmental documents of the executive departments, including most general publications, annual reports, rules and decisions, circulars, and catalogs in the *Checklist of United States Public Documents, 1789–1909* (the "1909 Checklist") except those in the Serial Set (departmental annual reports and materials submitted to Congress). *CIS Index to U.S. Executive Branch Documents, 1910–1932* is an annotated bibliography of executive documents not included in other CIS indexes, including those issued by bureaus, offices, and independent agencies. CIS sells companion microfiche collections.

The working documents of the White House are somewhat inaccessible. Goehlert and Martin emphasize that other than "the published papers of the executive branch, there is no published record of the White House staffers, such as policy and political advisors, the legislative liaison, press secretaries, and special counsels and consultants."[19]

Other Presidential Documents

Other types of presidential documents of legal effect, including presidential determinations, administrative orders, reorganization plans, and memoranda, also appear in the *Federal Register* and are compiled in Title 3 of the *Code of Federal Regulations.* A president uses reorganization plans to change executive-branch structure by combining, abolishing, or transferring agencies. Reorganization plans are transmitted to Congress as executive orders, published in the *Congressional Record* and *Federal Register,* printed as House or Senate Documents for inclusion in the Serial Set, and printed in the House and Senate Journals. Reorganization plans automatically become law unless disapproved by Congress before a specified deadline, and are cumulated in Title 3 of the *Code of Federal Regulations,* in Title 5 of the *U.S. Code,* as well as in the *Statutes at Large.* DeToro recommends the *U.S. Code* as the best source for reviewing enacted reorganization plans, where they are published "following the specific reorganization acts by which they are authorized, together with associated presidential messages and executive orders."[20]

ADDRESSES

The National Security Archive, Gelman Library, George Washington University, 2130 H Street, NW, Suite 701, Washington, DC 20037; e-mail: nsarchiv@gwis2.circ.gwu.edu; (202) 994-7000; Fax: (202) 994-7005; <http://www.seas.gwu.edu/nsarchive>.

Presidential Libraries and Collections:

A directory of Presidential Libraries of the National Archives System is available at <http://www.nara.gov/nara/president/address.html>

The Nixon Presidential Materials Project, National Archives at College Park, 8601 Adelphi Road, College Park, MD 20740-6001; e-mail: nixon@arch2.nara.gov; (301) 713-6950; Fax: (301) 713-6916

The President John F. Kennedy Assassination Records Collection, Access and FOIA Staff, Room 6350, National Archives at College Park, 8601 Adelphi Road, College Park, MD 20740-6001; (301) 713-6620; Fax: (301) 713-7480; e-mail inquiries may be addressed to NARA's general e-mail address, inquire@nara.gov; <http://www.nara.gov/nara/jfk/>

The Richard Nixon Library and Birthplace, 18001 Yorba Linda Blvd, Yorba Linda, CA 92686-3949; (714) 993-5075; Fax: (714) 528-0544; Catalog (800) USA-8865; <http://www.chapman.edu/nixon/>

FREEBIES

The following Subject Bibliographies are free from: Stop: SSOP, Washington, DC 20402; U.S. Fax Watch: (202) 512-1716:

106.   Presidents <http://www.access.gpo.gov/su_docs/sale/sb-106.html>

204.   Economic Policy <http://www.access.gpo.gov/su_docs/sale/sb-204.html>

210.   Foreign Relations of the United States <http://www.access.gpo.gov/su_docs/sale/sb-210.html>

Congressional Budget Office—copies of most CBO publications are free to the public: Publications Office, Office of Intergovernmental Relations, Congressional Budget Office, Ford

House Office Bldg., Second and D Streets, S.W., Washington, DC 20515; (202) 226-2809.

From Product Sales Section (NWPS), National Archives and Records Administration, 700 Pennsylvania Ave., NW, Washington, DC 20408:

> General Information Leaflet No. 64, "Presidential Libraries of the National Archives System." (AE 1.113:64).

FURTHER READING

Blanton, Tom, ed. *White House E-mail: The Top Secret Computer Messages the Reagan/Bush White House Tried to Destroy.* New York: The National Security Archive, 1995.

> Saved from the "delete" button by a six-year legal battle, these White House e-mail messages provide fascinating reading.

Congressional Quarterly, Inc. *CQ Guide to Current American Government.* Washington, DC: Congressional Quarterly, Inc., 1991.

> Clearly written overviews of the three branches of government include a discussion of the presidency.

Encyclopedia of the American Presidency, ed. by Leonard W. Levy and Louis Fisher. 4 vols. NY: Simon and Schuster Academic Reference, 1994.

> This is the winner of the 1995 Dartmouth Medal for reference works.

"The FDR Tapes: Secret Recordings Made in the Oval Office of the President in the Autumn of 1940" *American Heritage* (February/March 1982): entire issue.

> When Professor R.J.C. Butow joked about listening to "FDR tapes" during a visit to the Roosevelt Library, an archivist hauled out 16 forgotten recordings.

Haldeman, H.R. "The Nixon White House Tapes: The Decision to Record the Presidential Conversations." *Prologue* 20 (Summer 1988): 79-87. (AE 1.111:20/1).

> An insiders' account of the Nixon Oval Office recording system.

Herman, Edward. *The Federal Budget: A Guide to Process and Principal Publications.* Ann Arbor, MI: The Pierian Press, 1991.

> An in-depth review of the federal budget, related information sources, and tips for locating and interpreting information in the budget.

Library of Congress. *Presidents of the United States: Their Written Measure.* GPO, 1996. (LC 14.2:P 92).

> A bibliography of materials about the presidency, presidents' lives and careers, and their own writing about hobbies, interests, and everyday concerns.

Library of Congress. *Special Collections in the Library of Congress: A Selective Guide.* comp. by Annette Melville. Library of Congress, 1980. (LC 1.6/4:C 68).

> Describes the Presidential Papers Collection, which includes papers of 23 presidents, and guides to accessing materials in the collection.

Martin, Fenton S. and Robert U. Goehlert. *How to Research the Presidency.* Washington, DC: Congressional Quarterly, Inc., 1996.

> This guide to researching presidents and the presidency describes almanacs, bibliographical directories, encyclo-

pedias, indexes, electronic products and online services, databases, journals, newspapers, and news services.

National Archives. "Presidential Libraries of The National Archives System" <http://www.nara.gov/nara/president/overview.html> (November 10, 1997).

> An overview, with links to the individual presidential library home pages.

The National Commission on Presidential Sites and the University of North Carolina. The Presidential Sites—Specific Presidents. <http://sunsite.unc.edu/lia/president/pressites/PresidentS-list2.html> (November 15, 1997).

> Biographical information, historical sites, inaugural addresses, and more for learning about the presidents, although many of the links are dormant.

Nelson, Michael. *Guide to the Presidency.* 2nd ed. Washington, DC: Congressional Quarterly, Inc., 1996.

> Chapters written by scholars cover history, selection, and removal; presidential powers; relationship with the public, the executive branch, Congress, the Supreme Court, and the bureaucracy; and biographies of the presidents and vice presidents.

Price, Miles O. and Harry Bitner. *Effective Legal Research.* Boston: Little, Brown, and Co., 1953.

> The first edition of this title provided a listing of retrospective sources of proclamations and executive orders (pp. 143–48).

Senate Committee on Foreign Relations. *Treaties and Other International Agreements: the Role of the United States Senate.* GPO, 1993. (S.Prt. 103–53) (Y 4.F 76/2:S.PRT.103–53).

> Answers to all your questions about treaties.

NOTES

1. Arnold Hirshon, "The Scope, Accessibility and History of Presidential Papers," *Government Publications Review* 1 (1974): 363–90.

2. Robert U. Goehlert and Fenton S. Martin, *The Presidency: A Research Guide* (Denver, CO: ABC-Clio Information Services, 1985), p. xix.

3. Raymond Geselbracht, "The Four Eras in the History of Presidential Papers," *Prologue* 15 (Spring 1983): 37–42. (AE 1.111: 15/1).

4. Geselbracht, p. 37; a detailed summary of the fate of papers of individual presidents is given in *Nixon v. United States* 978 F.2d 1269 (D.C.Cir. 1992):1287-1299.

5. Geselbracht, p. 39.

6. Richard Sloane. "Finding Presidential Power." *New York Law Journal* 205 (February 19, 1991): 4.

7. Donald B. Schewe, "Establishing a Presidential Library: The Jimmy Carter Experience," *Prologue* 21 (Summer 1989) p. 125. (AE 1.111: 21/2).

8. Schewe, p. 125.

9. The Presidential Records and Materials Act of 1974 appropriated Nixon's tapes and other documents dealing with "abuses of governmental power" or public property of "general historical significance." Seizure of Nixon's records left no time to separate personal (and therefore private) from presidential (official) material. Thus, for more than two decades, public access has been hobbled by lawsuits. Under restric-

tions imposed by Nixon lawyers after years of litigation, no copies can be made until the year 2000, and no transcripts are available. Litigation continues over compensation to Nixon's estate for confiscation of his records. A proposed out-of-court settlement would bill the government $26 million, convert the privately run Nixon library in California into a federal facility, and ship all his papers and tapes there. They are now housed at the National Archives in College Park under a provision of the 1974 law saying they must be kept in the Washington, DC, area.

10. *Report of the Advisory Committee on Historical Diplomatic Documentation to the United States Department of State*. Department of State, 1997. <http://www.fas.org/sgp/advisory/hac96.html> (November 20, 1997).

11. Volumes issued for 1958–60 were the first published only as departmental, rather than congressional, documents.

12. *American Foreign Policy: Current Documents* continues the State Department series begun in 1950 with *A Decade of American Foreign Policy: Basic Documents, 1941–49*, and the subsequent 1957 publication of *American Foreign Policy, 1950–1955: Basic Documents*. Between 1956 and 1967, annual volumes entitled *American Foreign Policy: Current Documents* were issued. No further volumes were published until *American Foreign Policy: Basic Documents, 1977–1980* (1983), followed by annual volumes of *American Foreign Policy: Current Documents*.

13. Morris L. Cohen, Robert C. Berring, and Kent C, Olson, *How to Find the Law*, 9th ed. (St. Paul, MN: West Publishing Co., 1989), p. 458.

14. Jennifer DeToro, "A Guide to Information Sources," in *Studying the Presidency*, ed. by George C. Edwards and Stephen J. Wayne (Knoxville, TN: University of Tennessee Press, 1983), p. 140.

15. "Senate Foreign Relations Committee Opens Bulk of Archival Records," *Prologue* 18 (Summer 1986): 139. (AE 1.111: 18/2).

16. Loch K. Johnson, *The Making of International Agreements: Congress Confronts the Executive* (New York: New York University Press, 1984), p. 6.

17. National Study Commission on Records and Documents of Federal Officials. *Final Report of the National Commission on Records and Documents of Federal Officials* (GPO, 1977), p. 13. (Y 3.R 24/2:1/977).

18. DeToro, p. 142.

19. Goehlert and Martin, p. xx.

20. DeToro, p. 139.

EXERCISES

1. The United States is party to the Patent Cooperation Treaty (PCT), providing reciprocal patent protection and filing rights for member countries. Locate the text of this treaty and citations to its legislative history.

2. Find President Clinton's statement upon signing the GPO Electronic Information Access Enhancement Act of 1993 (P.L. 103–40).

3. When President Clinton signed Executive Order 12958 on April 17, 1995, releasing 1.5 billion pages of classified documents for declassification review, he launched the least restrictive classification standards since the Cold War. Find EO 12958.

Retrospective Searching:

4. Where would you find the first presidential proclamation, issued by George Washington in 1789 to declare "a day of public thanksgiving and prayer"?

5. Following World War II, Allied reconnaissance teams shipped tons of captured Nazi documents to the United States. To handle the flood of German documents, President Truman issued Executive Order 9568, establishing the Office of the Publication Board. Locate the text of Truman's executive order.

CHAPTER 11
Judicial Information Sources

There is no liberty if the power of judging be not separated from the legislative and executive powers. —C. S. Montesquieu

WHAT

The United States has two judicial systems: state and federal. At the pinnacle of each are supreme courts, below which are appellate (circuit) courts and trial courts (called U.S. district courts at the federal level). In addition, special courts have been established to consider particular issues. The federal judiciary is headed by the nine-member Supreme Court, and includes courts of appeals, district courts, and various special courts.

WHY

The United States courts were established by Congress under authority of the Constitution; state and local courts function under the authority of individual state governments.

WHO

Federal judgeships are presidential appointments, requiring Senate approval for confirmation. The federal judiciary has been called "an anomaly" in our democratic society, with nonelected judges holding office not for a specific time, but contingent upon "good behaviour."[1]

HOW

Growing numbers of court decisions are electronically available soon after release: on the Internet, through online and CD-ROM databases, and on computer bulletin boards. Printed court rulings may be published ("reported") in both official (government-published) and unofficial (commercially published) reporters considerably later than the electronic releases.

We are the only branch of government that explains itself in writing every time it makes a decision. —Byron R. White, Associate Justice, U.S. Supreme Court

Alexander Hamilton observed that "laws are a dead letter without courts to expound and define their true meaning and operation." Judicial opinions (case law) are sometimes called judge-made law because they join statutes and administrative regulations/adjudications to constitute our nation's three primary sources of law. Court decisions interpret both statutory and administrative law, and are important for determining whether a law or presidential action is constitutional. (See figure 11.1.)

The doctrine of *stare decisis* dictates that judicial decisions be based upon legal precedent. As Michael Lavin points out, the "critical point to remember about legal research is that the past can never be ignored."[2] The uses of court reporters go beyond legal precedent, however. Fascinating historical information is tucked into federal court records, revealing Wyatt Earp's prosecution as a horse thief; bankruptcy papers of the H. J. Heinz Company which claimed "pickles and relish" as assets; and a "custody" battle between two companies claiming patent and trademark ownership of Raggedy Ann, the rag doll.[3]

Many, but not all, court rulings are published—primarily those breaking new ground or amplifying previous decisions. A general rule of thumb is that the higher the court, the more likely its decisions have been published. However, even at the federal level, publication is not comprehensive—not even the Supreme Court publishes all its decisions. Official court reporters are government documents, and many are available to depository libraries, allowing depository libraries to maintain basic legal collections. Unofficial reporters reprint

FIGURE 11.1: Legislative/Judicial/Executive Relationships.

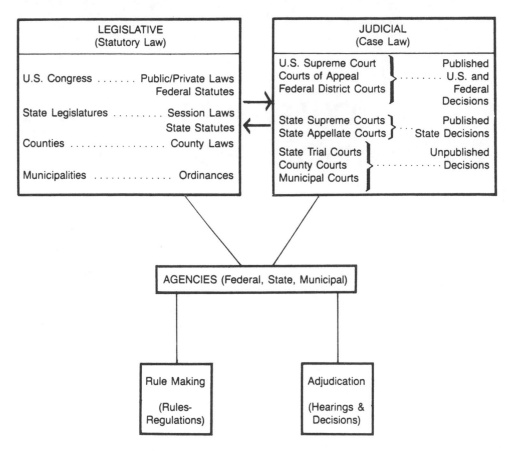

Source: *Finding the Law: A Workbook on Legal Research for Laypersons*, GPO, 1982 (I 53.2:L 41).

and enhance the official version by adding explanatory material and finding aids. Three leading commercial legal publishers are West Publishing Company (the most prominent American legal publisher), Lawyers Co-operative Publishing Company, and Shepard's/McGraw-Hill, Inc.

All federal courts file case documentation with their clerk of the court, including the initiating complaint, orders, answers, motions, and subpoenas. While not always published, this documentation is publicly available through on-site examination or requests for photocopies. (Fees are charged.) Each court establishes its own access procedures. Increasingly, individual courts have established their own free Internet sites to present court information. Many unpublished decisions are also available through online legal databases and free Internet sites, many maintained by law schools. The Administrative Office of the U.S. Courts manages the judiciary's Web site containing general information on the judiciary, publications, press releases, and proposed rules for public comment <http://www.uscourts.gov/>. Project Hermes is the wellspring of electronic Supreme Court opinions. Hermes (named after the Greek mes-

senger god) began in 1990 as an experiment in disseminating U.S. Supreme Court opinions electronically. The pilot was upgraded to an official dissemination mode in 1993, with the Supreme Court distributing its opinions to subscribers in WordPerfect or ASCII text.

The United States court system is like a pyramid, with the Supreme Court at the apex and the U.S. courts of appeals and U.S. district courts on the two levels below. This pyramidal structure allows the courts of appeals to correct errors made in trial courts and ensures uniformity through Supreme Court review.

For a court to render a valid judgment it must have the authority, or jurisdiction, to decide a case. The United States courts cannot decide all cases—only those qualifying as federal cases (thus the popular saying, "Don't make a federal case out of it," a warning not to overemphasize the importance of something). The Constitution and laws enacted by Congress prescribe what cases may be considered by the United States courts, leaving others to be tried in state courts.

Federal Court Reporters: Abbreviations	
Abbreviation	Reporter
F., F.2d, F.3d	Federal Reporter
F.Supp.	Federal Supplement
L. Ed., L. Ed. 2d	U.S. Supreme Court Reports, Lawyers Edition
S. Ct.	Supreme Court Reporter
U.S.	United States Reports

THE UNITED STATES SUPREME COURT: THE COURT OF LAST RESORT

As the nation's highest court, the Supreme Court is the final forum for appeal in the U.S. judicial system. Its decisions are final, creating legal precedents that guide lower court and subsequent Supreme Court decisions. Many view the Supreme Court as the most powerful entity in federal government—not only can it declare presidential actions illegal, it can also employ judicial review to strike down acts of Congress as unconstitutional.

The Supreme Court can preempt other courts and hear cases first (called "original jurisdiction") when foreign diplomats or states are involved. Fewer than six original jurisdiction cases are filed each term, making them the rarest of Supreme Court cases. More numerous are the appellate jurisdiction cases, in which the Court hears appeals from lower courts. Between the first Monday in October and sometime in June, some 4,000 cases thread their way up through state and federal courts to the Supreme Court. Except for a few cases that must be considered, the Supreme Court can opt to review lower court decisions or let them stand. Most are dismissed with a brief decision that the subject is either inappropriate or too insignificant for review. Only about 200 cases rate oral arguments before the Court each term, with another 100 or so decided without oral argument.

Between October and mid-May, the Court hears up to four one-hour arguments daily, three days a week. An attorney for each side is granted 30 minutes to make a presentation and answer questions from the bench. Limited visitor seating is available for the public, but cameras are forbidden. Audiotapes of oral arguments are stored in the National Archives in Record Group 267, Records of the Supreme Court of the United States. Recently, the Supreme Court authorized the National Archives to open these audiotapes of oral arguments to the public after a lag of a few months. Previously, the tapes were available only to federal employees and se-

rious scholars, and commercial reproduction was outlawed. Oyez Oyez Oyez, a multimedia database about the United States Supreme Court, makes selected oral arguments available on the Internet <http://court.it-services.nwu.edu/oyez/>. After the oral argument portion of the term, the Court takes the bench each Monday for "the release of orders and opinions," taking 15–30 minutes to decide cases. The daily *Journal—Supreme Court of the United States* summarizes Court proceedings (Ju 6.5:).

Although often used interchangeably, legal opinions and decisions can be differentiated: the decision tells whether the court upheld or reversed a lower court decision; the opinion explains why, giving the legal reasoning for the judgment. Although the majority rules in deciding cases, any justice may write a separate opinion to accompany the majority opinion. These may be concurring (in agreement with the majority, but for different reasons) or dissenting opinions (disagreeing with the majority).

Cases are decided by majority vote, with slip opinions reported both officially and unofficially—some searchable on the Internet and online through services such as LEXIS and WESTLAW. (See "Internet Supreme Court" Table, p 147.) The Supreme Court itself has no Web site, but Supreme Court decisions are available through Project Hermes. Case Western Reserve University, the first university law library to participate in the pilot project, maintains a Hermes archive at <ftp://ftp.cwru.edu/hermes/>, while the Cornell Legal Information Institute offers an enhanced archive at <http://supct.law.cornell.edu/supct/>. Supreme Court opinions and related documents from Hermes are also uploaded daily to the Federal Bulletin Board on GPO Access at <http://fedbbs.access.gpo.gov/court01.htm>. Selecting a court term opens a list of file libraries with a chronological list of decisions (date, names of parties, short description). The files, in WordPerfect 5.1 format, can be searched using the browser's Find command, or saved to a disk and then opened on a PC.

The people can change Congress but only God can change the Supreme Court.
—George W. Norris

The nine justices of the U.S. Supreme Court are appointed for life by the president of the United States, with the advice and consent of the Senate. In 200 years, the Senate has rejected roughly one out of every five Supreme Court nominees and has argued passionately about others. The decision is far-reaching—once confirmed, Supreme Court justices may be removed only by impeachment (something that has never happened).

Finding Court Cases		
Comprehensive	LC's "U.S. Judicial Branch Resources" http://lcweb.loc.gov/global/judiciary.html Select Judicial Opinions	Connects to sources of Supreme, state, or circuit court opinions
	CataLaw http://www.catalaw.com/region/Region.shtml	Supreme, district, or federal courts of appeals; foreign countries
	US Law Page http://www.farislaw.com/uscaselaw.html	Supreme, district, or federal courts of appeals
	DocLaw http://lawlib.wuacc.edu/washlaw/doclaw/doclaw5m.html	Gateway to statutory, case, and administrative law resources
	Law Journal Extra: Courthouse http://www.ljx.com/courthouse/index.html	Supreme, district, or federal courts of appeals, state courts; search full text of U.S. circuit courts of appeals decisions since 1994
	FindLaw http://www.findlaw.com/	Useful for locating press releases with party names, venue, etc.
Federal	House Internet Law Library "Federal Court Decisions and Rules" http://law.house.gov/6.htm	Supreme, district, or federal courts of appeals, links to key cases
	US Law Page http://www.farislaw.com/uscaselaw.html	Supreme, district, or federal courts of appeals
	Villanova Center for Information Law and Policy's Federal Court Locator http://www.law.vill.edu/Fed-Ct/fedcourt.html	Supreme, district, or federal courts of appeals
	FedLaw http://www.legal.gsa.gov/	Supreme, district, or federal courts of appeals, bankruptcy, and other courts
	Law Journal EXTRA! http://www.ljx.com/courthouse/index.html.	All federal circuit court decisions since 1994
States	The Villanova Center for Information Law and Policy's State Court Locator http://www.law.vill.edu/State-Ct/	Links to state judiciary home pages and opinions
	FindLaw, "U.S. State Government Resources" http://www.findlaw.com/11stategov/	Select a state and type of material search
	StateLaw http://lawlib.wuacc.edu/washlaw/uslaw/statelaw.html	State court opinions, laws
	Gryphon Goldlinks to Free Legal Resources on the Internet http://www.poseidon.com/links.html	State court opinions, laws

---

Biographical Information about Justices

Supreme Court:
<http://supct.law.cornell.edu/supct/index.html>
<http://court.it-services.nwu.edu/oyez/justices/ justice.pl>
The American Bench
Almanac of the Federal Judiciary
Judicial Yellow Book
Judicial Staff Directory

Supreme Court Reporters

Immediately after being handed down from the bench, a "bench opinion" is released electronically under Project Hermes, followed a few days later by the pub-

lished "slip opinion," an individually numbered pamphlet (Ju 6.8/B: and via the Federal Bulletin Board on GPO Access <http://fedbbs.access.gpo.gov/court01. htm>, or through the Supreme Court dialup bulletin board system). The name "slip opinion" harkens back to the days when opinions were temporary "slips" inserted into bound volumes until the updated cumulations appeared. Slip opinions may incorporate corrections or minor amendments to the bench opinion, with the addition of numbered pages for citing. The U.S. Supreme Court Electronic Bulletin Board System provides free access to the Court's automated docket, argument calendar, order lists, slip opinions, rules, bar admission forms, and instructions (202) 554-2570. The printed slip opinions are accumulated throughout the

Internet Supreme Court			
Scope	Source	Searchable By	Tips
Current court calendar	Project Hermes http://supct.law.cornell.edu/supct/index.html	Date	Grants and denials of certiorari, per curiam decisions, orders
Current term schedule of oral arguments	Project Hermes http://supct.law.cornell.edu/supct/index.html	Date, docket number, case (party) name	Use browser's Find function
Current term decisions	Project Hermes http://supct.law.cornell.edu/supct/index.html	Date	Use browser's Find function to locate month, case (party) name, docket no.; or use Supreme Court archive search engine
	Villanova Center for Information Law and Policy http://www.law.vill.edu/Fed-Ct/sct.html#flite	Date	Select month, then use browser's Find function to search for filing date, case (party) name, docket no.
Since October 1995	Villanova Center for Information Law and Policy http://www.law.vill.edu/Fed-Ct/sct.html#flite	Case name, *US Reports* volume, decision month; keyword	Search for decision date, case (party) name, docket no. Fax full text to area codes (215) or (610)
Since 1990 (slip opinions)	The Legal Information Institute Hermes http://supct.law.cornell.edu/supct/index.html	Search full opinions or syllabi (case summaries) by case (party) name or keywords; browse topics	Enclose phrases in quotes Case sensitive * = truncation Boolean = AND, OR, ANDNOT, XOR party/Nixon party/"United States"
	GPO Access Federal Bulletin Board http://fedbbs.access.gpo.gov/court01.htm	Select court term to get case list in reverse order by date	Use browser's Find function to locate case (party) name Case descriptions include decision date, case (party) name
Since 1906 (*US Reports* vol. 200)	FindLaw http://www.findlaw.com/casecode/supreme.html	Browsable by year and *US Reports* volume; full text searchable by keywords, citation, case title	Party name search: united states v. nixon or united states nixon Full text search: united states AND nixon
Key pre-1990 decisions	CD-ROM or abridged version via Project Hermes http://supct.law.cornell.edu/supct/cases/historic.htm	Select from a list of topics; case (party) name; justice who authored opinion	

Internet Supreme Court (*continued*)			
Scope	Source	Searchable By	Tips
1937–1975 *US Reports* vols 300–422 FLITE database	Villanova Center for Information Law and Policy http://www.law.vill.edu/Fed-Ct/sct.html#flite	*US Reports* volume, filing date, month, case (party) name, docket no., keyword (followed by party names, docket no.)	united states v. nixon united ADJ states *v.* nixon
	GPO Access http://www.access.gpo.gov/su_docs/supcrt/index.html	Keywords, case name or *US Reports* cite	"united states v. nixon" 416US232
	FedWorld http://www.fedworld.gov/supcourt/	Case name, *US Reports* volume, keyword	united states v. nixon united ADJ states v. nixon
Overruled decisions	http://www.access.gpo.gov/congress/senate/constitution/scourt.html	Overruling and overruled case names	Case name, using browser's Find function for case list, not full text
Audio of selected oral arguments	Oyez Oyez Oyez http://court.it-services.nwu.edu/oyez/	Cases arranged by decision date Case summary includes facts, decision, vote	Use browser's Find function to search date or party indexes by name; subject index by topic

term in official advance sheets called *Preliminary Prints* (Ju 6.8/a:), supplemented with headnotes or syllabi (summaries of significant legal issues in the case), names of counsel, indexes, and tables of cases.

The final, bound, "official" record of Supreme Court opinions is published in *United States Reports* some 12 to 18 months behind the electronic versions (Ju 6.8:). *United States Reports* lists justices on the bench and includes an index, a table of cases, a list of cases adjudged with dates of argument and decision and names of counsel, the opinion and the justice who delivered it, a list of orders on cases adjudged, and rules of civil and appellate procedure and bankruptcy rule. The *U.S. Reports* citation to volume and page (__ U.S. __) becomes its permanent or archival citation reference. Supreme Court opinions are also published unofficially, first as paperbound "advance sheets" containing several decisions, later replaced by bound volumes. Like their official counterparts, unofficial reporters include the text of opinions, but are augmented with annotations and supplemental information, and are available faster than the official reporters. Because of their speedy publication and editorial additions, most researchers prefer the unofficial versions to the *United States Reports*.[4]

Supreme Court Reporters	
Official	Commercial Counterparts
United States Reports	*United States Supreme Court Reports*
	West's *Supreme Court Reporter*

United States Supreme Court Reports from LEXIS-NEXIS has two series and may be searched online. The first series (cited as L. Ed.) covers opinions from volumes 1 to 351 of *United States Reports*. The second series (L. Ed. 2d) began with volume 352. (Multiple series are commonly used in court reporters to prevent unwieldy numbering.) The annually supplemented *Desk-Book to the United States Supreme Court Reports, Lawyers Edition, Second Series* contains tables of cases, laws, and regulations cited in L. Ed. 2d, information about Supreme Court justices since 1789, and an index to L. Ed. 2d annotations. *Supreme Court Reporter* (West Edition), part of the West Publishing Company's National Reporter System, is also searchable online. *Supreme Court Reporter* begins with volume 106 of the official set (1882) and omits cases reported in volumes 1–105.

The U.S. Air Force has released its 60-year file of Supreme Court opinions, called FLITE (Federal Legal Information Through Electronics), through both GPO Access <http://www.access.gpo.gov/su_docs/supcrt/index.html> and FEDWORLD <http://www.fedworld.gov/> (not well liked). Since the Air Force began FLITE as an experimental electronic database in 1963, its contents covering 1937 through 1975 were inaccessible to the public—until now.

Two weekly loose-leaf services are especially useful for tracing actions during the current Supreme Court term. Commerce Clearing House's weekly *U.S. Supreme Court Bulletin* reproduces the full text of the Court's opinions, with information on docketed cases and the Court's disposition of them. Its loose-leaf format allows fast reporting, an advantage shared by the daily legal reporting service, the Supreme Court section of *United States Law Week. U.S. Law Week* (USLW) which includes full texts of Supreme Court decisions along with status reports on developing cases—from docketing through denial or formal review. For tracing the disposition of a recent Supreme Court case using USLW, novices may find Maier's how-to discussion helpful.[5]

Legal digests are subject indexes to court decisions. *United States Supreme Court Digest* (West) and *United States Supreme Court Reports/Digest: General Index to Decisions, Annotations, and Digest* (Lawyers Co-operative) are complete indexes to Supreme Court decisions. The *Federal Practice Digest* covers the entire federal court system.

Legal Citations

To locate the text of a cited decision, consult the volume and page of the reporter abbreviated in the cite. The most respected guide to legal citing is the Harvard Law Review Association's *A Uniform System of Citation*, popularly known as "the Bluebook" because of its blue cover. The "preferred" citation for Supreme Court decisions is to *United States Reports*, the official reporter. Here is an example:

Roe v. Wade, 410 U.S. 113 (1973)

The case name is derived from the last names of the parties involved. The first name cited is the plaintiff; the second is the defendant. The "v." is an abbreviation for "versus."

Citation to volume 410, page 113 of *United States Reports* is where the text begins. The case was decided in 1973.

Cases are sometimes referred to only by the names of plaintiff and defendant. One way to locate the decision when you have a reference to the parties is to consult the alphabetical tables of cases in legal digests to locate citations to the case. The *United States Supreme Court Reports/Digest*, USC, *United States Code Annotated*, *United States Code Service*, and *Shepard's Acts and Cases by Popular Names: Federal and State* allow cross-referencing from a popular case name (the "Pentagon Papers" case, for example) to case citations (*New York Times Company v. United States*).

Parallel citations locate the same material in unofficial reporters. The unofficial reporters have cross-ref-

erence tables referring from official to unofficial citations. The Bluebook recommends West's *Supreme Court Reporter* as the "preferred unofficial" citation to use when the official publication is unavailable. The two unofficial reporters have their own numbering systems, but also give the *United States Reports* citation. West's copyrighted pagination system known as "star-pagination," also used by LEXIS under a licensing agreement, has been likened to "an atlas for the collective text of American law."[6] The American Bar Association has recommended a new universal, vendor-neutral citation system friendly to both electronic and print resources <http://www.abanet.org/ftp/pub/citation/home.html>.

Annotated Codes

Annotated codes are supplemented with citations and case notes for court and administrative agency decisions, with cross-references to the *Code of Federal Regulations*, and historical notes on the development of the law. Two unofficial annotated editions of federal statutes are the *United States Code Service* (USCS) and *United States Code Annotated* (USCA).

LOWER COURTS

Below the Supreme Court stand the United States courts of appeals, the intermediate appellate courts that review district court decisions. These federal appellate courts (circuit courts) render judgments affirming or reversing those of the lower district courts, and their decisions are final unless reviewed by the Supreme Court. The federal appeals courts are busy: over the last 30 years, the number of appeals has grown 16 times faster than the population. Since only about one percent of appealed cases rate Supreme Court review, the federal courts of appeals are the end of the judicial road for most Americans. As one federal appeals court judge explained: "Yes, the Supreme Court is above us, but in practice we are nearly always the final court of review."[7]

The United States is divided into 12 judicial circuits, each with a court of appeals that serves several states. (For a map with links, see <http://www.law.emory.edu/FEDCTS/>.) There is also a United States Court of Appeals for the Federal Circuit, with national jurisdiction. This court was created by merging the former U.S. Court of Claims with the U.S. Court of Customs and Patent Appeals. The resultant Court of Appeals for the Federal Circuit hears appeals from all district courts in patent and "Little Tucker Act" cases (claims against the United States) plus all appeals from the U.S. Claims Court, the U.S. Court of International Trade, the Boards of Contract Appeals, the Patent and Trademark Office, the Merit Systems Protection Board, and the International Trade Commission. There are also special national courts that handle specific types of cases. The U.S. Court of International Trade (formerly the U.S. Customs Court) deals with cases involving international trade and customs duties. The U.S. Claims Court, known as "the keeper of the nation's conscience," hears suits against the federal government for money damages. The U.S. Tax Court is a special court in the legislative branch which settles disputes between taxpayers and the Internal Revenue Service. The government publishes decisions of many special courts.

At the lowest rung of the federal court hierarchy are the United States district courts, the trial courts of the federal government, where cases are initially decided. Each state has at least one district court, with larger states having as many as four. (See figure 11.2.) Links to state court Web sites are given on the National Center for State Courts Web site <http://www.ncsc.dni.us/court/sites/courts.htm#state>.

Lower Court Reporters and Citators

A consortium of law schools, generally one from each circuit, provides free access to appellate slip opinions through each school's Internet Web site. Circuits were approached individually by the law schools about participating. The member law schools have complete responsibility for retrieving the opinions and uploading them to the Internet. The result is a wealth of material, but no uniformity in arrangement, appearance, search engines, indexing, or downloading procedures across the sites.[8] Each circuit court maintains its own Web site (Links are given in the Emory Law Library Federal Courts Finder <http://www.law.emory.edu/FEDCTS/>.) Internet resources are weak on historical material, however, with federal circuit court cases retrospective only to around 1992. Most state cases on the Web also lack a historical archive. Public access terminals located in the Clerk of the Court's office in appellate, district, and bankruptcy courts allow the public to quickly and easily access case and docketing information. The U.S. Federal Judiciary Web site's Directory of Electronic Public Access Services provides information on automated access to U.S. federal court information and records <http://www.uscourts.gov/>.

Although no official reporter exists for the U.S. courts of appeals or U.S. district courts, some are unofficially reported by West Publishing Company. West's National Reporter System's *Federal Reporter* 2d, documenting opinions from U.S. courts of appeals and some district courts, is available in print and online through WESTLAW. West's *Federal Supplement*, reporting opinions of the U.S. district courts, is also available in print or online. Both sets are issued first as advance sheets that are later bound. Jacobstein, Mersky, and Dunn emphasize that the *Federal Supplement* contains

only a small percentage of district court decisions and that others are published in special-subject loose-leaf services or available online.[9] The weekly *West's Federal Case News* summarizes Supreme Court and other federal decisions, plus selected cases from state courts. The *National Reporter Blue Book* refers from official citations to unofficial *National Reporter* citations.

Case citators document changes in the legal effect of court cases, identifying any subsequent legal action that may have reversed or overruled an earlier decision. Tracking the history of opinions is sometimes called "Shepardizing" a case, since *Shepard's Citations* is a popular citator. Citators are useful for determining the disposition of an appealed case, identifying interim opinions for the same case, locating parallel citations, tracing subsequent opinions, verifying the current status of an opinion, and obtaining subsequent cases, law review articles, or annotations citing the case. Novices to citators will find Shepard's Web tutorial a must <http://www.shepards.com/ccentral/tutorial/intro.htm>.

THE CONSTITUTION

Y 1.1/2:SERIAL 14152

http://www.access.gpo.gov/congress/senate/constitution

http://www.access.gpo.gov/su_docs/dbsearch.html

> *The Declaration of 1776 gave us our independence, but the Constitution of 1787 gave us our government.* —Frank G. Burke, former Archivist of the United States

Although not as familiar as Independence Day, September 17, 1787, is a milestone in our national history. On that day more than two centuries ago, 39 delegates from 12 states signed a document that began, "We the people of the United States"—the United States Constitution, the oldest written constitution on earth. With fully two-thirds of the world's constitutions adopted after 1970, only 15 other nations have constitutions penned before World War II.

The United States Constitution is the cornerstone of U.S. democracy. America claimed freedom on July 4, 1776, with the Declaration of Independence, but 11 years later the Constitution secured that freedom. That same year, Alexander Hamilton, James Madison, and John Jay issued the first of the Federalist Papers under a pseudonym. The Federalist Papers argued for the states' ratification of the proposed Constitution and are today considered among the most cogent constitutional explanations ever written. GPO Access is mounting a digital collection of the Core Documents of U.S. Democracy, including the Constitution, at <http://www.access.gpo.gov/su_docs/dpos/coredocs.html>.

FIGURE 11.2: U.S. Court System.

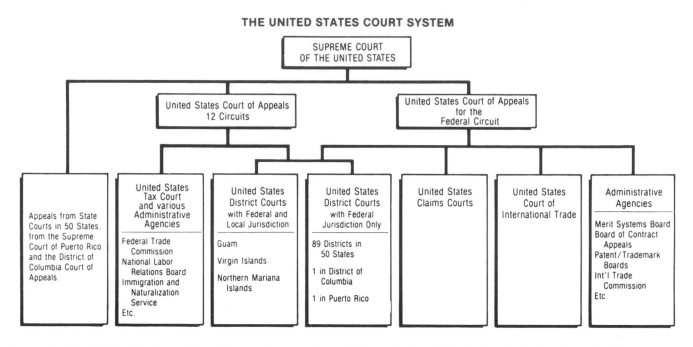

THE UNITED STATES COURT SYSTEM

Source: *The United States Courts: Their Jurisdiction and Work*, Administrative Office of the United States Courts, 1989 (Ju 10.2:C 83).

Annotated Constitution

Annotated constitutional texts provide judicial decisions that have interpreted or applied the Constitution, along with scholarly analysis. Examples are West's *United States Code Annotated: Constitution of the United States Annotated* and the Lawyers Co-operative Publishing Company's *United States Code Service: Constitution Volume.* The government-published *Constitution of the United States of America: Analysis and Interpretation: Annotations of Cases Decided by the Supreme Court of the United States to June 29, 1992* augments the charter with commentary, historical background, annotations to historic Supreme Court cases and decisions overruling previous decisions, and legal analysis (Y 1.1/2:SERIAL 14152). Often referred to as the "Annotated Constitution" or "Constitution Annotated," it also lists federal, state, and local laws deemed unconstitutional, and amendments with ratification dates. Hailed as "an indispensable constitutional law and history reference," its format is an article-by-article, amendment-by-amendment walk through the Constitution, with historical and legal commentary.[10] The *Constitution Annotated* is prepared by the Congressional Research Service, published as a Senate document, and revised each decade, with cumulative supplements every two years. (Cohen, Berring, and Olson point to this infrequent supplementation as the major weakness of this otherwise superb source.[11]) The 1996 edition, with annotations of Supreme Court cases through June 1992, is available on GPO Access at <http://www.access.gpo.gov/congress/ senate/constitution/>. The Web version of the hulking 2,468-page, nine-pound volume is searchable and browsable in both plain-text and Adobe Acrobat (.pdf) formats. The article/amendment arrangement spawns some very large files (over 1 megabyte in some cases).

STATE COURTS

The independent state courts in the 50 states are those with which citizens most often have contact. Located in towns and cities across the nation, the state courts are empowered to decide almost any type of case, subject only to limitations of state law. The blue pages in the Bluebook (*A Uniform System of Citation*) provide a directory of state courts. Many states publish slip opinions and advance sheets, often unofficially. The National Reporter System is one example, publishing state appellate court opinions according to a geographic breakdown of regional and state reporters.

FREEBIES

The following Subject Bibliography is free from: Stop: SSOP, Washington, DC 20402; U.S. Fax Watch: (202) 512-1716:

25. United States Reports <http://www.access.gpo. gov/su_docs/sale/sb-025.html>

From Public Information Office, U.S. Supreme Court of the United States, 1 First St., N.E., Washington, DC 20543; (202) 479-3211:

Supreme Court Slip Opinions: A few free copies of Supreme Court opinions are available immediately after their announcement

FURTHER READING

Administrative Office of the Federal Courts. *Understanding the Federal Courts*. 2nd ed. Washington, DC: The Office, 1996. JU 10.2:C 83/3/996 and <http://www.uscourts.gov/understanding_courts/899_toc.htm> (February 10, 1998).
> This detailed overview of the federal court system includes names of justices and a glossary.

Baum, Lawrence. *The Supreme Court*. 5th ed. Washington, DC: CQ Press, 1994.
> A thorough introduction.

Berring, Robert C. *Finding the Law*. St. Paul, MN: West Publishing Co., 1995.
> A standard legal textbook that thoroughly reviews legal literature from all levels of government.

Biskupic, Joan and Elder Witt. *Guide to the U.S. Supreme Court*. 3rd ed. Washington, DC: Congressional Quarterly, 1996.
> This reference guide to the Court's history, operation, and major decisions, with biographies of the justices, incorporates events through the July 1996 term.

Chicco, Guiliano J. "Surfing the Internet for High Court Cases." *New York Law Journal* 217 (March 17, 1997): S4, S6–S7.
> A profile of dozens of Internet and e-mail sources.

Christianson, Stephen G. and Lisa Paddock. *Great American Trials*. Detroit, MI: Visible Ink Press, 1994.
> Summaries of celebrated and significant trials spanning from the 1600s (Anne Hutchinson trials) to the Rodney King beating trial in 1993.

Congressional Quarterly. *Congressional Quarterly's Guide to the U.S. Supreme Court*. 2nd ed. Washington, DC: Congressional Quarterly, Inc., 1990.
> A key reference covering the history, procedures, and landmark decisions, with biographies of justices.

Epstein, Lee, et al. *The Supreme Court Compendium: Data, Decisions, and Developments*. 2nd ed. Washington, DC: Congressional Quarterly, 1996.
> The Court's history, justices' backgrounds, nominations, confirmations, and the Court's relationship with the public and government.

Geel, T. R. van. *Understanding Supreme Court Opinions*. 2nd ed. New York: Longman, 1997.
> A guide to reading and interpreting Supreme Court opinions.

Harrell, Mary Ann and Burnett Anderson. *Equal Justice under Law: The Supreme Court in American Life*. 6th ed. Washington, DC: The Supreme Court Historical Society, 1994.
> A simple introduction to the Supreme Court and its impact on American life.

Jost, Kenneth. *The Supreme Court Yearbook*. Washington, DC: Congressional Quarterly, 1990–. Annual.
> A review of the Court's most recent term, including summaries of every case.

Library of Congress. Global Legal Information Network. Guide to Law Online. <http://lcweb2.loc.gov/glin/worldlaw.html> (January 20, 1998).
> Hot links to world law resources.

Paddock, Lisa. *Facts about the Supreme Court of the United States*. New York: H. W. Wilson, 1996.
> A history that covers each Supreme Court from the 1790 Jay Court to the current Rehnquist Court, with important events, biographies of justices, and details of the key cases.

A Uniform System of Citation. 16th ed. Cambridge, MA: Harvard Law Review Association, 1996.
> The key reference for legal citation format, also called "The Bluebook."

Wolf, Gary. "Who Owns the Law?" *Wired* (May 1994): 98, 100–01, 138–39.
> While the text of decisions are in the public domain, West Publishing Company has the copyright to their citation style.

NOTES

1. Daniel Meador, *Consumers of Justice: How the Public Views the Federal Judicial Process* (Washington, DC: Federal Judicial Center, [1975]), p. 5.

2. Michael R. Lavin, *Business Information: How to Find It, How to Use It* (Phoenix, AZ: Oryx Press, 1987), p. 229.

3. Robert M. Warner, "The Law and American Society," *Prologue* 16 (Winter 1984): 212–13. (AE 1.111:16/4).

4. J. Myron Jacobstein, Roy M. Mersky, and Donald J. Dunn, *Fundamentals of Legal Research*, 6th ed. (Westbury, NY: Foundation Press, 1994), p. 44.

5. Elaine C. Maier, *How to Prepare a Legal Citation* (Woodbury, NY: Barron's Educational Series, Inc., 1986), pp. 38–40.

6. Thomas Scheffey. "A See-No-Evil Merger Probe?" *The Connecticut Law Tribune* 23 (February 24, 1997): p. 1.

7. Mary Ann Harrell, *Equal Justice under Law: The Supreme Court in American Life*, 4th ed. (Washington, DC: The Supreme Court Historical Society, 1982), p. 152.

8. Deborah M. Keene and William Morse. "Web Progresses as Source Of Primary Legal Material." *The National Law Journal* 18 (July 22, 1996): B10–11.

9. Jacobstein, Mersky, and Dunn, p. 51.

10. The Scout Report 1/17/97 <http://wwwscout.cs.wisc.edu/scout/report/> (July 20, 1997).

11. Morris L. Cohen, Robert C. Berring, and Kent C. Olson. *How to Find the Law*, 9th ed. (St. Paul, MN: West, 1989), p. 204.

EXERCISES

1. On June 26, 1997, in *Reno, Attorney General of the United States, et al. v. American Civil Liberties Union et al.*, the Supreme Court struck down provisions in the Communications Decency Act of 1996 that sought to protect minors from harmful material on the Internet. Locate this decision.

2. Ex-President Richard M. Nixon sued the government after Congress seized his presidential papers and tapes in 1974, charging that the confiscation was unconstitutional. In 1977, the Supreme Court upheld a lower-court decision denying Nixon's right to control his papers, overthrowing the 200-year precedent of presidential ownership and setting the stage for the Presidential Records Act of 1978. Identify this Supreme Court decision.

3. An article discussing the judicial opinion that "There simply is no first amendment right to receive a verbatim transcript of the proceedings of Congress" cites the following court case: *Gregg v. Barrett*, 771 F.2d 539 (D.C. Cir 1985). What court and source are being cited?

4. Which of the following are citations to Supreme Court decisions?
   798 F.2d.731
   116 S. Ct. 1091
   454 U.S. 812
   468 F.Supp. 927
   134 L.Ed.2d 167

CHAPTER 12
Statistics

In Washington the production of numbers is second only to the production of words.
—Peter Carlson, *Washington Post Magazine*

WHAT

Statistics are both an American tradition and a national resource. One of the federal government's major functions is collecting and analyzing data to satisfy legal requirements and emerging national needs. The United States, cranking out more statistics than any other entity in the world, has long been looked to as a source of reliable, consistent, and comparable data about national demographic, social, and economic trends. It is a task so complex that only the federal government has the facilities and funds to accomplish it.

WHERE

Federal statistical activity is decentralized, with more than 70 agencies authorized to collect and disseminate statistics. Three agencies supply the most used data in the nation: the Bureaus of the Census, of Economic Analysis, and of Labor Statistics. The remainder of federal statistical activity is scattered among other agencies whose statistical work supports their administrative, regulatory, or operating functions. Federal statistical activity is coordinated by the Office of Management and Budget (OMB).

WHY

Agencies collect statistics to support their missions and to satisfy legislative mandates requiring data collection. Eleven agencies have solely statistical missions, while others operate statistical programs in support of broader missions. Between one-half and three-quarters of the federal budget is allocated based on statistics and statistical formulas. The three primary uses of census data are redistricting within states and reapportionment of the House of Representatives, allocation of federal funds, and economic decision making in the public and private sectors.

HOW

Federal statistics are collected by federal agencies and relayed from state and local governments and private sources: vital statistics, for example, are compiled nationally based on state and local reporting.

The nation's statistical structure has long engendered concern about cost, coordination, comparability, and quality. Cost cutting, staff reductions, and sensitivity to respondent burdens are delicately balanced to maintain the quality, quantity, and utility of federal statistics.

WHEN

Federal data collection was launched with the constitutionally mandated decennial census and has been a national enterprise since the earliest days of our republic.

FINDING AIDS

FedStats

http://www.fedstats.gov

FedStats is a "one-stop shopping" terminus for federal agency statistics, linking to data from more than 70 agencies. Its search engine allows pursuing statistics without knowing which agency produces them. Information can be identified by using an A to Z index with 275 categories, by keyword searching that probes agency Web sites, by a "fast facts" linkage to frequently requested *Statistical Abstract* tables, and by direct links to agency contacts, news releases, and navigational/organizational aids. FedStats was developed as a multi-agency effort led by the Federal Interagency Council on Statistical Policy.

Unfortunately, a single index to all federal statistics does not exist. Individual agencies often publish guides to their own data, identifiable by searching their Web pages, the *Monthly Catalog*, or *American Statistics Index*. The Census Bureau Web site offers a User Manual with an alphabetical list of subjects <http://www.census.gov/main/www/man_main.html>. Andriot's *Guide to U.S. Government Statistics* lists key government statistical publications, with annotation, frequency, beginning and ending dates, depository item number, and SuDocs, OCLC, LC, LC card, ISSN, and Dewey numbers. It includes indexes by agency, title, area, and subject. To link to Internet sites, use the GPO Access "Browse Topics" and select "Statistics" <http://www.access.gpo.gov/su_docs/dpos/pathbrws.html>.

American Statistics Index (ASI)

American Statistics Index is a master guide to federally generated statistics. The ASI editorial staff scan every type of federal publication except highly scientific or technical ones: "If it contains statistics, it is indexed and described in ASI." Included are any federal publications that are wholly or partially statistical, with social, economic, demographic, or natural resources data, plus selected scientific and technical data. Coverage is comprehensive for the Census Bureau and Bureau of Labor Statistics, the National Center for Health Statistics, the National Center for Education Statistics, Energy Information Administration, and the Crop Reporting Board; and selective for other agencies. Coverage is retrospective to 1973, with indexing for key earlier publications dating back to the 1960s.

ASI covers tables of data, and also maps, charts, listings, and text that help locate statistics or clarify agency statistical activities. This coverage provides access to discussions of methodology, classification guides, directories, and bibliographies that include significant references to statistical materials. Print and Internet products are indexed in ASI by title, subject, issuing agency, name, and report number; and by geographic, economic, or demographic categories (a helpful timesaver). Index entries cite ASI accession numbers used to locate the full entry in the abstracts section, where the source document and individual tables are fully described. The ASI accession numbers that identify entries are useful only within ASI and should not be given as part of general bibliographic citations except to provide access to ASI microfiche. ASI provides SuDocs numbers, notes depository status, and includes prices and ordering information. Most titles can be purchased from Congressional Information Service (CIS) on microfiche, and many may also be used in depository libraries or purchased from the government. ASI is accessible online, on CD-ROM (Statistical Masterfile), or by using the print index.

Tip

Because agency annual reports usually recap agency activities using statistics, they are likely to be indexed and abstracted in ASI.

Statistical Reference Index (SRI)

Statistical Reference Index is a companion to ASI, focusing on U.S. statistics from nonfederal private and public organizations. It indexes and abstracts business, financial, and social statistical data from U.S. associations and institutes, businesses, commercial publishers, independent research centers, state governments, and universities. The publications indexed provide national, state, local, and foreign data. SRI indexes, abstracts, and sells microfiche copies of most of the documents listed and can be searched by subjects, names, categories, issuing sources, and titles. Coverage began in late 1979. *Statistical Reference Index* may be searched in print, online, or on CD-ROM (Statistical Masterfile).

Statistical Finding Aids

FedStats <http://www.fedstats.gov>
Census Bureau Web site, User Manual <http://www.census.gov/main/www/man_main.html>
STAT-USA/Internet <http://www.stat-usa.gov> (free in depository libraries)
American Statistics Index
Statistical Reference Index
Index to International Statistics
Sears and Moody, *Using Government Information Sources* 2nd ed., The Statistical Search, Chapters 29–44
Census Catalog and Guide
1990 Census of Population and Housing Guide (C 3.223/22:1990 CPH-R 1)

STATISTICAL STANDARDS

Because standard definitions and classifications increase statistical comparability and usefulness, several standards are used throughout government and in private and nonprofit organizations. In 1997, the Standard Industrial Classification (SIC) code for economic and industrial data was replaced by the North American Industry Classification System (NAICS—rhymes with "snakes"). The standard since the mid-1930s, the SIC that once described industries like trading-stamp redemption centers had difficulty wrapping itself around fin-de-siecle enterprises such as computer software, pet supply stores, and telemarketing. It had been revised numerous times, most recently in 1987. By more finely segmenting the economy and acknowledging new industries, NAICS promises a truer snapshot of today's economy. Unlike the SIC, for example, NAICS will unfurl the code for Eating Places (SIC 5812) by distinguishing between restaurants, hamburger stands, caterers, and tea rooms.

The new system also insures compatibility between the North American Free Trade Agreement partners—the United States, Canada, and Mexico—by replacing their separate systems for classifying industries with one uniform system. The NAICS code will employ six digits, in contrast to the four-digit SIC. Five digits will be shared across the three nations; the sixth will identify industries in individual countries. Thus, the five-digit level will be standardized internationally, but any six-digit code can be unique. Full implementation will take at least three years and will begin in the United States with the 1997 Economic Censuses. Like the SIC, NAICS will be used not only by government but also by business, trade, and professional organizations. A NAICS manual will be available to depository libraries under the SIC Manual item number and SuDocs stem (PREX 2.6/2:). The obsolete *Standard Industrial Classification Manual* (PREX 2.6/2:IN 27/987) can be searched by keyword or 4-digit SIC on the Internet <http://www.osha.gov/oshstats/sicser.html>.

The *Standard Occupational Classification Manual* provides a common language for categorizing occupations in social and economic programs (C 1.8/3:Oc 1/980). A new occupational classification system is under development for the next edition. The new SOC system will include all jobs in the national economy, including occupations in the public, private, and military sectors <http://stats.bls.gov/soc/soc_home.htm>. Similarly, SOC's companion source describing occupations, the *Dictionary of Occupational Titles* (L 37.2:Oc 1/2/991/v.1-2.) is being replaced by the Occupational Information Network, O*NET, a comprehensive system for data on job characteristics and worker attributes <http://www.doleta.gov/programs/onet/>.

Major Federal Statistical Agencies

Bureau of the Census: the central federal statistical agency and the nation's chief collector of economic and demographic data <http://www.census.gov/>

Bureau of Economic Analysis (Commerce Department): "the Nation's accountant" portrays the U.S. economy through data on economic growth, regional development, and America's stature in the world economy <http://www.bea.doc.gov/beahome.html>

Bureau of Justice Statistics: crime and criminal justice data <http://www.ojp.usdoj.gov/bjs/>

Bureau of Labor Statistics: the government's chief source of information on labor-related aspects of the economy, including employment and unemployment, prices, living standards, wages and benefits, industrial relations, and productivity <http://www.bls.gov/>

Bureau of Transporation Statistics: analysis of the use, performance, and consequences of the national transportation system <http://www.bts.gov/>

Economic Research Service (ERS): develops economic and statistical indicators for agriculture, food and consumer economics, natural resources and environment, rural economy, and energy <http://www.econ.ag.gov/>

Energy Information Administration: energy data and analysis to support energy decisions of government, industry, and the public <http://www.eia.doe.gov>

National Agricultural Statistics Service: national and state agricultural statistics, estimates, and forecasts <http://www.usda.gov/nass/#NASS>

National Center for Education Statistics: statistics about preschool through postsecondary education <http://www.ed.gov/NCES>

National Center for Health Statistics: health, population, health care, family changes, vital statistics <http://www.cdc.gov/nchswww/nchshome.htm>

IRS Statistics of Income Division, Internal Revenue Service: financial and tax data <http://www.irs.ustreas.gov/tax_stats/index.html>

CENSUSES

A census can count anything, from people and homes in the Census of Population and Housing to businesses, farms, governments, or even wild horses and burros (a census conducted by the Bureau of Land Management). Counting people is one of government's oldest activities. Evidence of Babylonian censuses have been dated as early as 3800 B.C., and in ancient China, food-conscious bureaucrats counted mouths instead of noses. Nine hundred years ago, a census resulted in the famous Domesday Book, when William the Conqueror counted the English under his rule.

Computerization has both streamlined modern censuses and unnerved respondents, making anti-census campaigns a sign of the times. In West Germany a census was finally taken in 1987, after a 17-year stalemate. West Germans had balked at the length and complexity of the questionnaire and feared leaks to government data banks. Opponents pressured for a census boycott under the slogan, "Only sheep let themselves be counted." Fear of "big brother" also struck in Holland, where a national census has been stalled on the drawing board since 1981. Since Holland's last census in 1971, the government has resorted to monitoring population growth through municipal residence records. In the United States, initial response to the 1990 census was sluggish, reflecting the public's changing attitudes, reluctance to tackle complicated questionnaires, and fear of "big brother." A "reformed" U.S. census is expected for 2000, using a combination of mailed questionnaires and follow-up statistical sampling to reap a more accurate population count than that obtained by the 1990 Census.

The Decennial Census

Since 1790, the nation has snapped a statistical family portrait every 10 years. Soon after the 13 colonies separated from England, a national head count was taken—not only to establish the House of Representatives, but also to divvy up the Revolutionary War debt among taxpayers. With a constitutional mandate to reapportion House of Representative's seats based on shifting population, the United States became the first nation to incorporate regular censuses into its Constitution. The decennial census of population and housing, which counts the entire population, is the cornerstone of our statistical system. This census, the nation's most comprehensive and costly data-gathering vehicle, is used not only in reapportioning the House of Representatives, but also in redistricting state and local legislatures, allocating government funding, completing site selections and market research, and supporting various other decisions made by bureaucrats and citizens.

> **How Ya Gonna Keep 'em Down on the Farm?**
> For the only time in history, Congress refused to reapportion the House of Representatives following the 1920 census. The 1920 count was the first to show city dwellers outnumbering those on farms, but Congress balked at launching a reapportionment that would have stripped 10 rural states of 11 congressional seats while bolstering urbanized states.[1]

The decennial census counts heads and gathers housing facts, providing a snapshot of social, demographic, and economic characteristics, with data on age, sex, race, household relationships, and home ownership. The census describes the nation as a whole, and its component regions, states, and metropolitan areas. Unlike other data-collection programs, the decennial census also provides statistics for small parcels like counties, congressional districts, cities, towns, and even neighborhood blocks. By including historical time series, each decennial census also allows comparison with previous censuses.

Unfortunately, decennial sample data are outdated by the time they are published some two years following the census, and their usefulness fades steadily throughout the decade. An ongoing American Community Survey (ACS) is poised to remedy this decade-long data decline. A monthly household survey, the American Community Survey will generate more accurate, annual (rather than decennial) demographic profiles. Annual ACS collection of social, economic, and housing data formerly on the long form will eventually allow the focus of the decennial census to return to the rudimentary head count mandated by the Constitution <http://www.census.gov/CMS/www/index_a.htm>.

> **Government Information in Action**
> In the time it takes to read this, eight more Americans will have been born. (Based on the Census Web site's POPClock.)

Selecting Census Questions

When attendees at a census conference were urged to describe their census-data questions, one asked how many Americans owned horses. The expectation that the census would probe into horse ownership highlights an important concept: although it may seem that the census asks every possible question, the questionnaire is actually painstakingly selective. Public input is solicited to select new questions and delete obsolete ones, mirroring the nation's shifting interests and data needs. Americans are no longer asked, for example, whether they own television sets: virtually every home now boasts at least one. Questions on appliance ownership, kitchen sinks, electric lights, and refrigerators were abandoned for similar reasons. Exploring "modern" trends, the 1990 census added questions about "blended families," asking about stepchildren, foster children, and grandchildren, and added solar heating to the list of home heating fuels. Some questions of limited use are never asked—horse ownership, for example. Others are reworded to reflect changing attitudes: the "head of household" concept, meaning the husband in a husband/wife household, was replaced in 1980 with the more neutral "person in column one."

As Ann Scott notes in *Census USA,* "choosing and wording of questions may well be the most fascinating part of census planning."[2] The impossibility of including every question useful to someone, somewhere, means careful choices must be made. "Over the years the Bureau has turned down appeals for statistics on dogs, cats, and parakeets, smoking, auto accidents, union membership, child spacing, boat ownership, and hundreds of other subjects of vital interest to some group or other."[3]

Question Suggestions Rejected by the Census Bureau[4]

Ask everyone's height and weight so you can determine the national obesity rate

How many people suffer from hay fever?

Do you take vitamins daily?

How many cigarettes do you smoke?

Have you ever had a paranormal or psychic experience?

Do you dream in color?

The left hand says "Cut," and the right hand says "Add more questions."
                                        —Philip L. Sparks, Census Bureau

Although the first census in 1790 asked only five questions, the head-count blueprint had already been beefed up by laws mandating a tally of free white men under or over 16, free white women, free blacks, and slaves. (See figure 12.1.) James Madison wanted occupational information gathered as well, but Congress balked. The 1790 census enumerated 3,929,214 Americans, but left

FIGURE 12.1: The First Census.

The Return for SOUTH CAROLINA having been made fince the foregoing Schedule was originally printed, the whole Enumeration is here given complete, except for the N. Weftern Territory, of which no Return has yet been publifhed.

DISTICTS	Free white Males of 16 years and upwards, including heads of families.	Free white Males under fixteen years.	Free white Females, including heads of families.	All other free perfons.	Slaves.	Total.
Vermont	22435	22328	40505	255	16	85539
N. Hampfhire	36086	34851	70160	630	158	141885
Maine	24384	24748	46870	538	NONE	96540
Maffachufetts	95453	87289	190582	5463	NONE	378787
Rhode Ifland	16019	15799	32652	3407	948	68825
Connecticut	60523	54403	117448	2808	2764	237946
New York	83700	78122	152320	4654	21324	340120
New Jerfey	45251	41416	83287	2762	11423	184139
Pennfylvania	110788	106948	206363	6537	3737	434373
Delaware	11783	12143	22384	3899	8887	59094
Maryland	55915	51339	101395	8043	103036	319728
Virginia	110936	116135	215046	12866	292627	747610
Kentucky	15154	17057	28922	114	12430	73677
N. Carolina	69988	77506	140710	4975	100572	393751
S. Carolina	35576	37722	66880	1801	107094	249073
Georgia	13103	14044	25739	398	29264	82548
	807094	791850	1541263	59150	694280	3893635
Total number of Inhabitants of the United States exclufive of S. Weftern and N. Territory.	Free white Males of 21 years and upwards.	Free Males under 21 years of age.	Free white Females.	All other Perfons.	Slaves.	Total
S. W. territory N. Ditto	6271	10277	15365	361	3417	35691

This page from the printed report of the 1790 census shows the five categories of information gathered in the first census.

Indians uncounted and recorded every five slaves as only three people. By the time the 10th census rolled around in 1880, questions had been added about the ages of white women, health, literacy, and employment. By 1890, the scope had expanded from five subjects to 235. To review questions from the first 20 population and housing censuses, consult *200 Years of U.S. Census Taking: Population and Housing Questions, 1790–1990* (C 3.2:T 93).

Many census questions are asked because they've been mandated by law or because of legal data requirements unattainable without the vast decennial census machinery. A mere handful of mandated items include age, sex, race, Hispanic origin, marital status, place of birth, education, and the newly legislated "grandparents as caregivers."[5] Most of the long-form sample questions are legally mandated. The long form was spawned in 1940 for Congress to assess the Depression's impact on employment, housing, and income. Over the years it "metastasized into something resembling a gigantic tabloid reporter."[6] It will probably be retired after Census 2000, displaced by the American Community Survey.

"There Ought to Be a Machine"

By 1890, census staff were overwhelmed by mountains of data spilling onto their desks. Hunched over bookkeeping and accounting ledgers, they tallied by hand on ruled sheets, stroke by stroke, like this: ⳞⳞⳀ. It was Dr. John Shaw Billings, head of Census Bureau Vital Statistics, who dreamed of mechanically counting the census and staged a contest to encourage inventors. The winner was young Herman Hollerith, a census office engineer whose tabulation machine would rescue the Bureau from the manual drudgery that had dogged the previous nine decades.

The Bureau leased 56 of Hollerith's machines, hoisted them outside the building to the third floor, and connected them by wires to primitive batteries in the basement. Census clerks, "nice-looking girls in cool white dresses," worked at long rows of counting machines that resembled pianos. (See figure 12.2.) It was a muggy July 1890, and while electric fans hummed, bells on the "statistical pianos" rang with every touch of the keys. For the first time in history, electricity was being used to count a population.[7]

FIGURE 12.2: The Census Machine.

Herman Hollerith's census tabulating machine saved the Census Bureau $5 million in two years, and created new jobs for women after men were found to be inferior at using Hollerith's machines (1904).

Profile: Herman Hollerith (1860–1929)

By the late 1880s, census enumeration had barely evolved from the ancient Babylonian tallies chipped onto clay tablets. The 1880 census was scarcely calculated before the 1890 census rolled around. Primitive counting methods, using pencil strokes on paper, inspired one observer to marvel that census clerks didn't go blind or crazy.

A contest was staged to find a "census machine" for computing the 1890 census. Herman Hollerith's entry, an electric, punched-card system, was pitted against the color-coded papers and hand-counted cards concocted by his two rival contestants. Hollerith's machine finished in 72 hours, beating his first and second runners-up by 39 and 72 hours.

A contemporary newspaper reporter predicted that since Hollerith's patents would only be useful to governments, Hollerith would "not likely get very rich." Nevertheless, Hollerith's Tabulating Machine Company netted $1,210,500 when he sold it in 1911 to the company that later became IBM.

Confidentiality

The Census Bureau is unique among federal agencies, enjoying specific legal protection of information gar-

nered from respondents, households, or firms, to ensure the data's use solely for statistical analysis. The classic challenge to Census Bureau confidentiality arose during World War II, when the War Department requested names and addresses to expedite the internment of Japanese Americans. The Census Bureau refused, turning over only publically available aggregate statistics describing the ethnic composition of neighborhoods. Similar refusals were issued when immigration authorities wanted addresses of people sought for deportation, and when the Labor Department requested names and addresses for a survey of all working women in Rochester, New York.

Only after enjoying a 72-year blackout are census records opened to scholars and researchers. When population schedules were first transferred from the Census Bureau to the National Archives in 1952, it was with the proviso that they stay closed for 72 years, the average American's life span in 1952.[8] When the National Archives unlocks the 1930 census records on April 1, 2002, a line of eager researchers will probably be waiting. The census schedules are the National Archives' most heavily used record group, shedding light on westward expansion, local history, immigration, and genealogy, plus providing proof of citizenship. The free National Archives General Information Leaflets, No. 5 "Using Records in the National Archives for Genealogical Research," and No. 7 "Military Service Records in the National Archives of the U.S." along with the *Guide to Genealogical Research in the National Archives* (nondepository, 1985) are recommended research aids. Don't overlook the National Archives' "Genealogy Page" <http://www.nara.gov/genealogy/genindex.html> and the more modest Census genealogy page <http://www.census.gov/genealogy/www/>.

The 1920 census records, unsealed in 1992, take up 3,400 miles of microfilm. The National Archives sells microfilmed census schedules from 1790 to 1920 and allows on-site searches of the files in Washington, DC, or at NARA's 13 regional archives.[9] Microfilmed copies of census schedules may be also be consulted at many libraries and genealogical societies, and through the National Archives Microfilm Rental Program (Box 30, Annapolis Junction, MD 20701-0030; [301] 604-3699). "Special List 24," a list of institutions owning copies of National Archives microfilmed census records, is free on microfilm from the National Archives. Four catalogs identify microfilm copies of the schedules: *Federal Population Censuses, 1790–1890* (GS 4.2:P 81/2/790–890), *1900 Federal Population Census* (GS 4.2:P 81/2/900), *The 1910 Federal Population Census* (GS 4.2:P 81/2/910), and *The 1920 Federal Population Census*. The inexpensive catalogs are available in libraries, on the Web <http://www.nara.gov/publications/microfilm/census/census.html>, and are for sale from the National Archives at (800) 234-8861 or <http://www.nara.gov/

publications/bookstore/microcat.html>. Census research often requires use of the Soundex system of phonetically coded indexes of surnames. An introduction is provided in National Archives General Information Leaflet No. 55, "Using the Soundex System" (AE 1.113:55), free from the National Archives.

Government Information in Action

In the closing chapters of *Roots*, Alex Haley described his quest to trace his family history. American and British Naval records helped Haley identify the ship which brought his ancestor, Kunta Kinte, to America in 1767. Poring through microfilmed census records from the 1800s, Haley found his great-aunt mentioned: "It was simply so uncanny sitting staring at those names actually right there in official U.S. Government records."

The 1990 Decennial Census

The founding fathers never said counting the population was going to be easy.
—Michael R. Darby,
Department of Commerce

The 200th anniversary of the decennial census was greeted halfheartedly by the 248,709,873 Americans it enumerated. As C-day approached, fully nine out of 10 realized the census was imminent, but after one month only about two-thirds had returned their questionnaires. Low response was attributed to "mailbox glut" from junk mail and surveys, the questionnaire's complexity, rising illiteracy, and changing attitudes. A *New York Times* poll of nonrespondents found half were too busy or "forgot" to answer census questions. Others called the census irrelevant or "none of the government's business." Despite assurances of confidentiality, nonrespondents and respondents alike worried that the Bureau would leak information to other agencies such as the IRS or Immigration and Naturalization Service.

Eventually, the 1990 census managed to tally 98.4 percent of the population, with concomitant expense, statistical weaknesses, and delays. Despite a heroic effort in the most costly census ever, more than 4 million people were missed (mostly Blacks and Hispanics living in big cities), making the 1990 enumeration the least accurate in history. Undercount lawsuits dragged the enumeration all the way to the Supreme Court.

The 1990 census morass illuminated the need for new ways to canvass the nation. Congress commissioned the National Academy of Sciences—National Research Council to explore cheaper, more accurate ways to take the decennial census.[10] Hindsight from 1990 foreshadowed the fruitlessness of trying to count everyone by mail and follow-up visits. (One-fifth of the 1990 census tab was spent on temporary enumerators trying to ferret out nonrespondents.) To make Census

2000 a "one number census," the panel prescribed simple, user-friendly forms and judicious sampling to fill in gaps.

Because the Census Accuracy Act requires that prospective questions be okayed by Congress three years before Census Day, the dust for Census 2000 started to fly in 1997. President Clinton vetoed emergency relief to the flood-ravaged Midwest partly because the bill harbored a prohibition against sampling in Census 2000. Public outcry induced Congress to rewrite the bill without a sampling ban, and Clinton signed the amended legislation.

Congress and the Census Bureau continued to butt heads over headcount-versus-sampling in Census 2000, however. Sampling, maintained the Census Bureau, would produce an accurate count and save up to $800 million. But many senators and representatives interpreted the requirement in Article I, section 2 of the Constitution for an "actual enumeration" as a headcount, and fought to maintain the two-century tradition.

User Aids

Lovers of cold, hard facts will find a fascinating vault of knowledge here at one of Uncle Sam's best Web offerings.   —Lycos, 1997

On the Census Bureau home page, consult "Subjects A-Z" for links to topics on the Census Web site <http://www.census.gov/main/www/man_subj.html>. Clicking on "Maps," for example, connects the requester to the TIGER Web page. Select "Search" from the Census home page to locate online documents and files by keyword, place names, zip codes, or by clicking on a map. To identify Census Bureau subject specialists, consult the free *Telephone Contacts for Data Users* (C 3.238/5: and <http://www.census.gov/contacts/www/contacts.html>).

Census Catalog and Guide

C 3.163/3:

http://www.census.gov/prod/www/
titles.html#genref

This annual publication is a mainstay for any user of census statistics. The Census Bureau calls it "the only one-stop guide to every Census Bureau data product and service," recommending it as "the book to buy before you buy any of our others." The *Catalog/Guide* helps users sort through thousands of data products and formats and to understand Census Bureau programs and services. Product summaries describe contents, scope, format, geographic coverage, and how to order. The *Catalog/Guide* includes telephone numbers of bureau specialists, plus lists of regional offices, State Data Centers, and other service centers. A free subscription to *Monthly Product Announcement* provides updates (also available on the Census Bureau Web site and as an e-mail subscription <http://www.census.gov/pub/mp/www/mpa.html>).

To identify Bureau of the Census publications from the first through 1972 censuses, consult *Bureau of the Census Catalog of Publications, 1790–1972* (C 56.222/2-2:790–972). Annual guides were issued throughout the balance of the 1970s. Information spanning 1980 to 1988 is cumulated in the 1989 *Census Catalog and Guide*, followed by the 1994 *Census Catalog and Guide*, covering 1988 to 1993, both of which should be kept as permanent references. All previous guides are available on microfiche or paper prints from Census Customer Services.

Factfinder for the Nation

C 3.252:

No user of census statistics should overlook the handy *Factfinder for the Nation* series. These concise, useful pamphlets explain sources of data for specific topics, summarize Census Bureau data gathering, and cite key references. Number 5 in the series, "Reference Sources," is an annotated bibliography of Bureau reference publications. The entire set costs about $5; single copies are free from Census Customer Services, and many are included as chapter introductions in the *Catalog and Guide*.

Factfinder for the Nation Titles	
No. 1	Statistics on Race and Ethnicity
No. 2	Availability of Census Records about Individuals <http://www.census.gov/ftp/pub/mp/www/pub/gen/msgen10h.html>
No. 3	Agricultural Statistics
No. 4	History and Organization
No. 5	Reference Sources
No. 6	Housing Statistics
No. 7	Population Statistics
No. 8	Census Geography: Concepts and Products
No. 9	Construction Statistics
No. 10	Retail Trade Statistics
No. 11	Wholesale Trade Statistics
No. 12RV.	Statistics on Service Industries (Revised)
No. 13	Transportation Statistics
No. 14	Foreign Trade Statistics
No. 15	Statistics on Manufactures
No. 16	Statistics on Mineral Industries
No. 17	Statistics on Governments
No. 18	Census Bureau Programs and Products
No. 19	Enterprise Statistics
No. 20	Energy and Related Statistics
No. 21	International Programs
No. 22	Data for Small Communities

Census and You

C 3.238:

http://www.census.gov/ftp/pub/prod/www/abs/msgen.html

This monthly newsletter announces new Census Bureau products, census and survey plans, and federal statistical developments and summarizes newsworthy statistics. Emphasis is on demographic, social, housing, and economic data developments for states and smaller areas. It also publishes key economic indicators. Although these contents may sound dry, the newsletter is interesting and well written. The December issue includes an index for the year. Issues since 1996 are available on the Census Bureau Web site where readers can sign up for automatic e-mail delivery of issues. A free companion source, the *Monthly Product Announcement*, spotlights new products.

Personal Assistance

The Census Bureau operates numerous outlets to help the public find and use statistics, including Regional Offices and State Data Centers in all 50 states (collecting data products for their own states). A directory is included in the *Census Catalog and Guide* or will be sent free from the Data User Services Division.

CENDATA: "The Census Bureau Online"

This online system available at a cost through commercial vendors provides current statistics, news releases, and ordering information. Most statistics are for the nation as a whole; many are for states, and a few cover counties, metropolitan areas, and cities. The *Census Catalog and Guide* summarizes CENDATA contents.

Decennial Downtime?

> *The Census Bureau is not like the mythical town of Brigadoon that magically appears once a decade. It's more like Santa's workshop, in a state of constant preparation.*
> —*American Demographics*, April 1996

People who imagine census staff napping or watching soap operas during the waxing of the decade underestimate the Bureau's mission. In fact, the Bureau never rests, planning the next decennial census years ahead, plus performing other censuses and interim sample surveys. Planning the decennial census begins mid-decade, and citizen input has long been a tradition. Alexander Graham Bell submitted 42 suggested questions about deafness for the 1890 census. For recent censuses, public meetings across the U.S. have allowed citizens and special-interest groups to propose questions and clarify their special needs. Field tests and "dress rehearsals" allow pretesting methods and technology to reveal problems that need solving before Census Day.

Other Censuses

Economic Census

Every five years the Census Bureau performs a monumental juggling act, simultaneously conducting censuses of Retail and Wholesale Trade; Service, Construction, and Mineral Industries; Manufactures; and Transportation that count establishments, employees, and payrolls for specific industries. Although the 1997 Economic Census sounds like a *fait accompli*, the data won't have been collected until early 1998; the results not released until 1999 and 2000. (These things take time—data from the 1992 Economic Census were still being released in 1996.) For a preview of the 1997 Economic Census, the first government program to adopt the North American Industry Classification System (NAICS), see the Census Web site <http://www.census.gov/epcd/www/ec97prev.html> or the publication C 3.252/2:EC 92-PR-1. Until 1999, users will rely on the 1992 Economic Census results on CD-ROM (C 3.277:CD-EC 92-nos.), the Web-based "1992 Economic Census Look-Up" <http://www.census.gov/epcd/econ/www/eclookup.html>, and Web "Summary of National Statistics" <http://www.census.gov/epcd/www/ecensus.html>.

User Aids: To identify additional PDF or HTML files on the Census Web site, select "Search" from the Census home page and submit "1992 Economic Census." *History of the Economic Censuses* provides background (C 3.253/3:992), and an overview, *Introduction to the 1992 Economic Census*, is free from Census Customer Services <http://www.census.gov/econ/www/econ_cen.html>. To link to Internet sites, use the GPO Access "Browse Topics," and select "Censuses of Business, Construction, Manufactures, Mineral Industries, and Transportation" <http://www.access.gpo.gov/su_docs/dpos/pathbrws.html>.

Census of Manufactures. Twice each decade since 1809, the census of manufactures has been part of the economic census, generating data about employment, payroll, supplementary labor costs, assets, capital expenditures, rents, depreciation, inventories, materials costs, fuels consumed, value of shipments, and value added by manufacture.

User Aids: *Factfinder for the Nation*, No. 15, "Statistics on Manufactures."

Census of Mineral Industries. Also a component of the economic censuses, the census of mineral industries provides statistics on number of establishments, employment, payroll, hours worked, materials costs, value added, capital expenditures, materials consumed, and products shipped.

User Aids: *Factfinder for the Nation*, No. 16, "Statistics on Mineral Industries."

Census of Transportation

The Census of Transportation, taken every five years since 1963, includes the truck inventory and use survey, and transportation industry statistics. Three other economic censuses also generate transportation statistics: the surveys of minority- and women-owned businesses, and the business enterprise statistics program.

User Aids: *Factfinder for the Nation*, No. 13, "Transportation Statistics."

Census of Governments

The census of governments focuses on state and local governments, gathering data on taxable property, number of employees, payrolls, revenues, expenditures, debts, and assets. To link to Internet sites, use the GPO Access "Browse Topics," and select "Census of Governments" <http://www.access.gpo.gov/su_docs/dpos/pathbrws.html>.

User Aids: *Factfinder for the Nation*, No. 17, "Statistics on Governments."

STATISTICAL COMPENDIA

> *Dear Gentlemen:*
> *I saw your census lady today. Why do you have to spend so much money to take the Census? You could get all the figures from the* World Almanac *for free.*
> *Yours truly,*
> *Mrs. Ethel _____, Ohio*
> *(a letter to the Census Bureau)*

Census Bureau statistics are probably the most quoted, and least credited, in the nation. Census data appear not only in almanacs, but also in books, encyclopedias, and newspaper articles. The fact is that most government statistics originate from the Census Bureau (by some estimates, 98 percent), even though other agencies sometimes release them.

When a statistical question arises, searching original census data may be inefficient. Many questions can be answered more quickly and easily using statistical compendia which digest data from numerous sources. Statistical compendia serve two purposes: data summary and referral to additional sources. When choosing a compendium, consider the special strengths of each, weighing the importance of subject versus geographic detail. Currency and time coverage should also be considered.

The Statistical Abstract of the United States

C 3.134:

C 3.134/7: (on CD-ROM)

http://www.census.gov/stat_abstract/

> *It's the best book the government publishes.*
> —Robert J. Samuelson, *Newsweek*

A government document that inspires testimonials? If you thought only blockbuster movies and best-selling novels could generate quotable praise, it's time to take another look at "Uncle Sam's Almanac." Since 1878, the *Statistical Abstract* (note that it's "Abstract," not "Abstracts") has been the single most authoritative source of facts about the American people, institutions, and economy. Daniel Boorstin, former Librarian of Congress, characterized it as "the standard national inventory which leaves no part of our lives untouched." It is so brimming with social, political, and economic facts that a Census Bureau advertising flier dared challenge: "Pick a question! The *Statistical Abstract* has just about all the answers!"

Ubiquitous Statistics

It's a rare library that doesn't own the *Statistical Abstract of the United States*. In 1997 it ranked 29th among the most-owned serials in the WorldCat database.[11]

Not only does the *Abstract* offer statistics, it also directs readers to more detailed data through chapter introductions, table source notes, and appendixes. An appendix lists key federal and commercial sources of statistics for topics. Other appendixes identify state and foreign government statistical abstracts. The sources cited include more information than can be summarized in the *Abstract's* tables and graphs, making the *Statistical Abstract* not just a fact source but also a reference to federal, international, and private data sources. ("Business" in the appendix, for example, lists not only the Bureau of Economic Analysis but also Dun & Bradstreet.) The CD-ROM version goes even further, providing links to the Internet and linking from tables to spreadsheets that can be manipulated with software like *Lotus 1-2-3*, *Microsoft Excel*, or *Quattro Pro*. For quick transport to the *Statistical Abstract* in PDF format, frequently requested tables, state rankings, and USA Statistics in Brief, use the FedStats "Fast Facts" linkage at <http://www.fedstats.gov>.

Historical Statistics of the United States, Colonial Times to 1970

C 3.134/2:H 62/970/pt.1,2

Historical Statistics of the United States is the venerable statistical synopsis of social, economic, political, and geographic development between 1610 and 1970. Coverage includes population, vital statistics, health, labor, prices, income, welfare, climate, agriculture, forestry, fisheries, minerals, construction, housing, manufactures, transportation, communications, energy, commerce, banking, and government. Data after 1970 are given in the *Statistical Abstract*, which includes an appendix linking each numbered *Historical Statistics* series to tables in the *Abstract* (Appendix IV, "Index to Tables Having Historical Statistics, Colonial Times to 1970 Series"). A CD-ROM edition of *Historical Statistics of the United States* from Cambridge University Press was produced in cooperation with the Census Bureau. Unfortunately, the Cambridge University Press imprint lobbed the product right out of the depository ballpark: not an official Census product, it's not available free to depository libraries.

To identify historical census publications from the first census through 1945, consult Kevin Cook's *Dubester's U.S. Census Bibliography with SuDocs Class Numbers and Indexes*. This enhancement of Henry J. Dubester's work is a comprehensive list of all materials issued by the Census Bureau and its predecessor organizations, with subject, title, series, report number, and SuDocs number indexes. Donald Dodd's *Historical Statistics of the United States: Two Centuries of the Census, 1790–1990* (Greenwood Press) supplements the government title and its updates in the *Statistical Abstract* and the annual *Agricultural Statistics* (A 1.47:), along with county-level data compiled by the Inter-University Consortium for Political and Social Research at the University of Michigan.

County and City Data Book

C 3.134/2-1:

http://www.census.gov/stat_abstract/ccdb.html

This *Statistical Abstract* supplement gives social and economic data for states, counties, cities, and census regions and divisions. Issued every five years, the latest is the 1994 edition, with the next expected in 1999. County data files appearing in the 1988 and 1983 editions are included in the *USA Counties* CD-ROM (C 3.134/6:). The Census Bureau's new CD-ROM series, CountyScope, offers data for specific counties. *Population of States and Counties of the United States: 1790 to 1990 from the Twenty-One Decennial Censuses* is a compendium of two centuries of state and county population statistics (C 3.2:P 81/26).

State and Metropolitan Area Data Book

C 3.134/5:

State and Metropolitan Area Data Book supplements the *Statistical Abstract* by providing data on states, metropolitan areas, and metropolitan counties. Published every five years, the next edition is slated for 1998. *USA Counties* is a CD-ROM *Statistical Abstract* supplement with county data published in the 1982, 1986, and 1991 editions of the *State and Metropolitan Area Data Book,* along with unpublished data (C 3.134/6:). For retrospective state data, consult *Population of States and Counties of the United States: 1790 to 1990 from the Twenty-One Decennial Censuses* (C 3.2:P 81/26).

U.S. Statistics at a Glance

This summary of demographic and economic indicators is included in issues of *Census and You* and online through CENDATA. It includes business, construction and housing, manufacturing, international trade, money, and other indicators as of this month, last month, and last year, with percent of change through time.

The White House Briefing Rooms

http://www.whitehouse.gov/fsbr

Some of the nation's most closely watched numbers are provided in the White House Internet Economic Statistics Briefing Room <http://www.whitehouse.gov/fsbr/esbr.html> and Social Statistics Briefing Room <http://www.whitehouse.gov/fsbr/ssbr.html>. The briefing rooms organize current releases of economic and social indicators by themes such as Output, Income, Employment, Production, Money, Prices, Transportation, International Statistics, Demographics, Education, Health, and Crime. Included in each theme are the most current release, graphic displays of the series over time, brief capsules of trends or noteworthy aspects of the release, and the agency that produced the statistic, with links to the source agency's Web site.

A Sampling of Statistical Compendia

While the *Statistical Abstract* and its supplements offer general data, other statistical compendia focus on particular topics.

> Agriculture:
> *Agricultural Statistics.* Annual. A 1.47: and <http://www.usda.gov/nass/pubs/agstats.htm>
> Business and Labor:

> *Survey of Current Business.* Monthly. C 59.11:
> *Economic Indicators.* Monthly. Y 4.Ec7:Ec7/date
> Communications:
> *Statistics of Communications Common Carriers.* Annual. CC 1.35:
> Criminal Justice:
> *Sourcebook of Criminal Justice Statistics.* Annual. J 29.9/6: and <http://www.albany.edu/sourcebook>
> *Uniform Crime Reports.* Annual. J 1.14/7: and <http://www.fbi.gov/ucr/crimeus/crimeus.htm>
> Earth Sciences:
> *Minerals Yearbook.* Annual. I 28.37:
> *United States Earthquakes.* Annual. I 19.65/2:
> Education:
> *Condition of Education.* Annual. ED 1.109: and <http://www.ed.gov/NCES/pubs/ce/index.html>
> *Digest of Education Statistics.* Annual. ED 1.326: and <http://www.ed.gov/NCES/pubs/D96/index.html>
> Energy:
> *International Energy Annual.* Annual. E 3.11/20: and <http://www.eia.doe.gov/>
> *Annual Energy Review.* Annual. E 3.1/2: (microfiche); GP 3.35:DOE_AER/date and on the Federal Bulletin Board
> Health:
> *Health, United States.* Annual. HE 20.6223: and <http://www.cdc.gov/nchswww/products/pubs/pubd/hus/2010/2010.htm>
> *Mental Health, United States.* Biennial. HE 20.8137:
> *Vital Statistics of the United States.* Annual. HE 20.6210:
> Libraries:
> *Academic Libraries.* Biennial. ED 1.328/3:L 61/3/ and <http://www.ed.gov/>
> *Public Libraries in the United States.* Annual. ED 1.328/3:L 61/2/ and <http://www.ed.gov/>
> Population:
> *World Population Profile.* Biennial. C 3.205/3:WP-yr. and <http://www.census.gov/ipc/www/world.html>
> Public Lands:
> *Public Land Statistics.* Annual. I 53.1/2:
> Transportation:
> *National Transportation Statistics.* Annual. TD 10.9: and <http://www.bts.gov/btsprod/nts/>
> *National Transportation Statistics, Annual Report.* Annual. TD 12.1/2:
> *FAA Statistical Handbook of Aviation.* Annual. TD 4.20:
> *Highway Statistics.* Annual. TD 2.23/2:
> Weather:
> *Monthly Climatic Data for the World.* Monthly. C 55.211:

Nothing Is as Simple as It Looks: Interpreting Tables

> *Ordinary reading ability is no more effective in reading a table than an ordinary can opener in*

FIGURE 12.3: *Statistical Abstract* Referral to Other Sources.

Excerpts from the Referral Information Provided
in Selected Statistical Abstract Tables

No. 95. Births to Unmarried Women, by Race and Age of Mother: 1950 to 1978

[Prior to 1960, excludes Alaska and Hawaii. Beginning 1970, excludes births to nonresidents of U.S. Includes estimates for States in which marital status data were not reported. No estimates included for misstatements on birth records or failures to register births. See also Appendix III and *Historical Statistics, Colonial Times to 1970*, series B 28–35] ← C

RACE AND AGE	1950	1955	1960	1965	1970	1973	1974	1975	1976	1977	1978
Total live births (1,000)	141.6	183.3	224.3	291.2	398.7	407.3	418.1	447.9	468.1	515.7	543.9
Percent of all births[1]	4.0	4.5	5.3	7.7	10.7	13.0	13.2	14.2	14.8	15.5	16.3
White (1,000)	53.5	64.2	82.5	123.7	175.1	163.0	168.5	186.4	197.1	220.1	233.6
Black and other (1,000)	88.1	119.2	141.8	167.5	223.6	244.3	249.6	261.6	271.0	295.5	310.2
Percent of total	62.2	65.0	63.2	57.5	56.1	60.0	59.7	58.4	57.9	57.3	57.0
Percent White of all White	1.7			2.3			6.4			7.7	

[1] For total births, see table 85. [2] Rate per 1,000 unmarried (never-married, widowed, and divorced) women aged 15–44 years, enumerated as of April 1 for 1950, 1960, and 1970, and estimated as of July 1 for all other years.

B ← Source: U.S. National Center for Health Statistics, *Vital Statistics of the United States*, annual, and unpublished data.

No. 101. Legal Abortions—Estimated Number, Rate, and Ratio by Race: 1972 to 1978

[Refers to women 15–44 years old at time of abortion. Minus sign (−) denotes decrease]

ITEM	1972		1975		1976		1977		1978	
	White	Black[1]	White	Black[1]	White	Black[1]	White	Black[1]	White	Black[1]
Total women, 15–44 yr old (1,000)	38,381	6,014	40,485	6,633	41,254	6,855	42,022	7,071	42,741	7,288
Number of abortions (1,000)	455.3	131.5	701.2	333.0	784.9	394.4	891.2	429.1	969.4	440.2
Annual pct. change	(x)		15.5	36.3		18.4	13.5		8.8	

A ← X Not applicable. [1] Includes other races.

Source: Alan Guttmacher Institute, New York, N.Y. unpublished data. Includes data from U.S. Bureau of the Census, U.S. National Center for Health Statistics, and U.S. Center for Disease Control, Atlanta, Ga.

In some cases general references are provided (arrow B); other references cite specific publications as the source of data (arrow A), or refer to additional data sources (arrow C). Source: Bureau of the Census. *Census '80: Projects for Students*, 1981.

opening a can of sardines, and if you go at it with a hammer and chisel you are likely to mutilate the contents.

—W. A. Wallis and H. V. Roberts,
Statistics, A New Approach

Statistical compendia appear quick and easy, but their detailed data compressed into concise tables demand sophisticated interpretation. Whether using statistical compendia or the original reports upon which they are based, hasty or careless reading can result in misinterpretation or selection of incorrect answers. Before attempting to extract data from statistical tables, review the introduction or preface, which summarizes data sources and important concepts, and read the notations and footnotes for individual tables. The extra time invested can make the difference between correctness and misinterpretation.

Pitfalls Aplenty: Interpreting Census Reports

An eighth of everyone in this country lives in California.   —Newspaper caption

When consulting census reports rather than summaries in compendia, reconnoitering can save time and prevent misinterpretation. First, determine whether the information sought was gathered in the census at all and whether it's available for the geographic area sought. Next, verify whether the question was in the population or housing component of the census questionnaire, and whether it was a complete count or a sample question. Answers to questions like these will determine which census reports to consult.

Since census reports are issued in state volumes and in national summary volumes, users should determine whether they want detailed state data or more general national data and should be aware that tables are numbered differently in the two types of publications. (Table-hopping among state volumes is simplified by the fact that subject tables use the same numbers for all states.) Once inside any census report volume, users should remember that general summary tables precede more detailed breakdowns and that each report includes a Table Finding Guide and Data Index.

1990 Census User Aids: A handy guide to census subjects is *Introduction to 1990 Census Products* in the *Census Catalog and Guide* and available free from Census Customer Services. *Subject Index to The 1990 Census of Population and Housing* is a detailed guide to tables in 1990 Census print and CD-ROM publications (Epoch Books, 1997). Lavin offers a detailed look at 1990 census-report coverage in his chapter on printed reports and maps.[12] *Subject Index to Current Population Reports* provides topical access to Series P–20, P–23, P–

25, P–26, P–60, and P–70 (C 3.186:P–23/174). And don't forget *American Statistics Index*, which provides detailed descriptions of census products. A list of all questions asked since the first census is provided in *200 Years of U.S. Census Taking: Population and Housing Questions, 1790–1990* (C 3.2:T 93). The Census Bureau Web site includes a guide to the 1990 Census <http://www.census.gov/main/www/cen1990.html> and the 1990 census questionnaire <http://www.census.gov/apsd/www/cqc.html>. The Congressional Information Service publishes a *Guide to 1990 U.S. Decennial Census Publications* and companion microfiche.

Definitions

Census nomenclature is precise. Terms have specific meanings that do not always reflect their popular usage, and definitions should not be guessed or assumed. What, for instance, is the term for an unmarried person? (It depends: has the person never married, or is he or she widowed, divorced, or separated?) How do census reports describe cohabiting unmarried couples? They're "unmarried-partners" if they have a close, personal relationship; "unmarried-couples" if they share living quarters but not hearts. Even seemingly obvious definitions should be verified: the term "person" seems unambiguous, but in 1790 American Indians were left uncounted because they paid no taxes, and five slaves were tallied as only three persons. Understanding terminology is essential for interpreting statistical tables. To verify Census Bureau definitions, consult Part B Glossary of the *1990 Census of Population and Housing Guide* (C 3.223/22:1990 CPH-R 1), the online "Glossary of Decennial Census Terms and Acronyms" <http://www.census.gov/dmd/www/glossary.html>, or appendixes in each published report.

Census vs. Samples

Census users should recognize differences between "complete-count" and sample data. A complete-count is a true census or headcount, in which everyone is counted. Complete-counts are also called "100 percent," indicating the target response rate. Samples, on the other hand, are estimates derived from a statistical sampling of the population. Intercensal surveys—those completed between regular censuses—are samples producing annual, quarterly, and monthly updates to the decennial census, primarily for large areas. Parallel complete-count and sample data sometimes provide different totals for the same component.

The 1990 short and long census questionnaires are embodiments of a census and a sample, respectively. The short form was sent to every household (a complete-count), while the additional 35 long-form questions were appended to one out of every six questionnaires (a sample). The Census Bureau estimated the 14 short-form questions each took about one minute to answer, with the 58-question long form demanding around 43 minutes of rapt attention. Census 2000 will mail a seven-question short form (the fewest since 1820) to five out of every six households, asking name, age, sex, race, Latino origin, household relationships, and home ownership.

Census vs. Survey		
	Census	Survey
Coverage	All	Sample
Frequency	Set by law	Varies
Geographic detail	Large and small areas*	Large areas only
Advantages	More detail, benchmark data	Economical, taken more frequently
Disadvantages	Costly, time consuming	Limited geography

*The decennial census of population and housing is the only national source of detailed population statistics for small geographic areas such as towns and school districts, and for population groups, such as Native Americans.

Summary Tape Files (STFs)

C 3.282:

STFs are decennial census computer-tape files, each presenting tables for specific geographic units. STFs 1 and 2 contain 100-percent data, while STFs 3 and 4 are sample data. STFs 1 and 3 report on smaller areas and offer less data detail than STFs 2 and 4. STFs 1 through 4 offer greater data detail than their 1980 equivalents. (Got that?)

Summary Tape Files (STFs)	
STF-1 100 %	STF-2 100 %
STF-3 Sample	STF-4 Sample
More data————>	
<————Smaller geography	

Public Use Microdata Sample (PUMS)

PUMS computer files are data from samples of long-form housing-unit records ("microdata") for large geographic areas. Microdata are "raw" records of individual responses, requiring computer manipulation to be meaningful. Microdata files are used to prepare customized tabulations and cross-tabulations. Each sample housing-unit record includes essentially all of the 1990 census data collected about each person in a sample household, along with housing unit characteristics. Any information that could identify an individual or housing unit is stricken to protect confidentiality.

Public Law 94–171

Public Law 94–171 requires complete-count data to be tabulated within the year for use in redistricting the 50 state legislatures. Public Law 94–171 data are early-release population counts required by law to be submitted to the president by the last day of December in a census year. P.L. 94–171 tabulations on CD-ROM include population data for states, counties, voting districts, minor civil divisions, places, American Indian/ Alaska Native areas, census tracts, block groups, and blocks (C 3.281:). As later, more detailed releases become available, they are superseded.

Census Geography

All census data are geographic. Census Bureau geographic units are either governmental (states, counties, cities) or statistical (census tracts, block groups, blocks). A glossary of census geographic terms is provided on the TIGER FAQ page <http://www.census.gov/ftp/ pub/geo/www/tiger/>. The larger the geographic area, the greater the number and detail of statistics published for it. Especially for small areas, more data are available electronically than in print. Letter suffixes to STF numbers indicate file types, differing in the geographic levels reported, but containing equal detail. To link to Internet sites, use the GPO Access "Browse Topics," and select "Census Tracts and Blocks" <http:// www.access.gpo.gov/su_docs/dpos/pathbrws.html>.

STF Geography		
	STF 1 100% Data	STF 3 Sample Data
Block Groups	1A	3A
Blocks	1B	
Zip Codes	None	3B
National	1C	3C
Congressional Districts	1D	3D
Census Tracts/BNAs	2A	4A
Counties/Places	2B	4B
National	2C	4C

Census mapping harkens back to the late nineteenth century when the first enumeration district maps were prepared. (These historic maps are preserved in NARA's Cartographic and Architectural Branch.) The 1990 cen-

sus witnessed a juncture in census mapping with the creation of TIGER, a coast-to-coast computerized map database <http://tiger.census.gov/>. Using TIGER, some 90,000 maps were created for the 1990 census, 10 times the number for the 1980 census. Some were issued on paper, while others are available on microfiche, CD-ROM, magnetic tape, and through census regional offices and State Data Centers. The Census Bureau sells periodic extracts of the TIGER database, known as the TIGER/Line files, to support creation of geographic information systems and other applications. TIGER is also repackaged and sold commercially by data vendors <http://www.census.gov/ftp/pub/geo/www/tiger>.

Free Online Maps and Data

In the Census Web site "Access Tools" section, select Map Stats to generate maps and census statistics such as state and county profiles <http://www.census.gov/ datamap/www/index.html>. Use the "1990 Census Lookup" to obtain STF3 (1990 Census Summary Tape File 3) sample count socioeconomic and demographic data or to manipulate 1990 Census Summary Tape File 1 (STF1) 100 percent count demographic variables. Use the "U.S. Gazetteer" to retrieve 1990 Census data and TIGER maps, generating a crisp place-profile in the process <http://venus.census.gov/cdrom/lookup>.

The public domain TIGER Map Service (TMS) can be used to create a graphic image for a Web page by downloading a screen image as a GIF file and creating a customized map, complete with multicolored pins and labels, for mounting on a Web page <http://tiger. census.gov/faq.html>. For greater detail, the GIF can be imported into a graphics program (like Paintbrush, Corel Draw, etc.) and edited. A TIGER Map Service bonus is the ability to plot 1990 Census data onto maps.

Hierarchy of Census Geography for Data Products
United States
Region
Division
State
County
Minor Civil Division/Census County Division
Place
Census Tract/Block Numbering Area
Block Group
Block

Source: *1990 Census of Population and Housing: Tabulation and Publication Program*, 1989, p. 11.

ELECTRONIC DATA

The Bureau anticipates paperless publication by Census 2000. As Robert J. Samuelson put it, the Census Bureau "is slowly going out of print," jettisoning printed reports in favor of electronic release, largely on the Internet or CD-ROM.[13] Depository libraries received CD-ROMs of 1990 census data, and all Census Bureau printed reports since 1996 are in PDF format on the Census Web site <http://www.census.gov/prod/www/titles.html>. As paper fades, the *Statistical Abstract* has expanded its coverage of waning subjects.

Census Bureau products can be purchased in numerous formats, including CD-ROM, magnetic tape, floppy disks, online, microfiche, maps, and printed reports <http://www.census.gov/mp/www/censtore.html>. Federal depository libraries are the primary hubs for free access to printed census reports, which until the 1990 Census were largely in paper and microform. To augment collections of Census Bureau publications in federal depository libraries, the Census Bureau sends copies of its publications to census depository libraries listed in the *Census Catalog and Guide*. The Bureau of the Census library in Suitland, Maryland, and the Department of Commerce Reference Room in Washington, DC, have the most extensive collections in the country.

The printed reports represent only the tip of the statistical iceberg, containing only about one-tenth of all 1980 and 1990 Census data: the bulk is computer-accessible only. Many depository libraries rely on State Data Centers for access to census computer tapes, while academic libraries may also refer to Inter-University Consortium for Political and Social Research (ICPSR) at the University of Michigan. The Census Bureau will download data from magnetic tapes to floppy disks for a fee.

Incremental migration of census data onto the Internet has made the Census Web site a data paradise. Users enjoy data access on the day of release and the option of accessing raw data for custom analysis. For notices of additions to the Web site, sign up for an e-mail announcement service <http://www.census.gov/mp/www/subscribe.html#SUB>. While most Census Bureau information on the Internet is free, CenStats provides interactive search-and-display for selected popular databases as a subscription service <http://www.census.gov/mp/www/index2.html>. Free in its pilot phase, it will evolve into a paid service but will remain free to depository libraries. Data Access and Dissemination System (DADS), on the drawing board for a 2001 debut, will be the hub for electronic access to all census statistics and will allow customized tabulations. People without Internet access can obtain data extracts from the electronic files on a reimbursable basis, provided on CD-ROM, floppy disks, or printouts.

EDGAR

Publicly traded corporations file many (but not all) forms electronically with the Securities and Exchange Commission (SEC), and those submissions that SEC requires to be electronically filed are added to the EDGAR database at <http://www.sec.gov/edgarhp.htm>. EDGAR contains electronic filings since 1994, including mandatory corporate 10-K and 10-Q filings of financial data such as earnings rate, long-term debt, and cash flow. EDGAR may be searched by such access points as Central Index Key, company ticker symbol, SIC code, zip code, filing date, or free text. A parallel site with slightly different search options is operated at New York University, the developers of the original EDGAR Internet project <http://allan.stern.nyu.edu/tools.shtml>.

NTIS

The National Technical Information Service is a reservoir of many government statistical data files, many of which are described on the NTIS Web site. NTIS's Federal Computer Products Center sells government software and datafiles <http://www.ntis.gov/fcpc/fcpc.htm>. Searches submitted on the Federal Computer Products Center Web site retrieve products from the entire NTIS Web site (but not from the NTIS Database). The monthly NTIS Alert on *Computers, Control & Information Theory* describes new software and datafiles added to the Federal Computer Products Center collection, with abstracts of research related to computers and information technology.

INTERNATIONAL DATA

The Census Bureau's International Programs Center (IPC) is a research group funded by government and private organizations which gathers and publishes demographic and economic data on world nations <http://www.census.gov/ipc/www/>. One of IPC's best-known publications is Series WP, the biennial *World Population Profile*, containing data on population, fertility, mortality, contraceptive use, and related demographics for the world, regions, and countries and territories populated by at least 5,000 souls (C 3.205/3:WP-yr. and <http://www.census.gov/ipc/www/world.html>). More information is available on the International Data Base (IDB) <http://www.census.gov/ipc/WWW/idbnew.html>, which can also be purchased from IPC. IDB includes figures since 1950 for population, age, sex, urban/rural residence, vital statistics, migration rate, and literacy, with projections to 2050. For a quick update on world population, check the "World POPClock" on the Census Web site.

The *Statistical Abstract* includes a "Comparative International Statistics" section in which world and national statistics are compared to U.S. data, and an appendix,"Guide to Foreign Statistical Abstracts."

INDEX TO INTERNATIONAL STATISTICS (IIS)

Index to International Statistics, from Congressional Information Service, indexes and abstracts data published since 1983 by major international intergovernmental organizations (IGOs). Covered are IGOs such as the United Nations, the European Community, and the Organization for Economic Cooperation and Development, the Organization of American States, commodity organizations, development banks, and other regional and special-purpose organizations. IIS may be searched in print, online, or on the Statistical Masterfile CD-ROM.

AGRICULTURE

Census of Agriculture

http://www.usda.gov/nass/census/census.htm

This enumeration generates agricultural data for the nation, the 50 states, and every county. Data are gathered on farming, ranching, land use, sales of agricultural products, poultry, livestock, crops, and energy costs. Beginning with the 1997 Census of Agriculture, responsibility was transferred from the Census Bureau to the National Agricultural Statistics Service. Known as "the Fact Finders of Agriculture," the National Agricultural Statistics Service (NASS) prepares estimates and reports on our agricultural economy, collecting data about every facet of U.S. agriculture.

User Aids: *Factfinder for the Nation, No. 3*, "Agricultural Statistics," *Guide to the 1992 Census of Agriculture and Related Statistics* (C 3.6/2:AG 8/2/992), and the Ag Census—USA home page <http://www.usda.gov/nass/census/census.htm>. To link to Internet sites, use the GPO Access "Browse Topics," and select "Census of Agriculture" <http://www.access.gpo.gov/su_docs/dpos/pathbrws.html>.

Another United States Department of Agriculture (USDA) statistical agency, the Economic Research Service (ERS), produces research, analysis, and economic and statistical indicators in five areas—commercial agriculture, food and consumer economics, natural resources and environment, rural economy, and energy and new uses <http://www.econ.ag.gov/>.

BUREAU OF ECONOMIC ANALYSIS (BEA)

http://www.bea.doc.gov/

The Commerce Department's Bureau of Economic Analysis calls itself "the Nation's accountant." BEA's economic accounts (or "indicators") profile economic growth, regional development, business trends, and the economy. Data appear first in news releases, and then in BEA's monthly journal of record, the *Survey of Current Business* (C 59.11: and via STAT-USA). Timely BEA data are available through STAT-USA and the Commerce Department's Economic Bulletin Board (EBB). The free *User's Guide to BEA Information* is an annotated list of publications, products, and services (C 59.8:B 89/ and <http://www.bea.doc.gov/bea/uguide.html>).

CRIMINAL JUSTICE

The National Institute of Justice (NIJ) is the Department of Justice's primary criminal justice research arm. NIJ is rare among federal agencies in requiring the deposit of data sets from funded research. Public-use data tapes and data sets are available from the National Archive of Criminal Justice Data, ICPSR/ISR/Univ of Michigan, Box 1248, 426 Thompson, Ann Arbor, MI 48106-1248; cdunn@icpsr.umich.edu; (800) 999-0960; <http://www.icpsr.umich.edu/NACJD/home.html>. To link to Internet sites, use GPO Access "Browse Topics," and select "Criminal Justice" <http://www.access.gpo.gov/su_docs/dpos/pathbrws.html>.

The National Criminal Justice Reference Service (NCJRS) is an international criminal justice information clearinghouse <http://ncjrs.org/homepage.htm>. NCJRS is a menage of clearinghouses within the U.S. Department of Justice's Office of Justice Programs: the National Institute of Justice, the Office of Juvenile Justice and Delinquency Prevention, the Bureau of Justice Statistics, the Bureau of Justice Assistance, the Office for Victims of Crime, and the Office of Justice Programs. The *National Criminal Justice Reference Service Document Data Base on CD-ROM* provides abstracts of books, articles, and reports published by federal, state, and local governments, international organizations, and the private sector. This document database of criminal justice literature is available in several formats, including distribution to depositories as a single workstation application (J 28.31/2:). The same information is available on the Web as NCJRS Abstracts Database <http://www.ncjrs.org/database.htm>. Users of NCJRS resources may wish to consult the *National Criminal Justice Thesaurus* used to index the NCJRS document database (J 28.28:). NCJRS also operates a library; provides information, referral, and distribution; and oversees clearinghouses on justice statistics, drug policies, juvenile delinquency and justice, crime victims, and statistics.

The Bureau of Justice Statistics (BJS), the nation's primary source for criminal justice statistics, is a hub for information on crime, offenders, victims, and the operation of federal, state, and local justice systems. The

NCJRS Electronic Bulletin Board System (NCJRS*BBS) posts BJS press releases, full-text publications, reports and statistics, news, announcements, and information about Office of Justice programs, agencies, and related clearinghouses <telnet://ncjrsbbs.aspensys.com>. Under the BJS wing is the Bureau of Justice Statistics Clearinghouse, providing easy access to crime and justice data. The clearinghouse distributes BJS publications, answers requests for statistics, and offers statistics information packages, referrals, and custom searches of the NCJRS database.

The nation's two major crime reports are the BJS's National Crime Victimization Survey (NCVS) and the FBI's Uniform Crime Reports (UCR). The National Crime Victimization Survey is BJS's largest statistical series and the government's second largest household survey (J 29.11/10: and <http://www.ojp.usdoj.gov/bjs/>). Administered annually for BJS by the Bureau of the Census, NCVS interviews ask about victimization by rape, robbery, domestic violence, assault, larceny, burglary, and auto theft. NCVS was redesigned in 1989, with improved questions and cues to trigger recall, and more explicit questions about sexual victimization. The first annual results from the redesigned survey were published for 1993.

NCVS complements the FBI's annual *Uniform Crime Reports*, also known as *Crime in the United States* (J 1.14/7: and <http://www.fbi.gov/publish.htm>). Unlike the crimes recounted in the victimization survey, these crimes were reported to local law enforcement agencies: homicide, rape, robbery, aggravated assault, burglary, larceny-theft, motor vehicle theft, and arson.

The Bureau of Justice Statistics also issues the *Sourcebook of Criminal Justice Statistics*, a one-volume compendium of data from more than one hundred sources (J 29.2: and <http://www.albany.edu/sourcebook>). Although issued in print only once yearly, the "Sourcebook On-line" is regularly updated with revised tables and new data sources as they will appear in the next edition.

To keep all of this straight, you might consult the National Clearinghouse for Criminal Justice Information Systems at <http://www.ch.search.org/>. The Clearinghouse is sponsored by the Bureau of Justice Statistics, U.S. Department of Justice, and is operated by SEARCH, The National Consortium for Justice Information and Statistics. The Clearinghouse Web site offers criminal justice publications such as the *FBI Law Enforcement Bulletin*, Opinions of the United States Supreme Court, reports, bulletins, and SEARCH-BBS access to several online database systems including the Automated Index of Criminal Justice Information Systems, Calendar of Events, Criminal Justice BBS List, National Employment Listing Service (employment listings in academics and research, community service and

corrections, institutional corrections, and law enforcement and security), Planning Abstract Listing Service (which provides information on programs, policies, and procedures developed by law enforcement agencies), Training Facilities Database (identifies computer labs and training centers where criminal justice organizations can host hands-on training for practitioners), and a Training Consultants Database. The SEARCH-BBS specializes in the exchange of public domain and shareware systems useful to criminal justice agencies.

EDUCATION

http://www.ed.gov/index.html

The federal government began gathering educational statistics in 1867, when it established the Department of Education. Calling itself "America's education factfinder," the Office of Educational Research and Improvement (OERI) is the Department of Education's primary statistical and research organ <http://www.ed.gov/offices/OERI/>. OERI collects statistics, disseminates information, reports on the condition of education, and sponsors R&D and library programs. The National Center for Education Statistics (NCES) is a subunit of OERI.

The National Center for Education Statistics collects statistics about U.S. and foreign education and disseminates print and electronic data <http://nces.ed.gov/>. The center's data collection programs cover public and private elementary and secondary education, higher education, vocational, and adult education. Statistical tables, charts, and studies are available on the Internet and in disk, tape, print, and special tabulations. The full text of reports and data products are provided in "NCES Products: Electronic Catalog and Online Library" <http://nces.ed.gov/ncespub1.html>. NCES provides Internet access to publication announcements, data sets, and full text publications from the National Data Resource Center (e-mail: ndrc@inet.ed.gov). Answers to questions about education statistics, research, publications, and data tapes may be obtained by contacting the OERI Information Office. *American Statistics Index* offers comprehensive coverage of NCES statistical publications. "Educational Statistics" in GPO Access "Browse Topics" links to Internet sites <http://www.access.gpo.gov/su_docs/dpos/pthbrws.html>.

ENERGY

The Energy Information Administration (EIA), the Department of Energy's statistical/analytical arm and information clearinghouse, is responsible for data about energy reserves, production, demand, consumption, distribution, and technology. EIA's *Energy InfoDisc* on CD-ROM offers the full text of EIA publications, databases, and software, with a search engine (E 3.60:). EIA's electronic bulletin board, EPUB, provides timely access to data in EIA statistical reports (202-586-2557 or through FEDWORLD at <http://www.fedworld.gov>). Instructions are provided in *Electronic Publishing System (EPUB) Quick Start Users Guide* (E 3.8:El 2), free from EIA's subunit, the National Energy Information Center (NEIC). The annual *EIA Publications Directory* (E 3.27: and <http://www.eia.doe.gov/index.html>), free from EIA, abstracts publications and computer data files and modeling programs sold through NTIS. EIA's *Annual Report to Congress* includes information on surveys, data collection, and publications, and is free from EIA (E 3.1:). "Energy and Related Statistics," No. 20 in the free *Factfinder for the Nation* series, is a guide to energy data collected in the censuses and surveys of agriculture, foreign trade, the economy, and government. *American Statistics Index* offers comprehensive coverage of Energy Information Administration statistical publications.

HEALTH

The National Center for Health Statistics (NCHS) collects and disseminates statistics about health and nutrition, illness and disability, health resources, health expenditures, and official vital statistics <http://www.cdc.gov/nchswww/nchshome.htm>. Vital statistics report life events, including births and deaths, health and disease, abortions, fertility, life expectancy, marriages, and divorces. These statistics are found in *Vital Statistics of the United States*, which has been called a "basic building block of demographic analysis."[14] Published annually in three volumes, it covers natality, mortality, and marriage/divorce (HE 20.6210:). The *Vital and Health Statistics Series* (HE 20.6209:) includes dozens of titles, covering numerous health topics. (See Subject Bibliography SB-121 <http://www.access.gpo.gov/su_docs/sale/sb-121.html> for a list of series titles for sale from GPO.) To locate health statistics online, use the Search option in Healthfinder <http://www.healthfinder.gov/> and select "Statistics."

The Congressional Information Service's *Index to Health Information: A Guide to Statistical and Congressional Publications on Public Health* (IHI) consolidates health-related citations and abstracts from *American Statistics Index*, *Statistical Reference Index*, *Index to International Statistics*, and *CIS/Index*. *American Statistics Index* offers comprehensive coverage of NCHS statistical publications.

THE BUREAU OF LABOR STATISTICS (BLS)

http://www.bls.gov/

The Bureau of Labor Statistics is the nation's chief factfinder for labor economics. BLS gathers data on topics such as the labor force, employment, hours and earnings, productivity, and foreign labor. BLS produces key economic indicators including the Consumer Price Index, the Producer Price Index, and Employment Situation. Many BLS economic indicators (prices, wages, employment) are available immediately through BLS's News Release Home Page <http://stats.bls.gov:80/newsrels.htm>. BLS Web pages, like the Consumer Price Indexes Home Page, provide overviews, FAQs, and data <http://stats.bls.gov/cpihome.htm>. The Commerce Department's Economic Bulletin Board subscription service includes timely statistics and economic news from the Bureau of Labor Statistics. *American Statistics Index* offers comprehensive coverage of BLS statistical publications.

The Commerce Department's Economic Bulletin Board (EBB) is composed of two complementary services: State of the Nation (information about the economy) and GLOBUS (business and trade). State of the Nation offers economic news from all federal statistical agencies, Federal Reserve reports, Bureau of Economic Analysis statistical files, and government economic reports. GLOBUS includes the *Commerce Business Daily*, daily agricultural and trade leads, and market research reports. Offered through STAT-USA/Internet, a product brochure for the subscription service is available at <http://www.stat-usa.gov/products.html>.

STAT-USA/Internet is a hub for business, economic, social, and environmental information from numerous federal agencies. While it's available to subscribers at "low cost," depository libraries have free subscriptions, each eligible to register for a single-station STAT-USA account, limited to one user at a time on a single-access workstation. Depositories must purchase site licenses for multi-user privileges. A quarterly *STAT-USA Newsletter* provides updates (C 1.91/2: and <http://www.stat-usa.gov/newsletter/>).

The *National Trade Data Bank* (NTDB) is the nation's most comprehensive source of international trade data and export promotion information and the government's best-selling CD-ROM. The *National Trade Data Bank* includes the full text of government publications (the *U.S. Industrial Outlook*, for example), tables, and statistics from numerous federal statistical agencies. Monthly NTDB discs can be used in depository libraries (C 1.88:) or the database can be accessed through STAT-USA/Internet, <http://www.stat-usa.gov>. As long as funding allows, GPO will continue to distribute paper and microfiche titles that also appear in the NTDB or on STAT-USA.

ADDRESSES

Census

Bureau of the Census, Customer Services, Washington, DC 20233; (301) 457-4100; Fax: (301) 457-4714; <http://www.census.gov/>

Criminal Justice

BJS Clearinghouse/NCJRS, P.O. Box 179, Annapolis Junction, MD 20701-0179; askncjrs@aspensys.com; (800) 732-3277.

National Criminal Justice Reference Service (NCJRS), P.O. Box 6000, Rockville, MD 20849-6000; E-mail: askncjrs@aspensys.com; (800) 851-3420 or (301) 251-5500; <http://www.ncjrs.org/ncjref.htm>

NCJRS Library, Box 6000, 2nd Floor, 2277 Research Blvd., Rockville, MD. 20850; E-mail: curr@ncjrs.org; (301) 519-5063; Fax: (301) 519-5212; <http://www.ncjrs.org>

NCJRS Bulletin Board System (NCJRS*BBS) is accessible through a computer and a modem by dialing (301) 738-8895 or <telnet://ncjrsbbs.aspensys.com>

Education

Department of Education, OERI/NCES, 555 New Jersey Avenue NW, Washington, DC 20208-5574; (800) 424-1616, (202) 219-1692; Fax: (202) 219-1696; <http://nces.ed.gov/>

OERI Electronic Bulletin Board: (800) 222-4922 or (202) 219-2011

OERI Information Office, National Library of Education, 555 New Jersey Ave. NW, Washington, DC 20208-5721; E-mail: Library@inet.ed.gov; (800) 424-1616; <http://www.ed.gov/offices/OERI/>

Energy

National Energy Information Center, NEIC/EIA, EI-231, 1000 Independence Ave SW, Washington, DC 20585; E-mail: infoctr@eia.doe.gov; (202) 586-8800; Fax: (202) 586-0727

Health

National Center for Health Statistics, 3700 East-West Hwy., Hyattsville, MD 20782; E-mail: nchsquery@cdc.gov; (301) 436-8500; <http://www.cdc.gov/nchswww/nchshome.htm>

FREEBIES

The following Subject Bibliographies are free from: Stop: SSOP, Washington, DC 20402; U.S. Fax Watch: (202) 512-1716:

83. Educational Statistics <http://www.access.gpo.gov/su_docs/sale/sb-083.html>

118. Annual Reports <http://www.access.gpo.gov/su_docs/sale/sb-118.html>

121. Vital and Health Statistics <http://www.access.gpo.gov/su_docs/sale/sb-121.html>

146. Census of Manufactures <http://www.access.gpo.gov/su_docs/sale/sb-146.html>

149. Census of Transportation <http://www.access.gpo.gov/su_docs/sale/sb-149.html>

152. Census of Business <http://www.access.gpo.gov/su_docs/sale/sb-152.html>

156. Census of Governments <http://www.access.gpo.gov/su_docs/sale/sb-156.html>

157. Census of Construction <http://www.access.gpo.gov/su_docs/sale/sb-157.html>

162. Agriculture <http://www.access.gpo.gov/su_docs/sale/sb-162.html>

181. Census of Population <http://www.access.gpo.gov/su_docs/sale/sb-181.html>

273. Statistics <http://www.access.gpo.gov/su_docs/sale/sb-273.html>

277. Census of Agriculture <http://www.access.gpo.gov/su_docs/sale/sb-277.html>

Agriculture

"How to Get Information from the U.S. Department of Agriculture" <http://www.usda.gov/news/howto/howto.htm>

Censuses

General Information Leaflet No. 55, "Using the Soundex System" (AE 1.113:55). National Archives General Information Leaflets (GIL) are free, by citing both title and GIL number, from Publications Distribution (NECD), National Archives, Room G9, Seventh and Pennsylvania Ave., NW, Washington, DC 20408; (202) 501-5235; Fax: (202) 501-7170; Fax-on-Demand: (301) 713-6905 (a list of Fax-on-Demand titles is available on the NARA Web site).

From Customer Services, Bureau of the Census, Washington, DC 20233; (301) 457-4100; Fax: (301) 763-4714; <http://www.census.gov/mp/www/censtore.html>

Factfinder for the Nation <http://www.census.gov/ftp/pub/mp/www/pub/gen/msgen10h.html>

Monthly Product Announcement is available on the Census Bureau Web site <http://www.census.gov/pub/mp/www/mpa.html> and as a free e-mail subscription by using the online subscription form or sending an e-mail message to majordomo@census.gov including "subscribe product-announce" followed by your e-mail address

Department of Commerce

From Economics and Statistics Administration, Washington, DC 20230; E-mail: stat-usa@doc.gov; (202) 482-2235; <http://www.doc.gov/agencies/esa/index.html>

User's Guide to BEA Information (C 59.8:B 89/ and <http://www.bea.doc.gov/bea/uguide.html>)

Education

From OERI Outreach and Customer Services Division, 555 New Jersey Ave. NW, Washington, DC 20208-5721; E-mail:

Library@inet.ed.gov; (800) 424-1616; <http://www.ed.gov/offices/OERI/>

> *OERI Bulletin*, a newsletter describing OERI priorities, publications, programs, research and statistics, competitions and events, and recent grants and contracts awarded by OERI program offices <http://www.ed.gov/newsletters.html#oeri>

Energy

From National Energy Information Center, El-231, Energy Information Administration, Room 1F-048, Forrestal Bldg.,Washington, DC 20585; E-mail: infocrt@eia.doe.gov; (202) 586-8800

> *EIA New Releases*, quarterly (E 3.27/4: and <http://www.eia.doe.gov/neic/newrel.html>)
>
> *EIA Publications Directory*
>
> *Energy Information Directory*

Health

From National Center for Health Statistics, 3700 East-West Hwy., Hyattsville, MD 20782; E-mail: nchsquery@cdc.gov; (301) 436-8500; <http://www.cdc.gov/nchswww/nchshome.htm>

> *Catalog of Publications, 1990-95* (HE 20.6216/4: and <http://www.cdc.gov/nchswww/data/catpub95.pdf>)

FURTHER READING

American Library Association, Government Documents Round Table. *DttP. Documents to the People*. Quarterly 1984–. March issue, "Bibliography on Documents Librarianship and Government Information."
> Includes a section on "Census."

Anderson, Margo J. *The American Census: A Social History*. New Haven, CT: Yale University Press, 1988.
> A history of the decennial census and its impact on the nation.

Bates, Mary Ellen. "Where's EDGAR Today? Finding SEC Filings Online." *Database* 19 (June 1996): 41+ (accessed 12/2/97 via NEXIS, ALLNEWS library).
> A thorough review of the government's Internet EDGAR and value-added commercial services.

Blake, Kelle. "First in the Path of the Firemen: The Fate of the 1890 Census." *Prologue* 28 (Spring 1996): 64–81. (AE 1.111:28/1).
> It took more than a fire to destroy the 1890 census schedules.

Lavin, Michael R. *Business Information: How to Find It, How to Use It*. 2nd ed. Phoenix, AZ: Oryx Press, 1992.
> Practical advice for finding and using statistics from the censuses, an introduction to statistical reasoning, plus overviews of economic and industry statistics.

———. *Understanding the Census: A Guide for Marketers, Planners, Grant Writers, and Other Data Users*. Phoenix, AZ: Oryx Press, 1996.
> This user-friendly guide explains census products, definitions, concepts, and practices with sample tables, examples, tips, and other user aids.

Morehead, Joe. "The Uses and Misuses of Information Found in Government Publications," in *Essays on Public Documents and Government Policies*. New York: The Haworth Press, 1986.
> A discussion of the need for intelligent interpretation of government statistics, with cautions about specific data weaknesses.

National Center for Education Statistics. *Data for Decisions: Resources from the National Center for Education Statistics* [videorecording 17 min., 13 sec.]. GPO, 1996. (ED 1.334/2:D 35/VIDEO).
> An introduction to NCES products and services.

"The North American Industry Classification System (NAICS)" <http://www.census.gov/epcd/www/naics.html> (June 18, 1998).
> The lowdown on NAICS and its expected impact, with SIC-NAICS translation tables.

Norwood, Janet L. *Organizing to Count: Change in the Federal Statistical System*. Washington, DC: The Urban Institute Press, 1995.
> A history of public and governmental inattention to the federal statistical system.

Schulze, Suzanne. *Population Information in Nineteenth Century Census Volumes*. Phoenix, AZ: Oryx Press, 1983.

———. *Population Information in Twentieth Century Census Volumes, 1900–1940*. Phoenix, AZ: Oryx Press, 1985.

———. *Population Information in Twentieth Century Census Volumes, 1950–1980*. Phoenix, AZ: Oryx Press, 1988.
> A subject index to data in decennial census volumes; especially useful for census volumes before 1940, which were published without guides.

Stratford, Jean Slemmons and Juri Stratford. *Major U.S. Statistical Series: Definitions, Publications, Limitations*. Chicago: American Library Association, 1992.
> An introduction to federal statistical measures for population, labor force, economic indicators, price indexes and inflation measures, GNP and production measures, foreign trade, and federal government finance.

U.S. Geological Survey. "Geographic Information Systems" <http://www.usgs.gov/research/gis/title.html> (November 3, 1997).
> A guide to GIS and how it is used.

NOTES

1. Ken Ringle. "Unearthing America's Urban Roots: Archive Releases Pivotal 1920 Census." *The Washington Post* (March 3, 1992): B1, column 6 and B6, column 4.

2. Ann Herbert Scott, *Census U.S.A.: Fact Finding for the American People, 1790–1970* (New York: Seabury Press, 1968), p. 121.

3. Scott, p. 121.

4. *Bureau of the Census, Census '80: Continuing the Factfinder Tradition* (GPO, 1980), p. 276.

5. Public Law 104–193.

6. Marc Peyser. "Question Time: What Will the 2000 Census Ask?" *Newsweek* (June 16, 1997): p. 14.

7. Geoffrey D. Austrian, *Herman Hollerith: Forgotten Giant of Information Processing* (New York: Columbia University Press, 1982), pp. 58–73.

8. More precisely, in 1952 the average white woman could anticipate living for 72.7 years; the overall average expected lifespan was 68.6 years.

9. Unfortunately, most of the 1890 census records were destroyed by fire. See Kellee Blake's "'First in the Path of the Firemen' The Fate of the 1890 Population Census" *Prologue* 28 (Spring 1996): 64-81. (AE 1.111:28/1).

10. Edmonston, Barry and Charles Schultze, eds. *Modernizing the U. S. Census.* Washington, DC: National Academy Press, 1995.

11. "Top 100 Serials in WorldCat." *OCLC Newsletter* No. 228 (July/August 1997): 20–21.

12. Michael R. Lavin, *Understanding the Census: A Guide for Marketers, Planners, Grant Writers, and Other Data Users.* (Phoenix, AZ: Oryx Press, 1996), pp. 195–227.

13. Robert J. Samuelson "Out of Print." *Washington Post* (September 6, 1995): A21.

14. Michael R. Lavin, *Business Information: How to Find It, How to Use It* (Phoenix, AZ: Oryx Press, 1987), p. 171.

EXERCISES

1. What is the population of the United States?
2. Using statistical reference tools, identify the answer or a probable answer source for the questions below. Cite the answer source and the reference you consulted to identify it.
   a. How scientifically literate are Americans?
   b. A magazine article mentions a 1991 Harris poll that found four out of five Americans to be concerned about threats to their personal privacy. Identify the survey.
   c. What percent of U.S. patents are granted to non-Americans?
   d. How can I get Charles McClure and Peter Hernon's report on depository library use of census data?

CHAPTER 13
Primary and Nonprint Sources

What is Past is Prologue.
 —Words from Shakespeare's *The Tempest*,
 carved on the National Archives building

WHAT

Primary sources are original, one-of-a-kind records that have survived from the past. Primary resources, forming what is called "the historical record," include photographs, films, books, personal papers, government documents, letters, oral histories, diaries, maps, reports, and artifacts. This chapter also offers an introduction to government audiovisuals and national museums.

WHERE

The nation's two citadels of historical materials are the Library of Congress and the National Archives. The big three of agencies distributing maps to depository libraries are the U.S. Geological Survey, National Imagery and Mapping Agency (NIMA), and National Ocean Service.

HOW

The Library of Congress, National Archives, and other federal wellsprings of primary materials have mounted some of their collections on the Internet. Most of their collections, however, remain accessible only on-site.

PRIMARY SOURCES

The National Archives

http://www.nara.gov/

The National Charters

The three icons of American history are here: the Declaration of Independence, the parchment copy of the Constitution, and the Bill of Rights. The originals are displayed in the National Archives rotunda in an atmosphere described as "distinctly High Church—buffed marble, shuffling feet, the occasional cough or whisper."[1] In 1952, after the Declaration of Independence and the Constitution were ceremoniously transferred from the Library of Congress, they were hermetically sealed in bulletproof cases that ascend each morning from a 55-ton vault of reinforced concrete and steel. Ultraviolet filters repel harmful light and an atmosphere of helium prevents deterioration of the parchment.[2]

Imagine a place where you can see the police report on Abraham Lincoln's assassination and President Nixon's letter of resignation, read journals of polar explorers and the passenger list for the *Lusitania*'s last voyage, examine Japanese surrender documents from World War II and a wanted poster for Butch Cassidy and the Sundance Kid, view Eva Braun's photo albums, and listen to the Nuremberg trials. You could experience all of this and more in the National Archives, the nation's memory. The National Archives records two centuries of U.S. history in documents, photographs, maps, films, recordings, and computer files. These records span the three branches of government, dating back to the First Continental Congress.

FIGURE 13.1: Before the National Archives.

When records were amassed for transfer to the new National Archives building in the 1930s, they were recovered from attics, abandoned theaters, warehouses, and the White House garage. More than half were damaged from neglect, fire, dirt, insects, or the elements. The photo above shows War Department records before their transfer to the archives.

Before the creation of our National Archives in 1934, the nation's records were haphazardly stored and generally inaccessible, not only to citizens but also to government. The documents of our history were scattered throughout the Capital in basements, attics, stables, and odd cubbyholes. (See figure 13.1.) Most agencies were so nonchalant about the moldering papers in their custody that many had already been lost or damaged by the time the National Archives opened its doors. Historians acknowledge that 1934 was "astonishingly late" to pull the nation's archives under one roof, especially compared with other Western countries whose archives date from the mid-nineteenth century.[4] When the cornerstone was laid in 1933, Herbert Hoover called the Archives building designed by John Russell Pope the "temple of our history." The neoclassical revival edifice in Washington, DC, and a glistening new facility in College Park, Maryland, are only part of a geographically scattered network that encompasses regional archives <http://www.nara.gov/nara/regional/nsrmenu.html>, federal records centers <http://www.nara.gov/nara/frc/frchome.html>, and presidential libraries (discussed in chapter 10)—all administered by the National Archives and Records Administration.

Twelve regional archives branches house basic archival collections, records of regional and local interest, plus copies of many NARA microfilm publications. Many branches offer basic collections of records, including those of U.S. district courts since the mid-1940s, the U.S. courts of appeals, the Bureau of Indian Affairs, the

Bureau of Customs, and the Office of the Chief of Engineers. A list of regional archives is given in the free booklet, "Regional Branches of the National Archives" (General Information Leaflet No. 22), from NARA. The holdings of regional archives are described in branch publications and in *The Archives: A Guide to the National Archives Field Branches* from Ancestry, Inc.

Although the motto inscribed on the Archives building reads "The Written Word Endures," the Archives began to gather not only government written records, but also films, sound recordings, photographs, maps, drawings, punch cards, and nongovernment material that illuminated U.S. history, including the everyday memorabilia of ordinary people. Within a few years, the Archives building was already two-thirds full. Solon J. Buck, second archivist of the United States, likened the surge of records to having a pet elephant: "its bulk cannot be ignored, its upkeep is terrific, and, although it can be utilized, uncontrolled it is potentially a menace." A stack of today's holdings in Washington and College Park, in regional archives, records centers, and the presidential collections would tower 378 miles high.

The Collections

The federal government now produces every four months a stack of records equal to all those produced in the 124 years between George Washington and Woodrow Wilson.
> —The National Coordinating Committee
> for the Promotion of History, 1989

If you've ever cleaned an attic, you can imagine the National Archives' task of culling the accumulated official papers of the nation—growing by billions of pieces each year. Federal records are those created as part of the business of government. Most are paper documents such as letters, completed forms, memos, directives, and reports. Records materialize in other forms such as photographs, maps, microfilm, motion pictures, sound recordings, and computer tapes or disks. Two key laws govern federal records management: the Federal Records Act of 1950, which established agency records management programs, and the Paperwork Reduction Act, which includes records management as part of overall federal information resources management. Federal records cannot be destroyed without authorization from the archivist of the United States, who oversees the preservation of those judged to have enduring value—about two to three percent each year. But preserving that tiny fraction has added up to billions of pages of text, millions of photographs, thousands of movie reels and sound recordings, maps, charts, and aerial photos. Just listening to all the sound recordings in the Archives would take 30,000 hours.

The National Archives also has the most inclusive permanent collection of federal government publications, about 2.4 million of them. The bulk of the collection was added in 1972, with the acquisition of the Superintendent of Documents collection, which has titles dating back to 1789. The Archives sells copies of these documents. An introduction to the Archives' government document collection is given in the free General Information Leaflet No. 28, "Looking for an Out-of-Print U.S. Government Publication?" (AE 1.113:28). The *Cumulative Title Index to United States Public Documents, 1789–1975*, compiled by Daniel Lester (U.S. Historical Documents Institute), is a listing of titles from the GPO collection now housed in the National Archives.

Access

An archives is not a library. While a library houses books . . . an archives houses the raw materials from which books are written.
> —Herman Viola,
> Museum of Natural History,
> Smithsonian Institution

Archival collections are not subject-classified or accessed through familiar library tools like card catalogs. Instead, they are organized according to their source of origin in "record groups," containing records of a single agency. The National Archives publishes guides, special lists, indexes, and other finding aids for researchers seeking specific records within the vast National Archives holdings. The free pamphlet "Publications from the National Archives" lists guides and indexes to specific collections, catalogs of microfilmed records, and special archival publications useful to scholars, archivists, historians, and researchers. An overview of National Archives collections is provided in the *Guide to Federal Records in the National Archives of the United States* (AE 1.108:G 94/V.1-3 and <gopher://gopher.nara.gov/11/inform/guide>). The long-awaited 1995 edition describes holdings through September 1, 1994. It's expected that this edition will be the last in paper—updates will be online and updated incrementally in *Prologue* and *The Record*. *Prologue* (as in "What is Past is Prologue"), the award-winning quarterly journal, offers fascinating articles and announcements (AE 1.111:). *The Record* is NARA's free newsletter about research, preservation, accessions and openings, declassifications, genealogy, regional archives, presidential libraries, and the National Historical Publications and Records Commission (AE 1.117/2:). *Resources for Research: A Comprehensive Catalog* is a comprehensive list of microfilmed federal records (AE 1.102:M 58/2/996 and <http://www.nara.gov/publications/microfilm/comprehensive/compcat.html> or <http://gopher.nara.gov:70/11/about/publ/micro/compre>).

Clio, the National Archives Information Server, is named in honor of the Greek muse of history. Clio currently encompasses Web and gopher sites, although the gopher files are being migrated to NARA's Web site. While some files will remain on the gopher, the most complete information can be found on NARA's Web site <http://www.nara.gov/>, ranked among the top three federal Web sites in a 1997 *USA Today* survey. NARA is exploring enhanced access options, including the possibility of an integrated online system that would make digital copies of high-interest documents available, allow online ordering, and support educational use of documentary material. The status of these initiatives is summarized in the free General Information Leaflet No. 65 "Online and Electronic Services from the National Archives and Records Administration" <http://www.nara.gov/nara/gil65.html>.

Already up and running is the NARA Archival Information Locator (NAIL), the prototype for an eventual online catalog of holdings in Washington, DC, the regional archives, and presidential libraries. Until the full catalog emerges, NAIL will serve as NARA's online information system. NAIL is a searchable database of information about selected NARA holdings across the country, allowing online retrieval of digital textual documents, photographs, maps, and sound recordings. Many NAIL records are accompanied by images (in thumbnails and full-size), tagged with red bullets. The NAIL pilot initially focused on audiovisual material from the Still Pictures Branch and the Motion Picture, Sound, and Video Branch, but all types of material are now described in NAIL. It will evolve into an online finding aid for all NARA holdings. Historical gems already digitized include the manuscripts of Dwight D. Eisenhower's D-Day invasion speech to the troops, Franklin D. Roosevelt's Day of Infamy speech, George Washington's first inaugural address, a private claim filed by Harriet Tubman, Civil War maps, and photos from the Kennedy White House.

To ensure preservation, NARA's unique records do not circulate or interlibrary loan. Photocopies of NARA documents and microfilm rolls may be purchased on-site or by mail, and many large research libraries also own copies. The National Archives research rooms are open to the public. Researchers should contact the User Services Division before visiting. "National Archives Primary Reference Contact List," free from NARA, lists archivists responsible for records on particular topics. General Information Leaflets No. 30, "Information about the National Archives for Researchers" <http://www.nara.gov/nara/dc/Archives1_info.html> and No. 63, "Information for Researchers [at the] National Archives at College Park" <http://www.nara.gov/nara/dc/Archives2_info.html> are free.

The Library of Congress

http://lcweb.loc.gov/

Tattered and torn, dog-eared, yellowed, crumbling and faded though some may be, these are the country's national memories, the pictures that made us laugh, songs that made us cry, words that made us free, maps that guided our way.
—Sarah Booth Conroy, *The Washington Post*

The Library of Congress (LC) celebrates its 200th anniversary in the year 2000. The cozy little reference room that began in 1800 with 740 books, four atlases, and three maps has mushroomed into the world's largest, most comprehensive library and one of the world's leading cultural institutions. Sometimes called Jefferson's legacy, LC arose from the ashes of the War of 1812 with Thomas Jefferson's book collection as its nucleus. Jefferson's encyclopedic interests set the regenerated library on a diverse course, collecting treasures such as a Gutenberg Bible (one of three perfect vellum copies in the world), flutes, a priceless collection of Stradivarius violins, pamphlets, drawings, films, manuscripts, prints, music, pho-

tographs, sound recordings, and videotapes. Having Congress "as its godfather" has made it "perhaps the most influential of all the national libraries of the world."[5] It simultaneously acts as Congress's library, the de facto national library, the nation's copyright agency, the hub for materials for the blind and physically handicapped, home base for America's poet laureate, library of last resort in all subjects except technical agriculture and clinical medicine, and the world's largest collection of maps, atlases, music, motion pictures, and television programs. *Special Collections in the Library of Congress* offers overviews of the Library's prized collections, including drawings, films, maps, prints, photographs, sound recordings, and videotapes <http://lcweb.loc.gov/spcoll/spclhome.html>. The Web version updates the now out-of-print 1980 edition (LC 1.6/4:C 68) with descriptions that retain its numbering system.

We can either become a museum of knowledge confined to our three buildings on Capitol Hill, or we can make the institution accessible to all Americans. We have chosen the latter option.
—Suzanne Thorin, Library of Congress

In a thrust to make its enormous riches "accessible to as many people as possible," the Library of Congress has harnessed the Internet to catapult its collections coast-to-coast and around the world. Mobilizing an evolving electronic repository of documents, films, photographs, graphics, sound recordings, music, manuscripts, pamphlets, and books collectively christened the National Digital Library, LC commandeered funding from government and corporate donors to support costly digitizing of material through the year 2000. The National Digital Library program frees primary historical material "from the page or shelf," piping unique collections of the Library of Congress and of libraries and archives throughout the world over the Internet. The Library of Congress's own initial contribution, called American Memory, spotlights treasures of Americana such as the Gettysburg Address, the rough draft of the Declaration of Independence, Walt Whitman's notebooks, and Mathew Brady's Civil War photographs, supplemented by interactive, electronic "exhibitions" to introduce the collections, as well as user guides, interpretive materials, and bibliographies <http://lcweb2.loc.gov/ammem/>.

PHOTOGRAPHS, PRINTS, AND MOTION PICTURES

We introduced Americans to America.
—Roy E. Stryker, director of the Farm Security Administration, 1935–43

Often overlooked as historical documentation, photographs form a hauntingly detailed record of times past. As primary sources, photographs often provide information unnoted by the written word. Studying Civil War images, for example, can furnish particulars about uniforms, equipment, battlefields, and camps. The Park Service's accurate restoration of Ford's Theatre might have been impossible without stereographic photos taken immediately after Lincoln's assassination <http://www.nps.gov/foth/index2.htm>.

From the late 1800s to the early 1930s, government staff photographers flourished, particularly during Franklin Roosevelt's administration, when photographs portraying the ravages of the Depression galvanized social change. A quarter of a million photos were taken by the Farm Security Administration (FSA) alone. The 1930s saw government photographs featured in books, pamphlets, magazines, newspapers, and even entered as evidence in congressional hearings.[6] In 1944, an executive order placed the archives of the Farm Security Administration's 1936–1942 "photo-documentation of America" file organized by Roy E. Stryker under the

FIGURE 13.2: Migrant Mother.

In the 1930s, Farm Security Administration photographers like Walker Evans, Gordon Parks, and Dorothea Lange produced some of the best known images of the twentieth century. It was FSA photographs that inspired John Steinbeck to write *The Grapes of Wrath*, after spending several days studying "those tragic, beautiful faces." "Migrant Mother," snapped by Lange in 1936, is the Library of Congress's most requested photo.

wing of the Library of Congress, along with another landmark federal photographic documentation project, the Office of War Information. A guide is Reference Aid #52, "Farm Security Administration/Office of War Information," free from the Library of Congress's Prints and Photographs Division. *Farm Security Administration, Historical Section: A Guide to Textual Records in the Library of Congress* is a finding aid to written records of the FSA photographic unit, including microfilmed office files, scrapbooks, captions, and photographic prints, negatives, and transparencies (LC 25.8/2:F 22). Except for the Farm Security Administration/Office of War Information Collection and the Historic American Buildings Survey/Historic American Engineering Record, however, the Library of Congress Prints and Photographs Division has only scattered government-produced images—look instead to the National Archives for these.

Pictures at the Library of Congress

Selected motion pictures, prints, and photographs are available for viewing through American Memory <http://lcweb2.loc.gov/ammem/>. The Library of Congress's Prints and Photographs Division is a cache of prints, negatives, transparencies, and stereographs produced with almost every photographic technology, old and new. Although the Division collects in five major areas, photography dominates. Nurtured by the Copyright Law of 1865 requirement that a copy of each copyrighted photograph, print, or engraving be deposited at the Library of Congress, the Prints and Photographs Division has amassed photographs, prints and drawings, posters, and architectural and engineering drawings. The collection provides unique visual documentation of U.S. history to the mid-1980s, spotlighting "the lives, concerns and achievements of its people, and of its place in the larger world." Copies from the collection, identified by reproduction number or call number, may be purchased through the Library's Photoduplication Service.

Although the Prints and Photographs reading room <http://lcweb.loc.gov/rr/print/> opens its photograph collections to visitors, "public awareness of the library's photographs has been indirect and random."[7] Frequent visitors include historians, picture researchers, photography students, authors seeking book illustrations, and people trying to identify their family photos. Although much of the collection remains uncataloged, a general introduction is given in *Library of Congress Prints and Photographs: An Illustrated Guide* (LC 1.6/4:P 93 and <http://lcweb.loc.gov/coll/print/guide/>). Few of the Prints and Photographs Division's older vertical files, card catalogs, and book publications will be retrospectively digitized. A portion of the Prints and Photographs Division's millions of images are described in LC's online catalog, LOCIS (catalog records only; no digitized images), but LOCIS covers only a fraction of the Division's total holdings. A guide to searching LOCIS for citations to images is given at <http://lcweb.loc.gov/rr/print/locisinx.html>. Many of the Internet records describe only groups of images rather than individual items, however. Information on descriptions and images available via the Internet is found in Reference Aid #182, "How to Find: Prints and Photographs Division (P&P) Materials over Internet," free from the Division.

Pictures at the National Archives

http://www.nara.gov/

The National Archives, custodian of U.S. government agency records, holds images made by and for the U.S. government. The National Archives is such a rich source of pictorial history it has been dubbed a "photographic time machine." Visitors to College Park, Maryland, may pursue picture research in the Archives' Still Picture Research Room. (Researchers should make advance arrangements.) The Still Picture Branch also boasts a definitive collection of federal posters, most produced during World Wars I and II to support the war effort. Among some 15,000 posters are images seared into the American consciousness: Uncle Sam asserting "I Want You" and Smokey Bear's reminder that "Only You Can Prevent Forest Fires." Reproductions of Still Picture Branch images and posters can be purchased. The *Guide to the Holdings of the Still Picture Branch of the National Archives and Records Administration* (AE 1.108:St 5) provides an overview of the collection. The free General Information Leaflet No. 38, "Information for Prospective Researchers about the Still Picture Branch of the National Archives," explains holdings and research procedures. The National Archives Motion Picture, Sound, and Video Research Room has images documenting America's history since colonial times, with emphasis on the nineteenth to mid-twentieth centuries. General Information Leaflet No. 33, "Motion Pictures and Sound and Video Recordings in the National Archives," explains holdings and the division of records between the two Archives buildings. NAIL, the NARA Archival Information Locator, is a searchable database of selected textual documents, photographs, maps, and sound recordings held in the Still Picture and Motion Picture, Sound, and Video Branches <http://www.nara.gov/nara/nail.html>. Specialized listings, such as "Military History Related Photographs Held by the National Archives Still Picture Branch," on the Center of Military History Web site, are also available <http://www.army.mil/cmh-pg/stillpic.htm>.

Agriculture and Forestry Collections

The National Agricultural Library's (NAL) Special Collections provides images of lovely rare botanical prints, and photos of not-so lovely plant diseases, along with forest firefighters, natural phenomena, and homesteads <http://www.nal.usda.gov/speccoll/>. The optical laser disc Photograph Collection of the USDA (PB90-504184) contains photographs illustrating broad areas of agriculture, food and nutrition, insects, plant and livestock diseases, forestry, and conservation. The Forest Service Photograph Collection, the world's largest forestry photo collection, begun in 1898, can be perused on-site at NAL or at selected Forest Service Units and Land-Grant libraries by browsing the Forest Service Photo Laser Disc, a word-searchable database of images and image information from the Forest Service Photo Browsing Collection at NAL (PB90-504192). It includes photos, slides, posters, illustrations, and maps. An accompanying database may be searched for additional information. Some Forest Service photos circulate, while others can be ordered as prints. The Agricultural Research Service maintains an Internet Image Gallery with photographs of plants, animals, fruits and vegetables, and more <http://www.ars.usda.gov/is/graphics/photos/index.html>.

The Smithsonian Institution Collection

An overview of the Smithsonian Institution's vast still photograph holdings of photonegatives, photoprints, phototransparencies, and direct positive processes is available in the *Guide to Photographic Collections at the Smithsonian Institution* (SI 3.10:P 56). Entries outline collections, dates of photos, origins, subjects, arrangement, captions, finding aids, and restrictions. Five volumes are planned; three have been completed. Smithsonian Photographs Online is a searchable Internet cache of work by Smithsonian photographers <http://photo2.si.edu/>. Arranged by topics from poisonous sea snakes to Washington's seldom-seen memorials, it's well worth browsing. The list, with images of air and space, science, technology, history, and current events, spotlights popular and important Smithsonian objects, events, exhibits, and interests, as seen through the viewfinders of its photographers.

U.S. Geological Survey (USGS) Collection

The USGS regional library in Denver, Colorado, includes the Photographic Library of photos taken since the 1860s by USGS scientists as part of their field studies, including pioneer photographers W.H. Jackson, T.H. O'Sullivan, C. Watkins, J.K. Hillers, T. Moran, A.J. Russell, E.O. Beaman, and W. Bell <http://www.usgs.

gov/library/denlib.html#Begin>. Photos include portraits of USGS personnel, earth science subjects, nineteenth-century mining, and people at work. Researchers may have the Photographic Library's files searched for photographs on topics of their choice, or those seen in USGS publications. Reproductions may be ordered at cost from the Photographic Library. Because the collection has more than 300,000 photographs, researchers are encouraged to visit in person. Three photo-CD-ROMs are sold by USGS to provide a collection overview: covering earthquakes, volcanoes, geologic hazards and other phenomena; historical mining operations in Colorado and Utah; and earth science photographs <http://pubs.usgs.gov/cdprods/mtoz.html>.

Aerial Photos

Attempts to photograph the Earth from above have evolved from attaching cameras to balloons, kites, and pigeons in the 1800s, to today's aerial photographs and satellite images. The U.S. Geological Survey Aerial Photography data set includes black-and-white photos taken since 1944 for mapping purposes <http://edcwww.cr.usgs.gov/glis/hyper/guide/usgsphotos>. USGS Earth Science Information Centers (ESIC) sell aerial photos, remotely sensed satellite images, and declassified photographs from early spy satellites. ESIC researchers help customers find USGS photos, imagery in other federal agency collections, and, in some cases, those of private companies. The U.S. Geological Survey Fact Sheet, Looking for an Old Aerial Photograph (Fact Sheet FS-127-96), provides guidance for tracking down aerial photos <http://mapping.usgs.gov/mac/isb/pubs/factsheets/fs12796.html>.

The National Aerial Photography Program is coordinated by the U.S. Geological Survey to acquire aerial photography of the 48 coterminous states every five years <http://edcwww.cr.usgs.gov/glis/hyper/guide/napp>.

The Library of Congress Panoramic Photograph Collection of American cities, landscapes, and group portraits is included in American Memory, Taking the Long View: Panoramic Photographs, ca. 1851–1991 <http://lcweb2.loc.gov/ammem/pnhtml/pnhome.html>. The subjects are wide ranging: farm life, beauty contests, disasters, bridges, canals and dams, fairs and expositions, military and naval activities, the oil industry, schools and college campuses, sports, and transportation.

MAPS

Maps are part of the understanding of all human-kind.
—Peter Steinhart,
contributing editor to *Audubon* magazine

For more than two hundred years, surveying, compiling, and publishing maps have been recognized as official obligations of government. Since our nation's infancy, the government has recognized map and chart making as vital to national development and defense. As early as 1777, General George Washington appointed a staff geographer and surveyor to make sketches and maps for the Continental Army. Later, major geographic features of the nation's new territories were delineated through public land surveys. The West was explored in government-sponsored expeditions like that of Lewis and Clark, and the nation's waterways were charted and surveyed to safeguard commercial and naval vessels. In 1807, Congress created the government's first scientific office, the Survey of the Coast (now embedded within the National Oceanic and Atmospheric Administration) to chart America's coastal waters. And in 1879, the army surrendered its role as the nation's chief mapper to a fledgling agency called the Geological Survey. But mapping had flourished on the continent long before the federalists took an interest in it: in 1869, when a U.S. Coast Survey geographer asked Chilkat Indians to describe the Sitka, Alaska, landscape, they spent three days drawing him a detailed, accurate map.

By some estimates, about 80 percent of all maps are officially published by national, state, county, or municipal governments. As a result, the most comprehensive map collections are found in official government agencies and in the world's national libraries. Numerous federal agencies collect and prepare cartographic data, creating maps not only for specific cartographic programs, but as working tools and for communicating information.

Cartographic Literacy

I'm at the corner of Walk and Don't Walk.
—Old joke

Are you cartographically literate? The United States recently placed sixth among eight nations in a National Geographic Society assessment of geographic knowledge. Americans came in dead last when 18- to 24-year-olds were compared across the globe. In other studies, one-third of college undergraduates studying geography couldn't find France or Japan on a map, and more than half were fuzzy on the whereabouts of Chicago. More than 14 percent of Americans interviewed couldn't locate the United States on a world map.[8]

Cobb and Seavey stress the need for librarians to be knowledgeable about maps in order to help users interpret them: "Almost never does one have to teach the patron how to read a book. This is not the case with maps. Often the patron will need assistance in actually interpreting the data presented by the cartographic format."[9]

A Cartographic Primer

Cartography is the science of mapmaking. Today this science uses geographic information systems (GIS) to create computerized maps <http://www.usgs.gov/research/gis/title.html>. Geographic information systems rely upon spatial data—data identified according to their locations. A pre-computer example can be seen in the Lascaux caves in France, where Cro-Magnon drawings of animals show track lines and tallies depicting migration routes. These prehistoric records incorporate the two-element structure of modern geographic information: a graphic file linked to an attribute database.[10]

Charts are maps that aid navigation in water, air, or space. Mapping and charting are not limited to Earth, but can also illustrate planets, satellites, and the rest of the heavens.

Atlases are collections of maps or charts, while national atlases focus on an entire country and are often government publications. The monumental *National Atlas of the United States of America*, published in 1970 by the U.S. Geological Survey, was the first and only U.S. national atlas ever produced (I 19.2:N 21a). The 400-page, 12-pound oversize volume included hundreds of maps depicting general, physical, historical, economic, sociocultural, and administrative aspects of the nation, along with sections on mapping, charting, and the world. Although the volume is now out of print, selected *National Atlas* maps, revisions of the original maps, and new maps published in *National Atlas* format are still sold by USGS for less than $10 <http://www.usgs.gov/atlas/index.html>. Refer to the free "National Atlas Maps" Fact Sheet FS-245-95 (from USGS Information Service, Box 25286, Denver, CO 80225) or <http://mapping.usgs.gov/mac/isb/pubs/factsheets/fs24595.html>. A revised, state-of-the-art CD-ROM edition is expected in 1998 <http://www.usgs.gov/atlas/index.html>.

Topographic maps depict natural and manmade landscapes, illustrating shape and elevation using contour lines (called "terrain relief"). With practice, a map reader can visualize hills and valleys from the contour lines on a topographic map. Symbols are the graphic language of maps, their shapes, sizes, locations, and color all having special meaning. On USGS topographic maps, a symbol's color indicates the feature represented: water is blue, human-made features like roads are black, wooded areas are green, while brown contour lines represent the earth. Planimetric maps do not show terrain relief.

Base maps are used to organize and display information which is "overlaid" on the base map. The USGS prepares base maps for the nation.

Thematic maps depict data through color and shading. The location and intensity of earthquakes, for example, could be depicted using defined colors on a map. (See figure 13.3.)

The map margin, the border around the map's outer edges, provides bibliographic information. Marginal information corresponds to a book's table of contents and introduction, noting how the map was made, by whom, and when. Like books, maps can be bibliographically described by title, publisher, and date, along with characteristics unique to maps, such as scale and contour.

Scale is the relationship between map distance and real distance, usually expressed as a ratio. A scale of 1:63,360, for example, means that one inch on the map represents 63,360 inches (one mile). When it comes to map scales, large is small: the larger the second number in the ratio, the smaller the map scale and the less detail shown.

Quadrangles are the most common map publication format. The most common scale for topographic maps is 1:24,000, called 7.5 ("seven-and-a-half") quadrangle maps because they cover 7.5 minutes of latitude and longitude. Quadrangle maps are fairly large-scale, showing details of natural and human-made features like buildings, campgrounds, ski lifts, water mills, bridges, fences, roads, and even drive-in theaters. To map the entire United States (excluding Alaska) requires a quilt of some 57,000 quadrangles. Smaller-scale maps (1:250,000 and smaller) show large areas and predominant features like boundaries, state parks, airports, major roads, and railroads. The USGS's National Mapping Program produces 7.5 quadrangle maps for each of the 50 states <http://mapping.usgs.gov/www/html/nmp_prog.html>. About 20 percent have been digitized into the emerging National Digital Cartographic Data Base.

Index maps are guides to maps of specific areas, using a base map with an overlaid grid that breaks the area into named segments.

Gazetteers are geographic dictionaries, alphabetical lists of places, with descriptions. The *National Gazetteer of the United States* is issued in separate volumes for selected states, all published as USGS Professional Paper 1200 and collectively dubbed The *National Gazetteer of the United States of America* (I 19.16:1200-state and <http://greenwood.cr.usgs.gov/propaper.html>). The *National Gazetteer of the United States of America—United States Concise 1990* volume covers the entire nation and its territories, describing significant features and places (I 19.16:1200-US). The entire database is also available on CD-ROM as the *Digital Gazetteer of the U.S.* (I 19.120:G 25/CD). A cooperative endeavor of the USGS and the U.S. Board on Geographic Names, the gazetteer provides a national standard for names of places, features, and areas.

FIGURE 13.3: Thematic Map.

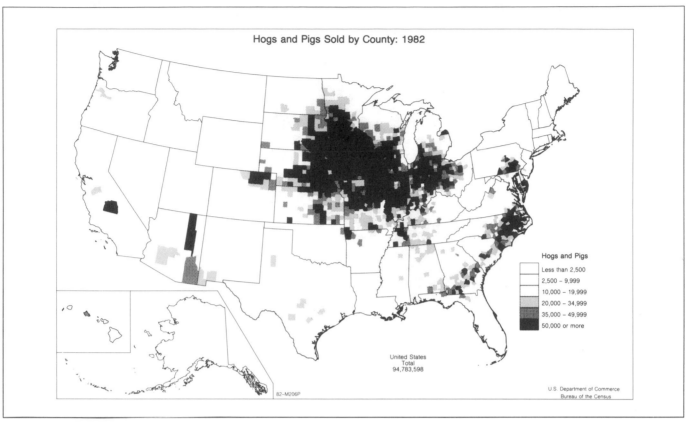

Source: Bureau of the Census.

> *The USGS folks put place names on maps, write them on lists, file them in drawers, talk about them at meetings and generally treat them like a 1955 set of mint condition Bowman Gum Co. baseball cards.*
>
> —Guy Gugliotta, *The Washington Post*

The *Gazetteer* is derived from the USGS's Geographic Names Information System (GNIS), the nation's official automated names repository. Federally sanctioned names of almost 2 million physical and cultural geographic features are identified ("Creek," by the way, is the most frequently used name), with state and county location and geographic coordinates, and references to the 1:24,000-scale USGS topographic map on which it is displayed. Also included are defunct features of special interest to genealogists, such as sites of long-forgotten churches and cemeteries. Fact Sheet FS-127-95, Geographic Names Information System, provides details <http://mapping.usgs.gov/mac/isb/pubs/factsheets/fs12795.html>. The entire GNIS database is searchable on the Web at <http://mapping.usgs.gov/www/gnis/index.html>.

Most Common U.S. Place Names

1. Midway
2. Fairview
3. Oak Grove
4. Five Points
5. Pleasant Hill

Source: *Geographic Names Information System* (I 19.120:G 25/CD).

The Nation's Primary Mapmakers

The three major distributors of maps to depository libraries are the U.S. Geological Survey, National Imagery and Mapping Agency (NIMA), and National Ocean Service. Other agencies join this triumvirate in sending maps to depository libraries, including the Forest Service, Soil Conservation Service, Central Intelligence Agency, Bureau of the Census, and National Park Service. Most maps arrive in depositories folded and cataloged, with SuDocs numbers assigned, and are listed in the *Monthly Catalog.* The *Federal Depository Library Manual* includes a chapter on maps, discussing issuing agencies, map types, indexes, handling, and processing.

U.S. Geological Survey

http://www.usgs.gov/

The U.S. Geological Survey is the nation's largest non-military mapping agency and largest earth science research and information agency. USGS is a source for information about water, energy, minerals, biological resources, and natural hazards such as earthquakes and floods. The USGS disseminates information in many formats, including books, maps, photographs, CD-ROMs, and computer files, working in cooperation with nearly 2,000 local, state, and federal agencies. An overview of USGS products is available in "Publications and Data Products" <http://www.usgs.gov/pubprod/index.html>. USGS maps are usually photo-revised every five to 10 years, and every major USGS map series is available to depositories. New topographic and thematic maps and charts are announced in the free, quarterly *New Publications of the Geological Survey* (I 19.14/4: and <http://pubs.usgs.gov/publications/index.html>). Search titles of thematic maps for sale on the USGS Web site at <http://greenwood.cr.usgs.gov/thmaps.html> and at <http://cpg.cr.usgs.gov/thmaps/thematic.htm>. An overview of products and services is available on USGS's "National Mapping Information" Web page <http://map.usgs.gov/>.

Government Information in Action

When Microsoft sought a terabyte (that's a 1 followed by 12 zeroes) of online data to exercise its skills in manipulating huge databases, the company turned to the U.S. Geological Survey. USGS easily supplied 3 terabytes of digital map data for one-fifth of the United States, depicting topography, roads, buildings, place names, and other features. In a partnership established in 1997, Microsoft will use its technology and software to manipulate USGS's gargantuan files, editing and packaging the maps so they can be searched on the Internet and downloaded from the average home computer. The result? By 1999, a map of "every backyard" will be available on the Internet.

The National Geologic Mapping Act of 1992 authorized a national program of geologic mapping to develop the information needed for informed decision-making regarding land use and resource identification and management <http://www.usgs.gov/reports/yearbooks/1992/geologic_map.html>. The emergent USGS National Geologic Map Database Project is being pursued cooperatively with state geological surveys, universities, and federal agencies. The project already offers a searchable catalog of paper and digital maps along with Internet access to archives of digital maps and data <http://ncgmp.usgs.gov/ngmdbproject/>.

The USGS Library System is one of the largest earth-science libraries in the world <http://www.usgs.gov/library/index.html>. A hub for information about geology, hydrology, cartography, biology, and related fields, the main USGS library is in Reston, Virginia; regional libraries are in Denver, Colorado; Menlo Park, California; and Flagstaff, Arizona.

National Imagery and Mapping Agency

http://www.nima.mil

In 1996, the National Imagery and Mapping Agency (NIMA) replaced the former Defense Mapping Agency, which had been known as the Pentagon's mapmaker. (Much government mapping in the United States and virtually every other modern nation relates to military operations.) The National Imagery and Mapping Agency offers little domestic mapping, focusing instead on maps and charts of all corners of the world to support the nation's defense and security. For national security reasons, only about one percent of NIMA maps, gazetteers, and charts are available to the public. Topographic maps, publications, and digital products are sold through the U.S. Geological Survey <http://164.214.2.59/poc/public.html>. Aeronautical, hydrographic, and topographic maps from the former Defense Mapping Agency are available through the Federal Depository Library Program.

National Ocean Service

http://www.nos.noaa.gov/

An agency within the National Oceanic and Atmospheric Administration (NOAA, pronounced "Noah"), the National Ocean Service (NOS) is responsible for domestic charting, both nautical (U.S. waters and navigable waterways) and aeronautical. Depository copies of National Ocean Service nautical and aeronautical charts are stamped "not to be used for navigation" since they may be outdated by the time they reach depository shelves. (NOS maps and charts are usually revised every 28–56 days.) The National Ocean Service's MapFinder is a one-stop gateway to maps, aerial photographs, and other spatial information <http://mapindex.nos.noaa.gov/>.

Because the law mandates that the Office of Coast Survey operate under a "cost recovery" program, NOS nautical charts themselves are not available over the Internet. In fact, no official government nautical charts are available free on the Internet. Instead, the latest chart editions are sold through a network of authorized NOAA chart agents (listed on the NOS Web site) and by the National Ocean Service's Distribution Division. Catalogs of nautical and aeronautical charts for sale are free from NOAA's Distribution Branch (C 55.418: and

C 55.418/2:) or consult the online NOAA Product Information Catalog <http://www.esdim.noaa.gov/synergy/pic.html>.

The Coast Survey <http://chartmaker.ncd.noaa.gov/>. NOAA's Coast Survey is the nation's only official chartmaker and our oldest scientific organization. After its establishment to chart America's coastal waters in 1807, it created maps of the United States' 5,000 miles of shoreline, plus islands, harbors, bays, headlands, lighthouses, and ocean. While topographers sketched prominent features of the shoreline, hydrographers gauged the depth and contour of the sea bottom and movements of the tides and currents. Then draftsmen and engravers would translate this field work into precise maps for mariners. The Coast Survey's collection of nineteenth-century maps and charts is being readied for digital access over the Internet and through selected NOAA Libraries <http://chartmaker.ncd.noaa.gov/ocs/text/MAP-COLL.htm>. The Historical Collection includes nautical charts, sketches of coastlines (including James Whistler's 1854 sketch of Anacapa Island); a Civil War collection; a Washington, DC, topographic series; and early Pacific Northwest exploration maps.

Whistler in Washington

In 1854, James McNeill Whistler accepted a post drawing and etching topographical maps for the U.S. Coast and Geodetic Survey. Although mapmaking is a factual craft demanding utmost accuracy for nautical safety, Whistler liked to jazz up his maps with sketches of people's faces. He also doodled on the walls of the building's stairway. Whistler's artistic enthusiasm and chronic lateness made him remembered, but not mourned, when he left the Survey after three months. One of the only two extant plates attributed to him is on the Coast Survey Web page <http://chartmaker.ncd.noaa.gov/ocs/historic/whist1s1.gif>. Note that the lower drawing on Whistler's chart of Anacapa Island, California, is enlivened with two flights of very nontopographical birds. The second surviving Whistler plate was donated to the Freer Gallery of Art.

The Census Bureau

http://www.census.gov

Accurate mapping is essential to conducting censuses. The Bureau keeps maps for all counties, incorporated villages, towns, cities, county subdivisions, census tracts, enumeration districts, and city blocks. The Census Bureau publishes outline maps showing names and boundaries of geographic areas, and statistical (thematic) maps, which illustrate data using color and shading.

Free online Mapping Services, TIGER Map Service <http://tiger.census.gov/cgi-bin/mapbrowse-tbl> and Map Stats <http://www.census.gov/datamap/www/>, are on the Census Web site. On the Census Bureau home page, consult "Subjects A-Z" for links to geographic topics such as "Maps" <http://www.census.gov/main/www/man_subj.html>. Number 8 in the Census Bureau's *Factfinder for the Nation* series, "Census Geography—Concepts and Products," is an excellent overview of census cartographic data and is free from Data User Services Division and reprinted in the *Census Catalog and Guide* <http://www.census.gov/prod/www/titles.html#genref>. *Census Catalog and Guide* includes a chapter on geography, describing reports and reference files. On GPO Access "Browse Topics," select "Census Tracts and Blocks (Maps)" to link to Internet sites <http://www.access.gpo.gov/su_docs/dpos/pathbrws.html>.

TIGER. Some 90,000 maps were computer-generated for the 1990 census using TIGER, "the Coast-to-Coast Digital Map Database." TIGER is the first computerized database to map the entire 3.6 million square miles of the nation. To create TIGER, the USGS scanned or manually digitized its 1:100,000-scale maps of the United States, which the Census Bureau then merged into a seamless map database. Selected TIGER files are available to the public on magnetic tape and CD-ROM. Census maps have been issued on paper, microfiche, CD-ROM, and computer tape. The regional census centers sell maps for their regions, and state data centers have copies of all their state's maps. The Census Bureau sells periodic extracts of the TIGER database, called TIGER/Line files, for use in geographic information systems or other geographic applications. TIGER/Line files are presented on maps that contain jurisdictional boundaries; detailed networks of roads, rivers, and railroads; census block group and tract polygons; and schools, hospitals, churches, cemeteries, airports, dams, and other landmarks. A list of TIGER/Line vendors is provided on the TIGER Web page <http://www.census.gov/geo/www/tiger/>.

LandView. The Census Bureau's LandView III is a CD-ROM atlas that can be overlaid with data from the Environmental Protection Agency, Bureau of Census, and NOAA (EP 1.104/4:CD-TGR 95-LV 3-*no.*) The result is a desktop mapper for depicting jurisdictional entities (states, counties, cities and towns, zip codes, congressional districts, and others), complete with roads, rivers, railroads, census block group and tract polygons, schools, hospitals, churches, cemeteries, airports, dams, and other landmarks, which then can be overlaid with social and demographic data from the 1990 Census, hazardous waste sites, pollution, etc. LandView III, with updated software and data, became available in 1997.

A tutorial is included (the LandView II tutorial is also available at <http://www.census.gov/geo/www/tiger/lv2tutor.html>). LandView III help is available at <http://cdserver.er.usgs.gov/cgi-bin/folioisa.dll/landview.nfo?> or from <http://cdserver.er.usgs.gov/default.htm>. LandView II, released in 1995, is available on CD-ROM (EP1.104/4:CD 92-LV 2-nos), and for download (single county) at <http://rtk.net/landview>. The discs depict detail down to the street level for U.S. regions. Disc 11 covers the entire country, but with streets depicted only for counties of the 12 largest metro areas.

More Historical Maps

Part XIV of the *CIS U.S. Serial Set Index,* Index and Carto-Bibliography of Maps, 1789–1969, describes more than 50,000 maps embedded in Serial Set volumes. The Carto-Bibliography can be searched by subject/geographic area, map title, personal names, and corporate names. The maps can be found folded into pockets in Serial Set volumes and in the CIS US Serial Set on Microfiche collection.

The Library of Congress panoramic map collection, the largest in North America, is available on the Internet as part of American Memory <http://lcweb2.loc.gov/ammem/pmhtml/panhome.html>. Popular during the late nineteenth and early twentieth centuries, panoramic maps depicted bird's-eye views of cities, showing streets, buildings, and major landscape features in perspective. LC's panoramic map collection is itemized in *Panoramic Maps of Cities in the United States and Canada: A Checklist of Maps in the Collections of the Library of Congress, Geography and Map Division* (LC 5.2:P 19).

Civil War Maps: An Annotated List of Maps and Atlases in the Library of Congress is a carto-bibliography of maps, charts, atlases, and sketchbooks depicting troop positions and movements, engagements, and fortifications, along with reconnaissance, theater of war, sketch maps, and coastal charts (LC 5.2:C 49/989). It includes indexes to short titles, battles, places, subjects, cartographers, surveyors, engravers, lithographers, publishers, printers, and other personal names. A related publication is *A Guide to Civil War Maps in the National Archives* (not depository).

Foreign Country Maps

When we take no joy in maps, we take no joy in distant places.
—Peter Steinhart,
contributing editor to *Audubon* magazine

The CIA, National Imagery and Mapping Agency, State Department, and USGS all publish world and foreign maps and charts, many of which are available to depository libraries. Other foreign maps and map-producing agencies may be identified using the *Monthly Catalog.* Earlier CIA maps were released through Doc Ex, and—since 1980—through NTIS or GPO. *CIA Maps and Publications Released to the Public* lists maps and publications released through Doc Ex since 1971, by country (note that recent releases are appended) <http://www.odci.gov/cia/publications/mapspub/index.html>.

The government's primary publisher of foreign gazetteers is the Board of Geographic Names within the National Imagery and Mapping Agency. Each gazetteer covers a country or geographic region and lists official place names approved by the federal government (D 5.319:). The Congressional Information Service's *Foreign Gazetteers of the U.S. Board on Geographic Names* is a microfiche file of country gazetteers (except the U.S.) since 1950.

Map Collections

Maps, like faces, are the signatures of history.
—Will and Ariel Durant,
The Story of Civilization

Library of Congress Map Collection

When the Library of Congress was established in 1800, its holdings included three maps and four atlases. Today the Library's Geography and Map Division boasts the world's largest and most comprehensive cartographic collection, containing not only maps and atlases, but also digital geographic data files, reference materials, globes, and three-dimensional plastic relief models <http://lcweb.loc.gov/rr/geogmap/gmpage.html>. The library's collections include familiar formats along with rarities: treasure maps taken from Spanish galleons by Sir Francis Drake; Micronesian charts fashioned from sticks, pebbles, and coconuts; Chinese maps painted on fans; neckerchief maps worn by British aviators in WW II; maps carved on gunpowder horns from the French and Indian War; and Pierre L'Enfant's original 1791 sketch of Washington, DC, with Thomas Jefferson's handwritten marginal notes. Some of the rarer holdings are tucked away in a temperature- and humidity-controlled 5,000-square-foot masonry vault. Selected Geography and Map Division treasures are available for viewing through the American Memory project at <http://lcweb2.loc.gov/ammem/>.

It has been estimated that the Library of Congress acquires copies of three-quarters of the world's unrestricted maps and charts. Because surveying and mapping are official functions of the federal government, many maps and atlases in the collection are deposited by official sources, such as the U.S. Geological Survey and the National Oceanic and Atmospheric Administration. Private and commercial cartographic works arrive via the Library of Congress's Copyright Office, while foreign maps are received by exchange or purchase. The collections are for on-site reference use only, with maps and atlases unavailable for public loan. Access is being expanded as the LC National Digital Library Program for Cartographic Materials scans Geography and Map Division materials to create digital images. And many map and atlas reproductions can be purchased through the Library of Congress's Photoduplication Service.

A peek at the Geography and Map Division collection is provided in *Library of Congress Geography and Maps: An Illustrated Guide* (LC 1.6/4:G 29). The Library's collections are reflected in several card and book catalogs, including the *Bibliography of Cartography* (G.K. Hall, 1976 and 1981 supplement), which shows photo-offset copies of cards from the Library's major reference tool, the Bibliography of Cartography Card File. The "B of C" is an author and subject index to books and journal articles about maps, mapmaking, interpretation, use, preservation, history, and map librarianship. *The National Union Catalog: Cartographic Materials* on microfiche (no SuDocs number) includes the complete Library of Congress map database, including entries for newly cataloged maps. Bibliographic records for the Geography and Map Division collection are part of LC's online catalog, LOCIS <http://lcweb.loc.gov>. Maps are included in *Special Collections in the Library of Congress* <http://lcweb.loc.gov/spcoll/spclhome.html>, with brief descriptions of the history, content, scope, subject strengths, and organization of the library's map collections.

The National Archives

NARA's Cartographic and Architectural Branch oversees a vast collection of maps, charts, aerial and satellite photographs, architectural drawings, patents, and plans for ships and aircraft, incorporating the nation's largest aerial photograph collection and second-largest U. S. and foreign map collection. Although published in 1971, *Guide to Cartographic Records in the National Archives* (GS 4.6/2:C 24) continues to be the key published guide to National Archives cartographic holdings. This title is supplemented by a corps of published and unpublished finding aids and the NARA Archival Information Locator (NAIL), a database of selected holdings, including maps <http://www.nara.gov/nara/nail.html>. The free General Information Leaflet No. 26, "Cartographic and Architectural Branch," describes holdings and research procedures.

Accessing Maps

On GPO Access "Browse Topics," select "Maps and Atlases" to link to Internet sites <http://www.access.gpo.gov/su_docs/dpos/pathbrws.html>. To identify map collections, consult *World Directory of Map Collections* from the International Federation of Library Associations and Institutions or the American Library Association's *Guide to U.S. Map Resources*, a comprehensive directory of the nation's map libraries and cartographic resources in public, private, state, and federal agencies. Federal depository libraries serve as map depositories by receiving maps from numerous agencies. In addition, U.S. Geological Survey Map Reference Libraries house selected USGS maps for public use. Their addresses are available from Earth Science Information Centers and from USGS Public Inquiries Offices, and are listed on the Index to Topographic Maps for each state. The U.S. Geological Survey offers select National Mapping Division digital products (known collectively as US GeoData) free over the Internet <http://edcwww.cr.usgs.gov/doc/edchome/ndcdb/ndcdb.html>. The free Fact Sheet, "US GeoData Available Through the Internet" (FS-124-95), provides details <http://mapping.usgs.gov/mac/isb/pubs/factsheets/fs12496.html>.

USGS sells and distributes about 3 million paper maps yearly. Topographic maps are among the most popular and versatile USGS products, favored by the public for outdoor/recreational pursuits and by scientists and engineers to support their research and technical applications. USGS maps may be purchased from Earth Science Information Centers, by mail from the USGS Denver Distribution Center, or from authorized local dealers listed on the USGS Web page <http://mapping.usgs.gov/esic/to_order.html>. The *Index to Topographic and Other Map Coverage [state]* includes a directory of map sales locations and addresses of USGS map libraries in the state (I 19.41/6-3:). Issued for individual states, the *Catalog of Topographic and Other Published Maps [state]* provides ordering information for topographic, U.S., state, satellite image, and world maps (I 19.41/6-2:). Maps from agencies other than USGS must be purchased from their issuing agencies or GPO. An index and inventory of topographic maps of the United States sold by USGS has been created by Thiry and Tassel at the Colorado School of Mines <http://magma.Mines.EDU/library/maproom/ftp.html>.

Earth Science Information Centers

http://mapping.usgs.gov/esic/index.html

A network of Earth Science Information Centers (ESICs, pronounced "ee-sicks") is the central source for USGS cartographic information and sales. Earth Science Information Centers provide information about the nation's mineral, land, and water resources; the earth's surface and interior; and even the space surrounding Earth. ESICs help to locate maps, charts, aerial and satellite photos and imagery, digital map data, earth science databases, and even nongovernment map data. A network of ESICs responds to questions by mail, e-mail, telephone (don't hold your breath), or walk-ins. (See Addresses at the end of this chapter.) State ESICs in state agencies and universities provide state and local information about earth science products and services, and some sell USGS products. A directory is provided on the federal ESIC Web site. The range of ESIC sales items is vast: aerial photos of your neighborhood, views of the earth taken from space, computer data, color slides, and out-of-print map reproductions are only a few examples. Three USGS photographic best-sellers are Apollo spacecraft and moon mission images showing the full moon, the whole Earth, and Astronaut and Flag on the Moon <http://www.nasm.edu/APOLLO/AS11/Apollo11_images.html>.

Finding the Right Map

Unlike books, many maps are uncataloged. Rather than using the library catalog as a finding tool, the map seeker uses techniques specially designed for maps. One of the most common finding aids is the map index. USGS map indexes divide the 50 states, Puerto Rico, Guam, American Samoa, and the Virgin Islands into named grids representing mapped quadrangles. Grids are named after a prominent place or natural landmark within their boundaries. After identifying a grid name, the corresponding map can be retrieved from alphabetically arranged map cabinets. To identify state grid maps, use the *Index to Topographic and Other Map Coverage [state]* (I 19.41/6–3:). A companion booklet, *Catalog of Topographic and Other Published Maps [state]*, is a catalog for ordering, with map prices and availability (I 19.41/6–2:). These map indexes and catalogs are free from Denver USGS Information Services. Additional map indexes are described in the maps chapter in the *Federal Depository Library Manual*.

Cobb and Seavey point out that atlases can serve as indexes to library map collections by helping identify the location to be searched on an index map: "'I know it's somewhere east of Magnetogorsk' can be pinned down very quickly using the gazetteer [place name index] that virtually all atlases have, or simply by scanning the small scale maps in the atlas itself."[11] Cobb and Seavey liken this approach to finding "the forest before looking for a specific tree."

Citations to maps appear in the *Monthly Catalog*, WorldCat, the NTIS database and Web site, and in *National Union Catalog (NUC): Cartographic Materials*. The *Monthly Catalog* concentrates on maps sent to de-

pository libraries, with sparse coverage of nondepository maps. Separate maps are rarely included in the NTIS collection, which emphasizes maps that are integral components of reports. When a map is available from NTIS, the keyword "Maps" is listed as a descriptor in the database, with "Mapping" used for reports describing how maps are made. An "Advanced Search" in WorldCat allows delimiting by type: to retrieve maps, select "Maps…..(map)." *NUC Cartographic Materials* is a quarterly microfiche publication that reproduces catalog records from the Library of Congress and contributing libraries, including the entire retrospective LC MARC database since 1969. It may be searched through any of five cumulative indexes: name, title, subject, series, and geographic classification code. *The Map Catalog: Every Kind of Map and Chart on Earth and Even Some above It*, commercially published, is a guide to maps and map products for the earth, sky, and water; introductions to dozens of map types; and advice on where to get them. David A. Cobb's *Guide to U.S. Map Resources* is a state and city directory of cartographic collections, including maps, atlases, globes, aerial photos, gazetteers, serials, books, relief models, manuscripts, and machine readable files.

Digital Maps

Today's federal cartography is propelled by computerized maps, known as geographic information systems (GIS). Digital maps are the greatest mapping revolution since Mercator depicted the Earth as round. Longitude-latitude coordinates, which provide a number code for every place on Earth, are easily computerized. Digital maps have simplified map storage and expanded versatility, allowing creation of customized maps on demand. U.S. Geological Survey topographic quadrangle maps are now issued on CD-ROM in digital raster graphic (DRG) format through a USGS partnership with the Land Information Technology Company of Colorado. Pennsylvania and Washington state are the first two available in a state-by-state series of digital topographic CD-ROM maps from USGS. Full coverage of the U.S. is expected by 1998 after some 57,000 USGS maps are converted to CD-ROM format. Each CD-ROM includes the USGS topographic maps for a 1-degree block. DRG versions of topographic maps can be combined with digital aerial photographs or terrain models to produce hybrids such as image maps and shaded relief maps.

As mentioned earlier, in 1997, the U.S. Geological Survey and Microsoft joined in a partnership to make detailed USGS-produced mapping data available free via the Internet. The quest to "put every backyard on the Internet" will eventually beam images of local neighborhoods to home computers where they can be downloaded over low-speed connections and manipulated for special needs. USGS has already stockpiled digital map data for about 20 percent of the country—roads, buildings, topography, place names, and other features. Microsoft will help edit and package these digital maps and images so that they can be searched on the Internet. Don't worry: USGS will continue publishing the paper topographic maps beloved by "planners, scientists, hikers, and hunters."

Agency GIS applications are widespread, currently focusing on natural resource management and environmental assessment. Two of the major federal digital map producers are USGS and the Census Bureau, creator of TIGER, the 1990 Census geographic database. Digital data and customized maps from both agencies are for sale to the public. USGS Earth Science Information Centers provide free information packages and Internet guides describing digital cartographic data. The Federal Geographic Data Committee, which oversees computerized federal mapping, envisions a National Geographic Data System that will pool spatial databases developed by government agencies.

ELECTRONIC INFORMATION

You can pick up a piece of paper that George Washington wrote and you can read it. But if you pick up a piece of computer tape and can't figure out the coding, you're going to have a big problem. —Mary Ronan, National Archives

For two centuries our government documented its activities on paper. Although paper still dominates, the U.S. government maintains the world's largest inventory of computer equipment, acquiring personal computers so quickly it can't keep track of their numbers. (More than four million have been counted, however.) Increasingly, the federal government uses computers for collection, maintenance, and dissemination of information. The prevalence of electronic agency records created with word processing and database management programs, spreadsheets, imaging, computer modeling, and e-mail is changing the way information is collected, stored, and disseminated. It has been predicted that by the year 2000, three-quarters of government transactions will be electronic, without paper counterparts.[12]

Electronic Records at the National Archives

Electronic records are those stored in a form that only a computer can process. This format encompasses many electronic media, including magnetic tape, CD-ROMs, and floppy disks. The National Archives and Records Administration oversees federal electronic record-keeping. Although the law forbids destroying federal records without the archivist's authorization, in reality key federal records have already been lost, electronically altered, or erased. The 1990 House Committee on Government Operations report, *Taking a Byte Out of History: The Archival Preservation of Federal Computer Records*, galvanized concern about the preservation of electronic archival records (Y 1.1/8:101–978). NARA has spent the last two decades sensitizing federal agencies to the importance of preserving the nation's machine-readable memory, taking custody of more than 30,000 of their data files.

Picture an electronic cache spanning back to World War II: punch cards, databases, weather and space data, magnetic tapes made under Presidents Bush and Reagan, and millions of e-mail missives that would curdle into gobbledygook unless transmission information about them was preserved. NARA's Center for Electronic Records maintains computerized government records, storing computer files and related documentation from Congress, the courts, and the Executive Office of the President; presidential commissions; and government agencies and their contractors <http://www.nara.gov/nara/electronic/>. The focus is on computer-generated records, not on retrospectively converting paper records into electronic format.

NARA does not provide online access to electronic records, but sells copies of most data sets on 9-track magnetic tape, 3480-class tape cartridge, or CD-ROM on a cost-recovery basis. The basic finding aid is the "Title List: A Preliminary and Partial Listing of the Data Files in the National Archives and Records Administration," free as a printout or available on the Internet <gopher://gopher.nara.gov:70/11/inform/dc/electr/titlelst>. The "Title List" is complemented by the Reference Reports and Handouts described on the Center's Web page. General Information Leaflet No. 37, "Information about the Center for Electronic Records in the National Archives for Prospective Researchers," is free (AE 1.113:26).

Technological obsolescence is the primary threat to the electronic historical record as future computer hardware and software lose the ability to read yesterday's records. Such obsolescence has already hobbled access to Department of Defense audiotapes made on Vietnam battlefields: the machinery to replay them is no longer available. Franklin Roosevelt's Oval Office tapes were recorded on a RCA machine that was never mass-produced. Luckily, RCA contacted the National Archives before dismantling the barren prototype, allowing master copies of FDR conversations to be duplicated. Even if obsolete hardware remains available, it is possible that no one will be able to run it and that no surviving instruction manuals will exist. Electronic databases cannot simply be printed—they must be transferred from deteriorating tapes and disks and freed from any obsolescent hardware and software on which they were created. To avoid this situation in the future, the Center for Electronic Records places electronic records in a format independent of any specific computer or program. Periodically, the Center recopies its electronic holdings into the latest technology, ensuring retrievability and readability.

Say It Ain't So, Joe.

Beware: the engaging story about the 1960 Census data tapes running on only two machines—one in the Smithsonian, the other in Japan—is apocryphal. In the late 1970s, the Census Bureau copied the 1960 summary tape files (microaggregation files), originally readable only on obsolete UNIVAC II-A tape drives, onto industry-compatible tapes.[13]

AUDIOVISUAL MATERIALS

The United States is the nation's biggest producer of audiovisual (AV) materials. In addition to legions of government-produced videotapes, audiotapes, posters, charts, maps, picture sets, and photographs have all been created—many of which are available to the public. Practically every government agency has created audiovisuals at one time or another, frequently by contracting out their productions. Government AV production is decentralized, without a central hub similar to GPO, and, except for maps, most agencies neglect to send copies to GPO for depository distribution. Although federal audiovisual productions are unique historical records, their preservation has been neglected.[14] Many federal films have been lost; posters have been poorly maintained. One agency that cranked out six to 12 posters yearly for 30 years did not keep a single copy.

Audiovisual Searches

It is important to realize that not only is there no governmentwide master list of AV materials, but many of the indexes relied upon for tracing printed documents are weak when it comes to AV. The *Monthly Catalog* lists printed guides to AV productions, such as the free National Audiovisual Center (NAC) subject brochures, but does not offer comprehensive coverage of AV resources themselves, emphasizing GPO/depository-distribution AV items like the posters listed in Subject Bibliography 57 <http://www.access.gpo.gov/su_docs/sale/sb-057.html>. An "Advanced Search" in WorldCat allows delimiting by type: to retrieve audiovisual material select "Media….. (med)."

To locate nondepository audiovisuals, several sources must be consulted. The National Audiovisual Center's *Media Resource Catalog* and database offer the broadest (although not completely comprehensive) coverage of federal AV output. To identify medical audiovisuals, use the National Library of Medicine AV catalogs.

National Audiovisual Center (NAC)

http://www.ntis.gov/nac/nac.htm

The National Audiovisual Center (NAC) is the government's primary audiovisual hub, with a collection among the largest and most diverse in the country. Now operated by NTIS, NAC serves as a central information and distribution source for sale of federally produced training and education audiovisuals. The NAC collection of some 9,000 active titles in some 600 subject areas emanates from more than 200 federal agencies. NTIS order numbers for audiovisuals begin with AVA: for example, AVA19357-VNB1INA.

The free *Media Resource Catalog* from NTIS (PR-1001) is an annotated bibliography of new and popular NAC videos, films, filmstrips, multimedia kits, and slide sets, but it reflects only a partial listing of NAC titles (AE 1.110/4:). The NAC collection can be searched from the NTIS Web site and on the NTIS Database. Free brochures on special subjects are announced on the NAC Web site (select Special Interest Collections) and in the free *NTIS Catalog of Products and Services* (PR-827) <http://www.ntis.gov/prs/pr827.htm>.

National Library of Medicine (NLM)

AVLINE, NLM's audiovisuals computer file, documents a wide-ranging biomedical audiovisual collection of videocassettes, videodiscs, audiocassettes, 16mm films, filmstrips, slides, x-rays, computer software, and CD-ROMs cataloged since 1975. AVLINE may be searched on MEDLARS and via the Internet (<telnet://locator.nlm.nih.gov> and login as locator). Most NLM audiovisuals are available through interlibrary loan by requesting items through your local library. Information is provided in the NLM Fact Sheet, "Access to Audiovisual Materials" <http://www.nlm.nih.gov/pubs/factsheets/avaccess.html>. For human assistance, contact Reference Section, NLM, 8600 Rockville Pike, Bethesda, MD 20894; (800) 272-4787; Fax: (301) 402-1384.

Agency Catalogs

Supplementing the NAC and NLM guides are numerous catalogs describing audiovisuals of specific agencies. Some agency catalogs can be identified using the *Monthly Catalog*, which lists bibliographies of audiovisuals, but often not the audiovisuals themselves.

Some agencies will provide free loans of their AV productions, even those in the NAC collection. Agency loans are best arranged directly through the agency or one of its field offices. Agencies may also arrange for commercial film distributors to lend some of their films without charge. Although the National Audiovisual Center does not lend materials, it can refer requesters to federal agency lending libraries and commercial loan sources.

National Union Catalog (NUC)

The *National Union Catalog. Audiovisual Materials* (LC 30.8/4:) is a quarterly microfiche listing of films, videos, filmstrips, transparency sets, and slide sets released in the United States or Canada and cataloged by the Library of Congress. The NUC register/index may be searched by name, title, subject, and series.

Hodgepodge

Archives

Washington, DC, is home to the country's largest concentration of archival records. The Smithsonian Institution (note that it's not Smithsonian *Institute*) has 10 distinct archives in areas as diverse as anthropology, space science, and the history of the Smithsonian itself. The Smithsonian archives brim with paper documents, still photographs, motion pictures, and video and audio recordings related to Smithsonian special collections. Some are profiled below, and all are described in a brochure available from the Smithsonian Institution Archives at (202) 357-1420, and through the Smithsonian Web site <http://www.si.edu/organiza/start.htm>. The Smithsonian Institution Research Information System (SIRIS) is a searchable online catalog shared by Smithsonian archival units, libraries, and research units <http://www.siris.si.edu/#Top>.

The National Air and Space Museum (NASM), the most-visited museum in the world, includes an Archives Division documenting air and space flight using photographs, motion pictures, videotape, and technical drawings <http://www.nasm.edu/NASMDOCS/ARCH/DEPT_archives.html>. A list of online resources is available from the NASM Collections and Research Web page <http://www.nasm.edu/FEATURES/NASMfeatures.html#special>.

The National Museum of American History, Archives Center, includes glass stereographs, color transparencies taken around the world, and black-and-white and color photographs by Arthur d'Arazien, a leading industrial and advertising photographer. Other photographic collections document specialized fields, such as the Hazen Collection of Band Photographs and Ephemera. Many of the manuscript and advertising collections include photographs <http://www.si.edu/organiza/museums/nmah/archives/ac-i.htm>. Audiovisual collections include phonodiscs and audiotapes in the Duke Ellington Collection, research and promotional films, audio field recordings of country music, the Computer Oral History Collection, the Lomas Col-

lection of Early Television Commercials, and Industry on Parade Film Collection. The National Museum of American History, Division of Photographic History, collects photographs directly related to the aesthetic, technical, or scientific history of photography. The Warshaw Collection of Business Americana, the largest and best-known collection in the Archives Center, includes advertising cards, posters, catalogs, pamphlets, labels, lithographs, invoices, letterheads, and business correspondence, primarily from the nineteenth and early twentieth centuries.

Want to go postal? The National Postal Museum tells the story of postal history in America <http://www.si.edu/postal/>. The museum's Library Research Center is among the world's largest philatelic and postal history research facilities, featuring a rare book reading room, an audiovisual room, U.S. Postal Service publications, and annual reports. In addition to its stamp collection, the museum has postal history material that predates stamps, postal stationery, mail delivery vehicles, mailboxes, meters, greeting cards, covers, and letters.

Animals

Yearning for a picture of a red-kneed tarantula? The National Zoo has an Internet Animal Photo Library of mammals, birds, reptiles & amphibians, and invertebrates <http://www.si.edu/organiza/museums/zoo/photos/photos.htm>. Images from the National Agricultural Library's Special Collections provides photos of plant pests, forest insects, and animals <http://www.nal.usda.gov/speccoll/>. For photographs of birds see the National Museum of Natural History, Division of Birds, Web site <http://www.nmnh.si.edu/vert/birds/brdphoto.html>.

Art

The National Museum of American Art (NMAA), Slide and Photograph Archives, collects slides, negatives, and photographs of American art and architecture and assists researchers in locating American paintings and sculptures <http://www.nmaa.si.edu/imgarch.html>. The NMAA inventories database contains records from the Inventory of American Paintings executed before 1914 and the Inventory of American Sculpture, focusing on indoor and outdoor works created by American artists <http://www.nmaa.si.edu/inventories.html>.

The National Museum of African Art, Eliot Elisofon Photographic Archives, is a research and reference center for visual materials illuminating the arts, peoples, and history of Africa <http://www.si.edu/organiza/museums/africart/elisofon.htm>. The holdings are divided into two major categories: art photographs, showing African works of art in museum and gallery settings; and field photographs, depicting life and art in Africa. The collection includes color transparencies, black-and-white photographs, original glass negatives, lantern slides, stereographs, postcards, engravings, maps, documentary feature films, and documentary and educational videotapes.

Medicine

Resources in the National Library of Medicine's History of Medicine Division include prints, photographs, historical audiovisuals, manuscripts, portraits, caricatures, pictures of institutions, genre scenes, and graphic art illustrating the social and historical aspects of medicine <http://www.nlm.nih.gov/hmd/hmd.html>. Internet access is through Images from the History of Medicine, offering nearly 60,000 images from the History of Medicine prints and photograph collection <http://wwwihm.nlm.nih.gov/>.

People

The National Portrait Gallery houses portraiture and statuary depicting people who have significantly molded the history, development, and culture of the United States—"heroes and villains, thinkers and doers, conservatives and radicals"—along with the artists who created such portraiture and statuary. The catalog of the Gallery's holdings, *National Portrait Gallery Permanent Collection Illustrated Checklist* (not depository), is sold in the Museum Shop. The Catalog of American Portraits (CAP), administered by the National Portrait Gallery, is a national reference center containing photographs and documentation for portraits of Americans, or for portraits by American artists <http://www.npg.si.edu/inf/cap.htm>. Digitized images being incorporated into the database began with images from the National Portrait Gallery's permanent collection <http://portraits.npg.si.edu./>. Photographs of individual portraits, in black and white or color, may be ordered from the Office of Rights and Reproductions at (202) 357-2791.

Within the National Museum of Natural History, the Department of Anthropology incorporates the Human Studies Film Archives of historic and contemporary film and video footage of human cultures, and the National Anthropological Archives, with photographs dating back to 1845.

Other, nongovernment archives in Washington include those of the American National Red Cross, Gallaudet University, George Washington University's Special Collections Division, Georgetown University's Special Collections Division, Howard University's Moorland-Spingarn Research Center, National Academy of Sciences, and Historical Society of Washington, DC.

How Do I Find More Agency Collections?

Good question. GPO Pathway Indexer searches of government Internet sites and GILS searches are currently

a little ragged for finding films, photographs, and archival materials. Exploration—Internet searching of government sites and reading agency publications—is still the best route to discovering these materials. Knowledge of agency missions supplements serendipity: consult the *U.S. Government Manual* on GPO Access <http://www.access.gpo.gov/nara/nara001.html>.

ADDRESSES

Library of Congress

Photoduplication Service, Library of Congress, Washington, DC 20540-5230. Phone: (202) 707-5640, Fax: (202) 707-1771. Users may visit the Photoduplication public service counter in the Adams Building, LM 120, Monday–Friday, 9:00 AM to 4:45 PM except holidays.

Prints and Photographs Division, Library of Congress, Washington, DC 20540-4840

National Archives

Researchers planning an Archives visit should write or telephone the appropriate unit beforehand.

Cartographic and Architectural Branch (NWDNC), National Archives at College Park, 8601 Adelphi Road, College Park, MD 20740-6001; E-mail: carto@arch2.nara.gov; (301) 713-7040; Fax: (301) 713-7488

Center for Electronic Records (NWRE), National Archives at College Park, 8601 Adelphi Road, College Park, MD 20740-6001; E-mail: cer@nara.gov; (301) 713-6630, (301) 713-6645 (Reference); Fax: (301) 713-6911; <http://www.nara.gov/nara/electronic/intro.html>

Motion Picture, Sound, and Video Branch (NWDNM), National Archives and Records Administration, 8601 Adelphi Road, College Park, MD 20740-6001; (301) 713-7060

Still Picture Branch (NWDNS), Room 5360, National Archives and Records Administration, 8601 Adelphi Road, College Park, MD 20740-6001; E-mail: stillpix@nara.gov; (301) 713-6660 (consultants), (301) 713-6795 (Research Room); Fax: (301) 713-7436; Fax-on-Demand: (301) 713-6905

User Services Branch (NWDTC), National Archives and Records Administration, 8601 Adelphi Road, College Park, MD 20740-6001; E-mail: inquire@nara.gov; (301) 713-6800; Washington (202) 501-5400; Fax: (301) 713-6920

National Audiovisual Center

National Audiovisual Center, NTIS, 5285 Port Royal Rd., Springfield, VA 22161; (800) 788-6282

National Imagery and Mapping Agency

National Imagery and Mapping Agency, Office of Congressional and Public Liaison, 8613 Lee Highway, Mail Stop A-11, Fairfax, VA 22031-2137; (800) 455-0899; <http://www.nima.mil>. To purchase maps, publications, or digital products, contact USGS Information Services, Map and Book Sales, Federal Center, Building 41, Box 25286, Denver, CO 80225; (800) 435-7627, (303) 202-4700; <http://164.214.2.59/poc/public.html>

U.S. Geological Survey

For information about USGS products and services call 1-800-USA-MAPS (often busy); E-mail: esicmail@usgs.gov; or Fax: (703) 648-5548; EARTHFAX fax-on-demand system: (703) 648-4888.

USGS Denver Distribution Center: USGS Information Services, Box 25286, Denver, CO 80225; E-mail: infoservices@usgs.gov; (800) HELP-MAP, (303) 202-4200; Fax: (303) 202-4188

FREEBIES

The following Subject Bibliographies are free from: Stop: SSOP, Washington, DC 20402; U.S. Fax Watch (202) 512-1716:

57. Posters and Prints <http://www.access.gpo.gov/su_docs/sale/sb-057.html>

73. Films and Audiovisual Information <http://www.access.gpo.gov/su_docs/sale/sb-073.html>

102. Maps and Atlases <http://www.access.gpo.gov/su_docs/sale/sb-102.html>

183. Surveying and Mapping <http://www.access.gpo.gov/su_docs/sale/sb-183.html>

From Customer Services, Bureau of the Census, Washington, DC 20233; (301) 457-4100; Fax: (301) 763-4714; <http://www.census.gov/mp/www/censtore.html>

"Maps and More: Your Guide to Census Bureau Geography"

National Archives

"Calendar of Events" (AE 1.117:) from N-POL, National Archives, Washington, DC 20408; also on the Internet <http://clio.nara.gov/nara/events/events.html>

The Record: News from the National Archives and Records Administration, a newsletter announcing news, accessions, openings, declassifications, publications, and grants, published five times yearly (September, November, January, March, and May): from Public Affairs (N-PA), National Archives and Records Administration, Room G6, 7th and Pennsylvania Avenue, NW, Washington, DC, 20408; E-mail: inquire@nara.gov; (202) 501-5525; Fax: (202) 208-6256.

Request General Information Leaflets (AE 1.113:) by citing both GIL title and number, from Product Sales Section (NWPS), National Archives and Records Administration, 700 Pennsylvania Ave., NW, Washington DC 20408; (202) 501-5235; Fax: (202) 501-7170; Fax-on-Demand: (301) 713-6905. (A list of Fax-on-Demand titles is available on the NARA Web site.)

"The National Archives of the United States," GIL Number 1

"Select List of Publications of the National Archives and Records Administration," GIL Number 3

"Information about the National Archives for Researchers," GIL Number 30

"The Regional Archives System of the National Archives," GIL Number 22; also on the Internet <gopher://gopher.nara.gov:70/00/about/publ/gil3.txt>

"Using Records in the National Archives for Genealogical Research," GIL Number 5

"Online and Electronic Services from the National Archives and Records Administration," GIL Number 65; also on the Internet <http://www.nara.gov/nara/gil65.html>

NOAA

From NOAA Distribution Branch, N/CG33, National Ocean Service, Room 105, 6501 Lafayette A, Riverdale, MD 20737-1199; (301) 436-6990; Fax: (301) 436-6829

Aeronautical Charts and Related Products (catalog)

U.S. Geological Survey

From Geologic Inquires Group, USGS, 907 National Center, Reston, VA 20192; E-mail: gig@usgs.gov; (703) 648-4383; Fax: (703) 648-6645

"U. S. Geological Survey World Wide Web Information" (Fact Sheet FS-121-96) <http://mapping.usgs.gov/mac/isb/pubs/factsheets/fs12196.html>

From USGS Information Services, Box 25286, Denver, CO 80225; E-mail: infoservices@usgs.gov; (800) HELP-MAP, (303) 202-4200; Fax: (303) 202-4188

Map indexes and catalogs.

From USGS New Publications, 903 National Center, Reston, VA 20192; E-mail: pburnworth@usgs.gov

New Publications of the Geological Survey (I 19.14/4: and <http://pubs.usgs.gov/publications/index.html>)

FURTHER READING

Bustard, Bruce I. "To Build an Archives." *Prologue* 27 (Summer 1995): 172–77. (AE 1.111:27/2).
How one of the most beautiful buildings in America was built.

Butler, Stuart L. and Graeme McCluggage. "Taking Measure of America: Records in the Cartographic and Architectural Branch." *Prologue* 23 (Spring 1991): 41–57. (AE 1.111:).
An introduction to the National Archives' Cartographic and Architectural Branch collection of maps, charts, and aerial photos, with a list of "Finding Aids Relating to Cartographic and Architectural Models."

General Accounting Office. *Smithsonian Institution: Better Care Needed for National Air and Space Museum Aircraft.* GAO/GGD- 96-9. GAO, 1995.
Aircraft restoration at NASM is remiss.

Hull, Theodore. "Reference Services and Electronic Records: The Impact of Changing Methods of Communication and Access." *Reference Services Review* 23 (Summer 1995):73–78.

A view from NARA's Center for Electronic Records.

Library of Congress. Women Come to the Front, Journalists, Photographers, and Broadcasters During World War II: Dorothea Lange. <http://lcweb.loc.gov/exhibits/wcf/wcf0013.html> (February 13, 1998).

This brief bibliography is hot-linked to photos by Lange.

McCoy, Donald R. *The National Archives: America's Ministry of Documents, 1934–1968.* Chapel Hill, NC: University of North Carolina Press, 1978.

A comprehensive history of the National Archives and presidential library system, with a lengthy bibliography.

National Archives. Internet exhibit: The Charters of Freedom <http://www.nara.gov/exhall/charters/charters.html> (December 3, 1997).

View some of the most highly detailed photographs ever made of the Declaration of Independence, the Constitution, and the Bill of Rights.

Sears, Jean L. and Marilyn K. Moody. *Using Government Information Sources: Print and Electronic.* (Phoenix, AZ: Oryx Press, 1994), pp. 494–500.

A chapter on "National Archives" describes a search strategy for accessing NARA records and lists microfilm catalogs and special subject guides.

Taylor, Paul Schuster. *The American West: The Magazine of the Western History Association.* 7 (May 1970): 41–47.

Dorothea Lange and Taylor, her husband, tell the story behind the "Migrant Mother" photo of Florence Thompson, who was 32 years old when Lange snapped her picture at a California pea-pickers camp.

Viola, Herman J. *The National Archives of the United States.* New York: Harry N. Abrams, Inc., 1984.

This dazzling volume of color photographs and vivid narrative recounts the history of the National Archives and gives the reader a taste of its collections.

NOTES

1. Alfred Meyer, "Daily Rise and Fall of the Nation's Revered Documents," *Smithsonian* 17 (October 1986): 134–43.

2. Although their 1951 state-of-the-art enclosures were slated to protect through the year 2051, the glass is deteriorating, and helium is now considered inferior to argon or nitrogen for blanketing rare documents.

3. Hugh T. Lefler, "Robert Digges Wimberly Connor," in *Keepers of the Past,* ed. by Clifford L. Lord (Chapel Hill, NC: University of North Carolina Press, 1965), p. 111.

4. Senate, Committee on Governmental Affairs, *National Archives and Records Administration Act of 1983: Hearings Before the Committee on Governmental Affairs, United States Senate 98th Congress First Session on S. 905 Entitled the "National Archives and Records Administration Act of 1983" July 29, 1983* (S. Hrg. 98-488) (GPO, 1984), p. 37. (Y 4.G 74/9: S. HRG. 98-488).

5. S. R. Ranganathan, "The Library of Congress Among National Libraries," *ALA Bulletin* (October 1950): 356.

6. Karin Becker Ohrn, *Dorothea Lange and the Documentary Tradition* (Baton Rouge: Louisiana State University Press, 1980).

7. Library of Congress, *A Century of Photographs, 1846–1946, Selected from the Collections of the Library of Congress* (LC, 1980), p. vii. (LC 1.2:P 56/5/846-946).

8. Connie Leslie, "Lost on the Planet Earth," *Newsweek* (August 8, 1988): 31; Dennis Kelly, "Getting Kids Acquainted with the Globe," *USA Today* (November 30, 1990): 10D.

9. David A. Cobb and Charles A. Seavey, *An Introduction to Maps in Libraries: Maps as Information Tools* (Chicago: Association of College and Research Libraries, [1982]), p. 19.

10. USGS. *Geographic Information Systems.* n.d. (I 19.2:G 29/26): no paging.

11. Cobb and Seavey, pp. 25–26.

12. House Committee on Government Operations, *Taking a Byte Out of History: The Archival Preservation of Federal Computer Records.* H. Rpt. 101-978 (GPO, 1990), p. 2. (Y 1.1/8:101-978).

13. Margaret O. Adams and Thomas E. Brown "Historical Narrative on Data from the 1960 Census" (April 3, 1996): <http://www.oclc.org:5046/OCLC/research/links/archtf/census_1960.html> (October 30, 1997); The Research Libraries Group. *Preserving Digital Information: Report of the Task Force on Archiving of Digital Information.* Washington, DC: The Commission on Preservation and Access, 1996, pp. 2–3. <http://www.rlg.org>.

14. National Archives and Records Administration, *The Management of Audiovisual Records in Federal Agencies: A General Report* (NARA, 1991).

EXERCISES

1. In 1941, the National Park Service hired Ansel Adams for $22.22 a day to photograph national parks for a Department of the Interior building photo mural. Although World War II halted the project after only a year, some of Adams's best-known photos bask in the public domain because they were taken while Adams was employed by the U.S. Government. Identify some of the Ansel Adams government photos.

2. How can I peruse the same Farm Security Administration photos that inspired John Steinbeck to write *The Grapes of Wrath*?

3. After the Presidential Commission on the Space Shuttle Challenger Accident (Rogers Commission) concluded its investigation, its records were transferred to the National Archives for permanent preservation. Included are reports, photographs, correspondence, memoranda, electronic datasets, transcripts, affidavits, videotapes, and sound recordings. How can researchers find out exactly which Rogers Commission records are available in the National Archives?

CHAPTER 14
Docs Populi: A Documents Toolkit

This chapter is a reference toolkit of federal, state, local, and foreign documents resources too broad to be discussed in topical chapters 1–13.

PROFESSIONAL UPDATE

LISTSERVS

GOVDOC-L.
> GOVDOC-L is a LISTSERV focusing on government information and the Federal Depository Library Program (FDLP). To subscribe, send a subscription message to govdoc-l@lists.psu.edu. The listserv archives are available through the server at Pennsylvania State University and through Resources of Use to Government Documents Librarians <http://www.lib.berkeley.edu/GODORT/>, which provides a GOVDOC-L Users Guide (also at <http://www.staff.uiuc.edu/~raeann/govdoc-l.html>).

Documents Technical Processing LISTSERV, DocTech-L.
> DocTech-L centers upon government documents technical processing, with emphasis on federal materials. To subscribe, send a message to maiser@library.lib.usu.edu with the message: Subscribe DocTech-L.[1]

Publications and Web Sites

American Library Association (ALA). Government Documents Roundtable (GODORT).
> GODORT is ALA's unit concerned with government documents at all government levels, including consideration of federal information policy, access to government information, and the impact of new technologies. The Resources of Use to Government Documents Librarians Web site chronicles GODORT activities, committees, and organization <http://www.lib.berkeley.edu>. The GODORT Handout Exchange offers handouts created by documents librarians on topics ranging from collection development policies to user guides <http://www.lib.umich.edu/libhome/Documents.center/godort.html>.

American Library Association. Government Documents Roundtable. *Documents to the People.* Chicago: American Library Association, 1972–. Bimonthly.
> Known as DttP, this information-packed newsletter has a no-frills format and a reasonable price. The index since Volume 18 (1990) is available through Resources of Use to Government Documents Librarians <http://www.lib.berkeley.edu/GODORT/> or <gopher://library.berkeley.edu:70/11/resdbs/gove/dodort/dttp>.

Government Information Quarterly: An International Review of Resources, Services, Policies, and Practices. Greenwich, CT: JAI Press, 1984–. Quarterly.
> Articles and columns cover government information dissemination, developments, and information resources. Tables of contents since Volume 1 are available on the Auburn Microform and Documents Department Web site <http://www.lib.auburn.edu/madd/docs/giq/conlink.html>.

Journal of Government Information: An International Review of Policy, Issues and Resources. New York: Pergamon Press, 1994–. Bimonthly.
> Articles and columns cover government information programs, policies, and U.S., foreign, and international government information resources. Tables of contents since Volume 1 are available on the Auburn Microform and Documents Department Web page <http://www.lib.auburn.edu/madd/docs/giq/conlink.html>. Formerly *Government Publications Review.*

University of California Berkeley Library Web. Resources of Use to Government Documents Librarians. <http://www.lib.berkeley.edu/GODORT/>.
> A documents mecca, with news, listservs, hot congressional materials, and (of course) more.

Recurring Columns

Journal of Government Information (See publication information above.)
> The November/December issue is devoted to notable documents of U.S., state, local, foreign, and international organizations. Regular columns spotlight theses in documents, news from Washington, technical reports,

computerized and networked government information (every other issue), and the annotated bibliography, "Recent Literature on Government Information" (twice yearly, generally in issues 2 and 5)—the best update around.

Library Journal. New York: R. R. Bowker, 1976–. Semimonthly except July–Aug. (monthly).

The annual "Notable Government Documents" (usually published in the May 15th issue), compiled by GODORT's Notable Documents Panel, lists noteworthy federal, state, local, and international titles useful in any type of library.

BIBLIOGRAPHIES

Andriot, Donna, ed. *Guide to U.S. Government Publications.* McLean, VA: Documents Index, Inc., 1973–. Annual.

"Andriot" (popularly known by its editor's name, pronounced "ANN-dree-ott") is the "bible" for identifying agency series and SuDocs number stems. Use it to verify document citations, current and historical SuDocs numbers, or publication history. Entries include SuDocs number stem (with SuDocs classification number history), depository item number, frequency, selected annotations, title changes, and ISSN. An "Agency Class Chronology" records the history of SuDocs classification stems and corresponding agencies.

Hoffmann, Frank W. and Richard J. Wood. *Guide to Popular U.S. Government Publications.* Englewood, CO: Libraries Unlimited, 1997. 4th ed.

Popular and best-selling titles are arranged topically, with annotations.

DOCUMENT CITATION GUIDE

Garner, Diane L., and Diane H. Smith. *The Complete Guide to Citing Government Information Resources: A Manual for Writers & Librarians.* rev. ed. Bethesda, MD: Congressional Information Service, 1993.

The style manual for citing federal, state, local, regional, and international publications.

DIRECTORIES

American Library Association. Government Documents Roundtable. *Directory of Government Documents Collections and Librarians.* Bethesda, MD: Congressional Information Service, 1974–. Irregular. (7th ed, 1997).

A state and city directory of documents libraries, collections, depository status, subject specialties, URLs, and staff names; with information about library school documents faculty; state documents authorities; names to know; subject terms; and agency names and acronyms.

Evinger, William, ed. *Directory of Federal Libraries.* 3rd ed. Phoenix, AZ: Oryx Press, 1998.

A worldwide listing of addresses, telephone numbers, contact people, special collections, database services, and electronic mail networks.

Office of the Federal Register. *U.S. Government Manual.* GPO, 1935–. Annual. (AE 2.108: and on GPO Access <http://www.access.gpo.gov/su_docs/dbsearch.html>).

The "official handbook of the federal government," *The U.S. Government Manual* (USGM) is a directory of agencies and personnel in the three branches of federal government. USGM summarizes agency responsibilities and gives addresses, telephone numbers (notoriously outdated), and names. It also gives information on quasi-official agencies, international organizations, boards, committees, and commissions. Appendixes cover abolished and transferred agencies, abbreviations and acronyms, and agencies appearing in the *Code of Federal Regulations.* An up-to-date link to Web sites (and names, addresses, telephone numbers) is GPO Access's Federal Agency Internet Sites <http://www.access.gpo.gov/su_docs/dpos/agencies.html>.

GUIDES TO REFERENCE MATERIALS

Government Reference Books. Littleton, CO: Libraries Unlimited, Inc., 1969–. Biennial.

A comprehensive, annotated subject guide to all types of government-published reference books issued during the previous two years.

Hardy, Gayle J. and Judith Schiek Robinson. *Subject Guide to U.S. Government Reference Sources.* Littleton, CO: Libraries Unlimited, Inc., 1997.

A selective, annotated bibliography of key government titles and Internet sites for general reference and in the social sciences, sciences, and humanities.

Sears, Jean L., and Marilyn K. Moody. *Using Government Information Sources: Print and Electronic.* 2nd ed. Phoenix, AZ: Oryx Press, 1994.

This essential award winner is arranged by type of search, with sources and search strategies thoroughly, yet concisely, explained.

TEXTBOOKS

Herman, Edward. *Locating United States Government Information: A Guide to Sources.* 2nd ed. Buffalo, NY: William S. Hein & Co., 1997.

A how-to guide for finding and using government publications, print and electronic.

Morehead, Joe. *Introduction to United States Government Information Sources.* 5th ed. Englewood, CO: Libraries Unlimited, 1996.

This title has been the classic guide to federal government publishing since it first supplanted Schmeckebier and Eastin's *Government Publications and Their Use* in 1975.

HISTORICAL SOURCES

Bernier, Bernard A. and Karen Wood, comps. *Popular Names of U.S. Government Reports: A Catalog*. 4th ed. Library of Congress, 1984. 272 p. (LC 6.2:G 74/984).

> This guide is a key to identifying official titles and issuing agencies when only the short, popular name of a federal report is known. Updated by: Bengtson, Marjorie C. "Popular Names of U.S. Government Reports: A Supplement" *Illinois Libraries* 69 (September 1987): 472–77; Bengtson, Marjorie C. "Popular Names of U.S. Government Reports: Second Supplement" *Illinois Libraries* 75 (April 1993): 161–65; Graf, Jeffrey and Louise Malcomb. "Identifying Unidentified U.S. Government Reports" *Journal of Government Information* (March/April 1994): 105–28.

Boyd, Anne M. *United States Government Publications*. 3rd ed. revised by Rae E. Ripps. New York: H. W. Wilson, 1949, reprinted 1952.

> "Boyd and Ripps" is a classic source of historical information about government printing, publishing, and distribution.

Schmeckebier, Laurence F. and Roy B. Eastin. *Government Publications and Their Use*. Washington, DC: Brookings Institution, 1969.

A key resource for tracing the history of documents in indexes, bibliographies, and catalogs.

STATE DOCUMENTS
State Depository Libraries

Although federal depositories are scattered coast to coast, each operates under the same federal laws. State depositories, on the other hand, are legally mandated by individual state legislatures, making each an independent system with varying quality and comprehensiveness. And some states have no depository laws, thus no depositories, whatsoever.

Bibliographies

The "Bibliography on Documents Librarianship and Government Information" in the March *Documents to the People* includes a section on "State and Local Governments."

State and Local Government on the Internet		
To Find	Use	URL
Meta-indexes and information sources	State and Local Governments (Library of Congress Internet resource page)	http://lcweb.loc.gov/global/state/stategov.html
Topics	U.S. State and Local Gateway	http://www.statelocal.gov/
	StateSearch	http://www.nasire.org/ss/
	PTI [Public Technology Inc.] Technology Links	http://pti.nw.dc.us/links.html
	WashLaw. StateLaw: State Government and Legislative Information	http://lawlib.wuacc.edu/washlaw/uslaw/statelaw.html
State agencies and local governments	State and Local Documents TF [Task Force] Web Resources at the University of Arizona (from GODORT)	http://dizzy.library.Arizona.EDU/library/teams/sst/arawan/godortz.html
	Yahoo - Government; U.S. States	http://www.yahoo.com/Government/U_S__States/
	State and Local Government on the Web (U. of Michigan Documents Center)	http://www.lib.umich.edu/libhome/Documents.center/state.html
	Internic. U.S. Government Internet Resources	http://ds.internic.net/ds/gov.html
	InfoSpace The Ultimate Government Guide	http://www.infospace.com/ Select "Government"
	Government Information Exchange	http://www.info.gov/ Select "State and Local Government"

Checklists

The Library of Congress's *Monthly Checklist of State Publications*, the most comprehensive national list of state publications, ceased publication in 1994 (LC 30.9:). Most states publish their own checklists of agency publications, with libraries often subscribing to their own state's checklist. State checklists vary from mere agency/title listings to full bibliographic citations, with their ease of use ranging from frustrating to friendly. Internet versions of state checklists and shipping lists are linked from StateList: The Electronic Source for State Publication Lists, from the Documents and Law Libraries at the University of Illinois <http://www.law.uiuc.edu/library/check/check.htm>. An update of Susan L. Dow's *State Document Checklists: A Historical Bibliography* (1990) is anticipated in 1998. Once identified, many state publications are available free from their issuing agencies (addresses can be garnered from state directories), but requesters must strike quickly before copies evaporate.

Directories and Legislative Manuals

State equivalents of the *U.S. Government Manual* are sometimes called blue books, red books, government manuals, or government handbooks. These state directories list agency personnel, describe state government processes and interactions with federal and local governments, and may be published officially or unofficially. They have been called "probably the best general reference available on state government organization."[2] FindLaw includes a state directories section <http://www.findlaw.com/11stategov/index.html>. State legislative manuals are directories of state legislatures, frequently giving organization, rules, procedures, names, and committee memberships.

Carroll's State Directory. Washington, DC: Carroll Publishing, three times yearly.
> A directory of executive, legislative, and judicial officials.

Hellebust, Lynn, ed. *State Reference Publications: A Bibliographic Guide to State Blue Books, Legislative Manuals and Other General Reference Sources*. Topeka, KS: Government Research Service, 1991/1992—. Annual.
> An annotated bibliography of state blue books; legislative handbooks, manuals, and directories; and general directories and statistical compilations.

State Yellow Book: Who's Who in the Executive and Legislative Branches of the 50 State Governments. New York: Monitor Leadership Directories, Quarterly.
> Names, addresses, and telephone numbers of state executive and legislative branch personnel.

Legislation, Regulations, Courts

Each state publishes session laws and annotated codes, either officially or unofficially (sometimes both), and many have mounted their legislative codes on the Internet. Unlike the federal government, however, many states never publish the background reports and hearings that seed legislation.

The Bluebook: A Uniform System of Citation. 16th ed. Cambridge, MA: Harvard Law Review Association, 1996.
> The Bluebook's blue pages list state statutory compilations, session laws, administrative registers and compilations, and court hierarchies. (The guides to legislative searching listed in the "Further Reading" section of chapter 8 also discuss state legislative materials.)

Hellebust, Lynn, ed. *State Legislative Sourcebook: A Resource Guide to Legislative Information in the Fifty States*. Topeka, KS: Government Research Service, 1985–. Annual.
> A comprehensive guide to legislative process and information sources in all 50 states.

Public Affairs Information Service. *PAIS International*. New York: PAIS, 1991–. Monthly.
> PAIS indexes all state legislative manuals and subject compilations of state laws received by The New York Public Library, a comprehensive collection of public affairs materials. State and local documents coverage is strongest for New York, New Jersey, and California, and New York City.

State regulations are not uniformly published and can be difficult to track down. Cohen, Berring, and Olson characterize their public announcement as "almost at the same primitive level as in the federal government before 1935."[3] While some states publish an equivalent to the *Federal Register* or *Code of Federal Regulations*, others require contacting agencies to identify regulations in force.

State judicial decisions are documented in official, or frequently unofficial, reporters. The National Reporter System covers the nation by regions (Northeastern Reporter, Pacific Reporter, etc.), printing state appellate court decisions. Shepard's [state name] Citations cite state court references to state laws, cases, court rules, ordinances, state constitutions, or jury instructions, and are available for each of the 50 states, District of Columbia, and Puerto Rico.

Reference Sources

The Book of the States. Lexington, KY: The Council of State Governments, 1935–. Biennial.
> This "encyclopedia of state government" provides information about state constitutions; executive, legisla-

State Law on the Internet		
To Find	Use	URL
State and multi-state sites and state courts	State and Local Government on the Net (from Piper Resources)	http://www.piperinfo.com/state/states.html
	The State Web Locator (from the Villanova Center for Information Law and Policy)	http://www.law.vill.edu/State-Agency/
	Government Information Web Page Template (from GODORT)	http://www.library.unt.edu/gpo/template/govinfo.html
	Indiana University School of Law—Bloomington	http://www.law.indiana.edu/law/v-lib/states.html
	Law Journal Extra: Courthouse	http://www.ljx.com/courthouse/index.html
State government databases and agencies, statutes, constitutions	State Materials [from lawmarks]	http://www.cclabs.missouri.edu/~tbrown/lawmarks/sd2.htm
Laws	House Internet Law Library, select U.S. State and Territorial Laws	http://law.house.gov/17.htm
	FedLaw	http://www.legal.gsa.gov/intro5.htm
Laws, by topic and by state	Legal Information Institute, Cornell Law School	http://www.law.cornell.edu/statutes.html
	FindLaw	http://www.findlaw.com/11stategov/index.html
	State Legislative Database Search	http://www.govaffs.com/states.html
	WashLaw. StateLaw: State Government and Legislative Information	http://lawlib.wuacc.edu/washlaw/uslaw/statelaw.html

tive, and judicial branches of state governments; elections, finances, management, activities, issues, and services; intergovernmental affairs; and statistics. Three supplemental state directories are issued by the Council of State Governments: *State Leadership Directory. Directory I, State Elective Officials; State Leadership Directory. Directory II. Legislative Leadership, Committees & Staff;* and *State Leadership Directory. Directory III, State Administrative Officials.*

Statistics

Bureau of the Census. *State and Metropolitan Area Data Book.* GPO, 1979–. Irregular. (C 3.134/5:).
A compendium of statistics for states, metropolitan areas, census divisions, and regions.

———. *Statistical Abstract of the United States.* GPO, 1878–. Annual. (C 3.134: and <http://www.census.gov/stat_abstract/>).
This compendium includes appendixes citing state statistical abstracts, with contact addresses and telephone numbers.

Congressional Information Service. *American Statistics Index.* Bethesda, MD: CIS, Inc., 1973–. Monthly with annual cumulation.
This is an index to federally generated statistics, with abstracts.

———. *Statistical Reference Index.* Bethesda, MD: CIS, Inc., 1980–. Bimonthly with annual cumulation.
This is an index to statistical data generated outside the federal government, including publications of state agencies. SRI abstracts and indexes social, governmental, economic, and demographic reports from the 50 states and the District of Columbia, as well as state statistical compendia, periodicals, and annual reports.

State and Local Statistics Sources. 2nd ed. Detroit: Gale Research, 1993.
Citations to sources of state and local statistics.

Maps

In plain truth, access to state and local maps "is very much a question of luck."[4] Some states operate a central map information center, similar to the United States

Geological Survey (USGS) Earth Science Information Centers, while others offer little help in tracking down maps. USGS index maps show named map quadrangles for sale for each state. To identify USGS state maps, use the *Index to Topographic and Other Map Coverage [state]* (I 19.41/6-3:). A companion booklet, *Catalog of Topographic and Other Published Maps [state]* (I 19.41/6-2:), is a catalog for ordering topographic, U.S., state, satellite image, and world maps. Both are free from USGS. The Library of Congress's Geography and Map Division collects state and county maps and atlases published in the nineteenth and early twentieth centuries, along with regional and state atlases published during the past four or five decades <http://lcweb.loc.gov/rr/geogmap/>.

LOCAL DOCUMENTS

Cities usually operate according to a municipal charter. The local legislature passes ordinances, some of which are published by the General Code Publishing Corporation. When indexes and regular publications are lacking, researchers must plow through records of key meetings, such as those of the city council, to identify actions taken, and then search records for amendments. Carroll Publishing issues two directories of local officials and administrators: *Carroll's County Directory* and *Carroll's Municipal Directory*.

Bureau of the Census. *County and City Data Book*. GPO, 1949–. Irregular. (C 3.134/2:C 83/2/yr.).
> Social and economic statistics for counties, metropolitan areas, and large cities are augmented by information about states, standard federal administrative regions, and census regions and divisions.

Index to Current Urban Documents. Westport, CT: Greenwood Publishing Group, Inc. 1972–. Quarterly.
> ICUD is an index to documents issued by large cities, counties, regional agencies, school districts, universities, and authorities in the U.S. and Canada. Subject terms are drawn from *Contemporary Subject Headings for Urban Affairs*. Most of the titles indexed are available in full text on microfiche from the Congressional Information Service's Urban Documents Microfiche Collection.

Local Government on the Internet		
To Find	Use	URL
City, county, and state governments	The Local Government Home Page	http://localgov.org/
	State and Local Government on the Net (Piper Resources)	http://www.piperinfo.com/state/states.html
	State and Local Government on the Web (U. of Michigan Documents Center)	http://www.lib.umich.edu/libhome/Documents.center/state.html
City and county government directories	FindLaw	http://www.findlaw.com/11stategov/directories/cities.html
	GovList	http://govt.net/govtlist/index.htm
Topical	Local Government Services (from Public Technology, Inc.)	http://world.localgov.org/services.html
	Local Government Departments Online (Select Departments from main menu)	http://www.ig.org/
County governments	County Government Web Sites (National Association of Counties)	http://www.naco.org/
Municipal codes	Municipal Codes Corporation	http://www.municode.com/database.html
	Municipal Codes Online, from the Seattle Public Library	http://www.spl.lib.wa.us/collec/lawcoll/municode.html
	WashLaw	http://lawlib.wuacc.edu/washlaw/cities.html

FOREIGN COUNTRIES/INTERNATIONAL DOCUMENTS*

Professional Update

INTL-DOC.

This listserv for international-document librarians and users of International Governmental Organizations (IGO) material, welcomes questions about the literature of foreign national governments and of international affairs. The United Nations Library uses INTL-DOC to post notices about the UN depository program and other matters. To subscribe, send the following message to listserv@listserv.acns.nwu.edu: Subscribe INTL-DOC yourfirstname yourlastname.[5]

Bibliographies

The "Bibliography on Documents Librarianship and Government Information" in the March *Documents to the People* includes sections on "Foreign National Governments" and "Intergovernmental Organizations." Browse Topics in GPO Access Pathway Services includes hot-linked resource lists for Africa, Asia, Bosnia, China, Europe, Latin America, Middle East, Pacific Rim, Russia, and South America, as well as Foreign Country Studies, and Intergovernmental Relations <http://www.access.gpo.gov/su_docs/dpos/pathbrws.html>.

American Library Association. Government Documents Roundtable. *Guide to Official Publications of Foreign Countries*. Bethesda, MD: Congressional Information Service, 1997.

Key publications of foreign governments are grouped by subject, with abstracts.

American Library Association. Government Documents Roundtable. *Guide to Country Information in International Governmental Organization Publications*. Bethesda, MD: Congressional Information Service, 1996.

A subject list of print and electronic publications issued by International Governmental Organizations about individual nations.

Balay, Robert. *Guide to Reference Books*. 11th ed. Chicago: American Library Association, 1996.

A section on Government Publications lists key national and international sources.

Hajnal, Peter I. *Directory of United Nations Documentary and Archival Sources*. New York: Kraus International, 1991.

An annotated bibliography of UN titles arranged by subject and type of resource.

———. ed. *International Information: Documents, Publications, and Electronic Information of International Governmental Organizations*. 2nd ed. Englewood, CO: Libraries Unlimited, 1997.

Publications, documentation of, and computerized information services of major international governmental organizations, such as the United Nations and the European Union.

Nurcombe, Valerie J. *Information Sources in Official Publications*. New Providence, NJ: Bowker-Saur, 1997.

A guide to official publications of nations and of regions of the world.

Reference Sources

Army. *Country Study Series*. GPO, irregular. (D 101.22:550-no. and <http://lcweb2.loc.gov/frd/cs/cshome.html/>).

Individual titles profile single countries, focusing on history, society, economy, government, and politics. Subject Bibliography 166 lists print titles for sale from GPO <http://www.access.gpo.gov/su_docs/sale/sb-166.html>. New titles are indexed and abstracted in *American Foreign Policy and Treaty Index* (consult AFPTI accession number 3700-2 in the abstracts). The series replaced the Area Handbooks.

Central Intelligence Agency. *World Factbook*. GPO, 1981–. Annual. (PREX 3.15/2: and <http://www.odci.gov/cia/publications/pubs.html>).

A source of maps and concise national profiles describing geography, people, government, economy, transportation, communications, and defense, especially for small and Third World countries.

Department of State. *Background Notes on (various countries)*. GPO, 1980–. Quarterly. (S 1.123: and <http://www.access.gpo.gov/state/state001.html> or <http://www.state.gov/www/background_notes/index.html>); also on the National Trade Data Bank, STAT-USA/Internet, and *U.S. Foreign Affairs on CD-ROM* (S 1.142/2:).

Short descriptions of the land, people, history, government, politics, economy, and foreign relations for countries, U.S. territories, and selected international organizations. *Background Notes* for new or emerging countries are not issued until the State Department considers them stabilized. The brief index lists all the countries alphabetically, with date of last issue in print (S 1.123/2:). Subject Bibliography 93 lists print titles available for sale <http://www.access.gpo.gov/su_docs/sale/sb-093.html>.

Public Affairs Information Service. *PAIS International*. New York: PAIS, 1991–. Monthly.

An index to public affairs publications covering foreign government documents in English, French, German, Italian, Portuguese, and Spanish, including international organizations' statistical publications, directories, studies, and reports related to public policy issues.

Statistics

Many countries publish statistical compendia or yearbooks of national demographic, economic, and social statistics, similar to the *Statistical Abstract of the United States*. In fact, many are cited in an appendix of the *Sta-*

*See chapter 15 for more complete coverage

tistical Abstract of the United States, along with contact addresses and telephone numbers.

In addition, many U.S. federal publications provide statistics about foreign nations. *American Statistics Index* (also described earlier in this chapter and in chapter 12) is an excellent source for identifying U.S. publications with statistics about foreign countries. The *Statistical Reference Index* (the Congressional Information Service's index to nonfederal U.S. statistics) indexes and abstracts world economic and demographic trends;

international finance, investment, and trade data; as well as social and economic data for foreign countries, frequently organized to allow comparison with U.S. data. *Index to International Statistics*, also from Congressional Information Service, indexes statistics issued by international intergovernmental organizations. (See chapter 12.) Finally, because Congress keeps tabs on international issues, *CIS/Index* is also a source for identifying statistics on foreign nations. Several of the statistical

Foreign Governments on the Internet (See also chapter 15)		
To Find	*Use*	*URL*
Links,	GODORT Documents Task Force	http://www.indiana.edu/~libgpd/idtf/home.html
Countries	Foreign Governments (GODORT and Northwestern U. Library)	http://www.library.nwu.edu/govpub/idtf/foreign.html
	U. of Michigan Documents Center: select "Foreign or International"	http://www.lib.umich.edu/libhome/Documents.center/
	Government Information Exchange	http://www.info.gov/ Select "Foreign/International"
Topics and countries	FindLaw, Foreign and International Resources	http://www.findlaw.com/
	The GODORT Handout Exchange	http://www.lib.umich.edu/libhome/Documents.center/godort.html Select "Foreign Governments or International Documents"
	GPO Access "Browse Topics"	http://www.access.gpo.gov/su_docs/dpos/pathbrws.html Select "Foreign Country Studies"
Officials	*Chiefs of State and Cabinet Members of Foreign Governments* (CIA)	http://www.odci.gov/cia/publications/chiefs/index.html PREX 3.11/2:
Embassies	*Foreign Consular Offices in the United States* (Dept. of State)	http://www.state.gov/www/travel/consular_offices/FCO_index.html S 1.69/2:
Law	GLIN/Law Library of Congress: Guide to Law Online	http://lcweb2.loc.gov/glin/worldlaw.html
IGOs	International Organizations (GODORT and Northwestern U. Library)	http://www.library.nwu.edu/govpub/idtf/igo.html
	Links from the Michigan State University Libraries	http://www.lib.msu.edu/publ_ser/docs/igos/igoorg.htm
	Federal Web Locator section on "Multilateral Organizations and Non-governmental Sites"	http://www.law.vill.edu/Fed-Agency/fedweb.new.html
Local governments & local government organizations	The International Local Government Home Page	http://world.localgov.org/

compendia listed in chapter 12 include international data.

Bureau of the Census. International Programs Center.
> This agency, discussed in chapter 12, disseminates demographic and economic data on foreign countries, publishing world population reports and producing the Census Bureau International Data Base <http://www.census.gov/ipc/www/>.

Central Intelligence Agency. *Handbook of International Economic Statistics*. GPO, 1992—. Annual. (PREX 3.16: and <http://www.odci.gov/cia/publications/pubs.html>).
> A source of statistics for all Communist countries and selected non-Communist countries, with maps, charts, and tables. Formerly *Handbook of Economic Statistics* (PREX 3.10/7-5:).

Maps

A national atlas is a source of valuable reference information about a country. Cobb and Seavey emphasize the value of national atlases, recommending that even libraries without map collections collect national atlases.[6] Several federal agency foreign map series are noted in chapter 13.

FREEBIES

The following Subject Bibliographies are free from: Stop: SSOP, Washington, DC 20402; U.S. Fax Watch: (202) 512-1716:

93. Background Notes <http://www.access.gpo.gov/su_docs/sale/sb-093.html>

102. Maps and Atlases <http://www.access.gpo.gov/su_docs/sale/sb-102.html>

150. Libraries <http://www.access.gpo.gov/su_docs/sale/sb-150.html>

166. Foreign Country Studies <http://www.access.gpo.gov/su_docs/sale/sb-166.html>

FURTHER READING

Elliot, Jeffrey M. *The State and Local Government Political Dictionary*. San Bernardino, CA: Borgo Press, 1995.
> A source of clear explanations of topics, political personalities, facts, institutions, and processes in state and local government.

Ratcliffe, John W. "International Statistics: Pitfalls and Problems." *Reference Services Review* 10 (Fall 1982): 93–95.
> Weaknesses and potential problems related to national statistics generated by foreign countries.

Rosenberg, Jim. "The Price Of Public Information." *Editor & Publisher Magazine* 130 (October 18, 1997): 13–14 <http://www.mediainfo.com> (December 5, 1997).
> As more state and local governments create electronic records, they are reducing costs by contracting with private firms to manage the databases.

NOTES

1. For more information, contact Camilla Williams, USU Merrill Library, Documents Department, Logan, UT 84322-3000, camwil@ngw.lib.usu.edu.

2. *State Bluebooks and Reference Publications: A Selected Bibliography* (Lexington, KY: The Council on State Governments, 1983), p. iv.

3. Morris L. Cohen, Robert C. Berring, and Kent C. Olson, *How to Find the Law*, 9th ed. (St. Paul, MN: West Publishing Co., 1989), p. 299.

4. Charles A. Seavey, "Government Map Publications: An Overview," in *Communicating Public Access to Government Information, Proceedings of the 2nd Annual Library Government Documents and Information Conference*, ed. by Peter Hernon. (Westport, CT: Meckler Publishing, 1983), p. 88.

5. The list owner and moderator is Mike McCaffrey-Noviss, International Documents Librarian, Northwestern University Library, Evanston, IL 60208-2300; E-mail: mmccaff@nwu.edu; (847) 491-2927; Fax (847) 491-8306.

6. David A. Cobb and Charles A. Seavey, *An Introduction to Maps in Libraries: Maps as Information Tools* (Chicago: Association of College and Research Libraries, [1982]), p. 26.

EXERCISES

1. Why does the SuDocs number for National Archives publications begin with AE?

2. Where can I get statistics on the ethnic composition of counties in my state?

3. Where can I get data about foreign countries?

4. What was the official title of the Nixon-era Watergate report?

CHAPTER 15
Foreign and International Documents

by Karen F. Smith

Foreign is a relative term; it depends on your vantage point. In this chapter the word "foreign" is used, not in a pejorative sense, but simply as a convenient way to refer to countries other than the United States. International is a broader term that refers to combinations of countries. The documents produced by foreign national governments and those issued by international governmental organizations (IGOs) fulfill, to an extent, the library's need for worldwide information. However, because each country of the world has a unique governmental structure and a unique publishing program (as does each international organization), it is impossible to describe them all here. This chapter will offer representative examples to establish some general approaches to finding foreign and international documents.

WHAT

International organizations whose members are countries, such as the United Nations, are known as international governmental organizations, or IGOs. Most IGOs are organized on a regional basis—for instance, the Organization of American States (OAS) and the Council of Europe. Others are bound together by common interests, such as the Organization of Petroleum Exporting Countries (OPEC) and the International Organization for Migration (IOM). Both IGOs and foreign governments issue official publications.

Foreign and international documents contain a wealth of information, not unlike U.S. government publications. They record the organizational structure and operations of government or international bodies. They describe and evaluate various social experiments and government programs, such as the value-added tax or child allowances. Like other government documents, those issued by foreign governments and international organizations are a rich source of demographic and economic statistics as well as scientific data and research

findings. Finally, the authoritative texts of laws, treaties, conventions, international agreements, and other legal materials are issued as official documents.

WHY

No nation is self-sufficient. Each must interact with, and thus have information from and about, other nations. For certain kinds of information, foreign and/or international documents may be the only source, the best source, or the least expensive source available.

WHERE

Although all types of libraries collect some foreign and international documents, academic and government libraries have the largest collections. Increasingly, however, one can go directly to the source as more and more governments and organizations put official information on the Internet.

WHO

All types of people may need foreign and international documents, from the high school student involved in Model United Nations competition to the scientist investigating the possibility of life on Mars.

Countless United States residents have ties to foreign countries through business, professional, or personal interest. Professors, students, business people, environmentalists, reporters, lawyers, government officials, and members of the intelligence community are among those interested in using foreign and international documents.

HOW

Accessing foreign and international documents is a challenge for both librarians and users. Access depends on the ability to determine what has been produced, the sources from which desired documents can be obtained, the appropriate organization of collections in libraries and on the Internet, and the availability of user-friendly reference and retrieval tools.

This chapter discusses how the librarian learns about, acquires, and organizes foreign and international documents, and how people can find these documents in the library or retrieve them from the Internet. Since describing the documents of just one country or organization could occupy a lifetime and fill a book, the discussion here will be quite general.

THE MOST IMPORTANT PRINCIPLE

The most important principle to be gleaned from this chapter is *know your government!* The more you know about how a country or IGO is organized and how it carries out its work, the more successful you will be in predicting where needed information will appear and the more efficient you will be in selecting and pursuing appropriate documents for use.

BIBLIOGRAPHIC IDENTIFICATION

Often people learn about new government documents by reading the newspaper. This fact is as true for foreign and international documents as it is for domestic documents. However, newspapers seldom provide an exact title or instructions for obtaining a copy, and so librarians and researchers must turn to more formal bibliographic sources for information.

Publishers' Catalogs

The researcher can use several ways to determine what foreign and international documents exist. Theoretically, the government (or the organization) will print its own bibliographic publications such as lists produced by a country's government printing office or by individual government agencies—the equivalent of the *Monthly Catalog*. In actuality, such lists may be slow in coming out, may be incomplete, or may not even exist. Unlike the United States, most countries do not maintain a centralized government printing office.

One way to verify the existence, name, and address of a country's government printing office is to use the *Europa World Year Book*.[1] A great deal of information is provided for each country in a standardized format. The country's government publishing house will be clearly identified at the end of the list of publishers. The structure of the government and the names and addresses of the various ministries or agencies are listed. Such information will be useful if you have to write and inquire about publication lists. Keep in mind, however, that since the names of the ministries have been translated into English, they do not provide exact terminology for Internet searches.

The description of an international organization in the *Europa World Year Book* includes a listing of major publications, including catalogs and publication lists. We don't always think of publishers' catalogs as reference tools, but in the case of international organizations, sales catalogs are invaluable. Because the library may use these catalogs behind the scenes and not catalog them for the stacks, the library user may be unaware of their existence. They are, however, readily available by writing to the organization and are often the best source of bibliographic information.

International organizations also use Web sites to promote and sell publications. For example, the World Conservation Bookstore <http://w3.iprolink.ch/iucnlib/bookstore/> sponsored by the IUCN[2] Library provides bibliographic data on all their publications past, present, and future, plus order numbers and prices for the "in print" titles. Thus the Bookstore combines a traditional library catalogue and an online "mail order" service. Over 1,300 titles spanning nearly 50 years can be searched by broad subject area, keyword, geographic term, author, title, ISBN, or year.

> **Searching the Library Catalog**
>
> To find a publisher's catalog or sales list, search under:
> [name of country]—**Government publications—Bibliography**
> [name of IGO]—**Bibliography—Catalogs**
> [name of IGO]—**Bibliography—Periodicals**
> **International agencies—Bibliography**
> **International agencies—Bibliography—Catalogs**
> **Catalogs, Publishers'**—[geographic area or country]

National Bibliographies

If a country has a recognized national bibliography published, it may include official government documents, often in a separate supplement or section. Works such as Barbara L. Bell's *An Annotated Guide to Current National Bibliographies*[3] and G.E. Gorman and J.J. Mills's *Guide to Current National Bibliographies in the Third World*[4] are useful for determining the existence, title, and scope of national bibliographies. However, in their quest to be comprehensive, national bibliographies are also apt to be slow in appearing. Thus, they are often more useful for historical research than for finding current information.

Searching the Library Catalog

To find a national bibliography, search under:
[name of country]—**Imprints**

To find a guide to or list of national bibliographies search under:
Bibliography, National—Bibliography

General Catalogs and Indexes

A catalog that includes documents from many countries is the *Bibliographic Guide to Government Publications—Foreign*[5], an annual publication produced from the cataloging records of The Research Libraries of the New York Public Library and the Library of Congress and published by G.K. Hall. The "foreign" designation in the title refers not just to foreign national documents but also to publications of international and regional agencies, foreign state and provincial governments, and major foreign cities, all of which are represented in this bibliographic guide.

Searching the Library Catalog

To find general catalogs and indexes, search under:
Government publications—Bibliography—Catalogs—Periodicals
International agencies—Bibliography—Periodicals

Specialized Catalogs and Indexes

Public Policy

Certain subject indexes cover foreign and international documents as well as commercial publications. PAIS[6], for example, provides access to public and social policy literature (articles, books, pamphlets, and government documents) and is available in a number of print and electronic formats and includes items published in English, German, French, Spanish, Italian, and Portuguese from 60 countries. Publications of international organizations and government documents are selected for their value as sources of factual information rather than as

records of governmental operations. Thus, reports of government investigations and significant policy developments are indexed. Routine administrative reports are not. The monthly issues of *PAIS International In Print* could be used as a current awareness tool. However, the cumulated annual Author Index is a more efficient, if less timely, source for identifying documents of national governments and international organizations because the entries appear just once and under the agency name rather than multiple times under various subject headings as they do in the monthly issues. Addresses of the publishers and distributors are listed in the front of each issue.

Statistics

A number of sources aid researchers in locating statistics. Princeton University's Office of Population Research seeks out census and demographic reports from the countries of the world to include in their *Population Index*.[7] Routine official statistical publications that do not contain substantive articles are cited in a special issue from time to time (for instance, see Vol. 61, No. 4, Winter 1995), but "Official Statistical Publications" is a regular section in every issue as well. The entire published database back to 1986 is available on the Internet at <http://popindex.princeton.edu> and can be searched by author, subject, geographical region, and year of publication.

For statistics published by international organizations, the *Index to International Statistics* (IIS),[8] published by Congressional Information Service, is the prime locating tool. IGO documents are a rich source of comparative information about countries, and IIS provides an especially detailed approach by name of country in the index volume. The documents indexed are available in a companion microfiche set[9] keyed to the abstract or entry number. IIS is one of the indexes included in the CD-ROM product Statistical Masterfile.[10]

Science and Technology

In the scientific and technical area, don't overlook the National Technical Information Service (NTIS). NTIS has been handling foreign government publications since World War II, when its predecessor, the Publication Board, was established to disseminate technical data captured from foreign sources during the war. NTIS acquires information from numerous foreign government departments and international organizations, especially those in Russia and the other countries of the former Soviet Union, Canada, Japan, and the European Union countries. Since *Government Reports Announcements and Index* (C51.9/3:) was discontinued in 1996, electronic versions of the NTIS database must be used to find relevant documents.[11] Publications added during the previous 30 days can be searched on the Internet: <http://www.ntis.gov/ordernow>.

Education and Library Studies

The Educational Resources Information Center (ERIC) can be a source of official publications dealing with education. It is particularly strong for UNESCO material and also includes reports of the International Federation of Library Associations (IFLA). The "Institution Index" in the print product, *Resources in Education* (ED1.30:), indicates the variety of foreign and international material to be found in the ERIC microfiche collection. The ERIC database[12] is searchable through various online and CD-ROM products.

Searching an ERIC Database

Search by name of country in the field for country of publication or geographic source.

Search for the word **foreign** or the word **international** in the field for level of government or governmental status.

Guides to the Literature

Aside from actual listings of publications, many countries and international organizations have guides to their official literature. Typically, these guides will explain how the government is organized; describe major series of publications; suggest useful bibliographic approaches; provide addresses; and list other books and articles for further reading.

Searching the Library Catalog

To find a "guide to the literature," look for the subheading—Government publications after
the name of the particular country or IGO:
   [name of country]—**Government publications**
   [world area]—**Government publications**
   [name of organization]—**Government publications**

Guide to Official Publications of Foreign Countries,[13] compiled by the International Documents Task Force of the American Library Association's Government Documents Roundtable, is the most comprehensive guide to the publications of foreign governments. For each of the 157 countries covered, standardized information is given concerning:

   Guides to Official Publications
   Bibliographies and Catalogs
   Sources of General Information on the Country

   Government Directories and Organization
     Manuals
   Statistical Yearbooks
   Laws and Regulations
   Legislative Proceedings
   Statements of Government Policy
   Economic Affairs
   Central Bank Publications
   Development Plans
   Budgets
   Census Results
   Health Titles
   Labor Titles
   Education Titles
   Court Reports

Emphasis is on titles published during the 1980s. Only the principal publications of the government are mentioned, but if the government has not produced a title in a particular category, a nonofficial publication is often included. Entries for most titles include a brief description of contents plus English translations of any titles or agency names not in English. This guide is invaluable for both reference and acquisitions work.

The best overall guide to IGO material is *International Information: Documents, Publications, and Information Systems of International Governmental Organizations*[14] edited by Peter I. Hajnal. It provides information on the organizational setting, bibliographic control, collection development, arrangement of collections, reference work, citation forms, microforms, and computerized information systems.

Pergamon Press publishes a series called "Guides to Official Publications." Number 1[15] in that series is a combined report of Vladimir Palic's *Government Publications: A Guide to Bibliographic Tools* (LC 1.12/2:G74) and *Government Organization Manuals* (LC 1.6/4: G74), both originally published by the Library of Congress. Palic describes the catalogs, bibliographies, and other sources for countries and international organizations. This book can be used as a starting point for finding out about foreign and international documents.

Guides to Primary Sources

Guides to individual types of primary source material are also very useful. For statistics issued by national statistical offices, the *Bibliography of Official Statistical Yearbooks and Bulletins,*[16] compiled by Gloria Westfall, is useful. Joan Harvey has produced guides to statistics for various areas of the world. Her *Statistics Africa,*[17] *Statistics America,*[18] *Statistics Asia and Australasia,*[19] and *Statistics Europe*[20] include nongovernmental as well as official publications. For statistics issued by international organizations, use *International Statistics Sources,*[21] sometimes referred to as *instat,* a comprehensive subject guide to the serial publications in which international statistical data can be found. It covers the full range of economic, political, business, and social statistics, plus many other areas of interest such as the environment, science and technology, defense, and climate.

Searching the Library Catalog

To find statistical compilations, search under:
    [name of country]—**Statistics**
    [topic]—**Statistics**
To locate guides to statistical publications, search under:
    Statistics—Bibliography

As mentioned earlier, the researcher's most important task in finding documents is to determine how the government or IGO is organized. The *Checklist of Government Directories, Lists and Rosters,*[22] from Meckler Publishing, is an annotated guide to the types of publications that provide a working knowledge of the organization, administrative scope, and personnel of national governments.

Searching the Library Catalog

Organization manuals can be tricky to find in the subject catalog. Some Library of Congress headings to search under are:
    Administrative agencies—[name of country]
    Legislative bodies—[name of country]
    [name of country]—**Executive departments**
    [name of country]—**Officials and employees**

Official gazettes are another important type of national publication. These "official journals" often combine information similar to that found in separate United States publications such as the *Congressional Record, Statutes at Large, Federal Register,* and the *Weekly Compilation of Presidential Documents.* The content will vary from country to country. Topics covered may include new legislation, regulations, orders and decisions, official announcements, texts of international agreements, court decisions, and legislative debates. The law library of the Library of Congress maintains an extensive collection of official gazettes and has issued *A Guide to Official Gazettes and Their Contents*[23] covering all the countries of the world.

Searching the Library Catalog

To find a guide that lists official gazettes, search under:
    Gazettes—Bibliography

To find official gazettes using the subject catalog, search under:
    [name of country]—**Politics and government**

Another tool that lists official gazettes and a whole lot more is *Foreign Law: Current Sources of Codes and Basic Legislation in Jurisdictions of the World.*[24] This work provides the legal researcher with relevant information on sources of foreign law, including complete bibliographic citations to legislation, the existence of English translations, and selected references to secondary sources in English. Each section begins with a narrative description of that country's legal history.

The Library Catalog

A library's own catalog may be helpful, not only for determining call numbers when bibliographic information is known, but also for determining the extent of that library's holdings for particular countries or international bodies. A library that has made an effort to collect elusive documents may be the only source for bibliographic information about them. More and more library catalogs from around the world are available for your exploration on the Internet. A useful list is available at <http://library.usask.ca/hywebcat/geographic.html>. Many libraries also subscribe to WorldCat for their patrons.[25] WorldCat, the public-use version of the OCLC cataloging database, gives users access to more than 20 million bibliographic records contributed by thousands of libraries.

Entries for official publications generally begin with the name of the country. It is fairly easy to browse through the cards filed under "France," for example, in a card catalog; perhaps is is less easy to browse through the entries retrieved in an online catalog when you enter "France" as author or corporate author. Entries under government agency or international organization names can be lengthy and complicated. They present many opportunities for the searcher to make mistakes whether by looking in the wrong place alphabetically or by typing in misspellings. That's why the Wordlist feature in WorldCat is so useful. Each part of the entry is listed separately.

> ### Searching the Library Catalog
>
> To find official publications in catalogs and indexes that use AACR cataloging rules, look first under the name of the country or IGO. In WorldCat, use a Corporate Name-bound phrase and search on the name of a country combined with a subject or author keyword:
>
> co=[name of country] **and au:Estadistica**
> co=[name of IGO] **and su:women**

Not only is it difficult to know whether you are searching correctly when dealing with government documents, but also the possibility exists that the library's holdings are not reflected in the general catalog. Documents may be in a separate catalog or the library may rely entirely on externally produced catalogs and indexes (print, CD-ROM, or online) for access to the documents collection, along with a simple shelflist to verify holdings.

Finding out about the existence of foreign and international documents may take some digging: bibliographic control for official publications has not been mastered by the world's libraries. Whether this failure is because government publishing is too decentralized, too voluminous, too varied, too changeable, or too much like archival material is an unanswered question. Although the problems are well known, the solutions remain to be found.

ACQUIRING FOREIGN AND INTERNATIONAL DOCUMENTS

Collection Development Policies

A library's holdings of foreign and international documents will be governed by its collection development policy and the needs of its patrons. When a library decides to collect foreign documents, it might first focus on English-language materials, such as those from Great Britain or Canada. Aside from a subject approach, documents can be collected in two main ways: by country and by type of material. Many libraries endeavor to collect a wide range of publications from a particular country. Others may collect certain specific types of material such as organization manuals and/or statistical abstracts from numerous countries.

Selection Tools

The *Journal of Government Information* (Tarrytown, NY: Pergamon, 1994—bimonthly) devotes the last issue of each year to notable documents. It is designed as a selection tool and as an alerting service for libraries interested in identifying significant new official publications from all levels of government and all countries.

Microform Collections

Some microform publishers, such as Inter Documentation Company AG, Chadwyck-Healey, Readex, and Micromedia Limited, offer attractive packages of foreign and international material for sale to libraries. The subject volume of the *Guide to Microforms in Print*[26] includes some 60 pages of foreign and international document listings under heading number 324: Official Government Documents. Norman Ross Publishing[27] is the leading distributor of foreign microforms in the United States, providing a convenient centralized service. Sometimes, however, microforms are only available directly from a country's government or from an international organization's sales outlet.

Interlibrary Loan

A library may decide not to collect foreign and international documents at all, but instead rely on interlibrary loan to satisfy the infrequent needs of its patrons. The British Library Document Supply Centre (BLDSC) receives about 30,000 requests a year for official publications. To contact their U.S. Service Centre, just call 1-800-932-3575. The main strength of the BLDSC collection lies in their holdings of British material, but they also have good collections of Australian, Canadian, foreign census material, and development plans.

The Center for Research Libraries in Chicago houses foreign documents for its members. The collection of several hundred thousand volumes from more than 100 foreign governments is particularly strong for Western Europe, Latin America, and Southeast Asia. An attempt is being made to catalog these documents, which are described in a general way in the Center's *Handbook.*[28] Libraries that are not Center members have limited borrowing privileges for a prepaid transaction fee. The Center's Web site can be accessed at <http://wwwcrl.uchicago.edu/>.

The *Directory of Government Documents Collections and Librarians*[29] shows which libraries collect documents from particular international organizations or foreign countries. The *Directory of Foreign Document Collections*[30] provides even more comprehensive and detailed descriptions of library holdings for foreign documents.

Verification

The first step in acquisitions is to identify the item bibliographically—sometimes a problem since bibliographic control for this material ranges from difficult to nonexistent. Use the sources described above or a cataloging utility such as OCLC or RLIN to verify bibliographic information before ordering. Foreign documents usually take from six months to a year to appear in OCLC with Library of Congress copy. Some never do appear. Since speed is important in acquiring government publications, you may be forced to order with incomplete information. For instance, it may be impossible to determine the price before ordering. Indeed, many government documents cost nothing. If you insist on a price quote before ordering, you risk a fatal delay, because documents are generally printed only in small quantities. You might specify a maximum price, asking that the order be canceled if the cost is higher.

Vendors

After you have pulled together pertinent bibliographic information—such as title, issuing body, date, and number of pages—the next step is to determine where to send your order. Some of the tools described above, like the *Guide to Official Publications of Foreign Countries*, include specific instructions and addresses for ordering the material. (A "List of Vendors by Region and Country" section appears in the front of the *Guide*.) For IGO publications, Bernan Associates[31] is the major distributor in the United States. The *International Literary Market Place*[32] has a list of major book dealers arranged by country. A letter of inquiry may be used to determine if a particular firm is capable of handling government documents or knows who will.

Without a vendor, libraries must deal directly with the issuing government or organization. Organization manuals, directories, telephone books, lists of publishers in national bibliographies, and the *Europa World Year Book* are sources for locating the proper addresses. Embassies are another—either the American embassy in the foreign country or the foreign embassy in this country. The private address and correspondence files built up by librarians over the years can be a very important acquisitions resource. Queries sent to ACQNET-L, a Listserv for acquisitions and collection development librarians,[33] may elicit help from other librarians who have more experience or better files. Another Internet resource is the AcqWeb site <http://www.library.vanderbilt.edu/law/acqs/acqs.html>, which provides links to information of value to acquisitions and collection development people. The scope is international and well worth exploring.

Embassies on the Internet

The Electronic Embassy <http://www.embassy.org>
Embassies Worldwide <http://www.xs4all.nl/~airen/index.html>
The Embassy Page <http://www.embpage.org>

Some foreign agencies prefer to receive requests written in their native language. Form letters can be translated into various languages. On college campuses native speakers from other countries can often be hired to translate. Some libraries maintain lists of local resource people by language. When it comes to coping with foreign languages, you may find a book like ALA's *The Language of the Foreign Book Trade*[34] handy to have nearby.

Payment

Paying for the item can present further problems. Since exchange rates are unstable, the price at the ordering stage may differ from the final price. If prepayment is required and your library is a public institution, you may have another problem. Librarians are often caught in the middle of a situation where one government requires the money before releasing the item and the other government requires the item before releasing the money. Sometimes deposit accounts can ameliorate this situation. One of the advantages of working with a vendor to buy documents is that business dealings are generally smoother.

Claiming

After the order is sent, experience will tell you when to expect receipt. If it doesn't come, send a follow-up request. If it still doesn't come, either follow up again, try another approach, or give up. Experience will indicate the point of diminishing returns. You may think you have set up a standing order for a foreign serial, but since government departments can be unreliable about maintaining mailing lists, to ensure receipt of an annual report or other serial publication you must write for it yearly around its issue date.

Special Methods of Acquiring Documents

Under certain circumstances, exchange agreements can be mutually advantageous for a pair of libraries in two different countries. Sometimes your own institutional publications can be used for barter. Sometimes university faculty members who work or travel in foreign countries collect materials for the library. Sometimes the librarian gets to go on buying trips.

Depository Arrangements

Depository libraries receive shipments of publications automatically, thus obviating much of the workload associated with acquiring publications. Except for Canada, few foreign countries maintain U.S. depositories, whereas international organizations have depositories all over the world. On the other hand, international organizations sometimes turn major publications over to private publishers, completely bypassing the depositories and making it difficult to keep track of what is available. Furthermore, some publications are produced through regional offices in the far corners of the world and are never even listed in the catalogs that emanate from headquarters, let alone distributed to depository libraries.

Recently, IGOs have been facing financial constraints severe enough to cause them to rethink their depository arrangements. In 1993, UNESCO reduced the number of depositories to one per member country. Former depositories now receive a 50 percent discount on new publications.

Sometimes the challenge for the foreign and international documents librarian is knowing what not to acquire; assessing how much the library can afford to process and store; setting up cooperative agreements with other libraries; knowing what can be borrowed; and knowing what will be used.

ORGANIZING FOREIGN AND INTERNATIONAL DOCUMENTS

Once the library acquires foreign and international documents, it must decide how to handle them. Where will they be shelved? How will they be classified? What level of cataloging will be provided for them?

Shelving

Libraries in the United States are about equally divided between those that keep documents in a separate collection and those that integrate them into the regular collection. Integrated collections keep subjects together but may scatter the publications of a particular nation or organization. A separate shelving sequence for documents makes it easier to keep all the publications of a body together, an arrangement often preferred by knowledgeable patrons, but it may increase the level of complexity facing the casual user of a library. Pemberton argues that every library should have a documents and reports collection because these materials constitute a third form of literature distinct from monographs and serials in that the source from which they emanate is of particular interest to the user. In addition to official publications, he would include the publications of political parties, pressure groups, and trade unions in the documents and reports collection.[35]

Classification

Unlike U.S. federal documents, some foreign and international documents have document classification num-

bers printed right on them. This numbering greatly facilitates processing and housing in a separate documents collection. The user who finds these numbers in printed indexes and catalogs can go directly to the shelves to retrieve the publication. Whether or not the documents come with numbers, the body may have developed an official classification scheme for its own documents that the library can adopt. Or the library may use an overall scheme into which it can fit all documents and reports. Several such systems are described in *The Bibliographic Control of Official Publications*[36] edited by John E. Pemberton. An important characteristic of a document classification system is that it groups together all the publications of a given country or a particular international organization.

Those who prefer a subject arrangement of documents have recourse to the Library of Congress, Dewey Decimal, or other classification system that the library uses. It should be noted, however, that documents can be classified by subject using the library's established system and still be kept in a separate documents collection (just as reference books are classified but shelved separately). Likewise, a library could modify its classification to provide a common class for all the publications of a particular country or organization so that they would stand together in the stacks.

Generally speaking, it is good practice to have a call number notation on every piece of library material so it can be retrieved from its proper place and be put back there. However, libraries have been known to shelve documents by agency name and title or by organization and then broad subject area. Sometimes color coding is used. Sometimes "filing" phrases are underlined on the cover of the document.

Cataloging

Whether and/or how documents are classified (and shelved) is an entirely independent issue from whether and/or how documents are cataloged. Bibliographic descriptions of the documents owned may be included in the library's general catalog, maintained as a separate documents catalog, or exist only in a shelflist. AACR2 rules are not particularly hospitable to the documents cataloger, which is why GODORT[37] produced a companion manual on documents cataloging.[38]

Many libraries trying to catalog and integrate documents into their regular collections get bogged down with processing and develop large backlogs that, in essence, become separate documents collections. Every library has hidden files and special collections that are not yet reflected in the catalog. Until they are, both users and librarians must remember to explore the possibility that alternative or additional resources exist.

USING FOREIGN AND INTERNATIONAL DOCUMENTS

How much are foreign and international documents actually used? One study in the field of international relations[39] found that citations to documents in journal articles were 19 percent of the total, and over half of the document citations were to publications of foreign governments or international organizations. Documents in foreign languages made up just over 10 percent of all documents cited. Use does, of course, vary by discipline.

Studies have shown that scholars often have their own means of acquiring documents and may not rely heavily on libraries. However, an international documents specialist at the Library of Congress receives some 65 questions a month that require extensive expertise to answer.[40] Often the answer or a clue to the answer comes from a personal filing cabinet. Sometimes a telephone call or e-mail message to another expert is required. Frequently, queries are in response to publicity in the newspaper about documents that are too new to have been received or cataloged. Although none of these problems are unique to foreign and international documents, they serve to emphasize the importance of the librarian being intimately familiar with the collection. The questions the librarian gets may be typical in that they can be grouped into categories, such as requests for statistics, legislation, development plans, or international agreements. However, handling them is seldom a routine matter. A request for the official election returns from Costa Rica may lead to a search for a statistical yearbook from the country, verification of the name of the agency responsible for elections (Tribunal Supremo de Elecciones), or frustration over the fact that indexing tools are not consistent in their use of terms, listing entries under both **Costa Rica—Elections** and **Elections—Costa Rica**. Some particular pitfalls of foreign and international document use, pitfalls that can be avoided by the alert and experienced librarian, are described below.

PECULIARITIES OF FOREIGN AND INTERNATIONAL DOCUMENTS

Language

Many international and some foreign documents are printed in more than one language, sometimes with parallel text in English and another language. If you do not spot the English text immediately, you may become confused, waste time, or even abandon the book needlessly. Dealing with parallel titles in several languages is one of the factors that makes cataloging more time-consuming for documents than for other material and makes finding such documents in the catalog more problematic and confusing.

However, more subtle problems than the simple inability to read foreign languages often arise. The English language is used differently in different countries and by different international organizations. This leads to subject heading variations in catalogs and indexes. Use of the wrong terminology leads to poor retrieval results.

Be aware of differences in terminology!

The press says: "Multinational corporations"

The United Nations uses the phrase: "Transnational corporations"

The Library of Congress subject heading is: "International business enterprises"

In the United States the word is "Antitrust" but in Canada the word is "Competition"

Library of Congress subject heading "Hijacking of aircraft" is what the United Nations Documents Index calls "Aerial interference"

United Nations uses the phrase "Human rights"
Library of Congress uses the phrase "Civil rights"

Types of Publications

Official publications are a reflection of the process of governing. As governing bodies differ, so do their documents. It is necessary to be open to learning about the importance of new types of publications when working with foreign and international documents. For instance, the United Nations carries on its work through the adoption of resolutions. Great Britain has its white papers (departmental policy statements), green papers (preliminary versions of the white papers), and blue books (commission reports).

Particularly with regard to international organizations, it is important to understand the distinction between publications and documents. Publications are materials produced for distribution to the public. They may be priced or unpriced, but generally some attempt is made to publicize them. Documents, on the other hand, are records of organization activity, produced primarily for the participants, not for public distribution. Examples include minutes, proceedings, and draft reports. Such documents may be cited but impossible to obtain.

Subject Matter

The documents of different nations reflect differing concerns. Foreign government documents may cover religious topics where a state religion exists, as in Israel. Countries with nationalized industries and crown corporations may issue very detailed business statistics and reports. Liechtenstein sponsors a gambling site on the

Web <http://interlotto.li>. International organizations grapple with problems of global significance not generally addressed by individual countries. So it is necessary to be open minded about the type of subject matter that may be covered by foreign and international documents.

Interpreting Citations

Librarians are wizards at deciphering bibliographic citations. However, not all librarians would be aware, for example, that the difference between Cmd.1 and Cmnd.1 in British documents is approximately 30 years. The British Command Papers series is a well-known and important part of that nation's parliamentary papers. Command Papers are numbered continuously, through several sessions of Parliament, from 1 to not more than 9999. The various series are distinguished by their prefix, as follows:

Years:	Cite as:
1833-1869	1 - 4222
1870-1899	C1 - C9550
1900-1918	Cd.1 - Cd.9239
1919-1956	Cmd.1 - Cmd.9889
1956-1986	Cmnd.1 - Cmnd.9927
1986-	Cm.1 -

The nuances of proper citation can be very important for the full identification of documents. A rule of thumb is to write down all the numbers located in a bibliographic search, rather than overlook the one number that may prove most important for document retrieval in a particular library.

ALTERNATIVE SOURCES OF INFORMATION

United States Documents

Foreign national documents are not the sole source of foreign country information. Indeed, few libraries collect documents from more than a few countries. United States documents, however, contain much valuable information about other nations. The Departments of Commerce, Defense, and State <http://dosfan.lib.uic.edu> are among the most prolific publishers in this regard. The Area Handbooks series, now called "Country Studies" (<http://lcweb2.loc.gov/frd/cs/cshome.html> or D101.22:550-no.), is especially valuable, as well as the *National Trade Data Bank CD-ROM* (C1.88: or on the Internet through STAT-USA) and the *World Factbook* (PREX3.15: also available from the CIA's homepage <http://www.odci.gov/cia/publications/pubs.html>.) The State Department's annual report on human rights practices (Y4.In8/16-15) is eagerly awaited each year. To view it on the Internet at <http://dosfan.lib.uic.edu>, select "Publications—Major Reports," then select "Human Rights Country Practices." Even the *Statistical Abstract of the United States* (C3.134/2:C83/2/yr) has a chapter on world statistics at the end.

The *American Foreign Policy and Treaty Index*[41] provides access not just to the publications of the U.S. Government that address foreign relations but also to those that provide information on the economic, social, and political conditions in foreign countries. It is a good general index to foreign country information in federal documents.

International Organization Publications

The publications of international organizations are a rich source of comparative information about countries. Member nations tend to be cooperative about releasing information to the IGOs, and the international organizations tend to be conscientious about publishing it in a consistent and comparable format. Much of this information is statistical in nature and available through *IIS* described earlier. However, the International Labor Office (ILO) monitors legislation dealing with labor and social security issues in all countries and prints the laws in the annual *ILO Legislative Series*.[42] A similar undertaking by the World Health Organization (WHO) results in the publication *International Digest of Health Legislation*.[43] The *Guide to Country Information in International Governmental Organization Publications*[44] is the first research tool and acquisition guide to survey all the major series and important monographs of these organizations that contain useful information on countries.

Commercial Publications

Commercial publications, ranging from textbooks and travelogues to expensive business loose-leaf services, also help fill the need for international information. The bimonthly *International Legal Materials*,[45] from the American Society of International Law, reprints or translates significant documents from all over the world. It includes judicial and similar proceedings, treaties and agreements, legislation and regulations, reports, and other documents.

Some information sources are hidden away in reference books that normally serve an entirely different purpose. For instance, one might easily overlook the foreign law digests in the last volume of the Martindale-Hubbell[46] directory of lawyers and law firms. These law digests provide understandable foreign legal information, which is probably exceeded only by the collections of the very best and largest law libraries.

Information about international governmental organizations may be located in *The Yearbook of International Organizations*,[47] which describes over 24,000 international organizations, only 5,000 of which are intergovernmental. (International organizations whose members are not countries, such as the International Federation of Library Associations, or IFLA, are known as nongovernmental organizations, or NGOs.) Entries include organization names (in all applicable languages); addresses, telephone, and telex; name of principal executive officer; main activities; history, goals, and structure; personnel and finances; technical and regional commissions; consultative relationships; memberships by country; publications; and interorganizational links. This book is the definitive source of information for international bodies.

ELECTRONIC ACCESS

Electronic access to bibliographic information about foreign and international documents has changed from dream to reality in recent years. Ready access is now available through cataloging utilities, online databases, CD-ROM products, and the Internet. For example, Chadwyck-Healey markets a CD-ROM index to the British government documents while the British Library provides online access to the same material,[48] and The Stationery Office (formerly HMSO[49]) has a Web site <http://www.the-stationery-office.co.uk> that offers searching, online ordering, and some full-text documents. To determine whether such a database exists for a particular country or organization, consult the *Gale Directory of Databases*.[50] It has a geographic index.

Exploring the Internet

Many Internet search engines, such as AltaVista <http://www.altavista.digital.com> and HotBot <http://www.hotbot.com>, allow you to search on elements of the URL. Limit your search to Web sites in a particular country by using the two-letter country code. For some English-speaking countries, limit to government sites by including the designation "gov."

domain:th (finds sites in Thailand)*

url:gov.au (finds government sites in Australia)

For a complete listing of country codes, use HotBot Super Search and click on domain and country code index.

PROFESSIONAL UPDATE SOURCES

Good sources for keeping up to date on foreign and international documents include *Documents to the People*,[51] *Government Information Quarterly*,[52] *Journal of Government Information*,[53] and the newsletter of the IFLA Official Publications Section.[54] Recently, a new

means of communication has gained popularity—discussion lists on the Internet. GOVDOC-L is a general documents forum, while INT-LAW[55] is specifically for exchanging information and talking about international legal issues, including documents of international organizations and foreign governments. Anything relating to acquisitions, reference work, databases, CD-ROM products, cataloging, classification, etc., can be discussed. The International Documents Task Force (IDTF)[56] has a Web site at <http://www.library.nwu.edu/govpub/idtf> that, among other services, provides links to official foreign and international Web sites. IDTF also sponsors a discussion list, INTL-DOC, primarily for individuals working with IGO documentation.[57]

CANADIAN GOVERNMENT DOCUMENTS

Canadian Documents in Libraries

Because Canada is our national neighbor and issues official publications in English (French too, of course), many U.S. libraries collect Canadian documents. The Canadian government has established 150 depository libraries outside Canada—40 in the United States. Selective depositories are entitled to select free copies of certain publications from the *Weekly Checklist of Canadian Government Publications*.[58] The Library of Congress, the only full Canadian depository in the United States, automatically receives weekly shipments of publications listed on the checklist.

Acquisition of Canadian Government Publications

Because of its timeliness, the *Weekly Checklist* is a good acquisitions tool. Nondepository libraries outside Canada can subscribe to it.[59] One can also search the *Weekly Checklist* on the Internet at <http://web2.ccg-gcc.ca/dsp-psd/Checklist/lists-e/html>. The *Weekly Checklist* includes both free and priced documents released by the Parliament of Canada, the federal departments, and Statistics Canada. URLs are given for the majority of items, and the full-text documents are hotlinked from the *Weekly Checklist* Web site.

Borrowing Canadian Documents through Interlibrary Loan

The National Library of Canada (NLC), the library of last resort for international ILL requests, accepts requests via OCLC's PRISM (enter "NLD" twice). NLC's Web site is at <http://www.nlc-bnc.ca/services/e-ill.htm>. AMICUS,[60] an online union catalog supported by the National Library of Canada, includes records generated by Canadian federal government libraries.

Guide to the Literature of Canadian Documents

Canadian Official Publications [61], written by Olga B. Bishop in 1981, is still the best guide to this material. She describes the types of publications issued by the Canadian government as well as the types of information to be found in particular documents.

Canada's Government Manual

The Canadian government no longer publishes *Organization of the Government of Canada* [62] (Canadian Class No. BT1-2), the guide to Canada's federal government that was very similar to our *U.S. Government Manual.* They do produce a guide that thoroughly describes government programs and where to go, write, or call for information. It is entitled *Info Source* [63] (Canadian Class No. BT51-3/1), but has no index or names. For telephone numbers, *Info Source: Directory of Federal Government Enquiry Points* [64] (Canadian Class No. BT51-3/15) is a handy tool. For information about people, a better source is the commercially produced *Canadian Parliamentary Guide.* [65] It contains biographical sketches, historical charts of office holders, and election results. The Web site for the Canadian government is at <http://canada.gc.ca>. [66]

Canada's Official Gazette

Canada's official gazette is called *The Canada Gazette* [67] (Canadian Class No. SP-1, SP-2, and SP-11). Part I of the *Canada Gazette* contains notices, proclamations, and other material required to be published; Part II contains regulations; and Part III contains the public acts (i.e., laws) that have received Royal Assent.

Canada's National Bibliography

The national bibliography of Canada is entitled *Canadiana* [68] (Canadian Class No. SN2-1). Official publications are intermixed in Part I with the other items published in Canada. Part II is foreign imprints; books about Canada published outside of Canada. *Canadiana* is a valuable aid for Canadian studies and is available in microfiche and on magnetic tape. A CD-ROM product is being developed.

Bibliographic Sources for Canadian Publications

The most important bibliographic tool for document reference purposes used to be *Government of Canada Publications,* [69] (Canadian Class No. IC6-1), a quarterly catalog that ceased publication in 1992. Now, one must rely on the searchable version of the *Weekly Checklist* on the Internet or use the Micromedia products described below.

Canadian Document Microforms

Micromedia Limited sells Canadian documents, both federal and provincial, on microfiche and provides a comprehensive index, formerly known as *Microlog* but now called *Canadian Research Index.* [70] Subscriptions are available for the CD-ROM version or for Internet access via Micromedia's ERL server, Voyageur.

Canadian Statistics

Like the U.S. Bureau of the Census, Statistics Canada collects and publishes numerical data on social and economic activity. Publications available for purchase from the agency are described in the annual *Statistics Canada Catalogue* [71] (Canadian Class No. CS11-204). A retrospective volume, the *Historical Catalogue of Statistics Canada Publications, 1918–1980* [72] (Canadian Class No. CS11-512), provides a complete record of the cataloged publications of Statistics Canada and its predecessor, the Dominion Bureau of Statistics.

Actual statistical tables are found in *Historical Statistics of Canada* [73] (Canadian Class No. CS11-516), most of them with time series data for approximately 50 years. More recent economic statistics are found in the monthly *Canadian Economic Observer* (Canadian Class No. CS11-010) and its *Historical Statistical Supplement* (Canadian Class No. CS11-021). [74] The *Canada Year Book* [75] (Canadian Class No. CS11-402), which is like a statistical abstract with pictures and text, has a broader range of social and cultural statistics. The CD-ROM edition of the *Canada Year Book* features an enhanced and expanded collection of tables and multimedia accessories to enrich and highlight areas of the text. Because only 10 percent or less of the data available from Statistics Canada are in printed form, online numeric databases such as CANSIM [76] are increasingly important.

Other statistical data can be tracked down using the *Bibliography of Federal Data Sources: Excluding Statistics Canada 1981* [77] (Canadian Class No. CS11-513) or *Canadian Statistics Index,* [78] published by Micromedia Ltd., which indexes both government and nongovernment statistics. As with other Micromedia indexes, a companion microfiche collection is available.

Classification of Canadian Publications

Canada prints the catalog number, which can be used as a classification number, in the document itself. Preprinted numbers facilitate the processing of documents by the library. An explanation of the system is available in *Government of Canada Publications: Outline of Classification*[79] (Canadian Class No. IC91-1984). This number is included in bibliographic records on the Micromedia Web site but not in their printed indexes.

Some Canadian libraries use CODOC, a system developed at the University of Guelph in 1967, which can be applied to the documents of all countries and any level of government.[80]

Professional Networking

A new electronic journal for document librarians, *Government Information in Canada* first appeared on the Internet in 1994 at <http://www.usask.ca/library/gic/index.html>. Canadian document librarians also have an active discussion list called GOVINFO.[81]

UNITED NATIONS PUBLICATIONS AND DOCUMENTS

The United Nations, while not the oldest international governmental organization, is probably the best known and the largest, with 185 member nations. The UN proper has six principal organs: the General Assembly, the Security Council, the Economic and Social Council, the Trusteeship Council, the International Court of Justice, and the Secretariat. Fourteen other organizations, known as the "specialized agencies," are related to the United Nations by special agreements and work through the coordinating machinery of the Economic and Social Council. These organizations, such as UNESCO and the World Bank, report annually to the United Nations but are separate, autonomous IGOs with separate lists of member countries and separate publishing programs. Thus, a library that collects United Nations documents does not necessarily have material from these other specialized agencies.

Guide to the Literature of the United Nations

The basic library guide for the United Nations proper is Peter Hajnal's book *Guide to United Nations Organization, Documentation and Publishing.*[82] It contains excellent tips for students, researchers, and librarians.

The United Nations' own guide, *Everyone's United Nations*[83] (United Nations Sales No. E.85.I.24), describes the structure and activities of the United Nations and the specialized agencies. It is also a handy place to find the Charter of the United Nations.

Also of value to the inexperienced user or librarian are two documents: *United Nations Documentation: A Brief Guide*[84] (ST/LIB/34/Rev.1) and *Instructions for Depository Libraries Receiving United Nations Material*[85] (ST/LIB/13/Rev.3).

Reference Tools for UN Research

The history of the United Nations is chronicled year by year in a series entitled *Yearbook of the United Nations.*[86] The *Yearbook*, which has extensive bibliographies and references to publications and documents, may often prove to be a more satisfactory bibliographic tool than the basic index, described below. However, several years may pass before the *Yearbook* comes out. For an even more highly condensed account of UN activities, see the *UN Fiftieth Anniversary 1945–1995: Special Edition of the Yearbook.*

The acronym for the UN's index varied over the years as UNDI, UNDEX, and, most recently, UNDOC, but the subtitle remained the same: *United Nations Documents Index.*[87] UNDOC, which ended in 1996, was a byproduct of the computer-based integrated online United Nations Bibliographic Information System (UNBIS).[88] The UN is reevaluating whether a paper index is needed at the present time. Meanwhile, it is experimenting with new products on the Internet such as the Optical Disk System (ODS) and UN-I-QUE.[89]

UNBIS files are available on *UNBIS Plus on CD-ROM*, a quarterly product created by the Dag Hammarskjold Library in cooperation with publisher Chadwyck-Healey. The retrospective file goes back to 1979. Readex also produces a CD-ROM index[90] soon to be an online product with the name *AccessUN* available through their Web site at <http://www.readex.com>.

Official Records of the United Nations

Most procedural information published by the United Nations is incorporated into the *Official Records* of the Economic and Social Council, the Security Council, and the General Assembly. (The Trusteeship Council has pretty much finished its work.) The *Index to Proceedings*[91] of each body provides very detailed access to procedural information. In fact, questions can be answered using the appropriate *Index to Proceedings* that cannot be answered using UNDOC or the other general UN indexes described above.

Current Information about the United Nations

References to recent publications and UN happenings can be found in the periodical *UN Chronicle.*[92] Even more current information and the full text of press releases are available on the United Nations Web site <http://www.un.org>. To find the Dag Hammarskold Library, click on "General Information."

Treaties Recorded by the United Nations

One of the most important functions of the United Nations is keeping track of multilateral treaties and international agreements. Authentic texts are found in the *Treaty Series*,[93] and a comprehensive list of signatures, ratifications, reservations, and objections is found in *Multilateral Treaties Deposited with the Secretary-General*.[94] These are the two parts of the UN Treaty Database on the Internet.

Statistics of the United Nations

Publications of the UN Statistical Office are extremely important. The most comprehensive compilation is called the *Statistical Yearbook*[95] (UN Document No. ST/ESA/STAT/ser.S). Updates to it on 60 subjects are provided by the *Monthly Bulletin of Statistics*[96] (UN Document No. ST/ESA/STAT/ser.Q). Many other specialized statistical sources are described on the UN Web site. One of particular interest is the *Demographic Yearbook*[97] (UN Document No. ST/ESA/STAT/ser.R) because each issue includes a lengthy article on a special topic in addition to the regular tables on population, mortality, natality, nuptiality, divorce, and migration.

United Nation Concerns

The *Yearbook on Human Rights*[98] is a country-by-country report on civil and political rights, economic and social rights, and freedom of information. Also in demand are the publications of the UN's Centre on Transnational Corporations, as is anything to do with developing countries.

United Nations Depository Libraries

The United Nations expects depository libraries to pay an annual fee. A complete list of depositories can be found on the Web at <http://www.un.org/MoreInfo/Deplib/>.

Acquisition of United Nations Publications

Publications for sale can be ordered from United Nations Publications, Room DC2-0853, New York, NY 10017, which will send a catalog of publications upon request. A standing-order service provides automatic receipt of documents by subject category or by serial title. Vendors such as Bernan Associates (formerly UNIPUB) also handle UN publications. Readex supplies microfiche of United Nations documents.

Classification of UN Materials

Not all UN publications are assigned document numbers. One numbering system is used for official records, another for documents, and another for sales publications—categories which are not mutually exclusive. The fact that a title can have more than one "official" number assigned to it can cause confusion, especially if the library wants to use official numbers to shelve UN materials.

EUROPEAN UNION (EU) PUBLICATIONS AND DOCUMENTS

The European Union (EU) is a regional international organization striving to become a national government by uniting the countries of Europe. The goal will have been achieved when national borders within Europe are no more a barrier to trade and free movement than state borders are within the United States. The next step in this process will be the adoption of a common currency, the euro.

Originally the EU was made up of three communities, the European Coal and Steel Community (ECSC), the European Economic Community (EEC), and the European Atomic Energy Community (EAEC or Euratom). The three were increasingly referred to, in the singular, as the European Community and then after 1992 as the European Union. Main entries in library catalogs tend to be under the original three community names or under the names of the common institutions. Lack of uniformity in the formation of these headings adds a degree of difficulty to the searching process.

Searching the Library Catalog

European Union material is found under headings such as:
   Commission of the European Communities
   Committee of the Regions of the European Communities
   Council of the European Union
   European Atomic Energy Community
   European Coal and Steel Community
   European Commission
   European Community Information Service
   European Economic Community
   European Parliament
   European Union
   Statistical Office of the European Communities

Phrases in subject headings include:
   European Communities
   European Economic Community Countries
   European Union Countries

Organization of the European Union

A useful guide to the organization of the EU is *Interinstitutional Directory—European Union*,[99] which outlines the structure of the EU and lists the names, addresses, and telephone numbers of officials. The EU Web site is found at <http://www.europa.eu.int/>.

European Union Depository Libraries

Although the United States is not, of course, a member, the European Union thinks it is important for Americans to be informed about and supportive of the EU's goals and accomplishments. Therefore, the EU is committed to maintaining a presence in the U.S. through a depository library system. The United States has 51 European Union depositories headed by the library of the Commission of the European Union Delegation to the United States in Washington, DC.

Magazines of the European Union

The Washington delegation issues a monthly journal called *Europe*,[100] which describes the current activities of the EU and includes an order form for new publications on the "EU Bookshelf" page. Each issue of *Europe* has a feature article on one of the EU's 15 member states. The Delegation of the European Commission Web site is accessible at <http://www.eurunion.org>.

The Secretariat General of the Commission puts out the *Bulletin of the European Union*,[101] a more formal publication that follows the activities and policies of the EU closely and has a section called "New Publications" each month. Supplements reprint official documents of the Commission such as communications to the Council, reports, and proposals.

Language in the European Union

When Great Britain joined the European Union in 1973, English became one of the official languages. At the present time, everything the EU publishes must be issued in 11 languages: French, English, German, Danish, Spanish, Italian, Portuguese, Dutch, Finnish, Swedish, and Greek. Many publications show parallel titles in all the languages on the title page of the piece. Since catalogers are instructed to use the first such title and since the English title is seldom the first one listed, the catalog records for these publications can be quite intimidating.

> **Tip**
>
> Don't automatically bypass foreign language titles, especially when searching for statistical information. Look for an English version of the title on the same record.

The standardized terminology of the EU is set out in *EUROVOC*,[102] an annex to the index of the *Official Journal of the European Communities*. Each language version of the latest edition consists of a permuted alphabetical section, a subject-oriented section, and a multilingual section.

Acquisition of European Union Material

The official distributor for EU publications in the United States is Bernan Associates/UNIPUB. Their free catalog[103] covers publications by and about the EU including monographs, yearbooks, periodicals, and document subscriptions in both paper and microfiche. Online ordering can be done through the Web site at <http://www.bernan.com>.

EU's official printer, the Office for Official Publications of the European Communities (EUR-OP), also has a free subject catalog of its popular publications entitled *The European Union as a Publisher*.[104]

Official Gazette of the European Union

The texts of legislation and other official acts of the EU are published in the *Official Journal of the European Communities*.[105] It is divided into several parts.

Legislation: The "L" section includes regulations, directives, and other binding acts. Texts of a temporary duration are printed in normal typeface; those with permanence in bold. Regulations are numbered consecutively from the beginning of each year with the number first, followed by the year, i.e., 222/89. Other acts, such as directives, are also done consecutively for each year, but the order is reversed, i.e., 89/222. A regulation is a law that is binding on all member states. A directive is binding as to the result to be achieved, but the choice of method is left to the individual states. Businesses affected by a directive must take account of the national implementing legislation as well as the directive.

Information and Notices: The "C" section includes nonbinding decisions, resolutions, and other communications requiring publication. Proposals and amendments issued by the Commission are usually published here but without the explanatory memorandum that appears only in the original mimeographed series of *COM Documents*.[106] Opinions and minutes of proceedings of the European Parliament appear here approximately three months after the plenary session.

Opinions of the Economic and Social Committee are grouped in particular issues. The operative text of each decision of the Court of Justice is published here. And this section is where you can find the ECU (European Currency Unit) exchange rate on a daily basis.

Supplement: The "S" section includes notices of invitations to tender for development contracts financed by the European Development Fund, public works and supply contracts of the member states open to bidding by companies within the Community, and procurement contracts open for bids under the GATT procurement code.

Annex: The annex prints the debates of the European Parliament. Reports of the European Parliament are issued separately as part of a series called *Session Documents*.[107]

Index: The alphabetical index to the *Official Journal*, issued monthly and cumulated annually, covers only the "L" section plus the decisions of the Court of Justice from the "C" section. The debates of the European Parliament in the Annex have their own index. The methodological index provides a way to find an *Official Journal* citation when you already know the number of a regulation or directive.

Ways the *Official Journal* has been cited*
in books and articles:

Official Journal 1979 No. L 50
OJL 13, 17.1.90 p34
OJ C 135/88
OJ 1985 L199
OJ Eur Comm. no.L209 (Aug. 2, 1988)

---

*This is not a style guide.

Guides to the Literature of the EU

The most recent guide to the literature of the EU is Barbara Sloan's *Researching the European Union*.[108] Ian Thomson's *The Documentation of the European Communities*[109] extends the historical information to be found in the earlier guide to the literature of the EC by John Jeffries, *A Guide to the Official Publications of the European Communities*.[110] The Jeffries guide has the following chapters:

1. Introduction
2. Publications of the European Communities
3. Commission—General publications
4. Commission—Nonstatistical publications
5. Eurostat—Publications of the Statistical Office of the European Communities
6. Council of Ministers
7. European Parliament
8. Court of Justice of the European Communities
9. Other bodies
10. Bibliographic aids

Appendix I. Addresses to which orders for publications should be sent.
Appendix II. European Documentation Centres and Depository Libraries.
Appendix III. Further reading on the European Communities.
Index

Reference Tools for EU Research

Except for a brief period during the mid-1980s, no one overall, cumulative, alphabetical index to documentation in paper has been available.[111] The *SCAD Bulletin*[112] comes out weekly, does not cumulate, and has a classified subject arrangement with a descriptor index in French. It covers official publications and documents of the EU, plus articles dealing with the work of the European Union that appear in commercially published periodicals. A SCAD database[113] can be searched online, which solves the noncumulating problem.

European Access[114] is a current awareness service published by Chadwyck-Healey which covers both EU documentation and material about the EU appearing in a wide assortment of books, journals, and newspapers. Here again a classified arrangement is used and no cumulation is available. However, each bimonthly issue also includes bibliographical review articles on EU policies and activities and descriptions of EU databases and how to use them.

Chadwyck-Healey is also responsible for the *EUROCAT CD-ROM*.[115] *EUROCAT* brings together over 850,000 records from four databases: CATEL, the database used by the Office for Official Publications to produce its catalogs and to index the *Official Journal;* ABEL, tables of contents of the *Official Journal* L series; CELEX, the official database of European Union law; and SCAD, including records of actual legislation, preparatory acts, Commission Final Documents, European Parliament working papers, and bibliographic records of publications distributed or published by the Office. Subject access is based on the *EUROVOC* thesaurus, enhanced with extensive cross-references to improve access.

Statistics of the European Union

The EU's statistical abstract is called *Basic Statistics of the European Union*.[116] It provides general statistical comparisons of the EU with other countries. This title and the many others produced by Eurostat (the Statistical Office of the European Communities) are indexed in detail by *IIS* described earlier. Eurostat has three numeric databases available to the general public: Cronos—macroeconomic time series data; Regio—regional breakdowns; and Comext—trade statistics.[117]

Classification of EU Publications

Although publications of the EU frequently have a "catalog number" printed on them and although that number may be included in the cataloging description, it is not a number that lends itself to being used as a shelf number. The EU itself uses the Universal Decimal Classification, which has not been adopted to any great extent in the United States. Consequently, libraries in the United States often classify EU documents by Library of Congress or Dewey systems and disperse them throughout the regular collection.

FURTHER READING

daConturbia, Sandra. "European Community Documents in American Libraries." *Technical Services Quarterly* 12 (1994): 9–21.

Eckman, Chuck. "Model United Nations Research." *Documents to the People* 22 (December 1994): 235–37.

Foote, Martha. "The *Canada Gazette.*" *Government Information in Canada* v1n4 (Spring 1995): <http://www.usask.ca/library/gic/v1n4/foote/foote.html> (June 18, 1998).

Hajnal, Peter I. "Access to Documents and Publications of International Organizations," in *Public Access to Government Information*, by Peter Hernon and Charles R. McClure, pp. 361–84. Norwood, NJ: Ablex Pub. Corp., 1984.

———. "User Study of Information from International Governmental Organizations," in *Reference Service for Publications of Intergovernmental Organizations*, edited by Alfred Kagan., pp. 23–29. Munchen; New York: K. G. Saur, 1991.

Hallewell, Laurence. "Government Publishing in the Third World." *Government Publications Review* 19 (January/February 1992): 23–58.

Harrison, Beverley J. "Treaty Research Demystified." *Canadian Law Libraries* 17 (April 1992): 51–53.

Innes, Stephen. "Acquiring Official Publications from Developing Countries: A South Pacific Perspective." *Australian Academic and Research Libraries* 25 (June 1994): 89–94.

Johnson, David G. "The British Library Lending Division and British Official Publications." *Government Publications Review* 3 (1976): 277–83.

Keck, Kerry A. and Barbara Stewart. "Cataloging Non-English Government Publications in a Medium Research Library." *Cataloging & Classification Quarterly* 17 (1993): 207–17.

Lopresti, Robert. "Analogous Reference Tools Produced by the U.S. and Canadian Federal Governments." *Government Publications Review* 18 (May/June 1991): 263–74.

Morton, Bruce. "Canadian Federal Government Policy and Canada's Electronic Information Industry." *Government Information Quarterly* 12 (1995): 251–95.

Nicholls, Paul. "Why Did You Think They Called It the World Wide Web?" *Searcher: The Magazine for Database Professionals* (May 1996): 20–27.

Piguet, Patrice. "Fifty Years of United Nations Publishing Activities." *IFLA Journal* 22 (1996): 91–97.

Price, M. Kathleen. "Linking Legislative Databases Into an International Legal Information Network." *Library Science with a Slant to Documentation and Information Studies* 30 (March 1993): 36–39 Paper F.

Rozkuszka, W. David. "The Art and Acquisition of Foreign Official Publications," in *Official Publications of Western Europe*, vol. 1, edited by Eve Johansson, pp. 1–11. London: Mansell, 1984.

Schaaf, Robert W. "Information Policies of International Organizations." *Government Publications Review* 17 (January/February 1990): 49–61.

Sittig, William J. "The Library of Congress and Western European Subnational Government Documents." *Collection Management* 15 (1992): 217–21.

Turner, David. "LC Seeks OK for Iraq Transactions: Publications Not Excluded from President's Embargo." *Library of Congress Information Bulletin* 49 (November 5, 1990): 370–71.

Windheuser, Christine S. "Government Mapping in the Developing Countries." *Government Publications Review* 10 (July-August 1983): 405–09.

Yeh, Thomas Y. "Government Publications of the People's Republic of China." *Government Publications Review* 14 (1987): 405–10.

NOTES

1. *Europa World Year Book.* 30th– 1989– (annual). (London: Europa Publications). Continues *Europa Year Book.*

2. Founded in 1948 as the International Union for Conservation of Nature and Natural Resources, the IUCN is now called the World Conservation Union.

3. Bell, Barbara L. *An Annotated Guide to Current National Bibliographies.* (Alexandria, VA: Chadwyck-Healey, 1986).

4. Gorman, G. E. and J. J. Mills, *Guide to Current National Bibliographies in the Third World*, 2nd rev. ed. (London: H. Zell, an imprint of K.G. Saur, 1987).

5. New York Public Library. Research Libraries. *Bibliographic Guide to Government Publications—Foreign.* 1975– (annual). (Boston: G. K. Hall).

6. *PAIS International In Print.* Vol.1, no.1– 1991– (monthly). (New York: Public Affairs Information Service, Inc.). *PAIS on CD-ROM.* 1972– (New York: Public Affairs Information Service). Also available from SilverPlatter Information, Inc. and EBSCO Publishing Co. *PAIS International Online* available from DataStar, DIALOG, OCLC, and RLG. *PAIS International on the Internet* available via DataStar, DIALOG, OCLC, and SilverPlatter ERL.

7. *Population Index.* Vol.3– 1937– (quarterly). (Princeton, NJ: Office of Population Research, Princeton University). Vol.52– 1986– also available at <http://popindex.princeton.edu/> (June 18, 1998). Cumulative indexes have been published by G.K. Hall & Co. for the years 1935–1968 and 1969–1981 under the title *Population Index Bibliography.*

8. *Index to International Statistics: IIS.* Vol.1– 1983– (monthly). (Washington, DC: Congressional Information Service).

9. *IIS Microfiche Library.* 1983– (Washington, DC: Congressional Information Service).

10. Statistical Masterfile. [CD-ROM] (Washington, DC: Congressional Information Service).

11. *NTIS Bibliographic Data Base.* Available online through BRS and DIALOG; CD-ROM versions available from DIALOG, SilverPlatter, and OCLC.

12. *ERIC.* Available online through BRS, OCLC EPIC, and DIALOG; CD-ROM versions available from DIALOG, OCLC, and SilverPlatter.

13. *Guide to Official Publications of Foreign Countries.* (Bethesda, MD: Congressional Information Service, 1990).

14. *International Information: Documents, Publications, and Electronic Information of International Governmental Organizations,* edited by Peter I. Hajnal. 2nd ed. (Englewood, CO: Libraries Unlimited, 1997).

15. Palic, Vladimir M. *Government Publications; A Guide to Bibliographic Tools, Incorporating Government Organization Manuals; A Bibliography.* (Oxford: Pergamon Press, 1977).

16. Westfall, Gloria. *Bibliography of Official Statistical Yearbooks and Bulletins.* (Alexandria, VA: Chadwyck-Healey, 1986).

17. Harvey, Joan M. *Statistics Africa.* 2nd ed. (Beckenham, Kent: CBD Research, 1978).

18. ———. *Statistics America.* 2nd ed. (Beckenham, Kent: CBD Research, 1980).

19. ———. *Statistics Asia and Australasia.* 2nd ed. (Beckenham, Kent: CBD Research, 1983).

20. ———. *Statistics Europe.* 5th ed. (Beckenham, Kent: CBD Research, 1987).

21. Fleming, Michael C. and Joseph G. Nellis. *International Statistics Sources: Subject Guide to Sources of International Comparative Statistics (Instat).* (London: Routledge, 1995).

22. *Checklist of Government Directories, Lists, and Rosters.* (Westport, CT: Meckler Pub., 1982).

23. Roberts, John E. *A Guide to Official Gazettes and Their Contents.* (Washington, DC: Library of Congress, 1985). (nondepository; Law Library of Congress general publications have SuDocs stem LC42.2:).

24. Reynolds, Thomas H. and Arturo A. Flores. *Foreign Law: Current Sources of Codes and Basic Legislation in Jurisdictions of the World.* (3v. loose-leaf) AALL Publications Series; no.33. (Littleton, CO: F. B. Rothman, 1989).

25. *WorldCat* is available through OCLC's First Search.

26. *Guide to Microforms in Print. Subject.* 1978– (annual). (Westport, CT: Microform Review Inc.).

27. For more information write to Norman Ross Publishing Inc., 330 West 58th Street, New York, NY 10019.

28. Center for Research Libraries. *Handbook.* 1969– (irregular; one published in 1996) (Chicago, IL: The Center).

29. *Directory of Government Document Collections & Librarians.* 1974– (Bethesda, MD: Congressional Information Service).

30. Turner, Carol A. *Directory of Foreign Document Collections.* (New York: UNIPUB, 1985).

31. UNIPUB and Bernan, both divisions of the Kraus Organization Limited, merged to become Bernan Associates.

For further information write to Bernan Associates, 4611–F Assembly Drive, Lanham, MD 20706-4391 or explore their Web site, Government Publications Network, <http://www.bernan.com> (June 18, 1998).

32. *International Literary Market Place.* 1971/72– (New York: Bowker).

33. To send postings, address them to: ACQNET-L@LISTSERV.APPSTATE.EDU. To subscribe, send an e-mail message to: LISTSERV@LISTSERV.APPSTATE.EDU saying SET ACQNET-L MAIL.

34. Orne, Jerrold. *The Language of the Foreign Book Trade; Abbreviations, Terms, Phrases.* 3rd ed. (Chicago: American Library Association, 1976).

35. *The Bibliographic Control of Official Publications.* Edited by John E. Pemberton. (Oxford: Pergamon, 1982), pp.151–52.

36. Ibid.

37. GODORT is the acronym for the Government Documents Roundtable of the American Library Association.

38. *Cataloging Government Documents: A Manual of Interpretation for AACR2.* Edited by Bernadine A. Hoduski. (Chicago: American Library Association, 1984).

39. Brill, Margaret S. "Government Publications as Bibliographic References in the Periodical Literature of International Relations: A Citation Analysis." *Government Information Quarterly* 7 (1990): 427–39.

40. Schaaf, Robert W. "International Organizations Documentation: Serving Research Needs of the Legal Community." *Government Publications Review* 13 (January-February 1986): 123–33.

41. *American Foreign Policy and Treaty Index.* Vol. 4, no.1– (1st quarter 1996–) (quarterly) (Bethesda, MD: Congressional Information Service, Inc.).

42. International Labor Office. *Legislative Series.* 1919– (annual). (Geneva: International Labor Office).

43. *International Digest of Health Legislation.* 1– 1948– (quarterly) (Geneva: World Health organization).

44. *Guide to Country Information in International Governmental Organization Publications,* edited by Marian Shaaban. (American Library Association, Government Documents Roundtable, 1996; distributed by Congressional Information Service).

45. *International Legal Materials.* Vol.1– 1962– (bimonthly). (Washington, DC: American Society of International Law).

46. *Martindale-Hubbell Law Directory.* 1932– (annual). (Summit, NJ: Martindale-Hubbell, Inc.). CD-ROM available from Bowker Electronic Publishing.

47. *Yearbook of International Organizations.* 11th– 1966/67– (irregular). Edited by Union of International Associations. (Munich: K.G. Saur).

48. *UKOP: Catalog of United Kingdom Official Publications.* [CD-ROM] 1980– (Cambridge: Chadwyck-Healey Ltd.). Available online through BLAISE-LINE and DIALOG.

49. The Stationery Office is a private company formed on October 1, 1996, following the privatization of HMSO, the United Kingdom Government Publisher. There is a residual body known as Her Majesty's Stationery Office which still handles Acts of Parliament and Statutory Instruments.

50. *Gale Directory of Databases.* 1993– (Detroit: Gale Research Inc.).

51. *DttP. Documents to the People*. 1972– (quarterly) (Chicago: American Library Association).

52. *Government Information Quarterly*. Vol.1, no. 1– 1984– (quarterly) (Greenwich, CT: JAI Press). Table of contents on the Web <http://www.lib.auburn.edu/madd/docs/giq/conlink.html> (June 18, 1998).

53. *Journal of Government Information*. Vol.21– 1994– (quarterly) (New York: Pergamon Press). Table of contents by e-mail alert (send message to alert@elsevier.com) or on the Web <http://www.lib.auburn.edu/madd/docs/jgi/title.html> (June 18, 1998).

54. International Federation of Library Associations and Institutions. Official Publications Section. *Newsletter - IFLA Official Publications Section*. No.1– 1978– (irregular). (London, The Section).

55. INT-LAW is moderated by Lyonette Louis-Jacques (llou@midway.uchicago.edu or 1-312-702-9612). To subscribe, send the following message to LISTSERV@TC.UMN.EDU: subscribe int-law Your Name.

56. The International Documents Task Force (IDTF) is a group within the Government Documents Roundtable (GODORT) of the American Library Association (ALA).

57. To subscribe to INTL-DOC, send the following message to listserv@listserv.acns.nwu.edu: Subscribe INTL-DOC yourfirstname yourlastname. The list owner and moderator is Mike McCaffrey-Noviss, International Documents Librarian at Northwestern University Library.

58. *Weekly Checklist of Canadian Government Publications*. 1978- (Ottawa: Canada Communication Group, Publishing Division).

59. The price of the *Weekly Checklist* is $78.00 (US) a year (in 1996). Orders should be addressed to the Canada Communication Group, Publishing Division, Ottawa, Canada K1A 0S9.

60. AMICUS is the bilingual fee-based information system of the National Library of Canada. Available through NLC, Information Technology Services, 395 Wellington St., Ottawa, ON, Canada K1A 0N4.

61. Bishop, Olga B. *Canadian Official Publications*. (Oxford: Pergamon Press, 1981).

62. *Organization of the Government of Canada*. 1990– (irregular) (Ottawa: Information Canada : Canadian Chamber of Commerce).

63. *Info Source: Sources of Federal Government Information*. 1990- (annual) (Ottawa: Government of Canada). *Info Source* is a series of publications and databases containing information about the Government of Canada, its organization and information holdings. It is a key reference tool to assist members of the public in exercising their rights under the "Access to Information Act" and the "Privacy Act."

64. *Info Source: Directory of Federal Government Enquiry Points*. 1995–1996– (Irregular) (Ottawa: Government of Canada, Treasury Board Secretariat, 1995).

65. *Canadian Parliamentary Guide*. 1909– (annual) (Toronto: Gale Canada).

66. For a review and comparison of Canadian Internet sites, see Cannon, Anita. "Finding Canadian Government Information on the Internet: A Look at Four Principal Sites and Their Initiatives." *Government Information in Canada* 2 (spring 1996) <http://www.usask.ca/library/gic/v2n4/cannon2/cannon2.html> (June 18, 1998).

67. Canada. *The Canada Gazette* Part I, v.104– Jan. 3, 1970– (weekly). Part II: Statutory Instruments, 1972– (bi-weekly). Part III: Statutes of Canada, v.1- Dec. 13, 1974– (monthly). (Ottawa, Queen's Printer).

68. *Canadiana*. Jan. 15, 1951– (monthly except July and August). (Ottawa: National Library of Canada).

69. *Government of Canada Publications: Quarterly Catalogue*. Vol.27–40, 1979–1992. (quarterly) (Ottawa: Canadian Government Publishing Centre).

70. *Canadian Research Index* (*Microlog*). 10– 1988– (monthly) (Toronto: Micromedia). *Microlog Microfiche Collections*. 1983– (monthly) (Toronto: Micromedia). *Microlog on CD*. 1979– (Toronto: Micromedia). Micromedia Web site: <http://www.micromedia.on.ca> (June 18, 1998).

71. Statistics Canada. *Statistics Canada Catalogue*. 1972- (annual). (Ottawa: Statistics Canada).

72. Statistics Canada. *Historical Catalogue of Statistics Canada Publications, 1918–1980*. (Ottawa: Statistics Canada, User Services Division, 1981).

73. *Historical Statistics of Canada*. 2nd ed. (Ottawa: Statistics Canada, 1983).

74. *Canadian Economic Observer*. 1988- (monthly). (Ottawa: Statistics Canada). *Canadian Economic Observer. Historical Statistical Supplement*. 1988– (annual). (Ottawa: Statistics Canada).

75. *Canada Year Book*. 1905– (irregular). (Ottawa: Communications Division, Statistics Canada).

76. *CANSIM Time Series Main Base*. 1946– Available online from Statistics Canada, Electronic Data Dissemination Division and a number of other vendors; CD-ROM available from Micromedia Ltd.

77. *Bibliography of Federal Data Sources: Excluding Statistics Canada 1981*. (Ottawa: Statistics Canada, User Services Division, Reference Products Section, 1982).

78. *Canadian Statistics Index*. 1985– (Toronto: Micromedia Ltd.).

79. *Government of Canada Publications; Outline of Classification*. 4th ed. (Ottawa: Canadian Government Publishing Centre, 1984).

80. Presser, Carolynne. "CODOC: A Computer Based Processing and Retrieval System for Government Documents." *College and Research Libraries* 39 (1978): 94–98.

81. To subscribe to GOVINFO, send the message SUBSCRIBE GOVINFO (YOUR NAME) to MAILSERV@SASK.USASK.CA. GOVINFO is not moderated. The contact person is Andrew Hubbertz, Head of Government Publications, Maps and Microforms, at the University of Saskatchewan Libraries.

82. Hajnal, Peter I. *Guide to United Nations Organization, Documentation and Publishing for Students, Researchers, Librarians*. (Dobbs Ferry, NY: Oceana Publications, 1978).

83. United Nations. *Everyone's United Nations*. 10th ed. (New York: United Nations, 1986).

84. United Nations. *United Nations Documentation: A Brief Guide* (New York: United Nations, 1981).

85. United Nations. Secretariat. *Instructions for Depository Libraries Receiving United Nations Material*. (New York: U.N. Secretariat, 1981).

86. United Nations. Office of Public Information. *Yearbook of the United Nations*. 1946/47– (annual). (New York: United Nations).

87. *UNDOC Current Index; United Nations Documents Index*. Vol.1–18, 1979–1996. (New York: United Nations, Dag Hammarskjold Library).

88. UNBIS records are accessible through the RLIN online service.

89. UN-I-QUE is a new electronic research tool that serves as a guide to symbols and/or sales numbers of tens of thousands of selected documents and publications from 1946 to the present. It is available on the Internet at <http://www.un.org/Depts/dhl/unique> (June 18, 1998).

90. *Electronic Index to United Nations Documents and Publications*. [CD-ROM] (New Canaan, CT: Readex).

91. *Index to Proceedings of the Economic and Social Council*. 1953– (irregular). (New York: United Nations). *Index to Proceedings of the General Assembly*. 5th session–1950/51– (irregular). (New York: United Nations). *Index to Proceedings of the Security Council*. 19th– 1964– (annual). (New York: United Nations). *Index to Proceedings of the Trusteeship Council*. 11th– 1952– (annual). (New York: United Nations).

92. *UN Chronicle*. Vol.12, no.4– Apr.1975– (quarterly). (New York: United Nations Office of Public Information).

93. *Treaty Series/United Nations*. Vol.1– 1946– (New York: United Nations).

94. Multilateral Treaties Deposited with the Secretary-General. 1980– (New York: United Nations). ST/LEG/SER.E or <http://www.un.org/Depts/Treaty> (June 18, 1998).

95. Statistical Yearbook. 1st– 19 (annual) (New York:

96. *Monthly Bulletin of Statistics*. 1947– (monthly). (New York: United Nations. Statistics Division).

97. *Demographic Yearbook*. 1st– 1948– (annual) (New York: Department of Economic and Social Affairs, Statistical Office, United Nations).

98. *Yearbook on Human Rights*. 1946–1988. (annual) (New York: United Nations).

99. *Interinstitutional Directory—European Union*. 1994– (irregular) (Luxembourg: Office for Official Publications of the European Communities).

100. *Europe*. 1979– (10 issues per year) (Washington, Delegation of the Commission of the European Communities). Subscription $19.95; student rate $14.95.

101. *Bulletin of the European Union*. 1994- (10 issues per year + index + supplements) (Brussels, Secretariat Gen-eral of the Commission). Subscription price ECU 144 or approximately $188 US includes 1st Supplement.

102. *EUROVOC: Annex to the Index of the Official Journal of the European Communities*. 3rd ed. (Luxembourg: Office for Official Publications of the European Communities, 1995).

103. *European Community Catalog of Publications*. Request from Bernan Associates/UNIPUB, 4611-F Assembly Drive, Lanham, MD 20706-4391.

104. Write to the Office for Official Publications of the European Communities, L-2985 Luxembourg for a free copy.

105. *Official Journal of the European Communities*. 1973- (Luxembourg: Office for Official Publications of the European Communities).

106. *COM Documents*. [microfiche] 1983– (Brussels: The Commission of the European Communities).

107. *Session Documents. Series A, Reports*. [microfiche] 1987– (Luxembourg: European Parliament).

108. Sloan, Barbara. *Researching the European Union*. (Washington, DC: European Commission, Office of Press and Public Affairs, 1996).

109. Thomson, Ian. *The Documentation of the European Communities: A Guide*. (London: Mansell, 1989).

110. Jeffries, John. *A Guide to the Official Publications of the European Communities*. 2nd ed. (London: Mansell, 1981).

111. The exception being *EC Index*. 1984–1986. (Maastricht, The Netherlands: Europe Data).

112. *SCAD Bulletin*. 1986– (weekly) (Brussels: SCAD : Washington, DC: European Community Information Service [distributor]).

113. *SCAD*. Available online through EUROBASES.

114. *European Access*. 1988– (bimonthly) (Cambridge: Chadwyck-Healey Ltd.).

115. *EUROCAT*. 1993– (quarterly) (Luxembourg: Office for Official Publications of the European Communities; Chadwyck-Healey; Ellis Pub.).

116. *Basic Statistics of the European Union*. 32nd– 1995– (annual) (Brussels: Statistical Office of the European Communities).

117. For further information contact the EUROSTAT Helpdesk, Telephone: 43014567 or Facsimile: 43014762.

APPENDIX 1
Publishers' Addresses and Web Sites

Andriot, see Documents Index, Inc.

BNA Online
The Bureau of National Affairs, Inc.
Box 40947
Washington, DC 20077-4928
E-mail: icustrel@bna.com
(800) 372-1033; Fax: (800) 253-0332
<http://www.bna.com/>

CCH INCORPORATED
4025 W. Peterson Ave.
Chicago, IL 60646-6085
(800) TELL CCH
<http://www.cch.com/>

Carroll Publishing
1058 Thomas Jefferson St. NW
Washington, DC 20007
E-mail: custsvc@carrollpub.com
(800) 336-4240, (202) 333-8620; Fax: (202) 337-7020
<http://www.carrollpub.com/>

Claitor's Law Books and Publishing Division
Box 261333
3165 S. Acadian at I-10
Baton Rouge, LA 70826-1333
E-mail: Claitors@claitors.com
(800) 274-1403; Fax: (504) 344-0480
<http://www.claitors.com>

The Council of State Governments
Box 11910
Lexington KY 40578-1910
(606) 244-8000; Fax: (606) 244-8001
<http://www.csg.org/>

DATA-STAR (Knight-Ridder Information Services, Inc.)
One Commerce Square
2005 Market St., Suite 1010
Philadelphia, PA, 19103
(800) 221-7754; Fax: (215) 587-2147
<http://www.dialog.com/> or
    <http://www.krinfo.com/>

DIALOG. See Knight-Ridder Information, Inc.

Documents Index, Inc.
7900 Sudley Road, Suite 405
Manassas, VA 20109
(800) 899-4988; Fax: (703) 257-4846
<http://www.andriot.com/>

ERIC Document Reproduction Service
7420 Fullerton Road
Suite 110
Springfield, VA 22153-2852
E-mail: service@edrs.com
(800) 443-ERIC, (703) 440-1400
<http://www.edrs.com>

European Patent Office
Erhardtstrasse 27
D-80331 Munich
<http://www.epo.co.at/epo/index.htm>

Government Research Service
214 S.W. 6th Avenue, Suite 301,
Topeka, KS 66603
E-mail: grs@cjnetworks.com
(800) 346-6898, (913) 232-7720; Fax: (913) 232-1615

Greenwood Publishing Group, Inc.
88 Post Road West
Box 5007
Westport, CT 06881-5007
(203) 226-3571; Fax: (203) 226-1502
<http://www.greenwood.com/>

Hein. See William S. Hein & Co., Inc.

Knight-Ridder Information, Inc.
2440 El Camino Real
Mountain View, CA 94040
(800) 334-2564; Fax: (415) 254-8123
<http://www.krinfo.com/>

Lawyers Cooperative Publishing
Aqueduct Building
Rochester, NY 14694
E-mail: information@lcp.com
(800) 762-5272, California (800) 313-9339; Fax: (716)
    546-4837
<http://www.lcp.com/>

LEGI-SLATE, Inc.
777 North Capitol Street, Suite 900
Washington, DC 20002-4239
E-mail: legislate@legislate.com
(800) 733-1131, (202) 898-2323
<http://www.legislate.com>

LEXIS-NEXIS
Box 933
Dayton, OH 45401-0933
(800) 227-4908
<http://www.lexis-nexis.com/>

NewsBank/Readex, Inc.
58 Pine St.
New Canaan, CT 06840
(800) 762-8182, (813) 263-6004; Fax: (813) 263-3004
E-mail: Sales@newsbank.com
<http://www.newsbank.com>

OCLC
6565 Frantz Rd.
Dublin, OH 43017-3395
(800) 848-5878, in Ohio (800) 848-8286
<http://www.oclc.org>

Oryx Press
P.O. Box 33889
Phoenix, Arizona 85067-3889
E-mail: info@oryxpress.com
800-279-6799, (602) 265-2651; Fax: 1-800-279-4663
<http://www.oryxpress.com/>

Ovid Technologies
333 Seventh Avenue
New York, NY 10001
(800) 950-2035, (212) 563-3006; Fax: (212) 563-3784

PAIS—Public Affairs Information Service, Inc.
521 West 43rd St.
New York, NY 10036-4396
E-Mail: inquiries@pais.org
(800) 288-7247, in New York City (212) 736-6629;
    Fax: (212) 643-2848
<http://www.pais.inter.net/>

Penny Hill Press
6440 Wiscasset Road
Bethesda, MD 20816
E-Mail: pennyhill@clark.net
(301) 229-8229; Fax: (301) 229-6988
<http://www.clark.net/pub/pennyhill/
    pennyhill.html>

Primary Source Media
12 Lunar Drive
Woodbridge, CT 06525
(800) 444-0799; Fax: (203) 397-3893
<http://www.psmedia.com/declass.htm

Readex Micro-print Corporation
58 Pine St.
New Canaan, CT 06840
(800) 762-8182, (813) 566-9122; Fax: (813) 566-9134

Research Publications
12 Lunar Drive
Woodbridge, CT 06525
(800) 444-0799, (203) 397-2600; Fax: (203) 397-3893
E-mail: sales@rpub.com
<http://www.thomson.com/rpub/default.html>

Shepard's
555 Middle Creek Parkway
Colorado Springs, CO 80921
(800) 743-7393, (719) 488-3000
<http://www.shepards.com/>

SIRS, Inc.
P.O. Box 2348
Boca Raton, FL 33427-2348
800-232-SIRS, (561) 994-0079; Fax: (561) 994-4704
<http://www.sirs.com/>

Staff Directories, Ltd.
Box 62
Mount Vernon, VA 22121-0062
E-mail: staffdir@staffdirectories.com
(800) 252-1722, (703) 739-0900; Fax: (703) 739-0234
<http://www.staffdirectories.com>

Thomson & Thomson
500 Victory Rd.
North Quincy, MA 02171-3145
(800) 692-8833, (617) 479-1600; Fax: (617) 786-8273
<http://www.thomson-thomson.com/>

University Publications of America
4520 East-West Hwy.
Bethesda, MD 20814-3389
E-mail: info@upapubs.com
(800) 692-6300, (301) 657-3200; Fax: (301) 657-3203
<http://www.upapubs.com/>

West Publishing Co.
620 Opperman Drive
Eagan, MN 55123
(800) 778-8090
E-mail: jennifer.moire@westgroup.com
<http://www.westpub.com/>

William S. Hein & Co., Inc.
1285 Main St.
Buffalo, NY 14209-1987
(800) 828-7571, Manhattan (212) 283-3528,
    Washington (202) 393-3938; Fax: (716) 883-8100
<http://lawlib.wuacc.edu/hein/heinhome.html>

World Intellectual Property Organization
UN Liaison Office
2 United Nations Plaza, Room 560
New York, NY 10017
(212) 963-6813; Fax: (212) 693-4801
<http://www.wipo.org/eng/index.htm>

APPENDIX 2
Citation Signposts

Here are some examples of types of citations that can stymie those unfamiliar with them. Fully numerical sequences are listed first; alphanumerical samples follow, listed alphabetically by their first letter.

I welcome your suggestions for additions to the next edition.

84.044 Five-digit *Catalog of Federal Domestic Assistance* number, identifying an agency and program

AD-M000 722 NTIS publication number

1 Agric. Dec. 472 (1942) Volume 1 of *Agriculture Decisions: Decisions of the Secretary of Agriculture Under the Regulatory Laws Administered in the United States,* page 472, published 1942 (A 1.58/A:)

AIB229 USDA Agricultural Information Bulletins

AR 86-1(9) (1/23/86) Acquiescence Ruling number 1 for 1986, published January 23, 1986; refers to a decision of the U. S. Court of Appeals for the 9th Circuit or AR 86-1(9)

B-239800, September 28, 1990 File number and date for an unpublished decision of the Comptroller General of the United States

1 Bevans 758 Volume 1, page 758 of *Treaties and Other International Agreements of the United States of America, 1776–1949,* edited by Charles Bevans (S 9.12/2:v.1-13)

40 CFR 211.10 (1978) Title 40, section 211.10 of the 1978 *Code of Federal Regulations* (See chapter 9.)

49 C. O. Bull. Copyright Office Bulletin no. 49; the official title is *Decisions of the United States Courts Involving Copyright* (LC 3.3/3:)

70 Comp. Gen. 4 (1990) Volume 70 *Decisions of the Comptroller General of the United States,* page 4, published 1990 (GA 1.5:)

CR D165 *Congressional Record,* Daily Digest section; probably cited in THOMAS (See chapter 8.)

CR E581 *Congressional Record,* Extensions of Remarks section; probably cited in THOMAS (See chapter 8.)

CR H765 *Congressional Record,* House of Representatives section; probably cited in THOMAS (See chapter 8.)

CR S1827 *Congressional Record,* Senate section; probably cited in THOMAS (See chapter 8.)

D377106 Design patent

DA PAM 25-30 *Consolidated Index of Army Publications and Blank Forms*

DE97000610 NTIS publication number

46 FR 3566 (1981) Volume 46, page 3566 of the 1981 *Federal Register* (See chapter 9.)

H1511 A Statutory Invention Registration (Patent Office)

HL *Congressional Record* section known as the Lobby List, listing individuals and organizations registered under the Lobbying Disclosure Act of 1995 and Federal Regulation of Lobbying Act of 1946

H.R. 668 House (of Representatives) bill (not to be mistaken for a House report: **H. Rept. 105-5**). (See chapter 8.)

MLC-001 Entries in issues of *Major Legislation of the Congress,* which ceased after the 1992 summary (LC 14.18:)

MP#1150 Agriculture miscellaneous publications, cited in *Index to USDA Miscellaneous Publications: Numbers 1-1479* (A 17.18/2:M 68)

860 O.G. 662 Volume 860 the *Official Gazette,* page 662

35 NRC 236 (1992) *Nuclear Regulatory Commission Issuances.* Cited in this format: volume 35 (1992) of *Nuclear Regulatory Commission Issuances,* p. 236.

304 NLRB No. 24 *Classified Index of National Labor Relations Board Decisions and Related Court Decisions.* Board decisions in Decisions and Orders of the National Labor Relations Board are cited by volume and folio number: volume 304 of Decisions and Orders of the National Labor Relations Board, advance sheet number 24. Decisions and Orders of the National Labor Relations Board includes a cross-reference table translating advance sheet numbers into page numbers in the Decisions volume.

PB97-965801 NTIS publication number

P.L. 95–261 Public Law 95–261, passed in the 95th Congress. (See chapter 8.)

PMID 9171061 A PubMed unique identifier; PubMed allows free MEDLINE searching

Q.B.—94-07 National Agricultural Library Quick Bibliographies (A 17.18/4:)

RE34813 Reissue patent

RG 287 A National Archives Record Group

Roll No. 3 The number of a congressional roll call vote

S. 15 Senate bill (not to be confused with S15, a citation to the *Congressional Record,* Senate section). (See chapter 8.)

SRB—94-01 National Agricultural Library Special Reference Briefs (A 17.24:)

SSR 87-23 (9/18/87) Social Security Ruling number 23 published September 18, 1987; or SSR 87-23 (C. E. 1987) referring to the *Cumulative Edition,* full title: *Rulings; Cumulative Edition; Social Security Rulings on Federal Old-Age, Survivors, Disability, Supplemental Security Income, and Black Lung Benefits.* (HE 3.44/2:) Social Security rulings with suffix "c" (such as SSR 80-1c) are based on court decisions; suffix "a" (SSR 80-1a) are based on decisions of the Appeals Council of the Office of Hearings and Appeals; suffix "p" (SSR 89-5p) are Policy Interpretation Rulings

97 Stat. 113 Volume 97, page 113 of the *Statutes at Large.* (See chapter 8.)

TB#1725 USDA Technical bulletins, cited in *Agricultural Information Bulletins, Numbers 1-649*

TIAS 6599 *Treaties and Other International Acts Series,* number 6599 (S 9.10:1501-nos.)

TS 593 Number 593 in the Treaty Series that begin with number 489 in 1908; these early treaties were published before 1945 by the State Department as pamphlets

672 UNTS 119 Volume 672, page 119 of the United Nations *Treaty Series*

43 USC 772 (1976) Title 43, section 772 of the 1976 *U.S. Code.* (See chapter 8.)

19 UST 7570 *United States Treaties and Other International Agreements* volume 19, page 7570 (S 9.12:)

APPENDIX 3
Answers to Exercises

SOLUTIONS TO EXERCISES FOR CHAPTER 2

1. *Mortgage Money Guide* (FT 1.8/2:SM).
   ANSWER: To request a free copy, first identify which issuing agency to contact. Since you have the SuDocs number, this step is a snap. The simplest approach is to look up the SuDocs number in the *List of Classes*. Or, you could locate the bibliographic citation in the *Monthly Catalog*, SPC, or WorldCat. Once you discover that FT is the SuDocs number for the Federal Trade Commission, you can get the FTC mailing address from the *U.S. Government Manual* or the FTC Web page (identify their URL using the GPO Access locator, "Federal Agency Internet Sites") <http://www.access.gpo.gov/su_docs/dpos/agencies.html>.

SOLUTIONS TO EXERCISES FOR CHAPTER 3

1. SuDocs number for the *Congressional Record*.
   ANSWER: Consult *U.S. Government Subscriptions*, alphabetically by title. This free quarterly pamphlet can be received automatically on standing request and is recommended as part of a basic free documents reference collection.

2. Sequencing SuDocs Numbers.
   ANSWER: The shelf order for the SuDocs numbers exercise is given below. Note that D 101.2.A 8 is an impostor: a SuDocs number lookalike that is actually a Library of Congress class number. Remember that each SuDocs number will have two distinguishing characteristics: a letter or letters at the beginning, and a colon in the middle. With its initial D, this LC number resembles a SuDocs number for the Department of Defense, but it lacks a colon.
   D 101.2:N 56
   I 19.81:40121-B 3-TF-024/991
   J 21.2/10:988
   J 21.22:1
   LC 3.4/2:62 a
   LC 3.4/2:62/991
   PR 41.8:P 96
   PREX 2.2:C 86
   Y 3.T 22/2:2 T 22/24/v.2/pt.2/China
   D 101.2.A 8 = Mayday, Mayday. This is a Library of Congress class number

SOLUTIONS TO EXERCISES FOR CHAPTER 4

1. *General Information Concerning Patents*.
   ANSWER: The *List of Classes* provides a quick answer. Because no title index is available, familiarity with government agencies and SuDocs numbers helps: the *List of Classes* appendix lists the Patent and Trademark Office as C 21. Skimming the document titles under PTO, you will find *General Information Concerning Patents* listed as Item 0256-A-02, SuDocs stem C 21.26/2: . Its presence in the *List of Classes* (coupled with an item number) confirms that it is a depository title.

SOLUTIONS TO EXERCISES FOR CHAPTER 5

1. What's the official title of "the Plum Book"?
   ANSWER: This Senate Committee Print is officially titled *United States Government Policy and Supporting Positions*, Y 4.G 74/7:P 75/6/[year]. It is also available via GPO Access at <http://www.access.gpo.gov/plumbook/toc.html/>. Published every four years following each presidential election, the "Plum Book" is issued alternately by the House Committee on Post Office and Civil Service and the Senate Committee on Governmental Affairs.
   TIPS: Although "Plum Book" is not this document's formal title, the record can be located in MOCAT (search full text for "plum book"), SPC, or WorldCat because it includes a note field for the popular title. The Internet version can also be located using GPO Access "Browse Electronic Titles" in the agency listing, under Congress.

2. Is *Basic Facts about Patents* on the PTO's Web site?
   ANSWER: It used to be.
   TIPS: A quick foray into the *Monthly Catalog* (use a fielded title search in the Web version) shows a URL in the summary record and in field 856 of the full record <http://www.uspto.gov/web/patbasic/toc.html>. Click on it, and you're transported to the electronic document on the PTO site, unless the URL in MOCAT is outdated, as it was in late 1997. If the link is moribund, go to the PTO home page, indicated in the root of the URL <http://www.uspto.gov/>. Select the "Site Index"; then "B" (for *Basic Facts about Patents*). If nothing is there, try GPO "Browse Titles," and select "Patent and Trademark Office." There, under *Basic Facts About*

Patents, is a note that the document has been replaced by *General Information Concerning Patents,* which is linked in Browse Titles below *Basic Facts.*

3. How much does the latest *Constitution of the United States of America: Analysis and Interpretation* cost?

ANSWER: $148 for a hardcopy volume from GPO (weighing nine pounds, by the way); free on the Internet via GPO Access.

TIPS: If this is a GPO sales title, SPC will list the price, so SPC is an efficient starting place. Use a fielded title search (enclosed in quotes) to locate the record. (This seems to work best with title only—omit subtitle.) But $148 is expensive. To check for an Internet version, take the GPO stock number (052-071-01157-9) into a Web MOCAT fielded search, and discover a record showing the free electronic version on GPO Access, and its presence in depository libraries [[1004-E]] and in the Serial Set (Y 1.1/2:SERIAL 14152). Anyone not wishing to pay $148 has plenty of alternatives. Why isn't the GPO Access Web version indicated in the SPC? Because SPC is a sales catalog and the Web version is free.

4. *Congressional Quarterly's Guide to Congress.*

ANSWER: Regularly revised, the last edition was in 1991. But that's not the point.

TIPS: Seeking this information in MOCAT or the SPC yields no hint of this publication. The reason is that its publisher, Congressional Quarterly, Inc., is not a federal entity, and therefore its publications will not be documented in the key federal bibliographies, MOCAT, or SPC. Use WorldCat as an ecumenical backup source, since it includes nongovernment publications.

5. Core depository titles.

POSSIBLE PITFALL: Mistaking citations to short GPO Subject Bibliographies (SB) about a title for cites to the title itself. Hints that you've found a SB are: 1) a SuDocs number identifying GPO as the issuing agency (GP 3.22/2:), 2) a collation of only a few pages, and 3) the phrase "Subject Bibliography" or an SB number.

TIP: Because most of the core depository titles are serials, they can be quickly identified using the CD-ROM *Monthly Catalog* Periodicals Supplement. The Periodicals Supplement gives open entries rather than citing individual issues as the regular *Monthly Catalog* will do.

Retrospective Sources

6. USDA "Farmers' Bulletins."

ANSWER: Pre-1976 USDA "Farmers' Bulletins" can be identified using the pre-MARC *Monthly Catalog.*

TIPS: In the older *Monthly Catalog,* series numbers follow the entry number and must be appended to the SuDocs stem to complete the SuDocs number. In the entry above, for example, the SuDocs number for *Beef Cattle, Dehorning, Castrating, Branding and Marking* is A 1.9:2141. The series number, 2141, must be added to the SuDocs stem listed at the head of the entry.

Farmers' bulletins. • Item 9	A.1.9:(nos.)

2214   2141.   Beef cattle, dehorning, castrating, branding and marking; (by R. T. Clark, A. L. Baker and George E. Whitmore). [Nov. 1959., slightly revised Dec. 1967.] [1967.] 16 p. il. ([Animal Husbandry Research Division. Agricultural Research Service.]) [Supersedes Farmers' Bulletin 1800.] • Paper, 10c.

2215   2152.   Slaughtering, cutting, and processing lamb and mutton on farm; [prepared by Animal Husbandry Research Division, Agricultural Research Service]. [Aug. 1960, slightly revised Dec. 1967.] [1967.] 16 p. il. [Supersedes Farmers' bulletin 1807, Lamb and mutton on farm.] • Paper, 10c.

2216   Growth country, living country, remarks by Secretary of Agriculture Orville L. Freeman at opening of rural industrialization meeting, History and Technology Building, Smithsonian Institution, Washington, D.C., Sept. 27, 1967. [1967.] 11 p. • (2859; USDA 3061-67.) ‡

---

7. Thomas Jefferson's Catalog.

ANSWER: Library of Congress. *Thomas Jefferson's Library: A Catalog with the Entries in His Own Order.* GPO, 1989. (LC 1.2:T 36).

TIPS: Again, this source predates the 1994 Web MOCAT. This information could have been identified using the *Monthly Catalog* Père subject index under the LCSH "Jefferson, Thomas—1743-1826—Library—Catalogs," or keyword index under "Thomas," "Library," or "Catalog" (89-14955). A WorldCat author search (Jeff,Tho) would also retrieve it (OCLC 19124971): note that the number 786 in Field 074 is the item number, indicating depository status.

This title was also listed in the hardcopy *Books in Print* under title and under the subject heading "Jefferson, Thomas, Pres. U.S., 1743–1826" (arrangement under the subject heading is alphabetical by authors' or editors' names; Gilreath, James is the editor). BIP did not list this under Thomas Jefferson as author. BIP lists the Library of Congress as publisher, but includes a GPO stock number (030-001-00130-0), which indicates that GPO, not the Library of Congress, sells the title. A check of SPC, however, indicates it's no longer for sale. BIP did not note its availability for free use in depository libraries or SuDocs number.

8. The KGB and the Library Target.

ANSWER: FBI. *The KGB and the Library Target, 1962–present.* FBI, [1988]. Not depository; no SuDocs number.

TIPS: This title was missed by both SPC and *Monthly Catalog.* A title search of WorldCat (kgb,an,th,l) located the document (OCLC 22544867), but indicated neither a SuDocs nor item number. The title was also located through an ERIC search, as *The FBI's Library Awareness Program: National Security vs. Government Intrusion into American Libraries [and] The KGB and the Library Target* (EJ 399470). The EJ number indicates a *Current Index to Journals in Education* cite to a journal article.

9. FBI Library Awareness Program.

ANSWER: House. Committee on the Judiciary. Subcommittee on Civil and Constitutional Rights. *FBI Counterintelligence Visits to Libraries.* GPO, 1989. (Y 4.J 89/1:100/123) Depository status.

TIPS: Because the item was released in late 1980s before the Web MOCAT, the *Monthly Catalog* Père should be consulted (89-12353). Because no author or title was provided, WorldCat could not be used handily. It is also indexed in PAIS, which identifies its SuDocs number (SD cat. no.) but gives no indication of depository status. Because the title is a hearing, it could also be located using resources discussed in chapter 8.

10. Depository library user study.
ANSWER: McClure, Charles R. and Peter Hernon. *Users of Academic and Public GPO Depository Libraries.* GPO, 1989. (GP 3.2:Us 2) Depository status.
TIPS: This information could have been identified using the *Monthly Catalog* Père (89-14241), or a WorldCat author search (OCLC 19866610).

SOLUTIONS TO EXERCISES FOR CHAPTER 6

1. NTIS *Environment Hightlights.*
ANSWER: In the GPO Web MOCAT, a search of "highlights AND ntis" locates the record for PR-868. Field 037a alerts that this is free from NTIS. It is also a depository item (field 074) and may also be downloaded from FedWorld.

2. Bibliographic Verification.
   a. *How to Get It.*
   ANSWER: Defense Technical Information Center. *How to Get It: A Guide to Defense-Related Information Sources.* NTIS, 1995. AD-A298 436 <http://www.dtic.mil/stinet/htgi/index.html>.
   SEARCH STRATEGY: Title searches can be performed in the NTIS Bibliographic Database or on the NTIS Web site (where a 1992 diskette version was found).
   b. *The Effects of Electronic Recordkeeping on the Historical Record of the U.S. Government.* NTIS, 1989. PB89-15221 (National Academy of Public Administration = performing organization).
   ANSWER: Identified on the NTIS Web site.
   c. Hasty, T.J. *Protection of Personal Privacy Interests Under the Freedom of Information Act.* NTIS, 1991. AD-A242 183 (Air Force Academy = performing organization).
   ANSWER: Identified on the NTIS Web site.
   d. *Managing Federal Information Resources: Annual Report Under the Paperwork Reduction Act of 1980.* 7th. NTIS, 1989. PB90-100173.
   ANSWER: This cite was identified on the NTIS Web site. Although issued almost a decade ago, it can still be purchased from NTIS.

While the citation omitted the SuDocs number (PREX 2.25:), a SuDocs number was included in the WorldCat record (9752396) along with notation of depository status (853-A-5 microfiche = item number).

3. PR-1001 *Media Resource Catalog.*
ANSWER: No search is necessary to answer this question. PR numbers indicate free brochures describing NTIS products and services. PR-1001 tells you that this is free from NTIS.

SOLUTIONS TO EXERCISES FOR CHAPTER 7

1. Patent Number Search.

ANSWER: If the number is above 3,930,270 (issued since 1976), an abstract is accessible on the PTO Web site, which allows searching by patent number <http://patents.uspto.gov/>. For older patents or a non-Internet approach, consult the *Official Gazette* weekly issue in which the patent number appeared. (Patent abstracts are listed in patent number order.)

2. Patent Name Search.
SEARCH STRATEGY: For recent patents, Cassis can be searched by inventor's name to identify patent number. Or conduct a fielded search on the PTO Web site <http://patents.uspto.gov/>. Select "Inventor Name (IN)," and format your query as a phrase inside quotation marks, with a semicolon separating last and first name: "lastname; firstname initial." Thus, David Golde's cellular patent would be searched: "Golde; David" or "Golde; David W."

For Cassis or the PTO Web site searches, no issue date is needed. A patent issue date streamlines use of the *Official Gazette*, however. Step One: to identify patent number, consult the annual *Index of Patents* (C 21.5/2:), "Part I, List of Patentees," for the year the patent was issued. Or, consult the microfiche *Patentee/Assignee Index* (C 21.27:) which lists patentees and assignees from the last five or six years, with corresponding patent numbers.

Step Two: the *Official Gazette* volume in which the patent number appears must be identified before the OG patent abstract can be located. To determine which OG issue the patent number appeared in, consult the table in Part II of the annual *Index of Patents*, "List of Patent, Design, Plant Patent, Reissue and Defensive Publication Numbers Appearing in the Individual Issues of the Official Gazette for [year]."
ANSWERS:
   a. #4,438,032 Unique T-Lymphocyte Line and Products Derived Therefrom *Official Gazette* (March 20, 1984).
   b. #4,704,583 Light Amplifiers Employing Collisions to Produce a Population Inversion *Official Gazette* (November 3, 1987).
   c. #4,736,866 Transgenic Non-Human Mammals *Official Gazette* (April 12, 1988).
   d. This 1947 patent is too old for Internet or Cassis searching. But wait! In a trademark-reference fluke, a boolean search for "slinky" retrieves Simon Cheng's Spring-Animated Toy Figure (#5,626,505, May 6, 1997), which references the earlier James patent in the "References Cited, U.S. Patent Documents": #2,415,012 Toy and Process of Use *Official Gazette* (January 28, 1947).
   e. Hollerith's 1889 computer patent predates Internet or Cassis search capabilities. #395,781 Art of Compiling Statistics *Official Gazette* (January 8, 1889).
   f. #4,259,444 Microorganisms Having Multiple Compatible Degradative Energy-Generating Plasmids and Preparation Thereof *Official Gazette* (March 31, 1981).

3. The author has mixed his metaphors: one does not "patent a trademark," nor can names or titles be patented. The name Bartlett was registered as a trademark. Such confusion often results with older items marked "Registered U.S. Patent Office," reflecting PTO's name until 1975.

4. National Technical Information Service registered trademarks, NTIS® and FedWorld®.
   ANSWER: FedWorld was registered on 1997-01-07 as a word mark; NTIS was registered 1996-12-17 as a word mark, both to the registrant NTIS. Both were also registered as service marks.
   SEARCH STRATEGY: Using the Cassis CD-ROM, Trademarks REGISTERED, select "Mark Combined Search" and search for FedWorld and NTIS.

SOLUTIONS TO EXERCISES FOR CHAPTER 8

1. OTA memoriam.
   ANSWER: *Congressional Record* September 28, 1995.
   SEARCH STRATEGY: Use THOMAS to search either the full text of the *Congressional Record* or the *Congressional Record Index*.
   Full text:
   a. Select 104th Congress
   b. In Keyword Search box, enter the Boolean search: #band(technology assessment close)
   c. Limit by House and Extensions of Remarks
   d. Limit by Houghton's last name to retrieve speeches, inserted remarks, or any appearance of member's name
   e. Limit by date typing 9/01/95 to 9/30/95 in the date-range boxes.
   Congressional Record Index:
   a. #band(technology assessment) retrieves a list of names and terms
   b. Select "Office of Technology Assessment"
   c. Under the heading "Remarks in House" is "Elimination, E1868-E1870 [28SE], E1886 [29SE]"
   d. Clicking on a page reference retrieves the full text of that page
   e. Use your browser's Find to locate Houghton's remarks
   f. Or select "Browse Alphabetical List of All Index Topics," selecting the alphabetic range containing Office of Technology Assessment
   g. Under the heading "Remarks in House" is "Elimination, E1868-E1870 [28SE], E1886 [29SE]"
   h. Clicking on a page reference retrieves the full text of that page
   i. Use your browser's Find to locate Houghton's remarks
   j. The "speech," was actually inserted in Extensions of Remarks, as evidenced by the page number: E1868.

2. Senate Report 104-114.
   SEARCH STRATEGY: In THOMAS, Select the "Senate Reports" radio box and enter report number (104-114). The full text of Senate Report 104-114, *Legislative Branch Appropriations, 1996* is retrieved. Select sections to read using the hot-linked Table of Contents. Note that the originating bill is given (H. R.1854).
   If the report number wasn't known, the report could be retrieved using a subject search: in THOMAS, click the radio button for House and Senate reports and enter the following Boolean search in the search box: #band(public printer electronic depository transition) to retrieve *Legislative Branch Appropriations, 1996* (Sen-

ate Report 104-114, ranked highly in the relevance list.)

3. Text of the Paperwork Reduction Act of 1995.
   ANSWER: The full text of the Paperwork Reduction Act of 1995, Public Law 104–13 (109 Stat. 163), enacted on May 22, 1995, is available on THOMAS.
   SEARCH STRATEGY: This kind of phrasing — __ Act of *year*—tends to refer to a law. In THOMAS, select "Bill Summary and Status" for the 104th Congress. Search "Word/Phrase: Paperwork Reduction Act," using the browser's Find to search for "law." Click on "S.244" to get a legislative history; then on "Law Text" for the full text of the law.
   Or read the slip law, the pamphlet version of this law printed soon after enactment. How could you identify this? Identify the SuDocs number for slip laws, using the *List of Classes* (to complete the SuDocs number, simply append the Public Law number following the colon—AE 2.110:104-13) or use MOCAT, searching by the law title to identify the slip law SuDocs number mentioned above. Or find the law in the *Statutes at Large* (109 Stat. 163).

4. H.R. 3802, the Electronic Freedom of Information Act Amendments of 1996.
   ANSWER: H.R. 3802 became Public Law 104–231.
   SEARCH STRATEGY: In THOMAS, select "Bills" in the 104th Congress (1995-96) and search by bill number in "Bill Summary & Status." The full text of the law and legislative history can be selected.

5. The most recent edition of *Citizen's Guide on Using the Freedom of Information Act and the Privacy Act of 1974 to Request Government Records.*
   SEARCH STRATEGY: Knowing that *Citizen's Guide on Using the Freedom of Information Act and the Privacy Act of 1974* is a House Report is the key. Search THOMAS, Committee Reports for the most recent Congress. Click on "Search word/phrase" and search for "citizen's guide" or "privacy act of 1974." *Citizen's Guide on Using the Freedom of Information Act and the Privacy Act of 1974 to Request Government Records* is returned, with House Report number prominent in the title paragraph. Clicking on hot-link retrieves the full text. Alternate sources: *Monthly Catalog* or *CIS/Index.*

6. The law governing the Federal Depository Library Program.
   SEARCH STRATEGY: Knowing that the depository law is in Title 44 of the *U.S. Code* (see chapter 4), enter "*44USC AND depository*" in the search box on the specialized U.S.C. search page on GPO Access. The full text of 44USC CHAPTER 19—DEPOSITORY LIBRARY PROGRAM is retrieved. To update the *U.S. Code* online, search public laws in THOMAS.

Retrospective Searches

7. Smokey Bear: Historical Search.
   ANSWER: S. 2322; P.L. 82–359, accompanied by H. Rpt. [82]-1512 and S. Rpt. [82]-1128; 66 Stat. 92.
   SEARCH STRATEGY: 1952 *Monthly Catalog* subject index, under "Smokey Bear," refers to *Monthly Catalog* entry numbers for both the law and the House and Senate reports.

1952 Senate *Journal*: "Smokey Bear" in index refers to H.R. 5790 in the "House Bills" section, which gives a legislative history and notes that S. 2322 was passed in lieu. In the "Senate Bills" section, the legislative history of S. 2322 notes Public Law number. Similar information could be located using the House *Journal*. The Smokey Bear of the 1990s also has a home page, which provides his history <http://www. odf.state.or.us/smokey/SMOKEY.HTM>.

Or, search the *Congressional Record Index*, vol. 98, subject search, or "History of Bills and Resolutions" under S. 2322.

8. NTIS Privatization.
ANSWER: House. Committee on Science, Space, and Technology. *Subcommittee on Science, Research and Technology. Hearing on the Privatization of the National Technical Information Service, and H. R. 812, The National Quality Improvement Award Act of 1987 100-1 March 4, 1987* (No. 5) (Y 4. Sci2:100/5).
SEARCH STRATEGY: Searching "National Technical Information Service" in *CIS/Index* or its online or CD-ROM equivalents nets citations to several NTIS privatization hearings. SuDocs numbers, depository status notation (Item No.), and CIS accession numbers facilitate access to the full text. Hearings are not included in the Serial Set. A *CIS/Index* subject search also unearths P.L. 100–519, the National Institute of Standards and Technology Authorization Act for FY89, which confirmed NTIS's protection from privatization.

Searching the *Monthly Catalog* subject index reveals citations to the hearings, but without abstracts.

9. Titanic Investigation: Historical Search.
ANSWER: During the 62nd Congress, the Senate issued Documents 726 and 933, and S. Rpt. 806.
SEARCH STRATEGY: These can be identified through subject searches of the *Congressional Record Index, CIS Congressional Serial Set Index*, or Congressional Masterfile 1 (which includes the CIS Committee Hearings Index), or the Document Catalog.

Although S. Doc. 726 was a hearing (hearings are not part of the Serial Set), it was ordered printed as a Senate Document, placing it in the Serial Set. Thus, S. Doc. 726 is cited in CIS's *Congressional Committee Hearings Index, Serial Set Index*, and Congressional Masterfile 1 on CD-ROM.

The *Congressional Record Index* cites the Senate Report and Documents plus numerous bills, speeches, and remarks in the *Congressional Record*, but they are not incorporated into the Serial Set because they were neither Reports nor Documents.

10. Hearings—FBI Library Awareness Program.
ANSWER: House. Committee on the Judiciary. Subcommittee on Civil and Constitutional Rights. *FBI Counterintelligence Visits to Libraries*. GPO, 1989. (Y 4.J89/1:100/123).
SEARCH STRATEGY: This information could have been identified through a subject search of *CIS/Index* or Congressional Masterfile 2 (1989 H521-64).

11. Disposal of Patent Models: Historical Search.
ANSWER: *Disposition of Old Patent Office Models*, S. Rpt. 1062 and H. Rpt. 1102 (both from the 68th Congress, 2nd session.) These will be in the Serial Set because they are congressional reports.
SEARCH STRATEGY: Report and serial numbers can be identified through a subject search of *CIS Congressional Serial Set Index* or Congressional Masterfile 1 (which also lists historical hearings and committee prints not in the Serial Set but cited in the CIS congressional hearings and committee prints indexes).

12. The Federal Information Resources Management Act of 1989.
ANSWER: It was never enacted into law, and died at the conclusion of the 101st Congress. (If enacted, the final statement in a legislative history will note public law number and approval date.)
SEARCH STRATEGY: Consult House *Calendars*, final edition for 101-2, "History of Bills and Resolutions" section under bill number: No action was taken on the bill after it was reported from the Senate Governmental Affairs Committee (S. Rpt. 101-487).

Similar information can be located by searching under S. 1742 in THOMAS or the 1990 editions of:

House or Senate *Journal*
Congressional Record Index

SOLUTIONS TO EXERCISES FOR CHAPTER 9

1. Snowbound *Federal Registers*.
ANSWER: Select the 1996 *Federal Register* on the specialized search page. Fill in the Issue Date in date range boxes—1/9/96 to 1/12/96—and in the Search Terms box, type "contents." Issues for January 8, 9, and 11 were lean, while January 10 was a normal size. The government shut down on Monday and Tuesday (January 8 and 9), with things getting back to normal by Wednesday. Issue size reflected these events with about a two-day lag. The storm topped off a 21-day partial government shutdown, however, which created a backlog possibly reflected in the issue of January 10.

2. Background information about the 1994 transfer of the National Audiovisual Center to NTIS.
ANSWER: 59 FR 35389 (1994).
SEARCH STRATEGY: You surmised that this question relates to regulations. But how and why? Search the 1994 *Federal Register* on the specialized search page, using the Search Terms: "National Audiovisual Center" AND technical. The text of the July 11, 1994, notice in Volume 59 is indexed as: fr11jy94 Notice of Transfer of Function to NTIS. Neither a regulation nor proposed rule, the announcement of the move was placed in the FR as a notice. Because it's in 1994, you have to patch in a page number. To identify the page, enter "fr11jy94 CONTENTS" using the Find command to search for "audiovisual." The index entry was: National Audiovisual Center; transfer of function to National Technical Information Service, 35389. The complete cite, then, is 59 FR 35389 (1994).

3. Find the 1997 *Federal Register* announcement that the North American Industry Classification System (NAICS) had replaced the Standard Industrial Classification (SIC).
ANSWER: 1997 North American Industry Classification System—1987 Standard Industrial Classification Replacement; Notice" 62 FR 17287-17337.

SEARCH STRATEGY: Select the 1997 *Federal Register* on the specialized search page. Search "standard industrial classification" or "industr* classification system*." The entries referring to "1997 North American Classification System—1987 Standard" are the ones sought. The citation to April 9, 1997, is abbreviated fr09ap97N 1997. Since it was in the Notices section, delimiting the search to Final Rules and Regulations would have missed the citation.

4. Thanksgiving or Mother's Day.
   SEARCH STRATEGY: Search on the *Federal Register's* specialized search page, selecting the year, a date range, and Presidential Documents. The proclamations also appear in Title 3 CFR the following January.

5. FR/CFR Citations.
   ANSWER: Since we're not looking for bits and pieces of amendments, the CFR is our main source for these—unless a complete revision of a rule has occurred during the last year. (This would be caught using the *Federal Register.*) Do subject searches in either the Web CFR, *CFR Index and Finding Aids*, or *CIS Index to the* CFR. A quick and dirty *Federal Register* search may identify the title and section needed, but only if the CFR was revised during the year.
   a. Patent models: 37 CFR 1.91 and 37 CFR 1.92
   b. Presidential gifts: 12 CFR 264b.3; 3 CFR 100.735-14
   c. Mayonnaise: 21 CFR 169.140
   d. Cottage cheese: 21 CFR 133.128
   e. Carry-on baggage: 14 CFR 91.523
   f. Child safety seats: 49 CFR 571.213

SOLUTIONS TO EXERCISES FOR CHAPTER 10

1. Patent Cooperation Treaty.
   ANSWER: PCT entered into force January 24, 1978; 28 UST 7645, TIAS 8733.
   SEARCH STRATEGY: If the treaty is still active, it will be described in the latest *Treaties in Force*, issued last January. The Patent Cooperation Treaty is listed under the subject "Patents," with references to the full text in UST (*United States Treaties and Other International Agreements*) and the numbered slip treaty in TIAS (*Treaties and Other International Acts Series*), ratification date, plus a list of nations party to PCT. The treaty text can be consulted in either 28 UST 7645 (volume 28, page 7645) or TIAS (by TIAS number).
   For background information, search for legislative history in *CIS/Index* or its electronic equivalents. Remembering that treaties can stagnate for years awaiting congressional action, search backwards from the ratification date (or, more quickly, by treaty title in Congressional Masterfile 2). The legislative history for Patent Cooperation Treaty, P.L. 94–131 (1975), lists a House and Senate report and a House hearing. (The House and Senate reports will be in the Serial Set.)

2. President Clinton's statement upon signing P.L. 103–40.
   SEARCH STRATEGY: In THOMAS, select "Public Laws By Law Number" for the 103rd Congress and search for P.L. 103–04. The legislative history for the original bill, S. 564, shows that the president signed it on June 8, 1993. The text of Clinton's statement appears in the *Weekly Compilation of Presidential Documents* and in *Public Papers of the Presidents* under that date. If the date were unknown, the subject indexes in these sources could have been used to ascertain the day the statement was issued.

3. E.O. 12958.
   SEARCH STRATEGY: The White House Web page Virtual Library includes Clinton's Executive Orders, with a search capability <http://www.whitehouse.gov/WH/Welcome.html>. Knowing the E.O. number allows direct retrieval of the full text of Executive Order 12958, Classified National Security Information, April 17, 1995.

Retrospective Searching

4. First Thanksgiving proclamation.
   SEARCH STRATEGY: Consult James D. Richardson's *A Compilation of the Messages and Papers of the Presidents, 1789–1897*. Volume 1, covering Washington's presidency, includes his "PROCLAMATION. A National Thanksgiving" (p. 56), signed in October in New York City.

5. Executive Order 9568.
   ANSWER: E.O. 9568, "Providing for the Release of Scientific Information," June 8, 1945.
   SEARCH STRATEGY: E.O. 9568 could quickly be identified using *CIS Index to Presidential Orders and Proclamations, 1789–1983*, by E.O. number, or by searching the subject index ("Demobilization," "Security Classification of Documents," or "Technology Transfer"). The section called "Index of Interrelated Orders and Proclamations" lists subsequent, related executive orders.
   Both the current Title 3 CFR and *Codification of Presidential Proclamations and Executive Orders, April 13, 1945–January 20, 1989* omit E. O. 9568. Why? Because Truman's executive order was later superseded, losing its legal effect. The "Disposition Tables" list E.O. 9568, citing later executive orders which superseded it. *Code of Federal Regulations*, Title 3—The President, 1936–1975 Consolidated Tables also lists it in the "Disposition Tables," as an inactive E.O.
   In libraries with hearty retrospective collections, the text could also be found in the 1945 *U.S. Code Congressional and Administrative News* (search index under "Executive Orders"), *Federal Register*, or in the 1943–1948 Compilation of 3 CFR, in chronological order under issue date.

SOLUTIONS TO EXERCISES FOR CHAPTER 11

1. Communications Decency Act.
   SEARCH STRATEGY: A search of the Federal Bulletin Board on GPO Access <http://fedbbs.access.gpo.gov/court01.htm> locates the bench opinion. Select "1996/1997 Opinions/ Decisions" and then use the Find command to locate *Reno v. ACLU.*

2. Nixon Papers.
   ANSWER: *Nixon v. Administrator of General Services*, 433 U.S. 425 (1977).
   SEARCH STRATEGY: We are seeking a Supreme Court decision rendered in 1977; Richard M. Nixon was the plaintiff, and the United States government was the defendant.

A search of the Cornell Law School Legal Information Institute's selected Historic Supreme Court Decisions—by Topic <http://supct.law.cornell.edu/supct/cases/historic. htm> using the terms "nixon v. administrator" yields four references to 433 U.S. 425 (1977). An alternate starting point would be a legal digest, with its indexes to Supreme Court decisions. Searching the "Table of Cases" in the *Digest of United States Supreme Court Reports, Lawyer's Edition* under "Nixon" locates a citation in *United States Reports: Nixon v. Administrator of General Services*, 433 U.S. 425. (It helps to realize that the Nixon materials were placed in the custody of the National Archives, at the time a division of the General Services Administration: see chapter 10.) To read the text of the decision, consult the official or unofficial Supreme Court reporter (the digest notes parallel citations in West and the Lawyers Edition). The full text is available on the Internet through FindLaw: select "Laws: Cases and Codes," then "Supreme Court Decisions" and type the citation in the Citation Search box.

3. Verbatim Transcripts 771 F.2d 539 (D.C. Cir 1985).
   ANSWER: Consult the "Federal Court Decisions" table in chapter 11. The abbreviation F.2d refers to decisions from U.S. courts of appeals reprinted in the Federal Reporter. The U.S. district courts comprise 12 circuits, one of which is the District of Columbia (D.C. Cir).

4. Supreme Court Citations.
   ANSWER: 116 S. Ct. 1091
   454 U.S. 812
   134 L.Ed.2d 167
   STRATEGY: Scan the citations to identify abbreviations for the official (U.S.) and unofficial (S. Ct. and L.Ed.2d) Supreme Court reporters.

SOLUTIONS TO EXERCISES FOR CHAPTER 12

1. Population of the U.S.
   ANSWER: The answer to this question is ever-changing.
   SEARCH STRATEGY: The easiest and quickest answer source is the Census Bureau Web site's population clock <http://www.census.gov/>. The White House Social Statistics Briefing Room provides a link to the Census Popclock under Demographic Statistics <http://www.whitehouse.gov/fsbr/ssbr.html>. Or consult the *Statistical Abstract of the United States*.

2. Identify Answers or Probable Answer Sources.
   a. Science literacy.
   ANSWER SOURCE: The White House Social Statistics Briefing Room, under "Education Statistics," provides a link called Science Proficiency <http://www.whitehouse.gov/fsbr/ssbr.html>. The *Statistical Abstract* index heading "Test Scores" offers one perspective on "literacy," which applies to school kids rather than adults. The *Statistical Abstract* Education section table, "Proficiency Test Scores for Selected Subjects, by Characteristic," provides science test results in the National Assessment of Educational Progress and another table of American College Testing (ACT) scores of college-bound seniors. Searching ASI under "Scientific

education," "Educational attainment," or "Educational tests" or using the Index by Categories (Demographic breakdowns-by age-education) directs you to the *Digest of Education Statistics*.
   b. 1991 Harris privacy poll.
   ANSWER: Harris-Equifax Consumer Privacy Survey 1991.
   ANSWER SOURCE: *Statistical Reference Index* (SRI). First, remember that polls = statistics. Because Harris polls are not government surveys, we are looking for statistics generated outside the federal government. A subject search ("Right to Privacy" or "Harris, Louis, and Associates") retrieves the report. (The SRI annotation mentions "level of concern regarding threats to privacy".)
   c. Patents granted to non-Americans.
   ANSWER SOURCE: *American Statistics Index* (ASI). A subject search ("Patents" or "Patent and Trademark Office") yields the PTO annual report (C 21.2:F yr.) and *Patents Issued by the Patent and Trademark Office*. Remember that because annual reports usually chronicle agency activities using statistics, they are likely to be indexed and abstracted in ASI. Another strategy is to refer to the PTO Web page, where patent grants by country are enumerated in the online PTO annual report and the Technology Assessment and Forecast (TAF) Program link.
   d. McClure and Hernon's report on depository use of census data.
   ANSWER: McClure, Charles R. and Peter Hernon. *Use of Census Bureau Data in GPO Depository Libraries: Future Issues and Trends*. 1990 (C 3.2:D 26/9) is available in depository libraries, and for sale from ASI on microfiche.
   SEARCH STRATEGY: ASI, author or subject search. ASI notes depository status (item number), SuDocs number, and ASI microfiche availability (ASI/MF/4). ASI was selected because this study was commissioned by the government. When unsure whether the title sought is federal or nonfederal, use Statistical Masterfile, which allows searching across both ASI and SRI for numerous years.

SOLUTIONS TO EXERCISES FOR CHAPTER 13

1. Ansel Adams photos.
   ANSWER: Because Adams's work was done under government auspices, it is likely to be in the National Archives. Search NAIL, the database of selected NARA holdings of photographs, documents, maps, and sound recordings, under "ansel adams" <http://www.nara.gov/nara/nail.html>. His photos appear in Record Group 79: Ansel Adams Photographs of National Parks and Monuments. The NAIL records tagged with red bullets are accompanied by thumbnail and full-size online images. Remember that NAIL documents are only a tiny fraction of NARA holdings.

2. Farm Security Administration photos.
   SEARCH STRATEGY: It helps to know that the Library

of Congress holds most of the FSA photos. A shotgun (broad) search of Farm Security Administration on WorldCat would retrieve *Farm Security Administration, Historical Section: A Guide to Textual Records in the Library of Congress* (LC 25.8/2:F 22), another way of pinpointing the photos as being in the Library of Congress. *Special Collections in the Library of Congress* describes the Farm Security Administration Collection, "probably the most famous pictorial record of American life in the 1930s," held in LC's Prints and Photographs Division.

A search of the National Archives' NAIL under Farm Security Administration uncovers Production Stills Made from Films Produced by the Documentary Film Section and Miscellaneous Photographs Taken by the Historical Section, ca.1935-ca.1943, which leads us to Record Group 96, Records of the Farmers Home Administration. The *Guide to the Holdings of the Still Picture Branch of the National Archives and Records Administration* (AE 1.108:St 5) loops to the same path, indicating that the National Archives also holds a collection of FSA photographs in Record Group 96, Records of the Farmers Home Administration.

3. *Challenger* Accident Archival Records.
SEARCH STRATEGY: Search NAIL, the database of selected NARA holdings of photographs, documents, maps, and sound recordings <http://www.nara.gov/nara/nail.html> under "challenger." The records, with control numbers like NWDNM(m)-220-CHC-1, indicate the records are in Record Group 220. A description of RG 220 is given in *Guide to Federal Records in the National Archives of the United States* (AE 1.108:G 94/V.1-3 and <gopher://gopher.nara.gov/11/inform/guide>). The *Challenger* records in Record Group 220: Records of Temporary Committees, Commissions, and Boards are scattered among several NARA units according to their media format. An index to the collection may be consulted at NARA or purchased on paper, microfiche, or computer tape. A handout describing *Challenger* records, "Information for Researchers: Records of the Presidential Commission on the Space Shuttle Challenger Accident," is free from NARA.

SOLUTIONS TO EXERCISES FOR CHAPTER 14

1. Why does the SuDocs number for National Archives publications begin with AE?
ANSWER: This question begs referral to Andriot's *Guide to U.S. Government Publications*, because it pertains to SuDocs number history. After discovering that

the AE scope note for National Archives Creation and Authority doesn't refer to the origins, try the Agency Index. The third agency reference, to National Archives Establishment, AE 1, provides the answer.

2. Ethnic composition of counties.
ANSWER: Consult the statistical compendium that focuses on county-level data: *County and City Data Book* (C 3.134/2:C 83/2/yr.). Another profitable source would be *American Statistics Index*, using the "Index by Categories" to locate tables broken down by 1) county, and 2) race. Remember that although ASI covers federally generated statistics, the federal government gathers statistics on diverse subjects and numerous geographic regions.

3. Foreign country data.
ANSWER: Search the Statistical Masterfile or ASI, using the "Index by Categories" to locate tables broken down by foreign countries. Such a search would locate statistical compendia such as the CIA *World Factbook*. Statistical Masterfile also incorporates *Index to International Statistics*, indexing statistics issued by international intergovernmental organizations. *PAIS International* indexes international organizations' statistical publications related to public policy issues. The *Statistical Abstract* includes a "Comparative International Statistics" section in which world and national statistics are compared to U.S. data, and an appendix,"Guide to Foreign Statistical Abstracts."

4. Official title of the Watergate report.
ANSWER: *Report, Watergate Special Prosecution Force*, (J 1.2:W 29) and *Final Report, Watergate Special Prosecution Force* (J 1.2:W 29/977). Consult Bernier and Wood's *Popular Names of U.S. Government Reports: A Catalog* (LC 6.2:G 74/984) to translate from the short, popular report name to its official title and issuing agency.
NOTE: the two titles cited in *Popular Names of U.S. Government Reports* are only two of numerous Watergate materials. A search of *CIS/Index* or Congressional Masterfile 2, for example, will yield citations to numerous impeachment hearings and related materials.

APPENDIX 4
Abbreviations and Popular Names

This potpourri supplements William Evinger's *Guide to Federal Government Acronyms* (1989) with additional agency notations, a few pronunciations, and documents-centric definitions not universally embraced throughout government. (When the full-blown name is rarely used, descriptions are given instead.) Additional resources for decoding abbreviations are the Library of Congress's Legislative Indexing Vocabulary (LIV) <http://lcweb.loc.gov/lexico/liv/brsearch.html> and Appendix A: Commonly Used Abbreviations and Acronyms in the *U.S. Government Manual* <http://www.access.gpo.gov/su_docs/dbsearch.html> (use Search Term: abbreviations).

The 1909 Checklist *Checklist of United States Public Documents,* 1789–1909, (GP 3.2:C 41/2)

ABBS Appellate Bulletin Board System (electronic access to appellate court decisions and other court information such as oral argument calendars, case dockets, local court rules, notices and reports, and press releases)

ACCESS Library of Congress's online catalog, a PC-based graphic interface

ACE Americans Communicating Electronically, public and private sector volunteers interested in promoting communication between the citizens and their government

ACIR Advisory Commission on Intergovernmental Relations, abolished in 1996 (Internet access is maintained at <http://www.library.unt.edu/gpo/acir/acir.html>)

AFPTI *American Foreign Policy and Treaty Index* (Congressional Information Service)

AFS formerly the Archive of Folk Song, now the Library of Congress's Archive of Folk Culture

AGRIS, a decentralized United Nations database maintained by the United Nations' Food and Agriculture Organization; its print counterpart is *Agrindex*

AIM *Abridged Index Medicus*

ALF The National Agriculture Library's electronic bulletin board, Agricultural Library Forum, discontinued in favor of WWW and Internet information delivery

"Andriot" *Guide to U.S. Government Publications,* Donna Andriot, editor

ANTS *Administrative Notes: Technical Supplement*

APS Patent and Trademark Office Automated Patent System

ASP American State Papers (reprints of documents from the first 14 congresses, 1789–1838); indexed in *CIS US Serial Set Index, 1989–1969*

ATPA American Technology Preeminence Act, mandates that federal agencies submit federally funded scientific, technical, and engineering information to NTIS (Public Law 102–245)

AVA19357–VNB1INA National Audiovisual Center order numbers

BBSs Electronic bulletin boards

BET Browse Electronic Titles (GPO Access)

Bevans *Treaties and Other International Agreements of the United States of America, 1776–1949* (S 9.12/2:2:v.1–13)

BGN U.S. Board on Geographic Names (USGS)

Bill Digest *Digest of Public General Bills and Resolutions*

BJS Bureau of Justice Statistics

BOA *Bibliography of Agriculture*

BOP Balance of payments

CAIM *Cumulated Abridged Index Medicus*

CAPNET An internal Congressional network accessible only to members of Congress

CBM *Current Bibliographies in Medicine* (National Library of Medicine)

CCE *Catalog of Copyright Entries*

Cd.[no.] British Command papers series (see chapter 15)

CDA Communications Decency Act of 1996

CDLs Census Depository Libraries

CFDA *Catalog of Federal Domestic Assistance*

CHAMPUS Civilian Health and Medical Program of the Uniform Services (DOD—Office of Civilian Health and Medical Program of the Armed Services)

CIM *Cumulated Index Medicus*

CIR *Current Industrial Reports*

CM [no.] British Command Papers series (see chapter 15)

CM2 Congressional Masterfile 2

Cmd. [no.] British Command Paper series (see chapter 15)

CMH Army Center for Military History

CMJ Code of Military Justice; also UCMJ; in 10 U.S.C. 801 ff (chapter 47)

Cmnd.[no.] British Command Papers series (see chapter 15)

CNIDR Center For Networked Information Discovery and Retrieval

COGI Coalition on Government Information, American Library Association, Washington Office. The Coalition focuses national attention on restricted access to government information and supports access enhancement.

CORDS Copyright Office Electronic Registration, Recordation and Deposit System

CPH Census of Population and Housing

CPI Consumer Price Index

CPI-U Consumer Price Index for All Urban Consumers

CPI-W Consumer Price Index for Urban Wage Earners and Clerical Workers

cri *Congressional Record Index* (A code such as cri94 in a GPO Access search of the *Congressional Record* indicates *Congressional Record Index*, 1994)

CWRU Case Western Reserve University, a participant in Project Hermes, the electronic dissemination of U.S. Supreme Court opinions

DADS Data Access and Dissemination System database (Census Bureau)

DCW *Digital Chart of the World*

Document Catalog *Catalogue of the Public Documents of the [53rd to 76th] Congress and of All Departments of the Government of the United States* (GP 3.6:)

DODISS *Department of Defense Index of Specifications and Standards*

DOSFAN The Department of State Foreign Affairs Network, established in cooperation with the University of Illinois at Chicago

DOT *Dictionary of Occupational Titles* (being replaced by the Occupational Information Network, O*NET <http://www.doleta.gov/programs/onet/>)

E & E *Employment and Earnings*

EDGAR The Securities and Exchange Commission's Electronic Data Gathering, Analysis, and Retrieval system of filings

EPO European Patent Office

EPRF *Exhausted GPO Sales Publications Reference File, 1980*

ERS Economic Research Service

ESBR Economic Statistics Briefing Room (White House)

Exec. Rept. 104-4 Senate Executive Reports on treaties (Y 1.1/6: and Serial Set)

FATUS *Foreign Agricultural Trade of the United States*

FBIS Foreign Broadcast Information Service

FDAC *Catalog of Federal Domestic Assistance*

FDLM *Federal Depository Library Manual*

FDLP Federal Depository Library Program

FEDBOP Federal Bureau of Prisons

FES *Firearms Evidence Sourcebook*

FIE Federal Information Exchange, Inc.

FNMA Federal National Mortgage Association, pronounced "Fannie Mae"

FRUS *Foreign Relations of the United States*

FSA Farm Security Administration

FTP Federal Theatre Project (the Library of Congress collection of U.S. Work Projects Administration records on deposit at George Mason University)

FTS Federal Telecommunications System

FWS Fish and Wildlife Service

FY Fiscal year

GATT General Agreement on Tariffs and Trade

GDP Gross Domestic Product

GII Global Information Infrastructure

GILS Government Information Locator Service

GLIN Global Legal Information Network of member countries, administered by the Library of Congress's Law Library

GLPTC Great Lakes Patent and Trademark Center

GNIS Geographic Names Information System (United States Geological Survey)

GNMA Government National Mortgage Association, pronounced "Ginnie Mae"

GODORT Government Documents Roundtable (American Library Association)

GPR *Government Publications Review;* new title is *Journal of Government Information* (JGI)

GRA&I *Government Reports Announcements and Index* (ceased in 1996; replaced by NTIS OrderNow <http://www.ntis.gov/ordernow/>)

"Green Book" *Background Material and Data on Major Programs within the Jurisdiction of the Committee on Ways and Means* <http://www.access.gpo.gov/congress/wm001.html>

H171/90 *Current Housing Reports, Supplement to the American Housing Survey for Selected Metropolitan Areas in 1990, H171/90*

HABS Historic American Buildings Survey

HAER Historic American Engineering Record or Historic Engineering Record; there are HAER collections in the Library of Congress and National Park Service

hob History of Bills (part of *Congressional Record Index*); a code such as hob95 in a GPO Access search indicates History of Bills, 1995

HS Harmonized Commodity Description and Coding System (from the Customs Co-operation Council, Brussels Belgium); replaced the SITC Schedule B (export) and TSUSA (import) Commodity Classifications

HUAC House Committee on Un-American Activities (pronounced "hugh-ack")

ICD-9-CM *International Classification of Diseases, 9th Revision, Clinical Modification*

ICPSR Inter-University Consortium for Political and Social Research

ICUD *Index to Current Urban Documents*

IFLA International Federation of Library Associations and Institutions

IFRs International Fishery Reports (National Marine Fisheries Service)

IGM Internet Grateful Med

IMM *International Mail Manual*

INID INID Codes on patents allow worldwide conformity of bibliographic information

IPC International Patent Classification System (World Intellectual Property Organization)

IRM Information Resources Management

ISOO Information Security Oversight Office (National Archives)

ISP-DP, Census Bureau Country Demographic Profiles series, now discontinued

JCP Congressional Joint Committee on Printing

JGI *Journal of Government Information* (formerly *Government Publications Review*)

KAV Unpublished and unnumbered treaties in *United States Current Treaty Index*, assigned numbers by Hein until the State Department numbers them

LCIB *Library of Congress Information Bulletin*

LCSH *Library of Congress Subject Headings*

LII Legal Information Institute (Cornell)

LIV Legislative Indexing Vocabulary (Library of Congress)

LJI *List of Journals Indexed in Index Medicus*

LSOA *Longitudinal Study of Aging* (Vital and Health Statistics Series 1, no. 28)

MARAD Maritime Administration

MCP *Mineral Commodity Profiles*

MEDOC was a bibliography of U.S. government publications in the biomedical sciences, produced by the University of Utah Health Sciences Library, that ceased in 1993

MeSH *Medical Subject Headings*

MHI Army Military History Institute

MLC *Major Legislation of the Congress;* MLC-001 = an entry number within an issue

MLR *Monthly Labor Review*

MMWR *Morbidity and Mortality Weekly Report*

MPA *Monthly Product Announcement* (Census Bureau)

MPEP *Manual of Patent Examining Procedure*, the "patent examiner's bible"

MUID MEDLINE unique identifier; attached to each MEDLINE citation

NACIC National Counterintelligence Center

NACJD National Archive of Criminal Justice Data

NAEP National Assessment of Educational Progress; regularly assesses achievement of 4th, 8th, and 12th graders in reading, math, writing, social studies, geography, and science

NASM National Air and Space Museum (Smithsonian Institution)

NASS National Agriculture Statistics Service

NCADI National Clearinghouse for Alcohol and Drug Information

NCHS National Center for Health Statistics

NCJRS National Criminal Justice Reference Service

NCVS National Crime Victimization Survey

NDL National Digital Library Program (Library of Congress)

Nec Not elsewhere classified

NEDI National Environmental Data Index

NESE-DB *National Economic, Social, and Environmental Data Bank* (ceased)

Nesoi Not elsewhere specified or included

NHIC National Health Information Center

NHIS National Health Interview Survey

NHPRC National Historical Publications and Records Commission

NIDR National Institute of Dental Research

NII National Information Infrastructure

NIJ National Institute of Justice

NIMA National Imagery and Mapping Agency

NIPA National Income and Products Accounts

NLE National Library of Education

NLS National Library Service for the Blind and Physically Handicapped

NMFS National Marine Fisheries Service

NNMS National Nutrition Monitoring System

NOHIC National Oral Health Information Clearinghouse (National Institute of Dental Research)

NPR National Performance Review

NPTS National Personal Transportation Survey (Federal Highway Administration)

NRMM *National Register of Microform Masters*

NSA National Security Archive

NST *New Serial Titles*

NTC National Translations Center, Library of Congress (defunct since 1993)

NTDB National Trade Data Bank

NTRS NASA Technical Report Server

NUCMC *National Union Catalog of Manuscript Collections*

OECD Organization for Economic Cooperation and Development

OG *Official Gazette of the United States Patent and Trademark Office: Patents*

OPRF *Out-of-Print GPO Sales Publications Reference File*

OSTI Office of Scientific and Technical Information (Department of Energy)

OWI Office of War Information

PACER Public Access to Court Electronic Records (dial-in to individual district or bankruptcy court computers to retrieve case information and court dockets)

PASS Procurement Automated Source System (SBA)

PMID a PubMed unique identifier

PRA Paperwork Reduction Act

PRF See SPC

"Price List 36" Popular title for *U.S. Government Subscriptions*

PRMPA Presidential Records and Materials Preservation Act of 1974 (P.L. 93–526) allowing seizure of Nixon's presidential materials

PTCS Patent and Trademark Copy Sales

PTDL Patent and Trademark Depository Libraries

PTDLP Patent and Trademark Depository Library Program

PUMS 1990 Census Public-Use Microdata Samples, *1990 Census of Population and Housing Census Public Use Microdata Files CD-ROM*

QCIM *Quarterly Cumulative Index Medicus*

RAL *National Union Catalog. Register of Additional Locations*

"Red book" *Library of Congress Subject Headings*, LCSH

RG Record Group (National Archives)

RIN Regulation Identifier Number; assigned to each regulatory action listed in the Unified Agenda published in the *Federal Register*

RMs Reference Materials

RRC Reports Required by Congress

RTECS *Registry of Toxic Effects of Chemical Substances*

S "Treaty Series" issued singly as pamphlets by the department of state until replaced in 1945 by TIAS

SAR Search and Rescue missions (Coast Guard)

SAR Student Aid Report

SASS *Schools and Staffing Survey*

Sc[i]³ The Sunnyvale Center for Innovation, a PTDL Partnership library

SCTB Online a Web-based version of the LC Science Tracer Bullet series <http://lcweb2.loc.gov/sctb>

SGML Standard Generalized Markup Language, prescribed by Federal Information Processing Standard 152

SIC Standard Industrial Classification code for economic and industrial data (replaced by NAICS, the North American Industry Classification System)

SIGCAT Special Interest Group on CD-ROM Applications and Technology; a worldwide user group

SIR Statutory Invention Registration (Patent Office)

SMF Statistical Masterfile (CIS)

SMT Survey of Manufacturing Technology series

SOC Manual *Standard Occupational Classification Manual*

SOCC *Statistics of Communications Common Carriers* (CC 1.35:)

SOD Superintendent of Documents

SPC *Sales Product Catalog* (formerly PRF, *Publications Reference File*)

SRH *U. S. Army Signals Intelligence in World War II: A Documentary History*

SRMs Standard Reference Materials

SS The Serial Set

SSBR Social Statistics Briefing Room (White House)

SSR *Social Security Ruling*

STAR *Scientific and Technical Aerospace Reports* (NASA); in PDF format since 1996 <http://www.sti.nasa.gov/Pubs/star/Star.html>

STEO Short-Term Energy Outlook

STF Summary Tape File (Census)

STIS Science and Technology Information System, National Science Foundation (NSF); an electronic dissemination system for accessing NSF publications

T-Search Trademark automation system (U.S. Patent and Trademark Office)

TAF Technology Assessment and Forecast (U.S. Patent and Trademark Office)

TIAS *Treaties and Other International Acts Series*

TIF *Treaties in Force*

TMEP *Trademark Manual of Examining Procedure*

TRI Toxics Release Inventory

UCR *Uniform Crime Reports* (FBI)

UNESCO United Nations Educational, Scientific and Cultural Organization

USBM U. S. Bureau of Mines; abolished in 1996 under P. L. 104–99, with NTIS maintaining a "legacy" collection of USBM publications from 1910–1995

USFAC *U.S. Foreign Affairs on CD-ROM*

USGPI *U.S. Government Periodicals Index*

USLW *U.S. Law Week*

USPC U.S. Patent Classification

UST *United States Treaties and Other International Agreements*

WCPD *Weekly Compilation of Presidential Documents*

WCUS *Waterborne Commerce of the United States*

WMCP Committee on Ways and Means Committee Print

WNC World News Connection (NTIS)

Z39.50 Information Retrieval Service Definition and Protocol Specifications for Library Applications

APPENDIX 5
Internet Addresses

Here are some of the key Internet sites described in this book, along with a few valuable sites not discussed at all. For publishers' Web pages, see Appendix 1, Publishers' Addresses and Web Sites.

ACCESS EPA
<http://www.epa.gov/Contacts/Access/>
or via the Federal Bulletin Board or EP 1.8/13:Ac 2/yr.

ACCESS ERIC
<http://www.aspensys.com/eric>

ACE (Americans Communicating Electronically)
<http://www.sba.gov/ace>

AcqWeb
<http://www.library.vanderbilt.edu/law/acqs.acqs.html>

Administrative Notes
<http://www.access.gpo.gov/su_docs/dpos/adnotes.html>
or unofficial version:
<http://www.du.edu/~ttyler/bdldhome.htm>

Administrative Notes: Technical Supplement
<http://www.access.gpo.gov/su_docs/dpos/techsup.html>
or searchable, full-text version
<http://www.lib.umich.edu/libhome/Documents.center/adnotes.html>
or unofficial version:
<http://www.du.edu/~ttyler/bdldhome.htm>

AgNIC (Agriculture Network Information Center), an electronic information network for accessing agricultural information and subject area experts
<http://www.agnic.org/>

Agricultural Statistics
<http://www.usda.gov/nass/pubs/agstats.htm>

ALIN (Agricultural Libraries Information Notes)
<http://www.nal.usda.gov/alin/>

American National Standards Institute
<http://www.ansi.org/>

Americans Communicating Electronically (ACE)
<http://www.sba.gov/ace>

Americans with Disabilities Act ADA Home Page (U.S. Department of Justice)
<http://www.usdoj.gov/crt/ada/dahom1.htm>

Annual Energy Review
on the Federal Bulletin Board at <http://fedbbs.access.gpo.gov/>

Army Center for Military History
<http://www.army.mil/cmh-pg>

AskERIC
<http://ericir.syr.edu >

Background Notes
<http://www.access.gpo.gov/state/state001.html>
or
<http://www.state.gov/www/background_notes/index.html>

Basic Facts about Trademarks
<http://www.uspto.gov/web/offices/tac/doc/basic/>
or
C 21.2:T 67/4/996

Browse Electronic Titles (GPO Access)
<http://www.access.gpo.gov/su_docs/dpos/btitles.html>

Budget of the U.S.
<http://www.access.gpo.gov/su_docs/budget/index.html>

Bureau of Economic Analysis
<http://www.bea.doc.gov/beahome.html>

Bureau of Justice Statistics
<http://www.ojp.usdoj.gov/bjs/>

Bureau of Labor Statistics
<http://www.bls.gov/>

Bureau of the Census
<http://www.census.gov>

Bureau of Transporation Statistics
<http://www.bts.gov/>

C-SPAN
<http://www.c-span.org>

Calendars of the House of Representatives
<http://www.access.gpo.gov/congress/
cong003.html>

Canadian Government
<http://canada.gc.ca>

Catalog of Federal Domestic Assistance
<http://www.gsa.gov/fdac/>

Census and You
<http://www.census.gov/ftp/pub/prod/www/
abs/msgen.html>

Census Bureau
<http://www.census.gov>

Census Catalog and Guide
<http://www.census.gov/prod/www/
titles.html#genref>

Center for Electronic Records, National Archives
<http://www.nara.gov/nara/electronic/>

Center for International Research (Census)
<http://www.census.gov/ipc/www/>

Center for Legislative Archives, National Archives
<http://www.nara.gov/nara/legislative/>

Center for Research Libraries
<http://wwwcrl.uchicago.edu/>

Center for the Book
<http://lcweb.loc.gov/loc/cfbook >

Center for the Study of Intelligence
<http://www.odci.gov/csi/>

Center of Military History
<http://www.army.mil/cmh-pg>

Centers for Disease Control and Prevention
<http://www.cdc.gov/>

*Chiefs of State and Cabinet Members of Foreign
Governments* (CIA)
<http://www.odci.gov/cia/publications/chiefs/
index.html>

CIA
<http://www.odci.gov/cia>

Classification Definitions
<http://patents.uspto.gov/CLASSES/
classes.html>

Clerk of the House's Legislative Resource Center
<http://clerkweb.house.gov/lrc/lrc.htm>

CNIDR
<http://www.cnidr.org>

Code of Federal Regulations
<http://law.house.gov/cfr.htm>
or

<http://www.access.gpo.gov/nara/CFR>
or
<http://www.access.gpo.gov/su_docs/
dbsearch.html>

Commerce Business Daily
<http://cbdnet.gpo.gov>

Condition of Education
<http://www.ed.gov/NCES/pubs/ce/
index.html>

Congress, E-mail Addresses for
<http://lcweb.loc.gov/global/legislative/
email.html>

Congressional Budget Office
<gopher://gopher.cbo.gov:7100/1>

Congressional Pictorial Directory, GPO Access
<http://www.access.gpo.gov/congress/
index.html>
or
Y 4.P 93/1:1 P/cong

Congressional Record Index
<http://thomas.loc.gov/>
or
<http://www.access.gpo.gov/su_docs/
dbsearch.html>

Constitution of the United States
<http://www.access.gpo.gov/congress/senate/
constitution>
or
<http://www.access.gpo.gov/su_docs/
dbsearch.html>

Consumer Centers (See Federal Consumer Centers)

Consumer Gateway (See U.S. Consumer Gateway)

Consumer Information Catalog
<http://www.pueblo.gsa.gov/cicform.htm>

Consumer Information Center
<http://www.pueblo.gsa.gov>

Copyright Office
<http://lcweb.loc.gov/copyright/>

Country Study Series
<http://lcweb2.loc.gov/frd/cs/cshome.html/>

County and City Data Book
<http://www.census.gov/stat_abstract/
ccdb.html>

CRS Reports
<http://www.house.gov/rules_org/
crs_reports.htm>

Crime in the United States
<http://www.fbi.gov/publish.htm>

Current Bibliographies in Medicine (CBM)
<http://www.nlm.nih.gov/pubs/
resources.html>

Daily Depository Shipping List
<http://ublib.buffalo.edu/libraries/units/cts/
acq/GPO/>

or
<http://febbbs.access.gpo.gov/fdlp01.htm>
or via GPO's FBB (downloadable only, can't be viewed)

Decisions of the Comptroller General of the U.S. (GAO)
<http://www.gao.gov/decisions/decision.htm>

Defense Technical Information Center
<http://www.dtic.mil>

DefenseLINK
<http://www.dtic.dla.mil/defenselink/index.html>

Delegation of European Commission (Washington)
<http://www.eurunion.org>

Department of Education
<http://www.ed.gov/>

Department of State
<http://www.state.gov/>
or
<http://fedbbs.access.gpo.gov/statedpt.htm>

Dictionary of Occupational Titles, last published in 1991 (L 37.2:Oc 1/2/991/v.1-2) has been replaced by O*NET, a comprehensive database on job characteristics and worker attributes
<http://www.doleta.gov/programs/onet/>

Digest of Education Statistics
<http://www.ed.gov/NCES/pubs/D96/index.html>

Dispatch
<http://www.state.gov/>
or
<http://fedbbs.access.gpo.gov/libs/dos_disp.htm>
or S 1.3/5:

DOE Reports Bibliographic Database
<http://apollo.osti.gov/dra/dra.html>

DOSFAN
<http://dosfan.lib.uic.edu/>

Duck stamps
<http://www.fws.gov/r9dso/index.html>

Earthquake information
<http://quake.wr.usgs.gov/>

Economic Report of the President
<http://www.access.gpo.gov/congress/index.html>

Economic Research Service
<http://www.econ.ag.gov/>

Economic Statistics Briefing Room (White House)
<http://www.whitehouse.gov/fsbr/esbr.html>

EDGAR
<http://www.sec.gov/edgarhp.htm>

Education sites
<http://www.ed.gov/free/>

Educational Resources Information Center
<http://ericir.syr.edu>

EIA Directory of Electronic Products
<http://www.eia.doe.gov/bookshelf/other.html>

EIA Publications Directory
<http://www.eia.doe.gov/index.html>

The Electronic Embassy
<http://www.embassy.org>

Embassies Worldwide
<http://www.xsall.nl/nairen/index/html>

The Embassy Page
<http://www.embpage.org>

Endangered Species Home Page (Fish and Wildlife Service)
<http://www.fws.gov/~r9endspp/endspp.html>

Energy InfoDisc
<http://www.eia.doe.gov>

Energy Information Administration (EIA)
<http://www.eia.doe.gov>

Environmental Protection Agency
<http://www.epa.gov>

EPA Toxics Release Inventory (TRI)
<http://www.epa.gov/opptintr/tri/>

ERIC (AskERIC)
<http://www.askeric.org/>

European Union home page
<http://www.europa.eu.int/>

An Explanation of the Superintendent of Documents Classification System
<http://www.access.gpo.g ov/su_docs/dpos/explain.html>

Fannie Mae
<http://www.fanniemae.com/index.html>

FDLP Administration
<http://www.access.gpo.gov/su_docs/dpos/fdlppro.html>

Federal Agency Internet Sites
<http://www.access.gpo.gov/su_docs/dpos/agencies.html>

Federal Bulletin Board
<http://fedbbs.access.gpo.gov/>

Federal Bureau of Investigation
<http://www.fbi.gov/>

Federal Computer Products Center
<http://www.ntis.gov/fcpc/fcpc.htm>

Federal Consumer Centers
<http://www.hud.gov/fedcentr.html>

Federal Depository Library Gateways
<http://www.access.gpo.gov/su_docs/aces/aaces004.html>

Federal Depository Library Manual
<http://www.access.gpo.gov/su_docs/dpos/93fdlm.html>

Federal Election Commission
<http://www.FEC.gov/>

Federal Information Center
<http://fic.info.gov>/

Federal Job Openings
<http://www.usajobs.opm.gov> (the U.S. Office of Federal Personnel Management's USA Jobs is the federal government's official job/employment information site)
or
<http://www.fedworld.gov/jobs/jobsearch.html>
or
Information Exchange <http://www.fie.com/>

Federal Population Censuses
<http://www.nara.gov/publications/microfilm/census/census.html>

Federal Register
<http://www.access.gpo.gov/nara/index.html>
or
<http://www.access.gpo.gov/su_docs/dbsearch.html>

Federal Register Thesaurus of Indexing Terms
<gopher://clio.nara.gov/00/register/thes.txt>

Federal Web Locator (Villanova)
<http://www.law.vill.edu/Fed-Agency/fedwebloc.html>

FedLaw
<http://www.legal.gsa.gov/intro5.htm>

FEDSTATS
<http://www.fedstats.gov>

FedWorld
<http://www.fedworld.gov>

FinanceNet
<http://www.financenet.gov/>

FindLaw
<http://www.findlaw.com/>

First Lady
<http://www.whitehouse.gov/WH/EOP/First_Lady/html/HILLARY_Home.html>

Ford's Theatre
<http://www.nps.gov/foth/index2.htm>

Foreign Consular Offices in the United States (Dept. of State)
<http://www.state.gov/www/travel/consular_offices/FCO_index.html>

Gateways, Federal Depository Libraries
<http://www.access.gpo.gov/su_docs/aces/aaces004.HTML>

General Accounting Office
<http://www.gao.gov>

General Services Administration
<http://www.gsa.gov>

GILS
<http://www.access.gpo.gov/su_docs/GILS/gils.html>

GILS Evaluation Project Web site
<http://www-lan.unt.edu/slis/research/gilseval/gilsdesc.htm>

Government Information in Canada
<http://www.usask.ca/library/gic/index.html>

GIX
<http://www.info.gov/>

Glossary of Senate Terms
<http://www.senate.gov/about/glossary.html>

GODORT
<http://www.lib.berkeley.edu/GODORT/>

Government Executive: The Independent Business Magazine of Government
<http://www.govexec.com/>

Government Information Exchange
<http://www.info.gov/>

Government Information in Canada, a quarterly electronic journal
<http://www.usask.ca/library/gic/>

GPO Access
<http://www.access.gpo.gov/su_docs/>

Grateful Med
<http://igm.nlm.nih.gov>

Gratefully Yours
<http://www.nlm.nih.gov/pubs/gyours/gyours.html >

Great American Web Site
<http://www.uncle-sam.com/preface.html>

GSA Federal Supply Service
<http://www.fss.gsa.gov>

GulfLINK
<http://www. dtic.dla.mil/gulflink/>

Health information
<http://www.healthfinder.gov>

Health, United States
<http://www.cdc.gov/nchswww/data/hus_95.pdf>

Healthfinder
<http://www.healthfinder.gov/>

Hermes
<ftp://ftp.cwru.edu/hermes/>
or
<http://supct.law.cornell.edu/supct/index.html>

History of Bills and Resolutions (*Congressional Record Index*)
<http://www.access.gpo.gov/congress/index.html>

Holocaust Memorial Museum
<http://www.ushmm.org/>

House *Calendars*
<http://www.access.gpo.gov/congress/cong003.html>

House Internet Law Library
<http://law.house.gov/>
or through
<http://www.house.gov/>
or
<http://143.231.180.66>

House of Representatives
<http://www.house.gov>

How Our Laws Are Made
<http://thomas.loc.gov/home/lawsmade.html>

Information Industry Association
<http://www.infoindustry.org/>

International Documents Task Force (IDTF)
<http://www.library.nwu.edu/govpub/idtf>

Internal Revenue Service
<http://www.irs.ustreas.gov/>

International Energy Annual
<http://www.eia.doe.gov/>

Inter-University Consortium for Political and Social Research (ICPSR)
<http://www.icpsr.umich.edu/index.html>

Iran/Contra Report
<http://fedbbs.access.gpo.gov/court01.htm>

IRS Statistics of Income Division
<http://www.irs.ustreas.gov/tax_stats/index.html>

Item Lister
<http://www.access.gpo.gov/su_docs/dpos/itemlist.html>

Jefferson's Legacy: A Brief History of the Library of Congress
<http://lcweb.loc.gov/loc/legacy/>

Judicial Branch Resources (Library of Congress Internet Guide)
<http://lcweb.loc.gov/global/judiciary.html>

Legal Information Institute, Cornell Law School
<http://www.law.cornell.edu>

Legislative Indexing Vocabulary (LIV), the thesaurus for searching "Bill Summary & Status" in THOMAS
<http://lcweb.loc.gov/lexico/liv/brsearch.html>

Library of Congress
<http://lcweb.loc.gov/>

Library of Congress Information Bulletin
<http://www.loc.gov/loc/lcib/>

Library of Congress Legislative Indexing Vocabulary (LIV)
<http://lcweb.loc.gov/lexico/liv/brsearch.html>

Library of Congress, Science and Technology Division
<http://lcweb.loc.gov/rr/scitech/trsover.html>

List of Classes
<http://fedbbs.access.gpo.gov/libs/class.htm>
or
<ftp://fedbbs.access.gpo.gov/gpo_bbs/class/listclas.txt>
or
<http://www.du.edu/~ttyler/locintro.htm>

LOCIS
<http://lcweb.loc.gov/catalog/>
or
<telnet://locis.loc.gov>

Los Alamos National Laboratory Research Library
<http://lib-www.lanl.gov>

Major Legislation of the Congress ceased after the 1992 summary

MARVEL
<gopher://marvel.loc.gov/>

MEDLINE
<http://www.nlm.nih.gov/nlmhome.html>
or
<http://www4.ncbi.nlm.nih.gov/PubMed/>

MEDTUTOR
<http://sis.nlm.nih.gov/tehpcl.htm>
or
<http://chid.nih.gov/>

Monthly Catalog
<http://www.access.gpo.gov/su_docs/>

Monthly Product Announcement (Census)
<http://www.census.gov/pub/mp/www/mpa.html>

Municipal Codes
<http://www.spl.lib.wa.us/collec/lawcoll/municode.html>

NAIL (National Archives)
<http://www.nara.gov/nara/nail.html>

NASA
<http://www.nasa.gov/>

NASA Patent Abstracts Bibliography (NASA PAB)
<http://www.sti.nasa.gov/Pubs/Patents/pat50.pdf>

NASA STI
<http://www.sti.nasa.gov>

NASA Technical Report Server
<http://www.sti.nasa.gov/RECONselect.html>

NASA Thesaurus
<http://www.sti.nasa.gov/nasa-thesaurus.html>

National Agricultural Library
<http://www.nal.usda.gov/>
National Agricultural Statistics Service
<http://www.usda.gov/nass/#NASS>
National AIDS Clearinghouse (CDC)
<http://www.cdcnac.org/>
National Archive of Criminal Justice Data (NACJD)
<http://www.icpsr.umich.edu/NACJD/home.html>
National Archives
<http://www.nara.gov/>
National Archives and Records Administration Audiovisual Information Locator (NAIL)
<http://www.nara.gov/nara/nail.html>
National Audiovisual Center
<http://www.ntis.gov/nac/nac.htm>
National Center for Education Statistics
<http://nces.ed.gov/>
National Center for Health Statistics
<http://www.cdc.gov/nchswww/nchshome.htm>
National Clearinghouse for Criminal Justice Information Systems
<http://www.ch.search.org/>
National Commission on Libraries and Information Science
<http://www.nclis.gov/info/info.html>
National Counterintelligence Center
<http://www.nacic.gov/>
National Crime Victimization Survey
<http://www.ojp.usdoj.gov/bjs/>
National Criminal Justice Reference Service
<http://ncjrs.org/ncjhome.htm>
National Digital Library Federation
<http://lcweb.loc.gov/loc/ndlf/digital.html>
National Energy Information Center
<http://www.eia.doe.gov/index.html>
National Film Registry
<http://lcweb.loc.gov/film/>
National Health Information Center
<http://nhic-nt.health.org/>
National Historical Publications and Records Commission (NHPRC)
<http://www.nara.gov/nara/nhprc/>
National Imagery and Mapping Agency
<http://www.nima.mil>
National Institute of Dental Research
<http://www.nidr.nih.gov/>
National Institute of Justice
<http://www.ncjrs.org/nijhome.htm>
National Institute of Mental Health
<http://www.nimh.hih.gov>

National Institute of Standards and Technology
<http://www.nist.gov/>
National Library of Canada
<http://www.nlc-bnc.ca/services/e-ill.htm>
National Library of Education
<http://www.ed.gov/NLE/>
National Library of Medicine
<http://www.nlm.nih.gov/>
National Museum of African Art
<http://www.si.edu/organiza/museums/africart/>
National Museum of American Art
<http://www.nmaa.si.edu/>
National Museum of Natural History
<http://www.nmnh.si.edu/>
National Ocean Service
<http://www.nos.noaa.gov/>
National Oceanic and Atmospheric Administration
<http://www.noaa.gov/>
National Park Service
<http://www.nps.gov>
National Portrait Gallery
<http://www.npg.si.edu/>
National Postal Museum
<http://www.si.edu/postal/>
National Register of Historic Places
<http://www.cr.nps.gov/nr/nrhome.html>
National Science Foundation
<http://www.nsf.gov>
National Technical Information Service
<http://www.ntis.gov/>
National Telecommunications and Information Administration
<http://www.ntia.doc.gov/>
National Trade Data Bank
<http://www.stat-usa.gov> (subscription)
Needs and Offers List
<http://docs.sewanee.edu/nando/nando.html>
New Products from the U.S. Government
<http://www.access.gpo.gov/su_docs/sale/market/prod001.html>
New Publications of the Geological Survey
<http://pubs.usgs.gov/publications/index.html>
NIOSH
<http://ftp.cdc.gov/niosh/nioshtic.html>
Nixon Presidential Materials Staff (the Nixon Project) at Archives II in College Park, MD
<http://sunsite.unc.edu/lia/president/nixon.html>
NLM Fact Sheets
<http://www.nlm.nih.gov/pubs/factsheets/>

NLM News
<http://www.nlm.nih.gov/pubs/nlmnews/nlmnews.html>

NTIS *Catalog of Products and Services*
<http://www.ntis.gov/prs/pr827.htm>

NTIS Database Search Guide
<http://www.ntis.gov/comserv.htm>

OERI Office of Educational Research and Improvement (Department of Education)
<http://www.ed.gov/offices/OERI/index.html>

Office of Disease Prevention and Health Promotion (ODPHP)
<http://odphp.osophs.dhhs.gov/>

Office of Management and Budget
<http://www.whitehouse.gov/WH/EOP/OMB/html/ombhome.html>

Office of Population Research (Princeton University)
<http://popindex.princeton.edu>

Office of the Federal Register
<http://www.nara.gov/fedreg/>

OMB
<http://www.whitehouse.gov/WH/EOP/omb>

OMB Circulars
<http://www.whitehouse.gov/WH/EOP/OMB/html/circular.html>

O*NET
<http://www.doleta.gov/programs/onet/>

OrderNow
<http://www.ntis.gov/ordernow/>

OTA Online former home page of Congress's Office of Technology Assessment, now mirrored at Princeton University's Woodrow Wilson School of Public and International Affairs
<http://www.wws.princeton.edu/~ota>

Oyez Oyez Oyez
<http://court.it-services.nwu.edu/oyez/>

Patent and Trademark Depository Library Directory
<http://www.uspto.gov/web/offices/ac/ido/cpti/ptdlib.htm>

Patent and Trademark Office
<http://www.uspto.gov>

Patent Bibliographic Database
<http://patents.uspto.gov/>

Patent *Products and Services* Catalog, see *Products and Services* Catalog (PTO)

Pentagon
<http://www.dtic.dla.mil/gulflink/>

Postal Service
<http://www.usps.gov>

President
<http://www.whitehouse.gov/WH/EOP/OP/html/OP_Home.html>

President John F. Kennedy Assassination Records Collection
<http://www.nara.gov/nara/jfk/>

Presidential Papers Collection (Library of Congress)
<http://lcweb2.loc.gov/ammem/presprvw/23pres.html>

Presidential Vetoes, 1789–1996: A Summary Overview
<http://www.house.gov/rules_org/97-163.htm>

PRF (now called SPC)
<http://www.access.gpo.gov/su_docs/sale/prf/prf.html>

Privacy Act Issuances Compilation
<http://www.access.gpo.gov/su_docs/aces/PrivacyAct.shtml>

Products and Services catalog (PTO)
<http://www.uspto.gov/web/uspto/patsales/patsales.html> or C 21.30:

Publications Reference File (now called *Sales Product Catalog*)
<http://www.access.gpo.gov/su_docs/sale/prf/prf.html>

Published Search Master Catalog (NTIS)
<http://www.ntis.gov/prs/pr186.htm>

Recreation on federal lands
<http://www.recreation.gov/>

Reports: Senate, House, and Executive
<http://www.access.gpo.gov/congress/index.html>

Resources for Research: A Comprehensive Catalog (National Archives)
<http://www.nara.gov/publications/microfilm/comprehensive/compcat.html>

Richard Nixon Library and Birthplace
<http://www.chapman.edu/nixon/>

Sales Product Catalog (formerly *Publications Reference File*)
<http://www.access.gpo.gov/su_docs/sale/prf/prf.html>

Scientific and Technical Aerospace Reports (STAR)
<http://www.sti.nasa.gov/Pubs/star/Star.html>

Securities and Exchange Commission
<http://www.sec.gov/> (includes EDGAR)

Selected Water Resources Abstracts (SWRA)
<http://water.usgs.gov/public/nawdex/swra.html>.

Senate Historical Office
<http://www.senate.gov/history/index.html>

Senate Manual
<http://www.access.gpo.gov/congress/senate/index.html> or Y 1.1/3:

Senators: Senate Historical Office List
<http://www.senate.gov/history/nameindex/a.htm>

Shipping List
<http://febbbs.access.gpo.gov/fdlp01.htm>
or by dial-in to GPO's FBB (downloadable only,
can't be viewed)

SIGCAT Conference
<http://www.sigcat.org>

Significant Features of Fiscal Federalism
<http://www.library.unt.edu/gpo/acir/
acir.html> (was Y 3.AD 9/8:18/, but is no longer
a government publication after ACIR, Advisory
Commission on Intergovernmental Relations, was
abolished in 1996

Smithsonian Institution
<http://www.si.edu>

Social Statistics Briefing Room (White House)
<http://www.whitehouse.gov/fsbr/ssbr.html>

Sourcebook of Criminal Justice Statistics
<http://www.albany.edu/sourcebook>

SPC
<http://www.access.gpo.gov/su_docs/sale/prf/
prf.html>

Standard Industrial Classification Manual
<http://www.osha.gov/oshstats/sicser.html>

STAT-USA
<http://www.stat-usa.gov>

State and Local Documents Task Force (GODORT)
<http://www.library.arizona.edu/users/
arawan/stat.html GODORT>

State and Local Government on the Web (U. of
Michigan Documents Center)
<http://www.lib.umich.edu/libhome/
Documents.center/state.html>

State Department
<http://www.access.gpo.gov/state/index.html>

StateList
<http://www.law.uiuc.edu/library/check/
check.htm>

StateSearch
<http://www.nasire.org/ss/>

Stationery Office (Great Britain, formerly HMSO)
<http://www.the-stationery-office.co.uk>

Statistical Abstract of the United States
<http://www.census.gov/stat_abstract/>
or FedStats "Fast Facts" linkage
<http://www.fedstats.gov>

Subject Bibliographies
<http://www.access.gpo.gov/su_docs/sale/
sale100.html>

Sunnyvale Center for Innovation
<http://www.sci3.com/>

Superintendent of Documents
<http://www.access.gpo.gov/su_docs/>

Superseded List
<http://www.access.gpo.gov/su_docs/dpos/
suplist.html>

Supreme Court Opinions
<http://supct.law.cornell.edu/supct/
index.html>
or
<http://fedbbs.access.gpo.gov/court01.htm>

Tax Forms (Internal Revenue Service)
<http://www.irs.ustreas.gov/basic/
forms_pubs/>

THOMAS
<http://thomas.loc.gov/>

TIGER
<http://www.census.gov/geo/www/tiger/>

Tracer Bullets (Library of Congress)
<http://lcweb.loc.gov/rr/scitech/>

Treasury Department
<http://fedbbs.access.gpo.gov/treasury.htm>

Treaties in Force
<http://www.acda.gov/state/>

Uncle Sam Migrating Government Publications
<http://www.lib.memphis.edu/gpo/mig.htm>

Uniform Crime Reports
<http://www.fbi.gov/ucr/crimeus/
crimeus.htm>

United Nations
<http://www.un.org>

U.S. Business Advisor
<http://www.business.gov/>

U.S. Code
<http://www.access.gpo.gov/congress/
index.html> or
<http://www.house.gov/Laws.html>

U.S. Code, "Tables" Volume
<http://law.house.gov/uscct.htm>

U.S. Consumer Gateway
<http://www.consumer.gov>

U.S. Federal Courts
<http://www.uscourts.gov/>

U.S. Geological Survey
<http://www.usgs.gov/USGSHome.html>

U.S. Government Manual
<http://www.access.gpo.gov/su_docs/
dbsearch.html>

U.S. Government Subscriptions
<http://www.access.gpo.gov/su_docs/sale/
subs001.html>

Vice President
<http://www.whitehouse.gov/WH/EOP/OVP/
html/GORE_Home.html>

Villanova Center for Information Law and Policy
<http://www.law.vill.edu/Fed-Agency/
fedwebloc.html>

Voting Records of Members of Congress
<http://lcweb.loc.gov/global/legislative/
voting.html#records>

WashLaw
<http://lawlib.wuacc.edu/washlaw/>

Weekly Checklist (Canadian)
<http://web2.ccg-gcc.ca/dsp-psd/Checklist/
lists-e/html>

*Where to Write for Vital Records . . . Births, Deaths,
Marriages, and Divorces*
<http://www.cdc.gov/nchswww/howto/w2w/
w2welcom.htm>

White House
<http://www.whitehouse.gov>

World Conservation Bookstore
<http://w3.iprolink.ch/iucnlib/bookstore/>

World Factbook
<http://www.odci.gov/cia/publications/
pubs.html>

World Intellectual Property Organization (WIPO)
<http://www.wipo.org/eng/index.htm>

World News Connection
<http://wnc.fedworld.gov/>

Zip codes
<http://www.usps.gov>

APPENDIX 6
Tips for Searching Old GRA&I Issues

To find the abstract for an index entry listed in pre-1980 issues, first locate the subject field and group numbers within the abstract section, and then find the report number in alphanumeric sequence within the subject field. A sample citation from the 1976 GRA & I annual index shows how these components were indicated:

GRA & I Index Entry Format:
Before 1980

Proceedings of the 1976 Army Numerical and Computer Analysis Conference Held at U.S. Army Research Office, Research Triangle Park, North Carolina, 11-12 February 1976.

AD-A028 492/7GI   76-22   9B   PC A23/MF A01

report no.   vol. 76-no. 22

field 9
group B

price
code

Between 1980 and 1983, the annual indexes referred to a GRA & I issue and page where the abstract would be found under NTIS order number, in alphanumeric sequence:

GRA & I Index Entry Format: 1980-1983

Photovoltaic Concentrator Technology Project.
DE82010947   83-08 1586 MF A01

NTIS order number

issue year-no.

page

price code

After 1984, the indexes referred to an abstract number within a particular biweekly issue:

GRA & I Index Entry Format: 1984 to Present

Cereals: Nutritional Value. 1972-June, 1984 (Citations from the Food Science and Technology Abstracts Data Base).
PB84-868470   16-442,426   PC N01/MF N01

NTIS order number
issue no.
abstract no.   price code

INDEX

by Kay Banning

Agriculture Network Information Center (AgNIC), 243
AGRINDEX, 65
AGRIS, 65
AIDS Bibliography, 67
AIDS Patent Database, 77
ALA (American Library Association), 4, 15, 195
Alaska, 181
Alaska Natives, 167
ALF, 66
ALIN (Agricultural Libraries Information Notes), 243
Almanac of American Politics, 108
Almanac of the Federal Judiciary, 146
AltaVista, 214
American Bar Association, 149
The American Bench, 146
American Civil Liberties Union, 9, 13, 15
American Community Survey (ACS), 157, 158
American Demographics, 161
American Dental Association, 63
American Foreign Policy: Current Documents, 136–37
American Foreign Policy and Treaty Index, 136, 137, 138, 139, 213
American Indians, 158, 166, 167
American Library Association (ALA), 4, 15, 195
American Memory historical collections, 110, 178, 181, 186
American National Red Cross, 192
American National Standards, 66
American National Standards Institute (ANSI), 66, 243
American Samoa, 188
American Spelling Book, 85
American State Papers, 111, 112
American Statistics Index (ASI)
 census statistics and, 166
 Energy Information Administration statistics and, 171
 Executive Office and, 140
 federal budget and, 134
 foreign and international information and, 202
 health statistics and, 171
 Index to Health Information and, 63
 labor statistics and, 171
 National Center for Education Statistics and, 155, 170
American Technology Preeminence Act (ATPA) of 1991, 53
American Treasures of the Library of Congress exhibit, 110
Americans Communicating Electronically (ACE), 243
Americans with Disabilities Act ADA Home Page, 243

Ames, John, 46, 112
AMICUS, 214
Anacapa Island, 185
Anderson, Terry, 14
Andriot, Donna, 155, 196
Animals, 191
Annals of Congress, 96
Annotated Constitution, 151
An Annotated Guide to Current National Bibliographies (Bell), 206
Annual Energy Review, 164, 243
Annual Index: Reports Issued in FY [year], 109
Annual Report to Congress (EIA), 171
"Annual update cycle," 31
ANSI (American National Standards Institute), 66, 243
Appellate courts, 86, 143, 144, 149–50, 176, 228
Appellate jurisdiction, 145
"Application for Assistance Under the Hague Convention on Child Abduction," 30
Appropriations bills, 134
APS (Automated Patent System), 76, 81
APS Image, 75, 76, 78
APS Text, 76, 78
The Archives: A Guide to the National Archives Field Branches, 176
Area Handbooks series, 213
ARL (Association of Research Libraries), 4
Army Center for Military History, 243
Aronsson, Patricia, 11
Art, 191–92
Arthur, Chester A., 128
ASCII, 30
ASI. *See American Statistics Index* (ASI)
AskERIC, 47, 243, 245
Association of Research Libraries (ARL), 4
Atlases, definition of, 182
ATPA (American Technology Preeminence Act) of 1991, 53
Auburn University Libraries Microforms and Documents Department (MADD), 48
Audiovisual materials. *See also* Nonprint sources
 freebies and, 193
 government information and, 6
 Monthly Catalog's exclusion of, 42
 NAIL and, 178, 180
 National Technical Information Service and, 53, 56
 as nonprint sources, 190–92
 presidential libraries and, 135
 search strategies/tips for, 190, 192
Australia, 209
Authorization bills, 134

Automated Index of Criminal Justice Information Systems, 170
Automated Patent System (APS), 76, 81
AV. *See* Audiovisual materials
AVLINE, 190

Babylonian censuses, 156, 159
Background Notes, 136, 201, 203, 243
Balay, Robert, 201
Base maps, 182
Basic Facts about Trademarks, 243
Basic Guide to Exporting, 57
Basic Statistics of the European Union, 219
Bass, Kenneth C., 10
Bates, Jim, 29
BEA (Economic Analysis Bureau), 154, 156, 169, 243
Beaman, E. O., 180
Bell, Alexander Graham, 53, 70, 161
Bell, Barbara L., 206
Bell, W., 180
Bench opinions, 146
Berlin Wall, 135
Bernan Associates, 210, 217, 218
Bernan Press, 133
Berne Convention for the Protection of Literary and Artistic Works, 85
Bernier, Bernard A., 197
Berring, Robert C., 138, 151, 198
"Bevans," 138, 139
Bevans, Charles, 138
BIA (Bureau of Indian Affairs), 176
Bible, 120
Bibliographic control
 of foreign and international information, 205–09, 211
 of government information, 4–5
 Government Printing Office and, 5
The Bibliographic Control of Official Publications (Pemberton), 211
Bibliographic Guide to Government Publications—Foreign, 206
Bibliographies. *See also* specific bibliographies
 audiovisual materials and, 190
 Canadian government documents and, 215
 Census Bureau and, 161
 foreign and international information and, 201
 government information and, 196
 Government Printing Office and, 20
 Library of Congress and, 178
 of maps, 186
 medicine and, 67
 MEDLINE and, 61
 Monthly Catalog as, 22, 36–44
 National Technical Information Service as, 42

patents and, 80
retrospective bibliographies, 44–46
search strategies/tips for, 46
of Serial Set maps, 112
state government information and,
197–98
statistics and, 155
trade bibliographies, 46
Bibliography of Agriculture, 63, 65
Bibliography of Cartography, 187
Bibliography of Cartography Card File,
187
*Bibliography of Federal Data Sources:
Excluding Statistics Canada 1981,*
215
Bibliography of Official Statistical Year-
books and Bulletins (Westfall), 207
Bibliography of Scientific and Industrial Research Reports, 54
"Bibliography on Documents
Librarianship and Government
Information," 197, 201
Bicameral action, 100
Bill of Rights, 175
Billings, John Shaw, 24, 61, 158
Billington, James H., 110
Bills. *See also* Legislative information
bicameral action and, 100
CIS/Index and, 100–01
committee reports and, 93, 94
Congressional Record and, 96–98
enrolled version of, 101
federal budget and, 134
floor action and, 95
hearings and, 92
introduction and preliminary
deliberations, 90
as laws, 102–04
legislative history of, 102, 104–07
number of, 93, 102, 106
presidential action and, 101–02
presidential messages and, 131
public versus private bills, 90
second chamber action and, 96
status of, 95
steps to becoming law, 91
THOMAS and, 90, 101
as type of legislation, 89–90
voting and, 95
*Biographical Directory of the United
States Congress, 1774–1989,* 107
Biographical sources
judicial information and, 146
legislative information and, 107–08
Bismarck, Otto von, 90
BJS (Justice Statistics Bureau), 156, 169–
70, 243
*Black Americans in Congress,
1870-1989,* 107
BLDSC (British Library Document Supply Centre), 65, 209

Blind/physically handicapped materi-
als, 178
BLJ Clearinghouse, 172
BLM (Land Management Bureau), 4,
156
BLS (Labor Statistics Bureau), 154, 155,
156, 171, 243
"Blue cover" reports, 109
*The Bluebook: A Uniform System of
Citation,* 198
Bluebook, 125, 149, 151, 198
BNA (Bureau of National Affairs), 86
BNA Online, 225
Boards of Contract Appeals, 149
Boggs, Hale, 96
Bok, Derek, 5
The Book of the States, 198–99
Books in Print, 46
Bookstores
GPO bookstores, 22–23, 27, 28
NTIS bookstore, 53
World Conservation Bookstore,
205, 251
Boorstin, Daniel, 110, 163
Bosenberg, Henry, 70
Boyd, Anne M., 197
Brady, Matthew, 178
Braun, Eva, 175
Brazil, 4
British Command Papers series, 213
British Library, 214
British Library Document Supply Cen-
tre (BLDSC), 65, 209
Brown, David, 4
"Browse Electronic Titles" page, 33, 38,
47, 243
Buck, Solon J., 176
*Budget of the United States Govern-
ment,* 7, 20, 24, 28, 134, 243
Bulletin boards
access to government information
and, 11
agriculture and, 66
Agriculture Department and, 54
Commerce Department and, 54,
169
of Consumer Information Center,
22
criminal justice and, 170
Depository Library Program and,
30
education and, 172
energy and, 171
FedWorld and, 54
government information and, 1, 3,
4, 30
GPO Access and, 2
judicial information and, 143
scientific information and, 50
Supreme Court and, 146
Bulletin of the European Union, 218
Burbank, Luther, 71

Bureau of Indian Affairs (BIA), 176
Bureau of National Affairs (BNA), 86
*Bureau of the Census Catalog of Publi-
cations, 1790–1972,* 161
Burke, Frank G., 150
Burma, 10
Burnham, David, 13
Burton, 128
Bush, George, 134–35, 137
Bush Presidential Library and Mu-
seum, 135
Bush Presidential Materials Project,
134–35
Business enterprise statistics program,
162

CAB Thesaurus, 63
*Calendars of the House of Representa-
tives*
bicameral action and, 100
committee membership and, 92
committee reports and, 95
federal budget and, 134
Internet address of, 244, 247
legislative history and, 107
legislative information and, 100
presidential action and, 101
second chamber action and, 96
California, 82
Canada
Canadian Government Internet
address, 244
depository systems and, 210
government documents of, 209,
214–16
government information policy
and, 4
National Technical Information
Service and, 206
North American Industry Classifi-
cation and, 156
trademarks and, 83
The Canada Gazette, 215
Canada Institute for Scientific and
Technical Information (CISTI), 65,
67
Canada Year Book, 215
Canadian Economic Observer, 215
Canadian Official Publications, 215
Canadian Parliamentary Guide, 215
Canadian Research Index, 215
Canadian Statistics Index, 215
Canadiana, 215
Canal Zone, 27
Cancer research, 5
CANSIM, 215
CAP (Catalog of American Portraits),
192
CAP (Current Awareness Publica-
tions), 58
Carlson, Peter, 154